THE CORE TEAM

ECONOMY, SOCIETY, AND PUBLIC POLICY

THE CORE TEAM

ECONOMY, SOCIETY, AND PUBLIC POLICY

Great Clarendon Street, Oxford, OX2 6DP,
United Kingdom

Oxford University Press is a department of the University of Oxford.
It furthers the University's objective of excellence in research, scholarship,
and education by publishing worldwide. Oxford is a registered trade mark of
Oxford University Press in the UK and in certain other countries

© CORE Economics Education 2019

The moral rights of the author have been asserted

Impression: 1
Version: 1.0.0

All rights reserved. No part of this publication may be reproduced, stored in
a retrieval system, or transmitted, in any form or by any means, without the
prior permission in writing of Oxford University Press, or as expressly permitted
by law, by licence or under terms agreed with the appropriate reprographics
rights organization. Enquiries concerning reproduction outside the scope of the
above should be sent to the Rights Department, Oxford University Press, at the
address above

You must not circulate this work in any other form
and you must impose this same condition on any acquirer

Published in the United States of America by Oxford University Press
198 Madison Avenue, New York, NY 10016, United States of America

British Library Cataloguing in Publication Data
Data available

Library of Congress Control Number: 2019947245

ISBN (print) 978-0-19-884984-1
ISBN (ebook) 978-1-5272-4374-3

Design and layout by Electric Book Works
Printed in Great Britain by Bell & Bain Ltd., Glasgow.

Links to third party websites are provided by Oxford in good faith and
for information only. Oxford disclaims any responsibility for the materials
contained in any third party website referenced in this work.

CONTENTS

	PREFACE	xi
	A NOTE TO INSTRUCTORS	xiii
	PRODUCING *ECONOMY, SOCIETY, AND PUBLIC POLICY*	xvii
1	**CAPITALISM AND DEMOCRACY: AFFLUENCE, INEQUALITY, AND THE ENVIRONMENT**	**1**
	1.1 Introduction	1
	1.2 Affluence and income inequality	3
	1.3 How did we get here? The hockey stick in real incomes	6
	1.4 Economic growth	10
	1.5 The permanent technological revolution: Engine of growth	19
	1.6 Another engine of growth: More machines and tools per worker	22
	1.7 The capitalist revolution	23
	1.8 Capitalism and growth: Cause and effect?	29
	1.9 Varieties of capitalism: Institutions and growth	34
	1.10 Varieties of capitalism: Growth and stagnation	35
	1.11 Capitalism, inequality, and democracy	37
	1.12 Capitalism, growth and environmental sustainability	40
	1.13 Conclusion	46
	1.14 Doing Economics: Measuring climate change	46
	1.15 References	47
2	**SOCIAL INTERACTIONS AND ECONOMIC OUTCOMES**	**49**
	2.1 Introduction	49
	2.2 Two types of social interaction	51
	2.3 Resolving social dilemmas	52
	2.4 Social interactions as games	55
	2.5 When self-interest works: The invisible hand	59
	2.6 When self-interest doesn't work: The prisoners' dilemma	61
	2.7 Free riding and the provision of public goods	66
	2.8 Social preferences and the public good	68
	2.9 Sustaining cooperation by punishing free riding	72
	2.10 How three kinds of social preferences address social dilemmas	76

2.11 Predicting economic outcomes: A Nash equilibrium	79
2.12 Which Nash equilibrium? Conflicts of interest and bargaining	81
2.13 Conflicts of interest in the global climate change problem	86
2.14 The economy and economics	90
2.15 Conclusion	92
2.16 Doing Economics: Collecting and analysing data from experiments	93
2.17 References	94

3 PUBLIC POLICY FOR FAIRNESS AND EFFICIENCY — 95

3.1 Introduction	95
3.2 Goals of public policy	98
3.3 Fairness and efficiency in the ultimatum game	100
3.4 Evaluating an outcome: Is it efficient?	105
3.5 Adding the option of transferring payoffs between players.	108
3.6 Evaluating an outcome: Is it fair?	111
3.7 Why are (some) economic inequalities unfair? Procedural and substantive judgements	115
3.8 Implementing public policies	120
3.9 Unintended consequences of a redistributive tax	124
3.10 Unintended consequences: Policies affect preferences	128
3.11 How do we find out if a policy will work?	131
3.12 Conclusion	135
3.13 Doing Economics: Measuring the effect of a sugar tax	136
3.14 References	137

4 WORK, WELLBEING, AND SCARCITY — 139

4.1 Introduction	139
4.2 Economic models: How to see more by looking at less	144
4.3 Decision making, trade-offs, and opportunity costs	146
4.4 Making decisions when there are trade-offs	148
4.5 Preferences	152
4.6 The feasible set	158
4.7 Decision making and scarcity	161
4.8 Hours of work and economic growth	164
4.9 Applying the model: Explaining changes in working hours	169
4.10 Applying the model: Explaining differences between countries	171
4.11 Is this a good model? Does it matter that people (mostly) do not really optimize?	172
4.12 Extending the model: The influence of culture and politics	173
4.13 Extending the model: Women, men, and the gender division of labour	174
4.14 Work and wellbeing as a social dilemma	176
4.15 Conclusion	182
4.16 Doing Economics: Measuring wellbeing	183
4.17 References	183

5 INSTITUTIONS, POWER, AND INEQUALITY — 185

5.1 Introduction	185
5.2 Institutions: The rules of the game	187
5.3 Production and distribution: Using a model	191
5.4 The rule of force: Bruno appears and has unlimited power over Angela	194
5.5 Property rights and the rule of law	200
5.6 Efficiency and conflicts over the distribution of the surplus	207
5.7 Property rights, the rule of law, and the right to vote	209
5.8 The lessons from Angela and Bruno's story	213
5.9 Measuring economic inequality	214
5.10 Comparing inequality across the world	220

	5.11 Conclusion	227
	5.12 Doing Economics: Measuring inequality: Lorenz curves and Gini coefficients	228
	5.13 References	228

6 THE FIRM: EMPLOYEES, MANAGERS, AND OWNERS — 229

- 6.1 Introduction — 229
- 6.2 Firms, markets, and the division of labour — 231
- 6.3 Power relations within the firm — 234
- 6.4 Other people's money: The separation of ownership and control — 238
- 6.5 Other people's labour: The employment relationship — 241
- 6.6 Why do a good day's work? Consider the alternative! — 244
- 6.7 Employment rents — 245
- 6.8 Work effort and wages: The labour discipline model — 249
- 6.9 The employer sets the wage to minimize the cost per unit of effort — 253
- 6.10 Why there is always involuntary unemployment — 257
- 6.11 Putting the model to work: Owners, employees, and public policy — 258
- 6.12 Why do employers pay employment rents to their workers? — 262
- 6.13 Another kind of business organization: Cooperative firms — 264
- 6.14 Another kind of business organization: The gig economy — 267
- 6.15 Principals and agents: Interactions under incomplete contracts — 268
- 6.16 Conclusion — 272
- 6.17 Doing Economics: Measuring management practices — 273
- 6.18 References — 273

7 FIRMS AND MARKETS FOR GOODS AND SERVICES — 275

- 7.1 Introduction — 275
- 7.2 Economies of scale and the cost advantages of large-scale production — 277
- 7.3 The demand curve and willingness to pay — 279
- 7.4 Profits, costs, and the isoprofit curve — 284
- 7.5 The isoprofit curves and the demand curve — 286
- 7.6 Gains from trade — 289
- 7.7 Price-setting, market power, and public policy — 294
- 7.8 Product selection, innovation, and advertising — 298
- 7.9 Buying and selling: Demand and supply in a competitive market — 300
- 7.10 Demand and supply in a competitive market: Bakeries — 307
- 7.11 Competitive equilibrium: Gains from trade, allocation, and distribution — 312
- 7.12 Changes in supply and demand — 316
- 7.13 The world oil market — 322
- 7.14 Conclusion — 327
- 7.15 Doing Economics: Supply and demand — 328
- 7.16 References — 329

8 THE LABOUR MARKET AND THE PRODUCT MARKET: UNEMPLOYMENT AND INEQUALITY — 331

- 8.1 Introduction — 331
- 8.2 Measuring the economy: Employment and unemployment — 334
- 8.3 The labour market, the product market and the aggregate economy: The WS/PS model — 337
- 8.4 The labour market and the wage-setting curve (firms and workers) — 338
- 8.5 The product market and the price-setting curve (firms and customers) — 344
- 8.6 Wages, profits, and unemployment in the aggregate economy — 353
- 8.7 Unemployment as a characteristic of equilibrium — 356
- 8.8 Why was unemployment higher in Spain than in Germany? — 357
- 8.9 Declining competition and increasing inequality in the US — 359

8.10	The labour and product market model and inequality: Using the Lorenz curve and Gini coefficient	361
8.11	Labour unions: Bargained wages and the union voice effect	364
8.12	Rising markups and profit share, weaker trade unions, and rising inequality	370
8.13	Labour market policies to address unemployment and inequality	372
8.14	Labour market policies: Shifting the Nash equilibrium	373
8.15	Looking backward: Baristas and bread markets	377
8.16	Structural and cyclical unemployment: The role of demand	381
8.17	Conclusion	383
8.18	Doing Economics: Measuring the non-monetary cost of unemployment	384
8.19	References	385

9 THE CREDIT MARKET: BORROWERS, LENDERS, AND THE RATE OF INTEREST — 387

9.1	Introduction	387
9.2	Income, consumption, and wealth	389
9.3	Borrowing: Bringing consumption forward in time	392
9.4	Reasons to borrow: Smoothing and impatience	396
9.5	Borrowing allows smoothing by bringing consumption to the present	400
9.6	Storing or lending allows smoothing and moving consumption to the future	402
9.7	Mutual gains and conflicts over their distribution in the credit market	406
9.8	Borrowing may allow investing: Julia's best hope	409
9.9	Balance sheets: Assets and liabilities	412
9.10	Credit market constraints: Another principal–agent problem	416
9.11	Inequality: Lenders, borrowers, and those excluded from credit markets	422
9.12	The credit market and the labour market	425
9.13	Conclusion	426
9.14	Doing Economics: Credit-excluded households in a developing country	427
9.15	References	427

10 BANKS, MONEY, HOUSING, AND FINANCIAL ASSETS — 429

10.1	Introduction	429
10.2	Assets, money, banks, and the financial system	431
10.3	Money and banks	436
10.4	Banks, profits, and the creation of money	439
10.5	The central bank, banks, and interest rates	444
10.6	The business of banking and bank balance sheets	446
10.7	How key economic actors use and create money: A summary so far	452
10.8	The value of an asset: Expected return and risk	454
10.9	Changing supply and demand for a financial asset	461
10.10	Asset market bubbles	463
10.11	Housing as an asset, collateral, and house price bubbles	469
10.12	Banks, housing, and the global financial crisis	470
10.13	The role of banks in the crisis	472
10.14	Banking, markets, and morals	474
10.15	Conclusion	478
10.16	Doing Economics: Characteristics of banking systems around the world	479
10.17	References	479

11 MARKET SUCCESSES AND FAILURES — 481

11.1	Introduction	481
11.2	The market and other institutions	483
11.3	Markets, specialization, and the division of labour	484
11.4	The 'magic of the market': Prices are messages plus motivation	485

11.5 Prices as messages — 488
11.6 Putting motivation behind the price message — 490
11.7 Market failure: External effects of pollution — 492
11.8 External effects and private bargaining — 497
11.9 External effects: Government policies and income distribution — 504
11.10 Property rights, contracts, and market failures — 509
11.11 Public goods, common pool resources, and market failure — 512
11.12 Missing markets: Insurance and lemons — 516
11.13 Market failure and government policy — 522
11.14 Conclusion — 524
11.15 Doing Economics: Measuring willingness to pay for climate change mitigation — 525
11.16 References — 526

12 GOVERNMENTS AND MARKETS IN A DEMOCRATIC SOCIETY — 527

12.1 Introduction — 527
12.2 The limits of markets: Repugnant markets and merit goods — 531
12.3 The government as an economic actor — 534
12.4 The government as a rent-seeking monopolist — 540
12.5 Competition can limit political rent-seeking — 546
12.6 Political monopoly and competition compared. — 549
12.7 Spending by democratic governments: Priorities of a nation — 552
12.8 The feasibility of economic policies — 555
12.9 Administrative feasibility: Information and capacities — 557
12.10 Political feasibility — 559
12.11 Policy matters — 562
12.12 The distributional impact of public policies: Early childhood education — 564
12.13 Free tuition in higher education: Can it be fair to non-students? — 566
12.14 The distributional impact of public policies: Rent control — 569
12.15 Conclusion — 574
12.16 Doing Economics: Government policies and popularity: Hong Kong cash handout — 575
12.17 References — 575

GLOSSARY — 577

BIBLIOGRAPHY — 589

COPYRIGHT ACKNOWLEDGEMENTS — 595

PREFACE

Welcome to CORE's *Economy, Society, and Public Policy* (*ESPP*).

In order to be well-governed, a democracy needs voters who are fluent in the language of economics and who can do some quantitative analysis of social and economic policy. We also need a well-trained cadre of researchers and journalists who have more advanced skills in these fields.

Many students in other disciplines are drawn to economics so that they can engage with policy debates on environmental sustainability, inequality, the future of work, financial instability, and innovation. But, when they begin the study of economics, they find that courses appear to have little to do with these pressing policy matters, and are designed primarily for students who want to study the subject as their major, or even for those going on to post-graduate study in the field.

The result: policy-oriented students often find they have to choose between a quantitative and analytical course of study—economics—that is only minimally policy oriented in content and that downplays the insights of other disciplines, or a policy and problem-oriented course of study that gives them little training in modelling or quantitative scientific methods.

Economy, Society, and Public Policy changes this.

It has been created specifically for students from social science, public policy, business and management, engineering, biology, and other disciplines, who are not economics majors. If you are one of these students, we want to engage, challenge, and empower you with an understanding of economics. We hope you will acquire the tools to articulate reasoned views on pressing policy problems. You may even decide to take more courses in economics as a result.

The book is also being used successfully in courses for economics, business, and public policy majors, as well as in economics modules for Philosophy, Politics and Economics (PPE), and masters' courses in Public Policy.

This textbook is the result of a worldwide collaboration among researchers, educators, and students who are committed to bringing the socially relevant insights of economics to a broader audience. We made it freely available online because we believe this understanding can contribute to richer participation of everyone—not just experts—in shaping our economies, and help to underpin an understanding of policy that is clearly based on evidence. We are grateful to the contributions of this entire team, and to the Nuffield Foundation for supporting the project financially.

MORE ABOUT CORE, OUR EBOOKS, AND OUR MISSION

If you want to know more about the content of this book and its companion text *The Economy* (https://tinyco.re/6612325), an ebook designed for economics majors, and how both differ from a conventional introduction to economics, you can find more detail here (https://tinyco.re/1812530).

For instructors who are considering adopting the book as the basis for either one-semester or two-semester courses, we have written a guide (page xiii) to help you use *Economy, Society, and Public Policy*.

Economy, Society, and Public Policy is intended to provide hands-on experience for students in using data to understand economic questions. For each unit there is an accompanying empirical project called *Doing Economics*. These address important policy problems using real data. *Doing Economics: Empirical Projects* is available as a free ebook (https://tinyco.re/1122412). We have also produced a guide to *Doing Economics* for instructors (https://tinyco.re/1353350).

The CORE team is a large and growing family. Join us! Let us know what you think of this book (https://tinyco.re/9001525) including things that we might improve.

Wendy Carlin, Samuel Bowles, Margaret Stevens, and Eileen Tipoe for the CORE team
August 2019

A NOTE TO INSTRUCTORS

Economy, Society, and Public Policy
by the CORE team

TARGET AUDIENCE
Our target audience includes:

- students at undergraduate and postgraduate level who are not taking economics as a major subject
- anyone who wants to learn how to use economics to understand and articulate reasoned views on some of the most pressing policy problems facing our societies: inequality, financial instability, the future of work, climate change, wealth creation, and innovation
- anyone who wants practical training in understanding and using data to measure the economy and policy effectiveness
- anyone interested in social and economic policy, who is taking a degree related to policy, or is hoping to have a policy-related job in the future.

PREREQUISITES

- no prior courses in economics or statistics are required
- familiarity with basic mathematical operations, percentages, decimals, 2-D graphs

CONTINUING IN ECONOMICS

- After taking the *ESPP* course, many students who would like to engage with major policy problems but have found standard economics courses unappealing may want to study some more economics.
- The course prepares students with a toolkit that will help those who wish to transition to more advanced economics courses to do so, if pathways are available.

COURSE DESIGN PRINCIPLES

- Students begin their study of economics by understanding that the economy is situated within society and the biosphere.
- Students study problems of identifying causation (not just correlation) through the use of natural experiments, lab experiments, and other quantitative methods.
- Social interactions (modelled using simple game theory) and incomplete information (modelled using a series of principal–agent problems) are introduced from the beginning of the course.
- A result is that phenomena studied by the other social sciences such as social norms and the exercise of power play a role. They are absent from typical economics courses.
- For similar reasons, the insights of diverse schools of thought—from Marx and the classical economists to Hayek and Schumpeter—play an integral part in the course.
- The way economists think about public policy is central to *ESPP*. This is introduced in Units 2 and 3, rather than later in the course.
- Tailored to *ESPP*: *Doing Economics*. This is a set of step-by-step hands-on empirical projects that use real data sets to address important problems arising in the course. Each project allows the student to produce a finished report using skills that are transferable to other courses, and to the workplace.

A NOTE TO INSTRUCTORS

FLEXIBLE COURSE DESIGN

Economy, Society, and Public Policy can be taught either as a one-term or one-semester course, or as a two-term or two-semester course. It introduces the key economic actors: firms, customers, employees, owners, borrowers, and lenders as well as government policy-makers, citizens as voters, and the central bank, plus their market and non-market interactions. A model of the aggregate economy is developed in Unit 8, which allows students to see how decisions made in the labour and product markets by owners, workers, and customers interact to determine unemployment and the distribution of income.

- For a 10-week course: The first 10 units provide a self-contained introduction to economic actors and markets within a framework that illuminates reasons for public policy intervention. A one-semester course with 12–13 weeks, can also take in Units 11 and 12.
- For a two-term or two-semester course to include macroeconomics: The instructor would combine Units 1–12 of *ESPP* with Units 13–17 from *The Economy*. Two weeks could be assigned for some of the units, to allow for data-based work.
- For a two-term or two-semester course with a focus on public policy (but not on macroeconomic policy): A course can be formed from Units 1–12 plus the following: the unit on the future of work from *The Economy* (Unit 16 'Technological progress, employment, and living standards in the long run', which does not rely on Units 13–15) and the four capstone units covering globalization (Unit 18), economic inequality (Unit 19), environmental sustainability (Unit 20), and innovation and the networked economy (Unit 21). There is plenty of material in these five units for a full term or semester of study.

ESPP AND DOING ECONOMICS AS PART OF A CONNECTED CURRICULUM

Doing Economics: Empirical Projects by Eileen Tipoe and Ralf Becker

These hands-on projects (https://tinyco.re/1122412) are designed so that they can either be used independently, in conjunction with the *ESPP* units, or in conjunction with units from *The Economy*.

If you are teaching a social science, engineering, business and management, or public policy program in which students have to take an economics course and a quantitative methods course, you can use *ESPP* and *Doing Economics* projects to connect these parts of the curriculum.

SUGGESTED COURSE STRUCTURES

Semester 1: Economy, Society, and Public Policy

Using units from *Economy, Society, and Public Policy*:

ESPP Unit	Title	*Doing Economics*
1	Capitalism and democracy: Affluence, inequality, and the environment	Empirical Project 1: Measuring climate change (datasets: Goddard Institute for Space Studies temperature data; US National Oceanic and Atmospheric Administration CO_2 data)
2	Social interactions and economic outcomes	Empirical Project 2: Collecting and analysing data from experiments (datasets: student-generated experimental data; Hermann et al. 2008)
3	Public policy for fairness and efficiency	Empirical Project 3: Measuring the effect of a sugar tax (datasets: Global Food Research Program's Berkeley Store Price Survey; Silver et al. 2017)
4	Work, wellbeing, and scarcity	Empirical Project 4: Measuring wellbeing (datasets: UN GDP data; Human Development Index)
5	Institutions, power, and inequality	Empirical Project 5: Measuring inequality: Lorenz curves and Gini coefficients (dataset: Our world in data)
6	The firm: Employees, managers, and owners	Empirical Project 6: Measuring management practices (dataset: World Management Survey)
7	Firms and markets for goods and services	Empirical Project 7: Supply and demand (dataset: US market for watermelons (1930–1951); taken from Stewart (2018))
8	The labour market and product market: Unemployment and inequality	Empirical Project 8: Measuring the non-monetary cost of unemployment (dataset: European Values Study)
9	The credit market: Borrowers, lenders, and the rate of interest	Empirical Project 9: Credit-excluded households in a developing country (dataset: Ethiopian Socioeconomic Survey)

SUGGESTED COURSE STRUCTURES

ESPP Unit	Title	Doing Economics
10	Banks, money, housing, and financial assets	Empirical Project 10: Characteristics of banking systems around the world (dataset: World Bank Global Financial Development Database)
11	Market successes and failures	Empirical Project 11: Measuring willingness to pay for climate change mitigation (dataset: German survey data, taken from Uehleke (2016))
12	Governments and markets in a democratic society	Empirical Project 12: Government policies and popularity: Hong Kong cash handout (datasets: University of Hong Kong Public Opinion Programme and the Hong Kong poverty situation report (published by the Hong Kong Census and Statistics Department))

Semester 2, option 1: Macroeconomic policy

Using units on the aggregate economy from *The Economy*:

Unit	Title
13	Economic fluctuations and unemployment (https://tinyco.re/7496156)
14	Unemployment and fiscal policy (https://tinyco.re/4227008)
15	Inflation, unemployment, and monetary policy (https://tinyco.re/8830985)
16	Technological progress, employment, and living standards in the long run (https://tinyco.re/5725158)
17	Capstone: The Great Depression, golden age, and global financial crisis (https://tinyco.re/7816209)

Semester 2, option 2: Economic Policies for innovation, sustainability, and fairness

Using units from *The Economy* on the future of work, globalization, inequality, environment, and innovation:

Unit	Title
16	Technological progress, employment, and living standards in the long run (https://tinyco.re/5725158)
18	Capstone: The nation and the world economy (https://tinyco.re/2583681)
19	Capstone: Economic inequality (https://tinyco.re/1108856)
20	Capstone: Economics of the environment (https://tinyco.re/3172610)
21	Capstone: Innovation, information, and the networked economy (https://tinyco.re/3673358)

xv

PRODUCING *ECONOMY, SOCIETY, AND PUBLIC POLICY*

Economy, Society, and Public Policy includes the work of the CORE team, who authored *The Economy* (https://tinyco.re/5656063). Content has been coordinated by Wendy Carlin, University College London, Samuel Bowles, Santa Fe Institute, Margaret Stevens, University of Oxford, and Eileen Tipoe, University of Oxford and researcher for the CORE EQuSS project.

ESPP has benefitted from the contributions of interns, reviewers, and writers. We are especially grateful for the participation of colleagues from disciplines outside economics. Tim Phillips is the editor, and Stella Yarrow is the project manager.

The main authors of the Units in ESPP are:
Unit 1: Samuel Bowles, Wendy Carlin, Arjun Jayadev, Margaret Stevens, Stephen Wright; Unit 2: Antonio Cabrales, Samuel Bowles, Wendy Carlin, Margaret Stevens; Unit 3: Samuel Bowles, Wendy Carlin; Unit 4: Margaret Stevens, Samuel Bowles, Robin Naylor, David Hope; Unit 5: Samuel Bowles, Wendy Carlin, Margaret Stevens; Unit 6: Samuel Bowles, Wendy Carlin, Margaret Stevens; Unit 7: Margaret Stevens, Samuel Bowles, Wendy Carlin; Unit 8: Wendy Carlin; Samuel Bowles; Unit 9: Wendy Carlin, Paul Segal, Stephen Wright, Samuel Bowles; Unit 10: Wendy Carlin, Paul Segal, Stephen Wright, Samuel Bowles; Unit 11: Margaret Stevens, Samuel Bowles, Rajiv Sethi; Unit 12: Samuel Bowles, Wendy Carlin, Tim Besley, Suresh Naidu.

CONTRIBUTORS
Gani Aldashev, Peter Backus, Simcha Barkai, Ralf Becker, Alvin Birdi, Clemens Blab, Antonio Cabrales, Bruce Chapman, Beatrice Cherrier, Jewel Conrad, Carlos Cortinhas, Manuela dal Borgo, Fiona Dawe, Matthew diGiuseppe, Mark Dodds, Marion Dumas, Robert Edwards, Jan Eeckhout, Stefano Falcone, Nancy Folbre, Florencia Gabriele, Richard Galletly, Stefan Gitman, Rachel Griffiths, Arthur Grimes, Gill Hammond, Agnar Freyr Helgason, David Hope, Girol Karacaoglu, Simon Khong, Humberto Llavador, Alaina Leggette, Ashley Litwin, Dunli Li, Deborah Mabbett, Davide Melcangi, Gordon Menzies, Helen Miller, Jeffrey Miller, Jennifer Miller, Michael Muthukrishna, Dohun Na, Adam Nadzri, Suresh Naidu, Antonio Neto, Max Roser, György Ruzicska, Paul Segal, Rajiv Sethi, Sanjna Shenoy, Christian Spielmann, Margaret Stevens, Erwin Van Sas, Guglielmo Volpe, Thomas West, Stephen Wright, Miao Xu, Oliver Yimeng Zhang, Shuting Zhang.

EDITORIAL, DESIGN, AND SOFTWARE DEVELOPMENT
This ebook edition is produced and maintained by the Electric Book Works team: Christina Tromp, Derika van Biljon, Janine Versfeld, Louise Steward, Klara Skinner, Dione Mentis, Jennifer Jacobs, Lauren Ellwood, and Arthur Attwell.

FUNDING
The project has been funded by the Nuffield Foundation, but the views expressed are those of the authors and not necessarily the Foundation. Visit www.nuffieldfoundation.org.

1
CAPITALISM AND DEMOCRACY: AFFLUENCE, INEQUALITY, AND THE ENVIRONMENT

Unequal scenes, Santa Fe, Mexico City

1.1 INTRODUCTION

- In the past 250 years there has been an unprecedented rise in global living standards. A minority of countries have achieved affluence, while a significant majority of the world's population has at least escaped from grinding poverty.
- At around the same time as the escape from poverty began, a new force was beginning to dominate the economy: capitalism.
- The capitalist revolution made the escape from poverty possible. It brought about advances in technology, increasing specialization, and massive increases in productive assets—capital. These three factors dramatically raised the amount that could be produced in a day's work.
- The capitalist revolution has also been accompanied by unprecedented global economic inequalities, and growing threats to our natural environment.
- In many countries, unequal access to growing affluence led to social unrest and demands for a new political system: democracy.
- Democracy brought greater political equality among the citizens of many of the countries that adopted it, and usually had some mitigating effect on economic inequality.

A South African story

When Cyril Ramaphosa, who in 2018 became the president of South Africa, was born in 1952, under the apartheid system of racial segregation he was excluded from the best schools, healthcare, and even public bathrooms. He had no right to vote.

In 2012, the year Ramaphosa became deputy president of South Africa, he had become the 29th-richest person in Africa, owning wealth of more than $700 million.

Under apartheid, the white minority prospered. They owned the mines, factories and farms that made South Africa the richest country on the continent, and some had achieved levels of affluence similar to that seen in the richest countries in the world. But the income *per capita* of black South African families in the late 1980s was around 11% of that of white families. It had been stuck at this level for at least 50 years.

Resistance to apartheid was brutally repressed. Nelson Mandela, the leader of the African National Congress (now South Africa's largest political party), which had been banned, was serving a life sentence in prison.

As leader of the mineworkers' union, Ramaphosa was part of a wave of strikes and community protests in the mid- and late-1980s that convinced many white business owners that apartheid had to go. Eventually, the government conceded defeat, releasing Mandela from prison.

Democracy, bringing the same legal rights, including voting, to people of all races, came late to South Africa. In 1994, South Africa's first democratic election made Mandela president. Ramaphosa was elected to parliament.

What economic changes have followed?

The abolition of apartheid and the transition to a democratic political system led to some clear economic gains for the black population. Legally-imposed racial separation of schools and healthcare was ended. Piped water and electricity became available to many more families. In many areas of the lives of South Africans, the indignities of racial exclusion became a thing of the past.

The nature of economic inequality in South Africa also changed.

Differences *between* the major population groups declined. So, if you took the income of a typical black citizen, it would be closer to that of a white citizen.

But inequalities *within* these groups increased dramatically. Ramaphosa's own experience is an extreme example.

The arrival of democracy with the abolition of apartheid meant that, measured by their political rights, all South Africans became equal. But the net effect of narrowing differences between racial groups and widening inequality within them, is that the inequality of the income that South Africans receive (after payment of taxes and receipt of government transfers like unemployment benefits and pensions) did not decline in the 20 years after the end of apartheid.

Looking ahead

In this and future units, we shall revisit many of the topics raised by South Africa's recent history, and indeed the personal experience of Cyril Ramaphosa as a political activist, union leader, business owner, and head of state.

In this unit, we first look beyond South Africa, and ask how a new form of economic organization called capitalism brought affluence, inequality, and threats to environmental sustainability as it spread across the world in the last 250 years, and how the emergence of democracy, which happened much later, both reflected and influenced the changes that capitalism brought, and is still making, to the way we live.

1.2 AFFLUENCE AND INCOME INEQUALITY

Measuring inequality

We know inequality when we see it—look at the unequal scenes (https://tinyco.re/5399771) in different parts of the world captured by flying a drone. We can guess that some countries or societies are more unequal than others. The drone's eye view dramatizes this by showing very rich and very poor neighbourhoods side by side. To be confident in making comparisons of incomes within and between countries and at different periods of time, we use statistics.

Using statistics, we can measure inequality in many ways, but one of the most powerful is to rank everyone in the world by income, from the richest to the poorest. When we do this, we can organize the information to get Figure 1.1. This allows you to place yourself in a three-dimensional visualization of the world.

This is a 3D visualization of global inequality, which we will call the 'skyscraper' figure. Countries in the world are lined up from poorest on the left, to richest on the right. For each country, the average income of the poorest 10% is the lowest bar in the front. The average income of the richest 10% is the highest bar for that country at the back. The width of the bar corresponds to the size of the population.

Take China, for example. Its block is wide because of its large population. Because countries are ordered by average income, the countries immediately to China's left and right have similar average incomes. But some have taller skyscrapers at the back, meaning a greater disparity between the top 10% and the rest of the population, whereas others have a less steep profile. China is coloured red, but its neighbours are yellow and green. We explain how the countries got their colours in Figure 1.1a (page 4). In Section 1.3 (page 6) we discuss how the data shown in the chart allows us to make meaningful comparisons between countries and across different time periods.

decile A subset of observations, formed by ordering the full set of observations according to the values of a particular variable and then splitting the set into ten equally-sized groups. For example, the 1st decile refers to the smallest 10% of values in a set of observations. *See also: percentile.*

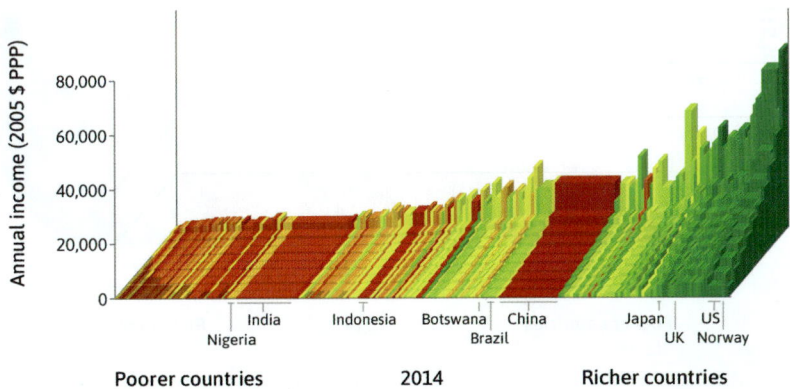

Figure 1.1 World income distribution in 2014: Countries are ranked by average incomes in US dollars at PPP (adjusting for the spending power of a dollar in different countries) from left to right. For each country the heights of the bars show average income for **deciles** of the population, from the poorest 10% in the front, to the richest 10% at the back. The width of the bar indicates the country's population.

GCIP 2015. Global Consumption and Income Project (https://tinyco.re/8468009). Bob Sutcliffe designed the representation of global inequality in Figure 1.1. A first version was published in: Robert B Sutcliffe. 2001. *100 Ways of Seeing an Unequal World*. London: Zed Books. See the interactive version of this graph on the Globalinc website (https://tinyco.re/7434364), where you can also download this data.

1 CAPITALISM AND DEMOCRACY: AFFLUENCE, INEQUALITY, AND THE ENVIRONMENT

Dissecting the skyscraper figure

There is a lot of information in Figure 1.1. In Figure 1.1a, we show alternative ways of looking at the skyscraper that allow you to make comparisons in a range of different ways, comparing both between and within countries, and seeing how the pattern of the global income distribution has changed over time.

To explore all of the slides in this figure, see the online version at https://tinyco.re/2942901.

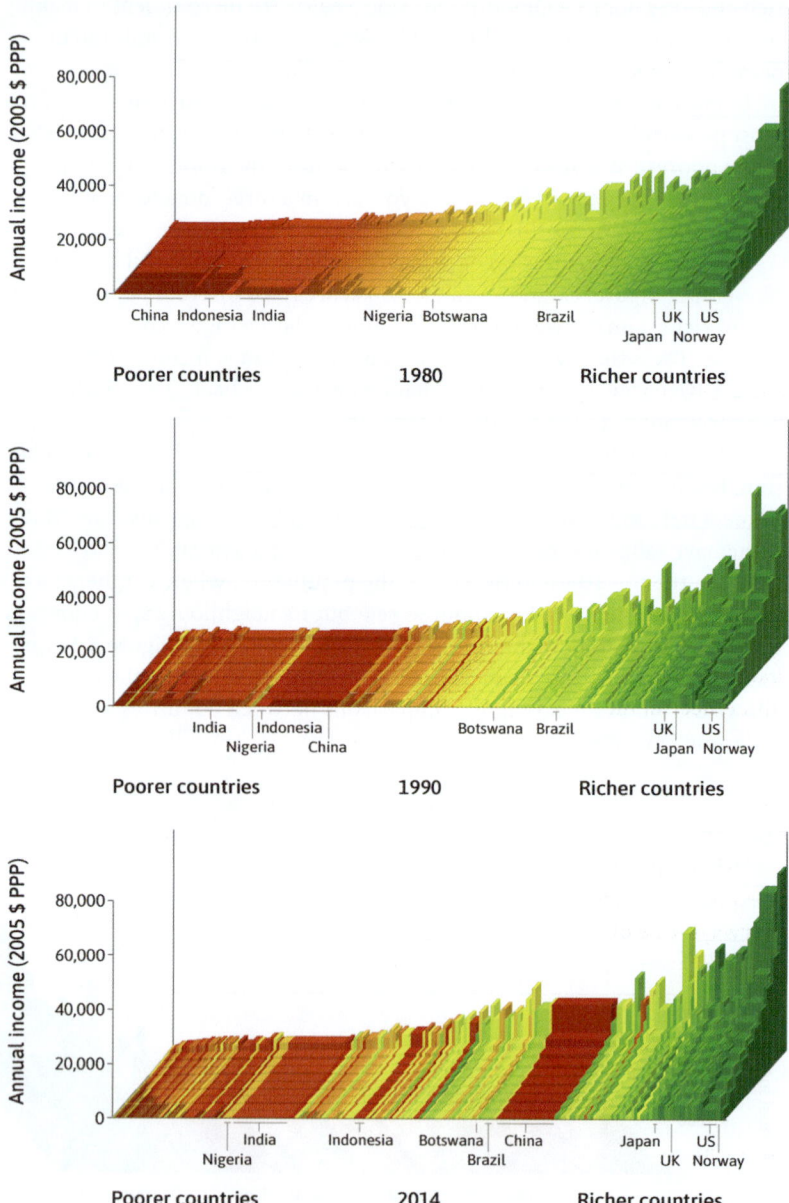

Figure 1.1a Dissecting the global income distribution.

1.2 AFFLUENCE AND INCOME INEQUALITY

1. Singapore and Niger
The average incomes of the poorest 10% to the richest 10% of the population are shown for Niger and Singapore, which are at opposite ends of the global income distribution.

2. Skyscrapers
The skyscraper bars in the back right-hand side of the figure are the richest 10% in some of the richest countries.

3. World income distribution in 1980
The poorest countries, coloured darkest red, were Lesotho and China. The richest (darkest green) were Switzerland, Finland and the US. At that time, the skyscrapers were not as tall as they would become by 2014. The differences between the richest 10% and the rest of a country's population were not as pronounced.

4. World income distribution in 1990
You can see that some countries changed ranking between 1980 and 1990. China (red) is now richer. Some taller skyscrapers have appeared, which means that inequality increased in many countries during the 1980s. If you use the interactive figure (https://tinyco.re/9553483), you can investigate individual countries, for example, to identify the country with the highest skyscraper.

5. World income distribution in 2014
By 2014, many countries had changed their ranking. China had grown rapidly since 1990. But the countries that were richest in 1980 (darkest green) were still rich in 2014.

6. Inequality within countries has risen
Income distributions have become more unequal in many of the richer countries. Some very tall skyscrapers have appeared. In the middle-income countries, too, there is a big step up at the back of the figure because the incomes of the richest 10% are now high relative to the rest of the population. For example, compare China in 1980 and 2014.

7. Skyscrapers
Norway and the US in 2014. Norway has the second-highest average income, but does not have a particularly tall skyscraper for the top decile. This is because income is more evenly distributed in Norway than in some other rich countries. Compare the heights of the top and bottom deciles in Norway with those in the US.

Inequality within and between countries

Two things are clear from the 2014 distribution. First, differences between the rich and the poor are huge *within* every country—the rich have *much* more than the poor. And secondly, there are huge differences in income *between* countries.

We can use the ratio between the heights of the front and back bars as one measure of inequality in a country. We will call it the rich/poor ratio, for obvious reasons.

Using this ratio, we can rank countries by how unequal they were in 2014. In this list, even Norway—one of the world's most equal countries on this measure—is probably less equal than you imagined.

The rich/poor ratio used here is similar to, but not exactly the same as, a commonly used measure of inequality called the 90/10 ratio (https://tinyco.re/7590416). The 90/10 ratio is defined as the ratio between the income of the two individuals at the ninetieth and tenth percentiles. We are instead taking the ratio of the average income of the tenth ('rich') and first ('poor') deciles. The tenth decile is made up of all the people with higher income than the person at the ninetieth percentile, so its average is larger than the income of that person. The first decile is made of all the people with income less than the person at the tenth percentile, and so its average will be lower than the income of that person. Therefore, our rich/poor ratio will be a higher number than the 90/10 ratio for the same country.

	Rich	Poor	Rich/Poor ratio
Botswana	24,523	169	145
Nigeria	4,449	203	22
India	4,446	223	20
US	60,418	3,778	16
Norway	45,302	8,325	5.4

Norway might be the most equal country on this list, but the average income in Norway is 19 times the average income in Nigeria. And the poorest 10% in Norway receive on average almost twice the income of the richest 10% in Nigeria.

While Figure 1.1 shows massive inequality in recent decades, it was not always the case.

A thousand years ago, the world was flat, economically speaking. Although there were differences in income between the regions of the world, the differences were small compared to what was to follow. We now ask, how did we get from that world to this one?

1.3 HOW DID WE GET HERE? THE HOCKEY STICK IN REAL INCOMES

Before we can answer this question, we need to consider how we measure income.

Real GDP per capita: Measuring incomes at different times, and different places

When we measure something in the real world by applying a rule or set of rules to data, the number we get is a known as a statistic. The most common statistic used to measure income is called **gross domestic product (GDP) per capita**.

People earn their incomes by producing and selling goods (these are things you can touch, like a loaf of bread) and services (which you can't touch, but which you buy, like Internet access). gross domestic product (GDP) is the total value of all the goods and services produced in a country in a given period, such as a year.

To make meaningful comparisons between countries and across time, we first need to make four adjustments to the GDP of a given country.

- First, and most crucially we need to divide a country's total GDP by its population, to derive GDP per capita: a measure of average annual income. A poor country with a large population like India may have total GDP many times higher than a rich country with a small population like Belgium—$2.66 trillion compared to $526 billion in 2017 (https://tinyco.re/3953235). But as economists, we are interested in the income of the *typical* inhabitant of a country, so correcting for population is a crucial first stage. In our example, Belgium, with a population of 11.38 million (https://tinyco.re/6100655), has a much larger GDP per capita than India, with a population of 1.34 billion—$46,169 compared to $1,987.
- Second, we need to correct for changes in spending power *within* the country. If GDP per capita rises by 10% in units of the country's currency, but the prices of goods and services have also risen by 10% (there has been 10% **inflation**), then in terms of actual spending power incomes have not risen: people can buy exactly the same goods and services with the money they earn. Economists say that in such a case, there has been no change in *real* incomes. So, in any historical comparison, we need to correct for inflation and calculate **real GDP** per capita (sometimes referred to as GDP at **constant prices**).

> **gross domestic product (GDP) per capita** A measure of the market value of the output of the economy in a given period (GDP) divided by the population.
> **inflation** An increase in the general price level in the economy. Usually measured over a year. *See also: deflation, disinflation.*
> **real GDP** An inflation-adjusted measure of the market value of the output of the economy in a given period. (GDP). *See also: inflation, constant prices, gross domestic product.*
> **constant prices** Prices corrected for increases in prices (inflation) or decreases in prices (deflation) so that a unit of currency represents the same buying power in different periods of time. *See also: purchasing power parity, real GDP.*

- Third, to compare GDP per capita between countries, we need to measure it in the same units. The US dollar is a commonly-used unit.
- Fourth, even after correcting for inflation, and converting into dollars, we also need to do one final adjustment, to reflect big differences in what $1 will buy in the local shops in different countries, even after it has been changed into local currency. We use a technique that is called **purchasing power parity**, or **PPP** for short.

No statistic shows the whole truth, and there are other ways to measure income (tax records, for example). There are also other ways to measure living standards (such as the wage of the person halfway up the income distribution). But GDP per capita has one big advantage: statisticians have calculated it using the same rules for many countries, and over long periods of time. And economists can use historical records to apply the same rules and estimate GDP per capita over periods that go back centuries.

purchasing power parity (PPP) A statistical correction allowing comparisons of the amount of goods people can buy in different countries that have different currencies. *See also: constant prices.*

The hockey stick

We have used GDP statistics and the adjustments described above to create the line graph in Figure 1.2. A line graph is a chart that shows the behaviour of a particular variable or variables over time. The height of each line is an estimate of average income, in terms of real spending power, in a given country at the date on the horizontal axis. Notice that the vertical axis is measured in units of real GDP per capita.

It helps us to understand the big differences between countries today. Some countries—Britain, Italy, and Japan in this figure—'took off' economically before 1900. They (and countries like them) are far to the right, at the richer end of the skyscraper in Figure 1.1.

If you have never seen an ice-hockey stick (or experienced ice hockey (https://tinyco.re/5637337)) this shape is why we call these figures 'hockey-stick curves'.

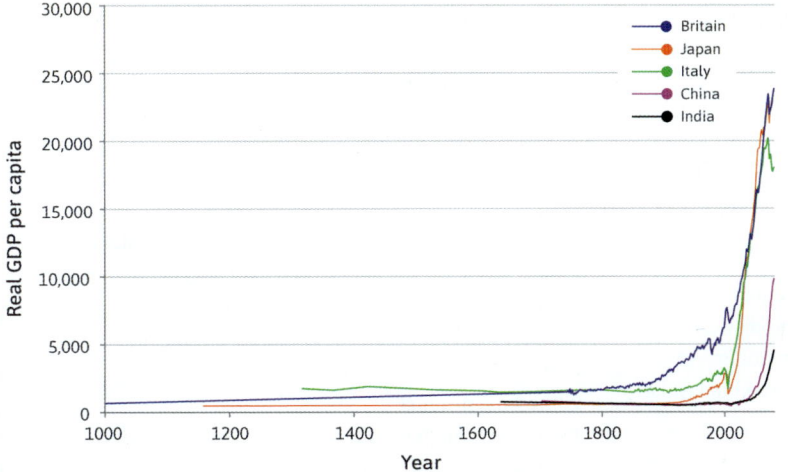

View this data at OWiD https://tinyco.re/3290463

Maddison Project Database (https://tinyco.re/5503002), version 2018. Jutta Bolt, Robert Inklaar, Herman de Jong and Jan Luiten van Zanden (2018), 'Rebasing 'Maddison': New income comparisons and the shape of long-run economic development' (https://tinyco.re/5386746), Maddison Project working paper 10.

Figure 1.2 History's hockey stick: Real gross domestic product per capita in five countries (1000–2016).

1 CAPITALISM AND DEMOCRACY: AFFLUENCE, INEQUALITY, AND THE ENVIRONMENT

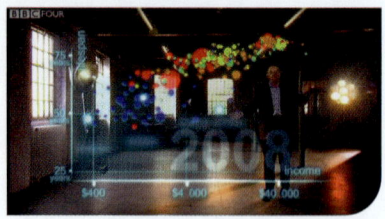

Hans Rosling's 200 Countries, 200 Years, 4 Minutes—The Joy of Stats
https://tinyco.re/3761488

But this happened recently. All countries spent most of the last thousand years in the flatlands to the left. If you want to know more, watch the short video by Hans Rosling, a statistician (https://tinyco.re/3761488). It presents an animated picture of the process by which the world became so unequal, with some countries taking off and others being left behind.

EXERCISE 1.1 INEQUALITY IN THE FOURTEENTH CENTURY
What do you think a 'skyscraper' figure like Figure 1.1 (page 3) would have looked like in the fourteenth century)?

EXERCISE 1.2 USING EXCEL: INCOME DATA AND THE RICH/POOR RATIO
You can see the interactive graph and download an Excel spreadsheet of data that we used to create Figure 1.2 by going to the Globalinc website (https://tinyco.re/9553483) and clicking 'xlsx' where it says, 'You can also download the data here …'.

Choose five countries that you are interested in.

1. For each one, calculate the rich/poor ratio in 1980, 1990 and 2014. (To do this in Excel, follow the step-by-step instructions in the walk-through in Figure 1.3 online (https://tinyco.re/1120058).
2. Describe the differences you find between countries and the changes over time.
3. Can you think of any explanations for these differences?

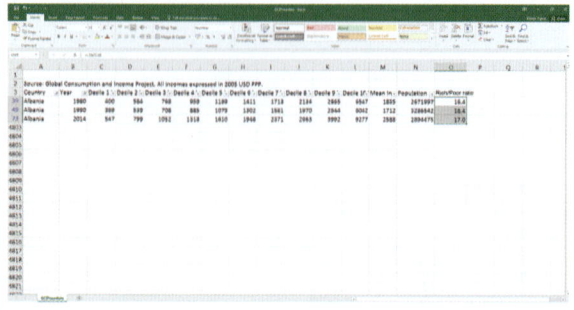

Figure 1.3 Income data and the rich/poor ratio.

1. The data
This is what the data looks like. Column A contains country names, column B contains the year, and columns C to L contain the average income in each decile. Column M contains the mean income in the population, which is the mean of columns C to L.

2. Filter the data to see only the country/countries we need
We apply a filter so that we see only the data we need. This makes the data easier to work with. We filter using the country names in column A.

3. Filter the data to see only the country/countries we need
After completing step 5, only the data for your selected country/countries is shown in the spreadsheet. Data for the other countries is still there, but it is now hidden.

4. Filter the data to see only the years we need
After completing step 6 your spreadsheet should look similar to the example above, with only the countries and years you want to see.

5. Calculate the rich/poor ratio for one row
We calculate the rich/poor ratio in a new column. Rather than calculating ratios manually, you can enter the calculation as a cell formula so Excel will do it for you.

6. Repeat this calculation for the rest of the rows
You don't need to type the same formula many times. Simply copy the formula to other cells to calculate the rich/poor ratio for other years.

7. Round the calculated values to one decimal place
Currently the calculations are not rounded to a given number of decimal places. To change the number of decimal places shown, we need to reformat the cells.

8. Round the calculated values to one decimal place
After step 15, the cell values will be displayed to one decimal place. Excel still stores the full number, but only shows the number of decimal places you specify.

9. The final product
The calculated rich/poor ratios are now rounded to one decimal place.

EXERCISE 1.3 USING EXCEL: LOOKING AT INCOME DISTRIBUTIONS

You will be using the same data as in Exercise 1.2 (https://tinyco.re/9553483) to understand the difference between the mean and the median. Follow the walk-through in Figure 1.4 online (https://tinyco.re/9712810) on how to do the Excel parts of this exercise.

Choose one country from this list (which we will refer to as Country A): Czech Republic, Finland, Netherlands, Norway, or Slovenia. Now choose one country from this list (we refer to this as Country B): Botswana, Central African Republic, Haiti, Jamaica, or Lesotho.

1. In Excel, filter the data so that only rows corresponding to these countries in 2014 appear.
2. The **median** is the 50th percentile (or Decile 5). You can think of everyone in the population lining up according to income, and picking the person who is right in the middle of the line. What is the median income in Country A? How about in Country B?
3. Suppose that the income in Decile 10 changed to $1 million. Would the median in either country increase, decrease, or stay the same? Why?
4. Plot a separate vertical bar chart (called a column chart in Excel) for Country A and Country B, showing the decile on the horizontal axis and income on the vertical axis. The **mean** is a summary statistic that we calculate by adding all values and dividing by the number of values. You can think of the mean as what would happen if everyone in their country brought their income to the same place, and all the money was put in a pile, and the money was then shared equally between everyone. The amount that each person got would be the mean.
5. Look at the bar charts from Question 4. In which decile would you guess that the mean amount would fall? Verify that your answer is similar to the mean income reported in Column M.
6. Column M (labeled 'Mean Income') shows the mean of Columns C to L. In a new column, calculate the mean using the AVERAGE function in Excel and verify that your answer is the same (rounded to the nearest dollar).
7. Suppose that the income in Decile 10 changed to $1 million. Would the mean income in either country increase, decrease, or stay the same? Why? Verify your answer in Excel by changing the value in the cells for Decile 10 and calculating the mean income.

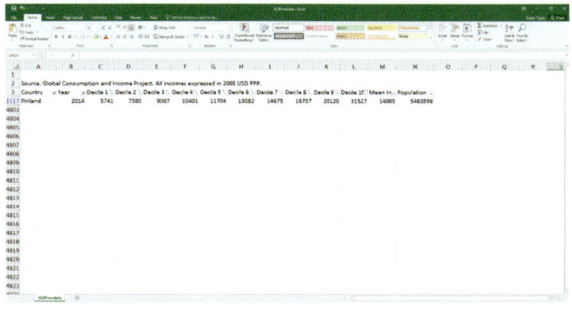

Figure 1.4 Mean and median, and bar chart.

1. The data
We are using the same data as in Exercise 1.2. Column A contains country names, Column B contains the year, and Columns C to L contain the average income in each decile. Column M contains the mean income in the population, which is the mean of Columns C to L. In this example, we have filtered the data to show the income deciles for our chosen country—Finland, in 2014. (See Exercise 1.2 (page 8) for how to do this).

2. Draw a column chart
Your column chart will look similar to the chart shown above, with income on the vertical axis and decile number (1 to 10) on the horizontal axis.

3. Add axis titles and a chart title
Excel's 'Add Chart Element' allows you to add axis titles and a chart title.

4. Calculate the mean income
Excel's AVERAGE function will calculate the mean of the selected cells.

1.4 ECONOMIC GROWTH

Between the years 1000 and 1600 in Figure 1.2, it's hard to see what's going on. The graph uses a 'linear' scale—this means that each 'unit' on the vertical axis represents the same amount (each $1,000 of income is represented by the same distance on the vertical axis).

In some ways, this scale doesn't represent the experience of real people well. For example, if you are in the poorest 10% in Niger and you earn an extra $1,000, your income is now $1,092. Your life is transformed. If you're in the poorest 10% in Singapore, and you earn an extra $1,000, your income is now $4,652. Your life is better, but mostly the same, because $1,000 is a smaller proportion of what you earn already.

Another way of looking at the data in Figure 1.2 is to consider, not just by how much income has grown over these years, but also how fast it has done so—in other words, the *rate* at which it has grown.

Calculating growth rates

In the media, you may have seen headlines about GDP growth, such as 'Country A's economy grew by 2% in 2016–2017' or 'Country B reports a GDP growth rate of 5% this year'. How do economists calculate these figures?

The (real) GDP growth rate is the percentage change in (real) GDP from one year to the next. National statistics agencies usually publish annual real GDP data, which is an estimate of real GDP, measured at the end of every year. Using this data, we can calculate the annual growth rate of real GDP in year t (let's call it g_t) as:

$$g_t \text{ (in \%)} = \frac{\text{GDP}_t - \text{GDP}_{t-1}}{\text{GDP}_{t-1}} \times 100\%$$

Example: If real GDP at the end of this year was $3 billion, and real GDP at the end of last year was $2.8 billion, then the annual growth rate of real GDP this year is:

$$g_t \text{ (in \%)} = \frac{3 - 2.8}{2.8} \times 100\% = 7.14\%$$

As before, a $1 billion increase in a country's real GDP would be very large if real GDP was $3 billion, but not if real GDP was $300 billion. For this reason, percentage changes allow us to compare real GDP growth of a country in different years. That's why we use percentages. If real GDP in Country A grew by 1% compared to 2% in Country B, we can say that Country B's economy grew faster than Country A's.

When we see growth reported, it is often reported as the average rate during a period of years. This is the case whether it is the growth of the economy (real GDP growth) or the growth of incomes (real GDP per capita). For example, knowing that real GDP per capita in China grew by an average of 2.97% per year between 1952 and 1978, and 8.12% between 1978 and 2007, is much more useful than knowing the number in any year. Calculating this statistic involves more advanced mathematics. If you want to learn how to work this out, see the 'Find out more' box about compound growth rates, below. The 'Find out more' box about the 'rule of 70' for growth rates gives a simple rule of thumb that lets you calculate how many years it takes for real GDP per capita to double when you know the compound growth rate.

1.4 ECONOMIC GROWTH

FIND OUT MORE

Compound growth rates

Once we've calculated the annual growth rate for a particular year, how can we tell if the country's economy has grown faster or slower than usual? One way is to compare the annual growth rate with the average annual growth rate (known as the compound annual growth rate or CAGR) over a given time period. For example, if real GDP per capita grew by 1% this year, but on average it grew by 2% between 1950 and 2010, then we can say that the economy's growth performance this year is below average.

To calculate the compound annual growth rate, we do not take averages, but instead use the principle of compounding. We usually calculate compound annual growth rates over long periods, such as decades. As the example below shows, failing to account for compounding would give vastly different growth rate figures.

Example: If real GDP per capita was $12,800 in 1950 and $42,300 in 2011, then the compound annual growth rate (CAGR) over these 61 years is:

$$\text{CAGR} = g \text{ (in \%)} = \left[\left(\frac{\text{GDP}_{2011}}{\text{GDP}_{1950}}\right)^{\frac{1}{61}} - 1\right] \times 100\%$$
$$= \left[\left(\frac{42,300}{12,800}\right)^{\frac{1}{61}} - 1\right] \times 100\%$$
$$= 2.0\%$$

If we instead take the average of the growth rate, then we would get:

$$g \text{ (in \%)} = \frac{1}{61}\left(\frac{\text{GDP}_{2011} - \text{GDP}_{1950}}{\text{GDP}_{1950}}\right) \times 100\%$$
$$= \frac{1}{61}\left(\frac{42,300 - 12,800}{12,800}\right) \times 100\%$$
$$= 3.8\%$$

In this example, failing to account for compounding gives an answer that is almost twice as large as the actual annual growth rate.

FIND OUT MORE

The rule of 70 for growth rates

Calculations involving compound growth rates are difficult to do mentally, but there is a handy rule of thumb that we can use for one particular situation. If the economy is growing at a constant rate, the number of years it will take for real GDP per capita to double is approximately 70 divided by the annual growth rate:

$$\text{number of years for real GDP per capita to double} = \frac{70}{\text{annual growth rate (\%)}}$$

For this reason, we refer to this approximation as the 'rule of 70'. The rule of 70 is useful if we are looking at growth rates over long periods of time, in which case the number in the denominator is the compound annual growth rate.

Example: If the compound annual growth rate of real GDP per capita is 2%, then it would take approximately 70/2 = 35 years for real GDP per capita to double.

If real GDP per capita was growing more slowly at a rate of 1%, then it would take approximately 70/1 = 70 years for real GDP per capita to double.

OPTIONAL EXERCISE 1.3.1 USING EXCEL: CALCULATING COMPOUND GROWTH RATES

Download and save the spreadsheet (https://tinyco.re/4744778) containing some of the GDP data used to make Figure 1.2.

1. Calculate the CAGR for China, Britain, Italy, and India between 1950 and 2011. Follow the walk-through in Figure 1.5 online (https://tinyco.re/9480674) on how to do this in Excel.

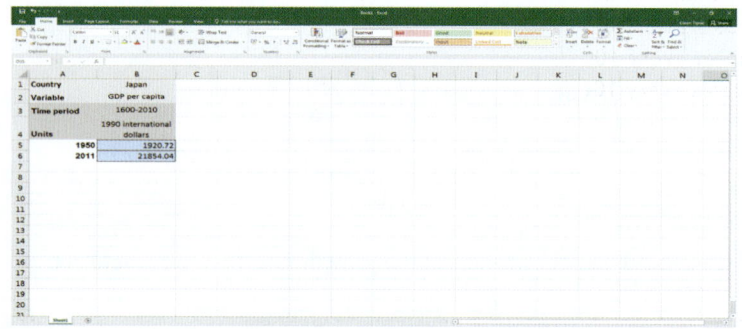

Figure 1.5 Calculating CAGR in Excel.

1. The data
Shown above is an excerpt of the data. In this example, we are using data from Japan for the years 1950–2011. Column A contains years, and Column B contains real GDP per capita values.

2. Calculate the difference in years
For the CAGR calculation, we need the values for real GDP per capita, and the difference in years (end year minus start year).

3. Calculate the CAGR
To calculate the CAGR, we will type the CAGR formula from 'Find out more: Compound growth rates' into Excel, using the cells containing GDP values in 1950 and 2011.

2. For each of these four countries, find the approximate number of years (rounding up) that it took for real GDP per capita to double its 1950 value.

Example: In Japan, real GDP per capita was 1,920.72 in 1950. Scrolling down the spreadsheet, we can see that real GDP per capita was 3,986.43 in 1960, which is approximately double the value in 1950. Therefore, it took Japan roughly 10 years for real GDP per capita to double its 1950 value.

3. Use the rule of 70 and the CAGR from Question 1 to calculate the approximate number of years required for real GDP per capita to double. Check that these numbers are close to your answer to Question 2.

A ratio scale

We can directly compare growth rates across countries over time if we plot the same hockey-stick data using a different scale on the vertical axis. In Figure 1.2, the scale went from 10,000 to 15,000 to 20,000 etc. by adding 5,000 at each step. Instead, in Figure 1.6, we go from 500 to 1,000 to 2,000, to 4,000 by doubling the number at each step. This is called a **ratio scale**. If you find this description confusing, just compare the numbers on the vertical axis of Figure 1.2 with those in Figure 1.6. Remember that we are using exactly the same data in each of these figures.

We say that the ratio scale captures growth rates. Why?

Using the ratio scale, if GDP grows by the same percentage every year, or every 100 years, the graph will be a straight line. So, if GDP doubles every 100 years, the line would be straight, sloping upwards. If, instead of doubling, the level quadrupled every 100 years, the line would still be straight, but it would be twice as steep. We say the growth rate was twice as high.

So, with a ratio scale:

- *A straight line* means a constant growth rate.
- *A steeper line* means a faster growth rate.

Using the ratio scale, we can immediately see something that was not obvious in Figure 1.2—when the hockey stick turns up, the lines for the latecomers Japan and China are much steeper than was the case in Britain or Italy. This means that their growth rates at that time were much faster.

> **ratio scale** A scale that uses distances on a graph to represent ratios. For example, the ratio between 3 and 6, and between 6 and 12, is the same (the larger number is twice the smaller number). In a ratio scale chart, all changes by the same ratio are represented by the same vertical distance. This contrasts with a linear scale, where the distance between 3 and 6, and between 6 and 9, is the same (in this case, 3). *Also known as a log scale (in for example, Microsoft Excel).*

EXERCISE 1.4 USING EXCEL: INTERPRETING GRAPHS DRAWN USING A RATIO SCALE

Figure 1.2 (page 7) uses a conventional scale for the vertical axis, and Figure 1.6 (page 14) uses a ratio scale.

1. For Britain, identify a period of time when its growth rate was increasing, and another period in which its growth rate was roughly constant. Which figure did you use, and why?
2. Identify a period during which real GDP per capita in Britain was shrinking (a negative growth rate) faster than in India. Which figure did you use and why?
3. Advanced: if you studied the optional 'Find out more: Compound growth rates' (page 11), use Figure 1.6 to identify whether Britain between 1800 and 1900 or Japan between 1900 and 2000 grew at a faster rate. Use the GDP data for Figure 1.2 (https://tinyco.re/4744778) to calculate the CAGR for Britain over the period 1800–1900, and for Japan over the period 1900–2000, and use these calculated growth rates to verify your answer.

1 CAPITALISM AND DEMOCRACY: AFFLUENCE, INEQUALITY, AND THE ENVIRONMENT

> **QUESTION 1.1 CHOOSE THE CORRECT ANSWER(S)**
> The GDP per capita of Greece was $22,494 in 2012 and $21,966 in 2013. Based on these figures, the growth rate of GDP between 2012 and 2013 (to two decimal places) was:
>
> ☐ −2.40%
> ☐ 2.35%
> ☐ −2.35%
> ☐ −0.24%

To explore all of the slides in this figure, see the online version at https://tinyco.re/7331841.
View this data at OWiD https://tinyco.re/3125412

Maddison Project Database (https://tinyco.re/5503002), version 2018. Jutta Bolt, Robert Inklaar, Herman de Jong and Jan Luiten van Zanden. 2018. 'Rebasing 'Maddison': New income comparisons and the shape of long-run economic development' (https://tinyco.re/5386746), Maddison Project Working Paper No. 10.

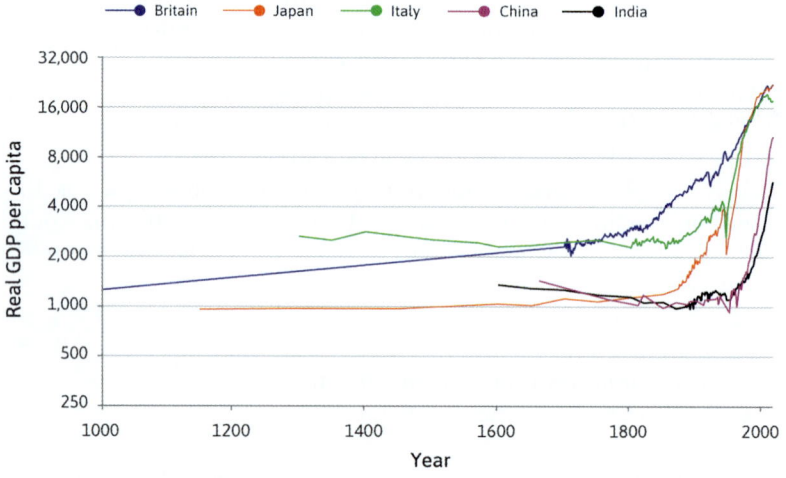

Figure 1.6 History's hockey stick: Living standards in five countries (1000–2016) using the ratio scale.

1. History's hockey stick
There were cultural changes and scientific advances in many parts of the world over the entire period shown in the figure, but living standards only began to rise in a sustained way from the eighteenth century (1700–1799) onwards. The figure looks like a hockey stick, and our eyes are drawn to the kink.

2. Before 1800, we have less information and so there are fewer data points (dots) in the graph
For the period before 1800, we have less information about GDP per capita, which is why there are fewer data points in that part of the figure.

3. A line is drawn through the data points
For each country the data points shown at the previous step have been joined with straight lines. Before 1800, we can't see how living standards fluctuated from year to year.

4. Britain
The bend in the hockey stick is not as abrupt in Britain, where growth began around 1650.

5. Japan
In Japan, the kink is more defined, occurring around 1870.

6. China and India
The kink for China and India happened in the second half of the twentieth century (post-1950). Real GDP per capita fell in India under British colonial rule from the early seventeenth century until the mid-nineteenth century. (An even sharper decline took place in China from the beginning of the sixteenth century until the Chinese revolution ended the domination of China's politics and economics by European nations).

7. Compare growth rates in China and Japan
The ratio scale makes it possible to see that recent growth rates in Japan and China were higher than elsewhere.

1.4 ECONOMIC GROWTH

QUESTION 1.2 CHOOSE THE CORRECT ANSWER(S)
The following graphs show the real GDP per capita of four countries, plotted according to the linear scale and ratio scale respectively.

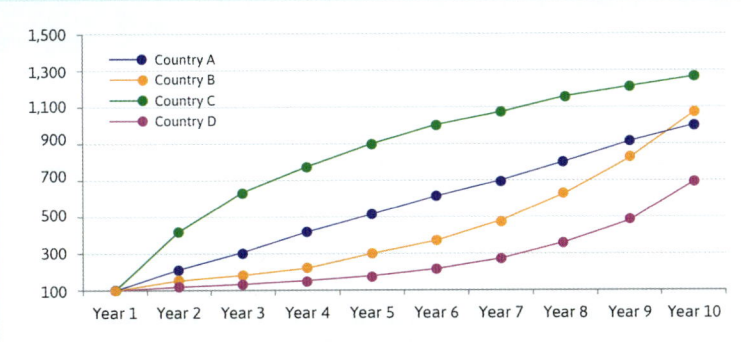

Figure 1.7 Real GDP per capita: Linear scale.

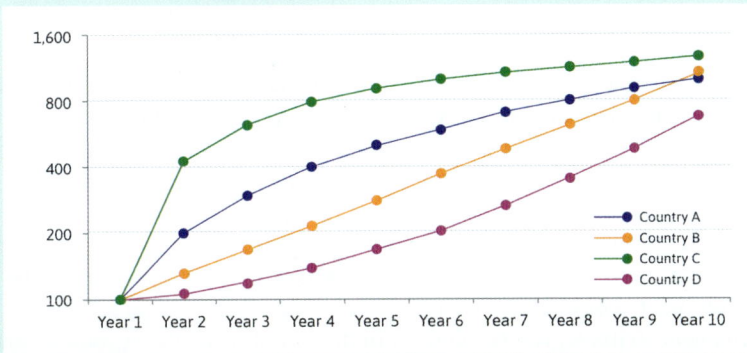

Figure 1.8 Real GDP per capita: Ratio scale.

Based on this information, which of the following statements are correct?

☐ Country B's real GDP per capita grew at a constant rate.
☐ Over the 10 years shown, Country A's real GDP per capita grew at the fastest rate, on average.
☐ Over the 10 years shown, Country D's real GDP per capita grew at the slowest rate, on average.
☐ Country C's real GDP per capita grew at a constant rate.

What influences growth and inequality?
From Figures 1.2 and 1.6, we learned three things about growth and inequality:

- For a very long time, living standards did not grow in any sustained way, anywhere.
- In some countries—India and China notably—per-capita income fell over long periods.

15

- When sustained growth occurred, it began at different times in different countries. It happened first in Britain, then in Italy and Japan (though at different rates), and finally in India and China. This led to vast differences in living standards around the world, as the video by Hans Rosling (https://tinyco.re/3761488) in Section 1.3 showed.

Why were there leaders and laggards?

In some economies (as illustrated in Figure 1.6 by China and India), substantial improvements in people's living standards did not occur until they gained independence from colonial rule or interference by European nations:

- *India:* According to Angus Deaton, an economist who specializes in the analysis of poverty, when 300 years of British rule of India ended in 1947: 'It is possible that the deprivation in childhood of Indians … was as severe as that of any large group in history'. In the closing years of British rule, a child born in India could expect to live for 27 years. Fifty years on, life expectancy at birth in India had risen to 65 years.
- *China:* It had once been richer than Britain, but by the middle of the twentieth century, GDP per capita in China was one-fifteenth that of Britain.
- *Latin America:* Neither Spanish colonial rule, nor its aftermath following the independence of most Latin American nations early in the nineteenth century, saw anything resembling the hockey-stick upturn in living standards experienced by the countries in Figures 1.2 and 1.3.

The emergence in the eighteenth century in Europe of a new way of producing goods and services, called **capitalism**, progressively came to be the dominant **economic system** in rich countries. This encouraged a 'permanent technological revolution'. In the rest of this unit, we look at how capitalism changed the world around us, and why, much later, it was followed by a new **political system**, **democracy**.

In the introduction, we explained how both capitalism and democracy influenced the lives of South Africans in the twentieth century.

South Africa was (and is) an economy in which capitalism plays a crucial role and its economy continued to grow, even during apartheid, fueled in part by the mineworkers that Ramaphosa's union represented. Whites benefited disproportionately. With the coming of democracy, many expected that the benefits of growth would be shared more equally. But we know that some stayed poor, and some did a lot better. The relationship between capitalism and democracy, and how well the economy functions, is not simple.

As we move through the units, we will help you to see how **governments** can, in principle, use well-designed policies to make economic outcomes better and fairer, but can be the cause of worse or unfair outcomes too.

First, we need to understand more about how a process of continuous growth emerged.

---

capitalism An economic system in which the method of producing goods and services is centred on firms, which own and control the capital goods that are used in production. Private property, markets, and firms all play an important role in capitalism.

economic system The institutions that organize the production and distribution of goods and services in an entire economy.

political system A set of principles, laws, and procedures that determine how governments will be selected, and how those governments will make and implement decisions that affect all or most members of a population.

democracy A political system, that ideally gives equal political power to all citizens, defined by individual rights such as freedom of speech, assembly, and the press; fair elections in which virtually all adults are eligible to vote; and in which the government leaves office if it loses.

Angus Deaton. 2013. *The Great Escape: health, wealth, and the origins of inequality* (https://tinyco.re/5750302). Princeton: Princeton University Press.

government Within a given territory, the only body that can dictate what people must do or not do, and can legitimately use force and restraints on an individual's freedom to achieve that end. *Also known as:* state.

1.4 ECONOMIC GROWTH

The nature and causes of economic growth

Understanding why and how growth has occurred in the way that it has, is one of the most important questions that economists have asked. The founder of modern **economics**, Adam Smith, gave his most important book the title, *An Inquiry into the Nature and Causes of the Wealth of Nations*.

economics The study of how people interact with each other and with their natural surroundings in providing their livelihoods, and how this changes over time.

GREAT ECONOMISTS

Adam Smith

Adam Smith (1723–1790) is considered by many to be the founder of modern economics. Raised by a widowed mother in Scotland, he went on to study philosophy at the University of Glasgow and later at Oxford.

Adam Smith. (1776) 2003. *An Inquiry into the Nature and Causes of the Wealth of Nations* (https://tinyco.re/9804148). New York: NY: Random House Publishing Group.

In *An Inquiry into the Nature and Causes of the Wealth of Nations*, published in 1776, Smith asked: how can society coordinate the independent activities of large numbers of economic actors—producers, transporters, sellers, consumers—often unknown to one another and widely scattered across the world? Previous notions of political and economic organization relied on rulers imposing order on their subjects. Smith's radical claim was that coordination among all of these actors might spontaneously arise, without any person or **institution** consciously attempting to create or maintain it.

Even more radical was his idea that this could take place as a result of individuals pursuing their self-interest, rather than attempting to coordinate, cooperate or care for one another: 'It is not from the benevolence of the butcher, the brewer, or the baker that we expect our dinner, but from their regard to their own interest,' he wrote.

In *The Wealth of Nations*, Smith introduced one of the most enduring metaphors in the history of economics—the 'invisible hand'. The businessman, he wrote, 'intends only his own gain, and he is in this, as in many other cases, led by an invisible hand to promote an end which was no part of his intention. Nor is it always the worse for the society that it was no part of it. By pursuing his own interest, he frequently promotes that of the society more effectually than when he really intends to promote it.'

Among Smith's insights is the idea that a significant source of prosperity is the **division of labour**, or **specialization**. Smith illustrated this idea in a famous passage on the pin factory: ten men undertaking to make an entire pin from start to finish separately and independently: 'certainly could not each of them have made twenty [pins], perhaps not [even] one pin in a day.' But where the ten men each fully specialized in one or two of 18 distinct operations involved in making pins, they could produce close to 50,000 pins a day. Specialization greatly increased productivity.

institution The laws and social customs governing the way people interact in society.
division of labour The specialization of producers to carry out different tasks in the production process. *Also known as: specialization.*
specialization This takes place when a country or some other entity produces a narrower range of goods and services than it consumes, acquiring the goods and services that it does not produce by trade.

> **market** A way of connecting people who may mutually benefit by exchanging goods or services through a process of buying and selling.

Smith also observed that such specialization is constrained by the 'extent of the **market**'; such an enormous number of pins would never be produced unless there were many buyers and those could only be found if the market extended far from their point of production. The pin makers themselves could not possibly need the vast quantity of pins they were able to produce. The construction of navigable canals and the expansion of foreign trade thus fostered specialization. And the resulting prosperity itself expanded the 'extent of the market', in a virtuous cycle of economic expansion.

But Smith did not think that people were guided entirely by self-interest, nor did he consider the market system perfect. In the same book in which he first used the phrase 'invisible hand', 17 years before *The Wealth of Nations*, he wrote:

> How selfish soever man may be supposed, there are evidently some principles in his nature which interest him in the fortunes of others, and render their happiness necessary to him, though he derives nothing from it except the pleasure of seeing it.

Adam Smith. 1759. *The Theory of Moral Sentiments* (https://tinyco.re/6582039). London: Printed for A. Millar, and A. Kincaid and J. Bell.

He also saw that the market system had some failings, especially if sellers banded together to form **monopolies**, so as to avoid competing with one another. Smith specifically targeted monopolies that were protected by governments, such as the British East India Company—a monopoly created by the government—that not only controlled trade between India and Britain, but also administered much of the British colony there.

He also agreed with his contemporaries that there was a role for government in a market system in protecting its nation from external enemies, and ensuring justice through the police and the court system. Smith was also an advocate of government investment in education and in public works, such as bridges, roads, and canals.

> **monopoly** A firm that is the only seller of a product without close substitutes. Also refers to a market with only one seller. *See also:* monopoly power, natural monopoly.

> **QUESTION 1.3 CHOOSE THE CORRECT ANSWER(S)**
> Which of the following statements regarding Adam Smith are correct?
>
> ☐ Adam Smith believed in the role of the government to improve societal welfare.
> ☐ Adam Smith believed that all markets were characterized by perfect competition.
> ☐ Adam Smith advocated that economic agents were guided entirely by self-interest.
> ☐ Adam Smith claimed that coordination among a large number of economic actors (producers, transporters, sellers, consumers), often unknown to one another, might spontaneously arise without any person or institution consciously attempting to create or maintain it.

1.5 THE PERMANENT TECHNOLOGICAL REVOLUTION: ENGINE OF GROWTH

Figure 1.2 (page 7) is flat for a long time, and then suddenly curves upward. We know that remarkable scientific and technological advances occurred at more or less the same time as the upward kink in the hockey stick in Britain in the middle of the eighteenth century.

In everyday usage, 'technology' refers to machinery, equipment, and devices developed using scientific knowledge. In the language of economics, **technology** is more specific. It is a process that takes a set of materials and other inputs—including the work of people and capital goods (such as machines)—and creates an output. For example, a technology for making a cake can be described by the recipe. It specifies the combination of inputs (ingredients such as flour, and labour such as stirring) needed to create the output (the cake).

The Industrial Revolution

The eighteenth century in Britain marked the beginning of a wave of technological advances and organizational changes that transformed an agrarian and craft-based economy into a commercial and industrial powerhouse. David Landes, an economic historian, wrote that the **Industrial Revolution** was 'an interrelated succession of technological changes' that transformed the societies in which these changes took place.

During the long flat portion of Figure 1.2, traditional craft-based techniques were used in most production processes, such as hand-weaving. Some of the earliest steps in the Industrial Revolution were in the production of textiles, such as the spinning jenny, a machine that enabled an individual to produce multiple spools of threads simultaneously. By the time the inventor, James Hargreaves died, there were over 20,000 spinning jennys in use across Britain. The power loom, which mechanized the process of weaving cloth, was developed in the 1780s. Important new technologies were introduced in energy and transportation as well as in textiles.

The cumulative character of these developments led to them together being called the Industrial Revolution. The new era brought new ideas, new discoveries, new methods and new machines, making old ideas and old tools obsolete. These new ways were, in turn, made obsolete by even newer ones.

While the Industrial Revolution was the impetus for the upturn of the hockey stick in Britain, it was not a one-off event: the process of technological innovation has been more or less continuous since then.

Technological progress

So far, we have looked at the world using incomes to compare countries, or the past with the present. This isn't the only way we can measure change. We can ask other questions, such as: How much work does it take to stay alive? How quickly can we communicate? (https://tinyco.re/1224757)

As **technological progress** revolutionized production, the time required to make a pair of shoes fell by half in only a few decades. The same was true of spinning and weaving, and of making cakes in a factory. This marked the beginning of a permanent technological revolution, where the amount of time required for producing most products fell generation after generation.

---

technology A process taking a set of materials and other inputs, including the work of people and capital goods (such as machines), to produce an output.

Industrial Revolution A wave of technological advances and organizational changes starting in Britain in the eighteenth century, which transformed an agrarian and craft-based economy into a commercial and industrial economy.

David S. Landes. 2003. *The Unbound Prometheus: Technological Change and Industrial Development in Western Europe from 1750 to the Present.* Cambridge: Cambridge University Press.

technological progress A change in technology that reduces the amount of resources (labour, machines, land, energy, time) required to produce a given amount of the output.

1 CAPITALISM AND DEMOCRACY: AFFLUENCE, INEQUALITY, AND THE ENVIRONMENT

Transformational technological change is still occurring. In his TED Talk, Hans Rosling claims that we should say, 'Thank you, industrialization' for creating the washing machine, a device that transformed the wellbeing of millions of women.
https://tinyco.re/7334115

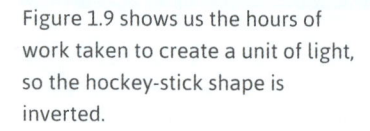

Figure 1.9 shows us the hours of work taken to create a unit of light, so the hockey-stick shape is inverted.

William Nordhaus. 1998. 'Do Real Output and Real Wage Measures Capture Reality? The History of Lighting Suggests Not' (https://tinyco.re/0949356). Cowles Foundation for Research in Economics Paper 1078.

Producing more with less work

If we need to work less to produce the basic things we need, technological changes can create significant increases in living standards.

Nobel prize-winner William Nordhaus measured this trend over thousands of years, by looking at the resources required to create light. Our distant ancestors typically had nothing brighter than a campfire at night. The first great technological breakthrough in lighting from campfire came 40,000 years ago, with the use of lamps that burned animal or vegetable oils. The Babylonians (1750 BC) used sesame oil. Three thousand years later, someone invented tallow candles. Since then, lighting has become more and more efficient through gas lamps, kerosene lamps, filament bulbs, fluorescent bulbs, and so on.

Today, the productivity of labour in producing light is half a million times greater than it was among our ancestors around their campfires. To put this in perspective, Figure 1.9 shows how much time it would have taken, starting 100,000 years ago, to produce the same amount of light as a modern low-energy lightbulb produces in one hour. It is in the shape of the hockey sticks that we saw when we were investigating growth of income, but now it is one that has been turned to face downwards, because the units (hours of work) are getting smaller. What would have taken a week's work 100,000 years ago now takes just a fraction of a second, at least in a modern economy like the US.

Time saved in creating light is time that can be used to produce other goods and services. This is an example of how growth happens.

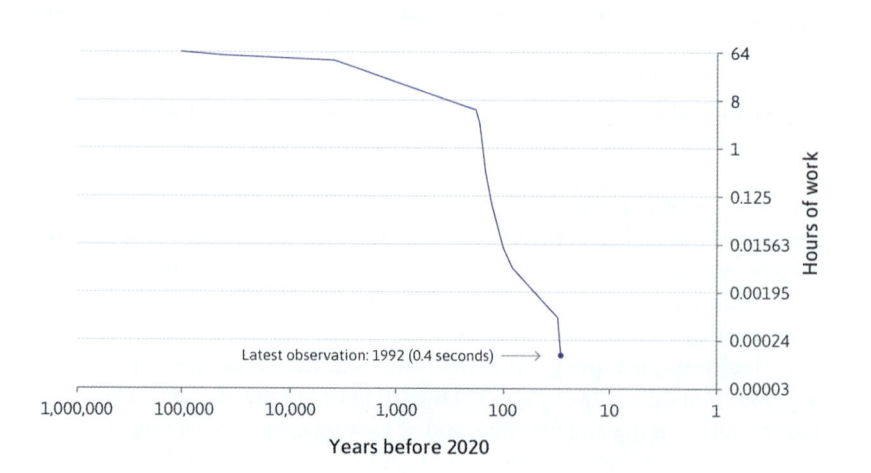

Figure 1.9 Hours of work required to produce 1,000 lumen-hours (roughly equal to the hourly light output of an 18 watt low-energy bulb). Note that the ratio scale is used for the horizontal axis as well as the vertical axis in this figure. This allows us to see more clearly what has happened in the last 200 years.

20

1.5 THE PERMANENT TECHNOLOGICAL REVOLUTION: ENGINE OF GROWTH

QUESTION 1.4 CHOOSE THE CORRECT ANSWER(S)

Figure 1.10 shows the productivity of labour in producing light, measured in lumen-hours per hour of labour, using different technologies.

Technology	Approximate date	Lumen-hours per hour of labour
Open wood fire	From earliest time	17
Animal or vegetable fat lamp	38000–9000 BC	20
Babylonian sesame oil lamp	1750 BC	24
Tallow candle	1800	186
Tallow candle	1830	333
Kerosene lamp	1875–1885	4,400
Town gas (Welsbach mantle)	1885–1895	12,000
Town gas (Welsbach mantle)	1916	83,000
Electric filament lamp	1930	96,000
Electric filament lamp	1940	182,000
Electric filament lamp	1950	530,000
Electric filament lamp	1960	980,000
Electric filament lamp	1970	1,800,000
Compact fluorescent	1992	8,400,000

Tables 15.2 and 15.3 from Gregory Clark. 2007. *A Farewell to Alms: A Brief Economic History of the World.* Princeton, NJ: Princeton University Press.

Figure 1.10 The productivity of labour in producing light.

Based on this information, which of the following statements is correct?

- ☐ The labour productivity of producing light increased roughly linearly over the years.
- ☐ The productivity of labour in producing light using compact fluorescent technology is half a million times greater than with the Babylonian sesame oil lamp.
- ☐ The kerosene lamp in the late 1800s was more than ten times more efficient in terms of labour productivity than the tallow candles in 1830.
- ☐ The labour productivity of producing light roughly doubled in almost every decade between 1930 and 1970.

1.6 ANOTHER ENGINE OF GROWTH: MORE MACHINES AND TOOLS PER WORKER

While Figure 1.9 paints a striking picture of how little labour is required to produce light in a modern economy, it is not a picture that applies to everyone in the world. For many people in poor countries, often with no access to grid electricity, providing even basic light in the home still absorbs a significant fraction of their incomes (https://tinyco.re/6549488). This is because the 'technology' of light—as defined by economists—is not useful unless it is combined with what we call 'technology' in everyday speech: light bulbs, power cables, power plants, and the resources to pay for and maintain them.

Economists call the goods required to produce other goods and services '**capital goods**'.

While the Industrial Revolution in Britain was driven by technology (in the economist's sense), it could only be *implemented* by a large increase in the amount of capital goods in the economy. This is shown in Figure 1.11, which shows the path traced by the increase in output per worker when capital goods per worker increased in Britain, starting in the middle of the eighteenth century.

capital goods The equipment, buildings, and other durable inputs used in producing goods and services, including where applicable any patents or other intellectual property that is used. Raw materials used in production are referred to as intermediate inputs.

To explore all of the slides in this figure, see the online version at https://tinyco.re/6555570.

Robert C. Allen. 2012. 'Technology and the Great Divergence: Global Economic Development Since 1820'. *Explorations in Economic History* 49 (1) (January): pp. 1–16.

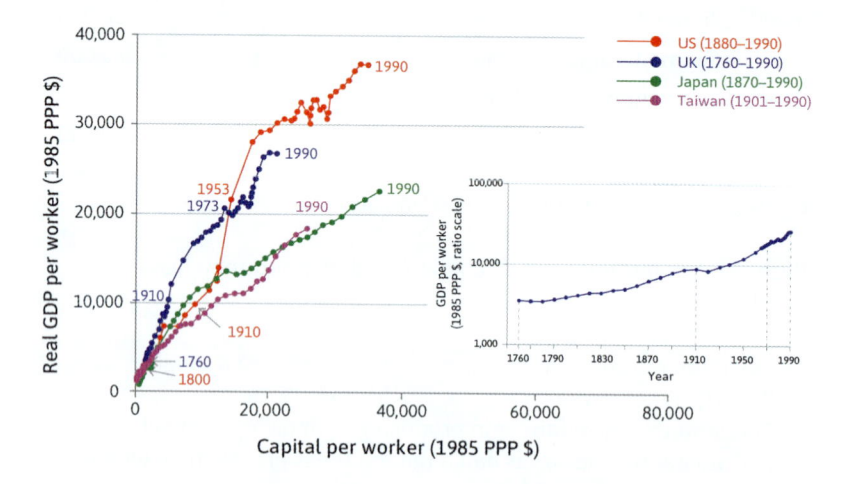

Figure 1.11 The hockey stick and the accumulation of capital.

1. The United Kingdom
The data begins in 1760 at the bottom corner of the chart, and ends in 1990 with much higher capital intensity and productivity.

2. GDP per worker
The right-hand side of the diagram shows the same points in the familiar hockey-stick curve for real GDP per worker, using the ratio scale.

3. The United States
In the US, productivity overtook the UK by 1910 and has remained higher since.

4. Japan and Taiwan
The paths of Japan and Taiwan show that moving along the hockey-stick curve of living standards requires capital accumulation and the adoption of new technology.

If we want to understand the hockey stick, it is important first to understand the nature of capital goods. First, because capital goods do not fall from the sky: all countries that have successfully moved from poverty to affluence have done so, of necessity, by accumulating large amounts of capital. We will also see that a crucial feature of capital*ism* is who *owns* and *controls* the capital goods in an economy.

1.7 THE CAPITALIST REVOLUTION

Capitalism is a way of organizing production—and with it, much of society—that began at around the time of the Industrial Revolution. Since then, we have seen that, the lives of much of humanity have been massively transformed. But capitalism, while it has produced affluence on an unprecedented scale, has also been associated with extraordinary inequalities, and threats to the quality of the natural environment.

Defining capitalism

Capitalism is an economic system characterized by a particular combination of institutions, by which we mean:

- *An economic system* is a way of organizing the production and distribution of goods and services in an entire economy.
- *Institutions* are the different sets of laws and social customs regulating production and distribution in different ways in families, private businesses, markets and government bodies.

We define a capitalist economy as one that combines three particular institutions:

- **private property**
- **markets**
- **firms**

'Capitalism'—in which, for the most part, capital goods are privately owned, can be contrasted with 'centrally planned' economies where the government owns all or nearly all of them, and is the key institution controlling production, and deciding how and to whom goods and services should be distributed. Central planning was the economic system in the Soviet Union, East Germany and many other eastern European countries prior to the end of Communist Party rule in the early 1990s.

Centrally planned economies describe one extreme, which has largely disappeared—almost the only exception is North Korea (Democratic People's Republic of Korea). The nature of what we shall describe as 'capitalist economies' varies considerably across the globe. How private property, markets, and firms combine with one another, and with families, governments, and other institutions, differs greatly between countries.

We shall, for example, refer to both China and the US as capitalist economies, because both share many of the characteristics of capitalism. But they differ greatly in the extent to which the government influences economic affairs (as well as in many other ways). Furthermore—and importantly—*no* economic system in the world today can be described as 'pure' capitalism. Even in the US, for example, only between two-thirds and three-quarters of GDP is produced by what we would call capitalist enterprises.

---

capitalism An economic system in which the method of producing goods and services is centred on firms, which own and control the capital goods that are used in production. Private property, markets, and firms all play an important role in capitalism.

private property The right and expectation that one can enjoy one's possessions in ways of one's own choosing, exclude others from their use, and dispose of them by gift or sale to others who then become their owners.

market A way of connecting people who may mutually benefit by exchanging goods or services through a process of buying and selling.

firm A business organization which pays wages and salaries to employ people, and purchases inputs, to produce and market goods and services with the intention of making a profit.

Private property

Over history, the extent of private property has varied. In some societies, such as the hunters and gatherers who were our distant ancestors, almost nothing except personal ornaments and clothing was owned by individuals. In others, crops and animals were private property, but land was not. In other economic systems, some human beings—slaves—were private property.

Private property may be owned by an individual, a family, a business, or some entity other than the government. Yet some things that we value are not private property—for example, the air we breathe and most of the knowledge we use cannot be owned, bought, or sold.

> **QUESTION 1.5 CHOOSE THE CORRECT ANSWER(S)**
> Which of the following are examples of private property?
>
> ☐ computers belonging to your college
> ☐ a farmer's land in the Soviet Union (under Communist Party rule)
> ☐ shares in a company
> ☐ a worker's skills

Markets

Markets are a means of transferring goods or services from one person to another:

- *They are reciprocated:* Unlike gifts and theft, one person's transfer of a good or service to another is directly reciprocated by a transfer in the other direction (either of another good or service as in barter exchange, or money, or a promise of a later transfer when one buys on credit).
- *They are voluntary:* Both transfers—by the buyer and the seller—are voluntary because the things being exchanged are private property. The fact that the exchange takes place means that it must be beneficial in the opinion of both parties. In this, markets differ from theft, and also from the transfers of goods and services in a centrally planned economy.
- *In most markets there is competition:* A seller charging a high price, for example, will find that buyers prefer to buy from other competing sellers.

Markets may be competitive, but they are also cooperative. Each of us, pursuing our private objectives, can work together, producing and distributing goods and services in a way that, while far from perfect, is in many cases better than the alternatives.

EXERCISE 1.5 THE POOREST MAN'S COTTAGE

'The poorest man may in his cottage bid defiance to all the forces of the Crown. It may be frail, its roof may shake; the wind may blow through it; the storms may enter, the rain may enter—but the King of England cannot enter; all his forces dare not cross the threshold of the ruined tenement.'— William Pitt, 1st Earl of Chatham, speech in the British Parliament (1763).

1. What does this tell us about the meaning of private property?
2. Does it apply to people's homes in your country?

EXERCISE 1.6 MARKETS AND SOCIAL NETWORKS

Think about a social networking site that you use, for example, Facebook. Now look at our definition of a market.

What are the similarities and differences between the social networking site and a market?

QUESTION 1.6 CHOOSE THE CORRECT ANSWER(S)

Which of the following are examples of markets?

☐ wartime food rationing
☐ auction websites such as eBay
☐ touts selling tickets outside concert halls
☐ sale of illegal arms

Firms

Private property and markets both predate the hockey stick by many centuries. So we need something else to help us understand the transition to rising living standards illustrated by the hockey stick: capitalism. In a capitalist economy, firms became the predominant organizations for the production of goods and services. Firms are created to make a profit and are owned by private individuals who pay others to work there.

An economist's definition of a 'firm' is not captured well by the segmentation of GDP data that records production in the economy. For example, according to the Bureau of Economic Analysis (https://tinyco.re/9779891), in 2017, 57% of US GDP was produced by nonfinancial corporate business, plus financial businesses; 75% was produced by what it calls the 'business sector', which also includes unincorporated businesses. The rest of GDP was produced by the household and nonprofit sectors, and state and local governments.

These organizations are some examples of what economists call firms: restaurants, banks, large farms that pay labourers to work on them, industrial establishments, supermarkets, and internet service providers.

These organizations are productive (and important), but are not firms: businesses in which most or all of the people who do the work are unpaid family members, non-profits, employee-owned cooperatives, and government-owned entities (in some countries, the railways, power or water companies are owned by the government).

share A part of the assets of a firm that may be traded. It gives the holder a right to receive a proportion of a firm's profit and to benefit when the firm's assets become more valuable. *Also known as: common stock.*

Continuous change

For working people, capitalism has increased the pace of change. One reason is that a successful firm can grow in a few years from just a few employees to a global company with hundreds of thousands of customers and employing thousands of people. They can do this because they are able to hire additional employees on another type of market: the labour market. They can borrow money or sell **shares** in the firm to finance the purchase of the capital goods they need to expand production.

Firms can die in a few years too. This is because a firm that does not make profits will not have enough money (and will not be able to borrow money) to continue employing and producing. The firm shrinks, and some of the people who work there lose their jobs.

Contrast this with a family farm, which is not a firm. If the farm is successful, the family will be better off than its neighbours, but expansion will be limited. If, instead, the family is not very good at farming, it will simply be less well off than its neighbours, but as long as the family can feed itself, it will not 'go out of business' in the way that a failing firm might. Government bodies also tend to be more limited in their capacity to expand if successful, and are usually protected from failure if they perform poorly.

The ability to adapt quickly has allowed an acceleration in one of the changes that was underway during Adam Smith's life, but has greatly accelerated since, namely specialization in the production of goods and services. As Smith explained, we become better at producing things when we each focus on a limited range of activities. This is true for the following reasons:

- *Learning by doing:* We acquire skills as we produce things.
- *Difference in ability:* For reasons of skill, or natural surroundings such as the quality of the soil, some people are better at producing some things than others.

But people will not specialize unless they have a way to acquire the other goods they need, thus we need the combination of firms and market.

Capitalism as an economic system

Figure 1.12 shows that the three parts of the definition of a capitalist economic system are nested concepts. The left-hand circle describes an economy of isolated families who own their capital goods and the goods they produce, but have little or no exchange with others.

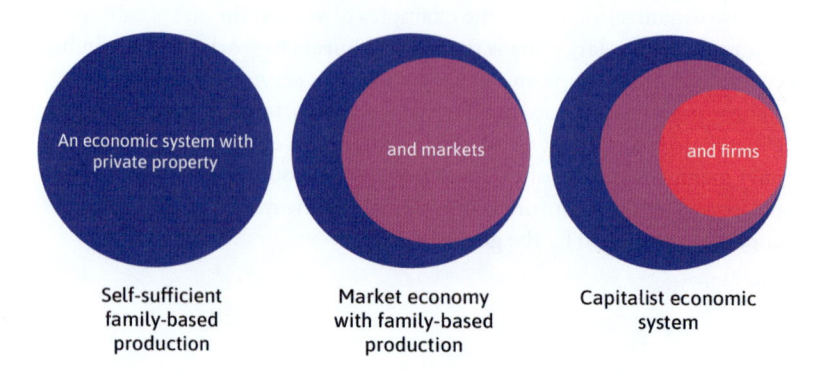

Figure 1.12 Capitalism: Private property, markets and firms.

Historically, economies like the left-hand circle have existed, but have been much less important than a system in which markets and private property are combined (the middle circle). Private property is an essential condition for the operation of markets: buyers will not want to pay for goods unless they can have the right to own them.

In the middle circle, most production is done either by individuals (shoemakers or blacksmiths, for example) or in families (for example, on a farm). Before 1600, many of the economies of the world were like this.

Only with the emergence of firms in the late eighteenth century were all the components of the capitalist system in place.

Capitalism is an economic system that can combine centralization with decentralization. On the one hand, it concentrates power in the hands of owners and managers of firms who are then able to secure the cooperation of large numbers of employees in the production process. On the other, it limits the power of those owners and other individuals, because they face competition to buy and sell in markets.

So, when the owner of a firm interacts with an employee, the owner is 'the boss'. But when the same owner interacts with a potential customer, they are simply another person trying to make a sale, in competition with other firms. It is this unusual combination of competition among firms, and concentration of power and cooperation within them, that accounts for capitalism's success as an economic system.

Capitalism is the first economic system in human history in which membership of the elite often depends on a high level of economic performance. As a firm owner, if you fail, you are no longer part of the club. Nobody kicks you out, because that is not necessary; you simply go bankrupt. Market competition provides a mechanism for weeding out those who underperform.

Of course, if they are initially very wealthy or very well-connected politically, owners and managers of capitalist firms survive and firms may stay in business despite their failures, sometimes for long periods or even over generations. Losers do sometimes survive, but there are no guarantees; staying ahead of the competition means constantly innovating.

Paul Seabright. 2010. *The Company of Strangers: A Natural History of Economic Life* (Revised Edition). Princeton, NJ: Princeton University Press.

> **EXERCISE 1.7 FIRM OR NOT?**
> Using our definition, explain whether each of the following entities is a firm by investigating if it satisfies the characteristics that define a firm. Research the entity online if you are stuck.
>
> 1. John Lewis Partnership (UK)
> 2. a family farm in Vietnam
> 3. your current family doctor's office or practice
> 4. Walmart (US)
> 5. an eighteenth-century pirate ship
> 6. Google (US)
> 7. Manchester United plc (UK)
> 8. Wikipedia

Capitalism and creative destruction

The first adopter of a new technology in a capitalist economy is called an **entrepreneur**. When we describe a person or firm as entrepreneurial, it refers to a willingness to try out new technologies and to start new businesses.

Joseph Schumpeter was an economist who argued that the dynamism of capitalism was due to the creation of technological improvements by entrepreneurs. The profits made by the first firm to produce a product at a lower cost, for example, or to bring a new product to the market will not last forever. Other firms, noticing that entrepreneurs are making more profits, will eventually adopt the new technology. They will also reduce their costs and their profits will increase.

As more firms introduce the new technology—say, for producing cloth—the supply of cloth to the market increases and the price will start to fall. This process will continue until everyone is using the new technology, at which stage prices will have declined to the point where no one is earning higher profits than in other lines of business. The firms that stuck to the old technology will be unable to cover their costs at the new lower price for cloth, and they will go bankrupt. Schumpeter called this **creative destruction**.

> **entrepreneur** A person who creates or is an early adopter of new technologies, organizational forms, and other opportunities.

> **creative destruction** Joseph Schumpeter's name for the process by which old technologies and the firms that do not adapt are swept away by the new, because they cannot compete in the market. In his view, the failure of unprofitable firms is creative because it releases labour and capital goods for use in new combinations.

GREAT ECONOMISTS

Joseph Schumpeter

Joseph Schumpeter (1883–1950) developed one of the most important concepts of modern economics: creative destruction.

Schumpeter brought to economics the idea of the entrepreneur as the central actor in the capitalist economic system. For Schumpeter, creative destruction was the essential fact about capitalism: old technologies and the firms that do not adapt are swept away by the new, because they cannot compete in the market by selling goods at a price that covers the cost of production. The failure of unprofitable firms releases labour and capital goods for use in new combinations.

This decentralized process generates a continued improvement in productivity, which leads to growth, so Schumpeter argued that it is virtuous.

Joseph A. Schumpeter. 1949. 'Science and Ideology' (https://tinyco.re/4561610). *The American Economic Review* 39 (March): pp. 345–59.

> Both the destruction of old firms and the creation of new ones take time. The slowness of this process creates upswings and downswings in the economy. Read Schumpeter's ideas and opinions in his own words and an online essay about his work by Robert Skidelsky, a historian of economic thought.
>
> Schumpeter was born in Austro–Hungary, but migrated to the US after the Nazis won the election in 1932 that led to the formation of the Third Reich in 1933. As a young professor in Austria, he had fought and won a duel with the university librarian to ensure that students had access to books. He also claimed that, as a young man, he had three ambitions in life: to become the world's greatest economist, the world's greatest lover, and the world's greatest horseman. He added that only the decline of the cavalry had stopped him from succeeding in all three.

Joseph A. Schumpeter. 1997. *Ten Great Economists*. London: Routledge.

Joseph A. Schumpeter. 1962. *Capitalism, Socialism, and Democracy*. New York: Harper & Brother.

Robert Skidelsky. 2012. 'Robert Skidelsky-portrait: Joseph Schumpeter' (https://tinyco.re/8488199).

Capitalism and the accumulation of capital goods

Just as the capitalist system provides strong incentives for innovation, it also rewards those who invest in the new machinery and other capital goods.

Because of the changing technologies, there were many profit opportunities for those producing using new technologies, as well as for those who financed and built the factories and machines embodying it. In this respect, capitalism differed not only in its dynamism, but also in the security of its property rights, so that those investing in the new capital goods could be confident that their property could not be confiscated either by the government or by others.

1.8 CAPITALISM AND GROWTH: CAUSE AND EFFECT?

We have seen that the institutions associated with capitalism have the potential to make people better off, through opportunities for both specialization and the introduction of new technologies. We have also seen that the permanent technological revolution coincided with (was associated with) the emergence of capitalism. This is strong circumstantial evidence—but can we conclude that capitalism actually caused the upward kink in the hockey stick?

We should be sceptical when anyone claims that something complex (capitalism) 'causes' something else (increased living standards, technological improvement, a networked world, or environmental challenges), just because we can see there is a correlation.

But we *do* want to make causal statements in economics if possible—to understand why things happen, or to devise ways of changing something so that the economy works better. We would like to be able to say that policy X is likely to cause change Y. For example, an economist might claim that: 'If the central bank lowers the interest rate, more people will buy homes and cars.'

In science, we support the statement that X causes Y by understanding the relationship between cause (X) and effect (Y), and we perform experiments to gather evidence that measure changes in X and in Y. But an economy is made up of the interactions of millions of people. We cannot measure and understand them all, and it is rarely possible to gather evidence by conducting experiments (although in Units 2 and 3, we will give examples of the use of experiments in economics).

If you want to explore how to distinguish causation and correlation in the real world, why not attempt a practical project from our online resource *Doing Economics* (https://tinyco.re/5421832)?

natural experiment An empirical study exploiting naturally occurring statistical controls in which researchers do not have the ability to assign participants to treatment and control groups, as is the case in conventional experiments. Instead, differences in law, policy, weather, or other events can offer the opportunity to analyse populations as if they had been part of an experiment. The validity of such studies depends on the premise that the assignment of subjects to the naturally occurring treatment and control groups can be plausibly argued to be random.

So how can economists explore cause and effect? Sometimes, the things we simply observe in the world—so-called '**natural experiments**'—can help us investigate.

Natural experiments to identify cause and effect

We can observe that capitalism emerged at the same time as, or just before, both the Industrial Revolution and the upward turn in our hockey sticks. This might suggest that capitalist institutions were among the causes of the upturn. Putting this in scientific language: *the observation would be consistent with the hypothesis that capitalist institutions were a cause of continuous productivity growth*. But the emergence of a free-thinking cultural environment known as The Enlightenment (https://tinyco.re/2577267) also predated or coincided with the upturn in the hockey sticks.

Figure 1.13 uses arrows to represent causal relationships. Before the eighteenth century, living standards were more or less the same every year. Afterwards, they grew constantly. Many economists and historians explain what happened in this way:

- The permanent technological revolution was the result of a change in both culture and institutions.
- The subsequent shift to growing affluence was the result of both capitalism and new technologies.

The arrows indicate causal relationships. So the picture represents the idea that institutions and culture were two of the causes of the permanent technological revolution that began in the Industrial Revolution. This simple picture is an example of what is called an 'economic model'.

So, was our growing affluence caused by institutions, culture, both, or something else? One method for investigating a question like this is called a 'natural experiment', in which we can identify two groups:

- A *'treatment' group*: This group undergoes a change. Other attributes of the group remain constant.
- A *'control' group*: This group was similar to the treatment group before the experiment, and the treatment does not occur in this group.

We can then compare what happened to the two groups. Natural experiments are used to test hypotheses in many fields of study, including the one that began the science of epidemiology (https://tinyco.re/8757564).

Economists and historians disagree on the causes of the Industrial Revolution. You can find out why they disagree by reading a discussion (https://tinyco.re/1164122) about why the Industrial Revolution happened first in the eighteenth century, and why it happened on an island off the coast of Europe.

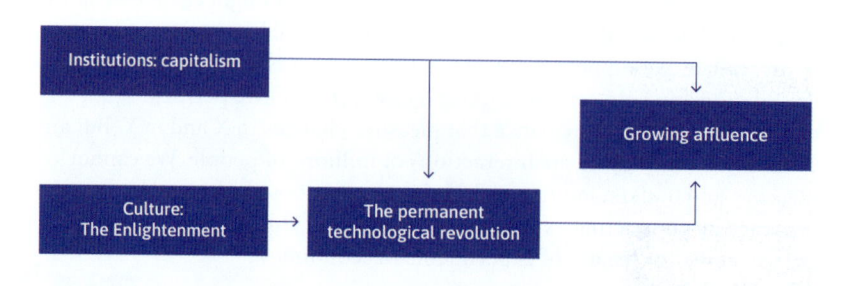

Figure 1.13 A possible explanation of the causes of growing affluence in the eighteenth and nineteenth centuries in Europe.

There is a natural experiment that has allowed us to evaluate whether capitalist institutions were indeed a cause of rapid economic growth. The setting for the natural experiment is the coexistence of two different economic systems in the west and east of Germany after the end of the Second World War.

Capitalism and central planning

In 1936, before the Second World War, living standards in what later became East and West Germany were the same, and firms in the East German provinces of Saxony and Thuringia were world leaders in automobile and aircraft production, chemicals, optical equipment and precision engineering.

At the end of the Second World War, Germany was divided into two countries. A political boundary, the 'Iron Curtain', as Winston Churchill, the British Prime Minister, described it in 1946, divided Germany. It separated two populations that until then had shared the same language, culture, and capitalist economy.

This separation introduced two different economic systems.

While West Germany returned to market-based capitalism, in East Germany the Communist Party introduced a system of centralized planning that saw private property, markets, and firms virtually disappear. Decisions about what to produce, how much, and in which plants, offices, mines, and farms were taken not by private individuals, but by government officials. The officials managing these economic organizations did not need to follow the principle of capitalism and produce goods and services that customers would buy at a price above their cost of manufacture.

Because of the imposition of different economic systems on these two parts of what had been the same country, this is a suitable setting for using the natural experiment method. West Germany is the control group, and East Germany the treatment group. The hypothesis is that imposing a planned economic system on East Germany would affect its performance relative to that of West Germany.

We can represent the logic of this natural experiment with a visual model, like the one in Figure 1.13. Figure 1.14 shows that in contrasting the two Germanies, one possible influence on their growth is 'held constant': German culture was common, but the institutions differed between East and West Germany. As in the previous figure, the arrows indicate causal relationships.

Because we cannot change the past, even if it were practical to conduct experiments on entire populations, we rely on natural experiments. In an interview (https://tinyco.re/8903951), Jared Diamond, a geographer, and James Robinson, a professor of government, explain the method.

You can read more about Winston Churchill's 'Iron Curtain' speech on history.com (https://tinyco.re/6053919).

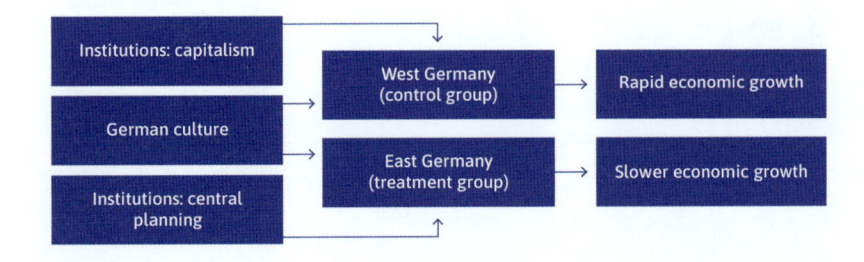

Figure 1.14 The logic of a natural experiment: East and West Germany.

Figure 1.15 shows the outcome of this natural experiment. It shows the different paths taken by them, and two other economies, from 1950. We have used a ratio scale to show the rate of growth.

The East German Communist Party forecast in 1958 that material wellbeing would exceed the level of West Germany by 1961. The failure of this prediction was one of the reasons that the Berlin Wall, which separated East and West Germany, was built in 1961. East Germany's planned economy never caught up with West Germany.

Notice from Figure 1.15 that West Germany did start from a more favourable position than East Germany in 1950, because the structure of the industries in East Germany was more disrupted by splitting the country than was the case in West Germany. But this difference was not mainly because of differences in the amount of capital goods, or skills per head of the population (and, as we noted above, before the war, living standards in the East and West had been similar).

So, following that disruption, we would have expected East Germany to have caught up with West Germany. But Figure 1.15 shows that, instead, the gap between the two lines widened (which on a ratio scale means that the ratio of incomes increased). By the time the Berlin Wall fell in 1989, and East Germany abandoned central planning, its real GDP per capita was less than half of that of capitalist West Germany.

The validity of this comparison as a natural experiment depends on the idea that East and West Germany differed in just one way that might affect their economic growth: their economic institutions. So, consider the second half of the twentieth century. Figure 1.15 suggests strongly that the imposition of central planning in East Germany—compared to what would have happened if East Germany had used the same capitalist system as West Germany—slowed the growth in income of East German people.

Hartmut Berghoff and Uta Andrea Balbier. 2013. 'From Centrally Planned Economy to Capitalist Avant-Garde? The Creation, Collapse, and Transformation of a Socialist Economy'. In *The East German Economy, 1945–2010: Falling behind or Catching Up?* Cambridge: Cambridge University Press.

View this data at OWiD https://tinyco.re/6997062

Conference Board, The. 2015. *Total Economy Database*. Angus Maddison. 2001. 'The World Economy: A Millennial Perspective' (https://tinyco.re/5310937). Development Centre Studies. Paris: OECD.

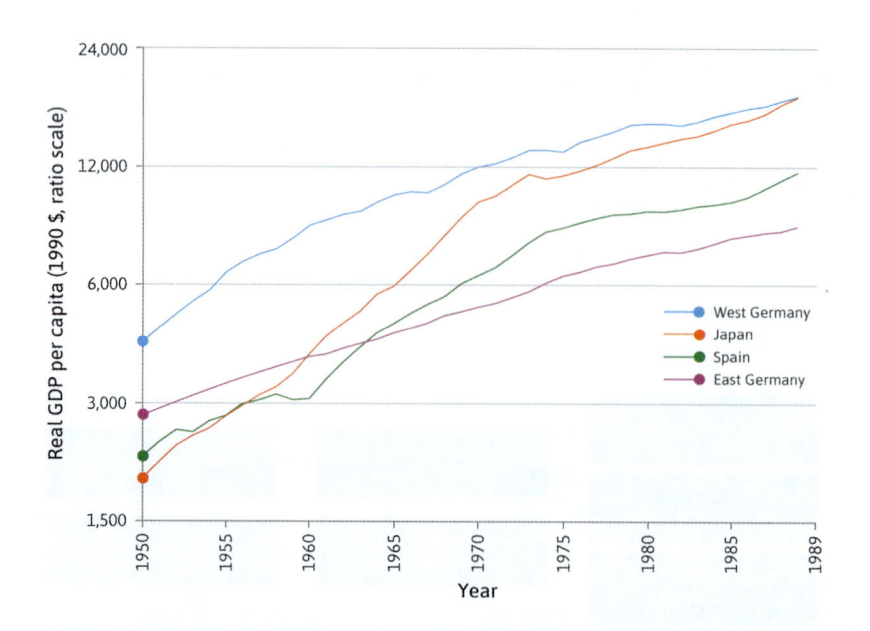

Figure 1.15 The two Germanies: Planning and capitalism (1950–89). West German real GDP grew faster than East German GDP between 1950 and 1989.

1.8 CAPITALISM AND GROWTH: CAUSE AND EFFECT?

We cannot conclude from the German natural experiment that capitalism *always* promotes rapid economic growth, or that central planning is always a cause of economic stagnation. There is evidence pointing in both directions:

- From Figure 1.15, we can see that some capitalist economies that had even lower real per capita income than East Germany in 1950 fared far better. By 1989, Spain had closed part of the gap, and the Japanese economy (which had also suffered war damage) had caught up to West Germany.
- But we will see in Figure 1.16 that the Soviet Union's centrally planned economy grew considerably faster between 1928 (when central planning was introduced there) and 1980 than the economies of many capitalist countries that were at similar levels of development in 1928.

But, while both comparisons are interesting, neither is a natural experiment: many factors influenced the outcomes in these countries, so we cannot isolate the impact of capitalism. Natural experiments in economics, in which two groups are similar beforehand, there is one treatment, and other factors are held constant, are rare. This is why, in economics, it is hard to make strong causal statements.

QUESTION 1.7 CHOOSE THE CORRECT ANSWER(S)

Look again at Figure 1.15, which shows a graph of real GDP per capita for West and East Germany, Japan and Spain between 1950 and 1990. Which of the following statements is correct?

- ☐ Having a much lower starting point in 1950 was the main reason for East Germany's poor performance compared to West Germany.
- ☐ The fact that Japan and West Germany have the highest real GDP per capita in 1990 implies that they found the optimal economic system.
- ☐ Spain was able to grow at a higher growth rate than Germany between 1950 and 1990.
- ☐ The difference in East and West Germany's performance proves that capitalism always promotes rapid economic growth, while central planning is a recipe for stagnation.

1.9 VARIETIES OF CAPITALISM: INSTITUTIONS AND GROWTH

Not every capitalist country is the kind of economic success story exemplified in Figure 1.2 (page 7) by Britain, later Japan, and the other countries that caught up, or in the post-Second World War catch-up shown in Figure 1.15. This explains why the left-hand end of the skyscraper diagram (Figure 1.1) is so much poorer than the right-hand end.

An example: In 1950, real GDP per capita in South Korea was the same as in Nigeria. Both were, on our broad definition, capitalist countries. By 2013, South Korea was ten times richer by this measure.

Many of the economies at the left-hand end of Figure 1.1 have been capitalist for many years, but remain poor. Why might this be?

Again, there are many causes. One of the most important is that there are many varieties, and qualities, of capitalism. Figure 1.16 tracks the fortunes of a selection of countries across the world during the twentieth century. It shows, for example that, in Africa, the success of Botswana in achieving sustained growth contrasts sharply with Nigeria's relative failure. Both are rich in natural resources (diamonds in Botswana, oil in Nigeria). Differences in the quality of their institutions—the amount of corruption and misdirection of government funds, for example—may help explain their contrasting trajectories.

South Korea's take-off in the middle of the twentieth century occurred under institutions and policies different from those in Britain in the eighteenth and nineteenth centuries. The most important difference was that the government of South Korea (along with a few large corporations) played a leading role in directing the process of development, explicitly promoting some industries, requiring firms to compete in foreign markets and also providing high-quality education for its workforce.

The term **developmental state** has been applied to the leading role of the South Korean government in its economic take-off, and now refers to any government playing this part in the economy. Japan and China are other examples of developmental states.

From Figure 1.16 we also see that, in 1928, when the Soviet Union's first five-year economic plan was introduced, GDP per capita was one-quarter of the level in Argentina, similar to Brazil, and higher than in South Korea. Central planning in the Soviet Union produced steady but unspectacular growth for nearly 50 years, such that real GDP per capita in the Soviet Union outstripped Brazil by a wide margin—and even overtook Argentina briefly—before Communist Party rule in the Soviet Union ended in 1990.

The contrast between West and East Germany demonstrates that one reason central planning was abandoned as an economic system was a failure to deliver the improvements in living standards that some capitalist economies had achieved. Yet the countries that had once made up the Soviet Union replaced central planning with many varieties of capitalism. These did not work so well either. We can see this from a sudden dip in real GDP per capita for the former Soviet Union after 1990.

---

developmental state A government that takes a leading role in promoting the process of economic development through its public investments, subsidies of particular industries, education and other public policies.

The World Bank. 1993. *The East Asian miracle: Economic growth and public policy* (https://tinyco.re/3040506). New York, NY: Oxford University Press.

QUESTION 1.8 CHOOSE THE CORRECT ANSWER(S)

Look again at Figure 1.16. Which of these conclusions is suggested by the graph?

☐ The Communist Party rule in the former Soviet Union before 1990 was a complete failure.
☐ The contrasting performances of Botswana and Nigeria illustrate that rich natural resources alone do not guarantee higher economic growth, but that higher-quality institutions (government, markets, and firms) may also be necessary.
☐ The impressive performance of South Korea's economy implies that other countries should copy their economic system.
☐ The evidence from the Russian Federation and the former Soviet Union after 1990 shows that the replacement of central planning by capitalism led to immediate economic growth.

1.10 VARIETIES OF CAPITALISM: GROWTH AND STAGNATION

The lagging performances of some of the economies in Figure 1.16 demonstrates that the existence of capitalist institutions is not enough, in itself, to create a dynamic economy—that is, an economy bringing sustained growth in living standards. Two sets of conditions contribute to the dynamism of the capitalist economic system:

- economic conditions
- political conditions—in other words, government and the way it functions.

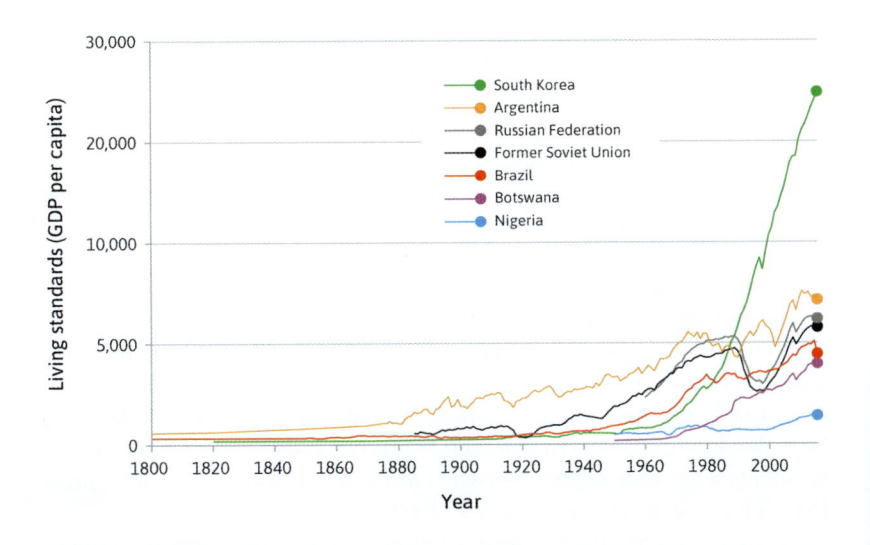

Figure 1.16 Divergence of GDP per capita among latecomers to the capitalist revolution (1928–2015). Between 1928 and 2015, the GDP of South Korea grew much more than that of Argentina, Russia and the former Soviet Union, Brazil, Botswana, and Nigeria.

View this data at OWiD https://tinyco.re/2023925

Maddison Project Database (https://tinyco.re/5503002), version 2018. Jutta Bolt, Robert Inklaar, Herman de Jong and Jan Luiten van Zanden. (2018).

'Rebasing 'Maddison': New income comparisons and the shape of long-run economic development' (https://tinyco.re/5386746), Maddison Project, Working Paper No. 10.

Some researchers question the validity (https://tinyco.re/2173358) of historical GDP estimates such as this one outside Europe, because the economies of these countries were so different in structure.

Economic conditions for capitalist dynamism

Where capitalism is less dynamic, economists usually look for failures in the three components of the capitalist system, private property, markets, and firms:

- *Private property must be secure:* There is less dynamism if there is weak enforcement of the rule of law and contracts, or expropriation either by criminal elements or by government bodies.
- *Markets must be competitive:* If markets fail to offer the carrots, and wield the sticks that make a capitalist economy dynamic through creative destruction, dynamism suffers.
- *Firms should not be owned and managed by people who survive because of their connections to government or their privileged birth:* Capitalism is dynamic when owners or managers succeed because they are good at delivering high-quality goods and services at a competitive price. This is more likely to be a failure when the other two factors above are not working well.

Combinations of failures of the three basic institutions of capitalism mean that individuals and groups often have more to gain by spending time and resources in lobbying, criminal activity, and other ways of shifting the distribution of income in their favour. They have less to gain from the direct creation of economic value.

Political conditions for capitalist dynamism

Government is also important. We have seen that in South Korea, for example, governments have played a leading role in the **capitalist revolution**. And in virtually every modern capitalist economy, governments are a large part of the economy. In some, their spending on goods and services as well as on transfers like unemployment benefits and pensions, accounts for more than half of GDP. But even where the government's role is more limited, as in Britain at the time of the Industrial Revolution, it still establishes, enforces, and changes the laws and regulations that influence how the economy works. Markets, private property and firms are all regulated by laws and policies.

For innovators to take the risk of introducing a new product or production process, their ownership of the profits must be protected from theft by a well-functioning legal system. Governments also adjudicate disputes over ownership and enforce the property rights necessary for markets to work.

Competition law and policy are also important. As Adam Smith warned, by creating or allowing monopolies such as the East India Company, governments may also dull the spur of competition. If a large firm is able to establish a monopoly by excluding all competitors, or if a group of firms is able to collude to keep the price high, the incentives for innovation and the discipline of prospective failure will be reduced. This is still true today. Some banks are considered to be **too big to fail** and are bailed out by governments when they might otherwise have failed, as was the case for banks in the global financial crisis of 2008–2009.

As well as supporting the institutions of the capitalist economic system, the government provides essential goods and services, such as physical infrastructure, education and national defence. In later units, we investigate why government policies may also make good economic sense in areas such

---

Daron Acemoglu and James A. Robinson. 2012. *Why Nations Fail: The Origins of Power, Prosperity, and Poverty*. New York, NY: Crown Publishing Group.

capitalist revolution Rapid improvements in technology combined with the emergence of a new economic system.

too big to fail Said to be a characteristic of large banks, whose central importance in the economy ensures they will be saved by the government if they are in financial difficulty. The bank thus does not bear all the costs of its activities and is therefore likely to take bigger risks. *See also: moral hazard.*

as sustaining competition, taxing and subsidizing to protect the environment, influencing the distribution of income, and the creation of wealth.

These are the conditions that together make possible a successful capitalist revolution that, first in Britain and then in some other economies, transformed the way that people interact with one another and with nature in producing their livelihoods.

In a nutshell, capitalism can be a dynamic economic system when it combines:

- *Private incentives for cost-reducing innovation:* These are derived from market competition and secure private property.
- *Public policy supporting these conditions:* Governments enforce laws and provide regulation.
- *Public policy that supplies essential goods and services:* These may not be provided in sufficient quantities by private firms, and include education and basic research.

> **QUESTION 1.9 CHOOSE THE CORRECT ANSWER(S)**
> Capitalism as an economic system can be dynamic and successful if:
>
> ☐ it allows failing firms to go bankrupt.
> ☐ it allows successful firms to gain market power.
> ☐ profits are claimed by the capitalists.
> ☐ the government is absent.

1.11 CAPITALISM, INEQUALITY, AND DEMOCRACY

The story of Cyril Ramaphosa that introduced this unit illustrates the complex relationship between capitalism, inequality, and democracy. After a quarter of a century of democratic rule by the African National Congress, overall inequality in South Africa had not fallen. While the different racial groups became more equal, this was offset by increasing inequality within groups, including the emergence of a rich and powerful black elite. Ramaphosa was a leader in the struggle for democracy. He then became a very successful capitalist. Since 2018, as president of South Africa, he faced the challenges of delivering higher living standards and more equal outcomes in a democratic country.

Capitalism and inequality

As the South African case shows, dynamic capitalism is a system of winners and losers. The creative destruction of the permanent technological revolution rewards successful innovators with wealth unknown even to royalty in the past. Those with wealth—whether acquired by inheritance, exploiting the trading opportunities of the new global trading system, or as the rewards for successful innovation—are in a position to hire labour to make a profit, thereby perpetuating and even enhancing their wealth before passing it on.

The result is that, in many countries for which data is available, capitalism ushered in an era of increasing inequality of wealth. We know how rich the very rich were at this time, because even centuries ago they needed to pay taxes, so someone recorded their incomes and wealth.

Facundo Alvaredo, Anthony B. Atkinson, Thomas Piketty, Emmanuel Saez, and Gabriel Zucman. 2016. *The World Wealth and Income Database (WID)* (https://tinyco.re/5262390).

Anthony B. Atkinson and Thomas Piketty, eds. 2007. *Top Incomes Over the Twentieth Century: A Contrast between Continental European and English-Speaking Countries*. Oxford: Oxford University Press.

economic inequality Differences among members of a society in some economic attribute such as wealth, income, or wages.

Thomas Piketty. 2014. *Capital in the Twenty-First Century*. Cambridge, MA: Harvard University Press.

Thomas Piketty: The long-run economics of wealth inequality
https://tinyco.re/8537633

Alfred Plummer. 1971. *Bronterre: A Political Biography of Bronterre O'Brien, 1804–1864*. Toronto: University of Toronto Press.

Figure 1.17 shows the fraction of all wealth held by the richest 1% for all countries on which long-run data is available. In most of the countries in Figure 1.17, you can see that wealth inequality increased until around the First World War.

In many countries around this time, first males without property and then women gained the right to vote. In all the countries shown in Figure 1.17, inequality of wealth began to fall following the advent of democracy.

In our 'Economist in action' video, Thomas Piketty, an economist and author of the bestseller *Capital in the Twenty-First Century*, examines **economic inequality** from the French Revolution until today, and explains why careful study of the facts is essential.

> **QUESTION 1.10 CHOOSE THE CORRECT ANSWER(S)**
> In the 'Economist in action' video, which of the following were NOT among the reasons that Piketty gave for the fall in the incomes of the very rich during the twentieth century?
>
> ☐ the First World War
> ☐ the Great Depression
> ☐ the Russian Revolution
> ☐ the Second World War

Inequality and democracy

In the nineteenth century, faced with increasing inequality, farmers, industrial workers, and the poor sought a way to protect their standards of living. They engaged in strikes (often brutally suppressed) and some wrecked the machines that had put them out of work. In 1848, there were attempted revolutions against the monarchy in Sicily, France, Germany, Italy, and the Austrian Empire. At the same time, Karl Marx was writing *The Communist Manifesto*, advocating revolution by workers to end the capitalist economic system.

Many demanded the right to vote as a means of gaining more influence over the government that, at the time, for the most part protected the economic interests of the well off. A greater share of political power, they reasoned, would allow them to claim a larger share of the output and wealth of the rapidly-growing economies.

One of the leaders of the movement to extend voting and other political rights to workers and the other less well off, James Bronterre O'Brien, told the people:

'Knaves will tell you that it is because you have no property, you are unrepresented. I tell you on the contrary, it is because you are unrepresented that you have no property …'

In the late nineteenth and early twentieth centuries, the wealthy in many countries concluded that extending democracy might be prudent, much as the leaders of the South African government were to conclude a century later.

Democracy is a political system, that ideally:

- *Gives equal political power to all citizens:* This power is defined by individual rights such as freedom of speech, assembly, and the press.
- *Selects political leaders by means of elections:* In these elections, virtually all adults are eligible to vote, and the governing party leaves office if it loses.

1.11 CAPITALISM, INEQUALITY, AND DEMOCRACY

In many societies throughout human history, the rich have elected representatives to govern them. This satisfied the second condition above, but is not considered democracy in the modern sense of the word because the less well off were typically excluded. This happened in ancient Athens, for example, where there were also many slaves.

Capitalism emerged in Britain, the Netherlands, and in most of today's high-income countries long before democracy. In no country were most adults eligible to vote prior to the end of the nineteenth century (New Zealand was the first).

Even in the recent past, capitalism has coexisted with undemocratic governments, as in South Africa before 1994, Chile from 1973 to 1990, in Brazil from 1964 to 1985, and in Japan until 1945.

The economies of contemporary China and Vietnam are very successful variants of the capitalist economic system, but their systems of government are based neither on the individual political rights nor the inclusive and fair elections that define democracy.

In many countries today, however, capitalism and democracy coexist, with each system influencing how the other works.

Figure 1.18 shows that democracy is a recent arrival in human history: in virtually all countries prior to the twentieth century, women and those without property were excluded from voting.

Democracy appeared in just a few countries at the beginning of the twentieth century, but has spread rapidly since then. In many cases, for example in South Africa, it was the threat of popular unrest and even revolution that pushed the wealthy and powerful to extend political rights and access to public services, such as education, to all groups.

As with capitalism, democracy comes in many forms, and these vary in the extent to which the democratic ideal of political equality among all citizens is realized. In some democracies, there are strict limits on the ways in which individuals can influence elections or public policy

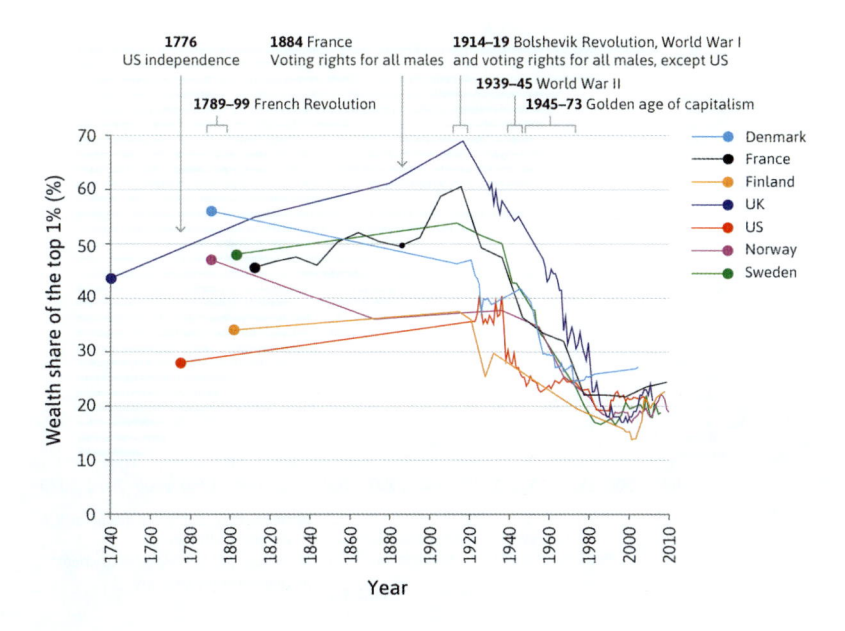

Figure 1.17 Share of total wealth held by the richest 1% (1740–2010).

Adapted from Figure 19 of Daniel Waldenström and Jesper Roine. 2014. 'Long Run Trends in the Distribution of Income and Wealth' (https://tinyco.re/8651400). In *Handbook of Income Distribution*: Volume 2a, edited by Anthony Atkinson and Francois Bourguignon. Amsterdam: North-Holland.

through their financial contributions. In others, private money has great influence through contributions to electoral campaigns, lobbying, and even illicit payments such as bribery.

The connections between capitalism, democracy, affluence and inequality are illustrated by the contrasting role of the government in four affluent, democratic, capitalist countries with modest levels of economic inequality:

- *Japan and South Korea:* Governments play an important role in setting the direction of their economies, but the amount collected in taxes and paid by the government to the less well off to reduce inequality is relatively low. The inequality of market incomes is relatively low in these countries.
- *Denmark and Sweden:* Payment of taxes (and benefits received from the government) reduce the inequality in how much money people have to spend by half.

1.12 CAPITALISM, GROWTH AND ENVIRONMENTAL SUSTAINABILITY

The capitalist revolution has also transformed our environment.

To sustain our livelihoods, humans have always relied on the physical environment and the biosphere, which provide essentials for life such as air, water, and food. The environment and biosphere—the collection of all living things—provide the raw materials that we use in the production of other goods, the air we breathe, our food—in short, the physical necessities of life.

Figure 1.19 shows that the economy is part of a larger social system, which is itself part of the biosphere. People interact with one another, and also with nature, in producing their livelihood.

Through most of our history, humans have regarded natural resources as freely available in unlimited quantities. But elements of the environment

Center for Systemic Peace. 2016. Polity IV annual time series (https://tinyco.re/3970843); Inter-parliamentary union. 2016. 'Women's Suffrage' (https://tinyco.re/8725984). Initial periods of democracy of less than five years are not shown in the chart.

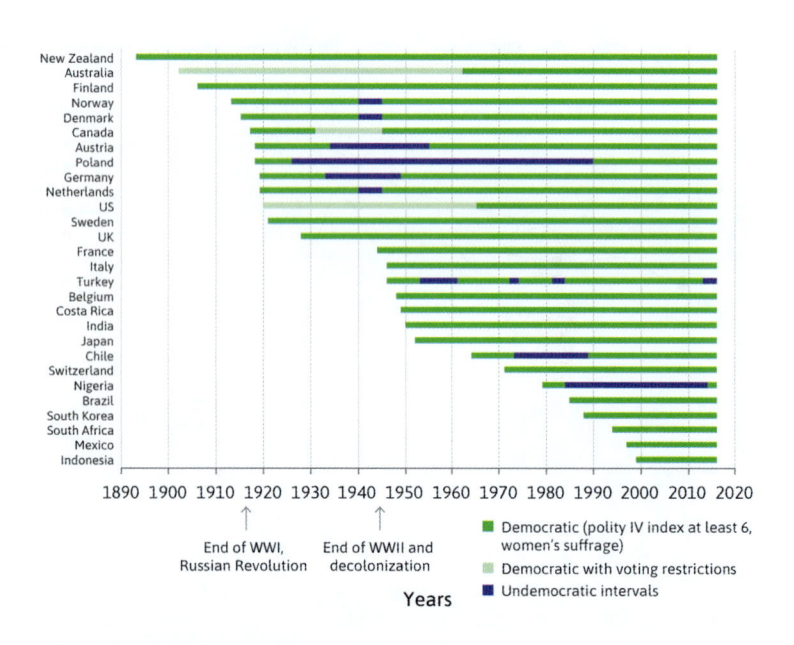

Figure 1.18 The advance of democracy in the world.

such as air, water, soil, and climate have been radically altered by how we have interacted with nature to produce our livelihoods.

Since the advent of capitalism, our impact on the environment has rapidly grown as we extract more from it, and introduce more into it. This has occurred as a byproduct of capitalism's success in raising material living standards, shown in the hockey sticks for real GDP per capita. Also contributing to our increased impact on the environment has been the ability of the capitalist economy to support a vast increase in the earth's population, which at over 7 billion in the early twenty-first century, was more than ten times higher than at the start of the eighteenth century. Projections shown in red in Figure 1.20 are that population will continue to grow but at a slower rate. Click through to the interactive chart (https://tinyco.re/5479221) to explore how world population has changed since the capitalist revolution.

Climate change and environmental sustainability

We say that something is sustainable if it can be continued indefinitely into the future. For example, we may say that a family's financial position is not sustainable if it is spending more than its income. Similarly, the environment may be unsustainable if the damage we are doing to it is not offset by its own capacity to restore itself, aided by policies to support environmental recovery.

The most striking effect of our activity on the natural environment is climate change. The authoritative source for research and data about climate change is the Intergovernmental Panel on Climate Change (https://tinyco.re/8844088). Figure 1.21 and 1.22 illustrate what has been happening.

We can see from Figure 1.21 that, while the average temperature of the earth fluctuates from decade to decade, there have been perceptible increases in the northern hemisphere's average temperatures from 1900 onwards.

The human causes and the reality of climate change are no longer widely disputed in the scientific community. These have mostly resulted from the CO_2 emissions associated with the burning of fossil fuels.

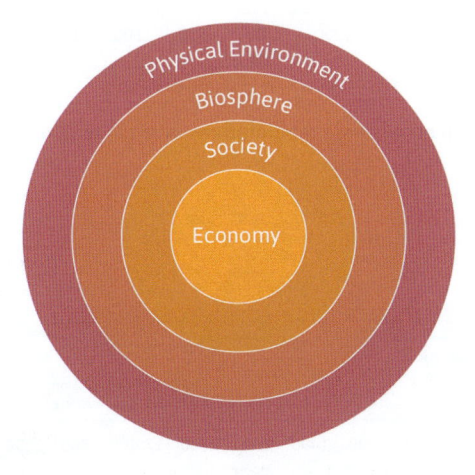

Figure 1.19 The economy is part of society, which is part of the biosphere.

Figure 1.22 presents evidence of our increased use of fossil fuels—coal, oil, and natural gas—and of a profound change in the natural environment. Figure 1.22 also shows that CO_2 emissions from fossil fuel consumption have risen dramatically since 1800.

View this data at OWiD https://tinyco.re/5479221

History Database of the Global Environment (https://tinyco.re/1405816); UN Population Division (2015 revision) Medium Projection (https://tinyco.re/7203152).

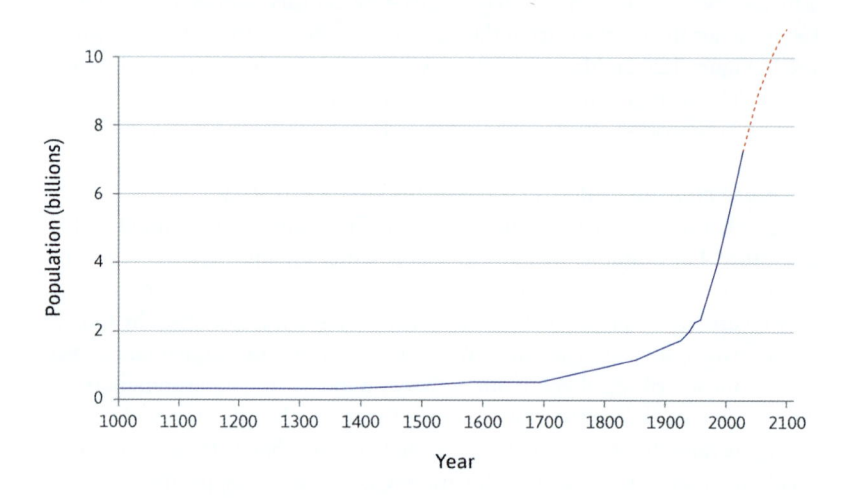

Figure 1.20 The global population hockey stick.

Michael E. Mann, Zhihua Zhang, Malcolm K. Hughes, Raymond S. Bradley, Sonya K. Miller, Scott Rutherford, and Fenbiao Ni. 2008. 'Proxy-based reconstructions of hemispheric and global surface temperature variations over the past two millennia' (https://tinyco.re/8992451). *Proceedings of the National Academy of Sciences* 105 (36): pp. 13252–13257.

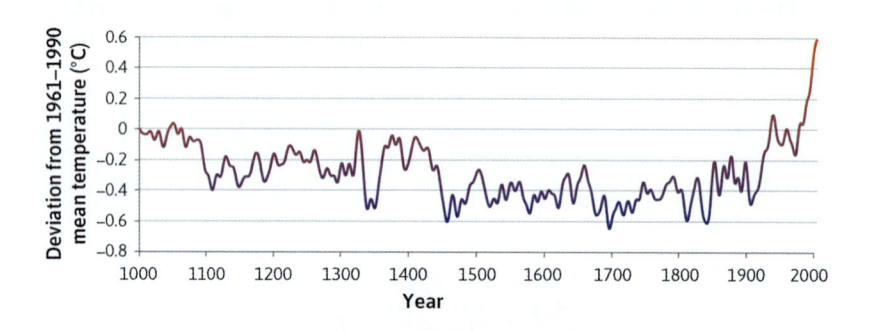

Figure 1.21 Northern hemisphere temperatures over the long run (1000–2006).

Years 1010–1975: David M. Etheridge, L. Paul Steele, Roger J. Francey, and Ray L. Langenfelds. 2012. 'Historical Record from the Law Dome DE08, DE08-2, and DSS Ice Cores'. Division of Atmospheric Research, CSIRO, Aspendale, Victoria, Australia. Years 1976–2010: Data from Mauna Loa observatory. Thomas A. Boden, Gregg Marland, and Robert J. Andres. 2010. 'Global, Regional and National Fossil-Fuel CO_2 Emissions'. Carbon Dioxide Information Analysis Center (CDIAC) Datasets.

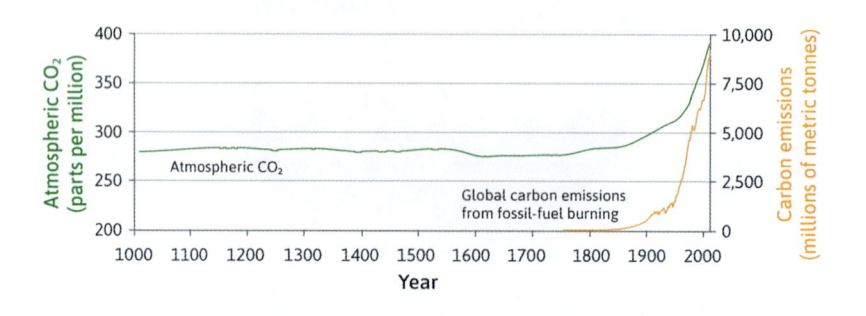

Figure 1.22 Carbon dioxide in the atmosphere (1010–2010) and global carbon emissions from burning fossil fuels (1750–2010).

The likely consequences of global warming are far-reaching—melting of the polar ice caps, rising sea levels that would put large coastal areas under water, and changes in climate and rain patterns that would destroy the world's food-growing areas.

> **EXERCISE 1.8 HOW MUCH DIFFERENCE DOES A COUPLE OF DEGREES MAKE?**
>
> Between 1300 and 1850, there were a number of exceptionally cold periods, as you can see from Figure 1.21. Research this so-called 'little ice age' in Europe and answer the following:
>
> 1. Describe the effects of these exceptionally cold periods on the economies of the affected countries.
> 2. Within a country or region, some groups of people were exceptionally hard hit by the climate change, while others were less affected. Provide examples.
> 3. How 'extreme' were these cold periods compared to the temperature increases since the mid-twentieth century and those projected for the future?

> **EXERCISE 1.9 USING EXCEL: PLOTTING LINE GRAPHS OF TEMPERATURE OVER TIME**
>
> A downloadable spreadsheet (https://tinyco.re/4744778) contains the temperature data used to make Figure 1.21. Using this data, recreate Figure 1.21. Follow the walk-through in Figure 1.23 online (https://tinyco.re/5133263) on how to draw this graph in Excel.
>
> **Figure 1.23** Plotting line graphs of temperature over time.
>
> **1. The data**
> This is what the temperature data looks like. Column A has time (in years), Column B has temperature deviations, and Column C contains the average northern hemisphere temperature. We will be using Columns A and B to make the line chart.
>
> **2. Draw a line chart**
> Your line chart will look similar to the chart shown, with temperature deviation on the vertical axis and time on the horizontal axis. Notice that the numbers for time are not correct (they should be years).
>
> **3. Change the horizontal axis variable to years**
> To change the horizontal axis labels to years, we need to add the values in Column A to the line chart.
>
> **4. Change the horizontal axis variable to years**
> The current horizontal axis labels are the numbers 1, 2, 3, and so on. To change these labels to years, we need to edit the labels.
>
> **5. Change the horizontal axis variable to years**
> After Step 10, the horizontal axis labels will be changed to the years 1000–2006.
>
> **6. Move the horizontal axis to the bottom of the chart**
> By default, the horizontal axis is positioned at the vertical axis value of 0. To move it to the bottom of the chart (as in Figure 1.21), we have to change the axis position. After Step 12, your chart will look similar to Figure 1.21.
>
> **7. Add axis titles and a chart title**
> Label the horizontal and vertical axes as in Figure 1.21, and give your chart the same title.

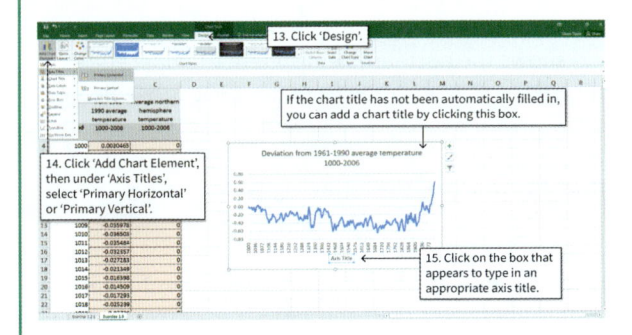

Technological progress can help

Figure 1.19 (page 41) shows the economy embedded in the biosphere and the physical environment. The relationship is two-way. We use natural resources in production, which may in turn affect the environment we live in and its capacity to support future production. But the permanent technological revolution, which brought about dependence on fossil fuels, may also be part of the solution to today's environmental problems.

Look back at Figure 1.9 (page 20), which shows the productivity of labour in producing light. The vast increases shown over the course of history and especially since the mid-nineteenth century occurred largely because the amount of light that could be produced per unit of heat (for example from a campfire, candle, or light bulb) increased dramatically.

In lighting, the technological revolution brought us more light for less heat, which conserved natural resources—from firewood to fossil fuels—used in generating the heat. In today's world, advances in technology may allow us to produce more of our energy from less-polluting sources, with a greater reliance on wind, solar, and other renewable sources.

> **QUESTION 1.11 CHOOSE THE CORRECT ANSWER(S)**
>
> Which of the following variables have followed the so-called 'hockey-stick' trajectory—that is, little to no growth for most of history followed by a sudden and sharp change to a positive growth rate?
>
> ☐ real GDP per capita
> ☐ labour productivity
> ☐ inequality
> ☐ atmospheric CO_2

> **QUESTION 1.12 CHOOSE THE CORRECT ANSWER(S)**
>
> Figure 1.21 (page 42) shows the northern hemisphere's temperature since year 1000, reported as the deviation from the 1961–1990 mean temperature.
>
> Based on this information, which of the following statements is correct?
>
> ☐ The 1961–1990 mean temperature was 0.2 to 0.6 degrees higher than the temperatures between 1450 and 1900.
> ☐ The negative numbers on the graph indicate that the temperature consistently fell between 1100 and 1900.
> ☐ A consistent rise in temperature is only a post-1980 phenomenon.
> ☐ The consistent rise in temperature after 1980 suggests that temperatures will continue to rise in every year following 2000.

1.12 CAPITALISM, GROWTH AND ENVIRONMENTAL SUSTAINABILITY

Democracy and the challenge of environmental sustainability

In many countries, the advent of democracy—and especially the extension of the vote to those without property and to women—saw a reduction in economic inequality because it gave more political power to the less well off. Organizations of the less well off—labour unions and political parties—used this power to alter laws and government policies so as to advance their own economic interests.

The relationship between democracy and the challenge of environmental sustainability is more complex than the one between democracy and addressing the problem of growing inequality. This is true for two reasons:

- *National costs and global benefits:* Democracy is a form of government of a nation, and while the citizens of a nation may adopt policies to protect the environment of that particular nation—its lakes and streams, its green spaces—they may have little incentive to protect the global environment, particularly if they will bear the costs and a great many others share in the benefits.
- *Effect on future generations:* Democratic citizens today are making decisions affecting people who may not be born for hundreds of years. These future generations do not have a vote.

Both reasons for why democracy may be limited in how it addresses the challenge of environmental sustainability are examples of something you will encounter throughout this course called external effects. **External effects** arise when an action taken by a person has consequences—benefits or costs—that are felt by others and which are not taken into account by the person taking the action.

In the light of the nature of the external effects—spilling across national borders and across generations—it is not surprising that we cannot show you a figure similar to Figure 1.12 (page 26) in which environmental damages declined following the extension of the vote to most adults in many countries. Nevertheless, many long-standing democratic nations—many in northern Europe, for example—are exemplary in the ways they have provided local environmental amenities and restricted carbon emissions.

Taking account of its level of income, Australia—where most people got the vote very early—stands out for its protection of the *local* environment (as shown, for example, by the data in Figure 20.25b (https://tinyco.re/7756070) in *The Economy*). This is something about which Australian voters have a direct interest and which parallels the reasons why democracy sometimes addresses the problems of inequality. Democracy can empower those who will benefit if inequality or local environmental damage is reduced. But Australia is far from exemplary in its CO_2 emissions, whose effects on the environment are global not local. The Australian case highlights the limits of national democratic governments in achieving global environmental sustainability.

> **external effect** When a person's action confers a benefit or cost on some other individual, and this effect is not taken account of by the person in deciding to take the action. It is external because it is not included in the decision-making process of the person taking the action. Positive effects refer to benefits, and negative effects to costs, that are experienced by others. A person breathing second-hand smoke from someone else's cigarette is a negative external effect. Enjoying your neighbour's beautiful garden is a positive external effect. *Also known as: externality. See also: incomplete contract, market failure, external benefit, external cost.*

1.13 CONCLUSION

Beginning with a look at **economic inequality**, both between and within countries, we have analysed hockey-stick trajectories for real GDP per capita, labour productivity, global climate change and its primary source, carbon emissions. The kinks in the hockey sticks occur at different times for different countries and are associated both with the emergence of the permanent technological revolution and the **capitalist revolution**. Affluence, global inequality, and environmental degradation have often accompanied change in the **economic system**.

Capitalism is an economic system defined by three nested characteristics: **private property**, **markets**, and **firms**. Firms and markets made the **division of labour** and **specialization** possible on an unprecedented scale. Further contributing to increases in the productivity of a day of work, the process of **creative destruction** incentivizes cost-reducing innovation.

Capitalism is a system of winners and losers both within nations and across the globe, and this, along with creative destruction, contributes to inequality.

The combination of centralization within firms and decentralization via competition in markets makes it a unique and dynamic system. Both economic and political conditions, including what the **government** does as an economic actor, contribute to a capitalist system's dynamism. Important conditions are the security of private property and the provision of basic research and education.

The rising inequality at the time of the capitalist revolution is a factor that contributed first to demands for and later to the spread of **democracy**, a **political system** characterized by the rule of law, civil liberties and inclusive fair elections. Various forms of capitalism exist—some dynamic and some not, some alongside democratic governments and others not.

We have introduced economic statistics and measures such as **real GDP per capita** and **purchasing power parity (PPP)**. We have seen how the **ratio scale** is useful for comparing growth rates in charts. To address the challenge of knowing when something like capitalism may cause something like economic growth, we have introduced a **natural experiment**, in which treatment and control groups occur outside the laboratory.

Capitalism and democracy continue to evolve, to change each other, to revolutionize the world, and to affect your everyday life. As a result of the environmental **external effects** of economic decisions, both capitalism and democracy are challenged to find ways to avert catastrophic climate change. **Economics** will help you understand these changes and show you ways that you—with others—can participate in this constant process of change.

1.14 *DOING ECONOMICS*: MEASURING CLIMATE CHANGE

In this unit, we discussed climate change as one of the effects of the rapid economic growth that happened in most countries since the Industrial Revolution. Climate change is an important issue for policymaking, since governments need to assess how serious the problem is and then decide how to mitigate it.

Suppose you are a policy advisor for a small island nation. The government would like to know more about the extent of climate change and its possible causes. They ask you the following questions:

1. How can we tell whether climate change is actually happening?
2. If it is real, how can we measure the extent of climate change and determine what is causing it?

Go to *Doing Economics* Empirical Project 1 (https://tinyco.re/3159330) to work on this problem.

> *Learning objectives*
> In this project you will:
>
> - use charts and summary measures to discuss the extent of climate change and its possible causes
> - use line charts to describe the behaviour of real-world variables over time
> - summarize data in a frequency table, and visualize distributions with column chart
> - describe a distribution using mean and variance
> - use scatterplots and the correlation coefficient to assess the degree of association between two variables
> - explain what correlation measures, and the limitations of correlation.

1.15 REFERENCES

Acemoglu, Daron, and James A. Robinson. 2012. *Why Nations Fail: The Origins of Power, Prosperity, and Poverty*. New York, NY: Crown Publishing Group.

Alvaredo, Facundo, Anthony B. Atkinson, Thomas Piketty, Emmanuel Saez, and Gabriel Zucman. 2016. *The World Wealth and Income Database (WID)* (https://tinyco.re/5262390).

Atkinson, Anthony B., and Thomas Piketty, eds. 2007. *Top Incomes Over the Twentieth Century: A Contrast between Continental European and English-Speaking Countries*. Oxford: Oxford University Press.

Berghoff, Hartmut, and Uta Andrea Balbier. 2013. 'From Centrally Planned Economy to Capitalist Avant-Garde? The Creation, Collapse, and Transformation of a Socialist Economy'. In *The East German Economy, 1945–2010: Falling behind or Catching Up?* Cambridge: Cambridge University Press.

Churchill, Winston. 1946. 'Iron Curtain' speech (https://tinyco.re/6053919).

Deaton, A. 2013. *The Great Escape: health, wealth, and the origins of inequality* (https://tinyco.re/5750302). Princeton: Princeton University Press.

Drèze, Jean, and Amartya Sen. 2013. *An Uncertain Glory: India and its Contradictions*. Princeton, NJ: Princeton University Press: p. 2.

Landes, David S. 2003. *The Unbound Prometheus: Technological Change and Industrial Development in Western Europe from 1750 to the Present*. Cambridge: Cambridge University Press.

Piketty, Thomas. 2014. *Capital in the Twenty-First Century*. Cambridge, MA: Harvard University Press.

Plummer, Alfred. 1971. *Bronterre: A Political Biography of Bronterre O'Brien, 1804–64*. Toronto: University of Toronto Press.

Schumpeter, Joseph. (1943) 2003. *Capitalism, Socialism and Democracy* (https://tinyco.re/4138375). pp. 167—72. Routledge.

Schumpeter, Joseph A. 1949. 'Science and Ideology' (https://tinyco.re/4561610). *The American Economic Review* 39 (March): pp. 345–59.

Schumpeter, Joseph A. 1997. *Ten Great Economists*. London: Routledge.

Seabright, Paul. 2010. *The Company of Strangers: A Natural History of Economic Life* (Revised Edition). Princeton, NJ: Princeton University Press.

Skidelsky, Robert. 2012. 'Robert Skidelsky-portrait: Joseph Schumpeter' (https://tinyco.re/8488199).

Smith, Adam. 1759. *The Theory of Moral Sentiments* (https://tinyco.re/6582039). London: Printed for A. Millar, and A. Kincaid and J. Bell.

Smith, Adam. 1776. *An Inquiry into the Nature and Causes of the Wealth of Nations* (https://tinyco.re/9804148). New York: NY: Random House Publishing Group.

World Bank, The. 1993. *The East Asian miracle: Economic growth and public policy* (https://tinyco.re/3040506). New York, NY: Oxford University Press.

2 SOCIAL INTERACTIONS AND ECONOMIC OUTCOMES

Playing xiangqi

2.1 INTRODUCTION

- When people choose to interact they do so because there is some opportunity for at least one of them to gain; but there is often a conflict about how these gains should be shared.
- We use game theory to show why the pursuit of self-interest can sometimes lead to results that are considered good by all participants, or outcomes that none of the participants would prefer.
- Social dilemmas like antibiotic misuse or environmental degradation occur when someone does not fully take account of the effects of their decisions on others.
- We collect data from experiments and use other evidence to show that both self-interest and social preferences—including a concern for others, feelings of reciprocity, and a preference for fairness—are all important motives that explain how people interact.
- We illustrate how the tools developed in this unit can be applied to a range of economic situations, including the global challenge of climate change.

Since the discovery of penicillin in 1928, the development of antibiotics has brought huge benefits to mankind. Diseases that were once fatal are now treated easily with medicines that are cheap to produce and widely available. But the World Health Organization has recently warned that we are heading for a 'post-antibiotic era' (https://tinyco.re/4578245) as many bacteria are becoming resistant to antibiotics: 'Unless we take significant actions to … change how we produce, prescribe and use antibiotics, the world will lose more and more of these global public health goods and the implications will be devastating.'

- Bacteria become resistant to antibiotics—turning into 'super-bugs'—when we use them too often, in the wrong dosage, or for conditions that are not caused by bacteria.
- Doctors recognize that leaving the allocation of antibiotics to the market has damaging consequences. In India, for example, antibiotics are easily available over the counter in pharmacies without a doctor's prescription and misuse is common.
- In these situations, people often use antibiotics when other treatments would be better. Even when antibiotics are appropriate, patients often stop taking the antibiotics to save money, when they feel a little better. These are exactly the patterns of use that will produce antibiotic-resistant pathogens.

social dilemma A situation in which actions, taken independently by individuals in pursuit of their own private objectives, may result in an outcome that is inferior to some other feasible outcome that could have occurred if people had acted together, rather than as individuals.

external effect When a person's action confers a benefit or cost on some other individual, and this effect is not taken account of by the person in deciding to take the action. It is external because it is not included in the decision-making process of the person taking the action. Positive effects refer to benefits, and negative effects to costs, that are experienced by others. A person breathing second-hand smoke from someone else's cigarette is a negative external effect. Enjoying your neighbour's beautiful garden is a positive external effect. *Also known as: externality. See also: incomplete contract, market failure, external benefit, external cost.*

For the patient, however, the treatment worked—or seemed to work—and the business of those supplying antibiotics will prosper. The overuse of antibiotics occurs because the user does not take account of the costs that will be imposed on others when superbugs proliferate.

The problem of misuse of antibiotics is far from unique. It is an example of what is called a **social dilemma**. Social dilemmas—like antibiotic misuse or environmental degradation—occur when people do not take adequate account of the effects of their decisions on others, whether these are positive or negative.

In Section 1.12 (page 40) of Unit 1, you learned that, because the effects on others are not fully taken into account, they are called **external effects** or externalities. The example used was how our decisions about what to consume, how to generate power and other environmentally sensitive choices affect our neighbours, those in other countries, and future generations.

Here, the external effect is that *my* misuse of an antibiotic may result in the superbug that kills *you*: overusing antibiotics for minor illnesses may allow the sick person to recover more quickly, but it also creates the external effect of antibiotic-resistant super bacteria that will kill many others. Similarly, traffic jams happen when our choice of a way to get around—for example driving alone to work rather than car-pooling—does not take account of the contribution to congestion and the longer commute times inflicted on others.

Social dilemmas occur frequently and diminish the quality of our lives and the lives of others. One of the tasks of public policies is to address social dilemmas, and economics has an important role in showing how this might be done.

2.2 TWO TYPES OF SOCIAL INTERACTION

Distinguishing between two types of **social interaction** helps us to understand the possible role of public policy. The key difference is whether external effects are present—as they are in a social dilemma.

The tragedy of the commons: A social dilemma

In 1968, Garrett Hardin, a biologist, published an article about social dilemmas in the journal *Science*, called 'The Tragedy of the Commons'. Hardin described a group of cattle herders, each raising ever-larger herds and eventually overgrazing their shared pastureland, driving it, their animals, and the herders themselves to ruin. Hardin's **tragedy of the commons** is a social dilemma.

He wrote that resources that are not owned by anyone (sometimes called 'common property' or 'common-pool resources'), such as the earth's atmosphere or fish stocks, are easily overexploited unless we control access in some way. The fishing industry would be more sustainable if each fishing boat were to catch fewer tuna in any given year, preserving stocks for the future catch. Humanity would be better off if businesses and individuals around the world would make choices limiting the emission of pollutants, or the use of antibiotics. But if you cut your own consumption, reduce your carbon footprint, or limit the number of tuna you catch, *you* will bear the costs, while *others* will enjoy the benefits today and in the future.

Examples of Hardin's tragedies and other social dilemmas are all around us: if you live with roommates, or in a family, you know just how difficult it is to keep a clean kitchen or bathroom. When one person cleans, everyone benefits, but it is hard work. Whoever cleans up bears this cost. The others are sometimes called **free riders**. If, as a student, you have ever done a group assignment, you understand that the cost of effort (to study the problem, gather evidence, or write up the results) is individual, yet the benefits (a better grade for the group project, higher class standing, or simply the admiration of classmates) go to all the members of group. A project member who does not care about the other members of the group may free ride; if all do this, the project will not amount to much and the grades of all project members will suffer.

The invisible hand: When self-interest works

Hardin's tragedy of the commons raised a warning flag against a common economic idea, namely the invisible hand, introduced by Adam Smith (page 17), the eighteenth-century founder of economics. Smith identified conditions under which individuals pursuing their own interest, without regard for the interests of others, can be consistent with the common good. He wrote that, under the right laws and economic institutions (private property, and competition among many economic actors), the economy would be guided, as if by an 'invisible hand' towards a socially beneficial outcome.

We will see in later units that there are conditions—competition and the absence of external effects—under which the mechanism discovered by Smith works, and how it can live up to his remarkable claim. But Hardin's example of the environmental degradation from the external effect of one herder placing an additional cow on the pasture, and many other similar social dilemmas, show that it is often not true. That's why Hardin called his 'tragedy' a 'rebuttal to the invisible hand'.

---

social interaction A situation in which the actions taken by each person affect other people's outcomes as well as their own.
tragedy of the commons A social dilemma in which self-interested individuals acting independently deplete a common resource, lowering the payoffs of all. See also: social dilemma.

Garrett Hardin. 1968. 'The Tragedy of the Commons' (https://tinyco.re/4834967). *Science* 162 (3859): pp. 1243–1248.

free ride Benefiting from the contributions of others to some cooperative project without contributing oneself.

Elinor Ostrom. 2008. 'The Challenge of Common-Pool Resources' (https://tinyco.re/0296632). *Environment: Science and Policy for Sustainable Development* 50 (4): pp. 8–21.

When we think about some economic or social or even biological problem, and how it might be resolved, we need to have in mind these two big ideas—the invisible hand and the tragedy of the commons. When we see a social interaction, we must ask whether it is a situation in which individuals, pursuing their own interests could, in principle, result in better outcomes for at least one person.

The answer will differ on a case-by-case basis, and so will the remedies. Some social dilemmas are resolved by communities, and some by government action. Some are avoided or at least moderated because humans have motives other than self-interest.

There is nothing new about social dilemmas. We have been facing them since prehistory.

More than 2,500 years ago Aesop, a Greek storyteller, wrote about a social dilemma in his fable *Belling the Cat*. A group of mice needs one of its members to place a bell around a cat's neck. Once the bell is on, the cat cannot catch and eat the other mice. But the outcome may not be so good for the mouse that takes the job. Each mouse would like to free ride on some other brave (or perhaps suicidal) mouse.

Aesop. 'Belling the Cat'. In *Fables*, retold by Joseph Jacobs. XVII, (1). The Harvard Classics. New York: P. F. Collier & Son, 1909–14; Bartleby.com (https://tinyco.re/6827567). 2001.

2.3 RESOLVING SOCIAL DILEMMAS

Social dilemmas can be avoided or minimized if people care sufficiently about how their actions affect others, or if society is organized so that people are constrained or motivated to act as if they did. We use the term '**social preferences**' to describe caring about others, and 'social institutions' to describe these constraints.

social preferences A person with social preferences cares not only about how her action affects her personally, but also about how it affects other people. Also known as: other-regarding preferences.

preference Pro-and-con evaluations of the possible outcomes of the actions we may take that form the basis by which we decide on a course of action.

Social Preferences: Caring about others

In a particular situation, people differ in their **preferences**—the way they compare alternatives as better or worse than each other, and use this evaluation as the basis of taking an action. For example, some people prefer coffee to tea, others prefer tea, and others do not like either. The available actions in question would be: 'have a cup of tea', 'have a cup of coffee', and 'don't have either coffee or tea'. Your preferences indicate which action you will take.

Our preferences may describe the food we like to eat, the importance we place on family as opposed to work, or how much we value free time as opposed to the money we would make if we worked more. We will see that preferences, along with other information, are part of our explanation of why people do the things they do.

To understand social dilemmas, and how they might be avoided, we distinguish between two classes of preferences:

- *Self-interested preferences:* When a person with self-interested preferences chooses to take some action, she only takes account of how it affects her personally, ignoring the effects on others.
- *Social preferences:* A person with these preferences cares not only about how her action affects her personally, but also about how it affects other people.

A person can simultaneously have self-interested preferences when making a menu choice in a restaurant, and social preferences when deciding how much effort to put in to keeping the family bathroom clean.

Social preferences are also called 'other-regarding' preferences because what happens to others is important to the person. In the same way, self-interested preferences are also called 'self-regarding'.

Social preferences are often expressed in social norms of good behaviour such as the principle found in many cultures, and in the social teachings of many religions, popularly known as the Golden Rule. This states that we should treat others as we would like to be treated ourselves.

Sometimes acting on one's social preferences is simply pleasurable, more like enjoying a good meal than conforming to some moral rule. This is what Abraham Lincoln, president of the US between 1861 and 1865, probably had in mind when he told his biographer: 'When I do good I feel good, when I do bad I feel bad, and that's my religion.'

Lincoln is not alone. There is a lot of evidence, including from neuroscience, that helping others even at a cost to oneself is a source of pleasure for many people. But if Lincoln felt good about doing good, does that mean that he was self-interested? No. What he felt good about was helping others, for example, by freeing slaves after the US Civil War. The preferences motivating him to do this were other-regarding.

The expression 'social preference' sounds like a good thing. But this need not be the case. Caring about what happens to others can also include wishing someone else harm, for example hating people of a different race or religion.

Social preferences are important in economics because they affect our behaviour in economically relevant ways, for example:

- *Paying taxes honestly:* One values the benefit to other people that the government's tax revenues will provide.
- *Changing one's lifestyle to help support a better environment:* This benefits future generations or perhaps other people who live in locations affected by air pollution.
- *Cooperating with others to achieve common objectives:* These may be a safer more pleasant neighbourhood, or demonstrating for a political cause, even when you would enjoy the benefits whether you participated or not.

Social preferences can help to resolve a social dilemma. If each of Hardin's herders, for example, cared about the wellbeing of each of the others, then each would have taken account of the damage done to all, and would have not placed additional animals on the pasture, where in this case the action is: 'place another animal on the pasture.'

The source of Hardin's social dilemma is the negative external effect of taking the action. This would be the cost borne by all the other herders when the pasture is overgrazed, which Hardin's self-interested individual herder does not consider. A herder with social preferences would take these negative external effects into account. That is to say, the herder would 'internalize' what would otherwise be an external effect.

Social institutions: The rules of the game

Social preferences are not the only way that societies resolve social dilemmas. Sometimes they can be resolved by government policies. For example, in the UK, the amount of waste that is dumped in landfills, rather than being recycled, has been dramatically reduced by a landfill tax (https://tinyco.re/8403762). The tax requires people to pay for the external costs they impose on others. Therefore it internalizes those costs, which changes their behaviour. In other cases, governments may simply prohibit actions that have negative external effects. For example, the use of strict quotas on fishing has averted the collapse of European North Atlantic stocks of cod (https://tinyco.re/3728803).

Local communities also create institutions to regulate behaviour. Irrigation communities need people to work to maintain canals that benefit the whole community by providing water. Individuals also need to use scarce water sparingly so that other crops will flourish, although this will lead to smaller crops for themselves. In Valencia, Spain, communities of farmers have used a set of customary rules for centuries to regulate communal tasks and to avoid using too much water. Since the Middle Ages, they have had an arbitration court called the *Tribunal de las Aguas* (https://tinyco.re/8410208) (Water Court) that resolves conflicts between farmers about the application of the rules. The ruling of the *Tribunal* is not legally enforceable. Its power comes only from the respect of the community, yet its decisions are almost universally followed.

Even present-day global environmental problems have sometimes been tackled effectively. The Montreal Protocol (https://tinyco.re/8364376) has been remarkably successful. It was created to phase out and eventually ban the chlorofluorocarbons (CFCs) that threatened to destroy the ozone layer that protects us against harmful ultraviolet radiation. The carbon emissions that result in global climate change have proven a more difficult challenge. We return at the end of the unit to global efforts to reach agreement about mitigating climate change.

QUESTION 2.1 CHOOSE THE CORRECT ANSWER(S)
Which of the following is an example of a social dilemma?

- ☐ dirty dishes piling up in the kitchen sink of your shared student accommodation
- ☐ dilemmas discussed on social media
- ☐ the problem of how to look after the elderly in society
- ☐ traffic jams due to people driving cars instead of car-pooling or taking public transportation

QUESTION 2.2 CHOOSE THE CORRECT ANSWER(S)
Which of the following is an example of free riding?

- ☐ fare dodgers on the subway
- ☐ small shareholders, having not read the accounts or the reports, benefit from the decisions of large investors, who have taken the time to gather information about the company
- ☐ fellow students benefitting from your efforts in a group work assignment
- ☐ fishermen in an overfished lake

EXERCISE 2.1 SOCIAL DILEMMAS
Using the news headlines from last week:

1. Identify two social dilemmas that have been reported (try to use examples not discussed above).
2. For each, explain why it is a social dilemma.

2.4 SOCIAL INTERACTIONS AS GAMES

In this unit, we will identify cases in which Adam Smith's reasoning about the invisible hand as a way of representing how people interact in the economy is a reasonable guide to public policy. We also study other cases that are more like Hardin's tragedy of the commons.

Introducing game theory

To distinguish between the two cases, we will use the tools of **game theory** to model social interactions.

On which side of the road should you drive? If you live in Japan, the UK, or Indonesia, you drive on the left. If you live in South Korea, France, or the US, you drive on the right. If you grew up in Sweden, you drove on the left until 5 p.m. on 3 September 1967, and at 5.01 p.m. you started driving on the right. The government sets a rule, and we follow it.

But suppose we just left the choice to drivers to pursue their self-interest and to select one side of the road or the other. If everyone else was already driving on the right, self-interest (avoiding a collision) would be sufficient to motivate a driver to drive on the right as well. Concern for other drivers, or a desire to obey the law, would not be necessary.

Devising policies to promote people's wellbeing requires an understanding of the difference between situations in which self-interest can promote general wellbeing, and cases in which it leads to undesirable results.

Not all social interactions lead to social dilemmas, even if individuals act in pursuit of their own interests. We will start with an example where the 'invisible hand' of the market channels self-interest so that individuals acting independently do reach a mutually beneficial outcome.

> **game theory** A branch of mathematics that studies strategic interactions, meaning situations in which each actor knows that the benefits they receive depend on the actions taken by all. See also: *game*.

Setting up a game

To see how game theory can clarify social interactions, imagine two independent farmers, who we will call Anil and Bala. Each faces a problem: should he grow rice or cassava, or both?

We assume that they have the ability to grow both types of crop:

- *They benefit from choosing one crop:* They could produce some of one crop and some of the other, but they benefit from specializing in one or the other crop because the knowledge and tools required for each differs.
- *Their land differs:* Anil's land is better suited for growing cassava, while Bala's is better suited for rice.

For these two reasons, they can do better by participating in a social interaction and specializing than by going it alone. Each farmer must decide which crop to produce. They decide this independently, which means they do not meet to discuss a course of action.

To model this problem using game theory, we use four terms:

- When people are engaged in a social interaction and are aware of the ways that their actions affect others, and vice versa, we call this a **strategic interaction**.
- A **strategy** is defined as an action (or a course of action) that a person may take when that person is aware of the mutual dependence of the results for herself and for others. The outcomes depend not only on that person's actions, but also on the actions of others.

> **strategic interaction** A social interaction in which the participants are aware of the ways that their actions affect others (and the ways that the actions of others affect them).
> **strategy** An action (or a course of action) that a person may take when that person is aware of the mutual dependence of the results for herself and for others. The outcomes depend not only on that person's actions, but also on the actions of others.
> **game** A model of strategic interaction that describes the players, the feasible strategies, the information that the players have, and their payoffs. See also: *game theory*.

- Models of strategic interactions are described as **games**.
- **Game theory** is a set of models of strategic interactions. It is widely used in economics and elsewhere in the social sciences, and even in biology and the training of military strategists.

Assuming independent decisions may seem odd in this model of just two farmers, but later we apply the same logic to climate change, in which hundreds or even millions of people interact, most of them total strangers to one another. Therefore, it is useful for us to assume that Anil and Bala do not come to some common agreement before taking action. This is called a non-cooperative game.

They both sell whatever crop they produce in a nearby village market.

- On market day, if they bring less rice to the market, the price will be higher.
- The same goes for cassava.

Figure 2.1 describes their interaction. We will refer to the interaction between Anil and Bala as the 'invisible hand game'. You will see why shortly.

Let's explain what Figure 2.1 means, because you will be seeing this a lot. You will become familiar with the terms used in game theory as we work through a variety of games in this unit.

Anil's choices are the rows of the table and Bala's are the columns. We call Anil the 'row player' and Bala the 'column player'.

To figure out how Anil and Bala might act in this situation, game theory asks us to engage in a series of 'what if?' questions. In Figure 2.1, each entry describes the outcome of a hypothetical situation. For example, the top left cell should be interpreted as: 'What would happen if (for any reason) Anil planted rice and Bala planted rice too?'

It does not matter that they may not choose to do this, the figure is just a way of exploring the possible outcomes of their interactions.

The entry in the top left cell indicates that since both are producing rice, there is a glut of rice on the village market, which will result in a low price, but a shortage of cassava. So, were they both to plant rice, neither of them would do very well. We also know that, because Anil is better at producing cassava than rice, he would do even worse than Bala.

There are four possible hypothetical situations. Figure 2.1 describes what would happen in each case.

To simplify the model, we assume that:

- There are no other people involved or affected in any way.
- The selection of which crop to grow is the only decision that Anil and Bala make.
- Anil and Bala will interact just once (because of this, it is called a **one-shot game**).
- They decide **simultaneously**. When a player makes a decision, that player doesn't know what the other person has decided to do (just like in the rock–paper–scissors game).

> **GAME**
> A description of a social interaction, which specifies:
> - *The players:* Who is interacting with whom
> - *The feasible strategies:* Which actions are open to the players
> - *The information:* What each player knows when making their decision
> - *The payoffs:* What the outcomes will be for each of the possible combinations of actions

> **one-shot game** A game that is played once and not repeated.
> **simultaneous game** A game in which players choose strategies simultaneously, for example the prisoners' dilemma. See also: *sequential game*.

	Bala	
	Rice	**Cassava**
Anil — Rice	Both produce rice: there is a glut of rice (low price) There is a shortage of cassava Anil not producing cassava, which he is better able to produce	No market glut High prices for both crops Both farmers producing the crop for which they are less suited
Anil — Cassava	No market glut High prices for both crops Both farmers producing the crop for which they are better suited	Both produce cassava: there is a glut of cassava (low price) There is a shortage of rice Bala not producing rice, which he is better able to produce

Figure 2.1 Social interactions in the invisible hand game.

Figure 2.2a shows the **payoffs** for Anil and Bala in each of the four hypothetical situations in a standard format that we call a **payoff matrix**.

- *Payoffs:* These are the incomes they would receive if the hypothetical row and column actions were taken.
- *A matrix:* This is just any rectangular (in this case square) array of numbers.
- Because the market price falls when it is flooded with one crop, they can do better if they specialize compared to when they both produce the same good.
- When they produce different goods, they would both do better if each person specialized in the crop that was most suitable for their land.

> **payoff** The benefit to each player associated with the joint actions of all the players.
> **payoff matrix** A table of the payoffs associated with every possible combination of strategies chosen by two or more players in a game.

2 SOCIAL INTERACTIONS AND ECONOMIC OUTCOMES

	Bala: Rice	Bala: Cassava
Anil: Rice	Anil gets 1, Bala gets 3	Both get 2
Anil: Cassava	Both get 4	Anil gets 3, Bala gets 1

Figure 2.2a The payoffs in the invisible hand game.

QUESTION 2.3 CHOOSE THE CORRECT ANSWER(S)

Which of the following statements are true? Use the payoff matrix in Figure 2.2a and the additional assumption that if they do not engage in a social interaction and instead operate as subsistence farmers consuming only what they produce, their payoff is 1.

☐ If Anil chooses Rice and Bala chooses Cassava, they both get a payoff of 4.
☐ The best outcome for both Anil and Bala is if both specialize in the crop that is most suitable for their land.
☐ Anil and Bala only benefit (each individual is strictly better off) from the interaction if they choose to produce different crops.
☐ If Anil and Bala choose the same crop, both of them would still be strictly better off than producing crops for their own use.

58

2.5 WHEN SELF-INTEREST WORKS: THE INVISIBLE HAND

Game theory describes social interactions, and it may also provide predictions about what will happen. To predict the outcome of a game, we need another concept: **best response**. This is the strategy that will give a player the highest payoff, given the strategies the other players select.

In Figure 2.2b we represent the payoffs for Anil and Bala in the invisible hand game in a payoff matrix. We have simplified the way we write a payoff matrix a little. The first number in each box is the reward received by the row player (whose name begins with A as a reminder that his payoff is first). The second number is the column player's payoff.

Think about best responses in this game. Suppose you are Anil, and you consider the hypothetical case in which Bala has chosen to grow rice. Which response yields you the higher payoff? You would grow cassava (in this case, you—Anil—would get a payoff of 4, but you would get a payoff of only 1 if you grew rice instead).

Work through the steps in Figure 2.2b to see that choosing Cassava is also Anil's best response if Bala chooses Cassava. Cassava is therefore Anil's **dominant strategy**: it will give him the highest payoff, whatever Bala does. You will also see that Bala has a dominant strategy too. The analysis gives you a handy method for keeping track of best responses by placing dots and circles in the payoff matrix.

Because both players have a dominant strategy, we have a simple prediction about what each will do: play their dominant strategy. Anil will grow cassava, and Bala will grow rice. This pair of strategies is a **dominant strategy equilibrium** of the game.

An **equilibrium** is a self-perpetuating situation: something of interest does not change. In this case, Anil choosing Cassava and Bala choosing Rice is an equilibrium because neither of them would want to change their decision after seeing what the other player chose.

If we find that both players in a two-player game have dominant strategies, the game has a dominant strategy equilibrium. As we will see later, this does not always happen. But when it does, we predict that these are the strategies that will be played.

Because both Anil and Bala have a dominant strategy, their choice of crop is not affected by what they expect the other person to do. But the payoff does. For example, if Anil is playing his dominant strategy (Cassava) he is better off if Bala plays Rice than if Bala plays Cassava as well.

In the dominant strategy equilibrium, Anil and Bala have specialized in producing the good for which their land is better suited. Simply pursuing their self-interest—choosing the strategy for which they got the highest payoff—resulted in an outcome that was:

- the best of the four possible outcomes for each player.
- the strategy that yielded the largest total payoffs for the two farmers combined.

> **best response** In game theory, the strategy that will give a player the highest payoff, given the strategies that the other players select.

> **dominant strategy** Strategy that yields the highest payoff for a player, no matter what the other players do.
> **dominant strategy equilibrium** An outcome of a game in which every player plays his or her dominant strategy.
> **equilibrium** A model outcome that does not change unless an outside or external force is introduced that alters the model's description of the situation.

2 SOCIAL INTERACTIONS AND ECONOMIC OUTCOMES

> **QUESTION 2.4 CHOOSE THE CORRECT ANSWER(S)**
> Which of the following statements is correct?
>
> ☐ A social interaction is a strategic interaction where people are aware of the ways that their actions affect each other.
> ☐ A dominant strategy is the strategy that gives the player the highest payoff, irrespective of the strategies selected by other players.
> ☐ A strategy is an action that a person may take when that person is unaware of the effect of their action on others.
> ☐ A best response is the strategy that results in the socially optimal outcome if all players choose it.

To explore all of the slides in this figure, see the online version at https://tinyco.re/3285498.

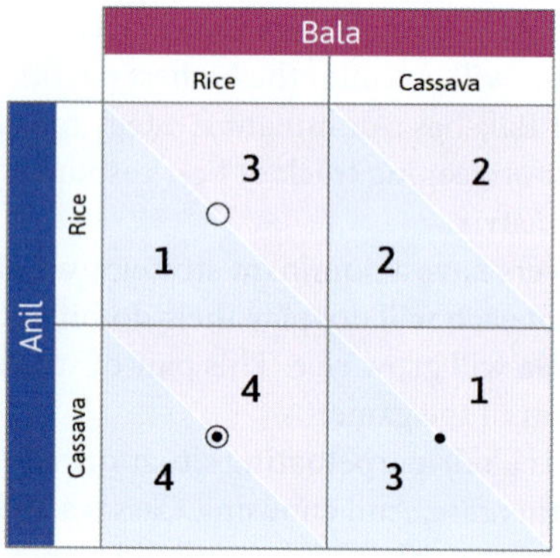

Figure 2.2b The payoff matrix in the invisible hand game.

1. Finding best responses
Begin with the row player (Anil) and ask, 'What would be his best response to the column player's (Bala's) decision to play Rice?'

2. Anil's best response if Bala grows rice
If Bala chooses Rice, Anil's best response is to choose Cassava—that gives him 4, rather than 1. Place a dot in the bottom left-hand cell. A dot in a cell means that this is the row player's best response.

3. Anil's best response if Bala grows cassava
If Bala chooses Cassava, Anil's best response is to choose Cassava too—giving him 3, rather than 2. Place a dot in the bottom right-hand cell.

4. Anil has a dominant strategy
Both dots are on the bottom row. Whatever Bala's choice, Anil's best response is to choose Cassava. Cassava is a dominant strategy for Anil.

5. Now find the column player's best responses
If Anil chooses Rice, Bala's best response is to choose Rice (3 rather than 2). Circles represent the column player's best responses. Place a circle in the top left cell.

6. Bala has a dominant strategy too
If Anil chooses Cassava, Bala's best response is again to choose Rice (he gets 4 rather than 3). Place a circle in the bottom left cell. Rice is Bala's dominant strategy (both circles are in the same column).

7. Both players will play their dominant strategies
We predict that Anil will choose Cassava and Bala will choose Rice because that is their dominant strategy. Where the dot and circle coincide, the players are both playing best responses to each other.

The invisible hand at work

In this example, the dominant strategy equilibrium is the outcome that each would have chosen if they had a way of coordinating their decisions. Although they independently pursued their self-interest, they were guided 'as if by an invisible hand' to an outcome that was in both of their best interests, and in this society of two people, produces the best social outcome. For this reason, we call the game the **invisible hand game**.

Adam Smith was writing about an economy far more complicated than our two-person game depicts. But our simplified version conveys one of Smith's lasting contributions to economics: the idea that the pursuit of self-interest can sometimes be a good thing.

The pursuit of self-interest without regard for others is sometimes considered to be morally bad, but the study of economics has identified cases in which it can lead to outcomes that are socially desirable.

There are other cases, however, in which the pursuit of self-interest leads to results that are not in the self-interest of any of the players. The **prisoners' dilemma** game, which we study next, describes one of these situations.

2.6 WHEN SELF-INTEREST DOESN'T WORK: THE PRISONERS' DILEMMA

Imagine that Anil and Bala are now facing a different problem. Instead of deciding which crop to grow, each is now deciding how to deal with pest insects that destroy the crops they cultivate in their adjacent fields. Each has two feasible strategies:

- *Use an inexpensive chemical called Terminator:* It kills every insect for miles around, both pests and beneficial insects. Terminator also leaches into the water supply that they both use.
- *Use integrated pest control (IPC) instead of a chemical:* A farmer using IPC introduces beneficial insects to the farm. The beneficial insects eat the pest insects.

There are, thus, four possible situations (two possibilities each for two farmers). Figure 2.3a describes what would happen in each of the four hypothetical situations:

- *If one farmer chooses Terminator and the other one chooses IPC:* There is some damage to insects and the water supply, but it is limited. (This describes the top right and bottom left cells).
- *If they both choose Terminator:* Water contamination becomes a serious problem, and they need to buy a costly filtering system (the bottom right cell).
- *If they both choose IPC:* Pest insects are eliminated, and the water supply is safe (the top left cell).

Both Anil and Bala are aware of these outcomes. Anil knows that his individual payoff depends not just on the choice of pesticide he makes, but also on the choice that Bala makes (and likewise for Bala). Like the invisible hand game, this type of situation is a strategic interaction.

---

invisible hand game A game in which there is a single Nash equilibrium and where there is no other outcome in which both players would be better off or at least one better off and the other not worse off. *See also:* Nash equilibrium, Pareto efficient.

prisoners' dilemma A game in which the payoffs in the dominant strategy equilibrium are lower for each player, and also lower in total, than if neither player played the dominant strategy.

EXERCISE 2.2 AMORAL SELF-INTEREST

Imagine a society in which everyone was entirely self-interested (cared only about his or her own wealth) and amoral (followed no ethical rules that would interfere with gaining that wealth). How would that society be different from the society you live in? Consider the following:
- families
- workplaces
- neighbourhoods
- traffic
- political activity (would people vote?)

2 SOCIAL INTERACTIONS AND ECONOMIC OUTCOMES

Using payoffs to predict the outcome in a strategic interaction

The payoff for Anil and Bala is their profit—the amount of money they will make at harvest time, minus the costs of their pest control strategy and the costs of installing water filtration, if that becomes necessary. Figure 2.3b shows the respective payoffs for Anil and Bala.

What will each of them choose to do? We can use the payoffs to predict the outcome. We can use the same method as in the invisible hand game (draw the dots and circles in the payoff matrix for yourself).

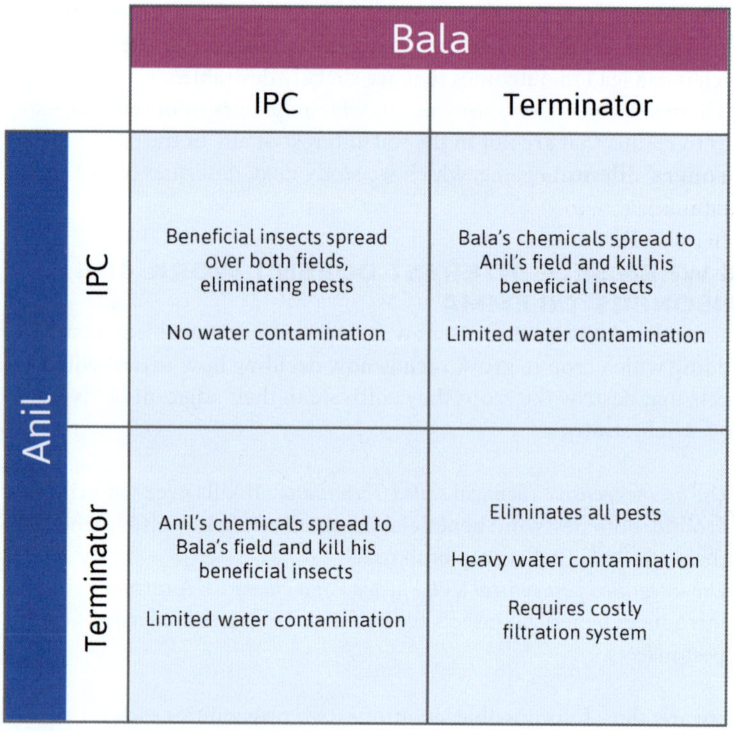

	Bala: IPC	Bala: Terminator
Anil: IPC	Beneficial insects spread over both fields, eliminating pests. No water contamination	Bala's chemicals spread to Anil's field and kill his beneficial insects. Limited water contamination
Anil: Terminator	Anil's chemicals spread to Bala's field and kill his beneficial insects. Limited water contamination	Eliminates all pests. Heavy water contamination. Requires costly filtration system

Figure 2.3a Social interactions in the pest control game.

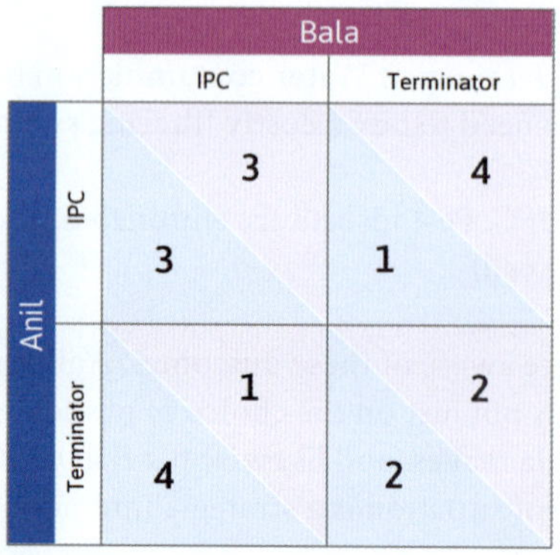

	Bala: IPC	Bala: Terminator
Anil: IPC	3 , 3	4 , 1
Anil: Terminator	1 , 4	2 , 2

Figure 2.3b Payoff matrix for the pest control game.

From Anil's point of view:

- *If Bala chooses IPC:* Anil's best option is to choose Terminator (payoff is 4, he gets cheap eradication of pests, and because he alone is using Terminator, there is little water contamination).
- *If Bala chooses Terminator:* Anil again does best to choose Terminator (he gets a greater payoff than if he chooses IPC because Terminator is cheaper and, in any event, Bala's Terminator chemicals would kill off the IPC's beneficial pests).

Terminator therefore is Anil's dominant strategy. From Bala's point of view:

- *If Anil chooses IPC:* Bala's best option is to choose Terminator (payoff is 4, he gets cheap eradication of pests, and because he alone is using Terminator, there is little water contamination).

You can check, similarly, that Terminator is also Bala's best response if Anil chooses Terminator. Bala's dominant strategy is therefore Terminator.

Because Terminator is the dominant strategy for both, we predict that both will use it. Where every player plays his or her dominant strategy in a game, this is called a **dominant strategy equilibrium** of the game.

> **dominant strategy equilibrium** An outcome of a game in which every player plays his or her dominant strategy.

QUESTION 2.5 CHOOSE THE CORRECT ANSWER(S)

Anna and Brian are discussing what to watch on TV tonight. There are two choices—a film or the snooker world championships. They can either watch one of the two programmes together, or watch different programmes in separate rooms. The following table represents the happiness levels (payoffs) of Anna and Brian, depending on their choice of programme (the top number is Brian's happiness level, while the bottom number is Anna's). Based on this information, which of the following statements are correct?

	Brian: Snooker	Brian: Film
Anna: Snooker	8 / 5	2 / 1
Anna: Film	6 / 2	4 / 4

Figure 2.4 Snooker or film?

☐ Anna's dominant strategy is to watch the film.
☐ Brian's dominant strategy is to watch snooker.
☐ There is no dominant strategy equilibrium.
☐ The dominant strategy equilibrium is for both to watch snooker.

2 SOCIAL INTERACTIONS AND ECONOMIC OUTCOMES

QUESTION 2.6 CHOOSE THE CORRECT ANSWER(S)

Alan and Beatrice have broken the rules and colluded in their coursework assignment, so the examiners are going to interview them. The interviews are taking place simultaneously and there is no communication allowed between the two. The students can either deny or confess to have colluded. The raw marks without penalty are 65 for Alan and 70 for Beatrice.

The examiners have decided on the following scheme: if they both deny, they will be penalised by 20 marks respectively; if one denies and the other confesses, then the denying student gets zero marks, while the confessing student retains their raw mark; if they both confess, then they both get the pass mark of 40. The possible outcomes are summarised in Figure 2.5.

	Beatrice Deny	Beatrice Confess
Alan Deny	50 / 45	70 / 0
Alan Confess	0 / 65	40 / 40

Figure 2.5 Deny or confess?

Based on this information which of the following statements is correct?

- ☐ The dominant strategy equilibrium will result in the highest aggregate mark.
- ☐ It is in the students' interests to deviate from the dominant strategy equilibrium.
- ☐ Denying is the dominant strategy.
- ☐ The examiners have managed to devise a scheme in which the students will definitely confess.

The prisoners' dilemma game

In our game, Anil and Bala each receive payoffs of 2, but both would be better off if they both used IPC instead. The *predicted* outcome is therefore not the *best feasible* outcome. The pest control game is a particular example of a game called the **prisoners' dilemma**. Another example is Hardin's tragedy of the commons, where the failure of cattle herders to take account of the impact of grazing on the common pool resource of the meadow led to the collapse of the ecosystem.

prisoners' dilemma A game in which the payoffs in the dominant strategy equilibrium are lower for each player, and also lower in total, than if neither player played the dominant strategy.

2.6 WHEN SELF-INTEREST DOESN'T WORK: THE PRISONERS' DILEMMA

FIND OUT MORE

The prisoner's dilemma
The name of this game comes from a story about two prisoners (we call them Thelma and Louise) whose strategies are either to Accuse (implicate) the other in a crime that the prisoners may have committed together, or Deny that the other prisoner was involved.

If both Thelma and Louise deny it, they are freed after a few days of questioning.

If one person accusing the other person, while the other person denies, the accuser will be freed immediately (a sentence of zero years), whereas the other person gets a long jail sentence (10 years).

Lastly, if both Thelma and Louise choose Accuse (meaning each implicates the other), they both get a jail sentence. This sentence is reduced from 10 years to 5 years because of their cooperation with the police. The payoffs of the game are shown in Figure 2.6. (Note: The payoffs are written in terms of years of prison—so Louise and Thelma prefer lower numbers.)

		Louise	
		Deny	Accuse
Thelma	Deny	1 / 1	0 / 10
	Accuse	10 / 0	5 / 5

Figure 2.6 Prisoners' dilemma (payoffs are years in prison).

For Anil and Bala, there are three aspects of their interaction that lead us to predict an unfortunate outcome in their prisoners' dilemma game:

- They did not place any value on the payoffs of the other person—Anil doesn't worry about the elimination of Bala's beneficial insects. If he did, he might take a different decision (see 'Social preferences: Caring about others' (page 52)).
- There was no way that Anil, Bala, or anyone else could make the farmer who used the insecticide pay for the harm that it caused.
- They were not able to make an agreement beforehand about what each would do. Had they been able to do so, they could have simply agreed to use IPC, or banned the use of Terminator.

If we can overcome one or more of these problems, the outcome preferred by both of them would sometimes result. Watch the clip from a TV quiz

A solution to a social dilemma on the show *Golden Balls*
https://tinyco.re/7018789

65

show called *Golden Balls* (https://tinyco.re/7018789), and you will see how one ordinary person ingeniously resolves the dilemma.

Ongoing relationships: Life may not be a one-shot game

In our model, the interaction between Anil and Bala was a one-shot game. But ongoing relationships are an important feature of social interactions; as owners of neighbouring fields, Anil and Bala are more realistically portrayed as interacting repeatedly.

Imagine how differently things would work out if we represented their interaction as a game to be repeated each season. This version of the game is called a **repeated** prisoners' dilemma.

Let's say that, in Season 1, Bala adopts IPC. What is Anil's best response if he knows there will be future seasons? He would reason like this: 'If I play IPC, then maybe Bala will continue to do so, but if I use Terminator—which would raise my profits this season—Bala would use Terminator next year. So, unless I am extremely impatient for income now, I'd better stick with IPC.' Bala could reason in exactly the same way. The result might be that they would then continue playing IPC forever.

The prisoners' dilemma is a situation in which there is something to gain for everyone by engaging with others in a common project such as pest control, maintaining an irrigation system, restricting the number of cattle on the pasture, or controlling carbon emissions. But there is also something to lose when others free ride.

Even if there is no ongoing relationship, Anil and Bala may choose IPC rather than Terminator because each places a value on the harm imposed on the other.

> **repeated game** A game in which the same interaction (same payoffs, players, feasible actions) may occur more than once.

> **EXERCISE 2.3 POLITICAL ADVERTISING**
> Many people consider political advertising (campaign advertisements) to be a classic example of a prisoners' dilemma situation.
>
> 1. Using examples from a recent political campaign with which you are familiar, explain whether this is the case.
> 2. Write down an example payoff matrix for this case.

2.7 FREE RIDING AND THE PROVISION OF PUBLIC GOODS

In contrast to the invisible hand game, the pursuit of self-interest is one reason for the unfortunate outcome in the prisoners' dilemma game. Now let's look at the second reason; there was no way that either Anil or Bala (or anyone else) could make whoever used the insecticide pay for the harm that it caused.

The public goods game

The problems of Anil and Bala are hypothetical and—unrealistically—there are just two people interacting. But their social dilemma captures the real challenges of free riding that many people around the world face. Take the case of climate change. The benefits of slowing global warming will be widely shared, but people will benefit even if they make no contribution themselves to reducing carbon emissions. At a more local level, as in Spain, many farmers in Southeast Asia rely on a shared irrigation facility to produce their crops.

2.7 FREE RIDING AND THE PROVISION OF PUBLIC GOODS

The system requires constant maintenance and new investment. Each farmer faces the decision of how much to contribute to these activities. These activities benefit the entire community and if the farmer does not volunteer to contribute, others may do the work anyway.

Imagine there are four farmers who are deciding whether to contribute to the maintenance of an irrigation project.

For each farmer, the cost of contributing to the project is $10. But when one farmer contributes, all four of them will benefit from an increase in their crop yields made possible by irrigation, so they will each gain $8. Contributing to the irrigation project is called a **public good**—when one individual bears a cost to provide the good, everyone receives a benefit.

As an example, let's focus on one of the farmers, called Kim. If two of the others contribute, Kim will receive a benefit of $8 from each of their contributions. If she makes no contribution herself, her total payoff is $16. This is shown in the top row of Figure 2.7 and by the red bar with '16' on top in Figure 2.8. If she decides to contribute, she will receive an additional benefit of $8 (and so will the other three farmers). But she will incur a cost of $10, so her total payoff is $14, as shown by the blue bar with '14' on top in Figure 2.8, and as calculated in Figure 2.7.

> **public good** A good for which use by one person does not reduce its availability to others. *Also known as: non-rival good. See also: non-excludable public good, artificially scarce good.*

Benefit from the contribution of others		16
Plus benefit from her own contribution	+	8
Minus cost of her contribution	−	10
Total		**$14**

Figure 2.7 Example: When two others contribute, Kim's payoff is lower if she contributes too.

Now, when Kim makes her decision, she has the information shown in Figure 2.8. This shows how her decision depends on her total earnings, but also on the number of other farmers who decide to contribute to the irrigation project. Note that the red bars are all higher than the blue ones—when Kim contributes, she earns less than when she free rides. This is a social dilemma.

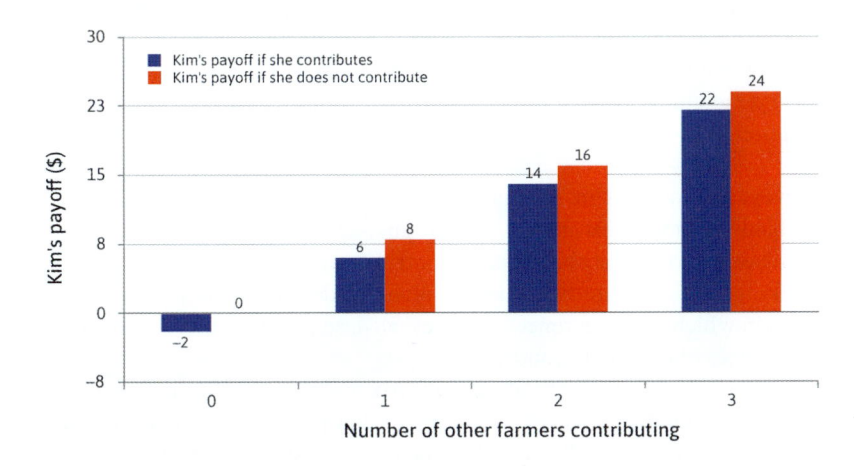

Figure 2.8 Kim's payoffs in the public goods game.

67

Whatever the other farmers decide to do, Kim makes more money if she doesn't contribute than if she does. Not contributing is a dominant strategy. She can free ride on the contributions of the others.

- This public goods game is a prisoners' dilemma in which there are more than two players.
- If the farmers care only about their own monetary payoff, there is a dominant strategy equilibrium in which no one contributes and their payoffs are all zero (as shown in Figure 2.8).
- On the other hand, if all contributed, each would get $22. Everyone would benefit if everyone cooperated, but irrespective of what others do, each farmer does better by free riding on the others.

Yet around the world, real farmers and fishing people have faced free rider situations in many cases with great success. The evidence gathered by Elinor Ostrom (page 70), a political scientist, and other researchers on common irrigation projects in India, Nepal, and other countries, shows that the degree of **cooperation** varies. In some communities, a history of trust encourages cooperation. In others, cooperation does not happen. In southern India, for example, villages with extreme inequalities in land and caste status had more conflicts over water usage. Less unequal villages maintained irrigation systems better—it was easier to sustain cooperation.

cooperation Participating in a common project that is intended to produce mutual benefits.

Elinor Ostrom. 2000. 'Collective Action and the Evolution of Social Norms' (https://tinyco.re/0059239). *Journal of Economic Perspectives* 14 (3): pp. 137–58.

2.8 SOCIAL PREFERENCES AND THE PUBLIC GOOD

The success or failure of communities in addressing the social dilemmas that they face often is determined by the extent and kinds of social preferences in the population. To better understand these cases and how to address the social dilemmas that we face, we need to find out more about social preferences; but until recently this has proven difficult.

Finding out about people's preferences

In the past, economists have learned about our preferences from:

- *Survey questions:* To determine political preferences, brand loyalty, degree of trust of others, or religious orientation.
- *Statistical studies of economic behaviour:* For example, by measuring how much purchases of two goods change when the relative price varies—to determine preferences for the goods in question. One strategy is to reverse-engineer what the preferences must have been, as revealed by purchases.

Surveys have a problem. Asking someone if they like ice cream will probably get an honest answer. But the answer to the question, 'How altruistic are you?' may be a mixture of truth, self-advertising, and wishful thinking. Statistical studies cannot control the decision-making environment in which the preferences were revealed, so it is difficult to compare the choices of different groups.

This is why economists, along with psychologists and other social scientists, sometimes use experiments so that people's behaviour can be observed under controlled conditions. In the next two sections, we report the results of experiments that have been carried out around the world—in the lab and among people facing social dilemmas in their working lives—that provide evidence about social preferences, and the way the people often take account of how their actions affect others.

Public goods experiments in real-world settings
In our 'Economist in action' video (https://tinyco.re/8347533), Juan Camilo Cárdenas, an economist at the Universidad de los Andes in Bogotá, Colombia, talks about his use of experimental economics in real-life situations. He performs experiments about social dilemmas with people who are facing similar problems to the farmer, Kim, such as overexploitation of a forest or a fish stock.

Juan Camilo Cárdenas: Invisible hands working together
https://tinyco.re/8347533

HOW ECONOMISTS LEARN FROM DATA
Laboratory experiments
Behavioural experiments have become important in the empirical study of preferences. Part of the motivation for economists undertaking experiments is that understanding someone's motivations (**altruism**, **reciprocity**, **inequality aversion** as well as self-interest) is essential to being able to predict how they will behave as employees, family members, custodians of the environment, and citizens. Each of these motivations is explored in more detail later in Section 2.10 (page 76) ('How three kinds of social preferences address social dilemmas').

Experiments measure what people *do* rather than what they *say*. Experiments are designed to be as realistic as possible, while controlling the situation by using these rules:

- *Decisions have consequences:* The decisions in the experiment may decide how much money the subjects earn by taking part. Sometimes the stakes can be as high as a month's income.
- *Instructions and rules are common to all subjects:* There is also a common treatment. This means that if we want to compare two groups, the only difference between the control and treatment groups is the treatment itself, so that its effects can be identified.
- *Experiments can be replicated:* They are designed to be implementable with other groups of participants.
- *Experimenters attempt to control for other possible explanations:* Other variables are kept constant wherever possible, because they may affect the behaviour we want to measure.

This means that, when people behave differently in the experiment, it is likely due to differences in their preferences, not in the situation that each person faces.

Economists have discovered that the way people behave in experiments can be used to predict how they react in real-life situations. For example, fishermen in Brazil who acted more cooperatively in an experimental game also practised fishing in a more sustainable manner than the fishermen who were less cooperative in the experiment.

behavioural experiment An experiment designed to study some aspect of human behaviour.
altruism The willingness to bear a cost in order to help another person. Altruism is a social preference. See also: social preferences.
reciprocity A preference concerning one's actions towards others that depends on an evaluation of the others' actions or character, for example, a preference to help those who have helped you or in some other way acted well (in your opinion), and to harm those who have acted poorly. It is considered a social preference. See also: social preferences.
inequality aversion A dislike of outcomes in which some individuals receive more than others. It is considered a social preference. See also: social preferences

Colin Camerer and Ernst Fehr. 2004. 'Measuring Social Norms and Preferences Using Experimental Games: A Guide for Social Scientists'. In *Foundations of Human Sociality: Economic Experiments and Ethnographic Evidence from Fifteen Small-Scale Societies*, edited by Joseph Henrich, Robert Boyd, Samuel Bowles, Colin Camerer, and Herbert Gintis. Oxford: Oxford University Press.

Steven D. Levitt and John A. List. 2007. 'What Do Laboratory Experiments Measuring Social Preferences Reveal About the Real World?' (https://tinyco.re/9601240). *Journal of Economic Perspectives* 21 (2): pp. 153–74.

Abigail Barr, Jean Ensminger, Clark Barrett, Alexander Bolyanatz, Juan Camilo Cardenas, Michael Gurven, Edwins Gwako, Natalie Henrich, Carolyn Lesorogol, Frank Marlowe, David Tracer, and John Ziker. 2006. 'Costly Punishment Across Human Societies' (https://tinyco.re/2043845). *Science* 312 (5781): pp. 1767–70.

For a summary of the kinds of experiments that have been run, the main results, and whether behaviour in the experimental lab predicts real-life behaviour, read the research done by some of the economists who specialize in experimental economics. For example, Colin Camerer and Ernst Fehr, Armin Falk and James Heckman, or the experiments done by Joseph Heinrich and a large team of collaborators around the world.

In Exercise 2.4, however, Steven Levitt and John List ask whether people would behave the same way in the street as they do in the laboratory.

EXERCISE 2.4 ARE LAB EXPERIMENTS A GOOD GUIDE TO WHAT PEOPLE DO?
In 2007, Steven Levitt and John List published a paper called 'What Do Laboratory Experiments Measuring Social Preferences Reveal about the Real World?' (https://tinyco.re/9601240). Read pages 158–171 of their paper (note that some of the language in the article is technical, and knowledge of it is not essential for answering the question).

According to their paper, why and how might people's behaviour in real life vary from what has been observed in laboratory experiments?

GREAT ECONOMISTS

Elinor Ostrom
The choice of Elinor Ostrom (1933–2012), a political scientist, as a co-recipient of the 2009 Nobel Prize surprised most economists. For example, Steven Levitt, a professor at the University of Chicago, admitted he knew nothing about her work, and had 'no recollection of ever seeing or hearing her name mentioned by an economist'.

Some, however, vigorously defended the decision. Vernon Smith, an experimental economist who had previously been awarded the Prize, congratulated the Nobel committee for recognizing her originality, 'scientific common sense', and willingness to 'listen carefully to data'.

Ostrom's entire academic career was focused on exploring the middle ground in an economy where communities, rather than individuals or formal governments, held property rights.

The conventional wisdom at the time was that informal collective ownership of resources would lead to a tragedy of the commons. That is, economists believed that resources could not be used efficiently and sustainably under a common property regime. Thanks to Elinor Ostrom, this is no longer a dominant view.

First, she made a distinction between resources held as common property and those subject to open access:

- Common property involves a well-defined community of users who are able in practice, if not under the law, to prevent outsiders from exploiting the resource. Inshore fisheries, grazing lands, or forest areas are examples.
- Open-access resources such as ocean fisheries or the atmosphere as a carbon sink, can be exploited without restrictions, other than those imposed by states acting alone or through international agreements.

Concentrating on common property, Ostrom drew on a unique combination of case studies, statistical methods, game theory models, and laboratory experiments to try to understand how tragedies of the commons could be averted.

She discovered great diversity in how common property is managed. Some communities were able to devise rules and draw on social norms to enforce sustainable resource use, while others failed to do so. Much of her career was devoted to identifying the criteria for success and using theory to understand why some arrangements worked well, while others did not.

Ostrom knew that sustainable use of common property was enforced by actions that clearly deviated from the hypothesis of self-interest. In particular, individuals would willingly bear considerable costs to punish those who violated rules or norms.

Ostrom developed simple game theory models in which individuals have social preferences, such as upholding social norms that supported cooperation. She also looked for the ways in which people faced with a social dilemma avoided tragedy by changing the rules so that the strategic nature of the interaction was transformed.

She worked with economists to run a pioneering series of experiments, confirming the widespread use of costly punishment in response to excessive resource extraction. Her work also demonstrated the power of communication and the critical role of informal agreements in supporting cooperation.

Social preferences like altruism partly explain why some communities avoid Garrett Hardin's tragedy of the commons. But communities may also find ways of deterring free-riding behaviour by punishing those who do not contribute, as Elinor Ostrom found. To better understand this, we will look in the next section at evidence of how people behave when playing experimental games.

> **QUESTION 2.7 CHOOSE THE CORRECT ANSWER(S)**
> Which of the following statements regarding social preferences are correct?
>
> ☐ Altruism is an example of social preferences.
> ☐ They are the preferences of society as a whole.
> ☐ 'Keeping up with the Joneses' is an example of behaviour that could be motivated by social preferences.
> ☐ An individual has social preferences if he cares about inequality in society.

> **QUESTION 2.8 CHOOSE THE CORRECT ANSWER(S)**
> According to Elinor Ostrom, which of the following statements about the problem of the tragedy of the commons are correct?
>
> ☐ One of Ostrom's major contributions was to provide empirical case studies explaining why the tragedy of the commons cannot be avoided.
> ☐ Agreements for cooperation must be enforced by governments.
> ☐ Individuals uphold social norms that support cooperation.
> ☐ Social norms can be drawn on to enforce sustainable resources, although it does not always succeed.

2.9 SUSTAINING COOPERATION BY PUNISHING FREE RIDING

Free riding today on the contributions of other members of one's community may have unpleasant consequences tomorrow or years from now. This is relevant to a wide range of social dilemmas, ranging from global ones like climate change and public health (for example antibiotic resistance and compliance with vaccination programmes for communicable diseases), to local dilemmas like the development of land on flood plains.

An experiment demonstrates that people can sustain high levels of cooperation in a public goods game, as long as they have opportunities to punish free riders once it becomes clear who is contributing less than the norm.

Worldwide public goods experiments

Figure 2.9a shows the results of laboratory experiments that mimic the costs and benefits from contribution to a public good in the real world. The experiments were conducted in cities around the world. In each experiment:

- Participants play ten rounds of a public goods game, similar to the one involving Kim and the other farmers that we just described.
- In each round, the people in the experiment (we call them subjects) are given $20.
- They are randomly sorted into small groups, typically of four people who don't know each other.

- They are asked to decide on a contribution from their $20 to a common pool of money.
- The pool is a public good. For every dollar contributed, each person in the group receives $0.40, including the contributor.

Imagine that you are playing the game and you expect the other three members of your group to each contribute $10.

- If you don't contribute, you will get $32 (three returns of $4 from their contributions, plus the initial $20 that you keep). The others have paid $10, so they only get $32 − $10 = $22 each.
- If you contribute $10, then everyone, including you, will get $22 + $4 = $26.
- Unfortunately for the group, you do better by not contributing because the reward for free riding ($32) is greater than for contributing ($26).
- And, unfortunately for you, the same applies to each of the other members.

After each round, the participants are told the contributions of other members of their group. In Figure 2.9a, each line represents the evolution over time of average contributions in a different location around the world. People are definitely not solely self-interested. If they were, and reasoned that everyone else was also self-interested, then they would not contribute.

As you can see, players in Chengdu contributed $10 in the first round, just as we described above. In every population where the game was played, contributions to the public good were high in the first period, although much more so in some cities (Copenhagen) than in others (Melbourne).

This is remarkable—if you care only about your own payoff, contributing nothing at all is the dominant strategy. In every city there must have been a substantial fraction of people with social preferences. But the figure also underscores the difficulty (or, as Hardin would have described it, the tragedy) of sustaining voluntary contributions to the public good. Everywhere, the contributions to the public good decreased over time.

Nevertheless, the results also show that, despite a large variation across societies, most of them still have high contribution levels at the end of the experiment.

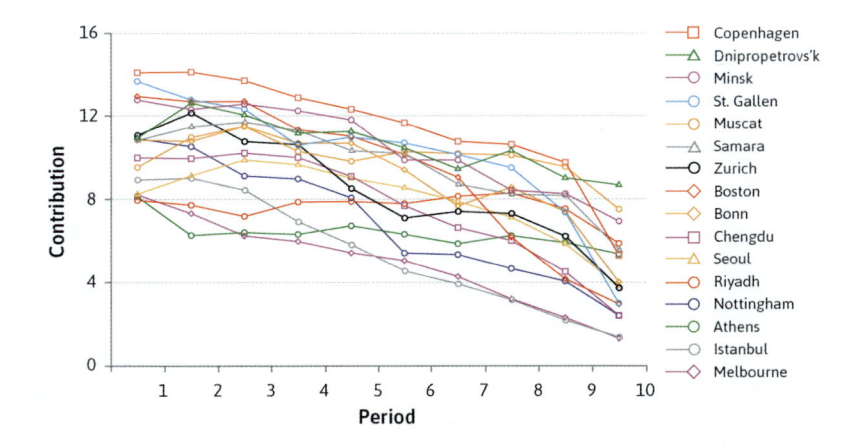

Figure 2.9a Worldwide public goods experiments: Contributions over 10 periods.

View this data at OWiD https://tinyco.re/3626220

Benedikt Herrmann, Christian Thoni, and Simon Gachter. 2008. 'Antisocial Punishment Across Societies'. *Science* 319 (5868): pp. 1362–67.

Introducing a punishment option in the public goods game experiment

To test this, the experimenters took the public goods game experiment shown in Figure 2.9a and introduced a punishment option. After observing the contributions of their group, individual players could pay to punish other players by making them pay a $3 fine. The punisher remained anonymous but had to pay $1 per player punished. The effect is shown in Figure 2.9b. For the majority of subjects, including those in China, South Korea, northern Europe, and the English-speaking countries, contributions increased when they had the opportunity to punish free riders.

View this data at OWiD https://tinyco.re/9711986

Benedikt Herrmann, Christian Thoni, and Simon Gachter. 2008. 'Antisocial Punishment Across Societies'. *Science* 319 (5868): pp. 1362–67.

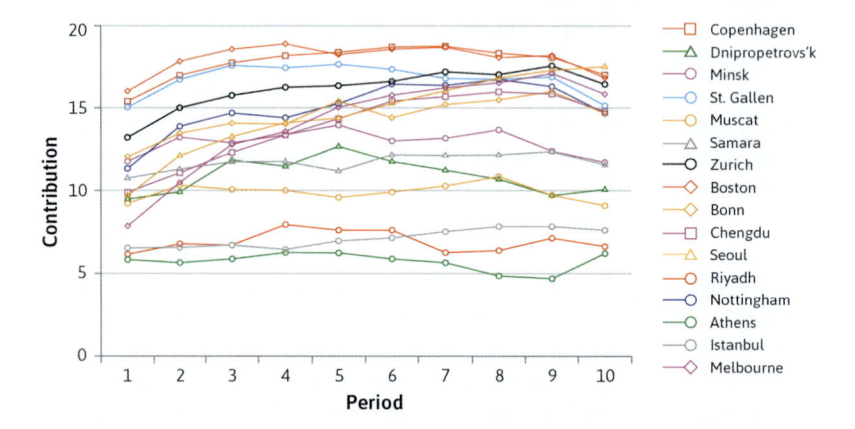

Figure 2.9b Worldwide public goods experiments with opportunities for peer punishment.

This experiment illustrates the way that, even in large groups of people, a combination of repeated interactions and social preferences can support high levels of contribution to the public good.

The public goods game, like the prisoners' dilemma, is a situation in which there is something to gain for everyone by engaging with others in a common project, such as controlling carbon emissions, pest control, and maintaining fish stocks. But there is also something to lose when others free ride.

EXERCISE 2.5 USING EXCEL: LOOKING AT DIFFERENCES IN CONTRIBUTIONS IN THE PUBLIC GOODS EXPERIMENTS

In this exercise, you will be using Excel to take a closer look at how contributions in the public goods experiments (shown in Figures 2.9a and 2.9b) have changed over the course of the game and after punishment was introduced.

Download and save the spreadsheet (https://tinyco.re/8088741) containing the data for Figures 2.9a and 2.9b.

1. Choose one figure (either 2.9a or 2.9b) and use the data to plot a line chart with contribution on the vertical axis and period on the horizontal axis. Follow the walk-through in Figure 2.10 online (https://tinyco.re/7681477) on how to do this in Excel.

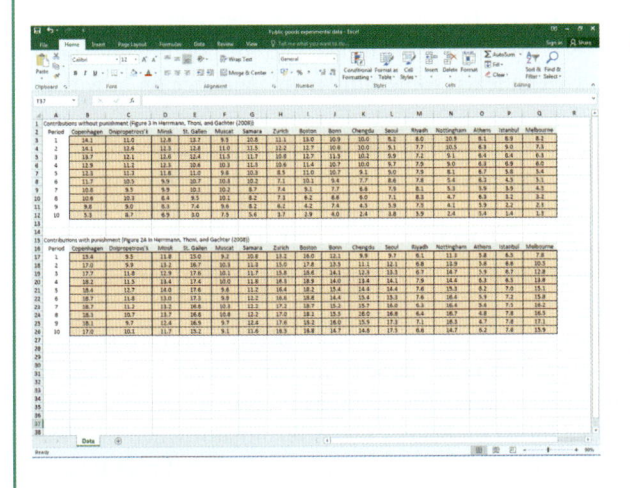

Figure 2.10 Plotting a line chart with multiple variables.

1. The data
This is what the data looks like. Each column has data for a particular country, and each row has data for a given time period (1 to 10). We will draw Figure 2.9a as an example; the steps to do Figure 2.9b are identical.

2. Draw a line chart
After completing step 3, the chart will look like this. Notice that the horizontal axis variable and vertical axis variables are not the same as Figure 2.9a (due to Excel's default setting).

3. Switch the horizontal and vertical axis variables
We can switch the horizontal and vertical axis variables in the 'Select Data' options.

4. Switch the horizontal and vertical axis variables
After step 7, the lines on your chart will look like those in Figure 2.9a or Figure 2.9b.

5. Move the legend to the right
After step 9, the legend will now be on the right-hand side of your chart. You can also experiment with the other positions to see which looks better.

6. Add axis titles and a chart title
After step 13, your chart will look like Figure 2.9a or Figure 2.9b.

2. For Figure 2.9a, calculate the difference between the starting and ending values. Which country had the largest/smallest change in contributions after ten periods? Do the same for Figure 2.9b. Did contributions increase, decrease, or stay the same when players could punish each other?
3. Now choose three countries in the data. Calculate and compare the difference between contributions in the game with and without punishment. Did subjects in your chosen countries contribute more in every period when there was punishment? Why would it be reasonable to think that the differences we see are due to the punishment option, rather than other explanations?

2.10 HOW THREE KINDS OF SOCIAL PREFERENCES ADDRESS SOCIAL DILEMMAS

What do these experiments tell us about social preferences and how they might sustain cooperation in an interaction that otherwise would be a social dilemma?

The first thing we learn is that while self-interested preferences are simple, social preferences are not. Three different kinds of social preference may explain how people around the world played the public goods game with punishment. All three express a person's concern about what other people get or experience. But they differ in important ways.

- **Altruism**: A willingness to help someone else at a cost to yourself.
- **Reciprocity**: A desire to help those who have (in your opinion) acted well, and to harm those who have acted poorly.
- **Inequality aversion**: A dislike of (aversion to) unequal outcomes even if you benefit from the disparities, but especially if others are doing better than you.

Altruism

To see how altruism could explain contributions in the public goods game recall that the prisoners' dilemma game is just a public goods game with only two players. So we can learn something from evidence on how that game is played.

When students play the one-shot prisoners' dilemma games in classroom or laboratory experiments, sometimes for large amounts of real money, many cooperate rather than opt for the dominant strategy—defect—that would give them the largest payoff. When students play the public goods game less than one-third typically adopt the dominant strategy, which is to contribute nothing.

An interpretation of these results is that some players are altruistic. In the pest control game, playing Terminator is the self-interested strategy no matter what the other player does. But if Anil had cared sufficiently about the harm that he would inflict on Bala by using Terminator when Bala was using IPC, then IPC would have been Anil's best response to Bala's IPC. And if Bala had felt the same way, then IPC would have been a mutual best response, and the two would no longer have been in a prisoners' dilemma.

In the example just given, Anil was willing to give up 1 payoff unit because that would have imposed a loss of 2 on Bala. The cost to him of choosing IPC when Bala had chosen IPC was 1, and it conferred a benefit of 2 on Bala, meaning that he had acted altruistically. And if Bala had felt the same way, then IPC would have been a mutual best response, and the two would no longer have been in a prisoners' dilemma. In the version of the IPC–Terminator case with these new payoffs, both Bala and Anil are motivated by altruistic preferences, which make them willing to bear a cost to help some other person.

Altruism could help to solve the free rider problem—if Kim cared about the other farmers, she might be willing to contribute to the irrigation project. Altruism could also explain why students in the global public goods game contributed a large amount in the first round of the game.

---

altruism The willingness to bear a cost in order to help another person. Altruism is a social preference. See also: social preferences.

reciprocity A preference concerning one's actions towards others that depends on an evaluation of the others' actions or character, for example, a preference to help those who have helped you or in some other way acted well (in your opinion), and to harm those who have acted poorly. It is considered a social preference. See also: social preferences.

inequality aversion A dislike of outcomes in which some individuals receive more than others. It is considered a social preference. See also: social preferences

2.10 HOW THREE KINDS OF SOCIAL PREFERENCES ADDRESS SOCIAL DILEMMAS

Reciprocity

But what explains why contributions to the public good declined in later rounds?

The most plausible explanation of the pattern is not altruism, but reciprocity. It is likely that contributors decreased their level of cooperation when they saw that others were contributing less, meaning that the others were free riding on them. It seems as if those who contributed more than the average had negative feelings toward the low contributors for their unfairness, or for violating a social norm of contributing.

This is an example of reciprocity: those violating a social norm should not benefit from their anti-social behavior, and if possible, they should be punished. A reciprocator may place a negative value on the payoffs of others (the opposite of altruism) and this may provide a sufficient motive even to pay in order to punish the free rider by reducing their payoffs.

But there is a problem facing the reciprocally motivated player in this game. Since the payoffs of free riders depend on the total contribution to the public good, the only way to punish free riders is to stop contributing. This is the most convincing reason why contributions fell so regularly in later rounds of this game.

And if you thought (correctly as it turns out) that the free rider would later contribute more to the public good, from which you would benefit, you could be motivated by self-interest. But note that in a large group your share of the increased public good would most likely be smaller than the cost of punishing.

Inequality aversion

If you could choose between either:

- you and another person both get a payment of $500 or
- you get $510 and the other person gets nothing,

which option would you pick? Another choice:

- you both get $500 or
- the other person gets $1,000 and you get $510.

In both cases, if you chose the first option you have inequality-averse preferences. Note that you would have more money in both cases if you took the second option. You are willing to sacrifice $10 to avoid an unequal outcome, even if the inequality would have benefited you compared to the other player, as in the first question.

How does inequality aversion affect play in the public goods game with punishment?

Remember everyone gets the same amount from the 'public good': it is just divided among all of the players equally. And your net payoff—what you go home with—is that amount minus how much you contributed. So the person who contributed nothing walks away with the largest payoff and the person who contributed the most has the smallest payoff.

In the experiment, you could spend $1 to fine someone else $3. So you could punish one of the ('rich') free riders reducing their income by much more than it reduced yours. The effect would be to reduce inequality among the players.

homo economicus Latin for 'economic man', referring to an actor assumed to adopt behaviours based on an amoral calculation of self-interest.

social norm An understanding that is common to most members of a society about what people should do in a given situation when their actions affect others.

Francis Ysidro Edgeworth. 2003. *Mathematical Psychics and Further Papers on Political Economy*. Oxford: Oxford University Press.

H. L. Mencken. 2006. *A Little Book in C Major*. New York, NY: Kessinger Publishing.

WHEN ECONOMISTS DISAGREE

Homo economicus *in question: Are people entirely selfish?*

For centuries, economists and just about everyone else have debated whether people are entirely self-interested or are sometimes happy to help others, even when it costs them something to do so. **Homo economicus** (economic man) is the nickname given to the selfish and calculating character that you find in economics textbooks. Have economists been right to imagine *homo economicus* as the only actor on the economic stage?

In the same book in which he first used the phrase 'invisible hand', Adam Smith also made it clear that he thought we were not *homo economicus*: 'How selfish soever man may be supposed, there are evidently some principles in his nature which interest him in the fortunes of others, and render their happiness necessary to him, though he derives nothing from it except the pleasure of seeing it.' (*The Theory of Moral Sentiments*, 1759)

But most economists since Smith have disagreed. In 1881, Francis Edgeworth, a founder of modern economics, made this perfectly clear in his book, *Mathematical Psychics*: 'The first principle of economics is that every agent is actuated only by self-interest.'

Yet everyone has experienced, and sometimes even performed, great acts of kindness or bravery on behalf of others in situations in which there was little chance of a reward. The question for economists is: Should the unselfishness evident in these acts be part of how we reason about behaviour?

Some say 'no'; many seemingly generous acts are better understood as attempts to gain a favourable reputation among others that will benefit the actor in the future.

Maybe helping others and observing **social norms** is just self-interest with a long-time horizon. This is what the essayist H. L. Mencken thought: '… conscience is the inner voice which warns that somebody may be looking.' Since the 1990s, in an attempt to resolve the debate on empirical grounds, economists have performed hundreds of experiments all over the world in which the behaviour of individuals (students, farmers, whale hunters, warehouse workers, and CEOs) can be observed as they make real choices about sharing, using economic games.

In these experiments, we almost always see some self-interested behaviour. But we also find that people are willing to help others even at a cost to themselves, to reciprocate kindness even if their payoffs would be greater otherwise, and other kinds of behaviour inconsistent with self-interest.

In many experiments, *homo economicus* is the minority. This is true even when the amounts being shared (or kept for oneself) amount to many days' wages.

Is the debate resolved? Many economists think so and now consider people who are sometimes altruistic, sometimes inequality averse, and sometimes reciprocal, in addition to *homo economicus*. They point out that the assumption of self-interest is appropriate for many economic settings, like shopping or the way that firms use technology to maximize profits. But it's not as appropriate in other settings, such as how we pay taxes, or why we work hard for our employer.

QUESTION 2.9 CHOOSE THE CORRECT ANSWER(S)
Consider the public goods experiment without peer punishment. Based on the information shown in Figure 2.9a, which of the following statements is correct?

☐ The evidence suggests that playing only one round ensures high contributions.
☐ The results prove that subjects are completely selfish.
☐ A disappointed expectation of reciprocity may be the reason for the falling contributions over the rounds.
☐ Repeating the game makes the subjects more altruistic in later rounds.

QUESTION 2.10 CHOOSE THE CORRECT ANSWER(S)
Which of the following is a difference between altruism and reciprocity?

☐ Suppose that given the choice of (a) you and another person both get $500 or (b) the other person gets $1,000 and you get $510, you prefer (b). We can then conclude that you have altruistic preferences but are unlikely to have inequality-averse preferences.
☐ Altruism promotes helping behaviour, while reciprocity may also motivate a desire to harm another.
☐ The helping behavior associated with altruism is unconditional, while the actions taken by a reciprocator are conditional on (depend on) the actor's judgement of the other's behaviour.
☐ Reciprocity is a form of inequality aversion, while altruism is not.

2.11 PREDICTING ECONOMIC OUTCOMES: A NASH EQUILIBRIUM

In the games we have been looking at until now, players could do as well as possible (get the highest payoff) regardless of what the other player did. There was a dominant strategy for each player, and hence a single dominant strategy equilibrium. This was true of the invisible hand game, the prisoners' dilemma, and public goods games.

But this is often not the case. We have already mentioned a situation in which it is definitely untrue—driving on the right or on the left. If others drive on the right, your best response is to drive on the right too. If they drive on the left, your best response is to also drive on the left. To predict what we will observe, even when there is no dominant strategy equilibrium, we need to extend our understanding of game theory.

In the US, everyone driving on the right is an equilibrium, in the sense that no one would want to change their strategy given what others are doing. In game theory, if everyone is playing their best response to the strategies of everyone else, these strategies are termed a **Nash equilibrium (NE)**.

In Japan, though, driving on the left is a Nash equilibrium. The driving 'game' has two Nash equilibria.

Many economic interactions do not have dominant strategy equilibria, but if we can find a Nash equilibrium, it gives us a prediction of what we should observe. We should expect to see all players doing the best they can, given what others are doing.

Nash equilibrium A set of strategies, one for each player in the game, such that each player's strategy is a best response to the strategies chosen by everyone else.

Even in simple economic problems, there may be more than one Nash equilibrium (as in the driving game). Suppose that, when Bala and Anil choose their crops, the payoffs are now as shown in Figure 2.11. This is different from the invisible hand game. If the two farmers produce the same crop, there is now such a large fall in price that it is better for each to specialize, even in the crop they are less suited to grow. Follow the steps in Figure 2.11 to find the two equilibria.

Note that a dominant strategy equilibrium, such as in the prisoners' dilemma game or the invisible hand game, is a particularly simple Nash equilibrium because:

- *Each player's best response does not depend on what the other player does:* Unlike in Figure 2.11, the dots are always in the same row, and the circles are always in the same column.
- *There is only one equilibrium.*

To explore all of the slides in this figure, see the online version at https://tinyco.re/5783942.

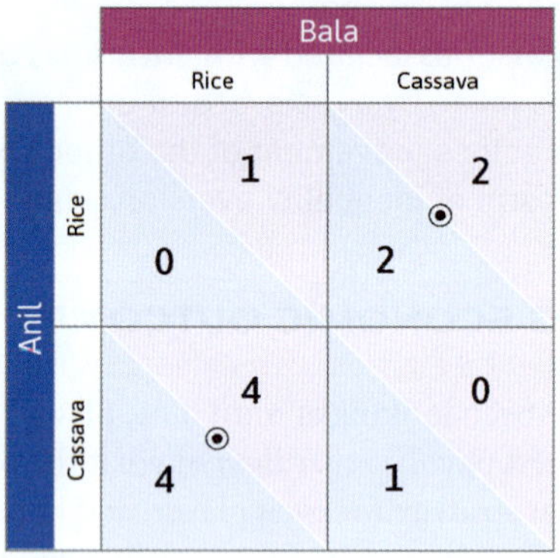

Figure 2.11 A division of labour problem with more than one Nash equilibrium.

1. Anil's best response to Rice
If Bala is going to choose Rice, Anil's best response is to choose Cassava. We place a dot in the bottom left-hand cell.

2. Anil's best response to Cassava
If Bala is going to choose Cassava, Anil's best response is to choose Rice. Place a dot in the top right-hand cell. Notice that Anil does not have a dominant strategy.

3. Bala's best responses
If Anil chooses Rice, Bala's best response is to choose Cassava, and if Anil chooses Cassava, he should choose Rice. The circles show Bala's best responses. He doesn't have a dominant strategy either.

4. (Cassava, Rice) is a Nash equilibrium
If Anil chooses Cassava and Bala chooses Rice, both are playing best responses (a dot and a circle coincide). This is a Nash equilibrium.

5. (Rice, Cassava) is also a Nash equilibrium
If Anil chooses Rice and Bala chooses Cassava, then both are playing best responses, so this is also a Nash equilibrium, but the payoffs are higher in the other equilibrium.

> **QUESTION 2.11 CHOOSE THE CORRECT ANSWER(S)**
> Which of the following statements regarding Nash equilibrium are correct?
>
> ☐ No player has an incentive to deviate from a Nash equilibrium.
> ☐ In a Nash equilibrium, all players choose their best response strategy given the other players' strategies.
> ☐ A Nash equilibrium is a dominant strategy equilibrium.
> ☐ A dominant strategy equilibrium is a Nash equilibrium.

2.12 WHICH NASH EQUILIBRIUM? CONFLICTS OF INTEREST AND BARGAINING

So far, we have seen examples in which, even though players act independently, they can achieve an outcome that is good for all of them:

- *The invisible hand:* Anil and Bala chose their crops in pursuit of their own interests. Their engagement in the village market resulted in a mutually beneficial division of labour where each specialized in the crop they were better at producing, and as a result, their incomes were higher than they would have been if they had not interacted through the market.
- *The repeated prisoners' dilemma:* When there is an ongoing relationship in the pest control game, Anil and Bala may refrain from using Terminator because they recognize the future losses they would suffer as a result of abandoning IPC.
- *The public goods game:* Players' willingness to punish others led to sustained high levels of cooperation in the experiments in many countries, without the need for agreements.

But in other cases, such as the one-shot prisoners' dilemma, we have seen that independent actions led to an unfortunate outcome. In these cases, the players could do better if they could reach an agreement.

Bargaining to resolve problems

People commonly try to do just this—they resort to negotiation to solve their economic and social problems. For example, international negotiation resulted in the Montreal Protocol, mentioned earlier, through which countries agreed to eliminate the use of chlorofluorocarbons (CFCs) in order to avoid a harmful outcome (the destruction of the ozone layer).

But negotiation does not always succeed, sometimes because of conflicts of interest over how the mutual gains of cooperation will be shared. The success of the Montreal Protocol in reducing the use of CFCs contrasts with the relative failure of the Kyoto Protocol (https://tinyco.re/2975858) and of the 2009 Copenhagen climate change summit. The reasons are partly scientific. The alternative technologies to CFCs were well developed and the benefits relative to costs for large industrial countries, such as the US, were much clearer and larger than in the case of greenhouse gas emissions. But one of the obstacles to agreement at the Copenhagen summit in 2009 was over how to share the costs and benefits of limiting emissions between developed and developing countries. The tools of game theory can help explain these different outcomes.

Situations with two Nash equilibria prompt us to ask two questions:

- Which equilibrium would we expect to observe in the world?
- Is there a conflict of interest because one equilibrium is preferable to some players, but not to others?

Whether you drive on the right or the left can be represented as a game with two Nash equilibria—everybody left, or everybody right. Which it will be is not a matter of conflict in itself, as long as everyone you are driving towards has made the same decision as you. We can't say that driving on the left is better for anyone, or for people in general, than driving on the right.

But in the division of labour game in Figure 2.11, it is clear that the Nash equilibrium with Anil choosing Cassava and Bala choosing Rice (where they specialize in the crop they produce best) is preferred by both farmers to the other Nash equilibrium.

Could we say, then, that we would expect to see Anil and Bala engaged in the 'correct' division of labour? Not necessarily. Remember, we are assuming that they take their decisions independently, without coordinating. Imagine that Bala's father had been especially good at growing cassava (unlike his son) and so the land remained dedicated to cassava even though it was better suited to producing rice. In response to this, Anil knows that Rice is his best response to Bala's Cassava, and so would have then chosen to grow rice. Bala would have no reason to switch to what he is good at—growing rice.

The example makes an important point. If there is more than one Nash equilibrium, and if people choose their actions independently, then an economy can get 'stuck' in a Nash equilibrium in which all players are worse off than they would be in the other equilibrium. Later in the course, we will see that this model helps explain phenomena like an economy getting stuck in a situation with low investment and high unemployment.

Nash equilibrium A set of strategies, one for each player in the game, such that each player's strategy is a best response to the strategies chosen by everyone else.

GREAT ECONOMISTS

John Nash

John Nash (1928–2015) completed his doctoral thesis (https://tinyco.re/8462257) at Princeton University at the age of 21. It was just 27 pages long, yet it advanced game theory (which was a little-known branch of economics back then) in ways that led to a dramatic transformation of the subject. He provided an answer to the question, 'When people interact strategically, what would one expect them to do?'. His answer, now known as a **Nash equilibrium**, is a collection of strategies, one for each player, such that if these strategies were to be publicly revealed, no player would regret his or her own choice. That is, if all players choose strategies that are consistent with a Nash equilibrium, then nobody can gain by unilaterally switching to a different strategy.

2.12 WHICH NASH EQUILIBRIUM? CONFLICTS OF INTEREST AND BARGAINING

There is hardly a field in economics that the development of game theory has not completely transformed, and this development would have been impossible without Nash's equilibrium concept. Remarkably, this was not Nash's only path-breaking contribution to economics—he also made a brilliantly original contribution to the theory of bargaining. In addition, he made pioneering contributions to other areas of mathematics, for which he was awarded the prestigious Abel Prize.

Nash would go on to share the Nobel Prize for his work. Roger Myerson, an economist who also won the prize, described the Nash equilibrium as 'one of the most important contributions in the history of economic thought.'

Nash originally wanted to be an electrical engineer like his father and studied mathematics as an undergraduate at Carnegie Tech (now Carnegie-Mellon University). An elective course in International Economics stirred his interest in strategic interactions, which eventually led to his breakthrough.

For much of his life, Nash suffered from mental illness that required hospitalization. He experienced hallucinations caused by schizophrenia that began in 1959. After what he described as '25 years of partially deluded thinking' (https://tinyco.re/6775628), he continued his teaching and research at Princeton. The story of his insights and illness are told in the book (made into a film starring Russell Crowe), *A Beautiful Mind*.

Sylvia Nasar. 2011. *A Beautiful Mind: The Life of Mathematical Genius and Nobel Laureate John Nash*. New York, NY: Simon & Schuster.

Conflicts of interest over which equilibrium will occur

So far, the problem facing our players has been to avoid getting trapped in an equilibrium that is worse for both, or all players. They experience mutual gains if they can cooperate and find a way to move to a different, mutually preferred outcome.

But players face other problems. When there is more than one equilibrium in a game, a conflict of interest occurs if players in a game would prefer *different* Nash equilibria. There may be mutual gains to getting to one or the other of these equilibria, but who gets the lion's share of these gains may differ among the outcomes.

Think of a couple in love but capable of only rudimentary speech in the other's native language. Which one is going to learn the other's language? Both speaking Greek and both speaking German are Nash equilibria, and both are preferable to neither learning the other's language, but they will probably differ in which each would prefer.

This fact underlies one of the key lessons of economics—when people interact, they may each benefit compared to what they could have had acting singly, but they will also face a conflict over who benefits more.

To see this, consider the case of Astrid and Bettina, two software engineers who are working on a project for which they will be paid. Their first decision is whether the code should be written in Java or C++ (imagine that either programming language is equally suitable, and that the project can be written partly in one language and partly in the other, although this would slow down their work).

Astrid wants to write in Java because she is better at writing Java code. While this is a joint project with Bettina, her pay will be partly based on how many lines of code were written by her. Unfortunately, Bettina prefers C++ for the same reason. The two strategies are therefore called Java and C++.

Their interaction is described in Figure 2.12a, and their payoffs are in Figure 2.12b.

From Figure 2.12a, you can work out three things:

- They both do better if they work in the same language.
- Astrid does better if the language is Java, while the reverse is true for Bettina.
- Their total payoff is higher if they choose C++.

How would we predict the outcome of this game?

If you use the dot-and-circle method, you will find that each player's best response is to choose the same language as the other player. In other words, there are two Nash equilibria. In one, both choose Java. In the other, both choose C++.

Can we say which of these two equilibria is more likely to occur? Astrid obviously prefers that they both play Java while Bettina prefers that they both play C++. With the information we have about how the two might interact, we can't yet predict what would happen.

In real social interactions, the outcome might be determined by such things as:

- *Which of the two has more power?* For example, if Astrid is Bettina's boss, they will probably end up using Java.
- *Who started work on the project first?* If Bettina has completed part of the project before her co-worker Astrid is brought onto the team, then they will probably continue with C++.

> **EXERCISE 2.6 CONFLICT BETWEEN ASTRID AND BETTINA**
> Predict the likely result of the game for each of the following scenarios:
>
> 1. Astrid can choose which language she will use first, and commit to it (just as the Proposer in the ultimatum game commits to an offer, before the Responder responds).
> 2. The two can make an agreement, including which language they use, and the size of a cash transfer from one to the other.
> 3. They have been working together for many years, and in the past they used Java on joint projects.

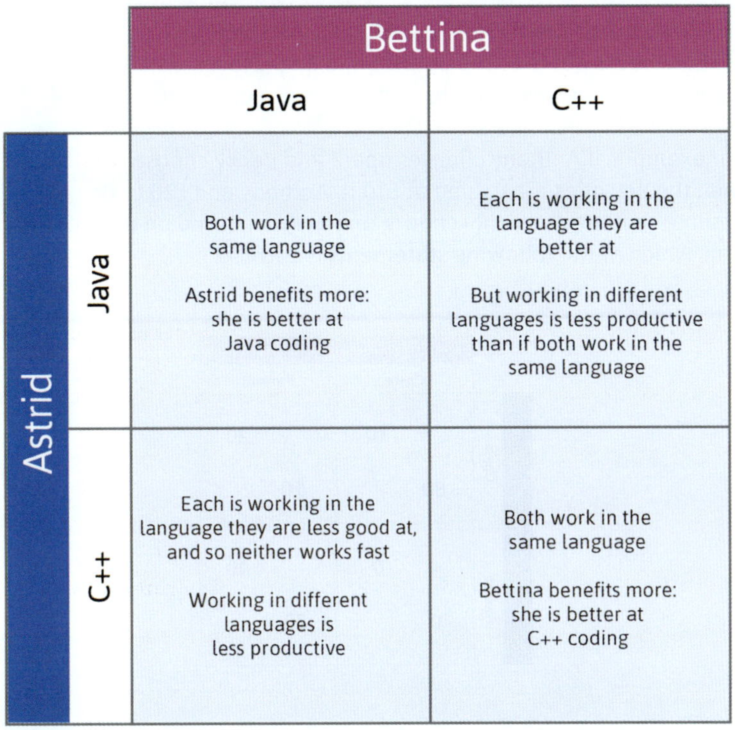

2.12 WHICH NASH EQUILIBRIUM? CONFLICTS OF INTEREST AND BARGAINING

	Bettina: Java	Bettina: C++
Astrid: Java	Both work in the same language. Astrid benefits more: she is better at Java coding	Each is working in the language they are better at. But working in different languages is less productive than if both work in the same language
Astrid: C++	Each is working in the language they are less good at, and so neither works fast. Working in different languages is less productive	Both work in the same language. Bettina benefits more: she is better at C++ coding

Figure 2.12a Interactions in the choice of programming language.

	Bettina: Java	Bettina: C++
Astrid: Java	Astrid 4, Bettina 3	Astrid 2, Bettina 2
Astrid: C++	Astrid 0, Bettina 0	Astrid 3, Bettina 6

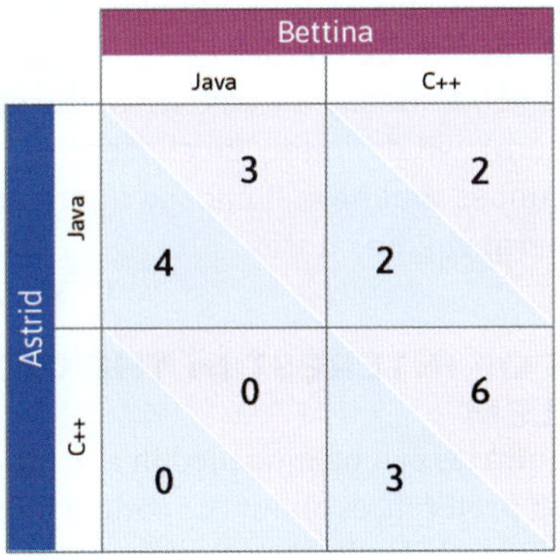

Figure 2.12b Payoffs (thousands of dollars to complete the project) according to the choice of programming language.

85

QUESTION 2.12 CHOOSE THE CORRECT ANSWER(S)
Anthony loves going to the opera while Becky loves watching football. Figure 2.13 is the payoff table for their choice of activity.

For example, if Anthony chooses opera and Becky chooses football, then the activities are valued at £10 to Anthony and £20 to Becky. Assume that they can only choose one activity. Based on this information, which of the following statements is correct?

	Becky: Opera	Becky: Football
Anthony: Opera	10 / 80	20 / 10
Anthony: Football	0 / 0	40 / 20

Figure 2.13 Opera or football?

☐ There are two Nash equilibria: (Opera, Opera) and (Football, Football).
☐ If Anthony offers £20 to Becky for coming to the opera with him, then (Opera, Opera) may be chosen.
☐ If Anthony offers £50 to Becky for coming to the opera with him, then (Opera, Opera) will definitely be chosen.
☐ If Anthony announces that he will choose opera and sticks to it, then (Opera, Opera) will be chosen.

2.13 CONFLICTS OF INTEREST IN THE GLOBAL CLIMATE CHANGE PROBLEM

Conflicts between countries can be modelled in a manner similar to Astrid and Bettina's differing preferences about the coding language. Here is an example, starting with a little background.

'The scientific evidence is now overwhelming: climate change presents very serious global risks, and it demands an urgent global response.'

This is the blunt beginning of the executive summary of the *Stern Review on the Economics of Climate Change*, released in 2006. The British Chancellor of the Exchequer (finance minister) commissioned a group of economists, led by Nicholas (now Lord) Stern, the former Chief Economist of the World Bank, to assess the evidence for climate change and to try to understand its economic implications. The *Stern Review* concludes that the benefits of early action to slow climate change will outweigh the costs of neglecting the issue.

However, this will not happen if we pursue what Stern referred to as 'business as usual'—a scenario in which people, governments, and businesses are free to pursue their own pleasures, politics, and profits without

2.13 CONFLICTS OF INTEREST IN THE GLOBAL CLIMATE CHANGE PROBLEM

taking adequate account of the effect of their actions on others, including future generations.

National governments disagree on the policies that should be adopted. Many nations in the developed world are pressing for strict global controls on carbon emissions; others have resisted these measures.

Think of the problem as a game between two countries, China and the US, considered as if each were a single individual. We do this to show that, depending on how the game is structured and the objectives of the participants, the outcomes may be very different.

Each country has two possible strategies for addressing global carbon emissions: Restrict (taking measures to reduce emissions, for example by taxing the use of fossil fuels) and BAU. BAU stands for 'business as usual', the strategy of not introducing policies to cut emissions.

Figure 2.14a describes the outcomes (top) and hypothetical payoffs (bottom), on a scale from best, through good and bad, to worst. This is called an ordinal scale because all that matters is the order—whether one outcome is better than the other—and not by how much it is better.

The worst outcome for both countries is that both persist with BAU, running a significant risk of human (and many other species') extinction. The best for each is to continue with BAU and let the other one Restrict. The only way to moderate climate change significantly is for both to Restrict.

The hawk–dove game

Figure 2.14a illustrates what is termed a **hawk–dove game**; acting like the aggressive species is one strategy in the game (the hawk is an aggressive species), and acting like the peaceful and sharing species (the dove) is the other strategy. Therefore, in the climate change version of the hawk–dove game, Doves Restrict and Hawks continue with Business as usual. The conflict of interest here is that each country does better if it plays Hawk while the other plays Dove.

> **hawk–dove game** A game in which there is conflict (when hawks meet), sharing (when doves meet), and taking (by a hawk when it meets a dove).

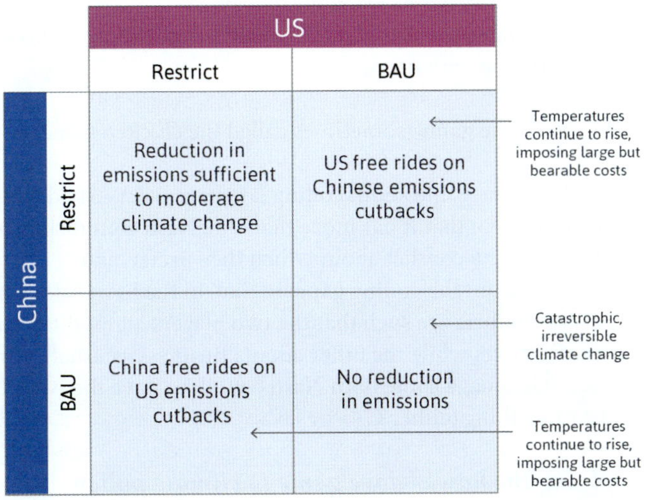

	US Restrict	US BAU
China Restrict	Reduction in emissions sufficient to moderate climate change	US free rides on Chinese emissions cutbacks ← Temperatures continue to rise, imposing large but bearable costs
China BAU	China free rides on US emissions cutbacks ← Temperatures continue to rise, imposing large but bearable costs	No reduction in emissions ← Catastrophic, irreversible climate change

Figure 2.14a The climate change game: Outcomes from the two strategies, Restrict and Business as usual (BAU).

One possible set of numerical payoffs for this game is illustrated in Figure 2.14b (bottom). We work through the game to find the predicted outcome.

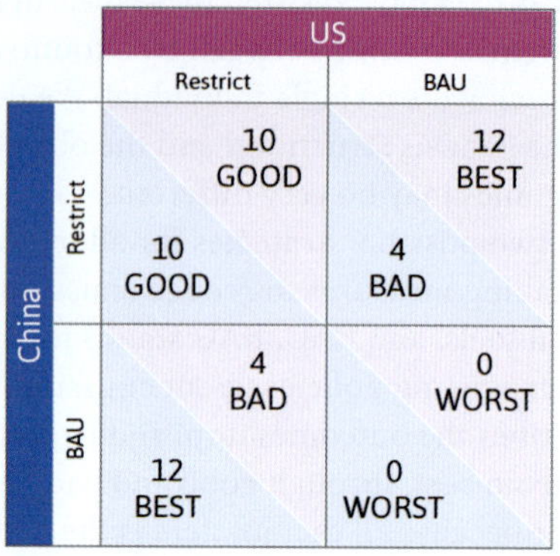

	US Restrict	US BAU
China Restrict	China 10 GOOD / US 10 GOOD	China 12 BEST / US 4 BAD
China BAU	China 4 BAD / US 12 BEST	China 0 WORST / US 0 WORST

Figure 2.14b The climate change hawk–dove game: Payoffs from the two strategies of Restrict and BAU (Business as usual).

First, consider China, the row player. If the US plays Restrict, then China's best response is BAU—place a dot in the bottom left cell. If the US plays BAU, then China, fearing human extinction, selects Restrict—place a dot in the top right cell. It is clear from this that China does not have a dominant strategy: what is best for China depends on what the US does.

By inspecting the payoff matrix, we can see that the game is symmetric. The same is true of the US—if China Restricts, the US will carry on with BAU. If China continues with BAU, then (like China in the previous case, fearing cataclysmic climate change for the entire planet) the US will Restrict. The circles will be in the bottom left and top right cells.

This is a social dilemma, but it differs from the prisoners' dilemma and the public goods game because:

- *Neither country has a dominant strategy.*
- *There are two Nash equilibria:* They differ on which country bears the cost of restricting emissions.

An example of the chicken game: in the 1984 film, Footloose (https://tinyco.re/7566753), two high-school students challenge each other by driving tractors towards each other, to see which one will 'chicken out' first.

The hawk–dove game (sometimes called the chicken game) is:

- similar to the game about coding languages that Astrid and Bettina are engaged in, in that it has more than one Nash equilibrium and the two players have a conflict about which they prefer, and
- different from the coding game in that, in the hawk–dove game, the two Nash equilibria are such that the two players adopt different strategies (one Restricts while the other adopts Business as usual), while in the coding language game both Nash equilibria have the two players doing the same thing (either C++ or Java).

Applying the hawk–dove game to climate policy

How do you think the hawk–dove game would be played in reality?

If the first country could commit itself to BAU so that the second country was certain that it would not consider any other strategy, then the second country would play Restrict (Restrict is a best response to BAU, to avoid catastrophe). But the same is true of the other country.

We can see that negotiations are bound to be difficult, since each country would prefer the other to take the lead on restricting carbon emissions. Among real countries (not the hypothetical players in our game) the situation is of course more complex—virtually all countries in the world are involved in the negotiations. The payoffs may look different to these varied players. For example, in 2015 China produced 30% of the world's total carbon emissions, the US was second with half of China's level, followed by India. On a per-capita basis, however, China produced less than half the emissions that the US did, and India less than an eighth.

The game represents the idea that no one wants to see catastrophic climate change, but each is waiting in order to see if others will move first.

There is another important aspect to this game—if we consider the numbers in the payoff matrix to be measures of the value of each possible outcome to the citizens of each country so that the total benefits of the two countries could be summed, then we can see that the best outcome for the world as a whole is that both Restrict (total payoffs = 20), followed by the two Nash equilibria with one country free riding on the other's Restrict policies (16), with BAU for both having the worst outcome.

Using public policy to change the game

How could the global social dilemma of climate change policy, as represented in this game, be solved?

Could the governments of the world simply prohibit or severely limit emissions that contribute to the problem of climate change? This would amount to changing the game by altering available strategies by making BAU illegal. But who would enforce this law? There is no world government that could take a government that violated the law to court (and lock up its head of state!).

If the climate change social dilemma is to be addressed, Restrict must be in the interests of each of the parties. Consider the bottom left corner (China plays BAU, US plays Restrict) equilibrium. If the payoffs China gets for playing Restrict were higher, when that is what the US is doing, then (Restrict, Restrict) might become an equilibrium.

Indeed, in the eyes of many climate change scientists and concerned citizens, the aim of global environmental policy is to change the game so that (Restrict, Restrict) becomes a Nash equilibrium. A number of mechanisms, aided by policy, could accomplish this:

- *Sustainable consumer lifestyles:* As a result of their concern for the wellbeing of future generations, people could come to prefer lifestyles that use fewer goods and services of the kind that result in environmental degradation. This would make the Restrict policy less costly and the BAU strategy less desirable.
- *Governments could stimulate innovation and the diffusion of cleaner technologies:* They might do this by, for example, raising the price of goods and services that result in carbon and other emissions, which would discourage their use. In the process, the use of these technologies would become cheaper, lowering the cost of Restrict. For example, renewable energy has become much cheaper. In some regions, it is now the cheapest energy option, which means Restrict is no longer more

expensive than BAU. Self-interested behaviour will result in lower carbon emissions.
- *A change in norms:* Citizens, non-governmental organizations (NGOs), and governments can promote a norm of climate protection and sanction or shame countries that do nothing to limit climate change. This would also reduce the attractiveness of BAU.
- *Countries can share the costs of Restrict more evenly:* This is possible if, for example, a country for whom Restrict is prohibitively expensive instead helps another country where it is less expensive to Restrict. An example would be paying countries in the Amazon basin to conserve the rainforest.

After intense negotiations following failed talks and a non-binding agreement in Copenhagen in 2009, the governments of all countries committed to eventual emission cuts at the United Nations Conference on Climate Change in Paris in December 2015, with the goal of stabilizing global temperatures at 2°C above pre-industrial levels. Almost all countries also submitted individual plans for cutting emissions.

Of course, there is no way that the Paris Agreement could be enforced. Although these plans are not yet consistent with this temperature stabilization goal, the Paris Agreement is widely seen as an important step in the right direction. It should:

- allow players to better understand the costs of restricting emissions
- encourage economic players to innovate in order to further lower the costs
- strengthen norms that reduce the attractiveness of BAU
- establish a base of trust to share some of the costs of Restrict and negotiate more ambitiously in the future.

2.14 THE ECONOMY AND ECONOMICS

Social dilemmas are unavoidable because of a basic fact of human existence: we are social animals. We interact directly and indirectly with thousands of people in a day. Take a single purchase that you have made today—perhaps a coffee—and create a mental map of all the people, their locations, and occupations involved in getting the coffee to the point at which you purchased it. We benefit hugely from our social nature in the friendships, families, exchanges of goods and services, knowledge, and other interactions of which we are a part. Life as a hermit would be impoverished by comparison. As a practical matter, human life in isolation would be impossible.

But our social nature poses an enormous challenge—how can we organize our interactions in such a way that the outcomes are acceptable—or even, by our own standards—good?

Although there are vast mutual gains to be had through interacting with others, there are also substantial conflicts among us about how these benefits will be shared.

In the eyes of many people, a desirable society is one that addresses the unavoidable social dilemmas that face us and also distributes the benefits and costs associated with our social interactions in a fair way. Economics has an important role to play in meeting these objectives.

Economics is the study of how people interact with each other and with their natural surroundings in producing their livelihoods, and how this changes over time. Therefore, it is about:

In the preface and chapter 1 of his history of economic life, Paul Seabright explains that *'Homo sapiens is the only animal that engages in elaborate task-sharing—the division of labour as it is sometimes known—between genetically unrelated members of the same species'*. Paul Seabright. 2010. *The Company of Strangers: A Natural History of Economic Life* (Revised Edition) (https://tinyco.re/2891054). Princeton, NJ: Princeton University Press.

economics The study of how people interact with each other and with their natural surroundings in providing their livelihoods, and how this changes over time.

- *How we come to acquire the things that make up our livelihood:* Things like food, clothing, shelter, or free time.
- *How we interact with each other:* Either as buyers and sellers, employees or employers, polluters and victims of climate change, citizens and public officials, parents, children, and other family members.
- *How we interact with our natural environment:* From breathing, to extracting raw materials from the earth.
- *How each of these changes over time.*

In Figure 1.19 (page 41) we showed that the economy is part of society, which in turn is part of the biosphere. Figure 2.15 shows the position of firms and families in the economy, and the flows that occur within the economy and between the economy and the biosphere. Firms combine labour with structures and equipment to produce goods and services that are used by households and other firms. The economy of households and firms depends on a healthy biosphere and stable physical environment.

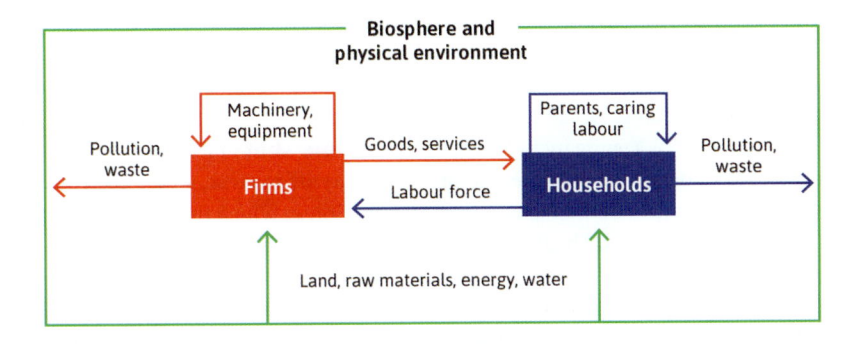

Figure 2.15 A model of the economy: Households and firms.

Production of goods and services also takes place within households, although, unlike firms, households may not sell their outputs in the market.

In addition to producing goods and services, households are also producing people—the next generation of the labour force. The labour of parents, caregivers, and others is combined with structures (for example, your home), and equipment (for example, the oven in that home) to reproduce and raise the future labour force working in firms and the people who will work and reproduce in the households of the future.

All of this takes place as part of a biological and physical system in which firms and households make use of our natural surroundings and resources, ranging from fossil fuels or renewable energy to the air we breathe. In the process, households and firms transform nature by using its resources, but also by producing inputs to nature. Currently, some of the most important of these inputs are the greenhouse gases, which contribute to climate change problems.

Humans have always relied on their environment—the physical environment and the biosphere, which is the collection of all forms of life on earth—for the resources they need to live and produce their livelihoods. The environment provides essentials for life, such as air, water, and food. It also provides the raw materials that we use in the production of other goods—such as wood, metals, and oil.

2.15 CONCLUSION

Our economy is shaped by millions of direct and indirect interactions among people. These **social interactions** offer opportunities for mutual gains, but conflicts frequently arise over how these gains should be distributed.

The individual pursuit of self-interest may lead to socially beneficial outcomes. But, in addition to these 'invisible hand' situations, there are interactions like the prisoners' dilemma and the **tragedy of the commons**, in which people would do better by cooperating rather than acting individually. These **social dilemmas** occur when people do not take into account the effects of their actions on others, called **external effects** or **externalities**.

And they give rise to the problem of **free riding**, where people benefit from the contributions of others to a **public good** or some other cooperative project without contributing themselves.

To understand how social dilemmas are sometimes resolved, we looked at **behavioural experiments**, which reveal the **preferences** that motivate people's actions. We find that, in addition to the self-interest exemplified by *homo economicus*, **social preferences** (such as **altruism**, **reciprocity**, and **inequality aversion**) and **social norms** also influence how we behave.

We have used **game theory** to study **strategic interactions** among people whose actions jointly determine the outcome. A **game** specifies the players, their feasible **strategies**, their information, and the possible payoffs. Characteristics of a game include whether it is a **one-shot** or a **repeated game**. We visualize the possible outcomes in a **payoff matrix**, where each entry describes the result of a hypothetical situation in which the players choose certain actions. The dot-and-circle method can help identify probable outcomes of the game.

Helpful concepts that have aided our analysis of games include that of a **best response** and a **dominant strategy**. We have seen that multiple **Nash equilibria** (mutual best responses) may occur, and that a **dominant strategy equilibrium** is a particularly simple example of a Nash equilibrium. Conflicts of interest arise when the players prefer different equilibria, and an economy may get 'stuck' in a Nash equilibrium where all of the participants are worse off.

Types of games (and corresponding examples) we have studied in this chapter are:

Game	Example	Characteristics
Invisible hand (page 60)	Crop specialization (Anil and Bala)	A single NE; no alternative that would benefit both players.
Prisoners' dilemma (page 62)	Pest control (Anil and Bala)	A single NE that is inferior for both relative to a feasible alternative
Public goods (page 67)	Irrigation project (Kim and farmers)	A single NE that is inferior for all relative to a feasible alternative
Coordination (page 80)	Crop specialization (Anil and Bala)	Two NE; one is better for both
Coordination/conflict (page 85)	Coding language (Astrid and Bettina)	Two asymmetric NE; one better for Astrid the other better for Bettina
Hawk–dove (page 88)	Climate Change (China and US)	Two asymmetric NE; one benefiting China the other, the US.

The issues discussed in this unit have helped us define economics as the study of how people interact with each other and with their natural surroundings to produce their livelihoods. Understanding these interactions can help us devise policies that yield desirable social outcomes that promote people's wellbeing.

2.16 *DOING ECONOMICS:* COLLECTING AND ANALYSING DATA FROM EXPERIMENTS

In Unit 2, we discussed how we could use experiments to investigate how people might behave in particular situations. Although we cannot perfectly predict how people would actually behave, the controlled environment of experiments allow us to isolate the effects of a given change and identify specific reasons for the observed behaviour. If we kept all conditions the same and only changed one thing, then we can be more certain that any differences we observe are due to that one change.

We will first learn more about how experimental data can be collected by playing a public goods game to collect our own data. Then we will look at ways to describe and analyse the experimental data from Figure 2.9a and 2.9b (page 73) in order to answer the following research questions:

1. What effect did the change in conditions (the punishment option) have on behaviour (average contributions)?
2. Are the differences in behaviour 'large enough' that we can attribute them to the change in conditions, rather than chance/coincidence?

Go to *Doing Economics* Empirical Project 2 (https://tinyco.re/3460318) to work on this problem.

> *Learning objectives*
> In this project you will:
>
> - collect data from an experiment and enter it into Excel
> - use summary measures, for example, mean and standard deviation, and line and column charts to describe and compare data
> - calculate and interpret the p-value
> - evaluate the usefulness of experiments for determining causality, and the limitations of these experiments.

2.17 REFERENCES

Aesop. 'Belling the Cat'. In *Fables*, retold by Joseph Jacobs. XVII, (1). The Harvard Classics. New York: P. F. Collier & Son, 1909–14; Bartleby.com (https://tinyco.re/6827567). 2001.

Camerer, Colin, and Ernst Fehr. 2004. 'Measuring Social Norms and Preferences Using Experimental Games: A Guide for Social Scientists'. In *Foundations of Human Sociality: Economic Experiments and Ethnographic Evidence from Fifteen Small-Scale Societies*, edited by Joseph Henrich, Robert Boyd, Samuel Bowles, Colin Camerer, and Herbert Gintis. Oxford: Oxford University Press.

Edgeworth, Francis Ysidro. 2003. *Mathematical Psychics and Further Papers on Political Economy*. Oxford: Oxford University Press.

Falk, Armin, and James J. Heckman. 2009. 'Lab Experiments Are a Major Source of Knowledge in the Social Sciences'. *Science* 326 (5952): pp. 535–538.

Hardin, Garrett. 1968. 'The Tragedy of the Commons' (https://tinyco.re/4834967). *Science* 162 (3859): pp. 1243–48.

Henrich, Joseph, Richard McElreath, Abigail Barr, Jean Ensminger, Clark Barrett, Alexander Bolyanatz, Juan Camilo Cardenas, Michael Gurven, Edwins Gwako, Natalie Henrich, Carolyn Lesorogol, Frank Marlowe, David Tracer, and John Ziker. 2006. 'Costly Punishment Across Human Societies' (https://tinyco.re/2043845). *Science* 312 (5781): pp. 1767–70.

Levitt, Steven D., and John A. List. 2007. 'What Do Laboratory Experiments Measuring Social Preferences Reveal About the Real World?' (https://tinyco.re/9601240). *Journal of Economic Perspectives* 21 (2): pp. 153–74.

Mencken, H. L. 2006. *A Little Book in C Major*. New York, NY: Kessinger Publishing.

Nasar, Sylvia. 2011. *A Beautiful Mind: The Life of Mathematical Genius and Nobel Laureate John Nash*. New York, NY: Simon & Schuster.

Ostrom, Elinor. 2000. 'Collective Action and the Evolution of Social Norms' (https://tinyco.re/0059239). *Journal of Economic Perspectives* 14 (3): pp. 137–58.

Ostrom, Elinor. 2008. 'The Challenge of Common-Pool Resources' (https://tinyco.re/0296632). *Environment: Science and Policy for Sustainable Development* 50 (4): pp. 8–21.

Seabright, Paul. 2010. *The Company of Strangers: A Natural History of Economic Life* (Revised Edition). Princeton, NJ: Princeton University Press.

3
PUBLIC POLICY FOR FAIRNESS AND EFFICIENCY

Goddess of Justice, Frankfurt

3.1 INTRODUCTION

- Public policies are evaluated on the basis of whether their intended outcomes are efficient and fair, and whether they can be implemented.
- People may consider an outcome to be unfair, either because who gets what is thought to be unjust, or because the rules of the game determining this distribution are seen as unfair.
- Experiments with a new game, the ultimatum game, show that people care about fairness, are willing to sacrifice their own material payoffs to avoid unfair outcomes, and are willing to punish unfair behaviour in others.
- Successful public policies such as taxes and subsidies change the circumstances in which people decide how to act, and in so doing create a new allocation that will not be sustained unless it is a Nash equilibrium.
- Understanding people's responses to policies so that we can better understand the likely outcomes of our policy choices is a major challenge for economists and policymakers.

In most countries and throughout human history, women have been underrepresented in positions of political leadership. We can argue that this affects the public policies that governments create. For example, countries in which women are more equally represented as members of parliament or heads of state have spent more to support the less well off.

But the fact that there are pro-poor policies when women are in powerful positions—as in Norway, Sweden, and the other Nordic countries—does not mean that electing women has caused these policies. It could be that countries that have values that lead them to support pro-poor policies are also more likely to elect women. In this case, they would enact the same pro-poor policies, even if women were not elected.

This raises the difficult problem of causation, introduced in Section 1.8 (page 29), where we compared economic growth under capitalist West Germany and centrally planned East Germany. The data in Figure 1.15 (page 32) indicated that the difference in their economic institutions was probably a cause (not just a correlate) of the divergent economic fortunes of the two Germanies. Economists are interested in what causes what, because we would like economic knowledge to be useful. One way it can be useful is if it contributes to the design of policies that would cause better outcomes to happen.

A study of changes in women's voting rights in the US, and the changes in public policy that followed, provides a similar opportunity to identify whether increased political power for women actually *caused* changes in policies. The US is a particularly useful laboratory for this kind of study because voting laws differ by state. As a result, women gained the right to vote at different times, starting in 1869 in Wyoming. In 1920, the Nineteenth Amendment to the US Constitution granted the vote to women in all of the remaining states that had not yet granted this right.

Grant Miller, an economist, has used the date at which women got the right to vote to do a before-and-after comparison of the actions taken by elected officials, public expenditures related to child health, and health outcomes for children.

Miller chose to focus on child healthcare policies because women had campaigned to expand health services for children. It is therefore reasonable to assume that women would have chosen different policies at this time than men would have chosen. During the nineteenth century and before, however, those who argued that only men should vote often claimed that women were represented through their husbands, brothers, and fathers.

Miller's study is a '**natural experiment**', and is similar to the case of the two Germanies:

- *It is an experiment:* The variable that interests us—the right to vote for women—was the only difference likely to affect public spending and child health. Other things that might have had an effect—the state's tax base, or improvements in medical knowledge, for example—are held constant by looking at the same state at roughly the same time, and at changes occurring in other states in which women did not have the right to vote.
- *It is natural:* It was not designed or conducted in a lab, but happened in the course of history.

The logic of a natural experiment is illustrated in this diagram, in which each arrow represents possible causes that Miller explored.

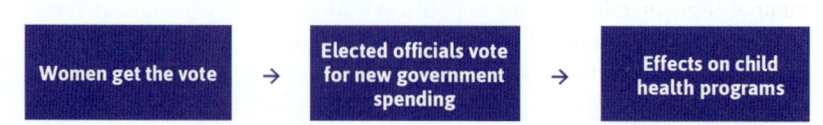

Women get the vote → Elected officials vote for new government spending → Effects on child health programs

Miller's research asked two questions: 'Did women's voting rights have a causal effect on what the government did?' (the first arrow), and 'Did the changes in government programs have any causal effect on children's wellbeing?' (the second arrow).

Grant Miller. 2008. 'Women's suffrage, political responsiveness, and child survival in American history' (https://tinyco.re/5731666). *The Quarterly Journal of Economics* 123 (3): pp. 1287–327.

natural experiment An empirical study exploiting naturally occurring statistical controls in which researchers do not have the ability to assign participants to treatment and control groups, as is the case in conventional experiments. Instead, differences in law, policy, weather, or other events can offer the opportunity to analyse populations as if they had been part of an experiment. The validity of such studies depends on the premise that the assignment of subjects to the naturally occurring treatment and control groups can be plausibly argued to be random.

To explore whether women's voting rights were a cause of the changes in spending and improved child health, Miller adopted what is called a '**difference-in-difference**' method. To identify the first arrow above as a **causal** relationship rather than just a correlation, he compared the difference in spending before and after the change in voting rights in the states in which this occurred, with changes in spending over the same period, but in states in which there was no change in voting rights.

If the difference was greater in the states where women had gained voting rights, he could conclude that the change in voting rights had *caused* the differences in spending.

The key assumption for the difference-in-difference method is that any relevant changes that took place in the state of Wyoming between 1868 and 1870 (when women were granted the vote), except the change in women's voting rights itself, were common to other states that did not grant women the right to vote during those years.

Here is what Miller found:

- *Social services increased:* Looking state-by-state at the date women got the right to vote, enfranchisement boosted social service spending by 24%. It had no apparent effect on public spending in other areas.
- *Spending on children increased:* Within a year of the passage of the Nineteenth Amendment, the US Congress voted for a substantial increase in public health spending aimed at children. A historian concluded that 'the principal force moving Congress was fear of being punished at the polls … by women voters.'
- *Child deaths decreased:* In 1900, one in five children in the US did not live to the age of five. The deaths of children under the age of nine fell by between 8% and 15%. This was primarily as a result of the public programs that had been adopted, especially large-scale door-to-door hygiene campaigns.

Healthcare programs, based on the recent revolution in scientific knowledge of bacteria and disease, prevented an estimated 20,000 child deaths per year. Votes for women helped to achieve this.

In many countries today, women participate much less in political life and leadership than do men, and political systems are often less responsive to the needs of women than men. But if we want to show that it makes a difference when women gain more political power, we must always distinguish, as Miller did, between causes and correlations.

India has provided an unusual laboratory to do this. In our 'Economist in action' video, Esther Duflo explains what happened when the government of India mandated that randomly selected villages elect a woman to head their local council.

The video shows that reserving positions for women to head village councils:

- increased public spending on the public services that women preferred, like wells
- reduced receipts of bribes by those in power
- transformed stereotypes, so that men in villages with women leaders perceived them more as leaders, rather than solely in domestic roles.

difference-in-difference A method that applies an experimental research design to outcomes observed in a natural experiment. It involves comparing the difference in the average outcomes of two groups, a treatment and control group, both before and after the treatment took place.

causality A direction from cause to effect, establishing that a change in one variable produces a change in another. While a correlation is simply an assessment that two things have moved together, causation implies a mechanism accounting for the association, and is therefore a more restrictive concept. *See also:* natural experiment, correlation.

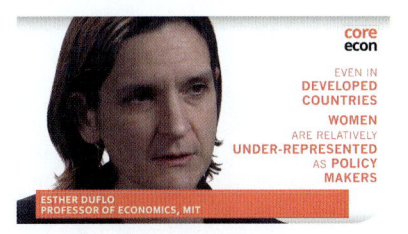

Esther Duflo: Representation for women in India https://tinyco.re/94993365

The reduction in child mortality in the US, and the changes in village council policies in India, illustrate the capacity of governments to provide solutions to problems arising in the economy.

In the US, for example, many children, particularly in poor families, no longer died from readily preventable diseases. The policies also limited the spread of communicable diseases among all members of the population.

In this case, the government provided a public good—better sanitation and public information about hygiene—that improved conditions for most Americans, and specially helped the least well off. These two objectives—promoting gains for all and correcting unfairness—are foremost among the standards by which we evaluate economic outcomes and policies to improve them.

> **QUESTION 3.1 CHOOSE THE CORRECT ANSWER(S)**
> According to the 'Economist in action' video featuring Esther Duflo:
>
> ☐ The reform of the panchayat (local council) was a natural experiment that enabled economists to attribute the changes in public goods investment to having women representation in the council.
> ☐ Duflo learned about villagers' attitudes towards women as policy-makers by asking them directly.
> ☐ A medium-term effect of the local council reform is that career aspirations of girls changed.
> ☐ A long-term effect of the local council reform is that girls were less likely to drop out of middle school.

3.2 GOALS OF PUBLIC POLICY

public policy A policy decided by the government. *Also known as: government policy*

To illustrate these two objectives of **public policy**—promoting gains for all and correcting unfairness—we return to the problem of free riding, as illustrated by the tragedy of the commons (page 51) introduced in the previous unit. Let's explore how public policy might avert the tragedy.

Here is how the tragedy of the commons unfolds, according to its author, Garrett Hardin:

Garrett Hardin. 1968. 'The Tragedy of the Commons' (https://tinyco.re/4834967). *Science* 162(3859): pp. 1243–1248.

> Picture a pasture open to all. … each herdsman … seeks to maximize his gain … [and] will try to keep as many cattle as possible on the commons. … he asks, 'What is the utility *to me* of adding one more animal …?' 1) The positive component … the herdsman receives all of the proceeds from the sale of the additional animal. 2) The negative component … the effects of overgrazing are shared by all of the herdsman [so] the negative utility for any decision-making herdsman is only a fraction of the total [negative effect].

The tragedy seems inevitable:

> The only sensible course for him to pursue is to add another animal to his herd. And another. But this is the conclusion reached by each and every … herdsman sharing a commons. Therein is the tragedy. Ruin is the destination towards which all men rush, each pursuing his own best interest. Freedom in the commons brings ruin to all.

Now think about how government policy might improve the situation.

Cows as common property

A policymaker might reason, as Hardin did, that the problem is that all herders have access to the pasture and they make their decisions independently—without taking account of the negative external effect on the other herders if they decide to put additional cows on the pasture. This suggests a solution. If they owned all of the cows jointly, they could decide together how many of them to put on the pasture. That way, there would be no external effects of placing too many cows on the pasture. The costs of overgrazing would be experienced by all members of the decision-making body.

If they owned the cows jointly, they would take care of the pasture. But, under this arrangement the cows would now be owned by everyone. So *who would take care of the cows*? Each of the herders would have an incentive to free ride on the others by letting somebody else tend the cattle. The tragedy of the commons has become the tragedy of the cows!

Private property averts the tragedy

Our policymaker might try a different approach. If one herder was given access to the pasture and the rest excluded, then this lucky herder would reason in a different way—'If I put an additional cow on the pasture, this gives me one more cow, but less pasture for the rest of *my own cows*. So, I should limit the size of my herd.'

The tragedy has been averted. Converting the pasture to the private property of the one lucky herder addresses the root of the problem, which was that each herder did not consider the effects of a decision on the other herders. Now there is only one herder, and they will take account of the damage that overgrazing might inflict on the pasture and the cattle on it.

Is this a fair allocation?

What about the herders who have been excluded from the pasture? Denying them access to the pasture hardly seems fair. An unfair outcome may not be sustainable in the long run, even if it provided an efficient solution to the initial problem.

Whether it is fishermen seeking to make a living while not depleting the fish stocks, or farmers maintaining the channels of an irrigation system, herders overgrazing a pasture, or two people dividing up a pie, we want to be able to both describe what happens and evaluate it—is it better or worse than other potential outcomes? The first involves facts; the second involves values.

We call the outcome of an economic interaction an **allocation**. Taking as an example the climate change game described in Unit 2 (page 86), each of the four outcomes *and* the resulting payoffs for the two players, the US and China, is called an allocation.

Our discussion of the tragedy of the commons has evaluated outcomes along two dimensions: ruining the pasture was not a sensible way to use the resource, but averting the tragedy by assigning the property right to the pasture to a single herder did not seem fair. We will illustrate these two objectives—which we will call efficiency and fairness—by a new kind of social interaction, which we call the ultimatum game. After we have played this game, we will explain these important terms in more detail.

> **allocation** A description of who does what, the consequences of their actions, and who gets what as a result (for example in a game, the strategies adopted by each player and their resulting payoffs).

3.3 FAIRNESS AND EFFICIENCY IN THE ULTIMATUM GAME

To study how the objectives of efficiency and fairness interact—sometimes in mutually supportive ways, but often in conflict—we turn to a new game, called the **ultimatum game**. It has been used around the world with experimental subjects including students, farmers, warehouse workers, and hunter-gatherers.

The subjects of the experiment play a game in which they will win some money. How much they win will depend on how they and the others in the game play. So, like the public goods game experiments in Unit 2 (page 72), it is a strategic interaction in which the payoffs of each depend on the actions of the others.

Real money is at stake in experimental games like these, otherwise we could not be sure the subjects' answers to a hypothetical question would reflect their actions in real life.

The rules of the game are explained to the players.

- They are randomly matched in pairs.
- One player is randomly assigned as the Proposer and the other the Responder.
- The subjects do not know each other, but they know the other player was recruited to the experiment in the same way.
- Subjects remain anonymous.

The Proposer is provisionally given an amount of money, say $100, by the experimenter, and instructed to offer the Responder part of it. Any split is permitted, including keeping it all, or giving it all away. We will call this amount the 'pie' because the point of the experiment is how it will be divided up.

The split takes the form 'x for me, y for you', where $x + y = \$100$.

- The Responder knows that the Proposer has $100 to split.
- After observing the offer, the Responder accepts or rejects it.
- If the offer is rejected, both individuals get nothing.
- If it is accepted, the split is implemented—the Proposer gets x and the Responder y.

For example, if the Proposer offers $35 and the Responder accepts, the Proposer gets $65 and the Responder gets $35. If the Responder rejects the offer, they both get nothing.

This is called a take-it-or-leave-it offer. It is the ultimatum in the game's name. The Responder is faced with a choice—accept $35 and let the other get $65, or get nothing and deprive the other player of any payoffs too.

A game tree

We start by thinking about a simplified case of the ultimatum game, represented in Figure 3.1 in a diagram called a game tree. The Proposer's choices are either the 'fair offer' of an equal split, or the 'unfair offer' of 20 (keeping 80 for herself). Then the Responder has the choice to accept or reject. The payoffs are shown in the last row. In the actual experiments, Proposers were not confined to these two fair and unfair options. Instead, they could choose any split they wished, including proposing to give everything or nothing to the other.

> **ultimatum game** An interaction in which the first player proposes a division of a 'pie' with the second player, who may either accept, in which case they each get the division proposed by the first person, or reject the offer, in which case both players receive nothing.

The game tree is a useful way to represent social interactions because it clarifies who does what, when they choose, and the results. We see that in the ultimatum game one player (the Proposer) chooses her strategy first, followed by the Responder. This is called a **sequential game** because each player knows the actions of the previous player before acting (unlike the prisoners' dilemma (page 61), for example).

A strategic interaction

What the Proposer will get depends on what the Responder does, so the Proposer has to think about the likely response of the other player. This is why it is called a strategic interaction. If you're the Proposer you can't try out a low offer to see what happens. You have only one chance to make an offer. How would you think this through if you were the Proposer?

1. *Put yourself in the place of the Responder in this game:* Would you accept (50, 50)? Would you accept (80, 20)?
2. *Now switch roles and suppose that you are the Proposer:* What split would you offer to the Responder? Would your answer depend on whether the other person was a friend, a stranger, a person in need, or a competitor?

We have some clues about how to answer these questions. Dividing something of value in equal shares (the 50–50 rule) is a social norm in many communities, as is giving gifts on birthdays to close family members and friends. Social norms are common to an entire group of people (almost all follow them) and tell a person what they should do in the eyes of most people in the community.

A Responder who thinks that the Proposer's offer has violated a social norm of fairness, or that the offer is insultingly low for some other reason, might be willing to sacrifice their own payoff to punish the Proposer.

> **sequential game** A game in which all players do not choose their strategies at the same time, and players that choose later can see the strategies already chosen by the other players, for example the ultimatum game. See also: *simultaneous game.*

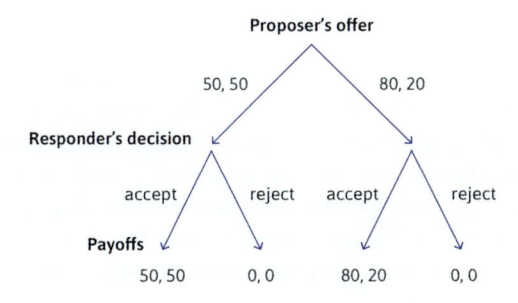

Figure 3.1 Game tree for the ultimatum game in which the only choices open to the Proposer are an even split, or to keep 80 while giving 20 to the Responder.

> **EXERCISE 3.1 ACCEPTABLE OFFERS**
> Look again at the ultimatum game shown in Figure 3.1.
>
> 1. *Suppose the Proposer received the $100 through some other means rather than being given $100 by the experimenter:* For example, she might have found it on the street, won it in the lottery, received it as an inheritance, or earned it through hard work. How might the Responder's perception of the ($80, $20) offer depend on the way that the Proposer acquired the $100?
> 2. *Suppose that the Proposer can offer more than $50 to the Responder, and the social norm in this society is 50–50:* Can you imagine anyone offering more than $50 in such a society? Why, or why not?

The problem of fairness and efficiency

If in the ultimatum game you were a Responder who cared only about your own payoffs, you would accept any positive offer, because something is better than nothing. But if you cared about fairness too, and the Proposer made you a very low offer that you considered to be unfair, you might decide to reject the offer. Neither you nor the Proposer would receive anything. This outcome—throwing away money!—cannot be efficient.

One way of eliminating this inefficiency would be to change the rules of the game so that a Responder, even one who cared very much about fairness, could not reject any offer. For obvious reasons, this is called the dictator game! There would never be money left on the table, but much like excluding all but one herder from using the pasture (in the tragedy of the commons), it would hardly be called fair.

People value fairness in practice

In a world composed only of self-interested individuals, in which everyone knew for sure that everyone else was self-interested, the Proposer would anticipate that the Responder would accept any offer greater than zero and, for that reason, would offer the minimum possible positive amount—one cent—knowing it would be accepted.

Does this prediction match the experimental data? No, it does not. As in the prisoners' dilemma studied in the previous unit, we don't see the outcome we would predict if people were entirely self-interested. One-cent offers get rejected. If it costs you just one cent to punish a selfish person—sending them away with nothing—it's not difficult to see why most people are happy to do so!

Let's see how Kenyan farmers and US students actually played the ultimatum game.

Look at Figure 3.2. Before playing the game, the researchers—a team of anthropologists and economists who conducted the same experiments throughout the world—asked their subjects to indicate (confidentially) the offers they would accept and which they would reject. The height of each bar indicates the fraction of Responders who were willing to accept the offer indicated on the horizontal axis. Offers of more than half of the pie were acceptable to all of the subjects in both countries, as one would expect.

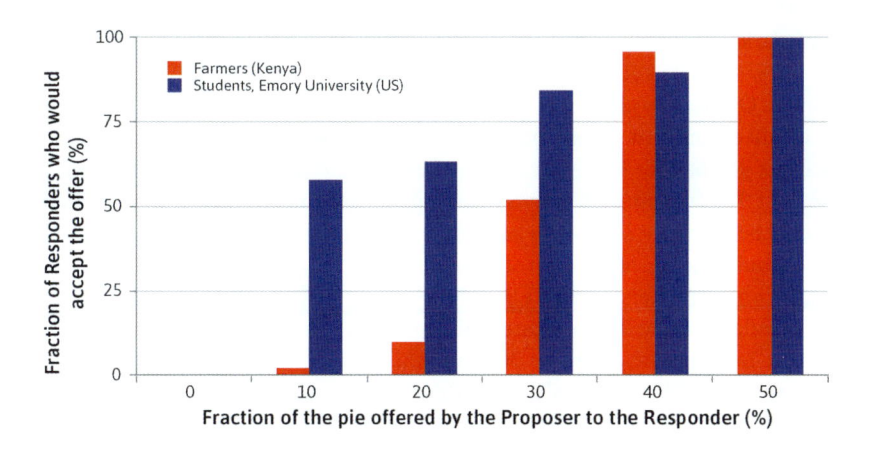

Adapted from Joseph Henrich, Richard McElreath, Abigail Barr, Jean Ensminger, Clark Barrett, Alexander Bolyanatz, Juan Camilo Cardenas, Michael Gurven, Edwins Gwako, Natalie Henrich, Carolyn Lesorogol, Frank Marlowe, David Tracer, and John Ziker. 2006. 'Costly Punishment Across Human Societies'. Science 312 (5781): pp. 1767–70.

Figure 3.2 Acceptable offers in the ultimatum game.

Notice that the Kenyan farmers are very unwilling to accept low offers, presumably regarding them as unfair, while the US students are much more willing to do so. For example, virtually all (90%) of the farmers would say no to an offer of one-fifth of the pie (the Proposer keeping 80%), while 63% of the students would accept such a low offer. More than half of the students would accept just 10% of the pie, but almost none of the farmers would.

Although the results in Figure 3.2 indicate that attitudes differ about the importance of fairness and what constitutes fairness, nobody in the Kenyan and US experiments was willing to accept an offer of zero, even though by rejecting it they would also receive zero.

Figure 3.3 shows another way of looking at these results. The full height of each bar in Figure 3.3 indicates the percentage of the Kenyan and American Proposers who made the offer shown on the horizontal axis when they actually played the game. For example, half of the farmers made proposals of 40%. Another 10% offered an even split. Only 11% of the students made such generous offers.

The Proposer's reasoning

But were the farmers really being generous? To answer, you should think not only about how much they were offering, but also what they must have reasoned when considering whether the Responder would accept the offer. If you look at Figure 3.3 and concentrate on the Kenyan farmers, you will see that very few proposed to keep the entire pie by offering zero (4% of them as shown in the far left-hand bar). This is no surprise, given that they must have reasoned that all of those offers would be rejected (the entire bar is dark).

On the other hand, looking at the far right of the figure, we see that for the farmers, making an offer of half the pie ensured an acceptance rate of 100% (the entire bar is light). Those who offered 30% were about equally likely to see their offer rejected as accepted (the dark part of the bar is nearly as big as the light part).

A Proposer who wanted to earn as much as possible would choose something between the extremes of trying to take it all, or dividing it equally. The farmers who offered 40% were very likely to see their offer accepted and receive 60% of the pie. In the experiment, half of the farmers chose an offer of 40%. This offer was rejected only 4% of the time, as can be seen from the tiny dark-shaded top part of the bar at the 40% offer in Figure 3.3.

Now suppose you are a Kenyan farmer and all you care about is your own payoff. Offering to give the Responder nothing is out of the question because that will ensure that you get nothing when they reject your offer. Offering half will get you half for sure—because the Responder will surely accept. But you suspect that you can do better. Something more than nothing but less than half would be your best bet. Given how likely the farmers were to reject low offers, you would maximize your payoffs on average if you offered 40%—this was the most common offer among Kenyan Proposers.

Similar calculations indicate that, among the students, the expected payoff-maximizing offer was 30%, and this was the most common offer among them. The students' lower offers could be because they correctly anticipated that lowball offers (even as low as 10%) would sometimes be accepted. They may have been trying to maximize their payoffs and hoping that they could get away with making low offers.

How do the two populations differ? Although many of the farmers and the students offered an amount that would maximize their expected payoffs, the similarity ends there. The Kenyan farmers were more likely to reject low offers. Is this a difference between Kenyans and Americans, or between farmers and students? Or is it something related to local social

To explore all of the slides in this figure, see the online version at https://tinyco.re/1191868.

Adapted from Joseph Henrich, Richard McElreath, Abigail Barr, Jean Ensminger, Clark Barrett, Alexander Bolyanatz, Juan Camilo Cardenas, Michael Gurven, Edwins Gwako, Natalie Henrich, Carolyn Lesorogol, Frank Marlowe, David Tracer, and John Ziker. 2006. 'Costly Punishment Across Human Societies'. *Science* 312 (5781): pp. 1767–70.

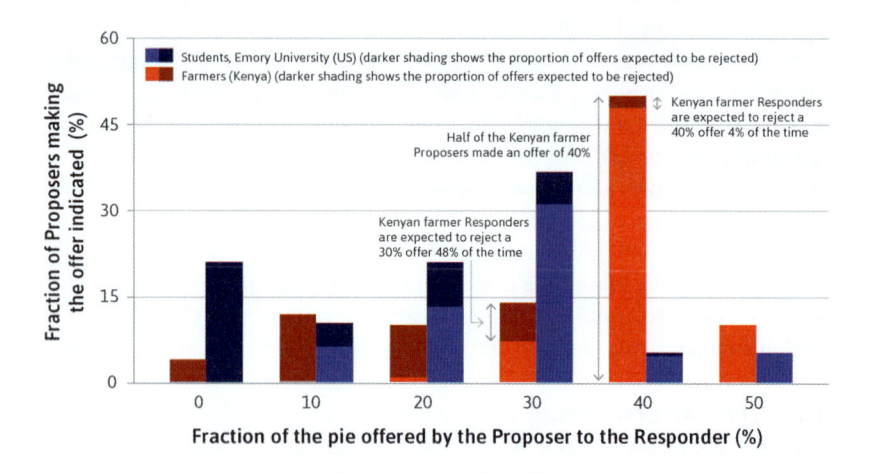

Figure 3.3 Actual offers and expected rejections in the ultimatum game.

1. What do the bars show?
The full height of each bar in the figure indicates the percentage of the Kenyan and American Proposers who made the offer shown on the horizontal axis.

2. Reading the figure
For example, for Kenyan farmers, 50% on the vertical axis and 40% on the horizontal axis means half of the Kenyan Proposers made an offer of 40%.

3. The dark-shaded area shows rejections
If Kenyan farmers made an offer of 30%, almost half of Responders would reject it. (The dark part of the bar is almost as big as the light part.)

4. Better offers, fewer rejections
The relative size of the dark area is smaller for better offers. For example, Kenyan farmer Responders rejected a 40% offer only 4% of the time.

norms, rather than nationality and occupation? Experiments alone cannot answer these interesting questions, but before you jump to the conclusion that Kenyans are more averse to unfairness than Americans, when the same experiment was run with people from rural Missouri in the US, they were even more likely to reject low offers than the Kenyan farmers. Almost every Proposer in the Missouri experiment offered half the pie.

> **EXERCISE 3.2 OFFERS IN THE ULTIMATUM GAME**
> In the ultimatum game shown in Figures 3.2 and 3.3:
>
> 1. Why do you think that some of the farmers offered more than 40%, and why do you think that some of the students offered more than 30%?
> 2. Why do you think that some offered less?

> **QUESTION 3.2 CHOOSE THE CORRECT ANSWER(S)**
> From the information shown in Figure 3.2, we can conclude that:
>
> ☐ Kenyan farmers place higher importance on fairness than US students.
> ☐ Kenyans are more likely than Americans to reject low offers.
> ☐ Both groups of Responders are neutral about accepting and rejecting an offer of receiving nothing.
> ☐ Just over 50% of Kenyan farmers rejected the offer of the Proposer keeping 30%.

3.4 EVALUATING AN OUTCOME: IS IT EFFICIENT?

When we consider alternative economic policies and we say that some outcome is 'better' or 'worse', there are two characteristics of the allocation that we will value:

- **efficiency**
- **fairness**

There are many other values that could be used to evaluate an economic outcome, including individual dignity and freedom, diversity, conformity to the prescriptions of one's religion or other values, and many more. But here we will focus on efficiency and fairness, as shown in Figure 3.4.

'Pareto efficiency'

In common use, the word 'efficiency' describes the absence of waste or the appropriate use of resources to accomplish something. A society would not be using its water resources efficiently, for example, if a lot of the water was wasted through leaky pipes.

We could also call it inefficient if some people did not have any access to clean drinking water, while others in the same community had well-watered desert golf courses. Why is this 'inefficient'? Perhaps because the golfers in the community would be less happy if their greens were less well watered, but only by a small amount compared to the increased happiness of the others if they suddenly had access to clean drinking water.

> **Pareto efficient** An allocation with the property that there is no alternative technically feasible allocation in which at least one person would be better off, and nobody worse off.
> **fairness** A way to evaluate an allocation based on one's conception of justice.

But in economics the word 'efficiency' has a simple and precise use—an outcome is efficient if there is no other outcome that would be preferred by everyone affected (or at least preferred by some, and not opposed by any). This use of the term is called Pareto efficiency after Vilfredo Pareto, an Italian economist and sociologist who developed the idea.

Saying that something is economically 'efficient' sounds profound. But this is not always so. Any division of a pie between two people —including one person getting all the pie—is Pareto efficient, as long as none of the pie is thrown away.

Returning to the golf course, in everyday language we might say: 'This is not a sensible way to utilize scarce water. It is clearly inefficient'. But in economics, Pareto efficiency means something different. A very unequal distribution of water can be **Pareto efficient** as long as the water is being used by a person who enjoys it even a little. This example emphasizes that the *efficiency* criterion says nothing about *fairness*, our other important value. We return to how fairness might be evaluated in the next section (page 108).

Now suppose that we want to use the concept of Pareto efficiency to compare two possible allocations, A and B, that may result from an economic interaction. Can we say which is better? Suppose we find that everyone involved in the interaction would prefer Allocation A, or some preferred A and none preferred B (some were neutral between A and B). Most people would agree that A is a better allocation than B. This criterion for judging between A and B is called the **Pareto criterion**.

Note that, when we say an allocation makes someone 'better off', we mean only that they prefer it. This implies that they would choose it rather than some other option, if both options were possible at that moment. So an allocation that makes you 'better off' than an alternative does not mean it makes you happier, or healthier, or mean you have more money, but just that you would choose it rather than the alternative. You may even choose it because of an addiction.

Pareto criterion According to the Pareto criterion, a desirable attribute of an allocation is that it be Pareto efficient. *See also: Pareto dominant.*

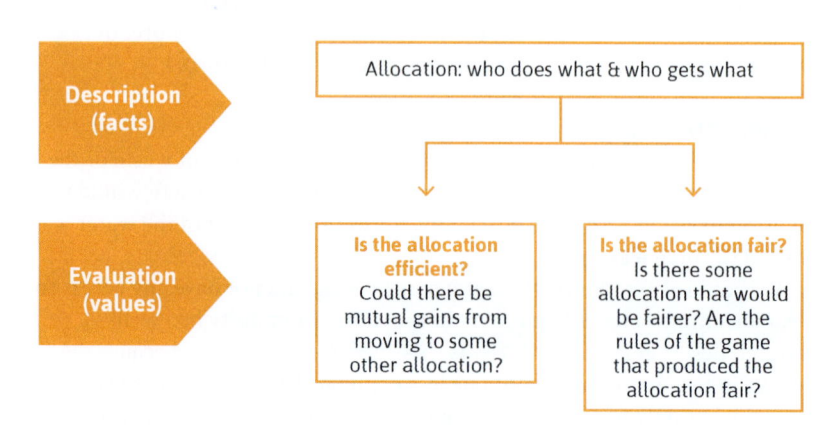

Figure 3.4 Description of allocations and their evaluation in terms of efficiency and fairness.

We now apply the language of Pareto efficiency to three possible ways of organizing the commons—open access (the reason for the tragedy), private ownership by a single herder, and joint determination by all of the herders to restrict access to the pasture as to achieve the highest income possible consistent with sustaining the pasture. We can say that:

- *Overgrazing the pasture under open access is not Pareto efficient:* All of the herders could have been better off if each had restricted the number of cows they pastured there.
- *Shifting from a regime of open access to one of jointly-agreed-upon restricted access would be a Pareto improvement:* This is an arrangement that **Pareto dominates** open access.
- *Both private ownership of the pasture by a single individual and joint restricted access by all the herders can be Pareto efficient.*
- *But shifting from jointly-agreed-upon restricted access to private ownership is not a Pareto improvement:* All of the herders except the one owner do worse under private ownership.
- *Shifting from private ownership by a single owner to jointly-agreed-upon restricted access is also not a Pareto improvement:* The single owner does worse as one of many joint owners.
- *The Pareto criterion would therefore recommend shifting from open access to joint restricted access:* It is a Pareto improvement. But it would not recommend whether to shift to private single ownership, or jointly determined access, because both are Pareto efficient.

Applying Pareto efficiency to the pest control game

Figure 3.5 uses the Pareto criterion to compare the four allocations in the pest control game that we studied in Unit 2 (page 61). In this example, we assume that Anil and Bala are self-interested, so they prefer allocations with a higher payoff for themselves. They each have two possible choices—use the chemical pesticide Terminator (T) or a non-chemical integrated pest control strategy (I). Recall that their payoffs describe a prisoners' dilemma. Both would be better off if both used I than if both used T, but without coordination, each would be better off by choosing T, regardless of what the other does.

In Figure 3.5, outcome (I, I) where they each get 3 Pareto dominates (T, T) where they each get 1. Visually this is true because point (I, I) lies above and to the right of (T, T). Follow the steps in Figure 3.5 to see more comparisons.

Likewise, we can see that moving from point (T, T) to point (I, I) is a Pareto improvement, meaning that the second point Pareto dominates the first.

You can see from this example that the Pareto criterion may be of limited help in comparing allocations. Here, it tells the policymaker or citizen only to rank (I, I) above (T, T).

> **Pareto dominant** Allocation A Pareto dominates allocation B if at least one party would be better off with A than B, and nobody would be worse off. *See also:* Pareto efficient.

Pareto this and Pareto that: Make sure you understand the terms Pareto efficient, Pareto dominate and Pareto improvement. The first is a characteristic of a single allocation, the second is a comparison between two allocations, and the third is about a move from one allocation to another.

3.5 ADDING THE OPTION OF TRANSFERRING PAYOFFS BETWEEN PLAYERS

The Pareto criterion is unhelpful to policymakers because:

- *Few Pareto improvements*: For major choices that policymakers and citizens face, there are very few changes that are truly win-win. And so, because there are losers from almost any policy change, a change in the status quo is almost never a Pareto improvement.
- *Compensation:* The Pareto criterion as we have applied it so far does not take account of the possibility that a game could have a second stage. In this stage, some of the payoffs of one player could be transferred to the other. This would more than compensate the other player for the loss in the first stage, leaving both of them better off than in the status quo.

To see how this could work, suppose the only two possible outcomes in the pest control game were option A, in which both used Terminator (T, T), or option B in which Anil used Terminator and Bala used IPC (T, I). The Pareto criterion does not rank the two outcomes: at (T, T), the two have identical payoffs, while at (T, I), Anil does much better and Bala worse. So if (T, T) were the status quo, then moving to (T, I) would not be a Pareto improvement.

To explore all of the slides in this figure, see the online version at https://tinyco.re/5967595.

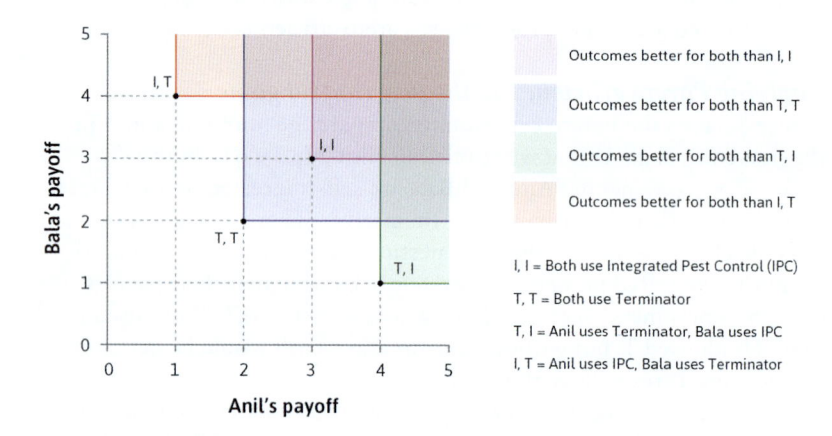

Figure 3.5 Pareto-efficient allocations: All of the allocations, except mutual use of the pesticide (T, T), are Pareto efficient.

1. Anil and Bala's prisoners' dilemma
The diagram shows the payoffs in the four possible allocations when Anil and Bala play the pest control game, a prisoners' dilemma.

2. A Pareto comparison
(I, I) lies in the rectangle to the northeast of (T, T), so an outcome where both Anil and Bala use IPC Pareto dominates one where both use Terminator, so (I, I) is Pareto efficient.

3. Compare (T, T) and (T, I)
If Anil uses Terminator and Bala IPC, then he is better off but Bala is worse off than when both use Terminator. The Pareto criterion cannot rank these two outcomes—neither allocation Pareto-dominates the other.

4. No allocation Pareto dominates (I, I)
None of the other allocations lie to the northeast of (I, I), so it is not Pareto dominated.

5. What can we say about (I, T) and (T, I)?
Neither of these allocations are Pareto dominated.

But a policymaker might set aside the Pareto criterion and just look at the total of the two payoffs, namely 4 at (T, T) and 5 at (T, I). If the policymaker could choose which outcome to implement, she might choose (T, I) with the proviso that Anil will pay Bala 1.5. Then both would receive 2.5, which is better for each than at (T, T). The transfer from Anil to Bala could take the form of a tax on Anil's income that would be transferred to Bala. Call this policy '(T, I) plus tax and transfer'. The result of this policy when implemented Pareto dominates the outcome (T, T). So the (T, I) plus tax and transfer outcome is Pareto efficient.

Variants of the tax and transfer policy would also Pareto dominate (T, T) as long as the amount transferred to Bala was at least 1 (so he would be better off than at (T, T)) and not greater than 2 (so that Anil would be better off than at (T, T)).

Applying a similar tax and transfer policy to the (I, T) outcome—with Bala paying Anil—would Pareto dominate (T, T).

Public policies often combine a change in the allocation (stage one of the game) followed by a transfer to compensate those whose payoffs were reduced in the new allocation (stage two).

For example, the reduction of import tariffs as part of international trade liberalization aims to create winners by making imported goods less expensive. The losers are those working in the industries that make goods that compete with similar imported goods. A policymaker might decide to compensate the losers by providing retraining and relocation opportunities for workers affected by factory closures, and some countries do this. But, in practice, trade liberalization polices have rarely been bundled with compensation policies that leave the losers no worse off as a result.

> **GREAT ECONOMISTS**
>
> *Vilfredo Pareto*
> Vilfredo Pareto (1848–1923), an Italian economist and sociologist, earned a degree in engineering for his research on the concept of equilibrium in physics.
>
> He is mostly remembered for the concept of efficiency that bears his name. Suppose that we want to compare two possible allocations, A and B, that may result from an economic interaction. Can we say which is better? Suppose we find that everyone involved in the interaction would prefer Allocation A. Then most people would agree that A is a better allocation than B. This criterion for judging between A and B is called the Pareto criterion. According to the Pareto criterion, Allocation A dominates Allocation B if at least one party would be better off with A than B and nobody would be worse off. Allocation A is called Pareto efficient if there is no other allocation that is feasible—given the available resources, knowledge, and technologies—and that dominates A.
>
> Pareto wanted economics and sociology to be fact-based sciences, similar to the physical sciences that he had studied when he was younger.

His empirical investigations led him to question the idea that the distribution of wealth resembles the familiar bell curve, with a few rich and a few poor in the tails of the distribution, and a large middle-income class. In its place he proposed what came to be called Pareto's law, according to which, across the ages and differing types of economy, there were very few rich people and a lot of poor people.

His 80–20 rule—derived from Pareto's law—asserted that the richest 20% of a population typically held 80% of the wealth. Were he living in the US in 2018 he would have to revise that to 90% of the wealth held by the richest 20%, suggesting that his law might not be as universal as he had thought.

QUESTION 3.3 CHOOSE THE CORRECT ANSWER(S)

Which of the following statements about the outcome of an economic interaction is correct?

- ☐ According to the Pareto criterion, a Pareto-efficient outcome is always fairer than an inefficient one.
- ☐ All participants are happy with what they get if the allocation is Pareto efficient.
- ☐ If the allocation is Pareto efficient, then you cannot make anyone better off without making someone else worse off.
- ☐ Each economic interaction only has one Pareto-efficient outcome.

QUESTION 3.4 CHOOSE THE CORRECT ANSWER(S)

Peter, John, and James are discussing how to share three apples and three oranges. Which of the following statements regarding Pareto-efficient allocations is correct?

- ☐ If all of them like both apples and oranges, there is only one Pareto-efficient allocation.
- ☐ Assuming that Peter likes both apples and oranges, it would be Pareto efficient if he had all the apples and oranges.
- ☐ It is always Pareto efficient for Peter, John, and James to have one apple and one orange each.
- ☐ Assuming that all of them like both apples and oranges, any allocation of three apples and three oranges between them is Pareto efficient.

3.6 EVALUATING AN OUTCOME: IS IT FAIR?

When combined with compensating those losing out from a policy change, the Pareto criterion can be used for a much wider set of policy problems.

Being fair does *not* mean automatically compensating losers. Imagine that it becomes possible for a hospital in Europe, funded by general taxation, to have its X-rays examined by qualified radiologists in Asia. This is cheaper for the hospital, which is short of funding. One group of losers would be well-paid radiologists in the hospital who lose a small part of their income as a result, and who ask that the government compensates them. It would be possible for the policymaker to replace this lost income to the hospital radiologists, and for the hospital to still save a small amount of money, although much less than before.

But policymakers faced with winners and losers may knowingly advocate a policy change that is not a Pareto improvement. Instead, they may advocate a policy on the grounds of fairness. This would be the case, for example, if those who gained were less well off and greatly in need of additional income, whilst those who lost, like the well-paid radiologists in the example, were wealthy. So far, our evaluation of outcomes has missed out fairness.

Too much inequality?

One of the reasons inequality is seen as a problem is that many people think there is too much of it.

Michael Norton, a professor of business administration, and Dan Ariely, a psychologist and behavioural economist, asked a large sample of Americans how they thought the wealth of the US should be distributed (https://tinyco.re/3629531). What fraction of US wealth, for example, should go to the wealthiest 20%? They also asked them to estimate what they thought the distribution of wealth actually was.

Figure 3.6 gives the results, with the top three bars showing the distribution that different groups of responders considered would be ideal, and the fourth bar showing the wealth distribution that they thought actually existed in the US.

The top bar shows that Americans thought that, ideally, the richest 20% should own a little more than 30% of total wealth—some inequality was desirable, but not a lot. Contrast this with the fourth bar (labelled 'Estimated'), which shows that they thought that the richest 20% owned about 60% of the wealth.

The bottom bar shows the actual distribution. In reality, the richest fifth owns 85% of the wealth. The actual distribution is much more unequal than the public's estimate—and contrasts sharply with the lower inequality they would like to see.

Different groups largely agree on the ideal distribution of wealth. Americans with an annual income greater than $100,000 thought that the share going to the top 20% should be slightly larger than those who earned less than $50,000 thought it should be. Democratic Party voters wished for a more equal distribution than Republican Party voters, and women preferred more equality than did men, although we have not shown this information in Figure 3.6 because the differences between these groups were small. Americans, whether rich or poor, Republican or Democrat, think that the distribution of wealth should be a lot more equal than it is.

Fair inequality or a tilted playing field?

Not all economic inequalities are unfair. Think of the difference in income between two identical twin brothers. The first is a poet who works part-time as a primary school teacher for a low wage, while preserving enough free time for his passion (poetry). The second is an engineer who puts in 60-hour weeks at a job that he does not enjoy so he can take home a high salary that supports his love of surfing holidays in exotic locations.

Both had opportunities for a good education. The poet dropped out after two years in university, while the surfer earned a postgraduate degree. The engineer-surfer earns three times what the poet lives on, but few people would think that the difference in income is unfair. This example shows there are more sources of inequality than the economic advantages resulting from the accidents of birth that people tend to think of as unfair.

The comparison of the brothers highlights the role of the choices made by two individuals who started at the same point on a level playing field. By making different choices, they end up with different incomes. Luck could also play a role. People will differ in their judgement about whether inequality arising from chance is fair or not.

Suppose we accept the idea that the kind of inequality that occurs between identical twins is not unfair. After all, they have the same parents and thus they win a similar prize in the lottery of accidents of birth. In our example, they grow up in the same neighbourhood, experience the same upbringing, share an identical genetic inheritance from their parents, and go to the same school.

The same reasoning applies to economic differences among identical twin sisters—but not between brother and sister twins because brother–sister differences in income could be the result of gender discrimination.

Adapted from Figures 2 and 3 in Michael I. Norton and Dan Ariely. 2011. 'Building a Better America—One Wealth Quintile at a Time' (https://tinyco.re/3629531). *Perspectives on Psychological Science* 6 (1): pp. 9–12.

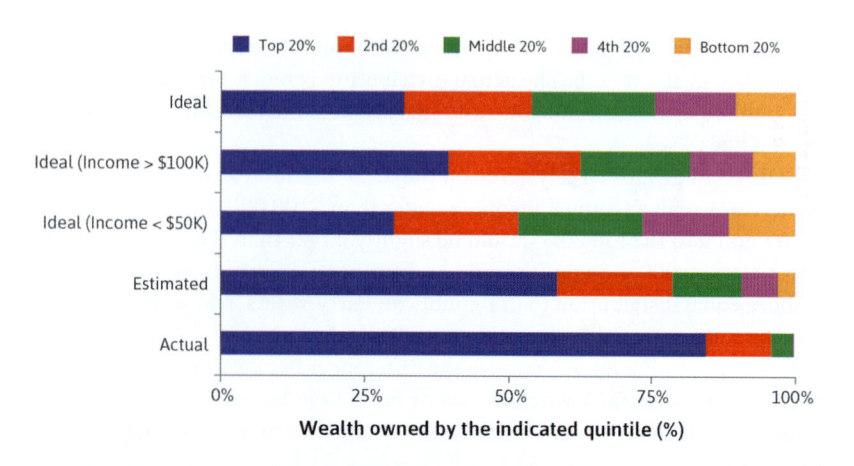

Figure 3.6 Americans' ideal, estimated, and actual distribution of wealth.

Christina Fong, an economist, wanted to know if people in the US think this way when it comes to their political support or opposition to policies to raise the incomes of the poor, financed by general taxation. An unusual survey from 1998 provided the data she needed; respondents were asked the usual questions about their economic situation, but also their opinion on why some people get ahead in life and succeed while others do not, and whether the government should introduce 'heavy **taxes**' to redistribute income to the poor.

She found that a person who thinks that hard work and risk-taking are essential to economic success is much less likely to support redistribution to the poor than a person who thinks that the key to success is inheritance, being white, your connections, or who your parents are.

The results of her study are in Figure 3.7. Notice that white people who think that being white is important to getting ahead strongly support redistribution to the poor—evidently because they think that the process that determines economic success is unfair.

tax A compulsory payment to the government levied, for example, on workers' incomes (income taxes) and firms' profits (profit taxes) or included in the price paid for goods and services (value added or sales taxes).

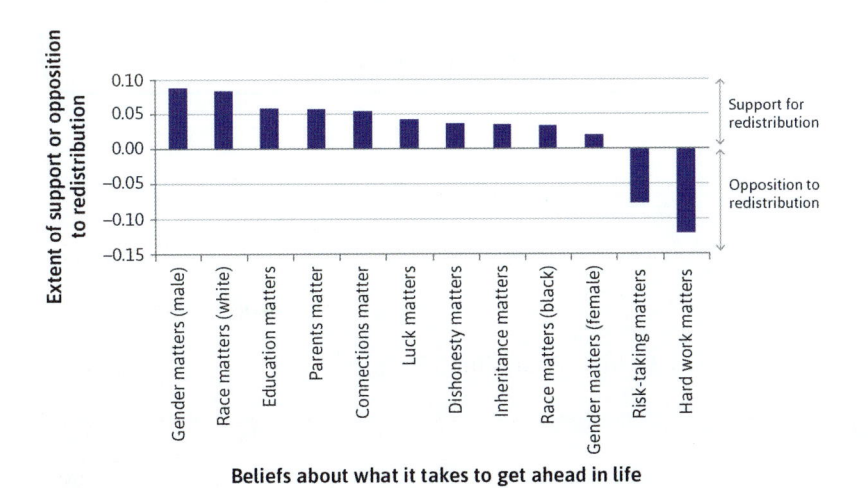

Figure 3.7 How Americans' beliefs about what it takes to get ahead predict their support or opposition to government programs to redistribute income to the poor.

Figure 5.3 in Samuel Bowles. 2012. *The New Economics of Inequality and Redistribution*. Cambridge: Cambridge University Press; Christina Fong, Samuel Bowles, and Herbert Gintis. 2005. 'Strong Reciprocity and the Welfare State'. In *Handbook of Giving, Reciprocity and Altruism*. Serge-Christophe Kolm and Jean Mercier Ythier (eds). Amsterdam: Elsevier.

EXERCISE 3.3 USING EXCEL: YOUR IDEAL INCOME DISTRIBUTION

Download and save the spreadsheet (https://tinyco.re/3355915) containing the data for Figure 3.6 (page 112).

1. Using the columns provided, fill in the row labelled 'Your own' according to your ideal income distribution for your own country. (For example, if you think the top 20% in your country should have 40% of the income, type 40.0 into cell B7.)
2. Plot your ideal income distribution alongside the other income distributions as a stacked bar chart in Excel. Follow the walk-through in Figure 3.8 online (https://tinyco.re/5539130) on how to do stacked bar charts in Excel. Is your ideal income distribution similar to or different from the Americans' ideal distribution (top three bars in Figure 3.6)?

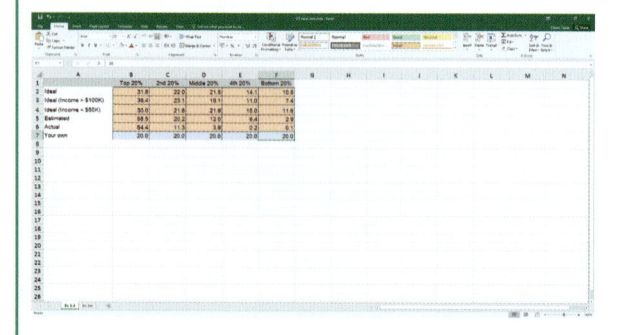

Figure 3.8 Making a stacked bar chart.

1. The data
We will be using this data to create a stacked bar chart. Each row contains a particular income distribution, and each column contains a particular group of society. The last row (cells shaded blue) contains an example of how you could fill in your ideal income distribution.

2. Draw a stacked bar chart
The stacked bar chart will look like the one shown above. If you selected the labels in Row 1, your legend would be labelled correctly. Otherwise, you have to change the labels manually.

3. Change the legend and horizontal axis labels
The bars corresponding to the quintiles are currently named 'Series 1', 'Series 2' and so on. We need to edit their names to correspond to those in Figure 3.6.

4. Change the legend and horizontal axis labels
After step 6, 'Series 1' will now be renamed as 'Top 20%'.

5. Change the legend and horizontal axis labels
After completing step 7, the bars in the chart legend will be labelled correctly.

6. Change the legend and horizontal axis labels
After completing step 9, the vertical axis will be labelled correctly.

7. Move the legend to the top of the chart
After step 10, the legend will now be at the top of your chart, as in Figure 3.6.

8. Add axis titles and a chart title
After step 14, your chart will look similar to Figure 3.6, but with the bars in a different order.

> **QUESTION 3.5 CHOOSE THE CORRECT ANSWER(S)**
> Figures 3.6 (page 112) and 3.7 (page 113) indicate that:
>
> ☐ In the US, people think there is less income inequality than there actually is.
> ☐ Aside from the ideal income of the top 20%, all Americans' ideal income distributions are quite similar.
> ☐ Aside from the allocation of income, people also care about the process by which that income is earned.
> ☐ Americans who believe that economic success depends on risk-taking are less likely to support redistribution, compared to those who believe that economic success depends on hard work.

3.7 WHY ARE (SOME) ECONOMIC INEQUALITIES UNFAIR? PROCEDURAL AND SUBSTANTIVE JUDGEMENTS

Inequalities among people go beyond economic differences, and concerns about fairness are not the only basis of objections to inequality.

When people express the view that there is too much inequality, they usually refer to differences among people in one or more of the following dimensions:

- *Income:* The reward in money (or some equivalent measure) of the individual's command over valued goods and services.
- *Hourly pay:* The income reward for a given amount of work.
- *Health status:* For example, longevity.
- *Happiness:* Economists, psychologists, and others have developed indicators by which subjective wellbeing can be measured.
- *Freedom:* The extent that one can do (or be) what one chooses without narrow socially imposed limits.
- *Respect, dignity or social status.*

Many people also object to economic inequalities—especially extreme disparities—whatever the source, on grounds other than fairness, including:

- *People should have second chances:* Mistakes made early in life—not working hard in school, for example—should not consign an individual to a lifetime of low income.
- *Economic inequalities may undermine democracy.*
- *Dignity and respect matter in society:* Large economic differences among people make it more difficult to achieve this.

But we will focus here on why some economic inequalities, notably of income and wealth, are considered to be unfair.

Andrew E. Clark and Andrew J. Oswald. 2002. 'A Simple Statistical Method for Measuring How Life Events Affect Happiness'. *International Journal of Epidemiology* 31 (6): pp. 1139–44.

Evaluating fairness using the veil of ignorance

The American philosopher John Rawls (1921–2002) devised a way to clarify our own ideas of fairness that can sometimes help us to find common ground on questions of values. Consider the following situation. You and a friend are walking down an empty street and you see a $100 note on the ground. How would you split your lucky find? We follow three steps:

1. *Fairness applies equally to all people taking part in the interaction:* Whatever the rule for dividing up the $100 is, it cannot involve the identity of one or the other of the players. (This principle, for example, would reject as unfair the rules of the game of a monarchy, in which a named person, say George III, is head of state; democratic constitutions specify *how* the head of state is to be selected, not *who* this will be.)
2. *Imagine a veil of ignorance:* Since fairness applies to everyone, including ourselves, Rawls asks us to imagine ourselves behind what he called a veil of ignorance, not knowing the position that we would occupy in the society we are considering. We could be male or female, healthy or ill, rich or poor (or with rich or poor parents), in a dominant or an ethnic minority group, and so on. In the $100 on the street game, we would not know if we would be the person picking up the money, or the person responding to the offer.
3. *From behind the veil of ignorance, we can make a judgement:* For example, the choice of a set of institutions—rules of the game that will determine who gets what—imagining that we will then become part of the society we have endorsed, with an equal chance of having any of the positions occupied by individuals in that society.

In making a judgement about fairness, the veil of ignorance assists you in doing something very difficult: putting yourself in the shoes of others quite different from you. You would then, Rawls argued, be better able to evaluate the constitutions, laws, inheritance practices, and other institutions of a society as an impartial outsider.

The veil of ignorance is a way of looking at problems of inequality and justice, it is not a statement about what is fair and what is not.

The two studies of Americans' attitudes towards fairness that we looked at in the previous section make a basic point about how people judge differences in these dimensions. Allocations can be judged unfair because of:

- *How unequal they are:* In terms of income, for example, or subjective wellbeing or the distribution of wealth, in Figure 3.6. These are **substantive judgements of fairness**.
- *How the inequalities came about:* For example, by force or racial discrimination, by competition on a level playing field, or by hard work, as in Figure 3.7. These are **procedural judgements of fairness**.

Substantive judgements

These are evaluations of the allocation itself—the shares of the pie. We know from the behaviour of ultimatum game experimental subjects (Figure 3.2 (page 103)) that many people would judge as unfair an allocation in which the Proposer took 90% of the pie. That is a substantive judgement about unfairness of an economic inequality.

---

substantive judgements of fairness
Judgements based on the characteristics of the allocation itself, not how it was determined. See also: procedural judgements of fairness.

procedural judgements of fairness
An evaluation of an outcome based on how the allocation came about, and not on the characteristics of the outcome itself, (for example, how unequal it is). See also: substantive judgements of fairness.

To make a substantive judgement about fairness, all you need to know is the allocation itself; you do not need to know the rules of the game and other factors that explain why this allocation occurred.

Suppose you lived in a society in which one segment of the population had limited access to medical care and as a result they had high rates of illness, high child mortality and limited life expectancy. Others in the same population had excellent medical care including access to cosmetic surgery and other vanity medical treatments. You might decide this situation was unfair.

But what is unfair about it?

One answer is that by reallocating medical personnel and facilities a vast improvement in the medical care of the disadvantaged group could be accomplished without any significant reduction of the health of the advantaged group. By this reasoning an unequal economic outcome is unfair if reducing the inequality would substantially increase the wellbeing of the poorer group, without inflicting significant reductions in wellbeing of the better-off group.

This view is based on a comparison of the wellbeing (or 'utility') of individuals and how it is affected by a change in the resources available to them. Its origins are with the utilitarian economist and philosopher, Jeremy Bentham (1748–1832). We could call this 'utilitarian unfairness' or Bentham-unfairness.

A second (and quite different) view of the unfairness of the inequality was put forward by John Rawls in an essay titled *Justice as Fairness*. Rawls held that in addition to equal rights and liberties, and equality of opportunity to better yourself, a just society is one in which the least well-off group are as well off as they can be. Where this is not true, we have what we will call 'Rawls-unfairness'.

John Rawls, 1985. 'Justice as Fairness: Political not Metaphysical' (https://tinyco.re/9065567). *Philosophy and Public Affairs* 14 (3): pp. 223–51.

This does not imply that economic inequalities can never be just, or that equality of income or wealth is the standard against which to judge unfairness. If paying doctors more than others is necessary to provide them with incentives to address the health needs of the poorest, then their higher incomes does not violate Rawls-unfairness.

Procedural judgements

These are ideas of fairness based on how the inequality came to be that focus not on *how* poor or rich someone is, but instead on *why* the person is poor or rich.

The rules of the game that brought about the inequality may be evaluated according to aspects such as:

- *Voluntary exchange of private property acquired by legitimate means:* Were the actions resulting in the allocation the result of free choices by the individuals involved? For example, did each person buy or sell things that they had come to own through inheritance, purchase, or their own labour? Or was fraud or force involved?
- *Equal opportunity for economic advantage:* Did people have an equal opportunity to acquire a large share of the total, or were they subjected to some kind of discrimination because of their race, sexual preference, gender, or who their parents were?
- *Deservingness:* Did the rules of the game that determined the inequality take account of the extent to which individuals need, or for some other reason deserve, the amounts they get?

We can use these differing judgements to evaluate an outcome in the ultimatum game. The experimental rules of the game will appear to most people's minds as procedurally fair:

- Proposers—who can expect to receive not less than half of the pie, and will probably receive more—are chosen randomly.
- The game is played anonymously, so who a person is (her name, or title, or some other aspect of her identity) cannot matter.
- All actions are voluntary. The Responder can refuse to accept the offer, and the Proposer is typically free to propose any amount.

These rules of the game are (procedurally) fair. But, as we have seen, the actions of Proposers are often seen as (substantively) unfair.

Now imagine that the person selected to be Proposer was based on ethnic origin and gender so that only males of European origin can be the Proposer. The game would be procedurally unfair by awarding the position that has the greatest income-earning prospects using a rule that discriminates against women and non-Europeans.

This suggests that, for many people, the question, 'How much inequality is too much?' cannot be answered unless we know why a family or person is rich or poor. Many people think it is unfair if income depends substantially on accidents of birth, such as your race, your sex, or your country. Inequalities based on hard work or taking risks are less likely to be seen as unfair.

A video (https://tinyco.re/8103838) of economist Helen Miller speaking to students at Manchester University in the UK in 2017 outlines some of the issues of tax fairness, starting with the question, 'What would be a fair tax rate for George Harrison?'. (George Harrison was lead guitarist for The Beatles during the 1960s and 1970s. The Beatles were the world's most famous pop group at the time. He was a high earner which meant that some of his income was taxed at a rate of 95%.)

Neither philosophy, economics, nor any other science, can eliminate disagreements about questions of value. But economics can clarify:

- *How the dimensions of unfairness may be connected:* For example, how the rules of the game that give special advantages to one or another group may affect the degree of inequality of income.
- *Trade-offs between the objectives of fairness and efficiency:* For example, are some kinds of unfairness essential for achieving efficient outcomes? Does unfairness (as in the ultimatum game) sometimes lead to inefficient outcomes (remember that the money is thrown away if the offer is rejected).
- *Public policies to address concerns about unfairness:* How can unfairness be reduced by the actions of governments and other bodies?
- *The effects of the introduction of new policies:* Economics can measure this once businesses, individuals, and other private economic actors have responded to the opportunities and constraints imposed by the new environment, and then use this information to make better policies in future.

The last bullet point poses our next challenge—will the intended outcomes of a government policy result once we take account of not only government actions, but also the reactions of private actors?

Helen Miller: 'Are the rich paying their fair share of taxes?'
https://tinyco.re/8103838

George Harrison had such a strong opinion about the unfairness of the 95% marginal tax rate that he wrote and recorded a song with the Beatles called 'Taxman' (https://tinyco.re/5087731) in 1966. It includes the lyrics, 'Let me tell you how it will be/There's one for you, 19 for me'.

EXERCISE 3.4 SUBSTANTIVE AND PROCEDURAL FAIRNESS, AND THE VEIL OF IGNORANCE

Consider the society you live in, or another society with which you are familiar.

1. To make society fairer (according to the substantive judgement of fairness), would you want greater equality of income, happiness, or freedom? Why? Would there be a trade-off between these aspects?
2. Are there other things that should be more equal to achieve greater substantive fairness in this society?
3. How fair is this society, according to the procedural judgement of fairness?
4. Suppose that, behind a Rawlsian veil of ignorance, you could choose to live in a society in which one (but only one) of the three procedural standards for fairness (voluntary exchange of property, equality of opportunity, and deservingness) would be the guiding principle for how institutions are organized. Which procedural standard would you choose, and why?

QUESTION 3.6 CHOOSE THE CORRECT ANSWER(S)

Which of the following statements regarding substantive judgements of fairness is correct?

☐ Fairness may depend on the individual's freedom to choose without socially-imposed limits.
☐ If all individuals receive an equal income, then this allocation cannot be made fairer.
☐ Since happiness cannot be objectively measured, it cannot be used to evaluate the fairness of an allocation.
☐ Two people making substantive judgements of fairness about the same situation must necessarily agree.

QUESTION 3.7 CHOOSE THE CORRECT ANSWER(S)

Which of the following statements regarding procedural judgements of fairness is correct?

☐ Consider an ultimatum game where only those with university degrees can be the Proposer. As the Proposer is free to propose any amount and the Responder's choice of response is voluntary, the game is procedurally fair.
☐ A transfer system where income earners are taxed to provide benefits to the unemployed may or may not be considered to be procedurally fair.
☐ Procedural fairness implies substantive fairness.
☐ Substantive fairness implies procedural fairness.

3.8 IMPLEMENTING PUBLIC POLICIES

Giving women the vote reduced child deaths in the US. Requiring randomly selected Indian villages to be headed by women changed spending priorities in ways that benefited women.

Governments implement policies through some combination of:

- *Prohibitions and directives*: Some actions can be simply directed by the government (sending your children to school) or prohibited (using leaded fuel for your car).
- *Incentives*: A policy changes the benefits or costs of alternative courses of action open to the individual.
- *Making information available*: People can use this information when they make decisions about which actions to take.

There is a limit to the extent that governments can order people around, and this is a problem for government policymakers. Even something simple, like imposing a speed limit on a highway, does not prevent people from driving fast. It just changes the environment in which the driver's decision about how fast to drive occurs.

For this reason, the outcome of a government policy is not something the government can dictate. Instead, it is the result of an interaction between the government's actions and the privately chosen actions of those affected.

To understand how government policies can change economic outcomes by changing what actions people decide to take, we will use game theory and the idea of a **Nash equilibrium**, introduced in Section 2.11 (page 79). Recall that a Nash equilibrium is a set of strategies adopted by players such that each is a best response to the others, so that none of the players have an incentive to change their strategy.

Nash equilibrium and Pareto efficiency are both concepts used in public policy analysis, but keep in mind that they refer to entirely different aspects of a social interaction. Figure 3.9 clarifies the relationship between the two concepts by using the invisible hand (crop selection) and pest control games.

Entries in the table are examples of the combinations indicated by the column and row names. The lower left cell, for example, indicates that three of the four outcomes in the pest control game—both use IPC, Bala uses Terminator and Anil uses IPC, and Anil uses Terminator and Bala uses IPC—are Pareto efficient, but none of the three is a Nash equilibrium.

Nash equilibrium A set of strategies, one for each player in the game, such that each player's strategy is a best response to the strategies chosen by everyone else.

	Pareto efficient	Not Pareto efficient
Nash equilibrium	Anil grows cassava, Bala grows rice (Invisible hand game) (page 60)	Both use Terminator rather than IPC (Pest control game) (page 62)
Not a Nash equilibrium	Both use IPC; or one uses Terminator, the other IPC (Pest control game) (page 62)	Bala grows cassava, Anil grows rice; or both grow the same crop (Invisible hand game) (page 60)

Figure 3.9 Pareto efficiency and Nash equilibrium contrasted, using two games.

Implementing fairness and efficiency in averting the tragedy of the commons

Let's return again to the tragedy of the commons and make things concrete (if somewhat unrealistic at this stage). The tragedy of the commons—as you saw in Unit 2 (Section 2.2) (page 51)—can be represented as a prisoners' dilemma in which overgrazing is the dominant strategy, even though restricting the amount of grazing would support higher payoffs for both players.

Let's say there are just two herders, and that they may each put either 10 or 20 cows on the communal pasture. The payoff table for their interaction is shown in Figure 3.10.

You can confirm that this is a prisoners' dilemma by noticing that whatever B does—restrict the cows she places on the commons to 10 or not—the highest payoff for A is to place 20 cows on the pasture. By pasturing more cows, she gets 12 rather than 10 if B has restricted his cows to 10, or 8 rather than 6 if he has pastured 20 cows.

The same is true of B. Whatever A does, the best for him is to put 20 cows on the pasture. Yet both A and B would be better off—getting 10 rather than 8—by both restricting the number of cows they put to pasture. Overgrazing is the Nash equilibrium.

An effective government policy might alter this situation by changing the Nash equilibrium. But how can this be done?

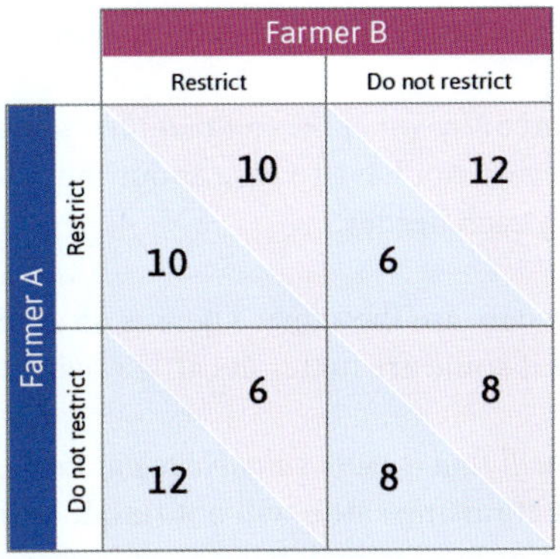

		Farmer B	
		Restrict	Do not restrict
Farmer A	Restrict	10, 10	12, 6
	Do not restrict	6, 12	8, 8

Figure 3.10 Overgrazing the commons.

A tax on overgrazing to change the Nash equilibrium

We saw at the beginning of this unit that one solution would be to give A access to the pasture and exclude B. This alters the game fundamentally. She would then pasture all 20 of her cows there, B would pasture none, and A would get a payoff of 20 (and B would get zero). While this solved the problem of overgrazing, it seemed unfair to B.

But the government could pursue a more even-handed approach. The problem of overgrazing, remember, arises because each herder, when deciding on how many cows to keep, thinks only of his or her own payoffs. Thus, when A compares pasturing 20 cows as opposed to 10 where B is pasturing only 10, she looks at how her own payoff is affected, rising from 10 to 12 as she adds the extra cows. She does not look at the fact that B has just seen his payoffs drop from 10 to 6. A has ignored the costs that her action imposed on B.

If A were altruistic, she might be concerned about the harm she caused B, and not overgraze. If the two were close friends or relatives, this might be enough to prevent overgrazing. Instead, let's imagine they are complete strangers and do not care at all for each other. As we saw in Unit 2 in the game with Anil and Bala (page 61), if there were really only two people involved, they probably would not be complete strangers, but we are using the two-person case as a simplification to understand what happens when there are dozens or even hundreds of herders, among whom many would be unknown to each other.

The government, however, could address the problem by adopting a policy that imposed a tax of 0.4 for any cow beyond 10 that a herder sent to pasture. We assume that the government uses the tax revenues for some purpose unrelated to the problem of overgrazing. This just means we do not have to think about what the tax is spent on. Under this new tax policy, for example, either herder would pay a tax of 4 if the herder sent 20 rather than 10 cows to pasture. The 'overgrazing tax' changes the payoff matrix, as shown in Figure 3.11.

The effect of the tax is to displace the Nash equilibrium from each herder putting 20 cows on the commons to both of them putting only 10. You can check that protecting the commons is now a Nash equilibrium—when one is putting only 10 cows on the commons the best response of the other is to also put only 10 cows on the commons.

The overgrazing tax has three valued features:

- *It treats both herders equally:* It averts the tragedy without introducing inequality among the herders and so, in this sense, it is both efficient and fair.
- *Each herder must take account of the cost that their overgrazing imposes on the other:* Note they do not have to care about the other herder because the cost is a tax on each herder.

We assumed both herders are the same. There is an additional feature of the tax that would occur if some are better at cattle raising than others.

- *The better herders will find it more valuable to put their cows on the pasture:* Those less skilled at raising cattle will not find it worth paying the tax. As a result, the better herders will have greater access to the pasture.

This solution is efficient—those who can make the best use of the land are using it. Any decision about whether this is fair or not would depend on additional facts that we have not discussed, for example, whether the not-so-good herders are better at something else, and whether they can make their living without herding.

But often it is more difficult to fashion a policy that will achieve its objectives, as the examples in the next two sections show.

> **QUESTION 3.8 CHOOSE THE CORRECT ANSWER(S)**
> Which of the following statements about the tragedy of the commons shown in Figure 3.11 is correct?
>
> ☐ The overgrazing tax changes the preferences of the herders, so that they now care about the costs they impose on each other.
> ☐ The overgrazing tax is only efficient and fair in certain situations.
> ☐ The amount of the tax is exactly equal to the cost that one herder imposes on the other.
> ☐ The overgrazing tax works by changing incentives and information available.

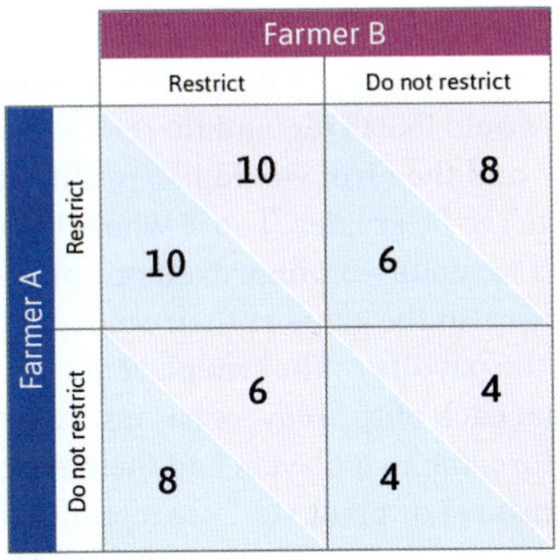

To explore all of the slides in this figure, see the online version at https://tinyco.re/3379949.

	Farmer B Restrict	Farmer B Do not restrict
Farmer A Restrict	10, 10	8, 6
Farmer A Do not restrict	6, 8	4, 4

Figure 3.11 An overgrazing tax averts the tragedy of the commons.

1. The original situation
In Figure 3.10 (page 121) (reproduced here), overgrazing occurred because each herder ignored the cost of their actions on the other herder. The Nash equilibrium is (Do not restrict, Do not restrict).

2. An overgrazing tax
Imposing the overgrazing tax reduces the payoffs for 'Do not restrict' by 4, making (Restrict, Restrict) the Nash equilibrium. The commons is protected.

3.9 UNINTENDED CONSEQUENCES OF A REDISTRIBUTIVE TAX

Suppose that a newly elected government wants to raise taxes on the profits of firms in order to fund high-quality public education and other new programs that will benefit middle- and low-income voters. At the current moderate tax rate, firms are making high after-tax profits. The new finance minister introduces a higher tax rate, calculating that it will raise revenue by 50%. Then he sets about planning how to spend the additional tax revenues, announcing popular improvements in pre-primary schooling.

The finance minister is not surprised when firm owners protest against the new tax rate. But he is dismayed when the head of the tax collection agency reports that tax revenues are falling. She estimates that the revenue from the profits tax will be 10% lower than it was the previous year. What has gone wrong?

The head of tax collection explains that when the tax rate went up, firms began hiring tax lawyers to exploit loopholes in the tax laws. The finance minister has failed to consider that a change in the tax regime may cause firms to change their strategies too.

The firms' response to government policy—hire lawyers to exploit tax loopholes—is commonly adopted in real life. Recall that George Harrison objected to the taxman saying, in his words, 'One for you, 19 for me,' in the 1960s. The Beatles hired an accountant who explained that if they formed a company, they would not have to pay the 95% marginal income tax, because company income was taxed at a lower rate than personal income. This is what they did.

Why firms hire tax lawyers

To understand the misjudgement made by our finance minister, we can represent the interaction between government policy and the strategies of firms as a game, which we will call the tax avoidance game, played by two hypothetical people—the 'Government' who will levy taxes and direct their uses, and the 'Firm owner' who will pay taxes on the profits accruing to the firm.

The Government would like taxes (and therefore its ability to improve schools) to be greater, and the Firm would like profits after the payment of taxes ('after-tax profits') to be greater. Those who will benefit from the expenditure of the tax revenue—on improved pre-primary centres, for example—are not players in the game as their role is entirely passive. Their actions do not affect the payoffs of the two players.

We will assume that each of the players has just two choices. In the games we studied before, the two players had the same two strategies to choose from—plant cassava or plant rice; use integrated pest management or use the Terminator pesticide; use C++ or use Java. Here, we recognize that the actors differ—the actions open to the Government are not the same as the actions open to a private citizen or the owner of the Firm:

- *The Government:* May levy either moderate taxes or high taxes on the Firm owner's profits.
- *The Firm:* Can either pay taxes at the statutory (government-intended) rate, or hire tax lawyers to exploit loopholes in the tax laws—finding accounting methods that will allow the Firm to 'earn' its profits in some other lower tax country, for example—so as to minimize its tax obligations.

The strategies available and the payoffs associated with each strategy are given in Figure 3.12. Consider first what happens when the owner pays tax at the statutory rate:

- *When the tax rate is moderate:* $100 million in tax is collected and the Firm's profits are $500 million (the upper left cell, A).
- *At the higher tax rate:* $150 million in tax is collected (lower left cell, B) and profits fall to $450 million. This is what the finance minister had expected to happen.

Now suppose that hiring legal advisors to find tax loopholes costs $20 million; the lawyers will be able to save the firm $15 million when the tax rate is moderate, and $60 million at the high tax rate. We can calculate the payoffs in cases C and D, as shown in Figure 3.12.

	Firm owner	
	Pay tax at statutory rate	**Engage tax lawyers to exploit tax loopholes**
Government — Moderate tax rate	A. Tax revenue $100 million; Profits after taxes $500 million	C. Tax revenue $85 million; Profits after taxes $495 million
Government — High tax rate	B. Tax revenue $150 million; Profits after taxes $450 million	D. Tax revenue $90 million; Profits after taxes $490 million

To explore all of the slides in this figure, see the online version at https://tinyco.re/5848054.

Figure 3.12 Payoffs in the tax avoidance game.

1. Cases A and B: No lawyers involved
If the Firm pays tax at the statutory rate, raising the tax rate from moderate to high increases the Government's revenue from $100 million to $150 million. The Firm's profits fall from $500 million to $450 million.

2. Case C
Avoiding taxes when the rate is moderate: When the tax rate is moderate, lawyers could reduce the tax paid by $15 million, to $85 million. But the Firm has to pay $20 million to the lawyers, so overall its profits would fall by $5 million, to $495 million.

3. Case D
Avoiding taxes when the rate is high: At the higher tax rate, lawyers could reduce the Firm's tax bill by $60 million—it falls from $150 million to $90 million. Taking into account the $20 million paid to the lawyers, the Firm's net gain from hiring lawyers would be $40 million. Its profits would therefore be $490 million rather than $450 million.

Figure 3.13 shows a useful way of representing the payoffs in this game. The Government's payoff (tax revenue) is shown on the horizontal axis, and the Firm's payoff (profits after taxes and lawyers' fees) on the vertical axis. Each of the four cases A, B, C and D in Figure 3.12 is marked as a point in this diagram.

Figure 3.13 tells the story of the newly elected government's redistributive tax policy. Initially, having 'inherited' the tax policies of the previous government, it finds itself at point A. Work through the steps in Figure 3.13 to see what happens next.

To explore all of the slides in this figure, see the online version at https://tinyco.re/8170256.

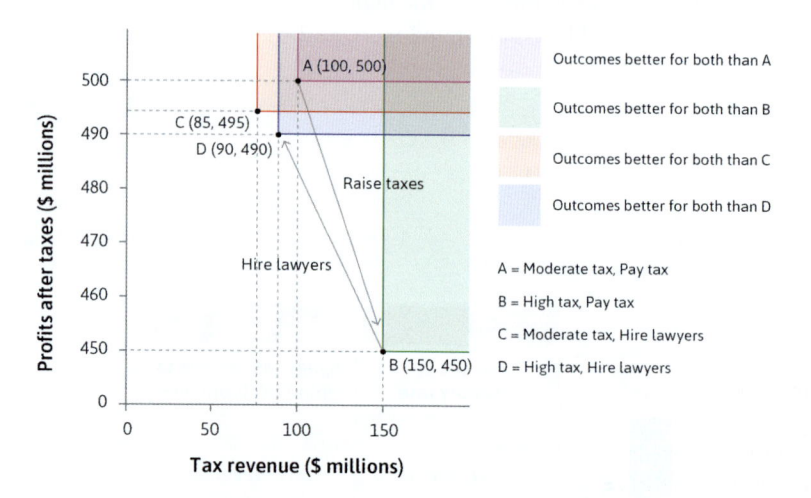

Figure 3.13 Payoffs in the tax avoidance game: How higher taxes may lead to less redistribution.

1. The payoffs in the four possible cases
The Government's payoff is shown on the horizontal axis, and the Firm's payoff on the vertical axis. The four points show the payoffs in each of the possible outcomes of the game.

2. When the Government comes into office, the tax rate is moderate
Initially the tax rate is moderate and the Firm pays the tax intended. The payoffs are shown by point A—100 for the Government and 500 for the Firm.

3. With a moderate tax rate, the Firm does not want to hire lawyers
Point C shows the payoffs if the Firm hires lawyers when the tax rate is moderate. Profits are lower at C than at A, so the Firm prefers to pay tax at the statutory rate.

4. Comparing payoffs
The pink-shaded area shows points where both players are better off than at point C. Point A lies inside this area—both the Government and the Firm are better off at A than C.

5. The Government raises the tax rate
The Government sets a high tax rate, hoping to move from A to B. At B, the Government is better off, but the Firm is worse off.

6. With a high tax rate, the Firm prefers to hire lawyers
Now that the tax has risen, the Firm re-evaluates the benefits of legal advice. Hiring lawyers would change the payoffs from B to D, where profits are higher. The Firm decides to hire lawyers.

7. In the end, both players are worse off
The decisions of the Government and the Firm have changed the payoffs from point A to point D. Both players have lower payoffs than they had at the beginning.

Can the game help us understand the challenge facing the Government? Notice first that, at the initial moderate tax rate, the Firm is not tempted to hire lawyers. It is better off at point A, paying tax at the statutory rate, than it would be at point C. But the strategies at point A are not a Nash equilibrium; given that the Firm is not hiring lawyers, the Government does better by raising taxes, taking it to point B.

But—and this is the key point—the strategies leading to outcome B, which the Government wishes to implement, are not a Nash equilibrium either! Given the higher tax rate, the Firm does better hiring tax lawyers. And so the outcome spirals downwards from point A to B to D—where they finally reach a Nash equilibrium. At this point, both players are doing the best they can, given the strategy chosen by the other player.

Point D is dominated by point A. Sadly, both players are worse off at the Nash equilibrium D than they would have been if they had remained at A, with moderate taxes and no lawyers. Because of their decisions, after-tax profits are lower and tax revenues are lower too.

A successful policy must be a Nash equilibrium

When government officials raise tax rates, the policy often succeeds. But our analysis illustrates that the outcomes of policies are determined by the decisions of private actors as well as those government officials. The outcome that the government wants must be a Nash equilibrium. Otherwise, like point B in Figure 3.13, it will not last.

This means that once the policy is implemented—say, a new tax—the intended outcome must be the result of everyone doing the best they can, given what everyone else is doing under the new tax. If that is not the case, then people will change what they are doing, and the intended outcome of the policy will not occur.

> **QUESTION 3.9 CHOOSE THE CORRECT ANSWER(S)**
> Which of the following statements about the tax avoidance game in Figure 3.13 is correct?
>
> ☐ The outcome due to the policy is a Nash equilibrium and is Pareto efficient.
> ☐ In Figure 3.13, there are three Pareto-efficient outcomes.
> ☐ If lawyers became more expensive to hire, then outcome B might be the final outcome.
> ☐ If the government closed the tax loopholes, then outcome B might be the final outcome.

3.10 UNINTENDED CONSEQUENCES: POLICIES AFFECT PREFERENCES

The tools we are developing are useful in many settings, not just so that governments can design policies. Consider the policy of an organization—a daycare centre—rather than a government.

Sometimes it is possible to conduct experiments 'in the field'; that is, to deliberately change the economic conditions under which people make decisions, and observe how their behaviour changes. An experiment conducted in Israel in 1998 demonstrated that behaviour may be very sensitive to the context in which decisions are made.

It is common for parents to rush to pick up their children from daycare. Sometimes, a few parents are late, making teachers stay extra time. What would you do to deter parents from being late?

Two economists ran an experiment that introduced fines in some daycare centres but not in others (these were used as controls). The 'price of lateness' went from zero to ten Israeli shekels (about $3 at the time). Surprisingly, after the fine was introduced, the frequency of late pickups doubled. The top line in Figure 3.14 illustrates this.

Why did putting a price on lateness backfire?

One possible explanation is that before the fine was introduced, most parents were on time because they felt that it was the right thing to do. In other words, they came on time because of a moral obligation to avoid inconveniencing the daycare staff. Perhaps they felt an altruistic concern for the staff, or regarded a timely pick-up as a reciprocal responsibility in the joint care of the child. But the imposition of the fine signalled that the situation was really more like shopping. Lateness had a price and therefore could be purchased, like vegetables or ice cream.

Samuel Bowles. 2016. *The Moral Economy: Why Good Incentives Are No Substitute for Good Citizens*. New Haven, CT: Yale University Press.

Uri Gneezy and Aldo Rustichini. 2000. 'A Fine is a Price' (https://tinyco.re/3450861). *The Journal of Legal Studies* 29 (January): pp. 1–17.

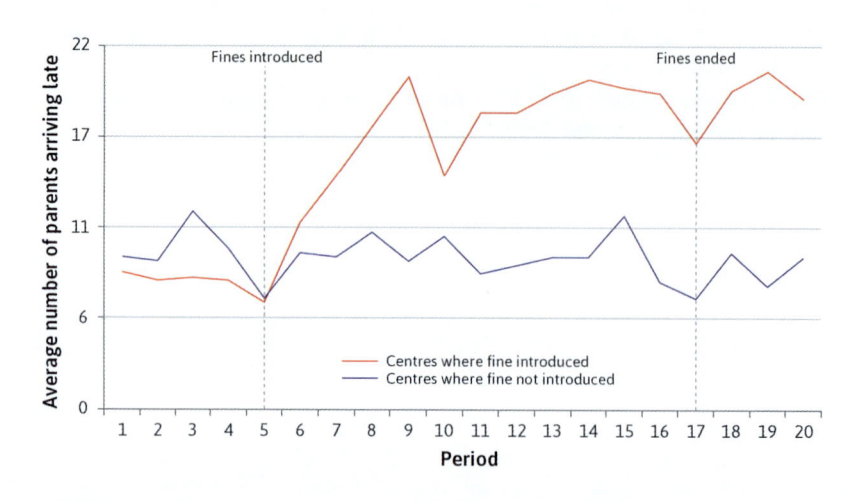

Figure 3.14 Average number of late-coming parents, per week.

3.10 UNINTENDED CONSEQUENCES: POLICIES AFFECT PREFERENCES

The use of a market-based incentive—the price of lateness—had provided what psychologists call a new 'frame' for the decision, making it one in which self-interest rather than concern for others was acceptable. Before the imposition of the fine, picking up your child late, though sometimes unavoidable was a violation of a social norm. The parents' social preferences told them to try to avoid this. The fine changed the frame: now coming late was something you could simply purchase, by paying the fine. The parent's self-interested preferences now said: coming late is OK as long as I pay the fine (and the fine is not too high).

When fines and prices have these unintended effects, we say that economic incentives have **crowded out** social preferences. Even worse, you can also see from Figure 3.14 that, when the fine was removed, parents continued to pick up their children late. The new frame—lateness is something you can buy—seems to have persisted even after the fine was removed.

If the policymaker ignores how people will respond to its actions, this policy is unlikely to have its intended effect.

Sections 3.9 and 3.10 illustrate some essentials of the policymaker's toolkit that will help to avoid unintended consequences. A good policymaker must make sure that:

- *The policy does not change people's preferences in unintended ways:* A change in preferences might mean that behaviour changes too, which may mean the policy fails to hit its target. This is what happened in the daycare centres in Israel.
- *The intended outcome is a Nash equilibrium:* Under the new policy, people must be motivated to act in ways that are consistent with the objective of the policymaker.

> **crowding out** There are two quite distinct uses of the term. One is the observed negative effect when economic incentives displace people's ethical or other-regarding motivations. In studies of individual behaviour, incentives may have a crowding-out effect on social preferences. A second use of the term is to refer to the effect of an increase in government spending in reducing private spending, as would be expected for example in an economy working at full capacity utilization, or when a fiscal expansion is associated with a rise in the interest rate.

> **QUESTION 3.10 CHOOSE THE CORRECT ANSWER(S)**
> Which of the following statements about the field experiment shown in Figure 3.14 are correct?
>
> ☐ The fine can be considered as the 'price' for collecting a child late.
> ☐ The introduction of the fine successfully reduced the number of late-coming parents.
> ☐ The crowding out of social preferences did not occur until the fines ended.
> ☐ The graph suggests that the experiment may have permanently increased the parents' tendency to be late.

EXERCISE 3.5 USING EXCEL: THE EFFECT OF DAYCARE CENTRE FINES

As in science experiments, we can think of the daycare centre experiment in terms of a 'treatment' and a 'control' group. Daycare centres who received fines were in the 'treatment' group, and those who did not were in the 'control' group.

Download and save the spreadsheet (https://tinyco.re/3355915) containing the data used to create Figure 3.14. You can see that Centres 1–6 are the 'treatment' group, while Centres 7–10 are the 'control' group.

Follow the walk-through in Figure 3.15 online (https://tinyco.re/9744480) to help you do this exercise.

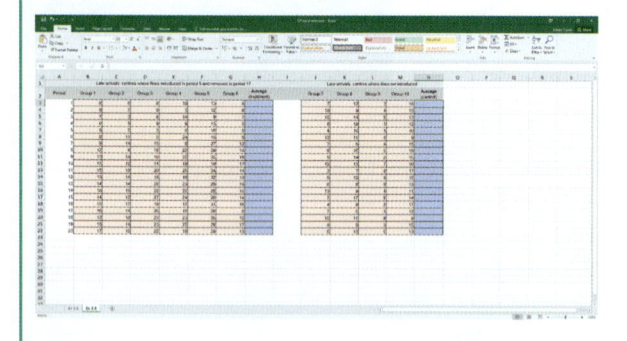

Figure 3.15 Making a line chart with labels.

1. The data
This is what the data looks like. Column A contains time periods, Columns B to G contain the number of late arrivals in centres where fines were introduced, and Columns J to M contain the number of late arrivals in centres where fines were not introduced.

2. Calculate averages for each group and time period
We will use Excel's AVERAGE function to calculate the average number of late arrivals for both groups, and put them in the shaded blue cells.

3. Draw a line chart
After completing step 6, your line chart should look like the one shown above.

4. Add dotted lines to show when fines were introduced and removed
Using Excel's 'Insert Shapes' option, you can add lines to your chart. To make a line dotted, you need to change its 'Dash type' using the options in the right-hand menu.

5. Add text boxes to label the dotted lines
Using Excel's 'Insert Shapes' option, you can add also text boxes and other shapes to your chart.

6. Add axis titles and a chart title
After step 15, your chart will look like Figure 3.14.

1. Fill in the columns 'Average (treatment)' and 'Average (control)' by taking the average separately for each group, for each period.
2. Plot a line chart of the 'Average (treatment)' and 'Average (control)'. Your chart should look similar to Figure 3.14. Label the lines as in Figure 3.14.
3. Calculate the difference in average lateness in Period 5 and in Period 17 ('Average (treatment)' minus 'Average (control)'). Relate these numbers to what you see in your chart or in Figure 3.14.
4. One explanation for the observed difference in Period 17 is that the treatment and control groups were initially different. Based on your answer to Question 3 and your Excel chart, do you think this explanation is plausible? What other aspects of the treatment and control groups do you think should be similar before the fines were introduced in order for us to infer that the fines 'caused' the increased lateness?
5. Why do you think that, after the fine was removed, parents in the treatment group still continued to pick up their children late?

3.11 HOW DO WE FIND OUT IF A POLICY WILL WORK?

We have seen that a policy works by changing a Nash equilibrium. In other words, it works by changing people's behaviour when they are doing the best they can, considering the new policy and what everyone else is doing (including the policymaker).

Thus, the policymaker faces another real-world policy design problem. When the policymaker pulls the policy lever, how do we work out the effect on outcomes? So far, we have simplified by assuming that our policymaker knows the possible futures with certainty—how the policy will shift the Nash equilibrium, and so what the outcome will be. This meant we could fill in the payoffs in the payoff matrix.

Policymakers sometimes talk of policy 'levers' or 'dials', but the connection between the policy and the effect is rarely as simple as these mechanical terms suggest.

If the policy makes something illegal, such as banning the use of lead in petrol, we can assume it will (broadly) be obeyed. But, in most cases, we do not know with this level of precision what the impact of a policy would be. If a tax is imposed on sugary drinks to discourage obesity and prevent diabetes, how do we know if people will drink tomato juice instead, or just switch to eating more chocolate to get their sugar? We also do not know how the effect might differ among, say, the rich and poor.

This is a challenge because the effect of a policy often depends on the actions taken by millions of people. We could ask each of them, 'If a soft drink were to cost you an additional euro per can, how would that change the amount you drink in a week?' But we should not be confident that we would get a reliable answer.

There are ways of narrowing the range of uncertainty about the effects of policies. Rather than asking people, economists typically look at what people do. First, we can examine the effects of similar policies adopted in the past, or by other bodies. This is why policymakers in India assumed that having women in political leadership in Indian villages would affect the decisions that were made.

But it is often difficult to distinguish between the effects of the policy under consideration, and the effects of other things that happened to take place at the same time. For example, see Figure 3.16.

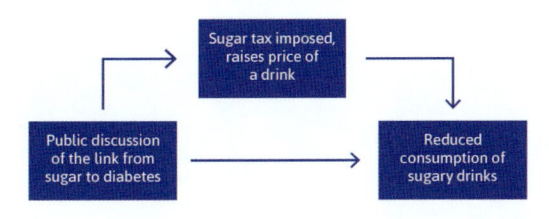

Figure 3.16 Identifying the causes of reduced consumption of sugary drinks: Prices or information?

Before introducing a sugar tax, a government may consult medical evidence about the problem of diabetes and its links to sugar consumption, and use it to explain to the public why it is considering the tax. Now imagine that sugary drink consumption falls following the tax. This might have happened because the drinks are more expensive. But it might also be because the public has new information about the effect of sugar, and this had the effect, not the higher price.

In this case, the correct policy would have been to provide information, not to impose the tax.

Here are two cases illustrating how researchers have estimated the effects of policies, starting with food taxes designed to reduce obesity.

The impact of taxes on food

Taxes on food will raise its price. The ability to measure how the amount sold varies in response to a change in price is essential for policymakers.

The effect of the tax will depend on what is termed the **price elasticity of demand**. This is the percentage change in demand (the amount sold) divided by the percentage change in price, made into a positive number (it will be negative, because demand goes down when prices go up).

- *If demand is highly elastic:* A small increase in price will cause a large reduction in sales, and the number is high (even greater than 1 in some cases). Typically, luxury or fun foods have elastic demand, because they are easier to do without.
- *If demand is inelastic:* Food which we consider essential for our diet has a low elasticity of demand, meaning that we continue to buy it in similar quantities when the price goes up. When demand is inelastic, the percentage change in demand is very low, and so elasticity is close to zero.

Note that policies applied to taxes on food (and all other goods that we buy, such as alcohol and petrol) have different effects depending on the price elasticity of demand:

- *Taxes on inelastic demand mostly raise government revenues:* A government wishing to raise tax revenue should choose to tax products with inelastic demand, because we will continue to buy them. For centuries, governments around the world—including France, Russia, China, and the British Empire (in India)—have taxed salt. Consumers do not cut back much on their salt consumption. Its demand is highly inelastic, so substantial revenues could be collected.
- *Taxes on elastic demand mostly change consumer behaviour:* A government wishing to change our food choices should choose to tax those foods and drinks with the most elastic demand. This is the reasoning behind a sugar tax.

price elasticity of demand The percentage change in demand that would occur in response to a 1% increase in price. We express this as a positive number. Demand is elastic if this is greater than 1, and inelastic if less than 1.

Anti-obesity taxes in practice

Several countries, including Mexico and France, have introduced taxes intended to reduce the consumption of unhealthy food and drink. A 2014 international study found worrying increases in adult and childhood obesity since 1980. In 2013, 37% of men and 38% of women worldwide were overweight or obese. In North America, the figures were 70% and 61% respectively, but the obesity epidemic does not only affect the richest countries—the corresponding rates were 59% of men and 66% of women in the Middle East and North Africa.

Matthew Harding and Michael Lovenheim used detailed data on the food purchases of US consumers to estimate elasticities of demand for different types of food, to investigate the effects of food taxes. They divided food products into 33 categories and used assumptions about how consumers make decisions to examine how changes in their prices would change the share of each category in consumers' expenditure on food, and hence the nutritional composition of the diet, taking into account that the change in the price of any product would change the demand for that product and other products too. Figure 3.17 shows the prices and elasticities for some of the categories.

You can see that the demand for lower-calorie milk products (category 31) is the most elastic. If their price increased by 10%, the quantity purchased would fall by 19.72%. But demand for snacks and candy is quite inelastic, which suggests that it may be difficult to deter consumers from buying them simply by imposing taxes.

Category	Type	Calories per serving	Price per 100 g ($)	Typical spending per week ($)	Price elasticity of demand
1	Fruit and vegetables	660	0.38	2.00	1.128
2	Fruit and vegetables	140	0.36	3.44	0.830
15	Grain, pasta, bread	1,540	0.38	2.96	0.854
17	Grain, pasta, bread	960	0.53	2.64	0.292
28	Snacks, candy	433	1.13	4.88	0.270
29	Snacks, candy	1,727	0.68	7.60	0.295
30	Milk	2,052	0.09	2.32	1.793
31	Milk	874	0.15	1.44	1.972

Matthew Harding and Michael Lovenheim. 2017. 'The effect of prices on nutrition: Comparing the impact of product- and nutrition-specific taxes' (https://tinyco.re/6153912). *Journal of Economics* 53(C): pp. 53–73.

Figure 3.17 Price elasticities of demand for different types of food. (Each food type is listed twice. See the 'Calories per serving' column to compare high- and low-calorie groups of each food type.)

Matthew Harding and Michael Lovenheim. 2017. 'The effect of prices on nutrition: Comparing the impact of product- and nutrition-specific taxes' (https://tinyco.re/6153912). *Journal of Economics* 53(C): pp. 53–73.

Harding and Lovenheim examined the effects of 20% taxes on sugar, fat, and salt. A 20% sugar tax, for example, would increase the price of a product that contains 50% sugar by 10%. A sugar tax was found to have the most positive effect on nutrition. It would reduce sugar consumption by 16%, fat by 12%, salt by 10%, and calorie intake by 19%.

> **EXERCISE 3.6 FOOD TAXES AND HEALTH**
> Food taxes intended to shift consumption towards a healthier diet are controversial. Some people think that individuals should make their own choices, and if they prefer unhealthy products, the government should not interfere. In view of the fact that those who become ill will be cared for at some public expense, others argue that the government has a role in keeping people healthy.
>
> In your own words, provide arguments for or against food taxes designed to encourage healthy eating.

The impact of intellectual property rights

Governments use intellectual property rights (IPR)—most often **patents** and **copyright**—to establish time-limited private monopolies for inventors or creators over the use of their ideas and inventions. This type of monopoly can mean greater profits for the inventor, as long as the protection lasts, because the government prevents others from copying the idea. In theory, this policy increases the incentive to innovate.

IPR in practice

patent A right of exclusive ownership of an idea or invention, which lasts for a specified length of time. During this time it effectively allows the owner to be a monopolist or exclusive user.

copyright Ownership rights over the use and distribution of an original work.

We can use historical data to learn whether IPR has actually boosted innovation. When Petra Moser, an economic historian, studied the number and quality of technical inventions shown at mid-nineteenth century technology fairs, she found that countries with patent systems were no more inventive than countries without patents. Patents did, however, affect the kinds of inventive activities in which countries excelled.

Petra Moser. 2013. 'Patents and Innovation: Evidence from Economic History' (https://tinyco.re/7074474). *Journal of Economic Perspectives* 27 (1): pp. 23–44.

But Moser came to a contrasting conclusion in another one of her studies. In our 'Economist in action' video, she explains that copyright protection for nineteenth-century Italian operas led to more and better operas being written, as long as the protection was not too broad, and not too long term.

Petra Moser. 2015. 'Intellectual Property Rights and Artistic Creativity' (https://tinyco.re/2212476). *VoxEU.org.* 4 November.

In her research into the quantity and quality of operas, we can be pretty sure that Moser had identified copyrights as the *cause* (not just a correlate), because she was able to use a natural experiment—some provinces in Italy had copyright protection because they had been invaded and ruled by Napoleonic France, and others that had not been under French rule did not have copyrights. As a result, what determined which provinces had intellectual property rights had nothing to do with how creative or music loving their populations were, but instead were accidents of geography and strategic priorities of the French forces.

Petra Moser: How copyright improved Italian opera
https://tinyco.re/3460846

> **EXERCISE 3.7 EFFECTIVE POLICYMAKING FOR INTELLECTUAL PROPERTY RIGHTS**
>
> Watch the 'Economist in action' video, in which Petra Moser discusses copyright protection for nineteenth-century Italian operas.
>
> 1. Outline Petra Moser's research question, and her approach to answering it.
> 2. What were Petra Moser's findings about patents and copyrights?
> 3. What factors should governments consider when deciding on the effective time period of IPR protection laws, such as patents and copyrights?

Policy evaluation

These two case studies highlight challenges economists face when seeking to evaluate the likely effect of a policy. This always involves the difficult problem of identifying causes rather than simply finding correlations.

- *Sugar tax:* Because detailed data on patterns of consumption is available, it is possible to design a well-targeted tax that would lead to a fall in obesity.
- *Intellectual property rights:* Modern governments can use natural experiments in history to find out whether patents and copyright encourage innovation, and how best to design these policies.

3.12 CONCLUSION

This unit has looked at how we can determine the **causal** effect of **public policies**. This is a difficult task, as it depends on the behaviour of thousands or millions of people and because there may be other factors that affect the outcome at the time the policy is introduced.

In our evaluation of economic outcomes, also called **allocations**, we have focused on the concepts of efficiency and **fairness**. An allocation is called **Pareto efficient** if there is no other feasible allocation that **Pareto dominates** it. In other words, there exists no other attainable outcome where at least one person would be better off and nobody worse off.

Substantive judgements of fairness consider how unequal an allocation is (based, for example, on income, wealth, or subjective wellbeing), whereas **procedural judgements of fairness** are concerned with how these inequalities come about (an uneven playing field due to discrimination, for instance).

Examples of institutions and policies we have looked at include women's suffrage and child health programs, anti-sugar **taxes**, and intellectual property rights in the form of **patents**. Yet we have also seen how incentives such as fines or paying people to do things may produce unintended results in behaviour, in which case incentives are said to crowd out social preferences.

We have expanded our game theory toolkit by introducing a game tree to model **sequential games**. Specifically, we have encountered two new games:

- *The **ultimatum game**:* In which the Proposer must consider how the Responder will react to the take-it-or-leave-it offer.
- *The tax avoidance game:* In which the government must consider the response of the private firm owners when deciding whether to levy moderate or high taxes.

While payoff diagrams are useful in visualizing whether allocations are Pareto efficient, the Rawlsian veil of ignorance is a concept that helps us evaluate the fairness of an allocation as impartial outsiders, not knowing the position we would occupy in the society we are considering.

The **price elasticity of demand** is useful for measuring how responsive consumers are to changes in prices of products, for instance as the result of an increase in taxation.

Economics can clarify how the rules of the game affect the degree of inequality in allocations and can help us design effective public policies that take into account potential trade-offs between the twin objectives of efficiency and fairness.

3.13 *DOING ECONOMICS:* MEASURING THE EFFECT OF A SUGAR TAX

In Section 3.11, we asked 'how do we find out if a policy will work?' One of the examples was the use of taxes on food as an anti-obesity policy.

In *Doing Economics* Empirical Project 3 we provide a step-by-step guide through the process of finding out the effects of the tax on sugar-sweetened beverages introduced in Berkeley in California in 2014. The introduction of the tax provides a natural experiment and we show how to construct treatment and control groups to test for the effects of the tax.

The project addresses two questions:

1. How did sellers change their prices for sugary beverages in response to the tax?
2. What was the effect of the tax on consumers' spending on sugary beverages?

Go to *Doing Economics* Empirical Project 3 (https://tinyco.re/3451308) to work on this problem.

> *Learning objectives*
> In this project you will:
>
> - use the differences-in-differences method to measure the effects of a policy or program, and explain how this method works
> - create summary tables using Excel's PivotTable option
> - use line and column charts to visualize and compare multiple variables
> - create summary tables to describe the data
> - interpret the p-value in the context of a policy or program evaluation.

3.14 REFERENCES

Bowles, Samuel. 2016. *The Moral Economy: Why Good Incentives Are No Substitute for Good Citizens*. New Haven, CT: Yale University Press.

Clark, Andrew E., and Andrew J. Oswald. 2002. 'A Simple Statistical Method for Measuring How Life Events Affect Happiness'. *International Journal of Epidemiology* 31 (6): pp. 1139–44.

Harding, Matthew, and Michael Lovenheim. 2017. 'The effect of prices on nutrition: Comparing the impact of product- and nutrition-specific taxes' (https://tinyco.re/6153912). *Journal of Economics* 53(C): pp. 53–73.

Miller, Grant. 2008. 'Women's suffrage, political responsiveness, and child survival in American history' (https://tinyco.re/5731666). *The Quarterly Journal of Economics* 123 (3): pp. 1287–1327.

Moser, Petra. 2013. 'Patents and Innovation: Evidence from Economic History' (https://tinyco.re/7074474). *Journal of Economic Perspectives* 27 (1): pp. 23–44

Moser, Petra. 2015. 'Intellectual Property Rights and Artistic Creativity' (https://tinyco.re/2212476). *VoxEU.org*. Updated 4 November 2017.

Rawls, John. 1985. 'Justice as Fairness: Political not Metaphysical'. *Philosophy and Public Affairs* 14 (3): pp. 223-51.

4
WORK, WELLBEING, AND SCARCITY

Clock mechanism

4.1 INTRODUCTION

- People value free time, but they also value what they can buy with their earnings from the time they spend at work.
- This is an example of the unavoidable trade-off we make when there is scarcity—satisfying one objective, such as having more free time, means satisfying other objectives less, such as having more possessions.
- An individual's choices may be understood using economic models, which are simplifications of situations that allow us to see more by looking at less.
- The two components of our model are a description of all of the outcomes that are possible, and the person's evaluation of each of these feasible outcomes.
- The model is based on the assumption that she will take the action that brings about the outcome—among those that are feasible—that she prefers most.
- This model helps explain differences in the hours worked by people in different countries, and the changes in hours of work as real GDP per capita rose in those countries, as we saw in Unit 1's hockey-stick charts (page 7).
- To maintain social status and respect, and to try to attain the consumption of the very rich, people may work longer hours. This may help explain why, as a nation gets richer, its citizens may not become happier.
- We ask, 'how good is the model?' We can better explain differences in working hours if we also consider differences between cultures and between men and women.

You are offered a job. It will pay you eight times as much, per hour, as you earn today. This is not just a short-term offer. You can expect to continue to earn at this rate for the rest of your life. Even better, you can choose to work as few or as many hours as you like while you earn this wage.

Let us consider the choices that this life-changing offer has given you:

- You could keep your working hours unchanged, and permanently increase the amount of goods and services you consume (and so pay for), to eight times your current level.
- At the opposite extreme, you could consume exactly what you consume today, and reduce your working hours to one-eighth of the current level, maybe about an hour a day. The rest of your time is now free.
- Or, in principle, you could increase both your consumption and free time. You cut back on your hours a little, but to a level at which you still earn more after your pay rise.
- Or, of course, you could really cash in. You could use this opportunity to work *more* hours. Your consumption would increase by more than a factor of eight.

Given how much you earn, how would you respond?

Now ask yourself whether your response would be different if you earned the median wage of a US graduate ($1,324 per week (https://tinyco.re/4130643)), or had the median income across the entire globe (around $50 per week at current PPPs (https://tinyco.re/8160050)).

In the absence of fairy godmothers, this seems like a pure thought experiment. An opportunity on this scale hardly ever happens.

But it is far from imaginary. While such a large change in circumstance rarely occurs to one person, such changes *did* occur over time to a typical worker in many rich countries, as those countries moved along the hockey-stick paths (page 14) we showed you in Unit 1. If the inhabitants of poor countries anticipate their income levels rising towards those in rich countries, changes of this magnitude, or even larger, will be a plausible prospect for a large fraction of the global population.

In 1930, John Maynard Keynes (https://tinyco.re/8099084), a British economist, predicted a future of free time in abundance, even warning of an embarrassment of riches in leisure. He published an essay entitled 'Economic Possibilities for our Grandchildren', in which he suggested that, over the next 100 years, technological improvements would make us, on average, about eight times better off.

John Maynard Keynes. 1963. 'Economic Possibilities for our Grandchildren' (https://tinyco.re/8213530). In *Essays in Persuasion*. New York, NY: W. W. Norton & Co.

What he called 'the economic problem, the struggle for subsistence' would be solved, and we would not have to work more than, say, 15 hours *per week* to satisfy our economic needs. The question he raised was, 'How would we cope with all the additional leisure time?'.

Keynes' prediction for the rate of technological progress in countries such as the UK and the US has been approximately right, and working hours have indeed fallen, although much less than he expected. It seems extremely unlikely that average working hours will be 15 hours per week by 2030, as Keynes predicted.

An article by Tim Harford (https://tinyco.re/5829245) in the 'Undercover Economist' column of the *Financial Times* examines why Keynes' prediction was wrong.

The hockey-stick charts in Unit 1 illustrated the dramatic increases in goods and services consumed in countries that have experienced the capitalist revolution. This prompts the question of whether economic progress always results in more free time as well as more goods. The answer is generally yes, but in different proportions in different countries.

Generally, but not always. In the year 1600, the average British worker worked for 266 days, which means taking roughly two days off a week.

This did not change much until the Industrial Revolution in the eighteenth century, when wages began to rise. But working time rose too—to 318 days in 1870. As wages rose for British workers, the number of days they took off work reduced by half!

In the US in the nineteenth century, hours of work initially increased for many workers who shifted from farming to industrial jobs. In 1865, the US abolished slavery, and former slaves used their freedom to work much less. From the late nineteenth century until the middle of the twentieth century, working time gradually fell. Figure 4.1 shows how annual working hours have fallen since 1900 in many countries.

> **EXERCISE 4.1 WORKING HOURS ACROSS COUNTRIES AND TIME**
> Use Figure 4.1 to answer these questions.
>
> 1. Looking at both Panel A and B, describe what happened to working hours over the period 1900–2000.
> 2. Compare working hours in the countries in Panel A with those in Panel B, and describe any differences you see.
> 3. What possible explanations can you suggest for why the decline in working hours was greater in some countries than in others?
> 4. Why do you think that the decline in working hours is faster in most countries in the first half of the century compared to the second half?
> 5. In recent years, is there any country in which working hours have increased? Why do you think this happened?

Figure 4.2 shows trends in income and working hours since 1870 in the Netherlands, the US and France.

As in Unit 1 (page 6), income is measured as real GDP per capita in US dollars. This is not the same as average earnings, but gives us a useful indication of average income for the purposes of comparison across countries and through time. In the late nineteenth and early twentieth centuries, average income approximately tripled, and hours of work fell substantially.

If you want to compare working hours in 1870 to those in the modern world, Michael Huberman and Chris Minns calculate them in their paper, 'The Times They Are Not Changin': Days and Hours of Work in Old and New Worlds, 1870–2000' (https://tinyco.re/2758271). *Explorations in Economic History* 44 (4): pp. 538–67.

An article gives more historical detail on the hours that people worked in the US: Robert Whaples. 2001. 'Hours of Work in U.S. History' (https://tinyco.re/1660378). *EH.net Encyclopedia*.

Michael Huberman and Chris Minns. 2007. 'The Times They Are Not Changin': Days and Hours of Work in Old and New Worlds, 1870–2000' (https://tinyco.re/2758271). *Explorations in Economic History* 44 (4): pp. 538–67.

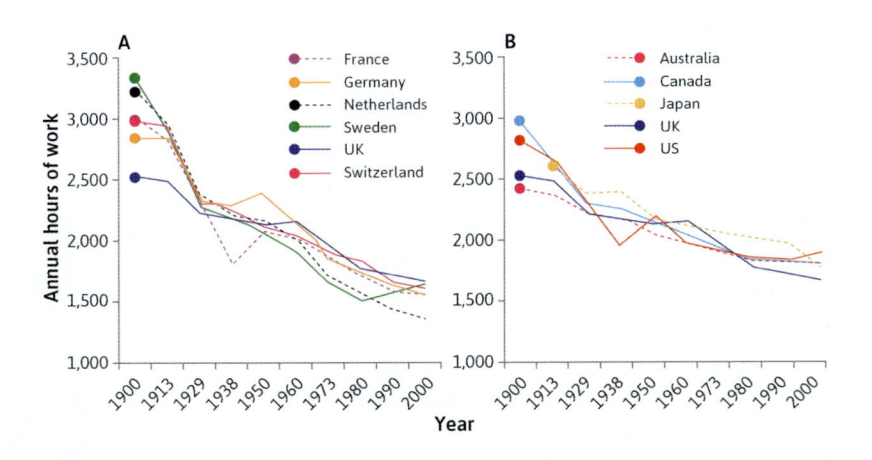

Figure 4.1 Annual hours of work (1900–2000).

During the rest of the twentieth century, income per head rose four-fold. Hours of work continued to fall in the Netherlands and France (albeit more slowly) but levelled off in the US, where there has been little change since 1960. At the end of this unit, we return to these cross-country differences.

While many countries have experienced similar trends, there are still differences in outcomes. Figure 4.3 illustrates the wide disparities in free time and income between countries between the years 2013–2017. Here, we have calculated free time by subtracting average annual working hours from the number of hours in a year. You can see that the higher-income countries seem to have lower working hours and more free time, but there are also some striking differences between them. For example, the Netherlands and the US have similar levels of income, but Dutch workers have much more free time. And the US and Turkey have similar amounts of free time, but a large difference in income.

In many countries, there has been a huge increase in living standards since 1870. But in some places, people have carried on working just as many hours as before but consumed more, while in other countries, people now have much more free time. Why has this happened? We will provide some answers to this question by studying a basic problem of economics—scarcity—and how we make choices when we cannot have everything that we want, such as goods and free time.

Study the model of decision making that we use in this unit carefully! It will be used repeatedly throughout the course, because it gives us an insight into a wide range of economic problems. Before developing our model, we need to ask why economists use models at all.

View this data at OWiD https://tinyco.re/0762342

Maddison Project Database, version 2018 (https://tinyco.re/5503002). Jutta Bolt, Robert Inklaar, Herman de Jong and Jan Luiten van Zanden (2018); 'Rebasing 'Maddison': new income comparisons and the shape of long-run economic development', Maddison Project Working paper 10 (https://tinyco.re/5386746); Michael Huberman and Chris Minns. 2007. 'The Times They Are Not Changin': Days and hours of work in Old and New Worlds, 1870–2000' (https://tinyco.re/2758271). *Explorations in Economic History* 44 (4): pp. 538–67; OECD Statistics (https://tinyco.re/7112802). GDP is measured at PPP in 1990 international Geary–Khamis dollars.

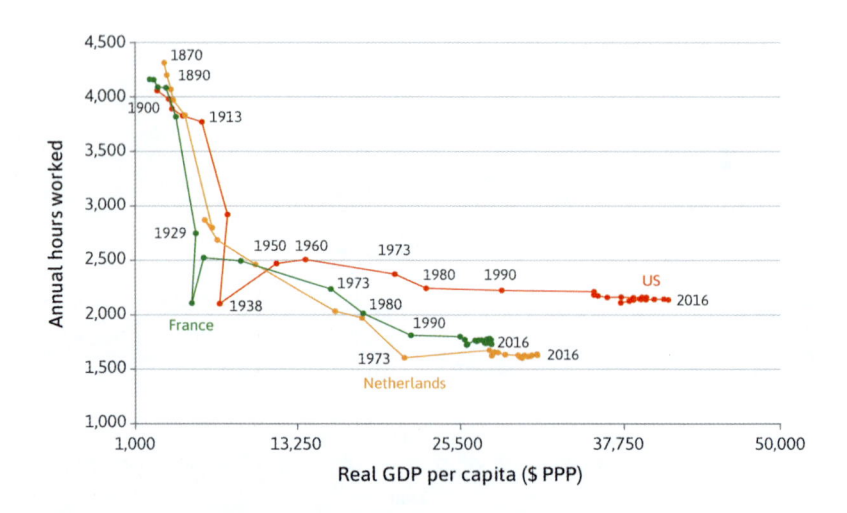

Figure 4.2 Annual hours of work and real income (1870–2016).

4.1 INTRODUCTION

QUESTION 4.1 CHOOSE THE CORRECT ANSWER(S)
Based on Figure 4.2, which of the following statements are true?

☐ An increase in real GDP per capita causes a reduction in the number of hours worked.
☐ The real GDP per capita in the Netherlands is lower than that in the US because the Dutch work fewer hours.
☐ Between 1870 and 2000, the French have managed to increase their real GDP per capita more than ten-fold, while more than halving the number of hours worked.
☐ On the basis of the evidence in the graph, the French will one day be able to produce a real GDP per capita of over $30,000 with less than 1,000 hours of work.

QUESTION 4.2 CHOOSE THE CORRECT ANSWER(S)
Based on Figure 4.3, which of the following statements are true?

☐ The chart gives strong evidence that workers choose to enjoy more free time as their living standards rise.
☐ Workers in the US and Turkey enjoy a similar amount of free time despite the huge disparity in income.
☐ If German workers worked as many hours as the Norwegians, they will be able to produce a similar level of real output per capita.
☐ Japanese workers require more hours of work to produce the same level of real output per capita as Korean workers.

View this data at OWiD https://tinyco.re/2903745

OECD. Level of GDP per capita and productivity (https://tinyco.re/8364498). Accessed March 2019.

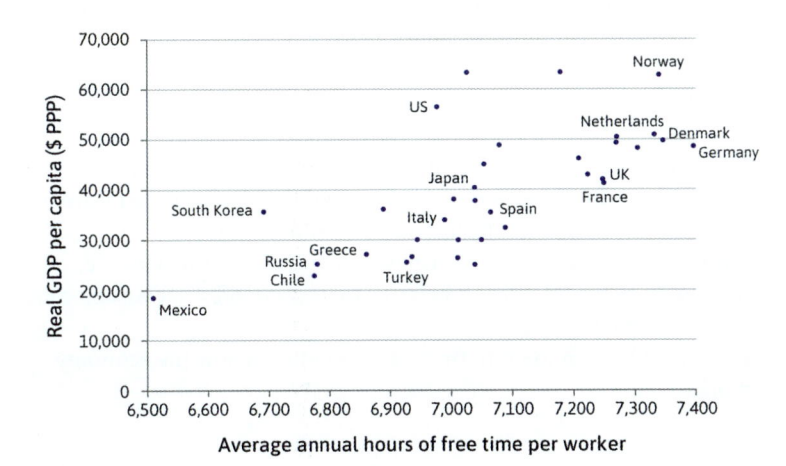

Figure 4.3 Average annual hours of free time per worker and real income (2013–2017).

143

4.2 ECONOMIC MODELS: HOW TO SEE MORE BY LOOKING AT LESS

What happens in the economy depends on what millions of people do, and how their decisions affect the behaviour of others. It would be impossible to understand the economy by describing every detail of how they act and interact. We need to be able to stand back and look at the big picture. To do this, we use models.

To create an effective model, we need to distinguish between the essential features of the economy that are relevant to the question we want to answer, which features should be included in the model, and which details are unimportant, and can be ignored.

Types of model

Models come in many forms—you have seen two of them already in Figures 2.1 (page 57) and 2.15 (page 91). For example, Figure 2.15 illustrated that economic interactions involve flows of goods (for example, when you buy a washing machine), services (when you purchase haircuts or bus rides), and also people (when you spend a day working for an employer). You have encountered still more models in the public goods game, the climate change game, and the ultimatum game.

Figure 2.15 is a diagrammatic model illustrating the flows that occur within the economy, and between the economy and the biosphere. The model is not 'realistic'—the economy and the biosphere don't look anything like it—but it nevertheless illustrates the relationships among them. The fact that the model omits many details—and in this sense is unrealistic—is a feature of the model, not a bug.

When we build a model, the process follows these steps:

1. We construct a simplified description of the conditions under which people take actions.
2. Then we describe in simple terms what determines the actions that people take.
3. We determine how each of their actions affects each other.
4. We determine the outcome of these actions. This is often an **equilibrium** (something is constant).
5. Finally, we try to get more insight by studying what happens to certain variables when conditions change.

A good model has five attributes:

- *It is clear:* It helps us better understand something important.
- *It identifies important relationships:* We need to have accurate information about these to evaluate alternative courses of action.
- *It predicts accurately:* Its predictions are consistent with evidence.
- *It improves communication:* It helps us to understand what we agree (and disagree) about.
- *It is useful:* We can use it to find ways to improve how the economy works.

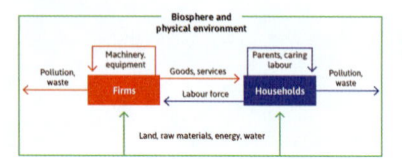

Models come in many forms such as those in Figures 2.1 (page 57) and 2.15 (page 91).

equilibrium A model outcome that does not change unless an outside or external force is introduced that alters the model's description of the situation.

Economic models often use mathematical equations and graphs, as well as words and pictures. Mathematics is part of the language of economics and can help us to communicate our statements about models precisely to others. Much of the knowledge of economics, however, cannot be expressed by using mathematics alone. It requires clear descriptions, using standard definitions of terms.

A model starts with some assumptions or hypotheses about how people behave, and often gives us predictions about what we will observe in the economy. Gathering data on the economy, and comparing it with what a model predicts, helps us to decide whether the assumptions we made when we built the model—what to include and what to leave out—were justified.

Governments, central banks, corporations, trade unions, and anyone else who makes policies or forecasts use some type of simplified model.

Bad models can result in disastrous policies. To have confidence in a model, we need to see whether it is consistent with evidence. We will see that the economic models used in later units pass this test—even though they leave many questions unanswered.

In this unit, we are going to build an economic model to help explain the trends in free time as incomes rose historically, and the variation across countries in these aspects of wellbeing.

The *ceteris paribus* assumption in models

As is common in scientific inquiry, economists often simplify an analysis by setting aside things that are thought to be of less importance to the question of interest, by using the phrase 'holding other things constant'. More often they use the Latin expression ***ceteris paribus***, meaning 'other things equal'. For example, later in the course we simplify an analysis of what people would choose to buy by looking at the effect of changing a price—ignoring other influences on our behaviour like brand loyalty, or what others would think of our choices. We ask, 'What would happen if the price changed, but everything else that might influence the decision was the same?'. These *ceteris paribus* assumptions, when used well, can clarify the picture without distorting the key facts.

In scientific experiments and in the experiments conducted by economists in the lab and in the field that we have considered in previous units, the experimental design holds many things constant in order to uncover the effect of X on Y. The *ceteris paribus* assumption refers to holding things constant in *thought* experiments.

> **ceteris paribus** Economists often simplify analysis by setting aside things that are thought to be of less importance to the question of interest. The literal meaning of the expression is 'other things equal'. In an economic model it means an analysis 'holds other things constant'.

> **EXERCISE 4.2 DESIGNING A MODEL**
> For a country (or city) of your choice, look up a map of the railway or public transport network. When designing this model, how do you think the modeller selected which features of reality to include?

4.3 DECISION MAKING, TRADE-OFFS, AND OPPORTUNITY COSTS

Alexei is a student who faces a dilemma. He wants both a higher grade and more free time. But, *ceteris paribus* (holding other things equal) he cannot increase his free time without getting a lower grade in the exam. Another way of expressing this is to say that free time has an **opportunity cost**—to get more free time, Alexei must forgo the *opportunity* of getting a higher grade. Whatever he decides to do, there is a *cost* to him. The opportunity cost of more free time is his dislike of getting a lower grade. We could also turn it around: the opportunity cost of getting a higher grade is how much he dislikes having less free time.

> **opportunity cost** The opportunity cost of some action A is the foregone benefit that you would have enjoyed if instead you had taken some other action B. This is called an *opportunity* cost because by choosing A you give up the opportunity of choosing B. It is called a *cost* because the choice of A costs you the benefit you would have experienced had you chosen B.

In everyday decision making, opportunity costs are relevant whenever we consider choosing between alternative and mutually exclusive courses of action. When we consider the cost of taking action A, we include the fact that if we do A, we cannot do B. So, forgoing the opportunity to do B becomes part of the cost of doing A. This is called an opportunity cost because doing A means forgoing the opportunity to do B.

Accountants think differently about costs. Imagine that an accountant and an economist have been asked to report the cost of going to a concert A in a theatre, which has a $25 admission cost. In a nearby park, there is concert B, which is free but happens at the same time. You cannot go to both.

ACCOUNTANT: The cost of concert A is your 'out-of-pocket' cost—you paid $25 for a ticket, so the cost is $25.

ECONOMIST: But what do you have to give up to go to concert A? You give up the $25, plus opportunity of enjoying the free concert in the park. So the cost of concert A for you is the out-of-pocket cost plus the opportunity cost.

Suppose that the most you would have been willing to pay to attend the concert in the park (if it wasn't free) is $15. The benefit of your next best alternative to concert A would be $15 of enjoyment in the park. This is the opportunity cost of going to concert A.

The total **economic cost** of concert A is the cost of the ticket plus the opportunity cost: $25 + $15 = $40. If the pleasure you anticipate from being at concert A is greater than the economic cost, say $50, then you will forego concert B and buy a ticket to the theatre. (The benefit of an action minus the economic cost is called its **economic rent**.)

> **economic cost** The out-of-pocket cost of an action, plus the opportunity cost.
> **economic rent** A payment or other benefit received above and beyond what the individual would have received in his or her next best alternative (or reservation option). See also: reservation option.

On the other hand, if you anticipate $35 worth of pleasure from concert A, then the economic cost of $40 means you will not choose to go to the theatre. In simple terms, given that you must pay $25 for the ticket, you will instead opt for concert B, pocketing the $25 to spend on other things and enjoying $15 worth of benefit from the free park concert.

Why don't accountants think this way? Because it is not their job. Accountants are paid to keep track of money, not to provide decision rules on how to choose among alternatives, some of which do not have a stated price. But making sensible decisions and predicting how sensible people will make decisions involve more than keeping track of money. An accountant might argue that the park concert is irrelevant.

ACCOUNTANT: Whether or not there is a free park concert does not affect the cost of going to the concert A. The cost to you is always $25.

ECONOMIST: But whether or not there is a free park concert can affect whether you go to concert A or not, because it changes your available options. If your enjoyment from concert A is $35 and your next best alternative is staying at home, with enjoyment of $0, you will choose concert A. However, if concert B is available, you will choose it rather than concert A.

The table in Figure 4.4 summarizes the example of your choice of which concert to attend. If something is a cost, the number is negative. If it is a benefit, the number is positive.

> **EXERCISE 4.3 OPPORTUNITY COSTS**
> The British government introduced legislation in 2012 that gave universities the option to raise their tuition fees. Most chose to increase annual tuition fees from £3,000 to £9,000.
>   From the viewpoint of an accountant, does this mean that the cost of going to university has tripled? What would an economist's viewpoint be?

> **QUESTION 4.3 CHOOSE THE CORRECT ANSWER(S)**
> You are a taxi driver in Melbourne who earns A$50 for a day's work. You have been offered a one-day ticket to the Australian Open for A$40. Being a big tennis fan, you value the experience at A$100. Based on this information, which of the following statements is true?
>
> ☐ The opportunity cost of the day at the Open is A$40.
> ☐ The economic cost of the day at the Open is A$40.
> ☐ The enjoyment minus economic cost of the day at the Open is A$10.
> ☐ You would be willing to pay up to A$100 for the ticket.

	A high value on concert A ($)	A low value on concert A ($)
Out-of-pocket cost (price of ticket for A)	−25	−25
Opportunity cost (foregone pleasure concert B)	−15	−15
Economic cost (sum of out-of-pocket and opportunity cost)	**−40**	**−40**
Enjoyment of concert A	+50	+35
Enjoyment minus economic cost	**+10**	**−5**
Decision	Go to concert A.	Go to concert B.

Figure 4.4 Opportunity costs and decision making: Which concert will you choose?

4.4 MAKING DECISIONS WHEN THERE ARE TRADE-OFFS

As a student, you choose how many hours to spend studying every day. There may be many factors influencing your choice—how much you enjoy studying, how difficult you find it, how much studying your friends do, and so on. Perhaps part of the motivation to devote time to studying comes from your belief that, the more time you spend studying, the higher the grade you will obtain at the end of the course. In this unit, we will construct a simple model of a student's choice of how many hours to work, based on the assumption that the more time spent working, the better the final grade will be.

We assume a positive relationship between hours worked and final grade, but is there any evidence to back this up? A group of educational psychologists looked at the study behaviour of 84 students at Florida State University to identify the factors that affected their performance.

Elizabeth Ashby Plant, Karl Anders Ericsson, Len Hill, and Kia Asberg. 2005. 'Why study time does not predict grade point average across college students: Implications of deliberate practice for academic performance' (https://tinyco.re/7875663). *Contemporary Educational Psychology* 30 (1): pp. 96–116.

At first sight, there seems to be only a weak relationship between the average number of hours per week the students spent studying and their grade point average (GPA) at the end of the semester. This is in Figure 4.5.

The 84 students have been split into two groups of 42 students each, according to their hours of study. The average GPA for those with high study time is 3.43—only slightly more than the GPA of those with low study time.

Elizabeth Ashby Plant, Karl Anders Ericsson, Len Hill, and Kia Asberg. 2005. 2005. 'Why study time does not predict grade point average across college students' (https://tinyco.re/7875663). *Contemporary Educational Psychology* 30 (1): pp. 96–116. Additional calculations were conducted by Ashby Plant, Florida State University, in June 2015.

	High study time (42 students)	Low study time (42 students)
Average GPA	3.43	3.36

Figure 4.5 Study time and grades.

Using the ceteris paribus *assumption*

Looking more closely, we discover this study is an interesting illustration of why we should be careful when we make *ceteris paribus* assumptions. Within each group of 42 students, there are many potentially important differences. The conditions in which they study would be an obvious difference to consider—an hour working in a busy, noisy room may not be as useful as an hour spent in the library.

In Figure 4.6, we see that students studying in poor environments are more likely to study longer hours. Of these 42 students, 31 of them have high study time, compared with only 11 of the students with good environments. Perhaps they are distracted by other people around them, so it takes them longer to complete their assignments than those students who work in the library.

Elizabeth Ashby Plant, Karl Anders Ericsson, Len Hill, and Kia Asberg. 2005. 'Why study time does not predict grade point average across college students' (https://tinyco.re/7875663). *Contemporary Educational Psychology* 30 (1): pp. 96–116. Additional calculations were conducted by Ashby Plant, Florida State University, in June 2015.

	High study time	Low study time
Good environment	3.63 (11 students)	3.43 (31 students)
Poor environment	3.36 (31 students)	3.17 (11 students)

Figure 4.6 Average GPA in good and poor study environments.

Now look at the average GPAs in the top row—if the environment is good, students who study longer do better. You can see in the bottom row that high study time pays off for those who work in poor environments too. This relationship was not as clear when we didn't consider the effect of the study environment.

After considering environment and other relevant factors (including the students' past GPAs and the hours they spent in paid work or partying), the psychologists estimated that an additional hour of study time per week raised a student's GPA at the end of the semester by 0.24 points on average. If we take two students who are the same in all respects except for study time, we predict that the one who studies for longer will have a GPA that is 0.24 points higher for each extra hour—in other words, study time raises GPA by 0.24 per hour, *ceteris paribus*.

> **EXERCISE 4.4 CETERIS PARIBUS ASSUMPTIONS**
> You have been asked to conduct a research study at your university, similar to the one done at Florida State University.
>
> 1. What factors do you think should be held constant in a model of the relationship between study hours and final grade?
> 2. What other information about the students, in addition to study environment, would you want to collect?

> **QUESTION 4.4 CHOOSE THE CORRECT ANSWER(S)**
> Based on Figure 4.6, which of the following statements are true?
>
> ☐ More students that spend a longer time studying do so in a bad environment rather than in a good environment.
> ☐ High study time is associated with a better grade.
> ☐ All students who spend a longer time studying attain a higher grade on average than those who study fewer hours.
> ☐ Grades vary with the amount of time spent studying, but not with the type of study environment.

Introducing the production function

Now imagine Alexei is a student who can vary the number of hours he spends studying. We will assume that, as in the Florida State University study, the hours he spends studying over the semester will increase the percentage grade that he will receive at the end, *ceteris paribus*. This relationship between study time and final grade is represented in the table in Figure 4.7. In this model, study time refers to all the time that Alexei spends learning, whether in class or individually, measured per day (not per week, as for the Florida students). The table shows how his grade will vary if he changes his study hours, if all other factors—his social life, for example—are held constant.

This is Alexei's **production function**. In general, a production function tells us how much of a good or service is produced, given the inputs into the production process. In Alexei's case, it translates the number of hours per day spent studying (his input of labour) into a percentage grade (his output). In reality, the final grade might also be affected by unpredictable events (in everyday life, we normally lump the effect of these things together and call it 'luck'). You can think of the production function as telling us what Alexei will get under normal conditions, if he is neither lucky nor unlucky.

production function A graphical or mathematical expression describing the amount of output that can be produced by any given amount or combination of input(s). The function describes differing technologies capable of producing the same thing.

If we plot this relationship on a graph, we get the curve in Figure 4.7. Alexei can achieve a higher grade by studying more, so the curve slopes upward. At 15 hours of work per day he gets the highest grade he is capable of, which is 90%. Any further time spent studying does not affect his exam result (he will be so tired that studying more each day will not achieve anything), and the curve becomes flat.

Alexei's **marginal product** is the increase in his grade from increasing study time by one hour. Follow the steps in Figure 4.7 to see how to calculate the marginal product.

At each point on the production function, the marginal product is the increase in the grade from studying one more hour. The marginal product corresponds to the slope of the production function.

marginal product The additional amount of output that is produced if a particular input was increased by one unit, while holding all other inputs constant.

diminishing marginal product A property of some production functions according to which each additional unit of input results in a smaller increment in total output than did the previous unit.

The concept of diminishing returns

Alexei's production function in Figure 4.7 gets flatter the more hours he studies, so the marginal product of an additional hour falls as we move along the curve. The marginal product is **diminishing**. The model captures the idea that an extra hour of study helps a lot if you are not studying much, but if you are already studying a lot, then studying even more does not help very much.

Notice that, if Alexei was already studying for 15 hours a day, the marginal product of an additional hour would be zero. Studying more would not improve his grade. As you might know from experience, a lack of either sleep or time to relax could even lower Alexei's grade if he worked more than 15 hours a day. If this were the case, then his production function would start to slope downward, and Alexei's marginal product would become negative.

Marginal change is an important and common concept in economics. You will often see it marked as a slope on a diagram. With a production function like the one in Figure 4.7, the slope changes continuously as we move along the curve. We have said that when Alexei studies for 4 hours a day the marginal product is 7, the increase in the grade from one more hour of study. Because the slope of the curve changes between 4 and 5 hours on the horizontal axis, this is only an approximation of the actual marginal product. More precisely, the marginal product is the rate at which the grade increases, per hour of additional study. In Figure 4.7, the true marginal product is the slope of the line that just touches the curve at 4 hours. In this unit, we will use approximations so that we can work in whole numbers, but you may notice that sometimes these numbers are not quite the same as the slopes.

> **QUESTION 4.5 CHOOSE THE CORRECT ANSWER(S)**
> Based on Figure 4.7, which of the following statements are true?
>
> ☐ The marginal product at 4 hours of study is approximately 7.
> ☐ The marginal product decreases beyond 15 hours of study.
> ☐ The horizontal production function beyond 15 hours means that studying for more than 15 hours is detrimental to Alexei's performance.
> ☐ The marginal product at 7 hours of study is higher than at 10 hours of study.

4.4 MAKING DECISIONS WHEN THERE ARE TRADE-OFFS

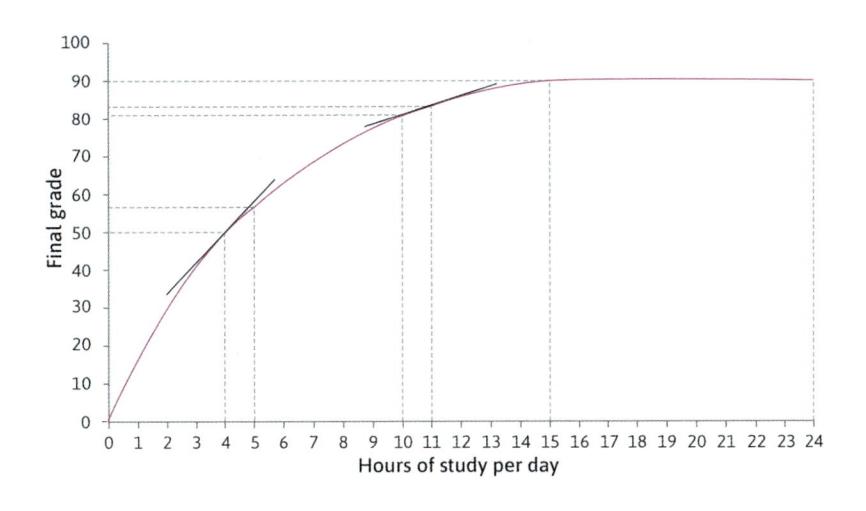

To explore all of the slides in this figure, see the online version at https://tinyco.re/1040823.

Study hours	0	1	2	3	4	5	6	7	8	9	10	11	12	13	14	15 or more
Grade	0	20	33	42	50	57	63	69	74	78	81	84	86	88	89	90

Figure 4.7 How does the amount of time spent studying affect Alexei's grade?

1. Alexei's production function
The curve is Alexei's production function. It shows how an input of study hours produces an output, the exam grade.

2. Four hours of study per day
If Alexei studies for 4 hours, his grade will be 50.

3. Ten hours of study per day
If he studies for 10 hours, he will achieve a grade of 81.

4. Alexei's maximum grade
At 15 hours of study per day, Alexei achieves his maximum possible grade, 90. After that, further hours will make no difference to his result—the curve is flat.

5. Increasing study time from 4 to 5 hours
Increasing study time from 4 to 5 hours raises Alexei's grade from 50 to 57. Therefore, at 4 hours of study, the marginal product of an additional hour is approximately 7.

6. Increasing study time from 10 to 11 hours
Increasing study time from 10 to 11 hours raises Alexei's grade from 81 to 84. At 10 hours of study, the marginal product of an additional hour is approximately 3. As we move along the curve, the slope of the curve falls, so the marginal product of an extra hour falls. The marginal product is diminishing.

7. The marginal product
The marginal product is the slope of the line that just touches but does not cross the production function. The marginal product at 4 hours of study is approximately 7, which is the increase in the grade from one more hour of study. More precisely, the marginal product is the slope of the line at that point, which is slightly higher than 7. The marginal product at 11 hours of study is approximately 2.

preference Pro-and-con evaluations of the possible outcomes of the actions we may take that form the basis by which we decide on a course of action.

4.5 PREFERENCES

If Alexei has the production function shown in Figure 4.7, how many hours per day will he choose to study? The decision depends on his **preferences**. The term preferences describes pro-and-con evaluations of the possible outcomes of the actions we may take that are the basis of our deciding on a course of action. In this case, his preferences describe the benefits (a higher grade) and the cost (less free time) associated with studying any particular number of hours. If he cared only about grades, he should study for 15 hours a day. But, like other people, Alexei also values his free time—he likes to sleep, go out or watch TV. So he faces a trade-off—how many percentage points is he willing to give up in order to spend time on things other than study?

Indifference curves: Different combinations of goods that are equally ranked

We illustrate his preferences using Figure 4.8, with free time on the horizontal axis and final grade on the vertical axis. Free time is defined as all the time that he does not spend studying. Every point in the diagram represents a different combination of free time and final grade. Given his production function, not every combination that Alexei would want will be possible, but for the moment we will only consider the combinations that he would prefer.

We can assume:

- For a given grade, he prefers a combination with more free time to one with less free time. Therefore, even though both A and B in Figure 4.8 correspond to a grade of 84, Alexei prefers A because it gives him more free time.
- Similarly, if two combinations both have 20 hours of free time, he prefers the one with a higher grade.
- But compare points A and D in the table in Figure 4.8. Would Alexei prefer D (low grade, plenty of time) or A (higher grade, less time)? One way to find out would be to ask him.

utility A numerical indicator of the value that one places on an outcome, such that higher-valued outcomes will be chosen over lower-valued ones when both are feasible.

Suppose he says he is indifferent between A and D, meaning he would feel equally satisfied with either outcome. We say that these two outcomes would give Alexei the same **utility**. And we know that he prefers A to B, so B provides lower utility than A or D.

A systematic way to graph Alexei's preferences would be to start by looking for all the combinations that give him the same utility as A and D. We could ask Alexei another question, 'Imagine that you could have the combination at A (15 hours of free time, 84 points). How many points would you be willing to sacrifice for an extra hour of free time?'. Suppose that, after due consideration, he answers '9'. Then we know that he is indifferent between A and E (16 hours, 75 points). Then we could ask the same question about combination E, and so on until point D. Eventually, we could draw up a table like the one in Figure 4.8. Alexei is indifferent between A and E, between E and F, and so on, which means he is indifferent between all the combinations from A to D.

The combinations in the table are plotted in Figure 4.8 and joined together to form a downward-sloping curve, called an **indifference curve**, which joins together all the combinations that provide equal utility or 'satisfaction'.

If you look at the three curves drawn in Figure 4.8, you can see that the one through A gives higher utility than the one through B. The curve through C gives the lowest utility of the three. To describe preferences, we don't need to know the exact utility of each option; we only need to know which combinations provide more or less utility than others.

> **indifference curve** A curve of the points which indicate the combinations of goods that provide a given level of utility to the individual.

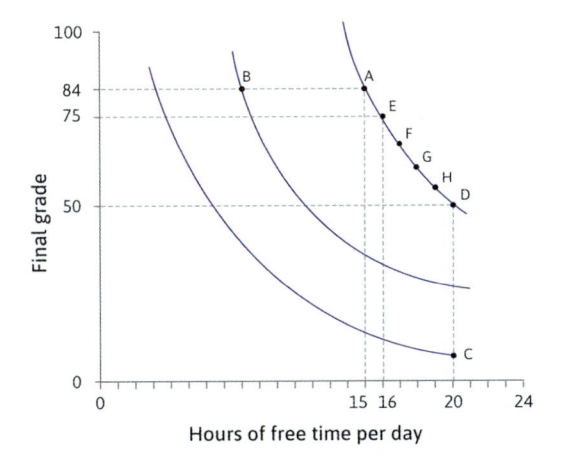

To explore all of the slides in this figure, see the online version at https://tinyco.re/8767511.

	A	E	F	G	H	D
Hours of free time	15	16	17	18	19	20
Final grade	84	75	67	60	54	50

Figure 4.8 Mapping Alexei's preferences.

1. Alexei prefers more free time to less free time
Combinations A and B both deliver a grade of 84, but Alexei will prefer A because it has more free time.

2. Alexei prefers a high grade to a low grade
At combinations C and D, Alexei has 20 hours of free time per day, but he prefers D because it gives him a higher grade.

3. Indifference
We don't know whether Alexei prefers A or E, so we ask him—he says he is indifferent.

4. More combinations giving the same utility
Alexei says that F is another combination that would give him the same utility as A and E.

5. Constructing the indifference curve
By asking more questions, we discover that Alexei is indifferent between all these combinations between A and D.

6. Constructing the indifference curve
These points are joined together to form an indifference curve.

7. Other indifference curves
Indifference curves can be drawn through any point in the diagram, to show other points giving the same utility. We can construct other curves, starting from B or C in the same way as before, by finding out which combinations give the same amount of utility.

Summary of indifference curves

The curves we have drawn capture our typical assumptions about people's preferences between two goods. In other models, these will often be **consumption goods**, such as food or clothing, and we refer to the person as a consumer. In our model of a student's preferences, the goods are 'final grade' and 'free time'. Notice that:

- *Indifference curves slope downward due to trade-offs:* Since resources (such as time or money) are limited, to get more of one good usually means giving up some of the other good(s). Therefore, if you are indifferent between two combinations, the combination that has more of one good must have less of the other good.
- *Higher indifference curves correspond to higher utility levels:* As we move up and to the right in the diagram, further away from the origin, we move to combinations with more of both goods.
- *Indifference curves are usually smooth:* Small changes in the amounts of goods don't cause big jumps in utility.
- *Indifference curves do not cross:* Work through Exercise 4.5 to understand why.
- *As you move to the right along an indifference curve, it becomes flatter.*

> **consumption good** A good or service that satisfies the needs of consumers over a short period.

> **QUESTION 4.6 CHOOSE THE CORRECT ANSWER(S)**
> Based on Figure 4.8, which of the following statements is correct?
>
> ☐ A is the student's most preferred choice as he would be attaining the highest grade.
> ☐ At A, the student is willing to give up 34 grade points for 5 extra hours of free time.
> ☐ If at B the number of free hours is 10, then the student is 50% happier at A than at B.
> ☐ The student strictly prefers a grade of 54 with 19 hours of free time to a grade of 67 with 18 hours of free time.

The marginal rate of substitution (MRS): Trade-offs between objectives

Look at Alexei's indifference curves, which are plotted again in Figure 4.9. If he is at A, with 15 hours of free time and a grade of 84, he would be willing to sacrifice 9 percentage points for an extra hour of free time, taking him to E (remember that he is indifferent between A and E). We say that his **marginal rate of substitution (MRS)** between grade points and free time at A is nine; it is the reduction in his grade that would keep Alexei's utility constant following a one-hour increase of free time.

We have drawn the indifference curves as becoming gradually flatter because it seems reasonable to assume that, the more free time and the lower the grade he has, the less willing he will be to sacrifice further percentage points in return for free time, so his MRS will be lower. In Figure 4.9, we have calculated the MRS for some combinations along the indifference curve. You can see that, when Alexei has more free time and a lower grade, the MRS—the number of percentage points he would give up to gain an extra hour of free time—gradually falls.

> **marginal rate of substitution (MRS)** The trade-off that a person is willing to make between two goods. At any point, this is the slope of the indifference curve. *See also: marginal rate of transformation.*

The MRS is the slope of the indifference curve; it falls as we move to the right along the curve. If you move from one point to another in Figure 4.9, you can see that the indifference curves get flatter if you increase the amount of free time, and steeper if you increase the grade. When free time is scarce relative to grade points, Alexei is less willing to sacrifice an hour for a higher grade—his MRS is high and his indifference curve is steep.

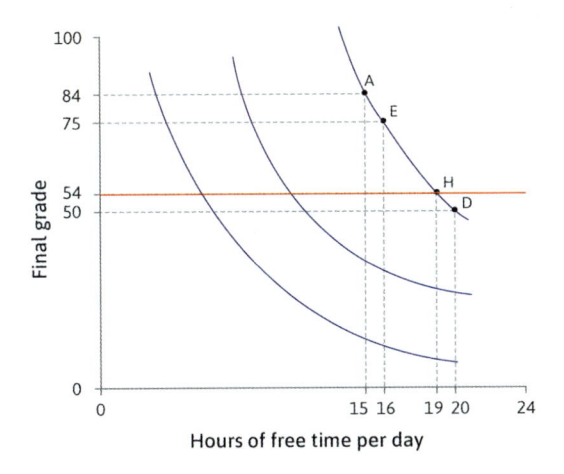

To explore all of the slides in this figure, see the online version at https://tinyco.re/7404294.

Figure 4.9 The marginal rate of substitution.

1. Alexei's indifference curves
The diagram shows three indifference curves for Alexei. The curve furthest to the left offers the lowest satisfaction.

2. Point A
At A, he has 15 hours of free time and his grade is 84.

3. Alexei is indifferent between A and E
He would be willing to move from A to E, giving up 9 percentage points for an extra hour of free time. His marginal rate of substitution is 9. The indifference curve is steep at A.

4. Alexei is indifferent between H and D
At H he is only willing to give up 4 points for an extra hour of free time. His MRS is 4. As we move down the indifference curve, the MRS diminishes, because points become scarce relative to free time. The indifference curve becomes flatter.

5. All combinations with 15 hours of free time
Look at the combinations with 15 hours of free time. On the lowest curve, the grade is low and the MRS is small. Alexei would be willing to give up only a few points for an hour of free time. As we move up the vertical line, the indifference curves are steeper—the MRS increases.

6. All combinations with a grade of 54
Now look at all the combinations with a grade of 54. On the curve furthest to the left, free time is scarce and the MRS is high. As we move to the right along the red line, he is less willing to give up points for free time. The MRS decreases, the indifference curves get flatter.

As the analysis in Figure 4.9 shows, if you move up the vertical line through 15 hours, the indifference curves get steeper—the MRS increases. For a given amount of free time, Alexei is willing to give up more grade points for an additional hour when he has a lot of points compared to when he has few (for example, if he was in danger of failing the course). By the time you reach A, where his grade is 84, the MRS is high; grade points are so plentiful here that he is willing to give up 9 percentage points for an extra hour of free time.

You can see the same effect if you fix the grade and vary the amount of free time. If you move to the right along the horizontal line for a grade of 54, the MRS becomes lower at each indifference curve. As free time becomes more plentiful, Alexei becomes less and less willing to give up grade points for more time.

EXERCISE 4.5 WHY INDIFFERENCE CURVES NEVER CROSS

In Figure 4.10, IC_1 is an indifference curve joining all the combinations that give the same level of utility as A. Combination B is not on IC_1.

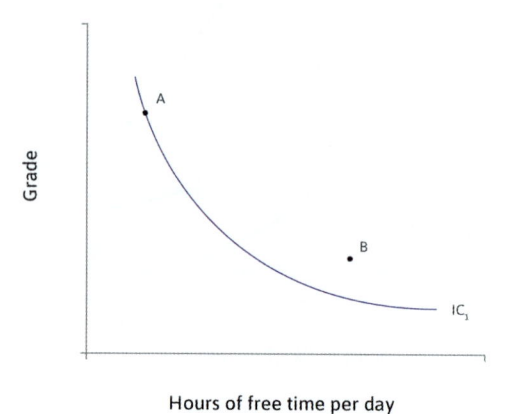

Figure 4.10 The trade-off between grades and work.

1. Does combination B give higher or lower utility than combination A? How do you know?
2. Draw a sketch of the diagram, and add another indifference curve, IC_2, that goes through B and crosses IC_1. Label the point at which they cross as C.
3. Combinations B and C are both on IC_2. What does that imply about their levels of utility?
4. Combinations C and A are both on IC_1. What does that imply about their levels of utility?
5. According to your answers to (3) and (4), how do the levels of utility at combinations A and B compare?
6. Now compare your answers to (1) and (5) and explain how you know that indifference curves can never cross.

EXERCISE 4.6 YOUR MARGINAL RATE OF SUBSTITUTION

Imagine that you are offered at job at the end of your university course that requires you to work for 40 hours per week. This would leave you with 128 hours of free time per week. Estimate the weekly pay that you expect to receive (be realistic!).

1. Draw a diagram with free time on the horizontal axis and weekly pay on the vertical axis, and plot the combination corresponding to your job offer, calling it A. Assume you need about 10 hours a day for sleeping and eating, so you may want to draw the horizontal axis with 70 hours at the origin.

Now imagine you were offered another job requiring 45 hours of work per week.

2. What level of weekly pay would make you indifferent between this and the original offer?
3. By asking yourself more questions about the trade-offs you would make, plot an indifference curve through A to represent your preferences.
4. Use your diagram to estimate your marginal rate of substitution between pay and free time at A.

QUESTION 4.7 CHOOSE THE CORRECT ANSWER(S)

Based on Figure 4.8 (page 153), which of the following statements are true?

☐ Alexei prefers C to B because at C he has more free time.
☐ Alexei is indifferent between the grade of 84 with 15 hours of free time, and the grade of 50 with 20 hours of free time.
☐ Alexei prefers D to C, because at D he has the same grade for more free time.
☐ At G, Alexei is willing to give up 2 hours of free time for 10 extra grade points.

QUESTION 4.8 CHOOSE THE CORRECT ANSWER(S)

The marginal rate of substitution (MRS) is:

☐ The ratio of the amounts of the two goods at a point on the indifference curve.
☐ The amount of one good that the consumer is willing to trade for one unit of the other.
☐ The change in the consumer's utility when one good is substituted for another.
☐ The slope of the indifference curve.

4.6 THE FEASIBLE SET

Now we return to Alexei's problem of how to choose between high grades and free time. Free time has an opportunity cost in the form of lost percentage points in his grade (equivalently, we might say that percentage points have an opportunity cost in the form of the free time Alexei gives up to obtain them). But before we can describe how Alexei resolves his dilemma, we need to work out precisely which alternatives are available to him.

From the production function to the feasible set

To answer this question, we look again at the production function. This time, we will show how the final grade depends on the amount of free time, rather than study time. There are 24 hours in a day. Alexei must divide this time between studying (all the hours devoted to learning) and free time (all the rest of his time). Figure 4.11 shows the relationship between his final grade and hours of free time per day—the mirror image of Figure 4.7 (page 151). If Alexei studies solidly for 24 hours, that means zero hours of free time and a final grade of 90. If he chooses 24 hours of free time per day, we assume he will get a grade of zero.

In Figure 4.11, the axes are 'final grade' and 'free time', the two goods that give Alexei utility. If we think of him choosing to consume a combination of these two goods, the curved line in Figure 4.11 shows the boundary of what is feasible. The line is his **feasible frontier**—the highest grade he can achieve given the amount of free time he takes, and the area inside the frontier is the **feasible set**.

Follow the analysis of Figure 4.11 to see which combinations of grade and free time are feasible, and which are not, and how the slope of the frontier represents the opportunity cost of free time.

Any combination of free time and final grade that is on or inside the frontier is feasible. Combinations outside the feasible frontier are said to be infeasible given Alexei's abilities and conditions of study. On the other hand, even though a combination lying inside the frontier is feasible, choosing it would imply Alexei has effectively thrown away something that he values. If he studied for 14 hours a day, then according to our model, he could guarantee himself a grade of 89. But he could obtain a lower grade (70, say), if he just stopped writing before the end of the exam. It would be foolish to throw away points like this for no reason, but it would be possible. Another way to obtain a combination inside the frontier might be to sit in the library doing nothing—Alexei would be taking less free time than is available to him, which again makes no sense.

By choosing a combination inside the frontier, Alexei would be giving up something that is freely available—something that has no opportunity cost. He could obtain a higher grade without sacrificing any free time, or have more time without reducing his grade.

The feasible frontier is a constraint on Alexei's choices. It represents the trade-off he must make between grade and free time. At any point on the frontier, taking more free time has an opportunity cost in terms of grade points foregone, corresponding to the slope of the frontier.

> **feasible frontier** The curve made of points that defines the maximum feasible quantity of one good for a given quantity of the other. See also: feasible set.
>
> **feasible set** All of the combinations of the things under consideration that a decision-maker could choose given the economic, physical or other constraints that he faces. See also: feasible frontier.

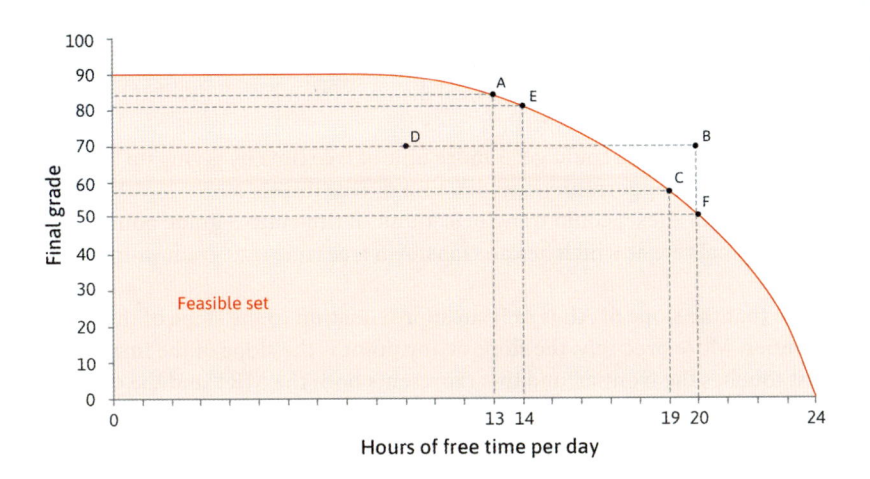

4.6 THE FEASIBLE SET

	A	E	C	F
Free time	13	14	19	20
Grade	84	81	57	50
Opportunity cost		3	7	

Figure 4.11 How does Alexei's choice of free time affect his grade?

1. The feasible frontier
This curve is called the feasible frontier. It shows the highest final exam grade Alexei can achieve, given the amount of free time he takes. With 24 hours of free time, his grade would be zero. By having less free time, Alexei can achieve a higher grade.

2. A feasible combination
If Alexei chooses 13 hours of free time per day, he can achieve a grade of 84.

3. Infeasible combinations
Given Alexei's abilities and conditions of study, under normal conditions he cannot take 20 hours of free time and expect to get a grade of 70 (remember, we are assuming that luck plays no part). Therefore, B is an infeasible combination of hours of free time and exam grade.

4. A feasible combination
The maximum grade Alexei can achieve with 19 hours of free time per day is 57.

5. Inside the frontier
Combination D is feasible, but Alexei is wasting time and/or points in the exam. He could get a higher grade with the same hours of study per day, or have more free time and still get a grade of 70.

6. The feasible set
The area inside the frontier, together with the frontier itself, is called the feasible set. (A set is a collection of things—in this case, all the feasible combinations of free time and grade.)

7. The opportunity cost of free time
At combination A, Alexei could get an extra hour of free time by giving up 3 points in the exam. The opportunity cost of an hour of free time at A is 3 points.

8. The opportunity cost varies
The more free time he takes, the higher the marginal product of studying, so the opportunity cost of free time increases. At C, the opportunity cost of an hour of free time is higher than at A—Alexei would have to give up 7 points instead of 3.

9. The slope of the feasible frontier
The opportunity cost of free time at C is 7 points, corresponding to the slope of the feasible frontier. At C, Alexei would have to give up 7 percentage points (the vertical change is –7) to increase his free time by an hour (the horizontal change is 1). The slope is –7.

159

marginal rate of transformation (MRT) A measure of the trade-offs a person faces in what is feasible. Given the constraints (feasible frontier) a person faces, the MRT is the quantity of some good that must be sacrificed to acquire one additional unit of another good. At any point, it is the slope of the feasible frontier. See also: feasible frontier, marginal rate of substitution.

The marginal rate of transformation (MRT): Trade-offs in what is feasible

Another way to express the same idea is to say that the feasible frontier shows the **marginal rate of transformation (MRT)**—the rate at which Alexei can transform free time into grade points. Look at the slope of the frontier between points A and E in Figure 4.11.

- *The slope of AE:* This is the vertical distance from A to E divided by horizontal distance from A to E. It is −3.
- *At point A:* Alexei could get 1 more unit of free time by giving up 3 grade points. The opportunity cost of a unit of free time is 3.
- *At point E:* Alexei could transform 1 unit of time into 3 grade points. The marginal rate at which he can transform free time into grade points is 3.

Note that the slope of AE is only an approximation to the slope of the frontier. More precisely, the slope at any point is the slope of the line that just touches the frontier, and this represents both the MRT and the opportunity cost at that point.

The two trade-offs

Note that we have now identified two trade-offs:

- *The marginal rate of substitution (MRS) is about a person's objectives:* In the previous section, we saw that the MRS measures the trade-off that Alexei is *willing* to make between exam grade and free time. The MRS is the slope of an indifference curve, which is almost always blue in the figures.
- *The marginal rate of transformation (MRT) is about the constraints a person faces:* In contrast to the MRS, the MRT measures the trade-off that Alexei is *constrained* to make by the feasible frontier. The MRT is the slope of the feasible frontier which is almost always red in the figures.

As we shall see in the next section, the choice Alexei makes between his grade and his free time will strike a balance between these two trade-offs.

> **QUESTION 4.9 CHOOSE THE CORRECT ANSWER(S)**
> Figure 4.11 shows Alexei's production function, which describes how his final grade (the output) depends on the number of hours spent studying (the input). Free time per day is given by 24 hours minus the number of hours of study. Based on this information and the figure, which of the following statements is true?
>
> ☐ To find the feasible set, one needs to know the number of hours that Alexei sleeps per day.
> ☐ The feasible frontier is a mirror image of the production function.
> ☐ If the production function is horizontal after 15 hours of study per day, the feasible frontier is horizontal between 0 and 10 hours of free time per day.
> ☐ The marginal product at 10 hours of study equals the marginal rate of transformation at 14 hours of free time.

> **QUESTION 4.10 CHOOSE THE CORRECT ANSWER(S)**
> Consider a student whose final grade increases with the number of hours spent studying. Her choice is between more free time and higher grades, both of which are 'goods'. Which of the following are the same as her marginal rate of transformation between the two goods?
>
> ☐ the opportunity cost of free time
> ☐ the number of percentage points the student would gain by giving up another hour of free time
> ☐ the slope of the student's feasible frontier
> ☐ the number of percentage points the student would lose by taking another hour of free time

4.7 DECISION MAKING AND SCARCITY

The final step in this decision-making process is to determine the combination of final grade and free time that Alexei will choose. Figure 4.12a brings together his feasible frontier (Figure 4.11) and indifference curves (Figure 4.9 (page 155)). Recall that the indifference curves indicate what Alexei prefers, and their slopes show the trade-offs that he is willing to make; the feasible frontier is the constraint on his choice, and its slope shows the trade-off he is constrained to make.

Figure 4.12a shows four indifference curves, labelled IC_1 to IC_4. IC_4 represents the highest level of utility because it is the furthest away from the origin. No combination of grade and free time on IC_4 is feasible, however, because the whole indifference curve lies outside the feasible set. Suppose that Alexei considers choosing a combination somewhere in the feasible set, on IC_1. By looking at the analysis of Figure 4.12a, you will see that he can increase his utility by moving to points on higher indifference curves until he reaches a feasible choice that maximizes his utility.

Alexei maximizes his utility at point E, at which the slope of his indifference curve is equal to the slope of the feasible frontier. The model predicts that Alexei will:

- choose to spend 5 hours each day studying, and 19 hours on other activities
- obtain a grade of 57 as a result.

We can see from Figure 4.12a that at E, the feasible frontier and the highest attainable indifference curve IC_3 touch but do not cross. At E, the slope of the indifference curve is the same as the slope of the feasible frontier. Remember that the slopes represent the two trade-offs facing Alexei:

- *The slope of the indifference curve is the MRS*: It is the trade-off he is willing to make between free time and percentage points.
- *The slope of the frontier is the MRT*: It is the trade-off he is constrained to make between free time and percentage points because it is not possible to go beyond the feasible frontier.

Alexei achieves the highest possible utility where the two trade-offs just balance (E). His best combination of grade and free time is at the point where the marginal rate of transformation is equal to the marginal rate of substitution.

4 WORK, WELLBEING, AND SCARCITY

constrained choice problem This problem is about how we can do the best for ourselves, given our preferences and constraints, and when the things we value are scarce. *See also: constrained optimization problem.*

Figure 4.12b lists the MRS (slope of indifference curve) and MRT (slope of feasible frontier) at the points shown in Figure 4.12a. At B and D, the number of points Alexei is willing to trade for an hour of free time (MRS) is greater than the opportunity cost of that hour (MRT), so he prefers to increase his free time. At A, the MRT is greater than the MRS so he prefers to decrease his free time. And, as expected, at E the MRS and MRT are equal.

We have modelled the student's decision of study hours as what we call a **constrained choice problem**—a decision-maker (Alexei) pursues an objective (utility maximization in this case) subject to a constraint (his feasible frontier).

To explore all of the slides in this figure, see the online version at https://tinyco.re/1689095.

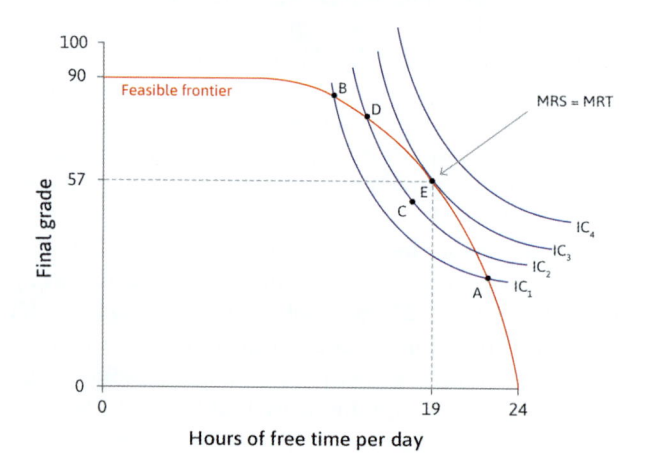

Figure 4.12a How many hours does Alexei decide to study?

1. Indifference curves and the feasible frontier
The diagram brings together Alexei's indifference curves and his feasible frontier.

2. Feasible combinations
On the indifference curve IC$_1$, all combinations between A and B are feasible because they lie in the feasible set. Suppose Alexei chooses one of these points.

3. Could do better
All combinations in the lens-shaped area between IC$_1$ and the feasible frontier are feasible, and give higher utility than combinations on IC$_1$. For example, a movement to C would increase Alexei's utility.

4. Could do better
Moving from IC$_1$ to point C on IC$_2$ increases Alexei's utility. Switching from B to D would raise his utility by an equivalent amount.

5. The best feasible trade-off
Alexei can raise his utility by moving into the lens-shaped area above IC$_2$. He can continue to find feasible combinations on higher indifference curves, until he reaches E.

6. The best feasible trade-off
At E, he has 19 hours of free time per day and a grade of 57. Alexei maximizes his utility—he is on the highest indifference curve obtainable, given the feasible frontier.

7. MRS = MRT
At E, the two curves touch but do not cross. The marginal rate of substitution (the slope of the indifference curve) is equal to the marginal rate of transformation (the slope of the frontier).

In our example, both free time and points in the exam are scarce for Alexei because:

- *Free time and grades are goods:* Alexei values both of them.
- *Each has an opportunity cost:* More of one good means less of the other.

In constrained choice problems, the solution is the individual's best choice. If we assume that utility maximization is Alexei's goal, the best combination of grade and free time is a point on the feasible frontier at which:

$$MRS = MRT$$

The table in Figure 4.13 summarizes Alexei's trade-offs.

> **EXERCISE 4.7 EXPLORING SCARCITY**
> In our model of decision making, grade points and free time are scarce. Describe a situation in which Alexei's grade points and free time would not be scarce. Remember, scarcity depends on both his preferences and the production function.

	B	D	E	A
Free time	13	15	19	22
Grade	84	78	57	33
MRT	2	4	7	9
MRS	20	15	7	3

Figure 4.12b How many hours does Alexei decide to study?

	The trade-off	Represented as	Equal to
MRS	Marginal rate of substitution: The number of percentage points Alexei is willing to trade for an hour of free time	The slope of the indifference curve	
MRT, or opportunity cost of free time	Marginal rate of transformation: The number of percentage points Alexei would gain (or lose) by giving up (or taking) another hour of free time	The slope of the feasible frontier	The marginal product of labour

Figure 4.13 Alexei's trade-offs.

> **QUESTION 4.11 CHOOSE THE CORRECT ANSWER(S)**
> Figure 4.12a shows Alexei's feasible frontier and his indifference curves for final exam grade and hours of free time per day. Suppose that all students have the same feasible frontier, but their indifference curves may differ in shape and slope depending on their preferences.
>
> Use the diagram to decide which of the following statements are true.
>
> ☐ Alexei will choose a point where the marginal rate of substitution equals the marginal rate of transformation.
> ☐ C is below the feasible frontier, but D is on the feasible frontier. Therefore, Alexei may select point D as his best choice.
> ☐ All students with downward-sloping indifference curves, whatever the slope, would choose point E.
> ☐ At E, Alexei has the highest feasible ratio of final exam mark per hour of free time per day.

4.8 HOURS OF WORK AND ECONOMIC GROWTH

New technologies raise the output produced per hour of labour. This is called the **average product** or labour productivity. We now have the tools to analyse the effects of increased productivity on living standards, specifically on incomes and free time.

A farmer's production function

So far, we have considered Alexei's choice between studying and free time. We now apply our model of constrained choice to Angela, a self-sufficient farmer who chooses how many hours to work. We assume that Angela produces grain to eat and does not sell it to anyone else. If she produces too little grain, she will starve.

What is stopping her producing more than enough grain? Like the student, Angela also values free time—she gets utility from both free time and consuming grain.

As a result, her choice is constrained. Producing grain takes labour time, and each hour of labour means Angela foregoes an hour of free time. The hour of free time sacrificed is the opportunity cost of the grain produced. Like Alexei, Angela faces a problem of scarcity. She has to make a choice between her consumption of grain and her consumption of free time.

Technological progress

To understand her choice and how it is affected by **technological progress** (as in Unit 1 (page 20)), we need to model her production function and her preferences.

Figure 4.14 shows the initial production function before the change occurs, which is the relationship between the number of hours worked and the amount of grain produced. Notice that the graph has a similar concave shape to Alexei's production function. The marginal product of an additional hour's work, shown by the slope, diminishes as the number of hours increases.

A technological improvement—such as seeds with a higher yield, or better equipment that makes harvesting quicker—will increase the amount of grain produced in a given number of hours. The analysis in Figure 4.14 demonstrates the effect on the production function.

---

average product Total output divided by a particular input, for example per worker (divided by the number of workers) or per worker per hour (total output divided by the total number of hours of labour put in).

technological progress A change in technology that reduces the amount of resources (labour, machines, land, energy, time) required to produce a given amount of the output.

4.8 HOURS OF WORK AND ECONOMIC GROWTH

Notice that the new production function is steeper than the original one for every given number of hours. The new technology has increased Angela's marginal product of labour. At every point, an additional hour of work produces more grain than under the old technology.

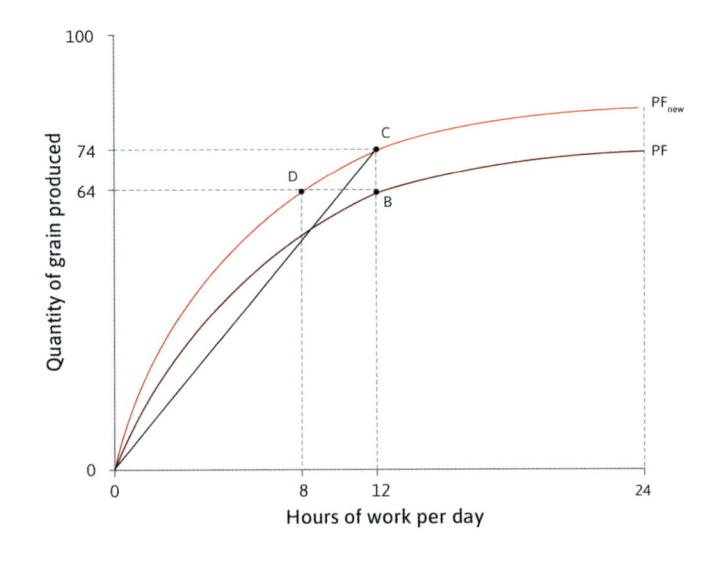

To explore all of the slides in this figure, see the online version at https://tinyco.re/9284679.

Working hours	0	1	2	3	4	5	6	7	8	9	10	11	12	13	18	24
Grain	0	9	18	26	33	40	46	51	55	58	60	62	64	66	69	72

Figure 4.14 How technological change affects the production function.

1. The initial technology
The table shows how the amount of grain produced depends on the number of hours worked per day. For example, if Angela works for 12 hours a day, she will produce 64 units of grain. This is point B on the graph.

2. A technological improvement
An improvement in technology means that more grain is produced for a given number of working hours. The production function shifts upward, from PF to PF$_{new}$.

3. More grain for the same amount of work
If Angela works for 12 hours per day, she can produce 74 units of grain (point C).

4. Same amount of grain, less work
Alternatively, by working 8 hours a day, she can produce 64 units of grain (point D), which previously took 12 hours.

5. The average product of labour
The average product at a particular point is the slope of the ray from that point to the origin. For example, at point B, Angela's average product is 64/12 = 5.33 units per hour.

6. Technological improvement raises the average product
After technological improvement, Angela's average product from working the same number of hours is now 74/12 = 6.17 units per hour.

165

> **QUESTION 4.12 CHOOSE THE CORRECT ANSWER(S)**
> Based on Figure 4.14, which of the following statements about marginal and average product are true?
>
> ☐ The marginal product and average product are approximately the same for the initial hour.
> ☐ For 2 hours of work, the average product is less than the marginal product.
> ☐ The average product is the same for 11 and 12 hours of work.
> ☐ Both the average product and marginal product are diminishing.

From the production function to the feasible frontier

Figure 4.15 shows Angela's feasible frontier, which is just the mirror image of the production function, for the original technology (FF), and the new one (FF$_{new}$).

As before, what we call free time is all the time that is not spent working to produce grain—it includes time for eating, sleeping, and everything else that we don't count as farm work, as well as her leisure time. The feasible frontier shows how much grain can be consumed for each possible amount of free time. Points B, C, and D represent the same combinations of free time and grain as in Figure 4.14. The slope of the frontier represents the MRT (the marginal rate at which free time can be transformed into grain) or, equivalently, the opportunity cost of free time. You can see that technological progress expands the feasible set, giving her a wider choice of combinations of grain and free time.

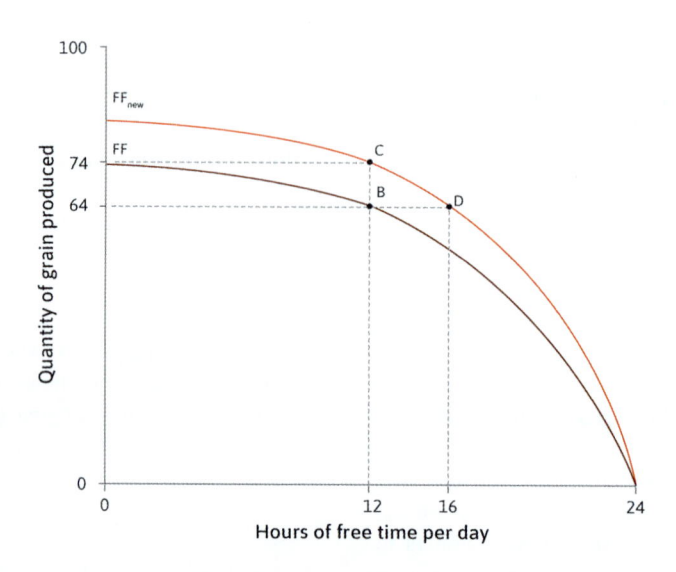

Figure 4.15 An improvement in technology expands Angela's feasible set.

4.8 HOURS OF WORK AND ECONOMIC GROWTH

The two trade-offs again

Now we add Angela's indifference curves to the diagram, representing her preferences for free time and grain consumption, in order to find which combination in the feasible set is best for her. Figure 4.16 shows that her best choice under the original technology is to work for 8 hours a day, giving her 16 hours of free time and 55 units of grain. This is the point of **tangency**, where her two trade-offs balance out—her marginal rate of substitution (MRS) between grain and free time (the slope of the indifference curve) is equal to the MRT (the slope of the feasible frontier). We can think of the combination of free time and grain at point A as a measure of her standard of living.

Follow the analysis of Figure 4.16 to see how her choice changes as a result of technological progress.

Technological change raises Angela's standard of living—it enables her to achieve higher utility. Note that in Figure 4.16, she increases both her consumption of grain and her free time.

> **tangency** When a line touches a curve, but does not cross it.

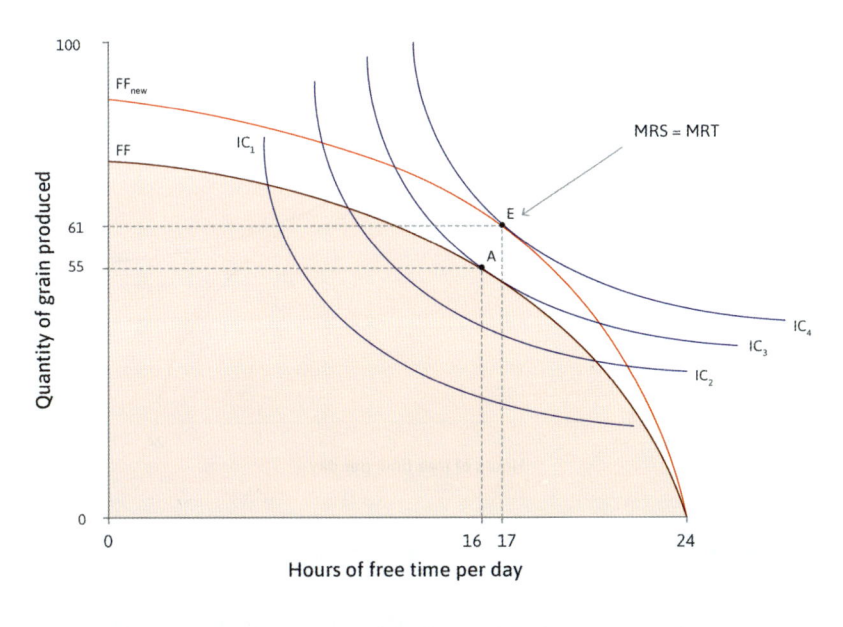

To explore all of the slides in this figure, see the online version at https://tinyco.re/8764909.

Figure 4.16 Angela's choice between free time and grain.

1. Maximizing utility with the original technology
The diagram shows the feasible set with the original production function and Angela's indifference curves for combinations of grain and free time. The highest indifference curve she can attain is IC₃ at point A.

2. Her best choice is point A on the feasible frontier
She enjoys 16 hours of free time per day and consumes 55 units of grain. At A, her MRS is equal to the MRT.

3. Technological progress
An improvement in technology expands the feasible set. Now she can do better than at A.

4. Angela's new best choice
When the technology of farming has improved, Angela's best choice is point E, where FF_new just touches indifference curve IC₄. She has more free time and more grain than before.

167

It is important to realize that this is just one possible result. Had we drawn the indifference curves differently, Angela's trade-offs would have been different. We can say that the improvement in technology definitely makes it feasible to both consume more grain and have more free time, but whether Angela will choose to have more of both depends on her preferences between these two goods, and her willingness to substitute one for the other.

To understand why, remember that technological change makes the production function steeper—it increases Angela's marginal product of labour. This means that the opportunity cost of free time is higher, giving her a greater incentive to work. But also, now that she can have more grain for each hour of free time, she may be more willing to give up some grain for more free time—that is, to reduce her hours of work.

These two effects of technological progress work in opposite directions. In Figure 4.16, the second effect dominates and she chooses point E, with more free time as well as more grain.

EXERCISE 4.8 YOUR PRODUCTION FUNCTION

Think back to the constrained choice problem of final grade and study hours.

1. What could bring about a technological improvement in your and your fellow students' production functions?
2. Draw a diagram to illustrate how this improvement would affect your feasible set of grades and study hours.
3. Analyse what might happen to your choice of study hours, and the choices that you might make.

QUESTION 4.13 CHOOSE THE CORRECT ANSWER(S)

The following diagram shows a farmer's choice between free time and grain before and after an improvement in technology.

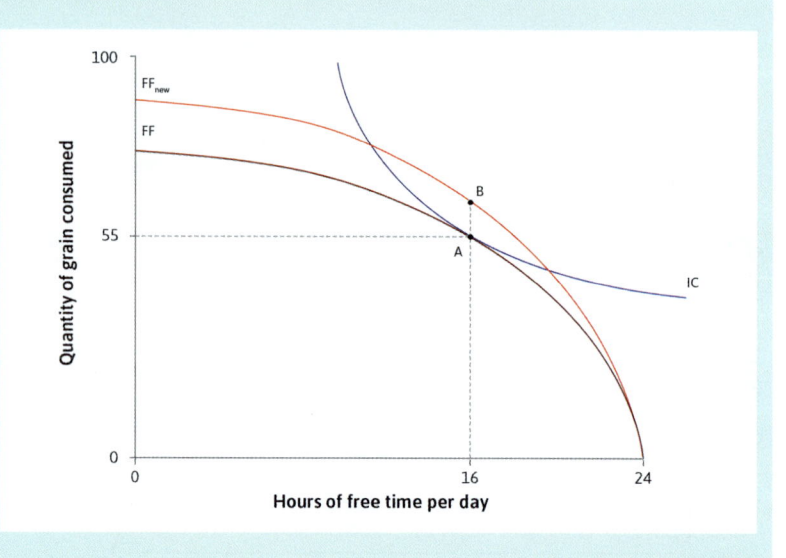

Figure 4.17 A farmer's choice between free time and grain.

Based on this information, which of the following statements are correct?

☐ If the MRS of the indifference curve at B is larger than the MRS of the indifference curve at A, then the farmer will have an incentive to take more free time after the technology improvement.
☐ The MRT of the new feasible frontier at B is larger than the MRT of the old feasible frontier at A. This gives the farmer an incentive to take more free time after the technology improvement.
☐ The farmer may choose a point to the left of B after the technology improvement.
☐ The farmer may choose a point to the right of B after the technology improvement.

4.9 APPLYING THE MODEL: EXPLAINING CHANGES IN WORKING HOURS

We can apply the model to help us understand how the technological change and rising incomes described in Unit 1 (page 22) affected the trade-off faced by workers. Higher wages meant it was possible to have both higher consumption and more free time. And, like Angela, workers wanted more of both. In economics, the term **normal good** is used when more of something is demanded as income rises. Using this definition, both consumption and free time are normal goods. (A good whose consumption falls when income rises, like an inexpensive but not very tasty source of carbohydrates, is called an **inferior good**.)

We use the idea of the two effects of technological progress on Angela's choice of free time to explore what has happened to working hours over the past 250 years.

When technological progress flows through to higher hourly wages, there are two effects:

- *Income effect* (of higher hourly wages): The higher income from every hour of work has made workers better off. This is called the **income effect**—since free time is a normal good, the income effect means that workers want to have more hours of free time (as well as more consumption).
- *Substitution effect* (of higher hourly wages): The higher reward from working an extra hour has increased the incentive to work. This is called the **substitution effect**—it has the effect of reducing hours of free time as workers *substitute* away from free time towards what is now higher-paying work.

> **normal good** A good for which demand increases when a person's income rises, holding prices unchanged.
> **inferior good** A good whose consumption decreases when income increases (holding prices constant).
> **income effect** The effect, for example, on the choice of consumption of a good that a change in income would have if there were no change in the price or opportunity cost.
> **substitution effect** The effect for example, on the choice of consumption of a good that is only due to changes in the price or opportunity cost, given the new level of utility.

Before 1870
Let's consider first the period before 1870 in Britain, when wages increased due to technological progress, and working hours rose.

- *Income effect:* At this time, there was a relatively low level of consumption. The income effect resulting in the choice of more free time was small.
- *Substitution effect:* Workers were paid more, so each hour of work brought more rewards than before in the form of goods, increasing the incentive to work longer hours. The substitution effect resulting in the choice of less free time was large.
- *The substitution effect dominated:* Work hours rose, which can be interpreted as saying that the substitution effect (free time falls) was bigger than the income effect (free time rises).

During the twentieth century
During the twentieth century, we saw rising wages but falling working hours. Using the same concepts, we can account for this change as follows:

To see how to use a diagram to represent the income and substitution effects, see Section 3.7 of *The Economy* (https://tinyco.re/1035741).

- *Income effect:* By the late nineteenth century, workers had a higher level of consumption and valued free time relatively more, so the income effect of a wage increase was larger.
- *Substitution effect:* This increased the incentive to work longer hours.
- *The income effect dominated:* When the income effect began to outweigh the substitution effect, working time fell.

4 WORK, WELLBEING, AND SCARCITY

Robert William Fogel. 2000. *The Fourth Great Awakening and the Future of Egalitarianism: The Political Realignment of the 1990s and the Fate of Egalitarianism.* Chicago: University of Chicago Press.

The future
What about the future?

The high-income economies will continue to experience a major transformation—the declining role of work in the course of our lifetimes. We start working at a later age, stop working at an earlier age, and spend fewer hours at work during our working years. Robert Fogel, an economic historian, estimated the total working time in the past, including travel to and from work and unpaid work at home, which economists call 'home production'. He made projections for the year 2040, defining what he called 'discretionary time' in a day as 24 hours minus the amount we all need for biological maintenance (sleeping, eating, and personal hygiene). Fogel calculated leisure time as discretionary time minus working time.

Fogel estimated that, in 1880, lifetime leisure time was just a quarter of lifetime work hours. In 1995, lifetime leisure time exceeded lifetime working time. He predicted that lifetime leisure would be three times lifetime working hours by the year 2040. His estimates are shown in Figure 4.18.

It is possible that Fogel overstated the future decline in working time, as Keynes once did. But he raises the challenging possibility that one of the great changes brought about by the technological revolution could be a vastly reduced role of work in the life of an average person.

QUESTION 4.14 CHOOSE THE CORRECT ANSWER(S)

In the period before 1870 in Britain, both wages and hours worked rose, while in the twentieth century, working hours fell even though wages continued to rise. Based on this information, which of the following statements are correct?

☐ The marginal rate of transformation between consumption and free time rose from the pre-1870s to the twentieth century.
☐ In the period before 1870, the substitution and income effects of rising wages led to workers taking less free time.
☐ From the pre-1870s to the twentieth century, the substitution effect of a rise in the wage rate on the hours of free time changed from negative (less free time) to positive (more free time).
☐ In the twentieth century, the substitution effect dominated the income effect, so that hours of free time rose.

Robert William Fogel. 2000. *The Fourth Great Awakening and the Future of Egalitarianism. The Political Realignment of the 1990s and the Fate of Egalitarianism.* Chicago: University of Chicago Press.

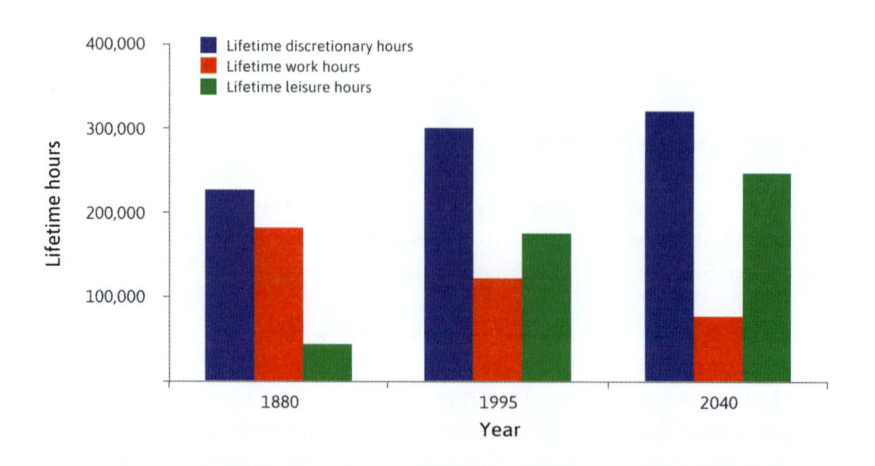

Figure 4.18 Estimated lifetime hours of work and leisure (1880, 1995, 2040).

4.10 APPLYING THE MODEL: EXPLAINING DIFFERENCES BETWEEN COUNTRIES

Figure 4.3 (page 143) showed that, in countries with higher income (real GDP per capita), workers tend to have more free time; it also showed that there are big differences in annual hours of free time between countries with similar income levels. The table in Figure 4.19 shows our calculations of the disposable income of an average employee per hour worked, his or her free time per day, and the maximum amount that could be consumed per day. The figures are shown for five countries.

Brian Burgoon and Phineas Baxandall explore the differences between the average hours that people spend at work in different developed countries and argue that cultural and economic differences have created three different 'worlds' in this paper: Brian Burgoon and Phineas Baxandall. 2004. 'Three Worlds of Working Time: The Partisan and Welfare Politics of Work Hours in Industrialized Countries.' *Politics & Society* 32 (4): 439–73.

From the data in Figure 4.19, we see that average free time in Mexico and South Korea was virtually the same, although the wage was much higher in South Korea than in Mexico. People from the Netherlands and the US have about as much to spend per day, but the Dutch have around one hour less of free time.

Could it be that South Koreans have the same preferences as Americans, so that, if the wage increased in South Korea, they would make the same choice? This seems unlikely—the substitution effect would lead them to consume more goods and take less free time; it is implausible to suppose that the income effect of a wage increase would lead them to consume fewer goods. More plausible is the hypothesis that South Koreans and Americans (on average) have different preferences.

In particular, the idea that South Koreans work exceptionally hard is consistent with the hypothesis that the average American is willing to give up more units of daily goods for an hour of free time than the average South Korean.

Country	Wage (disposable income per hour worked)	Free time per day	The most that could be consumed per day
US	34.02	19.12	165.91
South Korea	17.39	18.45	96.41
Netherlands	36.90	20.07	144.87
Turkey	9.23	18.92	46.90
Mexico	6.79	17.82	41.96

OECD. Average annual hours actually worked per worker (https://tinyco.re/6892498). Accessed June 2016. Net income after taxes calculated in US dollars using PPP exchange rates.

Figure 4.19 Free time and consumption per day across countries (2013).

4.11 IS THIS A GOOD MODEL? DOES IT MATTER THAT PEOPLE (MOSTLY) DO NOT REALLY OPTIMIZE?

We have looked at three different contexts in which people decide how long to spend working—a student (Alexei), a farmer (Angela), and wage earners in different countries and periods. We have used a model of preferences and feasible sets in which their best (utility-maximizing) choice is the level of working hours at which the slope of the feasible frontier is equal to the slope of the indifference curve.

You may have been thinking that this is not what people do in real life!

Billions of people organize their working lives without knowing anything about MRS and MRT (if they did make decisions that way, perhaps we would have to subtract the hours they would spend making calculations). And even if they did make their choice using mathematics, most of us can't just leave work whenever we want to. So how can this model be useful?

Remember that models help us 'see more by looking at less'. Lack of realism is an intentional feature of any model.

Is it possible that a model that ignores how we think is a good model of how we choose?

Milton Friedman, an economist, explained that, when economists use models in this way, they do not claim that we actually think through these calculations (such as equating MRS to MRT) each time we make a decision. Instead, we each try various choices (sometimes not even intentionally) and we tend to adopt habits, or rules of thumb, that make us feel satisfied and not regret our decisions.

In his book, *Essays in Positive Economics,* Friedman described this as similar to playing billiards (pool):

> Consider the problem of predicting the shots made by an expert billiard player. It seems not at all unreasonable that excellent predictions would be yielded by the hypothesis that the billiard player made his shots as if he knew the complicated mathematical formulas that would give the optimum directions of travel, could estimate accurately by eye the angles, etc., describing the location of the balls, could make lightning calculations from the formulas, and could then make the balls travel in the direction indicated by the formulas.
>
> Our confidence in this hypothesis is not based on the belief that billiard players, even expert ones, can or do go through the process described. It derives rather from the belief that, unless in some way or other they were capable of reaching essentially the same result, they would not in fact be expert billiard players.

Milton Friedman. 1953. *Essays in Positive Economics.* (7th ed.) Chicago: University of Chicago Press.

Similarly, if we see a person regularly choosing to go to the library after lectures instead of going out, or not putting in much work on their farm, or asking for longer shifts after a pay rise, we do not need to suppose that this person has done the calculations we set out. If that person later regretted the choice, next time they might go out a bit more, work harder on the farm, or cut their hours back. Eventually, we could speculate they might end up with a decision on work time that is close to the result of our calculations.

This is why economic theory can help to explain—and sometimes even predict—what people do, even though those people are not performing the mathematical calculations that economists make in their models.

4.12 EXTENDING THE MODEL: THE INFLUENCE OF CULTURE AND POLITICS

A second unrealistic aspect of the model is that usually employers (and not individual workers) choose working hours, and employers often impose a longer working day than workers prefer. As a result, the hours that many people work are regulated by law, so that neither the employee nor the employer can choose to work beyond the maximum amount. In this case, the government has limited the feasible set of hours and goods.

- Cultures differ. Some northern European peoples highly value their vacation times, while South Korea is famous for the long hours that employees put in.
- Legal limits on working time differ. In Belgium and France, the normal work week is limited to 35–39 hours, while in Mexico the limit is 48 hours, and in Kenya even longer.

This explanation stresses culture (meaning changes in preferences or differences in preferences among countries) and politics (meaning differences in laws, or trade union strength and objectives). Culture and politics certainly help to explain differences in working hours between countries.

Employers have an incentive to take account of these differences. For example, employers who advertise jobs with the working hours that most people prefer may find they have more applicants than other employers offering too many (or too few) hours.

Remember, we also judge the quality of a model by whether it provides insight into something that we want to understand. You can make a judgement as to whether our model of the choice of hours of work helps us understand why working hours differ so much between countries and why they have changed over time.

EXERCISE 4.9 ANOTHER DEFINITION OF ECONOMICS

Lionel Robbins, an economist, wrote in 1932 that 'Economics is the science that studies human behaviour as a relationship between given ends and scarce means which have alternative uses'.

1. Give an example from this unit to illustrate the way that economics studies human behaviour as a relationship between 'given ends and scarce means with alternative uses'.
2. Are the 'ends' of economic activity—that is, the things we desire—fixed? Use examples from this unit (study time and grades, or working time and consumption) to illustrate your answer.
3. The subject matter that Robbins refers to—doing the best you can in a given situation—is an essential part of economics. But is economics limited to the study of 'scarce means which have alternative uses'? In answering this question, include a contrast between Robbins' definition of economics and the one given in Section 2.14 (page 90). Note that Robbins wrote this passage at a time when 15% of the British workforce was unemployed.

Lionel Robbins. (1932) 1984. *An Essay on the Nature and Significance of Economic Science* (https://tinyco.re/4615466). (3rd ed.) New York: New York University Press.

4.13 EXTENDING THE MODEL: WOMEN, MEN, AND THE GENDER DIVISION OF LABOUR

A good model is like a structure made of LEGO: we can build on it, or take bits out and replace them by others without starting again. One way to build on the model of the choice of working hours is to consider differences between men and women. The trade-offs on which the model is based will look different, especially if we consider men and women who live in a household with children.

Most important we need to ask what we really mean by 'free time'. When we introduced the term, we explained it was about how Alexei 'values his free time—he likes to sleep, go out or watch TV'.

But suppose we want to understand the work choices of Alexa, not Alexei. Alexa is a mother of two children under the age of five, and is cohabiting with the children's father. For Alexa, the time that she is not working outside the home is hardly 'free,' because she lives in a society which is bound by a social norm that the mother is responsible for most of the childcare and home production.

The ways men and women differ in how they spend their work time is known as the **gender division of labour**. The greater importance of home production in a woman's day is an almost universal aspect of the gender division of labour in modern societies, though this differs markedly across nations and age groups.

So, let's divide Alexa's 24-hour day into three parts: working outside the home, home production, and free time. Alexei, too, may spend some time on home production.

As in the model of how much time to study, or to cultivate grain, Alexa and Alexei each face a trade-off. Each now has three objectives: more goods that can be purchased with the wages gained by working for pay, a cleaner house and better care for children, and more free time. In each case, achieving more of one objective implies getting less of the other objective. In other words, the opportunity cost of more time with the kids is either less free time, lower earnings to purchase goods, or both.

How could the choice of working hours model be extended to take account of the gender division of labour? Three important aspects of the problem missing from the model so far are:

- *Social norms*: These will have an important bearing on the choice of hours spent in unpaid work. If home production and childcare are considered to be 'women's work' this will affect the preferences of both men and women about doing that work.
- *Strategic interaction and joint decision making:* Both may be important. Whether cooperatively or in conflict, men and women raising children together will be aware that their wellbeing depends not only on their own choices, but also the choices of their partner. Understanding their decisions might require that we represent their interaction as a game (as in Unit 2 (page 55)) rather than as a single individual deciding how many hours to study or to produce grain.
- *Gender inequality in pay*: In most countries this will mean Alexa's opportunity cost of spending more time doing unpaid work in the home, and working less outside the home, is less than Alexei's—because her pay would be less than his.

> **gender division of labour** The ways men and women differ in how they spend their work time.

Figure 4.20 shows the amount of unpaid care work done by men and women in households with no children and with children under five. In all three countries, women spend more time in unpaid care work than men in households without children, and women's unpaid work rises by more in households with young children.

There are interesting differences across countries though. In Finland, with the lowest gap in pay between men and women, unpaid care work is shared more equally than in the other two countries. With young children, unpaid care work goes up in all three countries. The difference made by children is greatest in Finland—comparing the three countries, Finnish men and women spend the fewest minutes in unpaid care in households without children and the most when there are young children. Belgium is at the other extreme. Children are associated with only a modest increase in unpaid care time by women, and almost no extra time on the part of men.

Generous maternity and paternity leave in Finland (https://tinyco.re/5699313) help account for the increase in time spent in unpaid care work in households with young children. By contrast, in Belgium, the early age at which almost all children are in childcare outside the home (30 months) helps account for the lower amount of time spent in unpaid care work by both men and women than in Finland.

Among high income countries, the US is one of the least generous in terms of parental leave and provision of subsidized or free childcare places. Women frequently continue to work full time, adding a second shift of childcare in the home (https://tinyco.re/8376688).

Calculated from International Labour Office. 2018. *Care work and care jobs for the future of decent work* (https://tinyco.re/1154625). Geneva: ILO: pp. 67. Note: Latest year of available data is 2013 for Belgium, 2009 for Finland, and 2016 for the US.

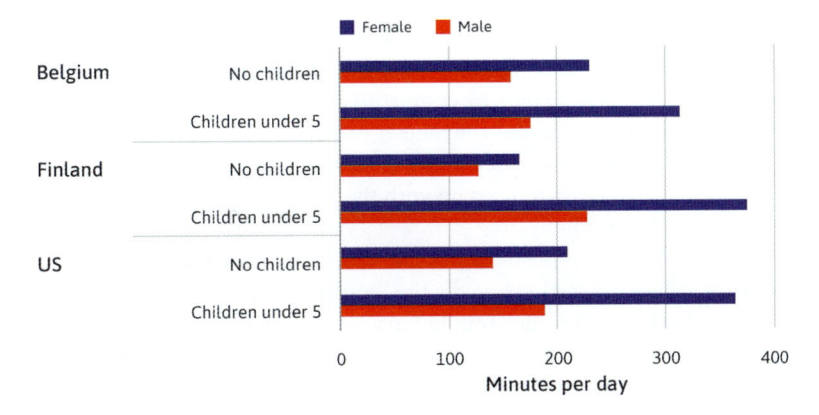

Figure 4.20 Total time spent doing unpaid care work by men and women in Belgium, Finland and the US (latest year of available data).

4.14 WORK AND WELLBEING AS A SOCIAL DILEMMA

We can also use the model to study questions of public policy concerning work, and the time we spend at work. One of the reasons a person may choose to work longer hours is to be able to show off their material success to others. Some goods—such as expensive cars, watches, and clothes—may be desired as status symbols. Their owners value these or other luxuries partly because ownership raises their status above that of other people.

Conspicuous consumption

Perhaps one of your motives when you buy a car, or a coat, is to demonstrate your wealth and superior style. Or perhaps you settle for a cheaper second-hand coat but feel envious, embarrassed, or disadvantaged at a job interview. Thorstein Veblen (1857–1929), an American economist and sociologist, described buying luxury items as a public display of social and economic status as **conspicuous consumption**. The process is more commonly described as 'keeping up with the Joneses'.

Veblen made an important point—when we work, buy, save, and engage in other economic activities, we are not only attempting to get things; we are also trying to be someone consistent with our own aspirations and the respect of others.

Expensive goods are a good way to communicate high income for the simple reason that poor people will not be able to compete on this terrain. The rich are the 'Joneses', whom people want to emulate.

Goods that are valued more because they are a symbol of status or income are an example of a larger class called **positional goods**. They are positional because they are based on status or power, which can be ranked as high or low. Our positions in this ranking, like the rungs of a ladder, may be higher or lower. But there is only a fixed amount of a positional good to go around. If Jo is on a higher rung of the ladder because of her new coat, somebody must now be on a lower rung.

Positional goods are sometimes called 'public bads'. Like public goods, they are 'available' to everyone—nobody in the neighbourhood can escape the fact that one of the neighbours is driving a BMW. But instead of a positive external effect on others, the effect is negative—envy.

To see how this leads to a social dilemma, consider the case of Sue Smith and her sister Jo Jones, each moving with their families to a new town. Each family has a choice between buying a luxury house or a more modest one. Their payoffs are represented in Figure 4.21. Since both families have limited funds, they would be better off if both bought modest houses than if both bought luxury ones, squeezing the rest of their budgets. But Sue is status-conscious and the two families are competitive when it comes to lifestyle. If the Smiths buy a modest house, the Joneses can benefit from feeling superior if they choose a luxury house. The Smiths, in turn, will feel miserable.

In short, Sue is trying to keep up with the Joneses, and Jo is trying to keep up with the Smiths.

You can see that this problem has the structure of a **prisoners' dilemma**. Whatever the Joneses do, the Smiths are better off with a luxury house. For both couples, choosing Luxury is a dominant strategy. They will achieve a payoff of 1 each, and the outcome is Pareto inefficient, because both would be better off if they each bought modest houses.

---

conspicuous consumption The purchase of goods or services to publicly display one's social and economic status.

positional good A good—such as high status, conspicuous consumption, or power—which, if enjoyed by one member of a community is experienced negatively by others. The more one person benefits from this good, the more others are harmed.

prisoners' dilemma A game in which the payoffs in the dominant strategy equilibrium are lower for each player, and also lower in total, than if neither player played the dominant strategy.

The root of this problem is the **external effect** that one family imposes on the other by choosing a luxury house. The price of the luxury house that Sue's family will buy does not include the positional externalities inflicted on her sister's family. If it did, Sue would not buy the luxury house, given the payoffs in the table.

What can they do to avoid the Pareto-inefficient outcome? We know from Unit 2 (page 76) that altruism would help, but Sue and Jo are more moved by sibling rivalry—these families are not altruistic about houses.

The 'keeping up with the Joneses' problem that Sue and Jo face arises because people care not only about what they have, but also about what they have *relative to* what other people have. This is sometimes called a **Veblen effect**.

> **external effect** When a person's action confers a benefit or cost on some other individual, and this effect is not taken account of by the person in deciding to take the action. It is external because it is not included in the decision-making process of the person taking the action. Positive effects refer to benefits, and negative effects to costs, that are experienced by others. A person breathing second-hand smoke from someone else's cigarette is a negative external effect. Enjoying your neighbour's beautiful garden is a positive external effect. Also known as: externality. See also: incomplete contract, market failure, external benefit, external cost.
>
> **Veblen effect** A negative external effect that arises from the consumption of a positional good. Examples include the negative external effects imposed on others by the consumption of luxury housing, clothing, or vehicles.

Taxing a positional good to address a social dilemma

The Nash equilibrium that is the outcome of this social dilemma will be that both families purchase a luxury house, when both would have been better off with more modest accommodation. If the only people trapped in the 'keeping up with the Joneses' dilemma were really sisters, we might expect them to contain their sibling rivalry sufficiently to agree that both would buy a modest house. But our story about the sisters is really a parable about entire communities, even on a global level; a face-to-face conversation, eye contact, and a handshake might have worked among sisters, but will not solve the problem.

		Joneses	
		Modest	Luxury
Smiths	Modest	2, 2	2.5, 0.5
	Luxury	0.5, 2.5	1, 1

Figure 4.21 Keeping up with the Joneses.

A government policymaker might devise a policy that would address the social dilemma, however. Recall from the previous unit that policies change outcomes by altering the Nash equilibrium of the relevant interaction. So, in this case, the policymaker would have to think of a way to make both families buying a modest home into a Nash equilibrium.

The policymaker could do this simply by passing a law prohibiting luxury housing. A more acceptable policy might be to impose a tax on luxury housing. You can see from the payoff matrix in Figure 4.21 that in order to make (Modest, Modest) a Nash equilibrium, a tax of just a little more than 0.5 on luxury housing would accomplish the objective. (This is similar to imposing a tax on placing additional cows on the pasture in the tragedy of the commons game in Section 3.8 (page 120).) Be sure that you understand what the new payoff matrix (with the tax) would look like, and why it would solve the social dilemma.

> **EXERCISE 4.10 TAX ON A POSITIONAL GOOD**
> Consider the situation in Figure 4.21.
>
> 1. Suppose the government imposed a tax of 0.6 on luxury housing. Draw the new (after-tax) payoff matrix and use game theory concepts to explain why this tax solves the social dilemma.
> 2. How large would the tax have to be in order to completely account for the Veblen effect? Draw the new payoff matrix (with this tax) and explain, with reference to external effects, why a tax of this size also solves the social dilemma.

Positional goods, inequality and the overwork rat race

Veblen effects can be especially important in economies in which 'the Joneses' are very rich, so that keeping up with them requires people to work long hours or to shift their expenditure away from necessities—like food consumed privately—and into conspicuous consumption.

Veblen effects help to explain two facts about modern economies:

- *People work longer hours in countries in which the very rich receive a larger fraction of the income:* Figure 4.22 shows some of the data for a large number of rich countries over the entire twentieth century. For example, the US has both higher hours of work and a higher income share of the very rich than Germany, France, Sweden, and the Netherlands. A century ago, American workers worked fewer hours than workers in all these countries. But over the past 100 years, the share of income going to the very rich declined in all these countries. Sweden, for example, went from one of the most unequal countries (by this measure) to one of the more equal. (For more on this topic, watch Juliet Schor's 'Economist in action' video (https://tinyco.re/8362335).)
- *As a nation gets richer, its citizens often do not become happier:* When an individual gets a wage increase or loses a job, there is a large effect on how happy that individual claims to be. But economists have also found that a change in our income has a much smaller effect if most of our acquaintances also got the same rise, or also lost their job. When an entire nation gets richer, the effect on individual happiness is small, if there is one at all.

Another reason that, as a nation gets richer, its citizens may not become happier is that people may become habituated to their recent standard of living, and so their happiness reverts back to previous levels if they do not keep becoming ever richer.

The situation in which nations become richer but their citizens become no happier—due either to the effects of income relativities or of habituation, or adaptation, as it is often known—is known as the 'Easterlin Paradox', in honour of the economist who made the argument in 1974.

Betsey Stevenson and Justin Wolfers, among other economists, produce alternative evidence that the link between happiness and higher incomes is not broken, even for the most developed countries.

When Veblen effects are present, the conspicuous consumption of the well off is a positional good, which has a negative external effect. If conspicuous consumption is experienced by everyone, reducing their satisfaction with their own situation, it is a public bad.

Richard A. Easterlin. 1974. 'Does economic growth improve the human lot?' (https://tinyco.re/7453951) In M Abramovitz, P David, and M Reder (Eds.). *Nations and Households in Economic Growth: Essays in Honor of Moses Abramovitz*. New York: Academic Press.

Betsey Stevenson and Justin Wolfers. 2008. 'Economic growth and subjective well-being: Reassessing the Easterlin paradox' (https://tinyco.re/7219387). *Brookings Papers on Economic Activity*: pp. 1–87.

Michael Huberman. 2004. 'Working hours of the world unite? New international evidence of worktime'. *Journal of Economic History* 64, 964–1001 and Andrew Leigh. 2007. 'How closely do top incomes shares track other measures of inequality?' *Economic Journal* 117, 619–33.

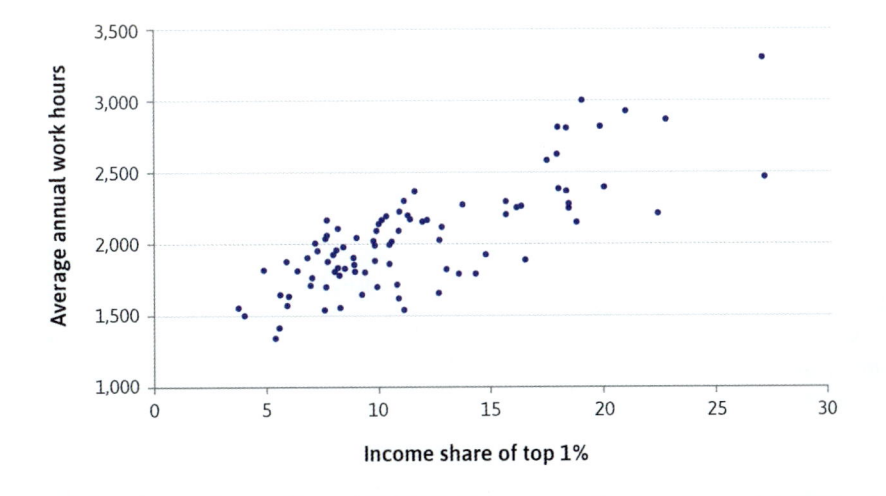

Figure 4.22 The relationship between average annual work hours and income share of the very rich (twentieth century).

EXERCISE 4.11 USING EXCEL: CORRELATION OR CAUSATION?

Figure 4.22 is a scatterplot of average annual work hours and income share of the top 1%, using data from 10 OECD countries. Download and save the spreadsheet (https://tinyco.re/4012073) containing the data for Figure 4.22.

1. Make a scatterplot similar to Figure 4.22, showing data for each country in a different colour. Follow the full walk-through in Figure 4.23 online (https://tinyco.re/7892481) on how to compile a scatterplot diagram in Excel. Are there any patterns you see for particular countries that are different from the overall pattern shown in Figure 4.22?

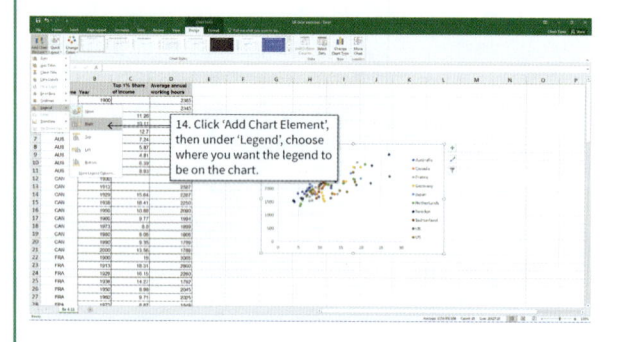

Figure 4.23 Making a colour-coded scatterplot.

1. The data
This is what the data looks like. Column A has country names, Column B has years, Column C has the percentage of total income earned by the top 1% in the population, and Column D has average annual working hours.

2. Draw a scatterplot with data for one country
After step 3, your scatter chart will look like the one shown above.

3. Add the other countries to the scatterplot
The scatterplot currently has data for Australia only. Now we will add the other countries to the scatterplot one by one, so they will each be shown in a different colour.

4. Add the other countries to the scatterplot
The section on the left lists all the data series currently plotted on the chart. We need to add the other countries as separate data series, so they will appear in different colours.

5. Add the other countries to the scatterplot
After step 8, the data for the country added will appear on the scatterplot in a different colour.

6. Add the other countries to the scatterplot
After completing step 9, your scatterplot will look like the one shown above, with each country represented by a different colour.

7. Add axis titles and a chart title
After step 13, your chart will look similar to Figure 4.22.

8. Add a chart legend
We will add a legend so it is easy to see which colour represents each country. You can see that the relationship between average annual working hours (vertical axis) and income share owned by the top 1% is positive for all countries, but clearer for some countries compared to others.

2. Calculate the correlation coefficient between average annual work hours and income share of the top 1%, using data from all countries. (Visit Doing Economics for a walk-through on how to calculate the correlation coefficient in Excel (https://tinyco.re/2327629).) What does this coefficient tell us about the strength of the association between these two variables?

3. Now calculate the correlation coefficient for each country separately. Which country has the highest correlation coefficient, and which country has the lowest? Suggest some explanations for why the relationship between income share and work hours differs in strength between countries.

4. In this unit, we presented one explanation for what we observe in Figure 4.22, namely that the conspicuous consumption of the top 1% may motivate people to work more ('keep up with the Joneses'). Can you think of an explanation for why higher average annual working hours would lead to a higher income share of the top 1%? What other factors could be responsible for the observed relationship? Based on your answers, discuss whether we can conclude from Figure 4.22 that a higher income share of the top 1% causes higher average annual work hours.

Changing preferences

When interpreting changes in working hours, we should also consider the possibility that preferences change over time. If you look carefully at Figure 4.1 (page 141), you can see that, in the last part of the twentieth century, hours of work rose in the US, even though wages hardly increased. Hours of work also rose in Sweden during this period.

Why? Perhaps Swedes and Americans came to value consumption more over these years. In other words, their preferences changed (in diagrammatic terms, this would be a flattening of the indifference curves.) This may have occurred because, in both the US and Sweden, the share of income gained by the very rich increased considerably and the lavish consumption habits of the rich set a higher standard for everyone else. According to this explanation, Swedes and Americans were 'keeping up with the Joneses' and the Joneses got richer, leading everyone else to change their preferences.

The combined political, cultural and economic influences on our choices may produce some surprising trends. In our 'Economist in action' video, Juliet Schor, a sociologist and economist who has written about the paradox that many of the world's wealthiest people are working more despite gains in technology, asks what this means for our quality of life, and for environment sustainability.

Juliet Schor: Why do we work so hard? https://tinyco.re/8362335

EXERCISE 4.12 VEBLEN EFFECTS AND POLICY
1. The example of Veblen effects above concerns houses. Can you think of any other examples where Veblen effects are present?
2. Why do Veblen effects cause inefficiency?
3. Describe in what way Veblen effects are similar to (or different from) pollution?
4. Discuss whether the government should adopt policies to address this market failure and, if so, what might they be?

QUESTION 4.15 CHOOSE THE CORRECT ANSWER(S)
Watch the 'Economist in action' video of Juliet Schor. Which of the following statements were *not* mentioned in the video?

☐ Technological advancement does not necessarily mean shorter working days.
☐ Workers can choose jobs but not their working hours.
☐ There has been a definite divergence recently in working hours across countries.
☐ Countries with longer working hours tend to have higher carbon footprints.

4.15 CONCLUSION

Technological improvements have enabled people to increase their consumption of goods and services and also to enjoy more free time. The extent to which higher wages have led to decreased working hours varies across time and between countries, reflecting the fact that **preferences** may change over time and that they are shaped by different cultural factors.

Using the key concept in economic modelling of *ceteris paribus*, we have built a **constrained choice** model to study an individual's choice between different combinations of consumption and free time.

Constraint: The feasible set	Preferences: Indifference curves
The **production function** translates inputs (like hours of work) into outputs (like grades or grain.) **Diminishing marginal product** means that, for each additional unit of input, the resulting increase in output becomes smaller. For some given level of input, the **marginal product** is the slope of the production function, while the **average product** is the slope of the ray from the origin to a given point on the production function.	**Indifference curves** join together all combinations of goods (like free time and consumption) that provide the same level of **utility**. Indifference curves are based on our **preferences**, that is on the benefit or cost that we associate with each possible outcome. To reflect the trade-off between two things that we value positively ('goods'), indifference curves slope downwards.
The **feasible frontier** gives the maximum amount of one good (grain) that can be obtained for a given amount of another (free time). The trade-off in what is feasible is represented by its slope, the **marginal rate of transformation (MRT)**. This shows the **opportunity cost** of, for example, increasing free time by one hour in terms of the grain the individual must forgo.	The trade-off between objectives is represented by the slope of an indifference curve and is called the **marginal rate of substitution (MRS)**, and it represents the trade-off between the two goods, namely, how much more of one good would be required to offset the subtraction of one unit of the other good.

Optimal choice: **MRT** = **MRS**

Technological progress can be modelled as an upward shift of the production function.

This expands the feasible set (in this case just the mirror image of the production function).

We have distinguished between two effects of a wage increase:

- *The substitution effect:* The amount by which leisure hours fall due to their higher opportunity cost in terms of foregone income.
- *The income effect:* The amount by which free time increases as a result of higher income, assuming that, like income, free time is a normal good.

Finally, we have considered how the **conspicuous consumption** of **positional goods** as a status symbol may lead to a Pareto-inefficient outcome in which one person's luxury consumption inflicts negative **external effects**, called **Veblen effects**, on others.

4.16 *DOING ECONOMICS:* MEASURING WELLBEING

In Unit 1 and in this unit, we have used real GDP per capita to compare living standards across countries or measure progress in living standards over time. The rationale is that higher income/expenditure means a greater ability to spend on goods and services, which in turn increases material wellbeing. Since material wellbeing can contribute to non-material wellbeing, we might also expect countries with higher real GDP per capita to have higher non-material wellbeing. But how do we measure non-material wellbeing? And does a higher real GDP per capita necessarily mean a higher non-material wellbeing?

In the *Doing Economics* Empirical Project 4 we answer these questions. The project shows how different variables can be summarized into an index by looking at real GDP and its components. We will then learn how indices of non-material wellbeing are constructed, and compare an index of material wellbeing (real GDP per capita) with an index of non-material wellbeing (the Human Development Index).

Go to *Doing Economics* Empirical Project 4 (https://tinyco.re/4523278) to work on this problem.

> *Learning objectives*
> In this project you will:
>
> - check datasets for missing data
> - generate new variables using cell formulae
> - sort data and assign ranks based on values
> - distinguish between time series and cross sectional data, and plot appropriate charts for each type of data
> - calculate the geometric mean and explain how it differs from the arithmetic mean
> - construct indices using the geometric mean, and use index values to rank observations
> - explain the difference between two measures of wellbeing (real GDP per capita and the Human Development Index)

4.17 REFERENCES

Easterlin, Richard. 1974. 'Does economic growth improve the human lot?' (https://tinyco.re/7453951) In M Abramovitz, P David & M Reder (Eds.), *Nations and Households in Economic Growth: Essays in Honor of Moses Abramovitz*. New York: Academic Press.

Fogel, Robert William. 2000. *The Fourth Great Awakening and the Future of Egalitarianism: The Political Realignment of the 1990s and the Fate of Egalitarianism*. Chicago: University of Chicago Press.

Friedman, Milton. 1953. *Essays in Positive Economics*. (7th ed.) Chicago: University of Chicago Press.

Harford, Tim. 2015. 'The rewards for working hard are too big for Keynes's vision' (https://tinyco.re/5829245). *The Undercover Economist*.

Huberman, Michael, and Chris Minns. 2004. 'The Times They Are Not Changin': Days and Hours of Work in Old and New Worlds, 1870–2000' (https://tinyco.re/2758271). *Explorations in Economic History* 44 (4): pp. 538–67.

Keynes, John Maynard. 1963. 'Economic Possibilities for our Grandchildren' (https://tinyco.re/8213530). In *Essays in Persuasion*. New York, NY: W. W. Norton & Co.

Leigh, Andrew. 2007. 'How closely do top incomes shares track other measures of inequality?' *Economic Journal* 117: pp. 619-33.

Plant, E. Ashby, Karl Anders Ericsson, Len Hill, and Kia Asberg. 2005. 'Why study time does not predict grade point average across college students: Implications of deliberate practice for academic performance' (https://tinyco.re/7875663). *Contemporary Educational Psychology* 30 (1): pp. 96–116.

Robbins, Lionel. (1932) 1984. *An Essay on the Nature and Significance of Economic Science* (https://tinyco.re/4615466). (3rd ed.) New York: New York University Press.

Stevenson, Betsey, and Justin Wolfers. 2008. 'Economic growth and subjective well-being: Reassessing the Easterlin paradox' (https://tinyco.re/7219387). Brookings Papers on Economic Activity: pp. 1–87.

Whaples, Robert. 2001. 'Hours of work in U.S. History' (https://tinyco.re/1660378). *EH.net Encyclopedia*.

5
INSTITUTIONS, POWER, AND INEQUALITY

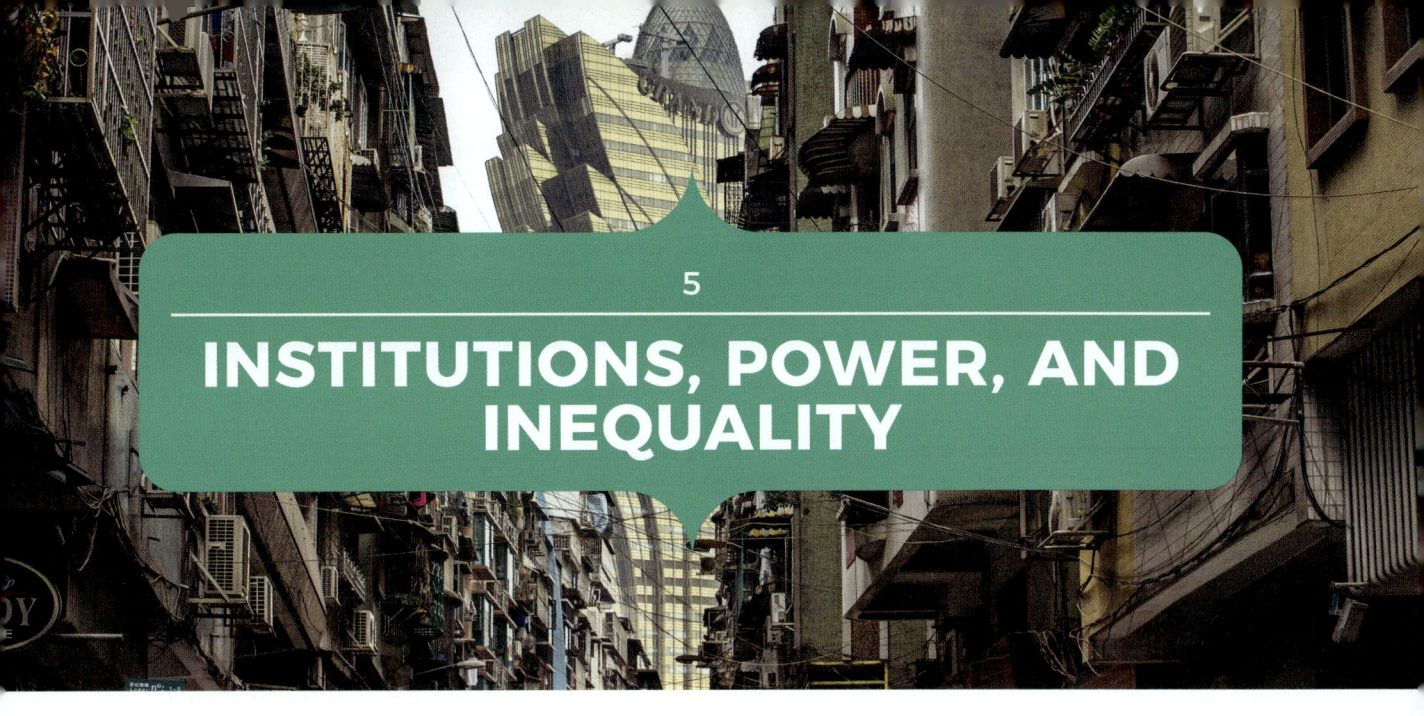

Macau old town

5.1 INTRODUCTION

- Institutions influence the balance of power among conflicting people or groups and affect the resulting level of inequality and other outcomes.
- Technology, biology, and people's preferences are also important determinants of economic outcomes.
- Power is the ability to do and get the things one wants in opposition to the intentions of others.
- Interactions between economic actors can result in mutual gains, but also in conflicts over how the gains are distributed, which affect inequality.
- Institutions influence the power and other bargaining advantages of actors.
- The degree of inequality can be measured and compared, both across societies and historical periods, and before and after the implementation of public policies.

Perhaps one of your distant ancestors considered that the best way to get money was by going to sea with a pirate like Blackbeard or Captain Kidd. If he had settled on Captain Bartholomew Roberts' pirate ship the *Royal Rover*, he and the other members of the crew would have been required to consent to the ship's written constitution. Figure 5.1 shows what the ship's constitution (called *The Royal Rover's Articles*) guaranteed.

The *Royal Rover* and its *Articles* were not unusual. During the heyday of European piracy in the late seventeenth and early eighteenth centuries, most pirate ships had written constitutions that guaranteed even more powers to the crew members. Their captains were democratically elected ('the Rank of Captain being obtained by the Suffrage of the Majority'). Many captains were also voted out, at least one for cowardice in battle. Crews also elected one of their number as the quartermaster who, when the ship was not in a battle, could countermand the captain's orders.

The example of the *Royal Rover* is taken from a fascinating article on the economic consequences of being a pirate. Peter T. Leeson. 2007. 'An-arrgh-chy: The Law and Economics of Pirate Organizations'. *Journal of Political Economy* 115 (6): pp. 1049–94.

If your ancestor had served as a lookout and had been the first to spot a ship that was later taken as a prize, he would have received as a reward 'the best Pair of Pistols on board, over and above his Dividend'. Were he to have been seriously wounded in battle, the articles guaranteed him compensation for the injury (more for the loss of a right arm or leg than for the left). He would have worked as part of a multiracial, multi-ethnic crew, of which probably about a quarter were of African origin, and the rest primarily of European descent, including Americans.

The result was that a pirate crew was often a close-knit group. A contemporary observer lamented that the pirates were 'wickedly united, and articled together'. Sailors of captured merchant ships often happily joined the 'roguish Commonwealth' of their pirate captors.

Another unhappy commentator remarked: 'These Men whom we term … the Scandal of human Nature, who were abandoned to all Vice … were strictly just among themselves.' If they were Responders in the ultimatum game that we explained in Unit 3, Section 3.3 (page 100), by this description they would have rejected any offer less than half of the pie!

Peter T. Leeson. 2007. 'An-arrgh-chy: The Law and Economics of Pirate Organizations'. *Journal of Political Economy* 115 (6): pp. 1049–94.

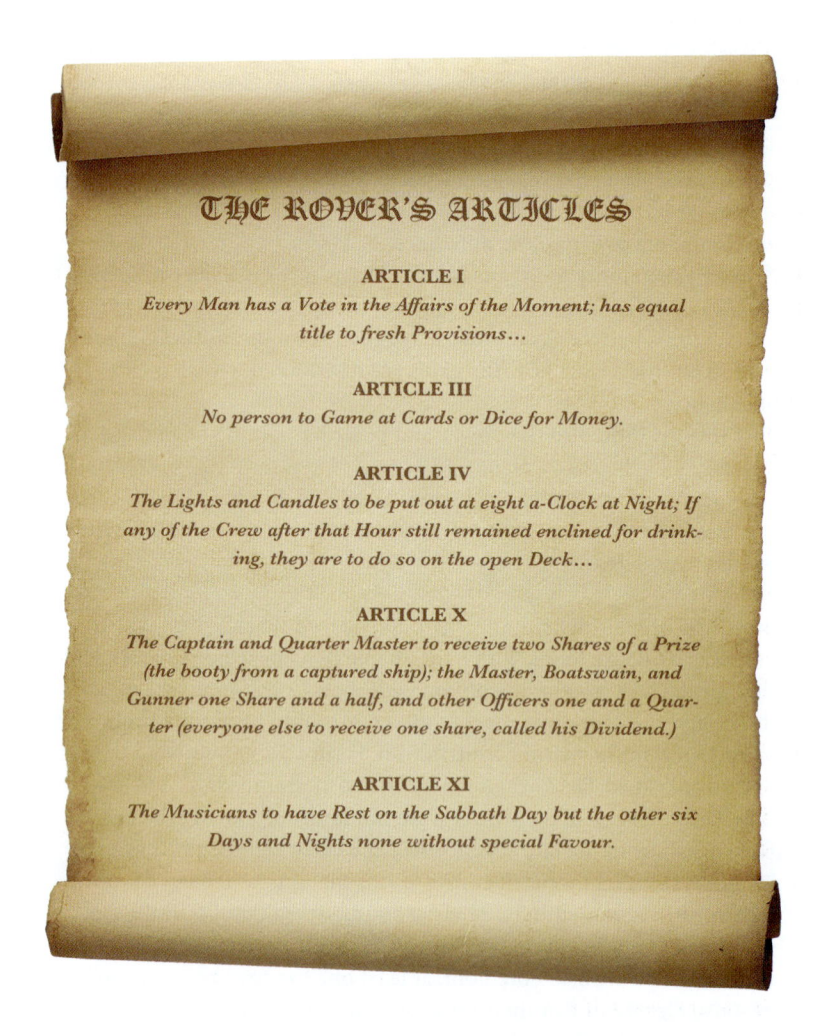

THE ROVER'S ARTICLES

ARTICLE I
Every Man has a Vote in the Affairs of the Moment; has equal title to fresh Provisions…

ARTICLE III
No person to Game at Cards or Dice for Money.

ARTICLE IV
The Lights and Candles to be put out at eight a-Clock at Night; If any of the Crew after that Hour still remained enclined for drinking, they are to do so on the open Deck…

ARTICLE X
The Captain and Quarter Master to receive two Shares of a Prize (the booty from a captured ship); the Master, Boatswain, and Gunner one Share and a half, and other Officers one and a Quarter (everyone else to receive one share, called his Dividend.)

ARTICLE XI
The Musicians to have Rest on the Sabbath Day but the other six Days and Nights none without special Favour.

Figure 5.1 *The Royal Rover's Articles.*

5.2 INSTITUTIONS: THE RULES OF THE GAME

In the late seventeenth and early eighteenth centuries, there was no country in the world that ordinary workers had the right to vote, to receive compensation for occupational injuries, or to be protected from arbitrary authority. These rights were taken for granted on the *Royal Rover*.

The Royal Rover's Articles laid down the understandings among the pirates about their working conditions. They determined who did what aboard the ship, and what each person would get. For example, the size of the helmsman's dividend compared to that of the gunner. There were also unwritten informal rules of appropriate behaviour that the pirates followed by custom, or to avoid condemnation by their crewmates, or punishment by the captain or quartermaster.

How the pirates interacted with one another was governed by their **institutions**.

Recall that institutions are the written and unwritten rules that regulate how people interact: this includes who meets whom, who does what tasks, with what rewards or penalties. On the *Royal Rover*, one rule was that the best pair of pistols would be given to the lookout who spotted a ship that was later taken. Another was that the captain and quartermaster would receive two shares, and ordinary crew one share, of the booty.

Private property is an economic institution that (as you learned in Unit 1 (page 23)), gives the owner of some object (a home, for example) the right to exclude others from its use, and to sell it to someone else.

Political institutions determine how a person may come to be a head of state (for example, a royal position inherited from a parent, or by election), and the kinds of things that government officials are permitted or prohibited from doing (for example, entering a private home without invitation or permission from the court system). Democracy (as you know from Unit 1 (page 37)) is an institution.

Marital institutions regulate who may marry whom (and who may not) as well as practices concerning the raising of children and the inheritance of property across generations. Monogamy—one spouse per person—is an institution. Primogeniture, under which inheritance passes to the eldest offspring—usually throughout history the eldest son—is another.

Two things to keep in mind about how we use the term 'institution':

- *Organizations are not institutions:* In common parlance, large organizations such as the University of Oxford and the Hyundai Motor Company are sometimes referred to as institutions. We will call an entity with a proper name an 'organization', and reserve the word 'institution' for a set of rules of the game, not for any particular example of those rules at work.
- *Institutions include social norms as well as laws:* Institutions can be formal (written and enforced) or informal. An example of a formal institution is the rule in football (soccer) that only goalkeepers may touch the ball with their hands while the ball is in play. An informal institution is the convention or social norm that if Team A kicks the ball off the pitch because there is an injury to a player on Team B, Team B always returns the ball to Team A from the restart. This is not written in any rule book and yet it is widely accepted, although less so in recent years. It is a social norm.

institution The laws and social customs governing the way people interact in society.

Institutions in models

Because we use games to represent how people interact, we naturally use the term 'rules of the game' to mean the same thing as 'institutions'.

Institutions directly affect inequality—the extent to which some people have more and others have less—as you can see by re-reading the *Royal Rover's* constitution (page 186).

The rules of the ultimatum game that you studied in Unit 3 (page 100) determine the ability of the players to obtain a high payoff (the extent of their advantage when dividing the pie), which is called **bargaining power**. A Proposer's right to make a take-it-or-leave-it offer gives her more bargaining power than the Responder, and usually results in the Proposer getting more than half of the pie.

Still, the Proposer's bargaining power is limited because the Responder has the power to refuse. Suppose we allow a Proposer simply to divide up a pie in any way, without any role for the Responder other than to take whatever he gets (if anything). Under these rules, the Proposer has all the bargaining power and the Responder none. There is an experimental game like this, called (you guessed it) the dictator game. 'Dictators' in this game typically make a lot more money than Proposers in the ultimatum game.

In experiments, the assignment of the role Proposer or Responder, and hence the assignment of bargaining power, is usually done by chance. In real economies, the assignment of power is definitely not random.

bargaining power The extent of a person's advantage in securing a larger share of the economic rents made possible by an interaction.

Institutions and power

In the labour market, the power to set the terms of the exchange typically lies with those who own the business—they are the ones proposing the wage and other terms of employment. Those seeking employment are like Responders, and since usually more than one person is applying for the same job, their bargaining power may be low. Also, because the place of employment is the employer's private property, the employer may be able to exclude the worker by firing her if her work is not up to the employer's specifications.

There are many past and present examples of economic institutions that are like the dictator game, in which there is no option to say no. Examples include today's remaining political dictatorships, such as The Democratic People's Republic of Korea (North Korea), and slavery, as it existed in the US prior to the end of the American Civil War in 1865.

Criminal organizations involved in drugs and human trafficking are another modern example, in which power takes the form of physical coercion or threats of violence. The term 'modern slavery' refers to relationships that migrants and sex workers are sometimes subject to, in which the worker is bound to the employer by physical threats, the employer seizing the worker's passport, and by other coercive means.

In a democratic society, however, institutions exist to protect people against violence and coercion, and to ensure that most economic interactions are conducted voluntarily.

As we saw in Unit 1 (page 40), India became a democracy in 1948. To provide a concrete case of institutions and how they change, we now look at how legislation in 1978 changed the institutions governing how a crop would be divided between the farmer who cultivated the land and the owner of the land.

How Operation Barga changed the rules of the game

In the Indian state of West Bengal, home to more people than Germany, many farmers work as sharecroppers ('bargadars' in the Bengali language), renting land from landowners in exchange for a share (that is, a percentage) of the crop.

The traditional contractual arrangements throughout this vast state varied little from village to village, with virtually all bargadars giving half their crop to the landowner at harvest time. This had been the social norm for at least five centuries.

But in the second half of the twentieth century many thought this was unfair, because of the extreme levels of deprivation among the bargadars. In 1973, 73% of the rural population lived in poverty, one of the highest poverty rates in India. The state and national government had generally supported the landlords. But in 1978, a democratic state election altered the balance of political power. The newly elected Left Front government of West Bengal adopted new laws, called Operation Barga.

The new laws benefited bargadars:

- *They could keep three-quarters of their crop:* The landlords' share was cut from one-half to one-quarter.
- *They were protected from eviction by landowners:* They were protected as long as they paid the newly legislated rent (one-quarter of the crop).

Both provisions of Operation Barga were advocated as a way of increasing output. There are certainly reasons to predict that the size of the pie would increase, as well as the incomes of the farmers:

- *They had a greater incentive to work hard and well:* Keeping a larger share meant that there was a greater reward if they grew more crops.
- *They had an incentive to invest in improving the land:* They were confident that they would farm the same plot of land in the future, so would be rewarded for their investment.

Did this dramatic change in institutions work?

Because the new law was implemented over many years, one village at a time (there are more than 20,000 villages in the state), economists have been able to isolate the effect of Operation Barga from other changes that were occurring at the same time (the weather, for example). By comparing the output of farms before and after the implementation of Operation Barga, researchers concluded that it improved work motivation, and increased investment.

One study estimated that Operation Barga was responsible for about 28% of the subsequent growth in output per farmer in the region. The empowerment of the bargadars also had positive spill-over effects as local governments became more responsive to the needs of poor farmers.

The result was that West Bengal experienced a dramatic increase in farm output per unit of land, as well as rising farming incomes.

Abhijit V. Banerjee, Paul J. Gertler, and Maitreesh Ghatak. 2002. 'Empowerment and Efficiency: Tenancy Reform in West Bengal' (https://tinyco.re/9394444). *Journal of Political Economy* 110 (2): pp. 239–80.

Ajitava Raychaudhuri. 2004. *Lessons from the Land Reform Movement in West Bengal, India* (https://tinyco.re/0335719). Washington, DC: World Bank.

Pareto criterion According to the Pareto criterion, a desirable attribute of an allocation is that it be Pareto efficient. *See also: Pareto dominant.*

Efficiency and fairness

Operation Barga was later cited by the World Bank as an example of good policy for economic development.

The evidence from Operation Barga indicates that, in this case, the pie got larger, and the poorest people got a larger slice.

In principle, the increase in the size of the pie means there could be mutual gains from the reforms, with both farmers and landowners being better off. In other words, there could be an improved allocation, according to the **Pareto criterion** as discussed in Section 3.3 (page 100).

The actual change in the allocation was not a Pareto improvement, however—landlords had strenuously opposed the legislation, but the bargadars and their allies far outnumbered them, so the Left Front's political power was secure in India's democratic political system. The incomes of some landowners fell following the legislated reduction in their share of the crop. Nevertheless, in increasing the income of the poorest people in West Bengal, many would judge that Operation Barga implemented an improvement in the allocation from the standpoint of fairness. We can assume that many people in West Bengal thought so, because they continued to vote for the Left Front alliance. It stayed in power from 1977 until 2011.

Operation Barga illustrates an important fact—institutions affect who has power, and this matters for who gets more and who gets less from the economy. To understand how institutions (the rules of the game) and the exercise of power affect the degree of inequality and other economic outcomes, we now present a model of that process.

> **QUESTION 5.1 CHOOSE THE CORRECT ANSWER(S)**
> Which of the following statements about institutions are correct?
>
> ☐ Institutions include organizations such as universities.
> ☐ Institutions must be written down.
> ☐ Institutions determine individuals' power to get what they want in interactions with others.
> ☐ Institutions are the rules of the game.

> **QUESTION 5.2 CHOOSE THE CORRECT ANSWER(S)**
> Which of the following statements regarding bargaining power are correct?
>
> ☐ In an ultimatum game, the Proposer has all the bargaining power.
> ☐ In an ultimatum game, increasing the number of Responders reduces the Proposer's bargaining power.
> ☐ In a dictator game, the Proposer has all the bargaining power.
> ☐ In a dictator game, increasing the number of Responders reduces the Proposer's bargaining power.

5.3 PRODUCTION AND DISTRIBUTION: USING A MODEL

Recall the model in Unit 4 (page 164) of the farmer, Angela, who produces a crop. We will extend that model by introducing a sequence of scenarios involving two characters, Angela and Bruno. We introduce them as people and we personify what they do and are trying to accomplish, even reporting on their conversations. We use two characters and the institutions governing how they interact to illustrate general facts about an entire society composed of many Angelas and Brunos. This story is an economic model simplifying reality to convey something important about how the much more complex world works.

Their story unfolds over a period of time in which they live under differing sets of institutions—different scenarios—as shown in the table (Figure 5.2). As you can see in the first scenario, Bruno is not in the picture and Angela gets everything she produces. In deciding how hard to work, she is facing a problem identical to the one we presented in Unit 4 (page 164). Next, we consider three scenarios involving Bruno, the owner of the land on which Angela works. In scenarios B, C, and D, what will happen—how many hours she will work and how much of what she produces she will get—depends on the ways in which the institutions characterizing these three scenarios give more or less bargaining power to Angela and Bruno.

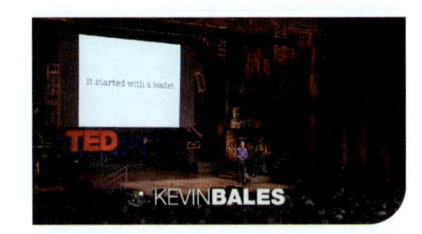

Kevin Bales: How to combat modern slavery https://tinyco.re/7492483

Scenario	In the model of Angela and Bruno	In the real world
A	*Independence:* Angela works the land on her own, and everything she produces is hers.	Independent farmers with access to land (either free, or because they own it) have been common in history ever since farming began.
B	*Rule of force:* Slavery. There is a second person, who does not farm, but is able to take some of the harvest. He is called Bruno. Bruno is heavily armed, and Angela is, effectively, his slave.	Also common throughout history: slavery and other forms of coerced labour in mines and plantations was the basis of much of the economy of North and South America after the arrival of Europeans. It persists today (https://tinyco.re/5817098)—among domestic workers and sex workers (https://tinyco.re/7492483)—though in most countries illegally. In the UK for example, the Modern Slavery Act (https://tinyco.re/7634403) was passed in 2015.
C	*Property rights and the rule of law:* Laws protect Angela from coercion but give Bruno ownership of the land. If she wants to farm his land, she must agree, for example, to pay him some part of the harvest. But she has the right to say no. He has to make her an offer that she will accept.	In manufacturing, farming, and other kinds of work, owners of land and other capital goods employ workers, or make their land available to the landless for rent, a common arrangement today and for thousands of years. The sharecropping in Bengal in India is an example.
D	*Property rights, the rule of law, and the right to vote:* the rules of the game are a bit more in Angela's favour. She and her fellow farmers achieve the right to vote and legislation is passed that increases Angela's claim on the harvest.	Capitalism and democracy in the twentieth century and today. Operation Barga in Bengal changed the rules and was the result of political pressure in a democracy.

Figure 5.2 Institutional arrangements in a model and in the world.

Pareto efficient An allocation with the property that there is no alternative technically feasible allocation in which at least one person would be better off, and nobody worse off.
indifference curve A curve of the points which indicate the combinations of goods that provide a given level of utility to the individual.
marginal rate of substitution (MRS) The trade-off that a person is willing to make between two goods. At any point, this is the slope of the indifference curve. *See also: marginal rate of transformation.*

In Figure 5.3, we depict how much bargaining power Bruno has over Angela.

For each of these scenarios, we will analyse the changes in terms of both Pareto efficiency and the distribution of income between Angela and Bruno. Remember that:

- If we have enough facts, we can probably agree on whether an outcome is **Pareto efficient** or not.
- Whether or not the outcome is fair depends on your own assessment of the problem, using the concepts of substantive and procedural fairness introduced in Unit 3 (page 115).

Angela values both grain and free time. Again, we represent her preferences as **indifference curves**, showing the combinations of grain and free time that she values equally. Remember that the slope of the indifference curve is called the **marginal rate of substitution (MRS)** between grain and free time.

An independent producer: Angela farms the land on her own

Figure 5.4 shows Angela's indifference curves and her feasible frontier. Remember: the indifference curves are about what Angela values. The feasible frontier is about what she can get. The steeper the indifference curve, the more Angela values free time relative to grain. You can see that the more free time she has (moving to the right), the flatter the curves—she values free time less.

In this unit, we make a particular technical assumption about Angela's preferences that you can see in the shape of her indifference curves. If she gets more grain, but her hours of free time do not change, then her MRS does not change either. For example, as you move up the vertical line at 16 hours of free time, the slope of each indifference curve crossing the line is the same. More grain does not change her valuation of free time relative to grain.

Why might this be? Perhaps she does not eat it all, but sells some and uses the proceeds to buy other things she needs. This is just a simplification that makes our model easier to understand. When drawing indifference curves for the model in this unit, remember to simply shift them up and down, keeping the MRS constant at a given amount of free time.

Angela is free to choose her typical hours of work to achieve her preferred combination of free time and grain. Go through the analysis of Figure 5.4 to determine the allocation.

To simplify the graphical exposition of the model, we assume that preferences are quasi-linear. To explore this further using calculus, see Leibniz 5.4.1 from *The Economy* (https://tinyco.re/L050401).

Scenarios	A. Angela's independence	D. Property rights, rule of law and democracy	C. Property rights and rule of law	B. Rule of force
Bruno's bargaining power	None (not applicable)	Limited (more equal to Angela's)	Great (compared to Angela's)	Total

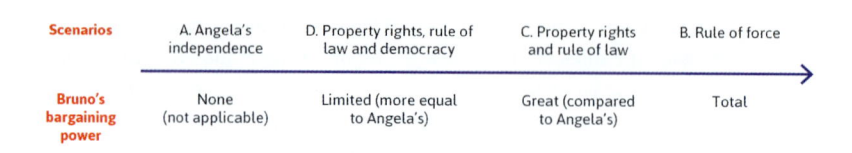

Figure 5.3 Bruno's bargaining power over Angela depends on the institutions in force in the four scenarios.

Figure 5.4 shows that the best Angela can do, given the limits set by the feasible frontier, is to work for 8 hours. She has 16 hours of free time and produces and consumes 9 bushels of grain. This is the number of hours of work where the marginal rate of substitution is equal to the **marginal rate of transformation**. She cannot do better than this! (If you're not sure why, go back to Unit 4 (page 164) and check.)

marginal rate of transformation (MRT) A measure of the trade-offs a person faces in what is feasible. Given the constraints (feasible frontier) a person faces, the MRT is the quantity of some good that must be sacrificed to acquire one additional unit of another good. At any point, it is the slope of the feasible frontier. See also: feasible frontier, marginal rate of substitution.

QUESTION 5.3 CHOOSE THE CORRECT ANSWER(S)
Based on Figure 5.4, which of the following statements are correct?

☐ The MRS is the trade-off between grain and free time that Angela is constrained to make.
☐ At a point to the left of Angela's optimal choice, the MRS is greater than the MRT.
☐ At a point to the right of Angela's optimal choice, she is less willing to trade grain for free time than at her optimal choice.
☐ Since all Angela's indifference curves have the same MRS at 16 hours of free time, any choice of grain at 16 hours of free time is optimal.

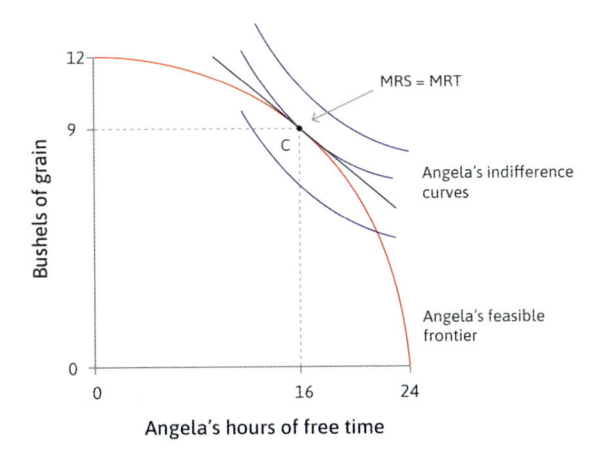

To explore all of the slides in this figure, see the online version at https://tinyco.re/3236848.

Figure 5.4 Scenario A: Independent farmer Angela's feasible frontier, best feasible indifference curve, and choice of hours of work.

1. The feasible frontier
The diagram shows Angela's feasible frontier, determined by her production function.

2. The best Angela can do
The best Angela can do, given the limits set by the feasible frontier, is to work for 8 hours, taking 16 hours of free time and producing 9 bushels of grain. At this point C, the marginal rate of substitution (MRS) is equal to the marginal rate of transformation (MRT).

3. MRS = MRT
The MRS is the slope of the indifference curve—the trade-off she is willing to make between grain and free time. The MRT is the slope of the feasible frontier—the trade-off she is constrained to make. At point C, the two trade-offs balance.

193

5.4 THE RULE OF FORCE: BRUNO APPEARS AND HAS UNLIMITED POWER OVER ANGELA

Angela now has company. The other person is called Bruno. He is not a farmer but is heavily armed and can claim some—even all—of Angela's harvest. We will study different rules of the game that explain how much is produced by Angela, and how it is divided between her and Bruno. For example, in one scenario, Bruno is the landowner and Angela pays some grain to him as rent for the use of the land. But we start with the rule of force.

Figure 5.5 shows Angela and Bruno's combined feasible frontier. The frontier indicates how many bushels of grain Angela can produce given how much free time she takes. For example, if she takes 12 hours of free time and works for 12 hours, then she produces 10.5 bushels of grain. One possible outcome of the interaction between Angela and Bruno is that 5.25 bushels go to Bruno, and Angela retains the other 5.25 bushels for her own consumption.

Work through the analysis of Figure 5.5 to find out how each possible allocation is represented in the diagram, showing how much work Angela does and how much grain she and Bruno each get.

To explore all of the slides in this figure, see the online version at https://tinyco.re/7655853.

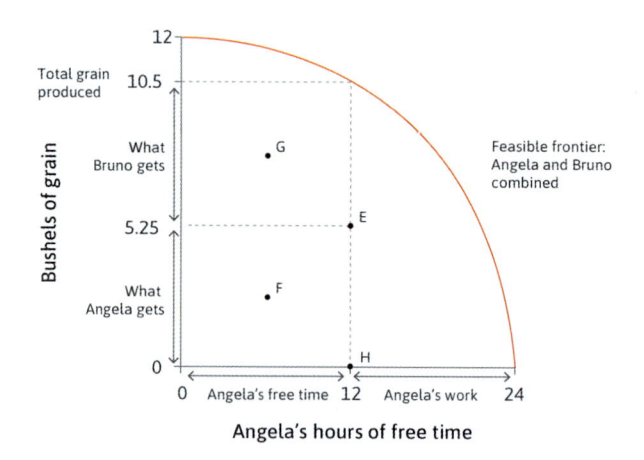

Figure 5.5 Feasible outcomes of the interaction between Angela and Bruno.

1. The combined feasible frontier
The feasible frontier shows the maximum amount of grain available to Angela and Bruno together, given Angela's amount of free time. If Angela takes 12 hours of free time and works for 12 hours, then she produces 10.5 bushels of grain.

2. A feasible allocation
Point E is a possible outcome of the interaction between Angela and Bruno.

3. The distribution at point E
At point E, Angela works for 12 hours and produces 10.5 bushels of grain. The distribution of grain is such that 5.25 bushels go to Bruno and Angela retains the other 5.25 bushels for her own consumption.

4. Other feasible allocations
Point F shows an allocation in which Angela works more than at point E and gets less grain. Point G shows the case in which she works more and gets more grain.

5. An impossible allocation
An outcome at H—in which Angela works for 12 hours a day, Bruno consumes the entire amount produced and Angela consumes nothing—which would not be possible; she would starve.

5.4 THE RULE OF FORCE: BRUNO APPEARS AND HAS UNLIMITED POWER OVER ANGELA

Which allocations are likely to occur? Not all of them are even possible. For example, at point H Angela works for 12 hours a day and receives nothing (Bruno takes the entire harvest), so Angela would not survive. Of the allocations that are at least possible, the one that will occur depends on the rules of the game.

> **QUESTION 5.4 CHOOSE THE CORRECT ANSWER(S)**
> Based on Figure 5.5, which of the following statements are correct?
>
> ☐ If Angela has very flat indifference curves, she may prefer G to the other three allocations.
> ☐ If Angela has very steep indifference curves, she may prefer F to the other three allocations.
> ☐ Allocation G is the best of the four for Bruno.
> ☐ It is possible that Angela is indifferent between G and E.

> **EXERCISE 5.1 AN ALLOCATION YOU HAVE KNOWN**
> Think of a job that you or someone you know has done (for example, a barista or an office worker).
>
> 1. Who are the parties involved in this economic interaction?
> 2. Describe the allocation—who does what, and who gets what?
> 3. Do you think the allocation is fair? Explain your answer.

How much can Bruno get?

As an independent farmer, Angela could consume (or sell) everything she produced. Now Bruno has arrived. He has the power to implement any allocation that he chooses. He is even more powerful than the dictator in the dictator game (in which a Proposer dictates how a pie is to be divided). Why? Bruno can determine the size of the pie, as well as how it is shared.

Unlike the experimental subjects in Unit 3 (page 100), in this model Bruno and Angela are entirely self-interested. Bruno wants only to maximize the amount of grain he can get. Angela cares only about her own free time and grain (as described by her indifference curves), just as she did in Unit 4 (page 164).

We now make another important assumption. If Angela does not work the land, Bruno gets nothing (there are no other prospective farmers that he can exploit). What this means is that Bruno's **reservation option** (what he gets if Angela does not work for him) is zero. As a result, Bruno thinks about the future—he will not take so much grain that Angela will starve. The allocation must keep her alive and physically able to work.

Angela's biological survival constraint in Figure 5.6 (page 197) shows the minimum amount of grain that she needs for each amount of work that she does; points below this line would leave her so undernourished or overworked that she would not survive. This constraint shows what is **biologically feasible**. Notice that, if she expends more energy working, she needs more food; that's why the curve rises from right to left from point Z as her hours of work increase. The slope of the biological survival constraint is the marginal rate of substitution between free time and grain in securing Angela's survival.

reservation option A person's next best alternative among all options in a particular transaction. Also known as: fallback option. See also: reservation price.

biologically feasible An allocation that is capable of sustaining the survival of those involved is biologically feasible.

The fact that Angela's survival might be in jeopardy is not a hypothetical example. During the Industrial Revolution, life expectancy at birth in Liverpool, UK, fell to 25 years—slightly more than half of what it is today in the poorest countries in the world. In many parts of the world today, farmers' and workers' capacity to do their jobs is limited by their intake of calories.

The biological survival constraint tells us the least amount that Angela can get under Bruno's rule of force while continuing to exist. But this constraint need not *literally* be biological. If Angela is receiving too little, she might choose to try to escape to a place where she could farm her own land and keep the entire crop. Or she might prefer the risk of trying to get his gun. In either case her relationship to him as a forced worker would change, just as if she had starved.

So, you can think of what we term the biological constraint as a sustainability constraint where what is being sustained is the relationship of forced labour between the two.

Next, we will work out the set of **technically feasible** combinations of Angela's hours of work and the amount of grain she receives—that is, all the combinations that are possible within the limitations of the technology (the production function) and biology (Angela must have enough nutrition to do the work and survive).

Figure 5.6 shows how to find the technically feasible set. We already know that the production function determines the feasible frontier. This is the technological limit on the total amount consumed by Bruno and Angela, which in turn depends on the hours that Angela works.

If Angela could consume everything she produced (the height of the feasible frontier) and choose her hours of work, her survival would not be in jeopardy, since the biological survival constraint is below the feasible frontier for a wide range of working hours. The question of biological feasibility arises because of Bruno's claims on her output.

In Figure 5.6, the boundaries of the feasible solutions to the allocation problem are formed by the feasible frontier and the biological survival constraint. This lens-shaped area gives the technically possible outcomes. We can now ask what will actually happen—which allocation will occur, and how does this depend on the institutions governing Bruno's and Angela's interaction?

> This extension of our model in which Angela takes action rather than submitting to the rule of force is not hypothetical. Rebellions of slaves and slaves driven to attempt escape because of their conditions are common in the history of that institution. They are probably more common than stories of starvation: slave owners had an interest in keeping a slave strong enough to work hard.

technically feasible An allocation within the limits set by technology and biology.

> **QUESTION 5.5 CHOOSE THE CORRECT ANSWER(S)**
> Based on Figure 5.6, which of the following statements are correct?
>
> ☐ If Angela works for 24 hours, she can survive.
> ☐ There is a technically feasible allocation in which Angela does not work.
> ☐ A new technology that boosted grain production would result in a bigger technically feasible set.
> ☐ If Angela did not need so much grain to survive, the technically feasible set would be smaller.

5.4 THE RULE OF FORCE: BRUNO APPEARS AND HAS UNLIMITED POWER OVER ANGELA

Given his power, Bruno makes his choice
With the help of his gun, Bruno can choose any point in the lens-shaped technically feasible set of allocations. But which will he choose?

He reasons like this:

BRUNO: For any number of hours that I order Angela to work, she will produce the amount of grain shown by the feasible frontier. But I'll have to give her at least the amount shown by the biological survival constraint for that much work, so that I can continue to exploit her. I get to keep the difference between what she produces and what I give her. Therefore, I should find Angela's working hours for which the vertical distance between the feasible frontier and the biological survival constraint (Figure 5.6) is the greatest.

Bruno first considers letting Angela continue to work for 8 hours a day, producing 9 bushels, as she did when she had free access to the land. For 8 hours of work, she needs 3.5 bushels of grain to survive. Therefore, Bruno could take 5.5 bushels without jeopardizing his future opportunities to benefit from Angela's labour.

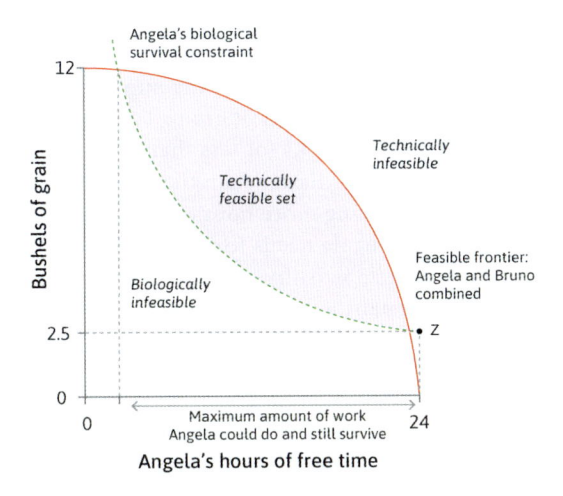

To explore all of the slides in this figure, see the online version at https://tinyco.re/5398086.

Figure 5.6 Technically feasible allocations.

1. The biological survival constraint
If Angela does not work at all, she needs 2.5 bushels to survive (point Z). If she gives up some free time and expends energy working, she needs more food, so the curve is higher when she has less free time. This is the biological survival constraint.

2. Biologically infeasible and technically infeasible points
Points below the biological survival constraint are biologically infeasible, while points above the feasible frontier are technically infeasible.

3. Angela's maximum working day
Given the feasible frontier, there is a maximum amount of work above which Angela could not survive, even if she could consume everything she produced.

4. The technically feasible set
The technically feasible allocations are the points in the lens-shaped area bounded by the feasible frontier and the biological survival constraint (including points on the frontier).

197

Bruno is studying Figure 5.6 and asks for your help. You have noticed that at 8 hours of work the MRS on the survival constraint is less than the MRT.

YOU: Bruno, your plan cannot be right. If you forced her to work a little more, she'd only need a little more grain to have the energy to work longer, because the biological survival constraint is relatively flat at 8 hours of work. But the feasible frontier is steep, so she would produce a lot more if you imposed longer hours.

You demonstrate the argument to him using the analysis in Figure 5.7, which indicates that the vertical distance between the feasible frontier and the biological survival constraint is the greatest when Angela works for 11 hours (13 hours of free time). If Bruno commands Angela to work for 11 hours, then she will produce 10 bushels and Bruno will get to keep 6 bushels for himself. We can use Figure 5.7 to find out how many bushels of grain Bruno will get for any technically feasible allocation.

The lower panel in the last step in Figure 5.7 shows how the amount Bruno can take varies with Angela's free time. The graph is hump-shaped, and peaks at 13 hours of free time and 11 hours of work. Bruno maximizes his amount of grain at allocation B, commanding Angela to work for 11 hours.

Notice how the slopes of the feasible frontier and the survival constraint (the MRT and MRS) help us to find the number of hours where Bruno can take the maximum amount of grain. To the right of 13 hours of free time (that is, if Angela works for less than 11 hours), the biological survival constraint is flatter than the feasible frontier (MRS < MRT). This means that working more hours (moving to the left) would produce more grain than Angela needs for the extra work. To the left of 13 hours of free time (Angela working more), the reverse is true—MRS > MRT. Bruno's **economic rent** is greatest at the hours of work where the slopes of the two frontiers are equal.

That is:

MRT of work hours into grain output =
MRS of work hours into subsistence requirements

economic rent A payment or other benefit received above and beyond what the individual would have received in his or her next best alternative (or reservation option). See also: reservation option.

> **QUESTION 5.6 CHOOSE THE CORRECT ANSWER(S)**
> Based on Figure 5.7, if Bruno can impose the allocation:
>
> ☐ He will choose the technically feasible allocation where Angela produces the most grain.
> ☐ His preferred choice will be where the marginal rate of transformation (MRT) on the feasible frontier equals the marginal rate of substitution (MRS) on the biological survival constraint.
> ☐ He will not choose 8 hours of work, because the MRS between Angela's work hours and subsistence requirements exceeds the MRT between work hours and grain output.
> ☐ He will choose 13 hours of free time for Angela, and consume 10 bushels of grain.

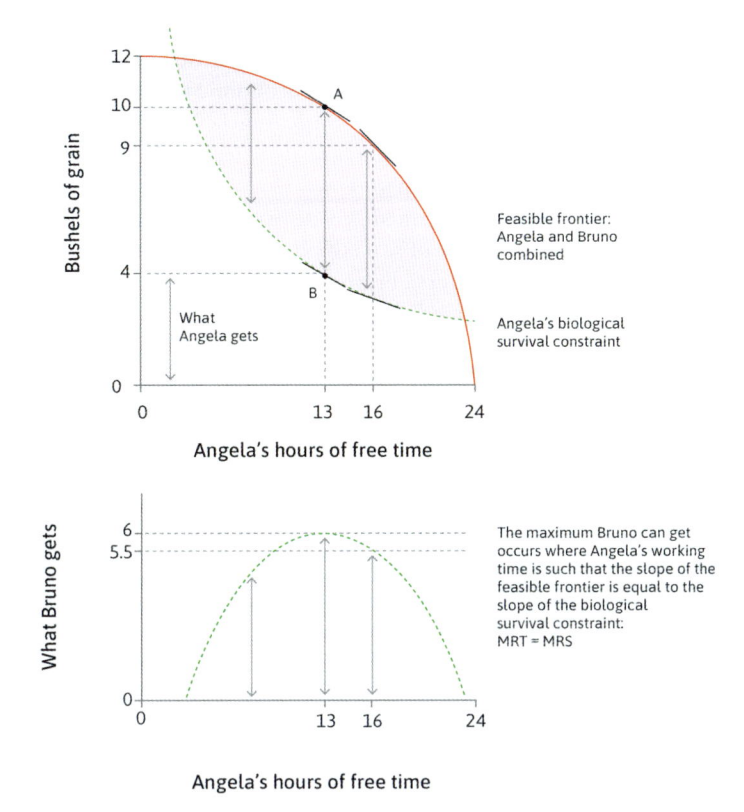

5.4 THE RULE OF FORCE: BRUNO APPEARS AND HAS UNLIMITED POWER OVER ANGELA

To explore all of the slides in this figure, see the online version at https://tinyco.re/2716237.

Figure 5.7 Scenario B: Coercion. The maximum technically feasible transfer from Angela to Bruno.

1. Bruno can command Angela to work
Bruno can choose any allocation in the technically feasible set. He considers letting Angela continue working for 8 hours a day, producing 9 bushels.

2. When Angela works for 8 hours
Bruno could take 5.5 bushels without jeopardizing his future benefit from Angela's labour. This is shown by the vertical distance between the feasible frontier and the survival constraint.

3. The maximum distance between frontiers
The vertical distance between the feasible frontier and the biological survival constraint is greatest when Angela works for 11 hours (13 hours of free time).

4. Allocation and distribution at the maximum distance
If Bruno commands Angela to work for 11 hours, she will produce 10 bushels, and needs 4 to survive. Bruno will get to keep 6 bushels for himself (the distance AB).

5. At higher working hours, the survival frontier becomes steeper
If Bruno makes Angela work for more than 11 hours, the amount he can take falls as working hours increase.

6. What Bruno gets
If we join up the points, we can see that the amount Bruno gets is hump-shaped, and peaks at 11 hours of work (13 hours of free time).

7. The best Bruno can do for himself
Bruno gets the maximum amount of grain by choosing allocation B, where Angela's working time is such that the slope of the feasible frontier is equal to the slope of the biological survival constraint: MRT = MRS.

199

5.5 PROPERTY RIGHTS AND THE RULE OF LAW

In the previous section, Bruno had the power to enslave Angela. If we move from a scenario of coercion to one in which there is a legal system that prohibits slavery and protects **private property** and the rights of landowners and workers, we can expect the outcome of the interaction to change.

In the example above, Angela was forced to participate, and Bruno chose her working hours to maximize his own economic rent. Next, we look at the situation where she can simply say no. Angela is no longer a slave, but Bruno still has the power to make a take-it-or-leave-it offer, just like the Proposer in the ultimatum game.

In Unit 1 (page 23), we defined private property as the right to use and exclude others from the use of something, and the right to sell it (or to transfer these rights to others). From now on, we will suppose that Bruno owns the land and can exclude Angela if he chooses. How much grain he will get as a result of his private ownership of the land will depend on the extent of his **power** over Angela in the new situation.

> **private property** The right and expectation that one can enjoy one's possessions in ways of one's own choosing, exclude others from their use, and dispose of them by gift or sale to others who then become their owners.
> **power** The ability to do (and get) the things one wants in opposition to the intentions of others, ordinarily by imposing or threatening sanctions.

The rule of law arrives and Angela can say no

We check back on Angela and Bruno, and immediately notice that Bruno is now wearing a suit and is no longer armed, at least not openly. He explains that his weapon is no longer needed because there is a government with laws administered by courts, and professional enforcers, called the police. Bruno now owns the land, and Angela must have permission to use his property. He can offer a contract allowing her to farm the land, and she can give him part of the harvest in return. But the law requires that exchange is voluntary—Angela can refuse the offer.

BRUNO: It used to be a matter of power, but now both Angela and I have property rights—I own the land, and she owns her own labour. The new rules of the game mean that I can no longer force Angela to work. She has to agree to the allocation that I propose.
YOU: And if she doesn't?
BRUNO: Then there is no deal. She doesn't work on my land, I get nothing, and she gets barely enough to survive from the government.
YOU: So you and Angela have the same amount of power?
BRUNO: Certainly not! I am the one who gets to make a take-it-or-leave-it offer. I am like the Proposer in the ultimatum game, except that this is no game. If she refuses, she goes hungry.
YOU: But if she refuses, you get zero?
BRUNO: That will never happen.

Why does he know this? Bruno knows that Angela, unlike the real subjects in the ultimatum game experiments (page 100), is entirely self-interested (she does not punish an unfair offer). If he makes an offer that is just a tiny bit better for Angela than not working at all and getting subsistence rations, she will accept it.

Now he asks you a question similar to the one he asked earlier.

BRUNO: In this case, what should my take-it-or-leave-it offer be?

You answered before by showing him the biological survival constraint. Now the limitation is not Angela's survival, but rather her agreement. You know that she values her free time, so the more hours he offers her to work, the more he is going to have to pay.

YOU: Why don't you just look at Angela's indifference curve that passes through the point where she does not work at all and barely survives? That will tell you how much is the least you can pay her for each of the hours of free time she would give up in order to work for you.

Point Z in Figure 5.8 is the allocation in which Angela does no work and gets only survival rations (from the government, or perhaps her family). This is her reservation option—if she refuses Bruno's offer, she has this option as a backup. Follow the analysis of Figure 5.8 to see Angela's **reservation indifference curve**—all the allocations that have the same value for her as the reservation option. Below or to the left of the curve, she is worse off than in her reservation option. Above and to the right, she is better off.

Angela's reservation indifference curve is above her biological survival constraint (except at point Z) because, at all points on the biological constraint, she might be close to starvation. The points differ in how many hours of free time she has. Being about to starve and not having to work is preferable to Angela than being about to starve and working 18-hour days. The points on her reservation indifference curve are combinations of free time and grain that are equally valued to Angela as doing no work and receiving 2.5 bushels of grain.

reservation indifference curve A curve that indicates allocations (combinations) that are as highly valued as one's reservation option. *See also: reservation option.*

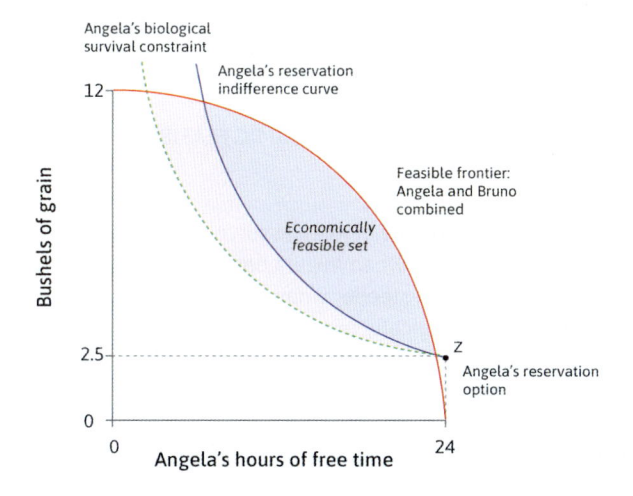

Figure 5.8 Economically feasible allocations when exchange is voluntary.

To explore all of the slides in this figure, see the online version at https://tinyco.re/4370054.

1. Angela's reservation option
Point Z, the allocation in which Angela does not work and gets only survival rations from the government, is called her reservation option.

2. Angela's reservation indifference curve
The curve showing all the allocations that are just as highly valued by Angela as the reservation option is called her reservation indifference curve.

3. The economically feasible set
The points in the area bounded by the reservation indifference curve and the feasible frontier (including the points on the frontiers) define the set of all economically feasible allocations.

The set of points bounded by the reservation indifference curve and the feasible frontier, is the set of all economically feasible allocations now that Angela has to agree to Bruno's proposal. Bruno thanks you for this handy new tool for figuring out the most he can get from Angela.

The biological survival constraint and the reservation indifference curve have a common point (Z)—at that point, Angela does no work and gets subsistence rations from the government. Other than that, the two curves differ. The reservation indifference curve is uniformly above the biological survival constraint. The reason, you explain to Bruno, is that, however hard she works along the survival constraint, she barely survives; and the more she works the less free time she has, so the unhappier she is. Along the reservation indifference curve, by contrast, she is just as well off as at her reservation option, meaning that being able to keep more of the grain that she produces compensates exactly for her lost free time.

We can see that both Angela and Bruno may benefit if a deal can be made. Their exchange—allowing her to use his land (that is, not using his property right to exclude her) in return for her sharing some of what she produces—makes it possible for both to be better off than if no deal had been struck:

- *Bruno is better off than if there is no deal:* This is true as long as Bruno gets some of the crop.
- *Angela can also benefit:* This is true as long as Angela's share makes her better off than she would have been if she took her reservation option, taking account of her work hours.

This potential for mutual gain is why their exchange need not take place at the point of a gun but can be motivated by the desire of both to be better off.

At this point, you decide, it would make it a lot easier to explain the situation to Bruno, if he were familiar with some basic terms from economics.

> **EXERCISE 5.2 BIOLOGICAL AND ECONOMIC FEASIBILITY**
> Using Figure 5.8:
>
> 1. Explain why a point on the biological survival constraint is higher (more grain is required) when Angela has fewer hours of free time. Why does the curve also get steeper when she works more?
> 2. Explain why the biologically feasible set is not equal to the economically feasible set.
> 3. Explain (by shifting the curves) how you would represent the effects of the following:
>   (a) an improvement in growing conditions, such as more adequate rainfall
>   (b) Angela having access to half the land that she had previously
>   (c) Angela having a better-designed hoe, making it physically easier to do the work of farming.

An economics lesson for Bruno

When people participate voluntarily in an interaction, they do so because they expect the outcome to be better than their reservation option—the next best alternative. The difference between the value of participating and the value of the next best alternative is called an **economic rent**. For example, if a deal with Angela results in Bruno getting 3 bushels of grain, he receives an economic rent of 3 bushels (since, if he does not interact with Angela, he gets nothing). Economic rents are also sometimes called **gains from exchange**, because they are how much a person gains by engaging in the exchange compared to not engaging.

The sum of the economic rents of the participants is termed the surplus (or sometimes the **joint surplus**, to emphasize that it includes all the rents). How much rent they will each get—how they will share the surplus—depends on their bargaining power. And that, as we know, depends on the institutions governing the interaction.

All the allocations that represent mutual gains are shown in the economically feasible set in Figure 5.8. Each of these allocations Pareto-dominates the allocation that would occur without a deal. In other words, Bruno and Angela could achieve a **Pareto improvement**.

This does not mean that both parties will benefit equally. If the institutions in effect give Bruno the power to make a take-it-or-leave-it offer subject only to Angela's agreement, he can capture the entire surplus (minus the tiny bit necessary to get Angela to agree). Bruno knows this already.

Once you have explained the reservation indifference curve to him, Bruno knows which allocation he wants. He maximizes the amount of grain he can get at the maximum height of the lens-shaped region between Angela's reservation indifference curve and the feasible frontier. This is where the MRT on the feasible frontier is equal to the MRS on the indifference curve. Figure 5.9a shows that this allocation requires Angela to work for fewer hours than she did under coercion.

Bruno would like Angela to work for 8 hours and give him 4.5 bushels of grain (allocation D). How can he implement this allocation? All he has to do is to make a take-it-or-leave-it offer of a contract, allowing Angela to work the land in return for giving him a share of the crop equal to 4.5 bushels per day. (This is a sharecropping contract, like the bargadars' contracts in West Bengal.) We could say that she rents the land from Bruno, but we will call the payment a crop share to avoid confusion between land rent and economic rent.

If Angela has to pay 4.5 bushels (CD in Figure 5.9a) then she will *choose* to produce at point C, where she works for 8 hours. You can see this in the figure; if she produced at any other point on the feasible frontier and then gave Bruno 4.5 bushels, she would have lower utility—she would be below her reservation indifference curve. But she can achieve her reservation utility by working for 8 hours, so she will accept the contract.

> **economic rent** A payment or other benefit received above and beyond what the individual would have received in his or her next best alternative (or reservation option). See also: reservation option.

> **gains from exchange** The benefits that each party gains from a transaction compared to how they would have fared without the exchange. *Also known as: gains from trade.* See also: economic rent.

> **joint surplus** The sum of the economic rents of all involved in an interaction. *Also known as: gains from exchange.*

> **Pareto improvement** A change that benefits at least one person without making anyone else worse off. See also: Pareto dominant.

> **EXERCISE 5.3 WHY ANGELA WORKS FOR 8 HOURS**
> Angela's income is the amount she produces minus the crop share she pays to Bruno.
>
> 1. Using Figure 5.9a, suppose Angela works for 11 hours. Would her income (after paying Bruno) be greater or less than when she works for 8 hours? Suppose instead, she works for 6 hours, how would her income compare with when she works for 8 hours?
> 2. Explain in your own words why she will choose to work for 8 hours.

Since Angela is on her reservation indifference curve, only Bruno benefits from this exchange. All the joint surplus goes to Bruno. His economic rent is the whole surplus.

Remember that, when Angela could work the land on her own, she chose allocation C. Notice now that she chooses the same hours of work when she has to pay Bruno. Why does this happen? Whatever the crop share Angela has to pay, she will choose her hours of work to maximize her utility, so she will produce at a point on the feasible frontier where the MRT is equal to her MRS. And we know that her preferences are such that her MRS doesn't change with the amount of grain she consumes, so it will not be affected by the crop share. This means that, if she can choose her hours, she will work for 8 hours, irrespective of the crop share (as long as this gives her at least her reservation utility).

To explore all of the slides in this figure, see the online version at https://tinyco.re/3546337.

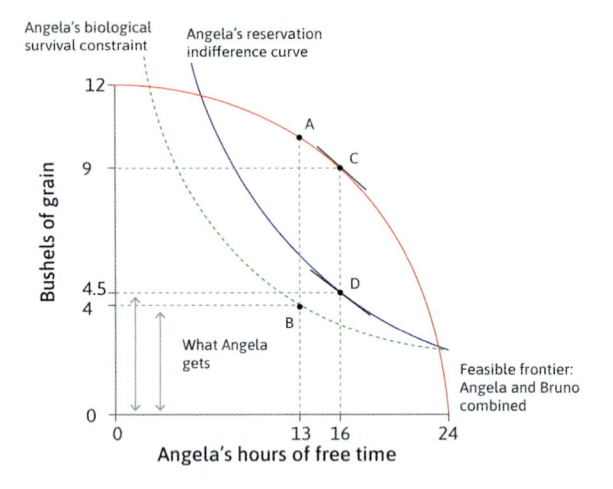

Figure 5.9a Scenario C: Bruno's take-it-or-leave-it proposal when Angela can refuse.

1. Bruno's best outcome using coercion
Using coercion, Bruno chose allocation B. He forced Angela to work for 11 hours and received grain equal to AB. The MRT at A is equal to the MRS at B on Angela's biological survival constraint.

2. When Angela can say no
With voluntary exchange, allocation B is not available. The best that Bruno can do is allocation D, where Angela works for 8 hours, giving him grain equal to CD.

3. MRS = MRT again
When Angela works for 8 hours, the MRT is equal to the MRS on Angela's reservation indifference curve, as shown by the slopes.

Figure 5.9b shows how the surplus (which Bruno gets) varies with Angela's hours. You will see that the surplus falls as Angela works for more or less than 8 hours. It is hump-shaped, like Bruno's rent in the case of coercion. But the peak is lower when Bruno needs Angela to agree to the proposal.

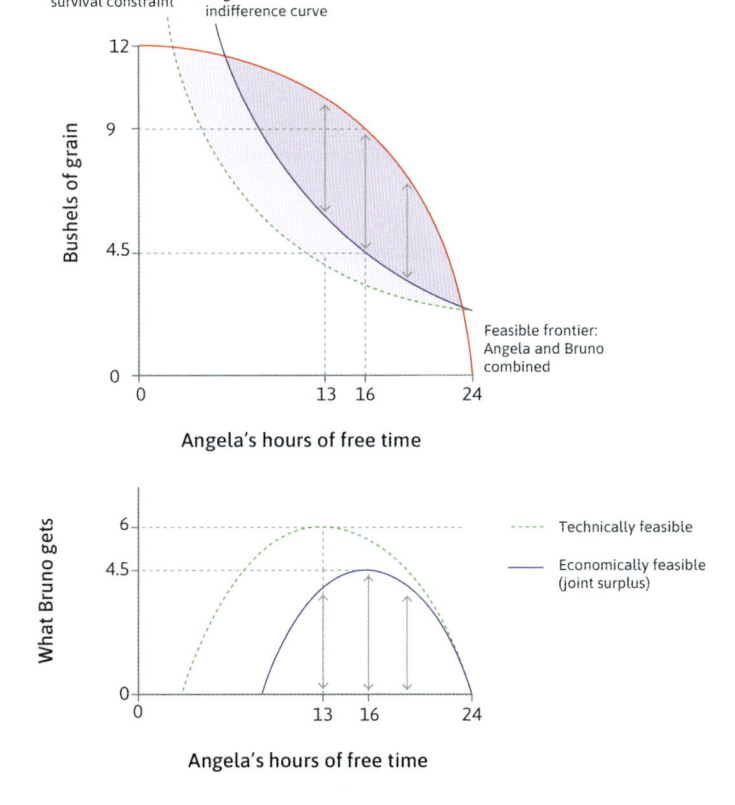

To explore all of the slides in this figure, see the online version at https://tinyco.re/7355244.

Figure 5.9b Scenario C: Bruno's take-it-or-leave-it proposal when Angela can refuse.

1. Angela's working hours when she was coerced
Using coercion, Angela was forced to work for 11 hours. The MRT was equal to the MRS on Angela's biological survival constraint.

2. Bruno's best take-it-or-leave-it offer
When Bruno cannot force Angela to work, he should offer a contract in which Angela pays him 4.5 bushels to rent the land. She works for 8 hours, where the MRT is equal to the MRS on her reservation indifference curve.

3. The maximum surplus
If Angela works for more or less than 8 hours, the joint surplus is less than 4.5 bushels.

4. Bruno's grain
Although Bruno cannot coerce Angela, he can get the whole surplus.

5. Technically and economically feasible peaks compared
The peak of the hump is lower when Angela can refuse, compared to when Bruno could order her to work.

EXERCISE 5.4 TAKE IT OR LEAVE IT?
1. Why is it Bruno, and not Angela, who has the power to make a take-it-or-leave-it offer?
2. Describe a situation in which the farmer, not the landowner, might have this power.

QUESTION 5.7 CHOOSE THE CORRECT ANSWER(S)
Bruno is a landowner and Angela is a farmer who pays a share of her grain output to Bruno for the use of the land. Suppose that Angela works for 8 hours a day and produces 10 bushels of grain. Angela's subsistence level of consumption is 4 bushels of grain. Based on this information, which of the following statements is correct?

- ☐ The surplus from production depends on Bruno and Angela's relative bargaining power.
- ☐ If Angela has all the bargaining power, then her gains from exchange is 10 bushels.
- ☐ The surplus from production is 6 bushels.
- ☐ If Bruno has all the bargaining power, then he will claim all 10 bushels.

QUESTION 5.8 CHOOSE THE CORRECT ANSWER(S)
Figure 5.9a shows Angela and Bruno's feasible frontier, Angela's biological survival constraint, and her reservation indifference curve. B is the outcome under coercion, while D is the outcome under voluntary exchange when Bruno makes a take-it-or-leave-it offer.

From this figure, we can conclude that:

- ☐ With a take-it-or-leave-it offer, Bruno's economic rent is equal to the joint surplus.
- ☐ Both Bruno and Angela are better off under voluntary exchange than under coercion.
- ☐ When Bruno makes a take-it-or-leave-it offer, Angela accepts because she receives an economic rent.
- ☐ Angela works longer under voluntary exchange than under coercion.

5.6 EFFICIENCY AND CONFLICTS OVER THE DISTRIBUTION OF THE SURPLUS

Given that she had the right to say no, Angela chose to work for 8 hours, producing 9 bushels of grain, both when she had to pay a share of the crop to Bruno and also when she did not. In both cases, there is a surplus of 4.5 bushels—the difference between the amount of grain produced, and the amount that would give Angela her reservation utility.

The two cases differ in who gets the surplus. When Angela had to pay a crop share, Bruno took the whole surplus, but when she could work the land for herself, she obtained all the surplus. Both allocations have two important properties:

- *All the grain produced is shared.*
- *MRS = MRT again:* The MRT on the feasible frontier is equal to the MRS on Angela's indifference curve.

This means that the allocations are **Pareto efficient**.

To see why, remember that Pareto efficiency means that it is impossible to change the allocation to make one party better off without making the other worse off; in other words, no Pareto improvement is possible.

The first property is straightforward—it means that no Pareto improvement can be achieved simply by changing the amounts of grain they each consume. If one consumed more, the other would receive less. On the other hand, if some of the grain produced was not being consumed, then consuming it would make one or both of them better off.

The second property, MRS = MRT, means that no Pareto improvement can be achieved by changing Angela's hours of work and hence the amount of grain produced.

If the MRS and MRT were not equal, it would be possible to make both better off. For example, if MRT > MRS, Angela could transform an hour of her time into more grain than she would need to get the same utility as before, so the extra grain could make both of them better off. But if MRT = MRS, then any change in the amount of grain produced would only be exactly what is needed to keep Angela's utility the same as before, given the change in her hours.

Figure 5.10 shows that there are many other Pareto-efficient allocations in addition to these two. Point C is the outcome when Angela is an independent farmer. Compare the analysis in Figure 5.10 with Bruno's take-it-or-leave-it offer to see the other Pareto-efficient allocations.

Figure 5.10 shows that, in addition to the two Pareto-efficient allocations we have observed (C and D), every point between C and D represents a Pareto-efficient allocation. CD is called the **Pareto efficiency curve**—it joins together all the points in the feasible set for which MRS = MRT. (You will also hear it called the contract curve, even in situations where there is no contract, which is why we prefer the more descriptive term Pareto efficiency curve.)

At each allocation on the Pareto efficiency curve, Angela works for 8 hours and there is a surplus of 4.5 bushels, but the distribution of the surplus is different—ranging from point D where Angela gets none of it, to point C where she gets it all. At the hypothetical allocation G, both receive an economic rent—Angela's rent is GD, Bruno's is GC, and the sum of their rents is equal to the surplus.

Pareto efficient An allocation with the property that there is no alternative technically feasible allocation in which at least one person would be better off, and nobody worse off.

PARETO EFFICIENCY AND THE PARETO EFFICIENCY CURVE
- A **Pareto-efficient** allocation has the property that there is no alternative, technically feasible allocation in which at least one person would be better off, and nobody worse off.
- The set of all such allocations is the Pareto efficiency curve. It is also referred to as the contract curve.

Pareto efficiency curve The set of all allocations that are Pareto efficient. Often referred to as the contract curve, even in social interactions in which there is no contract, which is why we avoid the term. *See also:* Pareto efficient.

QUESTION 5.9 CHOOSE THE CORRECT ANSWER(S)
Based on Figure 5.10, which of the following statements is correct?

- ☐ The allocation at C Pareto-dominates the one at D.
- ☐ Angela's marginal rate of substitution is equal to the marginal rate of transformation at all points on the Pareto efficiency curve.
- ☐ The mid-point of CD is the most Pareto-efficient allocation.
- ☐ Angela and Bruno are indifferent between all the points on CD, because they are all Pareto efficient.

To explore all of the slides in this figure, see the online version at https://tinyco.re/3708664.

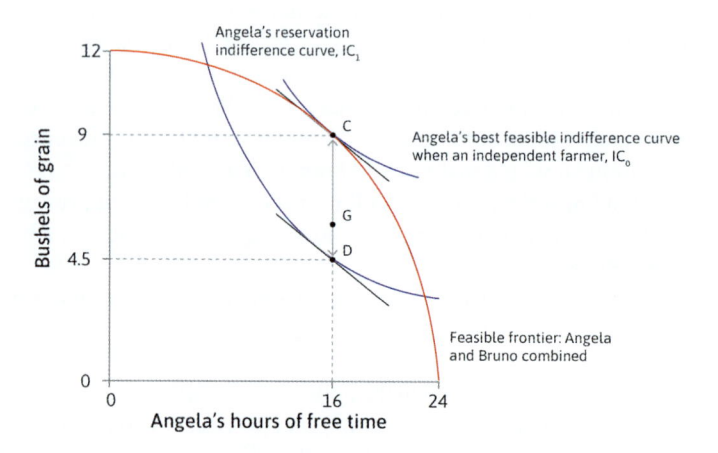

Figure 5.10 Pareto-efficient allocations and the distribution of the surplus.

1. The allocation at C
As an independent farmer, Angela chose point C, where MRT = MRS. She consumed 9 bushels of grain—4.5 bushels would have been enough to put her on her reservation indifference curve at D. But she obtained the whole surplus CD—an additional 4.5 bushels.

2. The allocation at D
When Bruno owned the land and made a take-it-or-leave-it offer, he chose a contract in which the crop share was CD (4.5 bushels). Angela accepted and worked for 8 hours. The allocation was at D, and once again, MRT = MRS. The surplus was still CD, but Bruno got it all.

3. Angela's preferences
Remember that Angela's MRS doesn't change as she consumes more grain. At any point along the line CD, such as G, there is an indifference curve with the same slope. Therefore, MRS = MRT at all these points.

4. A hypothetical allocation
Point G is a hypothetical allocation, at which MRS = MRT. Angela works for 8 hours, and 9 bushels of grain are produced. Bruno gets grain CG, and Angela gets all the rest. Allocation G is Pareto efficient.

5. The Pareto efficiency curve
All the points making up the line between C and D are Pareto-efficient allocations, at which MRS = MRT. The surplus of 4.5 bushels (CD) is shared between Angela and Bruno.

5.7 PROPERTY RIGHTS, THE RULE OF LAW, AND THE RIGHT TO VOTE

Bruno thinks that the new rules, under which he makes an offer that Angela will not refuse, are not so bad after all. Angela is also better off than she had been when she had barely enough to survive. But she would like a share in the surplus.

Fairness: Changing the law by democratic means

Angela and her fellow farm workers lobby for a new law that limits working time to 4 hours a day, while requiring that total pay is at least 4.5 bushels. They threaten to not work at all unless the law is passed.

BRUNO: Angela, you and your colleagues are bluffing.
ANGELA: No, we are not. We would be no worse off at our reservation option than under your contract, working the hours and receiving the small fraction of the harvest that you impose!

Angela and her fellow workers win, and the new law limits the working day to 4 hours.

How did things work out?

Before the short-hours law, Angela worked for 8 hours and received 4.5 bushels of grain. This is point D in Figure 5.11. The new law implements the allocation in which Angela and her friends work for 4 hours, getting 20 hours of free time and the same number of bushels. Since they have the same amount of grain and more free time, they are better off. Figure 5.11 shows they are now on a higher indifference curve.

Angela and Bruno's rents

To sum up, the introduction of the new law has increased Angela's bargaining power and Bruno is worse off than before. You can see that she is better off at F than at D. Because she is better off than she would be with her reservation option, she is now receiving an economic rent.

Remember the term 'economic rent' does not mean what you pay to your landlord, it means what you are getting above what you would get in your reservation position. Bruno's reservation position (if Angela runs away or starves to death) is to get zero. So, whatever he gets from Angela—the customary meaning of the term 'rent'—is also his economic rent.

Angela's economic rent can be measured, in bushels of grain, as the vertical distance between point J on her reservation indifference curve (IC_1 in Figure 5.11) and point F on the indifference curve she is able to achieve under the new legislation (IC_2). We can think of the economic rent in two equivalent ways:

- *What she would give up to live under a better law:* The rent is the maximum amount of grain per year that Angela would give up to live under the new law rather than in the situation before the law was passed.
- *What she would pay to pass a new law and keep it in force from year to year:* Angela is obviously political, and she devotes what spare time she has to trying to change the rules of the game. So you might think of her rent as the maximum amount she would be willing to pay per year to have the law passed and enforced.

We measure Angela's rent in bushels of grain because we can compare this to the rent that Bruno gets which, as we have explained above is just the amount she pays to Bruno. In this model, this happens to coincide with the everyday meaning of 'rent'.

Note that, when economists say 'the maximum amount' Angela would give up, this refers to the amount that would leave her in no worse a position under the new law. In reality, we would expect that she would give up less than the maximum, because she would want to be better off under the new law. This rather formal convention is useful because it allows us, for example, to show the rent precisely in the figure.

> **QUESTION 5.10 CHOOSE THE CORRECT ANSWER(S)**
> In Figure 5.11, D and F are the outcomes before and after the introduction of a new law that limits Angela's work time to 4 hours a day while requiring a minimum pay of 4.5 bushels. Based on this information, which of the following statements are correct?
>
> ☐ The change from D to F is a Pareto improvement.
> ☐ The new outcome F is Pareto efficient.
> ☐ Both Angela and Bruno receive economic rents at F.
> ☐ As a result of the new law, Bruno has less bargaining power.

To explore all of the slides in this figure, see the online version at https://tinyco.re/5732023.

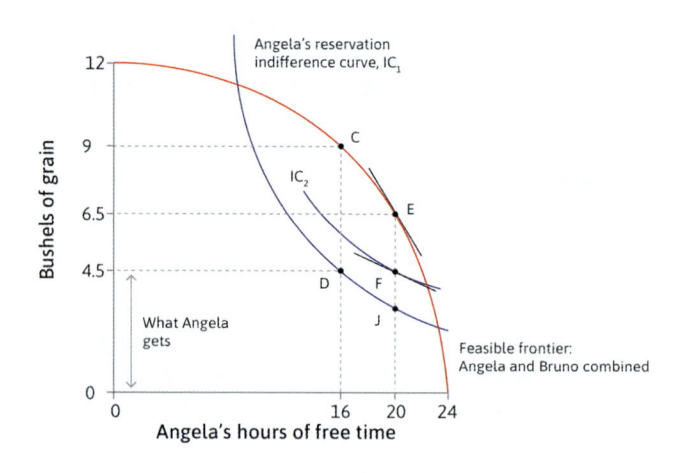

Figure 5.11 Scenario D: The effect of an increase in Angela's bargaining power through legislation.

1. Before the short-hours law
Bruno makes a take-it-or-leave-it offer, gets grain equal to CD, and Angela works for 8 hours. Angela is on her reservation indifference curve at D and MRS = MRT.

2. What Angela receives before legislation
Angela gets 4.5 bushels of grain. She is just indifferent between working for 8 hours and her reservation option.

3. The effect of legislation
With legislation that reduces work to 4 hours a day and keeps Angela's amount of grain unchanged, she is on a higher indifference curve at F. Bruno's grain is reduced from CD to EF (2 bushels).

4. MRT > MRS
When Angela works for 4 hours, the MRT is larger than the MRS on the new indifference curve.

5. Angela's economic rent
Angela's economic rent can be measured, in bushels of grain, as the vertical distance between point J on her reservation indifference curve (IC_1 in Figure 5.11) and point F on the indifference curve she is able to achieve under the new legislation (IC_2).

5.7 PROPERTY RIGHTS, THE RULE OF LAW, AND THE RIGHT TO VOTE

Efficiency: Bargaining to an efficient sharing of the surplus
Angela and her friends are pleased with their success. She asks what you think of the new policy.

YOU: Congratulations, but your policy is far from the best you could do.
ANGELA: Why?
YOU: Because you are not on the Pareto efficiency curve! Under your new law, Bruno is getting 2 bushels, and cannot make you work for more than 4 hours. So why don't you offer to continue to pay him 2 bushels, in exchange for agreeing to let you keep anything you produce above that? Then you get to choose how many hours you work.

The small print in the law allows a longer work day if both parties agree, as long as the workers' reservation option is a 4-hour day if no agreement is reached.

Now redraw Figure 5.11 and use the concepts of the joint surplus and the Pareto efficiency curve from Figure 5.10 to show Angela how she can get a better deal.

YOU: Look at Figure 5.12. The surplus is largest at 8 hours of work. When you work for 4 hours, the surplus is smaller, and you pay most of it to Bruno. If you increase the surplus, you can pay him the same amount and your own surplus will be bigger—so you will be better off. Follow the steps in Figure 5.12 to see how this works.

The move away from point D (at which Bruno had all the bargaining power and obtained all the gains from exchange) to point H where Angela is better off consists of two distinct steps:

1. *From D to F, the outcome is imposed by new legislation:* This was definitely not win–win. Bruno lost because his economic rent at F is less than the maximum feasible rent that he got at D. Angela benefitted.
2. *Once at the legislated outcome, there were many win–win possibilities open to them:* They are shown by the segment GH on the Pareto efficiency curve. Win–win alternatives to the allocation at F are possible by definition, because F was not Pareto efficient.

Bruno wants to negotiate. He is not happy with Angela's proposal of H.

BRUNO: I am no better off under this new plan than I would be if I just accepted the short-hours legislation.
YOU: But Bruno, Angela now has bargaining power, too. The legislation changed her reservation option, so it is no longer 24 hours of free time at survival rations. Her reservation option is now the legislated allocation at point F. I suggest you make her a counter offer.
BRUNO: Angela, I'll let you work the land for as many hours as you choose, if you pay me half a bushel more than EF.

They shake hands on the deal.

Because Angela is free to choose her work hours, subject only to paying Bruno the extra half bushel, she will work for 8 hours where MRT = MRS. Because this deal lies between G and H, it is a Pareto improvement over point F. Moreover, because it is on the Pareto-efficient curve CD, we know there are no further Pareto improvements to be made. This is true of every other allocation on GH—they differ only in the distribution of the mutual gains, as some favour Angela while others favour Bruno. Where they end up will depend on their bargaining power.

> **QUESTION 5.11 CHOOSE THE CORRECT ANSWER(S)**
>
> In Figure 5.12, Angela and Bruno are at allocation F, where she receives 3 bushels of grain for 4 hours of work. From the figure, we can conclude that:
>
> ☐ All the points on EF are Pareto efficient.
> ☐ Any point in the area between G, H and F would be a Pareto improvement.
> ☐ Any point between G and D would be a Pareto improvement.
> ☐ They would both be indifferent between all points on GH.

To explore all of the slides in this figure, see the online version at https://tinyco.re/7515393.

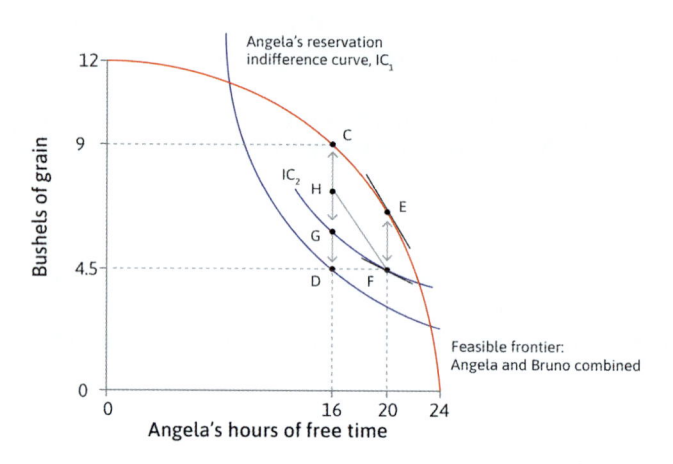

Figure 5.12 Bargaining to restore Pareto efficiency.

1. The maximum joint surplus
The surplus to be divided between Angela and Bruno is maximized where MRT = MRS, at 8 hours of work.

2. Angela prefers F to D
But Angela prefers point F implemented by the legislation, because it gives her the same amount of grain but more free time than D.

3. Angela could also do better than F
Compared to F, however, she would prefer any allocation on the Pareto efficiency curve between C and G.

4. Angela can propose H
At allocation H, Bruno gets the same amount of grain—CH = EF. Angela is better off than she was at F. She works longer hours but has more than enough grain to compensate her for the loss of free time.

5. A win–win agreement by moving to an allocation between G and H
F is not Pareto efficient because MRT > MRS. If they move to a point on the Pareto efficiency curve between G and H, Angela and Bruno can both be better off.

5.8 THE LESSONS FROM ANGELA AND BRUNO'S STORY

Angela's farming skills and Bruno's ownership of land provided an opportunity for mutual gains from exchange.

The same is true when people directly exchange, or buy and sell, goods for money. Suppose you have more apples than you can consume, and your neighbour has an abundance of pears. The apples are worth less to you than to your neighbour, and the pears are worth more to you. Therefore, it must be possible to achieve a Pareto improvement by exchanging some apples and pears.

When people with differing needs, property, and capacities meet, there is an opportunity to generate gains for all of them. That is why people come together in markets, online exchanges, or pirate ships. The mutual gains are what we call the surplus.

The allocations that we observe through history are largely the result of the institutions, including property rights and bargaining power, that were present in the economy. Figure 5.13 summarizes what we have learnt about the determination of economic outcomes from the succession of scenarios involving Angela and Bruno:

- *Technology and biology determine whether or not they are able to mutually benefit:* This is because they determine the technically feasible set of allocations in Section 5.4 (page 194). If Bruno's land had been so unproductive that Angela's labour could not produce enough to keep her alive, then there would have been no room for a deal.
- *Economically feasible allocations must be Pareto improvements of their reservation options:* Those reservation options may depend on institutions (such as Angela's survival rations from the government (Section 5.5 (page 200)) or legislation on working hours in Section 5.7 (page 209).
- *The outcome of an interaction depends both on what people want and their ability to get it:* Their preferences, and the institutions that provide their bargaining power, decide how the surplus is distributed in Section 5.7 (page 209).

The story of Angela and Bruno highlights that, if we have institutions under which people can jointly deliberate, agree on, and enforce alternative allocations, then it may be possible to achieve a fairer outcome that is also Pareto efficient. Angela and Bruno did this through a combination of legislation and bargaining between themselves (point H).

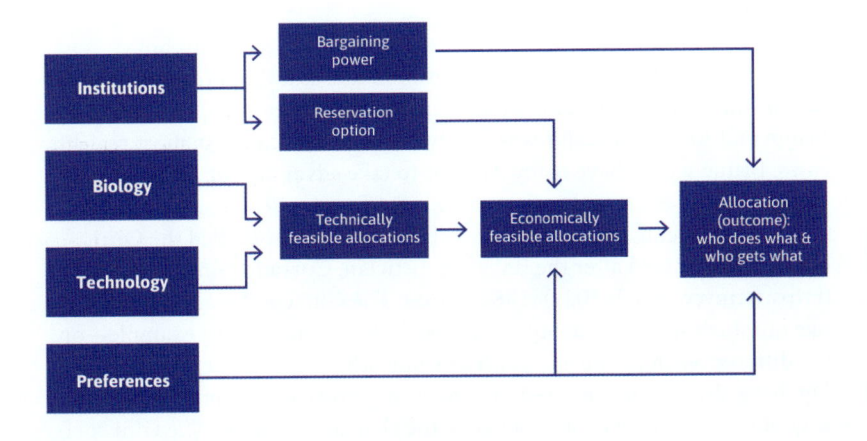

Figure 5.13 The fundamental determinants of economic outcomes.

5.9 MEASURING ECONOMIC INEQUALITY

In our analysis of the interaction between Angela and Bruno, we have assessed the allocations in terms of Pareto efficiency. We have seen that they (or at least one of them) can be better off if they can negotiate a move from a Pareto-inefficient allocation to one on the Pareto efficiency curve.

Fairness and inequality

But the other important criterion for assessing an allocation is fairness. We know that Pareto-efficient allocations can be highly unequal. In the case of Angela and Bruno, inequality resulted directly from differences in bargaining power, but also from differences in their **endowments**—what they each owned before the interaction (their initial wealth). Bruno owned land, while Angela had nothing except time and the capacity to work. Differences in endowments, as well as institutions, may in turn affect bargaining power.

endowment The facts about an individual that may affect his or her income, such as the physical wealth a person has, either land, housing, or a portfolio of shares (stocks). Also includes level and quality of schooling, special training, the computer languages in which the individual can work, work experience in internships, citizenship, whether the individual has a visa (or green card) allowing employment in a particular labour market, the nationality and gender of the individual, and even the person's race or social class background. *See also: human capital.*

The Gini coefficient

In our parable, summarized in Figures 5.2 (page 191) and 5.3 (page 192), Angela and Bruno lived under a series of four distinct institutional settings—Angela as an independent farmer; Bruno as the enforcer with unlimited power over Angela; both living under the rule of private property and voluntary transactions, first without and later with a democratic government. In the first—Angela as an independent farmer—Bruno was not in the picture, so she could enjoy everything she produced. But in the last three, Bruno's share of what Angela produced differed, resulting in differing levels of inequality between the two.

If we wanted to say *how unequal* the two were in the amount of grain they could consume, we could say that, under Bruno's rule of force (Figure 5.7 (page 199)), he got 6 bushels and she got 4, so the difference in what they got—the inequality—was 2 bushels of grain. But if we wanted to compare this measure of inequality with what some other enforcer and farmer—such as a farmer growing apples—were experiencing, we would run into trouble as we would be comparing 'apple-differences' with 'grain-differences'. To make the measures comparable, we could divide the difference—2 bushels of grain in the Angela and Bruno case—by the average amount of grain that each got—that is (6 + 4)/2 = 5. Our measure of inequality would be:

$$\frac{\text{difference in grain between the two}}{\text{average grain for the two}} = \frac{2}{5} = 0.4$$

This would work if there were just two people in the economy, but remember we introduced the two-person model as a simplification that will help us understand economies made up of a great many people. Even in the Bruno and Angela case, this was highly unrealistic because, in most real-life cases, Bruno would have many Angelas to take advantage of, just as the landlords in West Bengal each received rent from a great many bargadars.

To assess inequality, economists often use a measure called the **Gini coefficient**, named after the Italian statistician, Corrado Gini (https://tinyco.re/8561031) (1884–1965). The Gini coefficient is based—like our analysis of inequality in the above Bruno and Angela example—on the differences in incomes, wealth or some other measure between people. You have already encountered (in Unit 1 (page 6)) the rich/poor ratio as a way of measuring inequality between the rich and the poor. The Gini coef-

Gini coefficient A measure of inequality of any quantity such as income or wealth, varying from a value of zero (if there is no inequality) to one (if a single individual receives all of it).

ficient has the advantage that it includes information about everyone, not just the rich and the poor, but those 'in the middle' too.

To see what this means, consider the three-person population shown in Figure 5.14. The circles are people and the numbers within the circles are the income received. The numbers next to the arrows are the differences between the two people, indicated by the arrows. The Gini coefficient is calculated from two pieces of information:

- *The average of the differences between the people:* In the example, this is $(10 + 8 + 2)/3 = 20/3 = 6.67$
- *The average income of the people:* In the example, this is $(12 + 4 + 2)/3 = 6$

The Gini coefficient is equal to one-half times the first number (the average difference) divided by the second number (the average income). For the example, the Gini equals $0.5(6.67/6) = 0.56$. The Gini coefficient is equal to 1 if a single person owns all the income, and 0 if everyone has the same income.

- *If one person has all the income:* That is, 18, then the average of the differences would be $(18 + 18 + 0)/3 = 12$. The average income, as before, would be 6, so the Gini coefficient would be 1.
- *If they all have the same income:* Then there are no differences between any of the pairs, so the Gini coefficient must be zero.

In general, when we calculate the Gini coefficient, we obtain a number between 0 (perfect equality) and 1 (extreme inequality). The more unequally resources are distributed amongst the members of the population, the larger is the Gini coefficient.

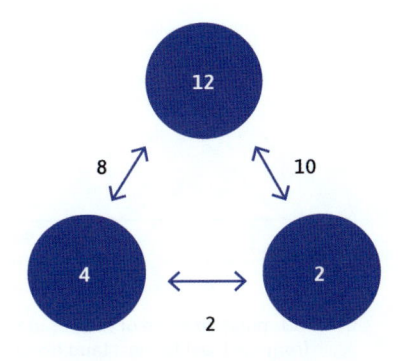

Figure 5.14 Income differences among pairs of households.

Lorenz curve A graphical representation of inequality of some quantity such as wealth or income. Individuals are arranged in ascending order by how much of this quantity they have, and the cumulative share of the total is then plotted against the cumulative share of the population. For complete equality of income, for example, it would be a straight line with a slope of one. The extent to which the curve falls below this perfect equality line is a measure of inequality. See also: Gini coefficient.

Max O. Lorenz. 1905. 'Methods of Measuring the Concentration of Wealth' (https://tinyco.re/0786587). *Publications of the American Statistical Association* 9 (70).

Measuring inequality—the Lorenz curve

A useful tool for looking at the entire distribution of income or wealth representing and comparing distributions of income or wealth across countries, is the **Lorenz curve** (invented in 1905 by Max Lorenz (1876–1959), an American economist, while he was still a student). It indicates how much disparity there is in income, or any other measure, across the population.

The Lorenz curve shows the entire population lined up along the horizontal axis from the poorest to the richest. The height of the curve at any point on the horizontal axis indicates the fraction of total income received by the fraction of the population given by that point on the horizontal axis.

To see how this works, imagine a village in which there are 10 landowners, each owning 10 hectares, and 90 others who farm the land as sharecroppers, but who own no land (like Angela in the model or a bargadar in Bengal). The Lorenz curve is the blue line in Figure 5.15. Lining the population up in order of land ownership, the first 90% of the population own nothing, so the curve is flat. The remaining 10% own 10 hectares each, so the 'curve' rises in a straight line to reach the point where 100% of people own 100% of the land.

If each member of the population owned one hectare of land—perfect equality in land ownership—then the Lorenz curve would be a line at a 45-degree angle, indicating that the 'poorest' 10% of the population have 10% of the land, and so on (although in this case, everyone is equally poor and equally rich).

The Lorenz curve allows us to see how far a distribution departs from this line of perfect equality. Figure 5.16 shows the distribution of income that would have resulted from the prize-sharing system described in the articles of the pirate ship, the *Royal Rover*, discussed in the introduction to this unit. The Lorenz curve is very close to the 45-degree line, showing how the institutions of piracy allowed ordinary members of the crew to claim a large share of income.

In contrast, when the Royal Navy's ships, *Favourite* and *Active*, captured the Spanish treasure ship *La Hermione*, the division of the spoils on the two British men-of-war ships was far less equal. The Lorenz curves show that ordinary crew members received about a quarter of the income, with the

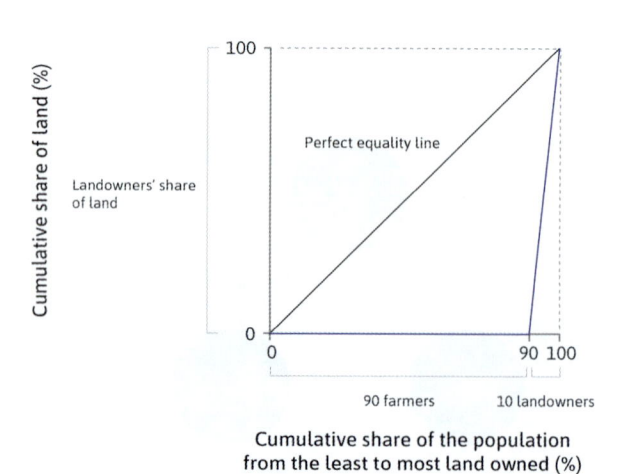

Figure 5.15 A Lorenz curve for wealth ownership.

remainder going to a small number of officers and the captain. You can see that the *Favourite* was more unequal that the *Active*, with a lower share going to each crew member. By the standards of the day, pirates were unusually democratic and fair-minded in their dealings with each other.

The Lorenz curve and the Gini coefficient

The Lorenz curve gives us a picture of the disparity of income across the whole population, and there is a very simple relationship between the Lorenz curve and the Gini coefficient. You can see that more unequal distributions have a greater area between the Lorenz curve and the 45-degree line. The Gini coefficient (or Gini ratio) introduced above, is calculated as the ratio of this area to the area of the whole of the triangle under the 45-degree line.

Using this new way of seeing the Gini coefficient, you can confirm (as you already learned) that, if everyone has the same income, (there is no income inequality), the Gini coefficient takes a value of 0. This is because the Lorenz curve would be the line of perfect equality itself, so there would be no area between the two. This is just as in the previous example under perfect equality there are no differences in the income of any pairs in the population.

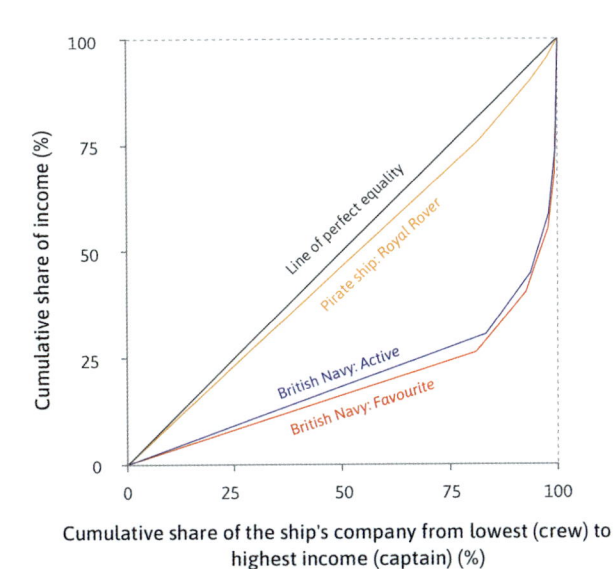

To explore all of the slides in this figure, see the online version at https://tinyco.re/3987590.

Figure 5.16 The distribution of spoils: Pirates and the Royal Navy.

1. The line of perfect equality
The Lorenz curve allows us to see how far a distribution departs from this line of perfect equality.

2. The Royal Rover
The Lorenz curve for the *Royal Rover* is very close to the line of perfect equality. Income was shared quite equally between crew members.

3. The British Navy ships
In contrast, the Lorenz curves for the British Navy's ships are much further away from the line of perfect inequality. Income was concentrated in a small group of senior officers, with ordinary crew members receiving a much lower share.

We can calculate the Gini for land ownership in Figure 5.17a as area A, between the Lorenz curve and the perfect equality line, as a proportion of area (A + B), the triangle under the 45-degree line:

$$\text{Gini} = \frac{A}{A + B}$$

Figure 5.17b shows the Gini coefficients for each of the Lorenz curves we have drawn so far.

Strictly speaking, this graphical method of calculating the Gini gives only an approximation. To calculate it precisely, we need to work out the average difference in income between every pair of individuals in the population, as we did in the example at the beginning of this section. We know that the Gini is equal to 1 when a single individual receives all the income, but you can see from Figure 5.17b that the area method would give a number slightly less than 1. The area approximation is accurate only when the population is large (https://tinyco.re/2558071).

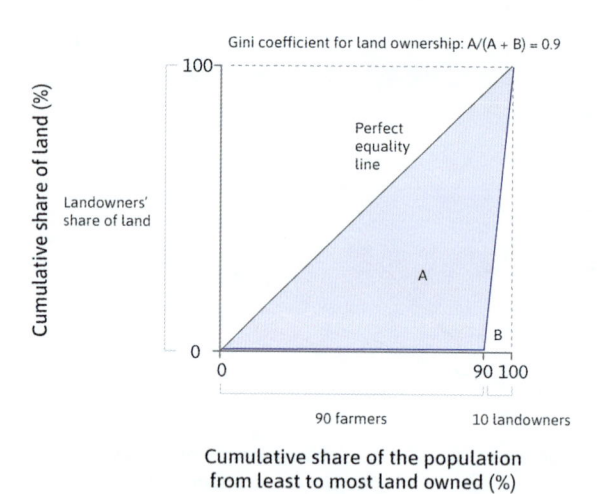

Figure 5.17a The Lorenz curve and Gini coefficient for wealth ownership.

Distribution	Gini
Pirate ship *Royal Rover*	0.06
British Navy ship *Active*	0.59
British Navy ship *Favourite*	0.60
The village with sharecroppers and landowners	0.90

Figure 5.17b Comparing Gini coefficients.

Varieties of inequality

The Gini coefficient measures inequality using a single number. But not all inequalities are equal!

Sometimes, we are interested in whether a society is highly unequal because there is a small number of exceptionally rich people—everyone else being moderately well off—or, instead, there are a small number of very poor people—everyone else being better off. These two societies could have the same Gini coefficient, but we would think of them as quite different in the nature of the inequality that they experience.

In Figure 5.18, we show two societies with the same Gini coefficient. The area A/(A + B) is the same in each Lorenz curve but the distribution of income is far from identical. In the society on the left, one-half of the total income is split among 90 farmers; the 10 landowners get the remaining half. In the society shown on the right, 50 poor farmers get one-tenth of the income to split between them and the richer 50 farmers split the remaining 90%.

> **EXERCISE 5.5 INCOME INEQUALITY AND ITS MEASUREMENT**
> Write a short description comparing the life of a farmer in the two societies shown in Figure 5.18. Do the same comparison for landowners. You should assume that the total income in each society is identical. In particular, consider what the schools, political systems, workplaces, and cities might look like.

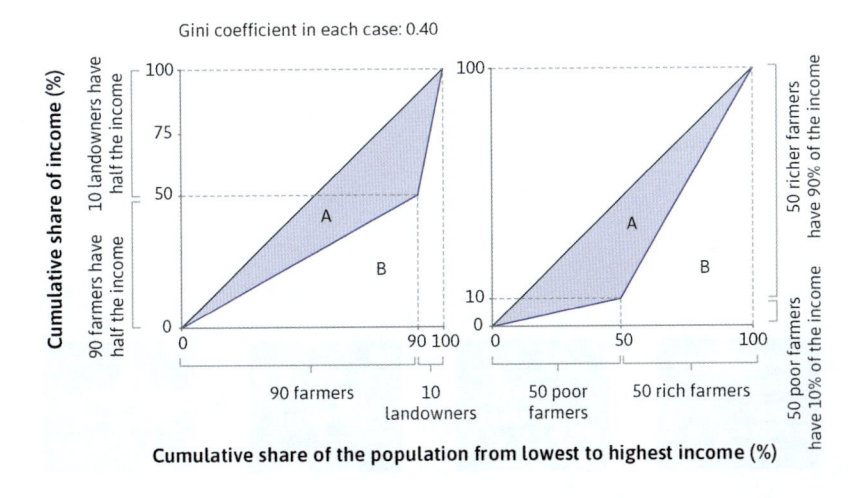

Figure 5.18 Two societies with the same Gini coefficient but different Lorenz curves.

disposable income Income available after paying taxes and receiving transfers from the government.

public policy A policy decided by the government. *Also known as:* government policy.

5.10 COMPARING INEQUALITY ACROSS THE WORLD

To assess income inequality within a country, we can either look at total market income (all income from employment, self-employment, savings and investments), or **disposable income**, which better captures living standards. Disposable income is what a household can spend without borrowing money, after paying tax and receiving transfers (such as unemployment benefit and pensions) from the government.

In Unit 1 (page 6), we compared inequality in the income distributions of countries using the rich/poor ratio. Lorenz curves give us a fuller picture of how distributions differ. Figure 5.20 shows the distribution of market income in the Netherlands in 2010. The Gini coefficient is 0.47, so by this measure it has greater inequality than the *Royal Rover*, but less than the British Navy ships.

The analysis of Figure 5.20 shows how redistributive **government policies** result in a more equal distribution of disposable income.

Notice that, in the Netherlands, almost one-fifth of the households have a near-zero market income, but most nonetheless have enough disposable income to survive, or even live comfortably—the poorest one-fifth of the population receive about 10% of all disposable income.

The Gini and the 90/10 ratio are widely used to measure income inequality, but they are not the only measure. Recall that we used the rich/poor ratio in Unit 1, which is similar but not precisely the same as the 90/10 ratio.

Figure 5.21 (page 222) compares the Gini coefficients for disposable and market income across a large sample of countries, ordered from left to right, from the least to the most unequal by the disposable income measure. The main reason for the substantial differences between nations in disposable income inequality is the extent to which governments can tax well-off families and transfer the proceeds to the less well off.

Notice that:

- The differences between countries in disposable income inequality (the top of the lower bars) are much greater than the differences in inequality of market incomes (the top of the upper bars).
- The US and the UK are among the most unequal of the high-income economies.
- The few poor and middle-income countries for which data is available are even more unequal in disposable income than the US, but …
- … (with the exception of South Africa) this is mainly the result of the limited degree of redistribution from rich to poor, rather than unusually high inequality in market income.

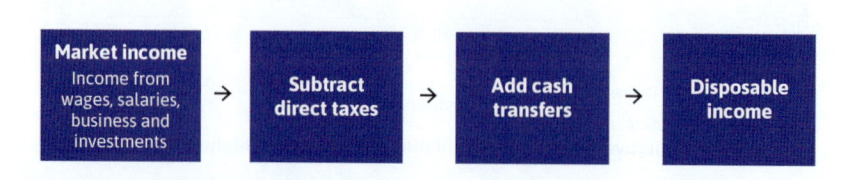

Market income (Income from wages, salaries, business and investments) → Subtract direct taxes → Add cash transfers → Disposable income

Figure 5.19 The difference between market and disposable income.

5.10 COMPARING INEQUALITY ACROSS THE WORLD

Two important questions arise from the figure—why is market income inequality so different between, say South Africa and South Korea? And, why do we see such a big difference in market income inequality and disposable income inequality—one measure of how much rich–to-poor redistribution the government does? You can see this by comparing China, India, and the US, on the one hand, with Sweden, Germany, and Hungary, on the other.

Because the Gini coefficient uses a single number to measure how unequal people are according to some economic indicator such as their income, it allows very intuitive statements about what this number means.

If we were to compare every possible pair in the population, the richer of the pair will have some multiple of the income or wealth of the poorer given by the following equation:

$$\frac{\text{income of the richer}}{\text{income of the poorer}} = \frac{1 + \text{Gini}}{1 - \text{Gini}}$$

For more on global income inequalities have a look at Hans Rosling's video, in which he demonstrates inequality using snowballs. https://tinyco.re/4876987

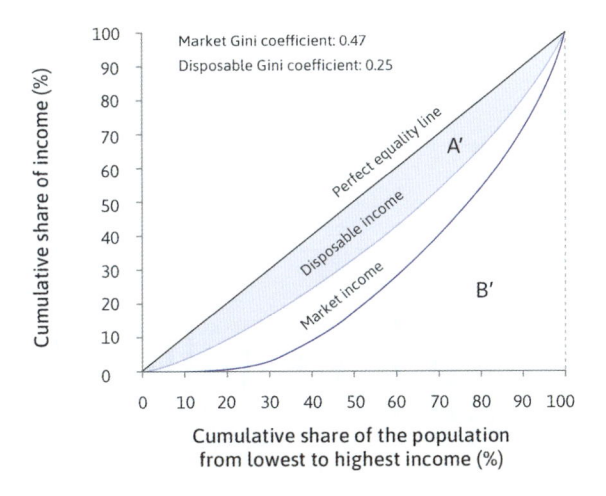

To explore all of the slides in this figure, see the online version at https://tinyco.re/5669154.
LIS. *Cross National Data Center* (https://tinyco.re/0525655). Stefan Thewissen (University of Oxford) did the calculations in April 2015. Household market (labour and capital) income and disposable income are equivalized and top- and bottom-coded.

Figure 5.20 Distribution of market and disposable income in the Netherlands (2010).

1. The Lorenz curve for market income
The curve indicates that the poorest 10% of the population (10 on the horizontal axis) receive only 0.1% of total income (0.1 on the vertical axis), and the lower-earning half of the population has less than 20% of the income.

2. The Gini for market income
The Gini coefficient is the ratio of area A (between the market income curve and the perfect equality line) to area A + B (below the perfect equality line), which is 0.47.

3. Disposable income
The amount of inequality in disposable income is much smaller than the inequality in market income. Redistributive policies have a bigger effect towards the bottom of the distribution. The poorest 10% have 4% of total disposable income.

4. The Gini for disposable income
The Gini coefficient for disposable income is lower. The ratio of areas A′ (between the disposable income curve and the perfect equality line) and A′ + B′ (below the perfect equality line) is 0.25.

221

So, if the Gini coefficient was 0.5, then the richer person is, on average, three times richer than the poorer person (1.5/0.5 = 3). This corresponds to the rich person getting three-quarters of the pie and the poorer person getting one-quarter.

Applying this to the Dutch income distribution, this means that if you randomly selected many pairs of people from the Dutch population on average the richer of the two would be (1 + 0.47)/(1 − 0.47) = 2.78 times as rich as the poorer.

The disposable income Gini coefficient of 0.25 means that on average the richer of the pairs randomly selected in a population will have 1.67 times the disposable income of the poorer (the ratio for market incomes was 2.78).

> **EXERCISE 5.6 COMPARING DISTRIBUTIONS OF WEALTH**
> Figure 5.22 shows three alternative distributions of land ownership in a village with 100 people and 100 hectares of land. Draw the Lorenz curves for each case.
>
> For cases I and III, calculate the Gini. For case II, show on the Lorenz curve diagram how the Gini coefficient can be calculated.

LIS. *Cross National Data Center* (https://tinyco.re/0525566). Stefan Thewissen (University of Oxford) did the calculations in April 2015.

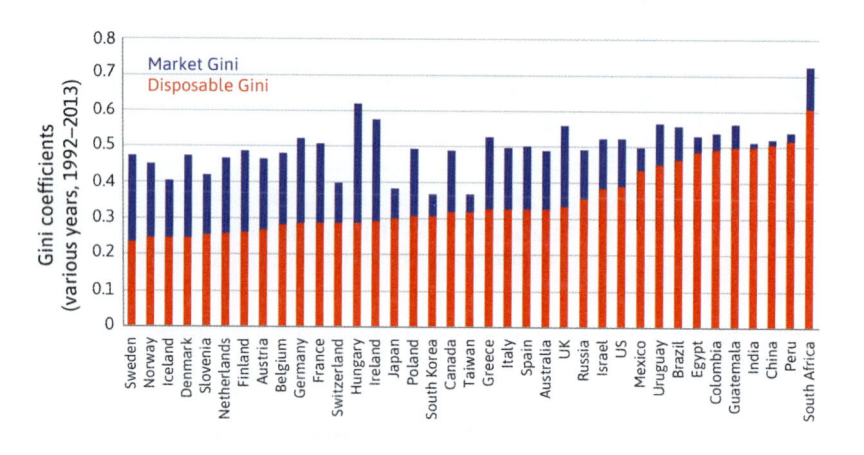

Figure 5.21 Income inequality in market and disposable income across the world.

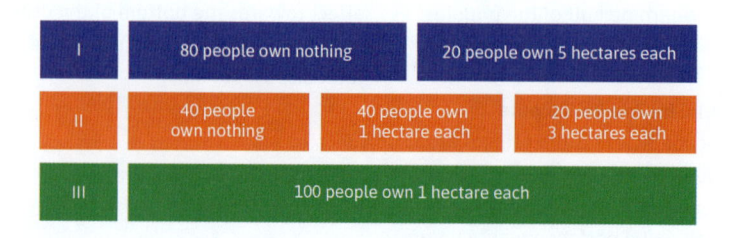

I	80 people own nothing	20 people own 5 hectares each
II	40 people own nothing	40 people own 1 hectare each	20 people own 3 hectares each
III	100 people own 1 hectare each

Figure 5.22 Three distributions of wealth (100 hectares of land).

QUESTION 5.12 CHOOSE THE CORRECT ANSWER(S)
Based on Figure 5.20 (page 221), which of the following statements are true?

☐ One-fifth of the Dutch population has virtually no market income.
☐ The Gini coefficient is larger for disposable income than for market income.
☐ The difference between market income and disposable income is taxes and cash transfers.
☐ The poorest one-fifth of the population receive about 20% of all disposable income.

QUESTION 5.13 CHOOSE THE CORRECT ANSWER(S)
Based on Figure 5.21, which of the following statements are true?

☐ Countries with lower Gini coefficients have less equal income distributions.
☐ Countries with a smaller difference between market income and disposable income Gini coefficients have more effective redistributive policies.
☐ The differences in market income Gini coefficients across countries are smaller than the differences in disposable income Gini coefficients across countries.
☐ Countries that have a higher degree of market income inequality also tend to have a higher degree of disposable income inequality.

FIND OUT MORE

The Gini coefficient as a measure of inequality
There are two other ways of looking at the Gini coefficient that will help you understand what the number means.

First, from the example in Figure 5.14 (page 215), if the richest person had an income of 10, then the average difference between all pairs divided by the mean income in the population would be twice the Gini coefficient. So, in this particular example where the Gini coefficient is 0.5, the average difference is the mean income itself. You can try another example for yourself by altering the numbers in the diagram in Figure 5.14.

Second, suppose there are just two people in a population and they are dividing a 'pie' representing total wealth. The portion received by the disadvantaged person is simply one-half of (1 − Gini). So in the example above where the Gini is 0.5, the poorer person gets a slice equal to one-quarter of the pie and the richer person gets three-quarters of the pie.

For another interpretation of the Gini coefficient, see Einstein 19.1 in *The Economy* (https://tinyco.re/4043896).

EXERCISE 5.7 USING EXCEL: INEQUALITIES AMONG YOUR CLASSMATES

1. Record the heights of you and your classmates in an Excel spreadsheet. Now, make a table with percentiles (0–100, in increments of 1) in one column and the corresponding cumulative share of the population in another column. Use this table to draw a Lorenz curve for height. Follow the full walk-through in Figure 5.23 online (https://tinyco.re/1936417) on how to draw a Lorenz curve in Excel.

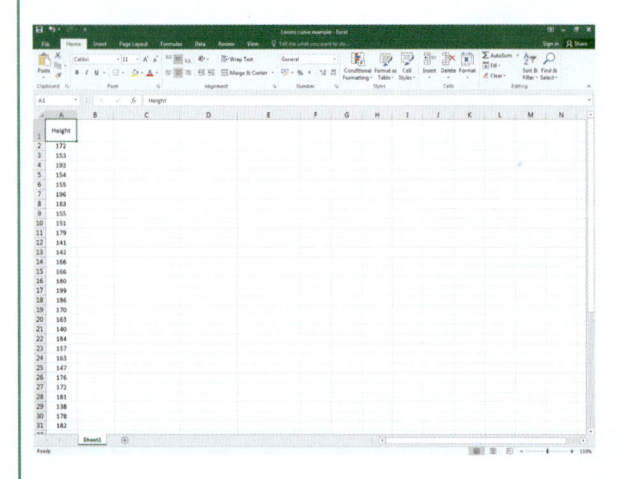

Figure 5.23 Drawing a Lorenz curve.

1. The data
We will be drawing a Lorenz curve of the height data in Column A (30 observations total, height measured in centimetres).

2. Calculate the heights corresponding to each decile
First, we will make a table with columns that correspond to the horizontal and vertical axis of the Lorenz curve diagram (Columns C and E respectively). We need Column D to calculate the values in Column E.

3. Calculate the cumulative share of height 'owned' by each decile
To calculate the values in Column E, we need to add up all the heights with values less than the corresponding value in Column D, and then divide by the sum of all heights in Column A.

4. Calculate the cumulative share of height 'owned' by each decile
The '$' signs in the formula shown ensure that the same range of cells is used, even when copying the formula to other cells. Without this sign, Excel would use a different range for each cell (e.g. the cell below would have A3:A32).

5. Draw a Lorenz curve (line chart)
After step 8, the line chart will look like the chart on the left above. The Lorenz curve is in orange, and the perfect equality line is in blue. The Gini coefficient is 5.79, indicating near perfect equality.

6. Another Lorenz curve
Our curve looks similar to the Lorenz curve from the Gini coefficient calculator (https://tinyco.re/8392848) website, shown here.

2. Using a Gini coefficient calculator (https://tinyco.re/8392848), calculate the degree of inequality of height (in cm) among your classmates. Check that your Lorenz curve looks like the one shown.
3. Explain any differences between the Gini coefficient you calculated for height, and those for market and disposable income in Figure 5.21 (page 222).

How Operation Barga changed the Lorenz curve and the Gini coefficient

Angela and Bruno live in the hypothetical world of an economic model, but real farmers and landowners face similar problems.

We do not have detailed information on the change in inequality that accompanied the implementation of Operation Barga described in Section 5.1 (page 185), but we can illustrate the effect of the land reform on the distribution of income in the hypothetical village of the previous section, with 90 sharecroppers and 10 landowners. Figure 5.24 shows the Lorenz curves. Initially, the farmers pay a rent of 50% of their crop to the landowners. Operation Barga raises the farmer's crop share to 75%, moving the Lorenz curve towards the 45-degree line. As a result, the Gini coefficient of income is reduced from 0.4 (similar to the US) to 0.15 (well below that of the most equal of the rich economies, such as Denmark). The 'Find out more' box at the end of this section shows you how the Gini coefficient depends on the proportion of farmers and their crop share.

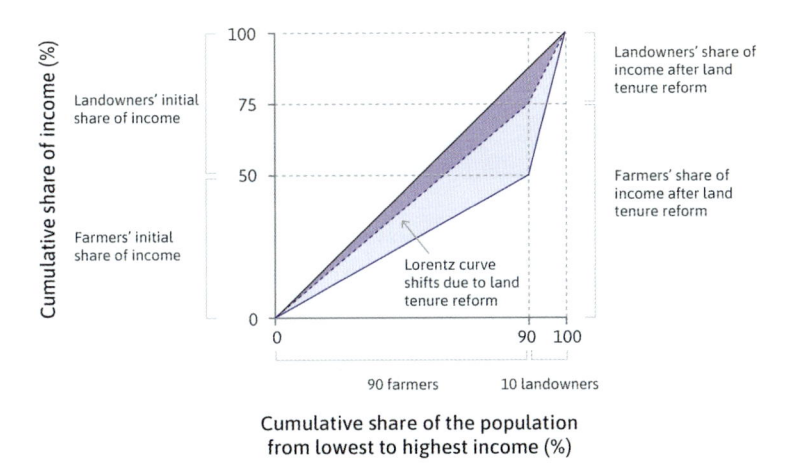

Figure 5.24 Bargaining in practice: How a land tenure reform in West Bengal reduced the Gini coefficient.

> **FIND OUT MORE**
>
> ### The Lorenz curve and the Gini coefficient in a class-divided economy with a large population
>
> Think about a population of 100 people in which a fraction, n, produces the output, and the others are employers (or landlords, or other claimants on income who are not producers).
>
> Take, as an example, the farmers and landlords in the text (in West Bengal). Each of the $n \times 100$ farmers produces q and they each receive a fraction, s, of this; so each of the farmers has income sq. The $(1 - n) \times 100$ employers each receive an income of $(1 - s)q$.
>
> Figure 5.25 presents the Lorenz curve and the perfect equality line, similar to Figure 5.24 in the text.
>
> **Figure 5.25** The Lorenz curve and the perfect equality line.
>
> The slope of the line separating area A from B_1 is s/n (the fraction of total output that each farmer gets), and the slope of the line separating area A from B_3 is $(1 - s)/(1 - n)$, the fraction of total output that each landlord gets. We can approximate the Gini coefficient by the expression $A/(A + B)$, where in the figure $B = B_1 + B_2 + B_3$.
>
> We can express the Gini coefficient in terms of the triangles and rectangle in the figure. To see how, note that the area of the entire square is 1, while the area (A+B) under the perfect equality line is 1/2. The area A is $(1/2) - B$. Then we can write the Gini coefficient as:
>
> $$g = \frac{(0.5 - B_1 + B_2 + B_3)}{0.5} = 1 - 2(B_1 + B_2 + B_3)$$
>
> We can see from the figure that:
>
> $$B_1 = \frac{ns}{2}$$
>
> $$B_2 = (1 - n)s$$
>
> $$B_3 = \frac{(1 - n)(1 - s)}{2}$$

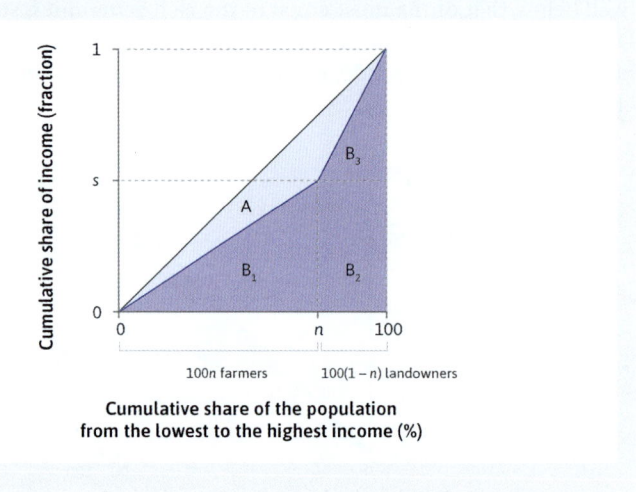

So

$$g = 1 - 2(\frac{ns}{2} + (1-n)s + \frac{(1-n)(1-s)}{2}$$
$$= 1 - (ns + 2s - 2ns + 1 - s + n + ns)$$
$$= n - s$$

This means that the Gini coefficient in this simple case is just the fraction of the total population producing the output (the farmers) minus the fraction of the output that they receive in income.

Inequality will increase in this model economy if:

- *The fraction of producers in the economy increases but the total share of output they receive remains unchanged:* This would be the case if some of the landlords became farmer tenants, each receiving a fraction, *s*, of the crop they produced.
- *The fraction of the crop received by the producers falls.*

5.11 CONCLUSION

Interactions among people are governed by political and economic **institutions**, which are the rules of the game in a society. Institutions comprise both formal rules (like laws and regulations) and informal customs (such as social norms), as well as the methods by which these are enforced.

The **economic rent** gained by each party to an interaction is how much better off they are with the interaction than they would have been without it, at their **reservation option**. When people voluntarily engage in an interaction, there must be economic rents. The sum of economic rents is the **joint surplus**.

Two important aspects of any interaction are the size of the joint surplus and how it is distributed among the parties. The latter depends on their **bargaining power**, which is influenced by institutions (such as property rights or how the government is selected) and conditions affecting the extent to which people cooperate rather than act individually.

In a democracy, **government policies** can increase the fairness of how the joint surplus is shared. An example studied is Operation Barga in India. Both government policies and private bargaining can implement a more efficient allocation.

We have used our constrained choice model toolkit to show that even the very powerful face limits as to how much they can get. The same model allows us to analyse how different institutional settings affect the degree of inequality in resulting allocations, by altering the balance of bargaining power between the parties engaging in the exchange.

While technology (the production function) determines the feasible frontier, subsistence requirements impose biological constraints. Together, these form the boundaries of the **technically feasible** set. With voluntary interactions under the rule of law rather than the rule of force, individuals' **reservation indifference curves** are a more binding constraint, defining the economically feasible set.

If (and only if) for some allocation, the **MRS** (slope of indifference curve—the trade-off between objectives) is equal to the **MRT** (slope of feasible frontier—the trade-off in what is feasible), then the allocation is

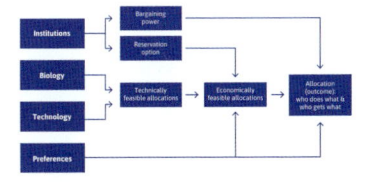

Figure 5.13 (page 213) showed the fundamental determinants of economic outcomes.

Pareto efficient. The set of all Pareto-efficient allocations is the **Pareto efficiency curve**.

The **Gini coefficient** is a measure of inequality based on differences in income, wealth, or some other economic indicator among all the members of an economy. The difference between the market income Gini and the **disposable income** Gini measures how taxes and transfers contribute to the redistributive effects of government policies in that country. The **Lorenz curve** gives us a picture of the disparity of income across the entire population and allows us to see that the nature of inequality may differ, even in countries with the same Gini coefficient.

5.12 *DOING ECONOMICS:* MEASURING INEQUALITY: LORENZ CURVES AND GINI COEFFICIENTS

To get hands-on experience constructing different measures of inequality and using a variety of data sources, go to *Doing Economics* Empirical Project 5 (https://tinyco.re/6741789). In this project, you will learn how to construct Gini coefficients and Lorenz curves from raw data. By constructing other measures of income inequality, the project shows how a country's income distribution can be summarized. A policymaker may wish to know how a proposed policy affects inequality as measured by these different summary indicators.

The project looks at how gender inequality can be measured and at how inequality can be accounted for in indices of wellbeing such as the Human Development Index.

> *Learning objectives*
> In this project you will:
>
> - draw Lorenz curves and interpret the Gini coefficient
> - calculate and interpret alternative measures of income inequality
> - research other dimensions of inequality and how they are measured.

5.13 REFERENCES

Banerjee, Abhijit V., Paul J. Gertler, and Maitreesh Ghatak. 2002. 'Empowerment and Efficiency: Tenancy Reform in West Bengal' (https://tinyco.re/9394444). *Journal of Political Economy* 110 (2): pp. 239–80.

Leeson, Peter T. 2007. 'An-arrgh-chy: The Law and Economics of Pirate Organizations'. *Journal of Political Economy* 115 (6): pp. 1049–94.

Lorenz, Max O. 1905. 'Methods of Measuring the Concentration of Wealth' (https://tinyco.re/0786587). *Publications of the American Statistical Association* 9 (70).

Raychaudhuri, Ajitava. 2004. *Lessons from the Land Reform Movement in West Bengal, India* (https://tinyco.re/0335719). Washington, DC: World Bank.

6

THE FIRM: EMPLOYEES, MANAGERS, AND OWNERS

At work

6.1 INTRODUCTION

- The firm is an actor in the capitalist economy, and also a stage on which interactions are played out among the firm's employees, managers, and owners.
- We explain why, like other economic interactions, working together in firms brings mutual gains.
- But, hiring workers is different from buying other goods and services. The contract between the two parties does not cover many things where the employee and the employer have conflicting interests, including how hard and how well the employee will work. Also, the employer cannot prevent the worker from quitting.
- Firms do not pay the lowest wages possible to get people to simply show up at their jobs. They set wages so that employees experience a cost if they lose their jobs. This motivates them to work effectively and stay with the firm, and it ensures that firms always have a large pool of job applicants.
- A consequence of firms setting wages to motivate workers in this way is that (even in equilibrium) there will always be unemployed people in the economy.
- Working in the gig economy, or in a worker-owned cooperative, is different from being an employee in a capitalist firm.

In March 2000, Terri Lawrence was driving her 1996 Ford Explorer SUV near Fort Lauderdale, Florida. 'All of a sudden', she said, 'there was this explosion'. One of her tyres had blown out. The Ford Explorer flipped over, and she was badly injured. By the summer of 2000, with similar reports of blowouts and overturned Explorers accumulating, Ford convened a 'war room' to deal with the public relations catastrophe. They quickly determined that the Firestone tyres used on most

Explorers were at fault. There were no unusual reports of blowouts on Explorers with Goodyear tyres.

In August 2000, in partnership with Ford, Firestone recalled 14.4 million tyres. According to the US National Highway Traffic and Safety Administration, blowouts of the Firestone tyres in question had resulted in crashes that took 271 lives. In the four months following the recall, the market value of Firestone shares on the stock exchange dropped by $9.2 billion, to less than half of their value before the crisis. But the cause of the spate of fatal blowouts remained a mystery.

High-speed stress tests confirmed that there was nothing wrong with the design of the tyres. An inconspicuous clue, however, pointed to 'the scene of the crime', if not its motive. On the sidewall of each of the blown-out tyres was a ten-digit tyre code, indicating the particular plant that had produced the tyre and the week of its production. Most of the faulty tyres had been produced at just one of Firestone's six plants, located in Decatur, Illinois.

For years, the Firestone Decatur plant had been in the news for other reasons. In 1994, the company had imposed a 12-hour shift that rotated between night and day for each worker, replacing the historic eight-hour shift. New hires' wages were reduced by 30%; vacations for more senior workers were cut by two weeks. On 12 July 1994, the United Rubber Workers union that represented the employees called a strike. The firm immediately hired 2,300 replacement workers, paying them 30% less than wages previously paid. Ten months later, the union called off the strike; returning workers accepted substantial pay cuts, a freeze in their pension benefits, and the 12-hour shifts. Bitterness toward the company and protests continued.

Building tyres at the time was a labour-intensive and skilled occupation. A number of the union workers blamed lack of training and experience among the replacement workers for the tyre blowouts. William Newton, a senior tyre builder in Decatur, reported that he 'saw a lot of people [working as replacements] who did not know how to build tyres'. But investigators looking at the detailed records of exactly when the faulty tyres were produced were in for a shock—virtually none of them had been produced during the strike, when Firestone was employing the replacement workers. Most of the faulty tyres had been produced by experienced union workers, both before the strike—when Firestone's pay cuts, 12-hour shift, and other new demands had been announced—and after the defeat of the strike, when the union workers returned.

While it cannot be proven, it seems likely that the permanent workers at the Decatur plant had retaliated against Firestone, devoting less effort to producing safe tyres, or even deliberately sabotaging production. The owners of Firestone discovered that they could indeed impose a 12-hour shift and a 30% pay cut, but they could not ensure that safe tyres would be produced if their employees were angry as a result.

Firms are major actors in the economy; we will use this and the next unit to explain how they work. A firm is often referred to as if it were a person—we talk about 'the price Firestone charges'.

But, while firms are actors—and in some legal systems are treated as if they were individuals—firms are also the stages on which the people who make up the firm act out their sometimes common, but sometimes competing, interests.

Alan B. Krueger and Alexandre Mas explain how economists analyzed the tyre defects at the Decatur plant in 'Strikes, Scabs, and Tread Separations: Labor Strife and the Production of Defective Bridgestone/Firestone Tires'. *Journal of Political Economy* 112 (2): pp. 253–89."

The people making up the firm—employees, managers, and owners—are united in their common interest in the firm's success because all of them would suffer if it were to fail. However, they have conflicting interests about how to distribute the profits from the firm's success among themselves (wages, managerial salaries, and owners' profits); they may also disagree about policies (such as conditions of work and managerial perks) and who makes the key decisions (such as whether it was a good idea to impose a 12-hour shift on the Firestone workers in Decatur and cut their vacation times).

In this unit, we focus on the firm as a stage and model the relationships among the key actors—employees, managers, and owners. We model how wages are determined when there are conflicts of interest between employers and employees, and look at what this means for the sharing of the mutual gains that arise in a firm. In Unit 7, we will look at the firm as an actor in its relationship with other firms and with its customers.

6.2 FIRMS, MARKETS, AND THE DIVISION OF LABOUR

The economy is made up of people doing different things, for example producing Apple iPhones or making clothing for export. Producing smartphones involves many distinct tasks, done by different employees within the companies that make components for Apple—Toshiba or Sharp in Japan, or Infineon in Germany.

Setting aside the work done in families, in a capitalist economy, the **division of labour** is coordinated in two major ways—**firms** and markets.

> **division of labour** The specialization of producers to carry out different tasks in the production process. *Also known as: specialization.*
>
> **firm** A business organization which pays wages and salaries to employ people, and purchases inputs, to produce and market goods and services with the intention of making a profit.

- Through firms, the components of goods are produced by different people in different departments of the firm and assembled to produce a finished shirt or iPhone.
- Components produced by groups of workers in different firms may also be brought together through market interactions between firms.
- By buying and selling goods on markets, the finished iPhone gets from the producer into the pocket of the consumer.

In this unit, we study firms. In the units to follow, we study markets. Herbert Simon, an economist, used the view from Mars to explain why it is important to study both.

Among the institutions of modern capitalist economies, the firm rivals the government in importance. John Micklethwait and Adrian Wooldridge explain how this happened.

John Micklethwait and Adrian Wooldridge. 2003. *The Company: A Short History of a Revolutionary Idea.* New York, NY: Modern Library.

Why do firms work the way they do? For example, why do the owners of the firm hire the workers, rather than the other way around? Randall Kroszner and Louis Putterman summarize this field of economics.

Randall S. Kroszner and Louis Putterman (editors). 2009. *The Economic Nature of the Firm: A Reader.* Cambridge: Cambridge University Press.

GREAT ECONOMISTS

Herbert Simon

Trained as a political scientist, Simon's desire to understand society led him to study both institutions and the human mind—to open the 'black box' of motivations that economists had come to take for granted. Herbert 'Herb' Simon (1916–2001) was celebrated in the disciplines of computer science, psychology, and, of course, economics, for which he won the Nobel Prize in 1978.

Imagine a visitor approaching Earth from Mars, Simon urged his readers. Looking at Earth through a telescope that revealed social structure, what would our visitor see? Companies might appear as green fields, he suggested, divisions and departments as faint contours within. Connecting these fields, red lines of buying and selling. Within these fields, blue lines of authority, connecting boss and employee, foreman and assembly worker, mentor and mentee.

Traditionally, economists had focused on the market and the competitive setting of prices. But to a visitor from Mars, Simon suggested:

> Organizations would be the dominant feature of the landscape. A message sent back home, describing the scene, would speak of 'large green areas interconnected by red lines.' It would not likely speak of 'a network of red lines connecting green spots'. ('Organizations and Markets', 1991)

A firm, he pointed out, is not simply an agent, shifting to match supply and demand. It is composed of individuals, whose needs and desires might conflict. Simon asked: In what ways could these differences be resolved? When would an individual shift from contract work (a 'sale' of a particular, predefined task) to an employment relation? An employment relation where a boss dictates the task after the sale is the relationship at the heart of a firm.

When the desired task is easy to specify in a contract, Simon explained that we could view this as simply work-for-hire. But high uncertainty (the employer not knowing in advance what needs to be done) would make it impossible to specify in a contract what the worker was to do and, in this case, the result would be an employer–employee relation that is characteristic of the firm.

This early work showcased two of Simon's lasting interests—the complexity of economic relations, where one might sell an obligation that was incompletely described, and the role of uncertainty in changing the nature of decision making. His argument demonstrated the emergence of the 'boss'.

Understanding how contract work turns into employment helps us understand a particular relationship between two members of an

---

Herbert A. Simon. 1991. 'Organizations and Markets' (https://tinyco.re/2460377). *Journal of Economic Perspectives* 5 (2): pp. 25–44.

Herbert A. Simon. 1951. 'A Formal Theory of the Employment Relationship' (https://tinyco.re/0460792). *Econometrica* 19 (3): pp. 293–305.

organization. We have yet to explain the firm as a whole—the Martian's green fields.

For Simon, the study of markets needed to be supplemented—even supplanted—by the study of institutions and governments better equipped to handle uncertainty and rapid change. These alternative 'authority mechanisms' draw on partially understood aspects of the human psyche: loyalty, group identification, and creative satisfaction.

By the time of his death in 2001, Simon had seen many of his ideas reach the mainstream. Behavioural economics has roots in his attempts to build economic theories that reflect empirical data. Simon's view from Mars shows that economics could not be a self-contained science; an economist needs to be both a mathematician—working with decision sets and utilities—and a social psychologist—reasoning about the motivations of human relationships.

The coordination of work

The way that labour is coordinated within firms is different to coordination through markets:

- *Firms represent a concentration of economic power:* This is placed in the hands of the owners and managers, who regularly issue directives with the expectation that their employees will carry them out. An 'order' in the firm is a command.
- *Markets are characterized by a decentralization of power:* Purchases and sales result from the buyers' and sellers' autonomous decisions. An 'order' in a market is a request for a purchase that can be rejected if the seller pleases.

The prices that motivate and constrain people's actions in a market are the result of the actions of thousands or millions of individuals, not a decision by someone in authority. Although the government can tax and regulate private property, the idea of private property specifically limits the things a government or anyone else can do with your possessions.

In a firm, by contrast, owners or their managers direct the activities of their employees, who may number in the thousands or even millions. The managers of Walmart, the world's largest retailer, decide on the activities of 2.2 million employees, a larger number of people than any army in world history before the nineteenth century. Walmart is an exceptionally large firm, but it is not exceptional in that it brings together a large number of people who work in a way coordinated (by the management) to make profits.

Like any organization, firms have a decision-making process and ways of imposing their decisions on the people in it. When we say that 'Fiat outsourced its component production' or 'the firm sets a price of €11,200', we mean that the decision-making process in the firm resulted in these actions.

Figure 6.1 shows a simplified picture of the firm's actors and decision-making structure.

These two books describe the property rights, authority structures, and market interactions that characterize the modern capitalist firm.

- Henry Hansmann. 2000. *The Ownership of Enterprise*. Cambridge, MA: Belknap Press.
- Oliver E. Williamson. 1985. *The Economic Institutions of Capitalism*. New York, NY: Collier Macmillan.

> **asymmetric information** Information that is relevant to all the parties in an economic interaction, but is known by some and not by others. *See also: adverse selection, moral hazard.*

The dashed upward green arrows represent a problem of **asymmetric information** between levels in the firm's hierarchy (owners and managers, managers and workers). Since owners or managers do not always know what their subordinates know or do, not all of their directions or commands (grey downward arrows) are necessarily carried out.

This relationship between the firm and its employees contrasts with the firm's relationship with its customers, which we study in the next unit. The bakery firm cannot text its customers to tell them to 'Show up at 8 a.m. and purchase two loaves of bread at the price of €1 each'. The firm could tempt its customers with a special offer, but unlike the relationship with its employees, it cannot require them to show up. When you buy or sell something, it is generally voluntary. In buying or selling, you respond to prices, not orders. The firm is different; it is defined by having a decision-making structure in which some people have power over others.

6.3 POWER RELATIONS WITHIN THE FIRM

Karl Marx, a philosopher and economist in the nineteenth century, was also interested in the power relations in a firm. He concluded that conflict between employers and workers was inevitable. Buying and selling goods in an open market is a transaction between equals—nobody is in a position to order anyone else to buy or sell. In the labour market, in which owners of capital are buyers and workers are the sellers, the appearance of freedom and equality was, to Marx, an illusion.

To explore all of the slides in this figure, see the online version at https://tinyco.re/4122225.

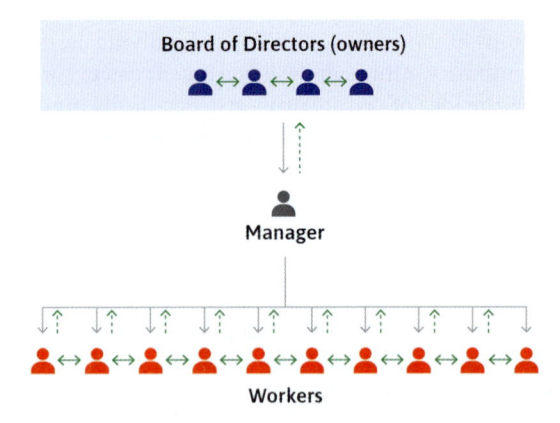

Figure 6.1 The firm's actors and its decision-making and information structures.

1. Owners decide long-term strategies
The owners, through their board of directors, decide the long-term strategies of the firm concerning how, what, and where to produce. They then direct the manager(s) to implement these decisions.

2. Managers assign workers
Each manager assigns workers to the tasks required for these decisions to be implemented and attempts to ensure that the assignments are carried out.

3. Flows of information
The green arrows represent flows of information. The upward green arrows are dashed lines because workers often know things that managers do not, and managers often know things that owners do not.

He reasoned that employers did not buy the employees' work, because this cannot be purchased. Instead, the wage allowed the employer to rent the worker and to command workers inside the firm. Workers were not inclined to disobey because they might lose their jobs and join the 'reserve army' of the unemployed (the phrase that Marx used in his 1867 work, *Capital*). Marx thought that the power wielded by employers over workers was a core defect of capitalism.

GREAT ECONOMISTS

Karl Marx

Adam Smith, writing at the birth of capitalism in the eighteenth century, was to become its most famous advocate. Karl Marx (1818–1883), who watched capitalism mature in the industrial towns of England, was to become its most famous critic.

Born in Prussia (now part of Germany), he distinguished himself only by his rebelliousness as a student at a Jesuit high school. In 1842, he became a writer and editor for the Rheinische Zeitung, a liberal newspaper, which was later closed by the government. After this, he moved to Paris and met Friedrich Engels, with whom he collaborated in writing *The Communist Manifesto* (1848). Marx then moved to London in 1849. At first, Marx and his wife Jenny lived in poverty. He earned money by writing about political events in Europe for the New York Tribune.

Marx saw capitalism as just the latest in a succession of economic arrangements in which people have lived since prehistory. Inequality was not unique to capitalism, he observed—slavery, feudalism, and most other economic systems had shared this feature—but capitalism also generated perpetual change and growth in output.

He was the first economist to understand why the capitalist economy was the most dynamic in human history. Perpetual change arose, Marx observed, because capitalists could survive only by introducing new technologies and products, finding ways of lowering costs, and by reinvesting their profits into businesses that would perpetually grow.

Marx also had influential views on history, politics, and sociology. He thought that history was decisively shaped by the interactions between scarcity, technological progress, and economic institutions, and that political conflicts arose from conflicts about the distribution of income and the organization of these institutions. He thought that capitalism, by organizing production and allocation in anonymous markets, created atomized individuals instead of integrated communities.

In recent years, economists have returned to themes in Marx's work to help explain economic crises. These themes include the firm as an arena of conflict and of the exercise of power (this unit), the role of technological progress that we analysed in Unit 1 (page 23), and the problems created by inequality that we saw in Unit 5 (page 214).

Capital, Marx's most famous work, is long and covers many subjects, but you can use a searchable archive (https://tinyco.re/9166776) to find the passages you need.

Karl Marx. (1867) 1906. *Capital: A Critique of Political Economy*. New York, NY: Random House.

Karl Marx. (1848) 2010. *The Communist Manifesto* (https://tinyco.re/0155765). Edited by Friedrich Engels. London: Arcturus Publishing.

George Bernard Shaw (1856–1950), a writer, joked that 'if all economists were laid end to end, they would not reach a conclusion.'

This is funny, but not entirely true.

Read the 'When economists agree' box to see how Marx and Ronald Coase of the University of Chicago—two economists from different centuries and political orientations—came up with similar ways of understanding the power relations between employers and their employees.

> ### WHEN ECONOMISTS AGREE
>
> *Coase and Marx on the firm and its employees*
> In the nineteenth century, Marx had contrasted the way that buyers and sellers interact on a market, voluntarily engaging in trade, with how the firm is organized as a top–down structure, one in which employers issue orders and workers follow them. He called markets 'a very Eden of the innate rights of man', but described firms as 'exploit[ing] labour-power to the greatest possible extent.'
>
> When Ronald Coase died in 2013, he was described by *Forbes* magazine as 'the greatest of the many great University of Chicago economists' (https://tinyco.re/6800200). The motto of *Forbes* is 'The capitalist tool', and the University of Chicago has a reputation as the centre of conservative economic thinking.
>
> Yet, like Marx, Coase stressed the central role of authority in the firm's contractual relations:
>
> > Note the character of the contract into which an [employee] enters that is employed within a firm ... for certain remuneration [the employee] agrees to obey the directions of the entrepreneur. (*The Nature of the Firm*, 1937)
>
> Coase founded the study of the firm as both a stage and an actor. In *The Nature of the Firm* he wrote:
>
> > If a workman moves from department Y to department X, he does not go because of a change in relative prices but because he is ordered to do so ... the distinguishing mark of the firm is the suppression of the price mechanism. (*The Nature of the Firm*, 1937)
>
> Coase sought to understand why firms exist at all, quoting his contemporary D. H. Robertson's description of them as 'islands of conscious power in this ocean of unconscious cooperation'.
>
> Coase pointed out that the firm in a capitalist economy is a miniature, privately owned, centrally planned economy. Its top–down decision-making structure resembles the centralized direction of production in entire economies that took place in many Communist countries (and in the US and the UK during the Second World War).

Ronald H. Coase. 1937. 'The Nature of the Firm' (https://tinyco.re/4250905). *Economica* 4 (16): pp. 386–405.

Dennis Robertson. 1923. *The Control of Industry*. Hitchen: Nisbet.

Ronald H. Coase. 1992. 'The Institutional Structure of Production' (https://tinyco.re/1636715). *American Economic Review* 82 (4): pp. 713–19.

Both Marx and Coase based their thinking on careful empirical observation, and they arrived at a similar understanding of the hierarchy of the firm. They disagreed, however, on the consequences of what they observed—Coase thought that the hierarchy of the firm was a cost-reducing way to do business; Marx thought that the coercive authority of the boss over the worker limited the employee's freedom. Over this, they disagreed. But they also advanced economics with a common idea.

HOW ECONOMISTS LEARN FROM DATA

Managers exert power
These three investigations, published as books, show the effect of the power that managers and owners exert.

- In *Nickel and Dimed: On (Not) Getting By in America*, Barbara Ehrenreich worked undercover for minimum wage in motels and restaurants to see how America's poor live.
- In *Hard Work: Life in Low-pay Britain*, Polly Toynbee, a British journalist, had previously done the same in the UK in 2003, taking jobs such as call centre employee and home care worker.
- In *Labor and Monopoly Capital: The Degradation of Work in the Twentieth Century*, Harry Braverman and Paul Sweezy provide a history of what they call the 'deskilling' process, and suggest how dumbing down jobs is a strategy for maximizing the employer's profits.

Barbara Ehrenreich. 2011. *Nickel and Dimed: On (Not) Getting By in America*. New York, NY: St. Martin's Press.

Polly Toynbee. 2003. *Hard Work: Life in Low-pay Britain*. London: Bloomsbury Publishing.

Harry Braverman and Paul M. Sweezy. 1975. *Labor and Monopoly Capital: The Degradation of Work in the Twentieth Century*. 2nd ed. New York, NY: Monthly Review Press.

Contracts and relationships

The difference between market interactions and relationships within firms is clear when we consider the differing kinds of written and unwritten **contracts** that form the basis of exchange.

A sale contract for a car transfers ownership, meaning that the new owner can now use the car and exclude others from its use. A rental contract on an apartment does not transfer ownership of the apartment (which would include the right to sell it); instead it gives the tenant a limited set of rights over the apartment, including the right to exclude others (including the landlord) from its use.

Under a **wage labour** contract, an employee gives the employer the right to direct him or her to be at work at specific times, and to accept the authority of the employer over the use of his or her time while at work.

The employer does not own the employee as a result of this contract. If the employer did, the employee would be called a slave. We might say that the employer has 'rented' the employee for part of the day. To summarize:

- *Contracts for products:* When sold in markets, they permanently transfer *ownership* of the good from the seller to the buyer.
- *Contracts for labour:* These contracts temporarily transfer *authority* over a person's activities from the employee to the manager or owner.
- *A contract does not have to be written:* It can be an understanding between the employer and the employee.

contract A legal document or understanding that specifies a set of actions that parties to the contract must undertake.

wage labour A system in which producers are paid for the time they work for their employers.

EXERCISE 6.1 THE STRUCTURE OF AN ORGANIZATION
In Figure 6.1 (page 234), we showed the actors and decision-making structure of a typical firm.

1. How might the actors and decision-making structure of the organizations Google, Wikipedia, and a family farm compare with this?
2. Draw an organizational structure chart in the style of Figure 6.1 to represent each of these entities.

QUESTION 6.1 CHOOSE THE CORRECT ANSWER(S)
Which of the following statements are true?

- ☐ A labour contract transfers ownership of the employee from the employee to the employer.
- ☐ According to Herbert Simon (page 232), a visitor approaching Earth from Mars with a telescope that reveals social structure would see a network of lines (market exchanges) connecting spots (firms and consumers).
- ☐ In a labour contract, one side of the contract has the power to issue orders to the other side, but this power is absent from a sale contract.
- ☐ A firm is a structure that involves decentralization of power to the employees.

6.4 OTHER PEOPLE'S MONEY: THE SEPARATION OF OWNERSHIP AND CONTROL

The firm's profits legally belong to the people who own the firm's assets, including its capital goods. The firm's owners direct the other members of the firm to take actions that contribute to the firm's profits. This, in turn, will increase the value of the firm's assets and improve the owners' wealth.

There are thus two aspects of ownership of a firm:

- *The owners direct the activities of other participants in the firm:* Usually through hiring managers.
- *The owners receive the firm's profits:* Namely, whatever remains after the revenues, which are the proceeds from sale of the products, is used to pay employees, managers, suppliers, creditors, and taxes.

residual claimant The person who receives the income left over from a firm or project after the payment of all contractual costs (for example the cost of hiring workers and paying taxes).

Profit is the *residual*. It is what's left of the revenues after these payments. The owners claim it, which is why they are called **residual claimants**. Managers and employees are not residual claimants (unless they have some share in the ownership of the firm).

This division of revenue has an important implication. If the firm's revenues increase because managers or employees do their jobs well, the owners will benefit, *but the managers and employees will not* (unless they receive a promotion, bonus, or salary increase). This is one reason we consider the firm as a stage, one on which not all the actors have the same interests.

6.4 OTHER PEOPLE'S MONEY: THE SEPARATION OF OWNERSHIP AND CONTROL

Owners delegate control to managers

In large corporations, there are typically many owners. Most of them play no part in the firm's management. The owners of the firm are the individuals and institutions (such as pension funds) that own the **shares** issued by the firm. By issuing shares to the general public, a company can raise capital to finance its growth, leaving strategic and operational decisions to a relatively small group of specialized managers.

These decisions include what, where, and how to produce the firm's output, or how much to pay employees and managers. The senior management of a firm is also responsible for deciding how much of the firm's profits are distributed to shareholders in the form of dividends, and how much is retained to finance growth. The owners benefit from the firm's growth because they own part of the value of the firm, which increases as the firm grows.

When managers decide on the use of other people's funds, this is referred to as the **separation of ownership and control**.

The separation of ownership and control results in a potential conflict of interest.

Conflict of interest between owners and managers

The decisions of managers affect profits, and profits decide the incomes of the owners. But the interests of owners and managers will be in conflict because managers' salaries and bonuses are paid from profits that would otherwise go to the owners. There are many things that managers can do to raise their pay at the expense of profits. For example, in firms listed on the stock market, managers' pay rises and falls with the firm's stock market performance over a period as short as a quarter or a year; there are many ways managers can boost the firm's short-term stock market performance but damage the firm's profitability in the long run.

Managers are in day-to-day control of the firm's assets and they may choose to take actions that benefit themselves, at the expense of the owners. An example is where managers seek to increase their own power and prestige through empire-building, even if that is not in the interests of shareholders.

Even sole owners of firms are not *required* to maximize their profits. Restaurant owners can choose menus they personally like, or waiters who are their friends. But, unlike managers, when they lose profits as a result, the cost comes directly out of their own pockets.

Although Adam Smith (page 17) had not seen the modern firm, he observed the tendency of senior managers to serve their own interests rather than those of shareholders. He said this about the managers of what were then called joint-stock companies:

> [B]eing the managers rather of other people's money than of their own, it cannot well be expected, that they should watch over it with the same anxious vigilance with which the partners in a [firm managed by its owners] frequently watch over their own … Negligence and profusion, therefore, must always prevail, more or less, in the management of the affairs of such a company. (*The Wealth of Nations*, 1776)

---

share A part of the assets of a firm that may be traded. It gives the holder a right to receive a proportion of a firm's profit and to benefit when the firm's assets become more valuable. *Also known as: common stock.*

separation of ownership and control The attribute of some firms by which managers are a separate group from the owners.

Aligning the interests of owners and managers

There are many ways that owners can incentivize managers to serve their interests. One is that they can structure contracts so that managerial compensation depends on the performance of the company's share price over a lengthy period of time.

Another is that the firm's board of directors, which represents the firm's shareholders and typically has a substantial share in the firm (like a representative of a pension fund), can monitor the managers' performance. The board has the authority to dismiss managers.

But although the shareholders, who are the ultimate owners, have the right to replace members of the board, they rarely do so. Shareholders are a large and diverse group that cannot easily coordinate to decide something. Occasionally, however, this **free-rider** problem is overcome and a shareholder with a large stake in a company may lead or coordinate a shareholder revolt to change or influence the board of directors and senior management.

In spite of the separation of ownership and control, when we model the firm as an actor, we often assume that it maximizes profits. This is a simplification, but a reasonable one for many purposes:

- *Owners have a strong interest in profit maximization:* It is the basis of their wealth.
- *Market competition tends to penalize or eliminate firms that do not make substantial profits for their owners:* We saw this process in Unit 1 (page 35) as part of the explanation of the permanent technological revolution, and it applies to all aspects of the firms' decisions.

free ride Benefiting from the contributions of others to some cooperative project without contributing oneself.

> **QUESTION 6.2 CHOOSE THE CORRECT ANSWER(S)**
> Which of the following statements about the separation of ownership and control are true?
>
> ☐ When the ownership and control of a firm is separated, the managers become the residual claimants.
> ☐ Managers always work to maximize the firm's profit.
> ☐ One way to address the problem associated with the separation of ownership and control is to pay the managers a salary that depends on the performance of the firm's share price.
> ☐ It is effective for shareholders to monitor the performance of the management, in a firm owned by a large number of shareholders.

6.5 OTHER PEOPLE'S LABOUR: THE EMPLOYMENT RELATIONSHIP

Most people who work outside the home have jobs in **firms**. Remember, a firm is a business organization that pays wages and salaries to employ people, and purchases inputs to produce and market goods and services with the intention of making a profit. A firm's profits (before the payment of taxes) are equal to the money the firm receives from the goods or services, minus the costs of producing these goods and services. The wages and salaries paid to the people a firm employs are a large fraction of its costs. The profits received by the owners of the firm depend—among many other things—on how hard and well those employees work.

In firms, the employer sets the wage, hours of work and working conditions. If you are an employee, the employer—whether an owner of the firm or a manager appointed by the owners—is the 'boss' who decides not only what you are to do on the job, but also whether you lose your job or are promoted.

But, as an employee, you also have some power in this relationship. You can quit your job, which will mean the employer has to incur the costs of hiring someone else. You can also decide how much effort to put into your work, which is very important to your employer.

The ongoing interaction between an employer and an employee in a firm is called the **employment relationship**. While the wage and the hours of work are governed by an employment contract, and some other aspects of the job (safety conditions for example) may be stipulated by public policy, the employer sets the hours and other conditions of work, and can terminate the job. The employee decides on her level of effort, and whether to remain in the firm.

Mutual gains and conflicts of interest

For an employer and an employee to remain in the employment relationship, both need to gain something compared to the next best alternative. For the firm this is to find, train and hire another worker. For the employee this is to find another job. We can infer two things from an employment relationship:

- *The employer prefers to keep this employee:* Owners need workers in order to produce and to make profits. The alternative is to replace this employee with another.
- *The employee prefers working in this firm*: The alternatives are seeking work elsewhere, or being unemployed.

It is clear that both employees and employers benefit from the employment relationship. But just as in Section 6.4 (page 238), where we found that there is conflict of interest between the owners of firms and their managers, there is also a conflict of interest between employers—owners and managers alike—and workers. The reason is that, in the simplest terms, owners want more employee effort at a lower wage, while workers want a higher wage for less effort.

In this section and the next sections, we explain the factors that affect the wage set by the employer. We start with a basic fact: employers cannot simply order the worker to work hard, as a slave-owner might have done. The employer will need not only to look at this decision from both the perspective of the employee and employer.

> **firm** A business organization which pays wages and salaries to employ people, and purchases inputs, to produce and market goods and services with the intention of making a profit.

> **employment relationship** The interaction between an employee and an employer in which the employer sets the hours and other conditions of work and the wage, directs the employee's activities and may terminate her employment, and the employee chooses how hard to work and whether to quit her job. The employee's level of effort, or her decision to remain in the firm, are determined by the choices made by the two parties—and are affected by the exercise of power by the employer and the social norms of both parties.

Why not pay workers piece rates?

If the employer cannot force the worker to work hard, why do employers not simply buy the employee's effort in the same way that they buy other inputs like energy or computers? If they could, they would pay employees using piece rates—for example, at a clothing factory the employers might pay $2 for each garment their workers finish. A piece rate is not a wage, because it is paid per unit of output (per piece) not per hour or day.

A **piece rate** provides the employee with an incentive to exert effort, because they take home more money if they make more garments.

In the late nineteenth century, the pay of more than half of US manufacturing workers was based on their output, but piece rates are not widely used in modern economies. At the turn of the twenty-first century, fewer than 5% of manufacturing workers in the US were paid piece rates and, outside the manufacturing sector, piece rates are used even less often.

Why do most firms not use piece rates?

- *It is very difficult to measure the amount of output an employee is producing in modern knowledge- and service-based economies:* Think about an office worker, or someone providing care at home for an elderly person.
- *Employees rarely work alone:* This means that measuring the contribution of individual workers is difficult, for example a team in a marketing company working on an advertising campaign, or the kitchen staff at a restaurant.

piece-rate work A type of employment in which the worker is paid a fixed amount for each unit of the product that the worker produces.

Susan Helper, Morris Kleiner, and Yingchun Wang. 2010. 'Analyzing Compensation Methods in Manufacturing: Piece Rates, Time Rates, or Gain-Sharing?' (https://tinyco.re/4437027). NBER Working Papers No. 16540.

A partial exception is today's **gig economy** (see Section 6.14 (page 267)). Consider the case of Uber, Lyft, Deliveroo, and other delivery and transportation services. Unlike modern office, hospital, school and factory work, the job is typically done by an individual, working alone. The task to be completed is subject to contract because it is easy to determine whether it has been completed—the package, for example, was either delivered or not.

But if piece rates are not practical in most of the economy, then production is carried out in firms with employees who have an employment contract under which payment is for time spent working, rather than for output. The employment contract is necessarily incomplete—after all, if a complete contract specifying every aspect of the worker's output were possible, labour input would be purchased on the market under a piece-rate system.

gig economy An economy made up of people performing services matched by means of a computer platform with those paying for the service. Workers are paid for each task they complete, and not per hour. They are not legally recognized as employees of the company that owns the platform, and typically receive few benefits from the owners, other than matching.

The employment contract is incomplete

From the firm's perspective, hiring employees is different from buying other goods and services. When an employer buys a fork-lift truck, or pays someone to audit the accounts, it is clear what the employer is purchasing. If the seller does not deliver, the employer either does not pay, or goes to court to get its money back.

But an employer cannot write an enforceable employment contract that specifies the exact tasks employees have to perform in order to get paid. This is for three reasons:

- *The employer cannot see the future*: Unforeseen future events mean the firm does not know exactly what it will require the employee to do at the time it draws up a contract of employment.
- *It is expensive, and may be impossible, to measure effort*: It is usually impractical to observe exactly how much effort each employee makes.

- *The contract may not be enforceable*: Even if the firm somehow acquired this information, it might not be able to use it in court.

To understand the last point, consider a restaurant that requires staff to serve customers in a pleasant manner. Imagine a court being asked to decide whether the owner can withhold wages from a waiter, because he had not smiled often enough.

An employment contract omits things that both the employees and the owner care about because they are central to the employment relationship—including how hard and how well the employee will work, and for how long the worker will stay. We call this an **incomplete contract**. As a result, paying the lowest possible wage is almost never the firm's strategy to minimize the cost of acquiring the labour effort it needs. To see why, we need to ask why a worker puts in a good day's work.

> **incomplete contract** A contract that does not specify, in an enforceable way, every aspect of the exchange that affects the interests of parties to the exchange (or of any others affected by the exchange).

> **QUESTION 6.3 CHOOSE THE CORRECT ANSWER(S)**
> Which of the following statements regarding employment contracts are correct?
>
> ☐ Employment contracts are incomplete as they can only specify things that both the employees and the business owner care about.
> ☐ The firm is required to state exactly what it needs the employee to do in an employment contract.
> ☐ Employees' effort levels cannot be the basis of an enforceable contract.
> ☐ The firm needs to specify exactly how much effort employees are expected to put into their jobs.

> **QUESTION 6.4 CHOOSE THE CORRECT ANSWER(S)**
> Which of the following are reasons why employment contracts are incomplete?
>
> ☐ The firm cannot contract an employee not to leave.
> ☐ The firm cannot specify every eventuality in a contract.
> ☐ The firm is unable to observe exactly how an employee is fulfilling the contract.
> ☐ The contract is unfinished.

> **EXERCISE 6.2 INCOMPLETE CONTRACTS**
> Think of two or three jobs with which you are familiar, perhaps a teacher, a retail worker, a nurse, or a police officer.
>
> In each case, indicate why the employment contract is necessarily incomplete. What important parts of the person's job—things that the employer would like to see the employee do or not do—cannot be covered in a contract, or if they are, cannot be enforced?

6.6 WHY DO A GOOD DAY'S WORK? CONSIDER THE ALTERNATIVE!

There are many reasons why people put in a good day's work. For many people, doing a good job is its own reward, and doing anything else would contradict their work ethic. Even for those not intrinsically motivated to work hard, feelings of responsibility for other employees or for one's employer may provide strong work motivation.

For some employees, hard work is the appropriate way to respond to the employer for providing a job with good working conditions. In other cases, firms use performance-related pay to reward hard work. It is sometimes possible to identify teams of workers whose output is readily measured—for example, the percentage of on-time departures for airline staff—and pay a benefit to the whole group, to be divided among team members. These employees have a reason to work hard—they are paid for it.

However, as we have seen, there is another reason to do a good job—the fear of being fired, or of missing the opportunity to be promoted into a position that has higher pay and greater job security.

Laws and practices concerning the termination of employment for cause (that is, because of inadequate or low-quality work, not due to insufficient demand for the firm's product) differ among countries. In some countries, the owners of the firm have the right to fire a worker whenever they choose, while in others, dismissal is difficult and costly. But, even in these cases, an employee has to fear the consequences of not meeting the standards that the employer sets. If this happened, she might lose her job if lower demand for the firm's products results in workers being laid off.

Do workers care whether they lose their jobs? They would have no reason to care if they could immediately get another job at the same wage and working conditions. If this is not the case, then there is a cost to losing your job, as well as some benefits from not working.

People who lose their jobs can typically expect help from family and friends while they are out of work. Also, in many economies, people who lose their jobs receive an **unemployment benefit** or financial assistance from the government. They may be able to earn a small amount in self-employment or by taking odd jobs.

Figure 6.2 sets out the costs and benefits from having a job and compares them with the costs and benefits of not having the job, all on a daily basis. This is a hypothetical exercise from the perspective of someone with a job.

In Column A are the monetary and non-monetary benefits and costs associated with having a job, and in column B, with losing that job. We use the concept of **utility** introduced in Unit 4. We can say that the worker's utility is increased by the goods and services she can buy with her wage, but reduced by the unpleasantness of going to work and working hard all day—the *disutility of effort*.

In the top row, if you lose your job, you would lose the wage and instead get some unemployment benefit and financial assistance from family and friends. Although you would not have to pay travel to work costs, you would incur costs of searching for a new job, including possible retraining and relocation expenses. Costs and benefits are about more than money. On one hand you gain by being rid of the disutility of effort—you no longer have to get up for work, and have more free time—but on the other hand you may lose the esteem that comes with the job. Some jobs come with medical and other benefits, which you would lose.

Read about the tactics used by some Japanese companies—in a culture of lifetime employment—to get unneeded employees to quit.

Hiroko Tabuchi. 2013. 'Layoffs Taboo, Japan Workers Are Sent to the Boredom Room' (https://tinyco.re/2026351). *The New York Times*, 16 August.

unemployment benefit A government transfer received by an unemployed person. *Also known as: unemployment insurance.*

utility A numerical indicator of the value that one places on an outcome, such that higher-valued outcomes will be chosen over lower-valued ones when both are feasible.

disutility of effort The degree to which doing some task (effort) is unpleasant.

6.7 EMPLOYMENT RENTS

Taking the employee's perspective of how hard to work, the employer looks at Figure 6.2 and would like to find a way to make the worker love having her job, at least compared to the alternative. Many of the items in columns A and B of the figure are beyond the control of the employer. But one is not.

The employer can set the wage so as to get a good day's work from the employee. Because the employee cannot literally be forced to work hard, this requires that the worker be motivated to provide adequate effort on the job. This motivation is provided by both a carrot and a stick.

- *The stick:* This is the employer's threat to sack the worker or to not promote her to a more secure job. Given the size of any stick, we will show that the effort that the worker puts in depends on the size of the carrot.
- *The carrot:* This is the value of the employment relationship to the worker or how much better off she is having the job, now and in the future, than she would be if she lost her job today. This quantity, called the **employment rent**, is the difference between how the employee will do in these two futures.

In Figure 6.2, the employee's employment rent depends on the difference in how much the worker values entries in the first and second columns, multiplied by the length of time that the person expects to remain unemployed if she loses her job.

To decide how much it is worth to her to keep the job at the wage offered in the employment contract, the worker has to think ahead: 'How hard will I have to work, what is the chance of being sacked or not promoted for slacking on the job, and what are my prospects if I lose my job? It takes time to get another job and during that time, an unemployed worker relies on unemployment benefits and may lose other job-related benefits like a sense of making a productive contribution or health insurance. Also, if I lose my job now, the next job I find may pay less.'

> **employment rent** The economic rent a worker receives when the net value of her job exceeds the net value of her next best alternative (that is, being unemployed). *Also known as: cost of job loss.*

	A. What if you keep your job?	**B. What if you lose your job?**
Income	Wage	Unemployment benefit; financial assistance from family and friends
Costs	Travel to work	Job search; perhaps including retraining and relocation
Subjective costs and benefits	Disutility of the effort of working; esteem from being valued at work	More free time; possibly social stigma or shame
Medical and other benefits	Many medical and other benefits are job related	More limited access to medical and other benefits

Figure 6.2 The daily costs and benefits of having and losing a job.

If there was no carrot (employment rent), the employee would be just as happy to lose her job as to keep it. So the stick would be ineffective. If the employment rent is big enough, the employer gets a 'good day's work' from the employee. Just as the owners of the firm protect their interests by linking management pay to the firm's share price, the manager uses incentives so that employees will work effectively.

Because the worker gets an employment rent (the carrot) and can lose her job (the stick), she does not want to lose her job or risk not being promoted and she will therefore exert effort on the job.

To understand the employment rent and its determinants, we look at its purely monetary aspects: the wage rate, the unemployment benefit and the length of time one may expect to remain unemployed if fired. A key to this analysis is what income the worker will get if she was fired (the first entry in column B in Figure 6.2). In most countries there are limits on the length of time one can receive unemployment benefits. In all countries, there are limits to how generous one's family and friends will be in supporting you while you are unemployed.

To capture this idea, we assume that the amount of income per week that you will receive if unemployed is some total sum B divided by the number of weeks in your spell of unemployment, i.e. the period that you are out of work, s. The per-week amount B/s divided by the number of hours worked per week (when employed) is called your **reservation wage** (b), that is, what you can expect to get instead of your hourly wage, while unemployed.

reservation wage What an employee would get in alternative employment, or from an unemployment benefit or other support, were he or she not employed in his or her current job.

In Figure 6.3 we illustrate the case of a worker called Maria who has an hourly wage of W and works h hours, and if she loses her job she can expect to be unemployed for s weeks. We assume this is 10 months (roughly 44 weeks), as was typical among OECD countries in 2016. So every week she loses $Wh - \frac{B}{s}$ in income, and her total loss of income occasioned by her spell of unemployment is this number times the number of weeks she will be out of work or

$$\text{Employment rent} = s(Wh - \frac{B}{s}) = sWh - B.$$

This is the shaded area in the figure. We can put some numbers to this area to quantify the size in dollars of Maria's employment rent. For example, if the hourly wage is $24, hours per week are 35 and the expected spell of unemployment is 44 weeks, then $sWh = 44 \times 24 \times 35 = \$36,960$. If we assume that the unemployment benefit is $600 per week and is limited to 30 weeks, then $B = \$18,000$. Hence, the employment rent = $36,960 − $18,000 = $18,960.

Even with the very generous provision of unemployment benefits that we assumed in the example, the cost of losing your job is substantial. And of course, we should include the social and psychological costs, as illustrated by this article about a former employee of the General Motors plant in Lordstown (Ohio, US) called Rick Marsh (https://tinyco.re/8775686). After 25 years, he lost his job building cars when the factory closed down in 2019, which led him to ask 'what am I?'

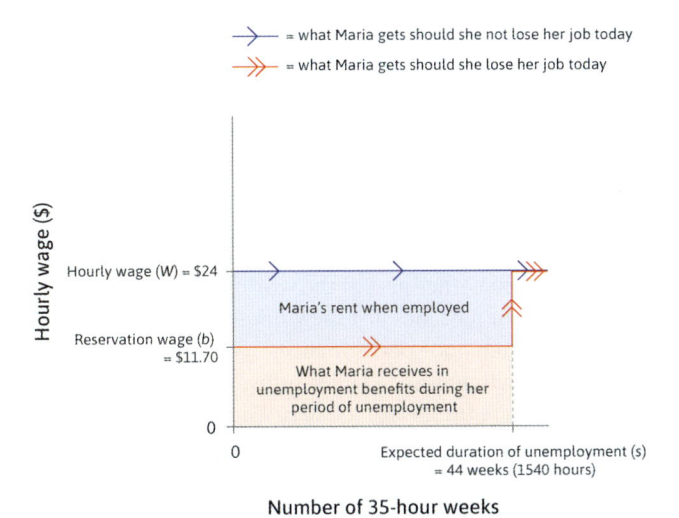

To explore all of the slides in this figure, see the online version at https://tinyco.re/8878779.

Figure 6.3 Employment rents: Maria compares her income from employment with what it would be, should she lose her job and be unemployed for 44 weeks (the employment rents shown are those at point J in Figure 6.5 (page 252)).

1. Maria's wage
Maria's hourly wage, after taxes and other deductions, is $24. Looking ahead from now (week 0), she will continue to receive this wage for the foreseeable future if she keeps her job, indicated by the horizontal line with blue arrows.

2. If Maria loses her job
If instead Maria were to lose her job in week 0, she would receive unemployment benefits equivalent to an hourly wage of $11.70. This unfortunate state would persist as long as she remains unemployed (which we assume to be 44 weeks, shown by the red lines and double arrows).

3. Maria finds a job
Maria expects to find another job at the same wage after 44 weeks.

4. Maria's employment rent
The blue shaded area is her employment rent, which would be the total cost of job loss from the spell of unemployment, were she to lose her job.

natural experiment An empirical study exploiting naturally occurring statistical controls in which researchers do not have the ability to assign participants to treatment and control groups, as is the case in conventional experiments. Instead, differences in law, policy, weather, or other events can offer the opportunity to analyse populations as if they had been part of an experiment. The validity of such studies depends on the premise that the assignment of subjects to the naturally occurring treatment and control groups can be plausibly argued to be random.

Lori G. Kletzer. 1998. 'Job Displacement' (https://tinyco.re/8577746). *Journal of Economic Perspectives* 12 (1): pp. 115–36.

Kenneth A. Couch and Dana W. Placzek. 2010. 'Earnings Losses of Displaced Workers Revisited'. *American Economic Review* 100 (1): pp. 572–89.

Louis Jacobson, Robert J. Lalonde, and Daniel G. Sullivan. 1993. 'Earnings Losses of Displaced Workers'. *The American Economic Review* 83 (4): pp. 685–709.

HOW ECONOMISTS LEARN FROM DATA

How can employment rents be measured in a real (rather than a model) economy?

Setting aside the undoubtedly large hard-to-measure psychological and social cost of losing one's job, estimating the cost of job loss (the size of the employment rent) is not simple.

Can we compare the economic situation of workers currently employed with the economic situation of unemployed people? No, because the unemployed are a different group of people, with different abilities and skills. Even if they were employed, they would be likely (on average) to earn less than people who currently have jobs.

An entire firm closing, or a mass layoff of workers, provides a **natural experiment** that can help. We could look at the earnings of workers before and after they lost their jobs during a major employment cutback. When a factory closes because the parent company has decided to relocate production to some other part of the world, for example, virtually all workers lose their jobs, not just the workers who were most likely to lose their jobs through poor performance.

Louis Jacobson, Robert Lalonde, and Daniel Sullivan used such a natural experiment to estimate the cost of job loss. They studied experienced (not recently hired) full-time workers hit by mass layoffs in the US state of Pennsylvania in 1982. In 2014 dollars, those displaced had been averaging $50,000 in earnings in 1979. Those who were fortunate enough to find another job in less than three months took jobs that paid a lot less, averaging only $35,000—being laid off meant that their earnings declined by $15,000.

Four years later, they were still making $13,300 less than similar workers who had been making the same initial wage, but whose firms did not lay off their workers. In the five years that followed their layoff, they lost the equivalent of an entire year's earnings.

Many, of course, did not find work at all. They suffered even greater costs.

The year 1982 was not a good time to be looking for work in Pennsylvania, but similar estimates (from the US state of Connecticut between 1993 and 2004, for example) suggest that, even in better times, employment rents are large enough that workers would worry about losing them.

QUESTION 6.5 CHOOSE THE CORRECT ANSWER(S)

Which of the following statements regarding employment rents are correct?

- ☐ Higher employment rents make workers more likely to quit their jobs.
- ☐ They are the costs you have to pay for your employment.
- ☐ It equals the wage you receive in your employment.
- ☐ Employers can use high employment rents to exert power over employees.

> **QUESTION 6.6 CHOOSE THE CORRECT ANSWER(S)**
> In which of the following employment situations would the employment rent be high, *ceteris paribus*?
>
> ☐ in a job that provides many benefits, such as housing and medical insurance
> ☐ in an economic boom, when the ratio of jobseekers to vacancies is low
> ☐ when the worker is paid a high salary because she is a qualified accountant and there is a shortage of accountancy skills
> ☐ when the worker is paid a high salary because the firm's customers know and trust her

> **EXERCISE 6.3 CALCULATING THE EMPLOYMENT RENT**
> 1. In the US, the unemployment benefit is typically about half of a worker's wage, and is restricted to 26 weeks. Using these numbers for the unemployment benefit, with the other numbers in the example in Figure 6.3, what is the employment rent?
> 2. If unemployment benefits are subject to income taxation (just like wages, as is the case in the US), what is the employment rent if the tax rate is 20%?

6.8 WORK EFFORT AND WAGES: THE LABOUR DISCIPLINE MODEL

When the cost of job loss (the employment rent) is large, workers will be willing to work harder in order to reduce the likelihood of losing the job. Holding constant other ways that it might influence the employment rent, a firm can increase the cost of job loss—and therefore the effort exerted by its employees—by raising wages. We refer to 'effort' as if it were a single thing, but of course what the firm needs to make profits is many dimensions of what an employee may do on the job, including physical effort, care, and not engaging in the kinds of vindictive sabotage that may have occurred in the Firestone plant in Decatur, Illinois (page 229).

We now represent this social interaction in the firm as a **game** played by the owners (through their managers) and the employees. This game is called the **labour discipline model**. It gets its name because it describes how carrots and sticks are used by the employer to provide workers with the incentive to work hard in order to avoid losing their job.

As with other models, we ignore some aspects of their interaction to focus on what is important, following the principle that sometimes we see more by looking at less.

On the stage of the firm, the cast of characters is just the owner (the employer) and a single worker, Maria. The game is sequential (one of them chooses first, like the ultimatum game that we saw in Section 3.3 (page 100)) and is repeated in each period of employment. Here is the order of play:

1. *The employer chooses a wage:* This is based on his knowledge of how employees like Maria respond to higher or lower wages, and informs employees that they will be employed in subsequent periods at the same

> **game** A model of strategic interaction that describes the players, the feasible strategies, the information that the players have, and their payoffs. See also: *game theory*.
> **labour discipline model** A model that explains how employers set wages so that employees receive an economic rent (called employment rent), which provides workers an incentive to work hard in order to avoid job termination. See also: *employment rent, efficiency wages*.

wage—as long as they work hard enough. This is the incomplete employment contract.
2. *Maria chooses a level of work effort:* This is in response to the wage offered, taking into account the costs of losing her job if she does not provide enough effort.

The payoff for the employer is the profit. The greater Maria's effort, the more goods or services she will produce, and the more profit he will make. Maria's payoff is how much she values the wage she receives, taking into account the effort she has expended.

This game describes the employment relationship between Maria and her employer.

If Maria chooses her work effort as a best response to the employer's offer, and the employer chooses the wage that maximizes his profit given that Maria responds the way she does, their strategies are a **Nash equilibrium**.

Employers typically hire work supervisors and may install surveillance equipment to keep watch over their employees, increasing the likelihood that the management will find out if a worker is not working hard and well. Here we will ignore these extra costs and just assume that the employer occasionally gets some information on how hard or well an employee is working. This is not enough to implement a piece-rate contract, but more than enough to fire a worker if the news is not good. Maria knows that the chance of the employer getting bad news decreases the harder she works.

To decide on the wage to set, the employer needs to know how the employee's work effort will respond to higher wages. We will consider Maria's decision first. In the next section, we consider the firm's decision and the Nash equilibrium in this game.

The employee's best response

Maria's effort can vary between zero and one. We can think of this as the proportion of each hour that she spends working diligently (the rest of the time she is not working). An effort level of 0.5 indicates she is spending half the working day on non-work-related activities, such as checking Facebook, shopping online, or just staring out of the window.

To find out Maria's reservation wage, we ask the hypothetical question: at what wage would she not care one way or the other if her job ended? We will assume that the answer in this case is $11.70 per hour because this is the unemployment benefit she would get (the amount of the benefit averaged over 35 hours), were her job to end. So, even if Maria put in no work whatsoever (and so endured no disutility of effort, spending all day on Facebook and daydreaming), if her job paid a $11.70 wage she would be no better off than being without work. Her best response to a wage of $11.70 would therefore be zero effort.

For Maria, effort has a cost (the disutility of work) and a benefit (it increases the likelihood of her keeping the job, and the employment rent she gets from it). In her choice of effort, she needs to find a balance between these two.

What if she were paid a higher wage?

A higher wage increases the employment rent and hence the benefit from effort, so it will lead her to choose a higher level of effort. Maria's best response (the effort she chooses) will increase with the level of the wage chosen by the employer.

> **Nash equilibrium** A set of strategies, one for each player in the game, such that each player's strategy is a best response to the strategies chosen by everyone else.

Figure 6.4 shows that Maria's employment rent increases when the wage increases, *ceteris paribus*. The area of the rent rectangle increases when she gets a higher wage, assuming that there is no change in the expected length of unemployment should she lose her job and no change in the unemployment benefit. Since her employment rent is higher, Maria will be more concerned about losing her job and will exert more effort. We can show Maria's effort in response to different wages in the 'best response diagram'.

Figure 6.5 shows the effort Maria chooses for each level of the wage, referred to as her **best response curve**, or **worker's best response function**. (Just like the production functions in Unit 4, it shows how one variable, in this case effort, depends on another, the wage.) Maria's best response to a wage offer depends on how long she would expect to be unemployed before getting a new job if she were to lose her job. We assume this is 44 weeks as in Figures 6.3 and 6.4.

The best response curve is concave, meaning that it becomes flatter as the wage and the effort level increase. This is because, as the level of effort approaches the maximum possible level, the disutility of effort becomes greater. In this case, it takes a larger employment rent (and hence a higher wage) to get a given amount of extra effort from the employee.

> **worker's best response function (to wage)** The amount of work that a worker chooses to perform as her best response to each wage that the employer may offer. *Also known as:* best response curve.

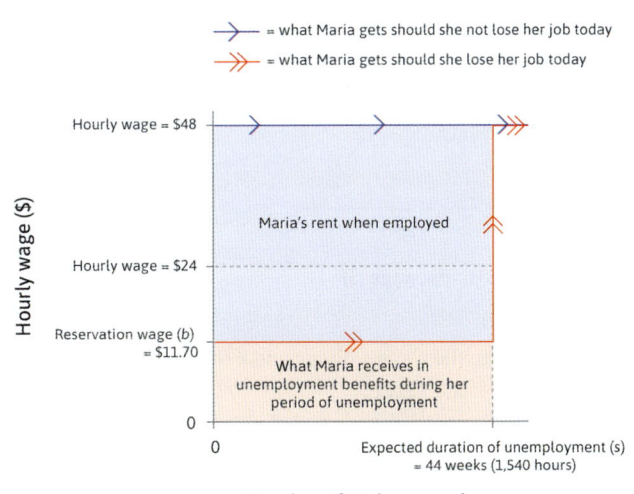

To explore all of the slides in this figure, see the online version at https://tinyco.re/3372875.

Figure 6.4 Maria's employment rent is higher when the wage doubles to $48 per hour (the employment rents shown for the $48 wage are those at point K in Figure 6.5).

1. Maria's wage doubles
Maria's hourly wage, after taxes and other deductions, increases to $48. Looking ahead from now (week 0), she will continue to receive this wage for the foreseeable future if she keeps her job, indicated by the horizontal blue line with arrows.

2. Maria's employment rent when her wage doubles
Ceteris paribus, Maria's employment rent shaded blue increases when her wage increases.

Seen from the standpoint of the owner or the employer, the best response curve shows how paying higher wages can elicit higher effort, but with diminishing marginal returns. In other words, the higher the initial wage, the smaller the increase in effort and output the employer gets from an extra $1 per hour in wages.

The best response curve is the frontier of the feasible set of combinations of wages and effort the firm can get from its employees, and the slope of the frontier is the marginal rate of transformation of wages into effort.

Why not pay the lowest wage?

The lowest wage the firm could set for Maria would be the reservation wage, $11.70, where the best response curve hits the horizontal axis and effort is zero. We can see that the firm would never offer the lowest wage possible, because she would not exert any effort at work.

To explore all of the slides in this figure, see the online version at https://tinyco.re/1731550.

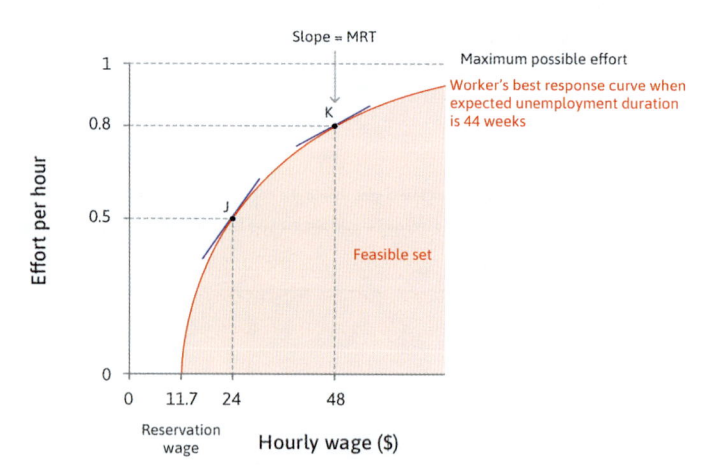

Figure 6.5 Maria's best response to the wage. Points J and K refer to the information in Figures 6.3 (page 247) and 6.4 (page 251).

1. Effort per hour
Effort per hour, measured on the vertical axis, varies between zero and one.

2. The relationship between effort and the wage
If Maria is paid $11.70, she does not care if she loses her job because $11.70 is her reservation wage. This is why she provides no effort at a wage of $11.70. If she is paid more, she provides more effort.

3. The worker's best response
The upward-sloping curve shows that when the wage increases from $24 to $48 shown on the horizontal axis, her effort rises from 0.5 to 0.8 (from point J to point K). Effort is higher when the wage is higher because a higher wage increases her employment rent, as we saw in Figure 6.4.

4. The effect of a small wage increase when effort is low
When the wage is low, the best response curve is steep—a small wage increase raises effort by a substantial amount.

5. Diminishing marginal returns
At higher levels of wages, however, increases in wages have a smaller effect on effort.

6. The employer's feasible set
The best response curve is the frontier of the employer's feasible set of combinations of wages and effort that it gets from its employees.

7. The employer's MRT
The slope of the best response curve is the employer's marginal rate of transformation of higher wages into more worker effort.

> **QUESTION 6.7 CHOOSE THE CORRECT ANSWER(S)**
> Figure 6.5 depicted Maria's best response curve when the expected duration of unemployment was 10 months. Which of the following statements are correct?
>
> ☐ If the expected unemployment duration increased to 11 months, Maria's best response to a wage of $24 would be an effort level above 0.5.
> ☐ If the unemployment benefit were reduced, then Maria's reservation wage would be higher than $11.70.
> ☐ Over the range of wages shown in the figure, Maria would never exert the maximum possible effort per hour.
> ☐ Increasing effort from 0.5 to 0.6 requires a larger wage increase than increasing effort from 0.8 to 0.9.

6.9 THE EMPLOYER SETS THE WAGE TO MINIMIZE THE COST PER UNIT OF EFFORT

Maria is not in the situation that Angela faced in Unit 5 (page 194), when Bruno could order her to work at the point of a gun. Maria has bargaining power because she can always walk away—an option that, initially, Angela did not have.

Maria chooses how hard she works. But the employer can determine the conditions under which she makes that choice. The owners and managers know that they cannot get Maria to provide more effort than is given by the best response curve shown in Figure 6.5. The fact that the best response curve slopes upwards means that employers face a trade-off. They can only get more effort by paying higher wages.

Employers maximize profits by minimizing costs of production

To maximize their profits, firms want to minimize the costs of production. In particular, they want to pay the lowest possible price for inputs. A company purchasing oil for use in the production process will look for the supplier that can provide it at the lowest price per litre. Likewise, Maria provides an input to production, and her employer would like to purchase it at the lowest price. But this does not mean paying the lowest possible wage. We already know that, if he paid the reservation wage, workers might show up (they wouldn't care one way or the other), but they would not work if they did.

The wage, W, is the cost to the employer of an hour of a worker's time. But what matters for production is not how many hours Maria provides, but how many units of effort—effort is the input to the production process. If Maria chooses to provide 0.5 units of effort per hour and her hourly wage is W, the cost to the employer of a unit of effort is $2W$. In general, if she provides e units of effort per hour, the cost of a unit of effort is W/e.

So, to maximize profits, the employer should find a feasible combination of effort and wage that minimizes the cost per unit of effort, W/e.

Another way to say the same thing is that the employer should maximize the number of units of effort (sometimes called **efficiency units**) that he gets per dollar of wage cost, e/W.

> **efficiency unit** A unit of effort is sometimes called an efficiency unit.

The firm's isocost curves for effort

The upward-sloping straight line in Figure 6.6 joins together a set of points that have the same ratio of effort to wages, e/W. If the wage is $24 per hour and a worker provides 0.5 units of effort per hour, the employer gets 0.021 efficiency units per dollar. Equivalently, a unit of effort costs $24/0.5 = $48. The employer would be indifferent between this situation and one in which the wage is $28.8 with an effort of 0.6, or the wage is $48 with an effort of 1 —the cost of effort is exactly the same at all points on the line.

We will call this an **isocost line** for effort. These lines join points (combinations of wage and effort) that have identical effects on the employer's costs, just like an isobar joins the points of identical atmospheric pressure on a map ('iso' is Greek for 'same'). We can also think of an isocost line as an indifference curve for the employer. Since the cost of effort is the same at all points on an isocost curve, the employer is indifferent between the points.

isocost line A line that represents all combinations that cost a given total amount.

To explore all of the slides in this figure, see the online version at https://tinyco.re/1765897.

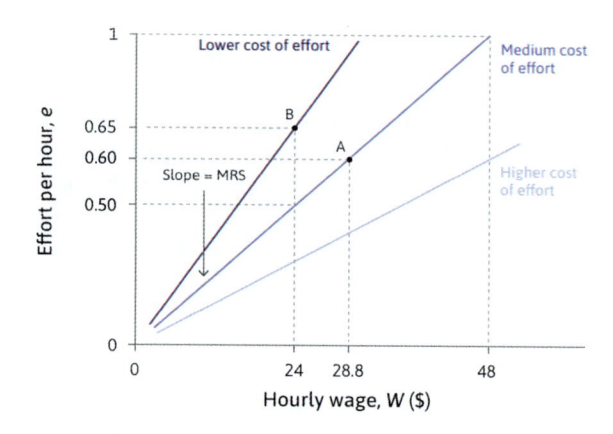

Figure 6.6 The employer's indifference curves: Isocost curves for effort.

1. An isocost line for effort
If $W = $24 and $e = 0.5$, $e/W = 0.021$. At every point on this line, the ratio of effort to wages is the same, for example at point A, $e/W = 0.6/28.8 = 0.021$. The cost of a unit of effort is $W/e = $48.

2. The slope of the isocost line
The line slopes upward because a higher effort level must be accompanied by a higher wage for the e/W ratio to remain unchanged. The slope is equal to $e/W = 0.021$, the number of units of effort per dollar.

3. Other isocost lines
On an isocost line, the slope is e/W, but the cost of effort is W/e. The steeper line has a lower cost of effort, and the flatter line has a higher cost of effort.

4. Some lines are better for the employer than others
A steeper line means lower cost of effort and hence higher profits for the employer. On the steepest isocost line, he gets 0.65 units of effort for a wage of $24 (at B), so the cost of effort is $24/0.6 = $40 per unit. On the middle line he only gets 0.5 units of effort at this wage, so the cost of effort is $48 and profits are lower.

5. The slope is the MRS
The employer is indifferent between points on an isocost line. Like other indifference curves, the slope of the effort isocost line is the marginal rate of substitution—the rate at which the employer is willing to increase wages to get higher effort.

6.9 THE EMPLOYER SETS THE WAGE TO MINIMIZE THE COST PER UNIT OF EFFORT

> **QUESTION 6.8 CHOOSE THE CORRECT ANSWER(S)**
> Consider isocost lines drawn on a graph with hourly wage on the horizontal axis and effort per hour on the vertical axis. Which of the following statements is correct?
>
> ☐ Isocost lines intersect the horizontal axis at the reservation wage.
> ☐ For an isocost line with a slope of 0.07, the cost of a unit of effort is $14.30.
> ☐ The slope of the isocost line is the employer's marginal rate of transformation of higher wages into worker effort.
> ☐ Steeper isocost lines represent higher costs per unit of effort.

To minimize costs, the employer will seek to reach the steepest isocost line for effort, where the cost of a unit of effort is lowest. (Remember, steeper isocost lines mean that a given increase in the wage will result in a larger increase in effort.) But the employer lacks the ability to dictate how much effort Maria puts into her work, and so has to pick some point on Maria's best response curve. From the employer's standpoint, the best response curve is the feasible frontier.

The best the employer can do is to set the wage at $24 on the isocost line that is **tangent** to Maria's best response curve (point J in Figure 6.7). Use the analysis in Figure 6.7 to see how the employer sets the wage.

The firm sets the 'efficiency' wage

In Figure 6.7, the employer will choose point A, offering a wage of $24 per hour to hire Maria, who will exert effort of 0.5. The employer cannot do better than this point—any point with lower costs, for example, point D, is infeasible.

The employer minimizes costs and maximizes profit at the point where the employer's **MRS** (the slope of the indifference curve or isocost line) equals the **MRT** (the slope of the best response curve, which is the employer's feasible frontier). This balances the trade-off the employer is willing to make between wages and effort against the trade-off the employer is constrained to make by Maria's response.

This is a **constrained choice problem**, similar to the one in Unit 4 (page 161). There, individuals maximizing utility chose working hours where MRS = MRT, and the slope of their indifference curve equalled the slope of the feasible frontier determined by the production technology.

When wages are set by the employer in this manner, they are sometimes called **efficiency wages** because the employer is recognizing that what matters for profits is e/W—the efficiency units (units of effort) per dollar of wage costs—rather than how much an hour of work costs (W).

What has the labour discipline model told us?

- *Equilibrium:* In the owner–employee game, the employer offers a wage and Maria provides a level of effort in response. Their strategies are a Nash equilibrium.
- *Rent:* In this allocation, Maria provides effort because she receives an employment rent that she might lose if she were to slack off on the job.
- *Power:* Because Maria fears losing this economic rent, the employer is able to exercise power over her, getting her to act in ways that she would not do without this threat of job loss. This contributes to the employer's profits.

---

tangency When a line touches a curve, but does not cross it.
marginal rate of substitution (MRS) The trade-off that a person is willing to make between two goods. At any point, this is the slope of the indifference curve. See also: marginal rate of transformation.
marginal rate of transformation (MRT) A measure of the trade-offs a person faces in what is feasible. Given the constraints (feasible frontier) a person faces, the MRT is the quantity of some good that must be sacrificed to acquire one additional unit of another good. At any point, it is the slope of the feasible frontier. See also: feasible frontier, marginal rate of substitution.
constrained choice problem This problem is about how we can do the best for ourselves, given our preferences and constraints, and when the things we value are scarce. See also: constrained optimization problem.
efficiency wages The payment an employer makes that is higher than an employee's reservation wage, so as to motivate the employee to provide more effort on the job than he or she would otherwise choose to make. See also: labour discipline model, employment rent.

EXERCISE 6.4 THE EMPLOYER SETS THE WAGE

Would any of the following affect Maria's best response curve or the firm's isocost lines for effort in Figure 6.7? If so, explain how.

1. The government decides to increase childcare subsidies for working parents but not for those unemployed. Assume Maria has a child and is eligible for the subsidy.
2. Demand for the firm's output rises as celebrities endorse the good.
3. Improved technology makes Maria's job easier.

To explore all of the slides in this figure, see the online version at https://tinyco.re/8590897.

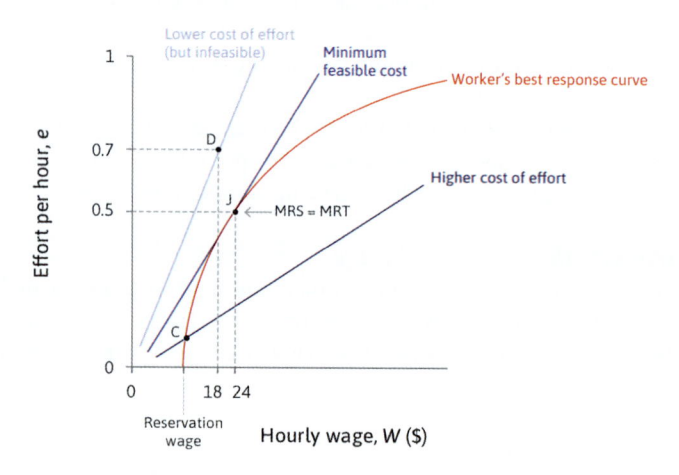

Figure 6.7 The employer sets the wage to minimize the cost of getting the worker to provide effort.

1. Minimizing the cost of effort
To maximize profits, the employer wants to obtain effort at the lowest cost, and will seek to get onto the steepest isocost line possible. But, without the ability to dictate the level of effort, the employer must pick some point on the worker's best response curve.

2. C is not the best the employer can do
Would the employer choose a point such as C? No. We shall see that, by paying more, the employer will benefit from a lower wage–effort ratio, because effort will increase more than proportionally to the wage.

3. Point J is the best the employer can do
The best the employer can do is to set the wage where the isocost line is just touching (tangent to) the worker's best response curve.

4. MRS = MRT
At this point, the marginal rate of substitution (the slope of the isocost line for effort) is equal to the marginal rate of transformation of higher wages into greater effort (the slope of the best response function).

5. Point D
Points on steeper isocosts, such as point D, would have lower costs for the employer but are infeasible. They are outside the feasible frontier shown by the worker's best response curve.

6. Minimum feasible costs
Therefore, $24 is the hourly wage that the employer should set to minimize costs and maximize profits.

QUESTION 6.9 CHOOSE THE CORRECT ANSWER(S)

Figure 6.7 depicts the efficiency wage equilibrium of a worker and a firm. According to this figure:

- ☐ Along the isocost line tangent to the best response curve, doubling of the per-hour effort from 0.5 to 1 would lead to an increased profit for the firm.
- ☐ The slope of each isocost line is the number of units of effort per dollar.
- ☐ At the equilibrium point, the marginal rate of transformation on the isocost line equals the marginal rate of substitution on the worker's best response curve.
- ☐ Points C and J both represent Nash equilibria because they are on the best response curve.

6.10 WHY THERE IS ALWAYS INVOLUNTARY UNEMPLOYMENT

When we think about the implications of the labour discipline model for the whole economy, it tells us something else, which may at first seem surprising:

There must always be **involuntary unemployment**.

Being unemployed involuntarily means not having a job, although you would be willing to work at the wage that other workers like you are receiving.

In developing our model, we *assumed* that Maria could expect to be unemployed for ten months before receiving another job offer at the same wage level. But the model implies that there *must be* an extended period of unemployment.

To see why, try to imagine an equilibrium in the game between Maria and her employer, in which the employer pays her a wage of $24 per hour and, if she loses her job, she could immediately find another at the same wage. In that case, Maria's employment rent would be zero. She would be indifferent between keeping the job and losing it. Therefore, her best response would be an effort level of zero. But this could not be an equilibrium—the employer would not pay $24 an hour to someone who did no work.

Now imagine there were plenty of jobs available in the economy at $24 per hour and no one was unemployed. Immediately, you can see that this situation could not last. Employers would *offer* higher wages, say an extra $8 per hour, to ensure that their workers had something to lose and would therefore work hard. But, after offering higher wages, they would not be able to offer as many jobs. Workers who lost their jobs would no longer be able to find new ones easily. Jobs would be scarce, and it might take weeks or months to find another. The economy would move to a new equilibrium with higher wages and involuntary unemployment. Employees would be earning $32 an hour and those who lost their jobs would be willing to accept another at $32, but they would not immediately be able to find one.

In equilibrium, both wages and involuntary unemployment have to be high enough to ensure that there is enough employment rent for workers to put in effort.

Unemployment is an important concern for voters, and so for the policymakers who represent them. We can use this model to see how policies that governments pursue to alter the level of unemployment, or to provide income to unemployed workers, will affect the profits of firms and the effort level of their employees.

> **involuntary unemployment** A person who is seeking work, and willing to accept a job at the going wage for people of their level of skill and experience, but unable to secure employment is involuntarily employed.

6.11 PUTTING THE MODEL TO WORK: OWNERS, EMPLOYEES, AND PUBLIC POLICY

Until now we have considered how the employer chooses a point on the best response function. But changes in economic conditions or public policies can shift the entire best response function, moving it to the right (or up) or to the left (or down).

The worker's incentive to choose a high level of effort depends on how much she has to lose (the employment rent), but also the likelihood of losing it. The position of the best response function depends on:

- the utility of the things that can be bought with the wage
- the disutility of effort
- the reservation wage
- the probability of getting fired when working at each effort level.

If there are changes in any of these factors, the best response curve will shift. Public policy can affect the position of the best response function.

Unemployment, and unemployment benefits, affect the wage that firms set

A higher unemployment rate
Imagine how an increase in the unemployment rate affects the best response curve. When unemployment is high, workers who lose their jobs can expect a longer spell of unemployment. Recall that unemployment benefits (including support from family and friends) are limited, so the longer the expected spell of unemployment, the lower the level of the unemployment benefit per hour (or per week) of lost work. An increase in the duration of a spell of unemployment has two effects:

- *It reduces the reservation wage:* This increases the employment rent *per hour*.
- *It extends the period of lost work time:* This increases the total cost of job loss and hence *total* employment rents.

The effect of a higher unemployment rate on employment rent at an unchanged wage is shown in Figure 6.8. A longer expected spell of unemployment (from s to s^*) increases the size of the shaded rectangle measuring the employment rent. Remember that the employment rent is:

$$\text{Employment rent} = s(Wh - \frac{B}{s}) = sWh - B.$$

By extending the length of time unemployed, the reservation wage ($b = B/(sh)$) falls. The rectangle of employment rent increases in area because the reservation wage is lower over the longer spell. Remember that unemployment and other government benefits are usually strictly time-limited, and help from family and friends will probably not last for ever.

A higher employment rent increases effort at any given wage, so that the best response function in Figure 6.9 shifts up. It also shifts to the left because of the fall in the reservation wage that accompanies the longer expected spell of unemployment.

6.11 PUTTING THE MODEL TO WORK: OWNERS, EMPLOYEES, AND PUBLIC POLICY

A higher unemployment benefit

Figure 6.9 can also be used to illustrate the implications of a rise in the unemployment benefit for the best response function. You can first show the effect on the employment rent in a version of Figure 6.3 (page 247) by shifting up the horizontal line at b, the reservation wage. Since greater benefit generosity lowers the employment rent (the shaded rectangle in your version of Figure 6.3 shrinks), the worker will supply less effort for a given wage and the wage at which there is zero effort is higher. Translating this into the best response diagram in Figure 6.9, the curve shifts downward and rightward.

Figure 6.9 shows the effects on the best response curve of a rise in unemployment, and also of a rise in unemployment benefits.

Economic policies affect the wage firms set

A rise in the level of unemployment shifts the best response curve to the left:

- For a given wage, say $36, the amount of effort that the worker will provide increases, improving the profit-making conditions for the employer.
- The wage that the employer would have to pay to get a given effort level, say 0.6, decreases.

A rise in unemployment benefits shifts the best response curve to the right, so it has the opposite effects.

Economic policies can alter both the size of the unemployment benefit and the extent of unemployment (and hence the duration of a spell of unemployment). These policies are often controversial.

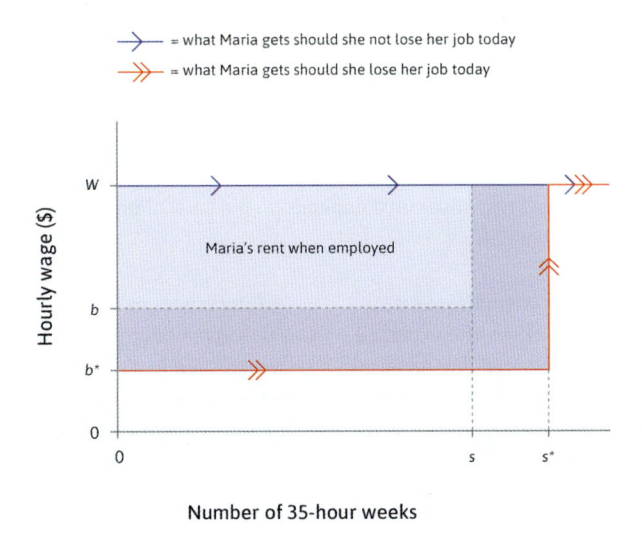

Figure 6.8 The effect on employment rent of a rise in the duration of unemployment.

259

- *Workers are favoured by a rightward shift of the worker's best response function:* This may be a result, for example, of more generous unemployment benefits which makes them less fearful of losing their job. Because this *reduces* their employment rents, the worker will put in less effort for any given wage.
- *Employers are favoured by a leftward shift:* This may be a result, for example, of higher unemployment. They will acquire the effort of their workers at a lower cost, raising profits. This is because the higher unemployment increases the worker's employment rent. When workers have more to lose, employers benefit.

To explore all of the slides in this figure, see the online version at https://tinyco.re/5847062.

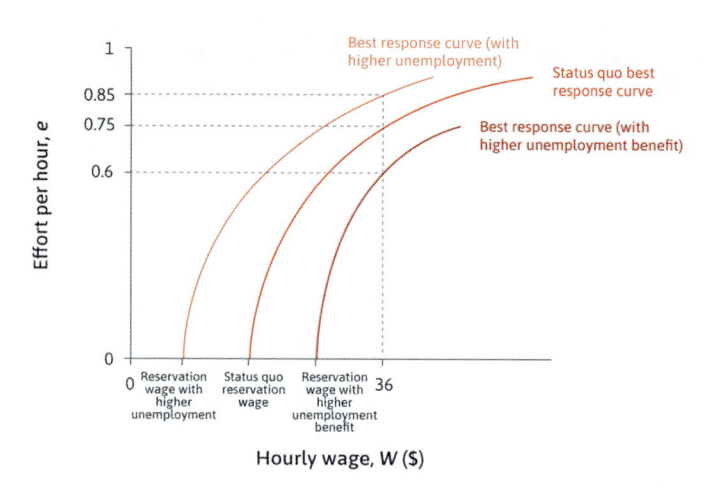

Figure 6.9 The best response curve depends on the level of unemployment and the unemployment benefit.

1. The status quo
The position of the best response curve depends on the reservation wage. It crosses the horizontal axis at this point.

2. The effect of unemployment benefits
A rise in the unemployment benefit increases the reservation wage and shifts the worker's best response curve to the right.

3. An increase in unemployment
If unemployment rises, the expected duration of unemployment increases. Therefore, the worker's reservation wage falls, and the best response curve shifts to the left.

4. Effort changes for a given wage
For a given hourly wage, say $36, workers put in different levels of effort when the levels of unemployment or unemployment benefit change.

6.11 PUTTING THE MODEL TO WORK: OWNERS, EMPLOYEES, AND PUBLIC POLICY

> **EXERCISE 6.5 EFFORT AND WAGES**
> Suppose that, with the status quo best response curve in Figure 6.9, the firm chooses the wage to minimize the cost of effort, and the worker's best response is an effort level of 0.6. If unemployment rose:
>
> 1. Would effort be higher or lower than 0.6 if the firm did not change the wage?
> 2. How would the firm change the wage if it wanted to keep the effort level at 0.6?
> 3. How would the wage change if the firm minimized the cost of effort at the new unemployment level?

HOW ECONOMISTS LEARN FROM DATA

Workers speed up when the economy slows down

The idea that employment rents are an incentive for employees to work harder is illustrated in a study by Edward Lazear (an economic advisor to former US President George W. Bush) and his co-authors. They investigated a single firm during the global financial crisis, to see how the managers and workers reacted to the turbulent economic conditions. The firm specialized in technology-based services—such as insurance-claims processing, computer-based test grading, and technical call centres—and operated in 12 US states. The nature of the work made it easy for the firm's management to track the workers' productivity, which is a measure of worker effort.

It also allowed Lazear and his colleagues to use the firm's data from 2006–2010 to analyse the effect on worker productivity of the worst recession since the Great Depression.

When unemployment rose, workers could expect a longer spell of unemployment if they lost their jobs. Firms did not use their increased bargaining power to lower wages as they could have, fearing their employees' reaction.

Lazear and his co-authors found that, in this firm, productivity increased dramatically as unemployment rose during the financial crisis. One possible explanation is that average productivity increased because management fired the least productive members of the workforce. But Lazear found that the effect was more due to workers putting in extra effort. The severity of the recession raised the workers' employment rent for any given wage, and they were therefore willing to work harder. We would predict from our model that the best response curve would have shifted to the left as a result of the recession. This meant that (unless employers lowered wages substantially) workers would work harder. Apparently, this is what happened.

Our model shows that employers could have cut wages, while sustaining an employment rent sufficient to motivate hard work. An earlier recession provided another insight that helps to explain their reluctance to reduce wages in the crisis. Truman Bewley, an economist, was puzzled when he saw only a handful of firms in the northeast of the US cutting wages during the recession of the early 1990s. Most firms, like the one Lazear's team studied, did not cut their wages at all.

Edward P. Lazear, Kathryn L. Shaw, and Christopher Stanton. 2016. 'Making Do with Less: Working Harder during Recessions'. *Journal of Labor Economics* 34 (S1 Part 2): pp. 333–60.

Truman F. Bewley. 1999. *Why Wages Don't Fall during a Recession*. Cambridge, MA: Harvard University Press.

Bewley interviewed more than 300 employers, labour leaders, business consultants, and careers advisors in the northeast of the US. He found that employers chose not to cut wages because they thought it would hurt employee morale, reducing productivity and leading to problems of hiring and retention. They thought it would ultimately cost the employer more than the money they would save in wages.

> **EXERCISE 6.6 LAZEAR'S RESULTS**
> Use the best response diagram to sketch the results found by Lazear and co-authors in their study of a firm during the global financial crisis.
>
> 1. Assuming that the employer did not adjust wages, draw a best response curve for each of the following years and explain what it illustrates:
>   *(a)* the pre-crisis period (2006)
>   *(b)* the crisis years (2007–2008)
>   *(c)* the post-crisis year (2009)
> 2. Is there a reason why a firm might not cut wages during a recession? Think about the research of Truman Bewley, and the experimental evidence about reciprocity in Unit 2 (page 72).

> **QUESTION 6.10 CHOOSE THE CORRECT ANSWER(S)**
> Which of the following statements are true?
>
> ☐ If unemployment benefits are increased, the minimum cost of a unit of effort for the employer will rise.
> ☐ If the wage doesn't change, employees will work harder in periods of high unemployment.
> ☐ If workers continue to receive benefits however long they remain unemployed, an increase in the level of unemployment will have no effect on the best response curve.
> ☐ If an employee's disutility of effort increases, the reservation wage will rise.

6.12 WHY DO EMPLOYERS PAY EMPLOYMENT RENTS TO THEIR WORKERS?

When a firm is deciding on how to run its operation, it looks for the lowest cost available as we saw in Section 6.9 (page 253). If we were to observe a firm paying €0.15 per kilowatt hour of electricity when it could be purchased for €0.11, we would conclude that, for some reason, the firm was not minimizing its costs and therefore could not be maximizing its profits. It would be throwing away money.

When workers receive employment rents, they value having their jobs more than their next best alternative (being unemployed and searching for and eventually taking some other job). This means that the employer is paying more than the minimum that would induce the worker to prefer taking the job over remaining unemployed.

Isn't this just a gift from employer to worker? How does this benefit employers?

6.12 WHY DO EMPLOYERS PAY EMPLOYMENT RENTS TO THEIR WORKERS?

We have explained one reason:

- *Employment rent is a powerful motivation for the employee to work hard and well*: It can be withdrawn by the employer (by firing the worker). This aligns the interests of the employer and the worker. An increase in the employment rent shifts power from the worker to the employer.

There are other ways that paying a rent to the worker contributes to the profits of the firm.

- *The rent makes the worker more likely to stay with the firm:* Worker turnover is costly to the firm. If she were to quit the job, the firm would bear the cost of recruiting and training someone else.
- *The rent expands the pool of job applications among whom the firm can choose:* If the unemployed are similar to the employees of the firm, the larger the rent received by workers, the more attractive the firm will be to currently unemployed workers. A result will be that, when the firm wishes to expand or replace workers who retire, quit, or are fired, they will be able to choose from a larger selection of job applicants.
- *The rent may be experienced as a gift that is reciprocated by the worker:* Though it benefits the owner of the firm (for the above reasons), the rent received by the worker may be experienced by the employee as an act of generosity that would be reciprocated by hard work and loyalty to the firm and its owners.

What, then, is the difference between labour and kilowatt hours, or office furniture, or any of the other non-labour inputs of the firm, or any of the other goods or services for which no firm would ever pay more than the minimum? The answer is simple—for electricity, all that matters is that the good or service is delivered to the firm.

But for the firm, making a profit is not as simple as getting the worker to show up for work, as Firestone Tire and Rubber Company discovered when the strikers at Decatur returned to work. Because the labour contract is incomplete, as we have seen in Section 6.4 (page 238), the worker must also be motivated to work hard, and stay with the firm.

QUESTION 6.11 CHOOSE THE CORRECT ANSWER(S)

Which of the following are correct explanations of why, when purchasing electricity, the firm will always seek the cheapest provider, but it will not pay an employee the lowest amount that would motivate the worker to accept the job?

- ☐ A rent provides a powerful motivation for the employee to work hard and well.
- ☐ There are many competitors supplying electricity, but this is not the case for labour.
- ☐ Electricity (or equivalent forms of power) represent a larger share of the firm's costs than does labour.
- ☐ Paying the employee more makes it more likely that she will remain with the firm.

6.13 ANOTHER KIND OF BUSINESS ORGANIZATION: COOPERATIVE FIRMS

Even in capitalist economies, some business organizations have an entirely different structure to the one we have been analysing—their workers are the owners of the capital goods and other assets of the company, and they select managers who run the company on a day-to-day basis. This form of business organization is called a **worker-owned cooperative** or **cooperative firm**.

One well-known example of a cooperative is the British retailer John Lewis Partnership (https://tinyco.re/2414644), founded in 1864 and held in trust for its employees since 1950. Every employee is a partner, and employee councils elect five out of seven members of the company board. The benefits for employees (pension, paid holidays, long-service sabbaticals, and social activities) are generous, and the business's profits are shared out as a bonus, calculated as a percentage of each person's salary every year.

> **worker-owned cooperative** A form of business in which a substantial fraction of the capital goods are owned by employees rather than being owned by those who are not involved in production in the firm; worker-owners typically elect a manager to make day-to-day decisions.
> **cooperative firm** A firm that is mostly or entirely owned by its workers, who hire and fire the managers.

Cooperatives have fewer supervisors

Worker-owned cooperatives are hierarchically organized, like conventional firms, but the directives issued from the top of the hierarchy come from people who owe their jobs to the worker-owners. Other than this, the main differences between conventional firms and worker-owned cooperatives are that the cooperatives need fewer supervisors and other management personnel to ensure that the worker-owners work hard and well. Fellow worker-owners will not tolerate a shirking worker because the shirker is reducing the profit share of the other workers. Reduced need for supervision is among the reasons that worker-owned cooperatives produce at least as much per hour (if not more) than their conventional counterparts.

During the twentieth century, worker-owned plywood producers successfully competed with traditional capitalist firms in the US.

John Pencavel. 2002. *Worker Participation: Lessons from the Worker Co-ops of the Pacific Northwest*. New York, NY: Russell Sage Foundation Publications.

There are typically fewer inequalities in wages and salaries within the company in worker-owned cooperatives than in conventional firms, for example between managers and production workers. And worker-owned cooperatives tend not to lay off workers when the economy goes into recession, offering their worker-owners a kind of insurance (often they cut back on the hours of all workers rather than terminating the employment of some).

The knowledge-based economy is creating new forms of firms, neither capitalist nor worker-owned.

Tim O'Reilly and Eric S. Raymond. 2001. *The Cathedral & the Bazaar: Musings on Linux and Open Source by an Accidental Revolutionary*. Sebastopol, CA: O'Reilly.

Case studies show that, in those unusual companies owned primarily by the workers themselves, work is done more intensely with less supervision. There have been many attempts to establish other types of business organization throughout recent history, but borrowing the funds to start and sustain worker-owned companies is often difficult because, as we will see in Unit 9, banks are often reluctant to lend funds (except at high interest rates) to people who are not wealthy.

> **EXERCISE 6.7 A WORKER-OWNED COOPERATIVE**
> In Figure 6.1 (page 234) we showed the actors and decision-making structure of a typical firm.
>
> 1. How do the actors and decision-making structure of John Lewis Partnership (https://tinyco.re/7059886) differ from that of a typical firm?
> 2. Redraw Figure 6.1 to illustrate your answer to Question 1.

QUESTION 6.12 CHOOSE THE CORRECT ANSWER(S)
Which of the following statements regarding a cooperative firm such as John Lewis are correct?

☐ The firm is owned by shareholders, some of whom are employees.
☐ Workers typically exert more effort, despite having less supervision.
☐ During a downturn, the firm tends to reduce working hours for all workers, rather than fire some workers.
☐ Profits are not paid out to the owners but retained within the firm for future investment.

EXERCISE 6.8 USING EXCEL: WHO OWNS THE FIRMS?
In this unit, we learned that owners are at the top of the ownership structure of a 'typical' firm, with managers in the middle and employees at the bottom of the hierarchy. We will now look at the characteristics of firm owners in different countries.

The data you will be using is from the 'Enterprise Surveys' (https://tinyco.re/6031672) compiled by the World Bank, which collect information about characteristics of firms around the world and the business environment they face.

Download the firm ownership data (https://tinyco.re/0058751). There are four variables related to ownership:

- proportion of private domestic ownership in a firm
- percentage of firms with at least 10% of foreign ownership
- percentage of firms with at least 10% of government/state ownership
- percentage of firms with legal status of sole proprietorship (these firms are not a legally separate entity from their owner, and cannot sell shares to raise funds for the business)

1. Choose two countries in the dataset and filter the data so that only the entries with 'All' for the variable 'Subgroup Level' are visible. For each country, plot a column chart showing these four variables, with percentages on the vertical axis and sector (manufacturing or services) on the horizontal axis. Make sure to include a legend and label the axes appropriately. (If your chosen country has more than one year of available data, plot a separate column chart for each year). For help on how to filter the data and draw a column chart, go back to Exercise 1.3 in Unit 1 (page 9).
2. The variable 'Subgroup' shows the same four variables, but for different subsectors, firm sizes, regions within a country, exporting behaviour, and gender of the top manager. Choose one subgroup and plot a separate column chart for each country, showing these four variables, with percentages on the vertical axis and the variable 'Subgroup Level' (containing the name of each subgroup) on the horizontal axis.
3. Suggest some explanations for any similarities or differences in firm ownership across countries and/or time that you observe in your charts from Questions 1 and 2. (You may find it helpful to research the institutions and policies related to business activity in your chosen countries.)

John Stuart Mill. (1859) 2002. *On Liberty* (http://tinyco.re/6454781). Mineola, NY: Dover Publications.

John Stuart Mill. (1848) 1994. *Principles of Political Economy* (https://tinyco.re/9348882). New York: Oxford University Press.

GREAT ECONOMISTS

John Stuart Mill

John Stuart Mill (1806–1873) was one of the most important philosophers and economists of the nineteenth century. His book, *On Liberty* (1859), parallels Adam Smith's *Wealth of Nations* in advocating limits on governmental powers, and is still an influential argument in favour of individual freedom and privacy.

Mill thought that the structure of the typical firm was an affront to freedom and individual autonomy. Mill described the relationship between firm owners and workers as an unnatural one:

> To work at the bidding and for the profit of another, without any interest in the work … is not, even when wages are high, a satisfactory state to human beings of educated intelligence … (*The Principles of Political Economy*, 1848)

Attributing the conventional employer–employee relationship to the poor education of the working class, he predicted that the spread of education, and the political empowerment of working people, would change this situation:

> The relation of masters and work-people will be gradually superseded by partnership … perhaps finally in all, association of labourers among themselves. (*The Principles of Political Economy*, 1848)

EXERCISE 6.9 WAS MILL WRONG?

Why do you think Mill's vision of a postcapitalist economy of worker-owned cooperatives has not yet occurred?

6.14 ANOTHER KIND OF BUSINESS ORGANIZATION: THE GIG ECONOMY

A 'gig' for a musician or comedian is a single appearance for which they will be paid not by the hour, but an agreed sum for the performance. The **gig economy** is not about jokes and tunes, however; it refers to the combined activities of Uber or Lyft drivers, TaskRabbits, Upworkers, Mechanical Turkers, and others who transport people and goods, home-assemble online purchased furniture, and perform other well-defined tasks for which they are paid a fixed rate.

Gig workers do their jobs independently, not as members of a team, and gain access to their 'gigs' by means of a two-sided digital platform that connects those who will pay for the work, and those who perform it.

The gig economy provides an illuminating contrast with the model of labour discipline studied in this unit. The key difference is that there is no labour discipline problem because the tasks performed are sufficiently well defined that a virtually complete contract is possible—if you want to go from your hotel to the airport, your Lyft driver does not get paid until that has happened. If you hire someone to assemble your flat-packed furniture, the TaskRabbit worker who was putting it together does not make any money until it is put together properly.

An important feature of the gig economy is that the only way that workers can get gigs is through the platforms owned by a few firms—for example Uber and Lyft for taxi services, TaskRabbit for tasks around the home, or Mechanical Turk for small administrative jobs. This means that those performing the gigs have no real bargaining power—if a TaskRabbit worker objects to the terms, there will always be another Tasker to do the job. The worker who refused the job will be unlikely to find better gigs on that platform.

The digital platform that allows those who need a gig performed to connect to those performing the gigs makes substantial mutual benefits possible by putting together gig workers—who have free time and the skills, a vehicle, or other equipment required—with those willing to pay for a completed gig. But because there are few platforms and many gig workers, they typically receive very little pay for often difficult and onerous work.

A result is that gig performers in this economy face extraordinary economic insecurity—they are not guaranteed a fixed schedule of hours and pay, nor do they receive health insurance benefits, maternity leave, holiday pay, or pension contributions through their employer.

Why does TaskRabbit, for example, not pay enough for gigs so that the Taskers receive an employment rent, as would be the case in the typical office or plant described by the labour discipline model? The answer is that they do not need to pay more than the gig worker's next best alternative. They do not need to motivate the worker to do the job—if it is not done, the worker will not be paid. A result is that the gig economy can often produce services at a lower cost and price than are available from conventional firms.

> **gig economy** An economy made up of people performing services matched by means of a computer platform with those paying for the service. Workers are paid for each task they complete, and not per hour. They are not legally recognized as employees of the company that owns the platform, and typically receive few benefits from the owners, other than matching.

What happens when your boss is an algorithm? Read this article in the *Financial Times* to find out.

Sarah O'Connor. 2016. 'When Your Boss is an Algorithm' (https://tinyco.re/8368823). *Financial Times*, 8 September.

6 THE FIRM: EMPLOYEES, MANAGERS, AND OWNERS

The gig economy affects employees in conventional firms
The gig economy is a small portion even of those high-income economies where, for example, ride services like Uber and Lyft have competed successfully against conventional taxi firms.

It has at least three effects on employees working in conventional firms:

- *They may benefit as consumers:* The firm may become more profitable by taking advantage of low-cost ways of getting tasks such as taxi services, deliveries or repairs, that had previously been done by conventional suppliers. This may be a positive effect for workers.
- *It may provide an additional source of income should the worker lose a job:* Working as an occasional Rabbit Tasker or Deliveroo rider, for example, is an alternative to unemployment benefits. This would be a positive effect, because it could improve the worker's reservation position.
- *The gig economy may make it more difficult for some types of worker to find re-employment:* For example, a driver for a delivery service, who loses a job under a conventional labour contract, may find fewer similar jobs will be open in future. This would be a negative effect, as it would be likely to extend the expected length of a spell of unemployment.

6.15 PRINCIPALS AND AGENTS: INTERACTIONS UNDER INCOMPLETE CONTRACTS

In the relationship between Maria and her employer, Maria's work effort matters to both parties but is not covered by the employment contract. This leads to the existence of employment rents. If they had been able to write a complete contract, the situation would have been quite different. The employer could have offered her an enforceable contract, specifying both the wage and the exact level of effort she should provide, and if these terms were acceptable to her, she would have agreed and worked as required. To maximize profit, the employer would have chosen a contract that was only just acceptable, so Maria would not have earned any rents.

This example is not unusual. In practice, all employment relationships are governed by incomplete contracts. Employment contracts often do not even bother to mention that the worker should work hard and well. By contrast, the way we have described the gig economy means that a gig worker does not have an employment contract with a firm. The nature of work in the gig economy is the subject of legal battles in many countries.

Why are contracts incomplete?
Thinking about some examples of economic interactions, we can see that there are several reasons for the absence of a complete contract:

- *Information is not verifiable:* For a contract to be enforceable, relevant information must be observable by both parties, but also *verifiable* by third parties such as courts of law. The court must be able to establish whether or not the requirements of the contract were met. Verifiable information is often unavailable; for example, it may be impossible to prove whether the poor condition of a rented apartment is due to normal wear and tear or the tenant's negligence.
- *The future is uncertain:* A contract is generally executed over a period of time—for example, specifying that Party A does X now and Party B does Y later. But what B should do later may depend on things that are unknown when the contract is written. People are unlikely to be able to

anticipate every possible thing that might happen in future—and trying to do so would probably not be cost effective.
- *Measurement may not be possible:* Many services and goods are inherently difficult to measure or describe precisely enough to be written into a contract. How would the restaurant owner measure how pleasantly his waiters interact with customers?
- *Absence of a judiciary:* For some transactions, there are no judicial institutions (courts or other relevant third parties) capable of enforcing contracts. Many international transactions are of this type.
- *Preference for incompleteness:* Even where the nature of the goods or services to be exchanged would permit a more complete contract, a less complete contract might be preferred. Intrusive surveillance of workers may backfire if the employer's distrust angers the workers, leading to less satisfactory work performance. You do not necessarily want to know the exact quality of a concert before you buy the ticket—discovering it may be part of the experience.

Principal–agent models

In the case of Maria and her employer, the employer is called the principal. The employer would like to offer Maria, the agent, an employment contract and she wants the job, but the amount of effort she will provide cannot be specified in the contract because it is not verifiable. The relationship between the two actors within the firm is an example of a **principal–agent relationship**.

> **principal–agent relationship** This is an asymmetrical relationship in which one party (the principal) benefits from some action or attribute of the other party (the agent) about which the principal's information is not sufficient to enforce in a complete contract. See also: incomplete contract. Also known as: principal–agent problem.

Our model of Maria's employment is an example of a principal–agent model, in which an action taken by the agent is 'hidden' from the principal, or 'unobservable'.

- *The agent:* This actor takes some action, such as working hard.
- *The principal:* This actor benefits from this action.
- *A conflict of interest:* This action is something the agent would not choose to do, perhaps because it is costly or unpleasant.
- *A hidden action:* Information about this action is either not available to the principal or is not verifiable.
- *An incomplete contract:* There is no way that the principal can use an enforceable contract to *guarantee* that the action is performed.

In short, a **hidden action problem** occurs when there is a conflict of interest, between a principal and an agent, over some action that may be taken by the agent, and this action cannot be subjected to a complete contract.

> **hidden actions (problem of)** This occurs when some action taken by one party to an exchange is not known or cannot be verified by the other. For example, the employer cannot know (or cannot verify) how hard the worker she has employed is actually working. Also known as: moral hazard. See also: hidden attributes (problem of).

Incomplete contracts are the rule, not the exception, in the economy

Using the lens of the principal–agent relationship, we can see many other ways in which we interact in the economy and society without a complete contract:

- *Banks lend money to borrowers in return for a promise to repay the full amount plus the stipulated interest:* But this may be unenforceable if the borrower is unable to repay.
- *Owners of firms would like managers to maximize the value of the owners' assets:* But managers also have things they like, which reduce the owners' wealth (such as flying first class, or really expensive office furniture). Managerial contracts often cannot specify an enforceable requirement to maximize the owners' wealth.
- *Landlords rent apartments to tenants who sign contracts that require they maintain the value of the property:* But aside from gross neglect, the liability for not maintaining the property is unenforceable.
- *Insurance companies ask people to sign contracts that require they should behave prudently:* Insurance contracts require (but typically cannot enforce) that people who are insured do not take unreasonable risks.
- *Families purchase education and health services in many countries:* But the quality of the service that will be provided to citizens is rarely specified in a contract (and would be unenforceable if it were).
- *Parents care for their children:* They hope their children will take care of them when they are old and unable to work, but our children do not sign a contract that ensures this will happen.

The table in Figure 6.10 identifies the principals and agents in the above examples.

Principal	Agent	Action taken by the agent that is hidden, and not covered in the contract
Employer	Employee	Quality and quantity of work
Banker	Borrower	Repayment of loan, prudent conduct
Owner	Manager	Maximization of owners' profits
Landlord	Tenant	Care of the apartment
Insurance company	Insured	Prudent behavior
Parents	Teacher/doctor	Quality of teaching and care
Parents	Children	Care in old age

Figure 6.10 Hidden action problems.

Emile Durkheim (1858–1917), the founder of modern sociology, observed that 'not everything in the contract is contractual'. There is usually something that matters to at least one of the parties that cannot be written down in an enforceable contract.

6.15 PRINCIPALS AND AGENTS: INTERACTIONS UNDER INCOMPLETE CONTRACTS

EXERCISE 6.10 PRINCIPAL–AGENT RELATIONSHIPS
For each of the following examples, explain who is the principal, who is the agent, and what aspects of their interaction are of interest to each and are not covered by a complete contract.

1. A company hires a security guard to protect its premises at night.
2. A charity wants to commission research to find out as much as possible about a new virus.

QUESTION 6.13 CHOOSE THE CORRECT ANSWER(S)
Which of the following statements correctly identify who is the principal and who is the agent?

- ☐ In a public limited company, the managers are the principals and the shareholders are the agents.
- ☐ In a contract between a football club and its star player, the club is the principal and the player is the agent.
- ☐ In an Airbnb contract, the owner and the traveller are both principals and agents.
- ☐ In a contract to buy an essay from an online provider, the essay writer is the principal and the student is the agent.

QUESTION 6.14 CHOOSE THE CORRECT ANSWER(S)
Which of the following are measures that can reduce principal–agent problems?

- ☐ paying part of the chief executive's bonus as company shares rather than cash
- ☐ a black box in the car that measures the speed of the driver
- ☐ travellers who submit an insurance claim must pay the first £100 of the amount claimed out of pocket (the insurer will not reimburse this £100)
- ☐ increasing the number of workers in a factory

6.16 CONCLUSION

In a capitalist economy, the **division of labour** is coordinated both by markets (which contribute to the decentralization of power) and by firms (which concentrate power in the hands of owners). To understand the role of the firm, we view it not only as an actor in markets, but also a stage on which owners, managers and employees interact in **principal–agent relationships**.

While the **separation of ownership and control** makes it possible for the objectives of owners and managers to diverge, incentive schemes may help align interests. The problem of **hidden actions** becomes especially evident in the worker–employer relationship, characterized by **incomplete contracts**. These arise due to the fact that employees' effort is neither perfectly observable nor verifiable, and their tasks depend on unforeseeable future events. It is this contractual incompleteness that causes the wages offered to workers to be above their **reservation wage**, giving rise to an **employment rent** that incentivizes them to exert effort.

Drawing on our game theory and constrained choice tools, we have developed the **labour discipline model** to study the worker–employer interaction as a sequential, repeated game where the employer offers a wage and the worker responds by choosing the amount of effort she exerts:

Worker	Employer
The **worker's best response function** shows the level of effort the worker chooses to exert at a given wage. It slopes upward because a higher wage increases employment rents (the **cost of job loss**), inducing the worker to put in more effort. It is concave because the **disutility of effort** is greater at higher effort levels, causing diminishing marginal returns to wages. Its slope is the marginal rate of transformation (**MRT**) of wages into effort.	**Isocost lines** can be seen as indifference curves. They join the set of points with the same ratio of effort to wages, which the employer seeks to maximize in order to minimize the wage cost per **efficiency unit**. A steeper isocost line represents a lower cost of effort. The slope of an isocost represents the rate at which the employer is willing to increase wages to get higher effort (the **MRS**).
Optimal Choice: MRT = MRS	

Figure 6.11 The labour discipline model.

The point of tangency represents a Nash equilibrium, and wages set this way are known as **efficiency wages**. The main implication for the broader economy is that there is always **involuntary unemployment** in equilibrium. We can analyse the effects of public policies by considering how these affect employment rents and the worker's best response function.

We have also looked at **worker-owned cooperatives**, where typically less supervision is necessary, and considered the implications of the modern **gig economy**, including for people currently working as employees in firms.

6.17 *DOING ECONOMICS*: MEASURING MANAGEMENT PRACTICES

In Section 6.2, we discussed the top-down decision-making structure in most firms, which involves managers directing the activities of their employees to implement the long-term strategies decided by owners. We might expect that firms where employees and production processes are managed well will be more productive than poorly-managed firms. However, defining and quantifying 'good' management practices is a challenge.

In *Doing Economics* Empirical Project 6, we look at some ways to measure the quality of a firm's management practices, and make comparisons across countries, industries, and types of firms, and discuss possible explanations for the patterns we observe.

Go to *Doing Economics* Empirical Project 6 (https://tinyco.re/9404029) to work on this project.

> *Learning objectives*
> In this project you will:
>
> - explain how survey data is collected, and describe measures that can increase the reliability and validity of survey data
> - use column charts and box and whisker plots to compare distributions
> - calculate conditional means for one or more conditions, and compare them on a bar chart
> - construct confidence intervals and use them to assess differences between groups
> - evaluate the usefulness and limitations of survey data for determining causality.

6.18 REFERENCES

Bewley, Truman F. 1999. *Why Wages Don't Fall during a Recession*. Cambridge, MA: Harvard University Press.

Braverman, Harry, and Paul M. Sweezy. 1975. *Labor and Monopoly Capital: The Degradation of Work in the Twentieth Century*. 2nd ed. New York, NY: Monthly Review Press.

Coase, Ronald H. 1937. 'The Nature of the Firm' (https://tinyco.re/4250905). *Economica* 4 (16): pp. 386–405.

Coase, Ronald H. 1992. 'The Institutional Structure of Production' (https://tinyco.re/1636715). *American Economic Review* 82 (4): pp. 713–19.

Couch, Kenneth A., and Dana W. Placzek. 2010. 'Earnings Losses of Displaced Workers Revisited'. *American Economic Review* 100 (1): pp. 572–89.

Ehrenreich, Barbara. 2011. *Nickel and Dimed: On (Not) Getting By in America*. New York, NY: St. Martin's Press.

Hansmann, Henry. 2000. *The Ownership of Enterprise*. Cambridge, MA: Belknap Press.

Helper, Susan, Morris Kleiner, and Yingchun Wang. 2010. 'Analyzing Compensation Methods in Manufacturing: Piece Rates, Time Rates, or Gain-Sharing?' (https://tinyco.re/4437027). NBER Working Papers No. 16540.

Jacobson, Louis, Robert J. Lalonde, and Daniel G. Sullivan. 1993. 'Earnings Losses of Displaced Workers'. *The American Economic Review* 83 (4): pp. 685–709.

Kletzer, Lori G. 1998. 'Job Displacement' (https://tinyco.re/8577746). *Journal of Economic Perspectives* 12 (1): pp. 115–36.

Kroszner, Randall S., and Louis Putterman (editors). 2009. *The Economic Nature of the Firm: A Reader*. Cambridge: Cambridge University Press.

Lazear, Edward P., Kathryn L. Shaw, and Christopher Stanton. 2016. 'Making Do with Less: Working Harder during Recessions'. *Journal of Labor Economics* 34 (S1 Part 2): pp. 333–60.

Marx, Karl. (1848) 2010. *The Communist Manifesto* (https://tinyco.re/0155765). Edited by Friedrich Engels. London: Arcturus Publishing.

Marx, Karl. 1906. *Capital: A Critique of Political Economy*. New York, NY: Random House.

Micklethwait, John, and Adrian Wooldridge. 2003. *The Company: A Short History of a Revolutionary Idea*. New York, NY: Modern Library.

Mill, John Stuart. (1848) 1994. *Principles of Political Economy* (https://tinyco.re/9348882). New York: Oxford University Press.

Mill, John Stuart. (1859) 2002. *On Liberty* (https://tinyco.re/6454781). Mineola, NY: Dover Publications.

O'Reilly, Tim, and Eric S. Raymond. 2001. *The Cathedral & the Bazaar: Musings on Linux and Open Source by an Accidental Revolutionary*. Sebastopol, CA: O'Reilly.

Pencavel, John. 2002. *Worker Participation: Lessons from the Worker Co-ops of the Pacific Northwest*. New York, NY: Russell Sage Foundation Publications.

Robertson, Dennis. 1923. *The Control of Industry*. Hitchen: Nisbet.

Simon, Herbert A. 1951. 'A Formal Theory of the Employment Relationship' (https://tinyco.re/0460792). *Econometrica* 19 (3).

Simon, Herbert A. 1991. 'Organizations and Markets' (https://tinyco.re/2460377). *Journal of Economic Perspectives* 5 (2): pp. 25–44.

Toynbee, Polly. 2003. *Hard Work: Life in Low-pay Britain*. London: Bloomsbury Publishing.

Williamson, Oliver E. 1985. *The Economic Institutions of Capitalism*. New York, NY: Collier Macmillan.

7 FIRMS AND MARKETS FOR GOODS AND SERVICES

Factory warehouse storage

7.1 INTRODUCTION

- Technological and cost advantages of large-scale production favour large firms.
- Firms producing differentiated products choose price and quantity to maximize their profits, taking into account the product demand curve and the cost function.
- Firms with fewer competitors have more power to set prices, and so achieve higher profit margins.
- When consumers and firm owners interact in markets, the gains from trade are shared, but when prices are set above marginal cost there is market failure and deadweight loss.
- The responsiveness of consumers to a price change is measured by the elasticity of demand.
- Economic policymakers use estimates of elasticities of demand to design tax policies, and reduce firms' market power through competition policy.
- In some cases, competition can determine a market equilibrium in which both buyers and sellers are price-takers. This is called a competitive equilibrium, and it ensures that all possible gains from trade are realized.
- Shifts in supply or demand, known as shocks, will cause a period of adjustment in prices.

Ernst F. Schumacher's *Small is Beautiful,* published in 1973, advocated small-scale production by individuals and groups in an economic system designed to emphasize happiness rather than profits. In the year the book was published, the firms Intel and FedEx each employed only a few thousand people in the US. Forty years later, Intel employed around 108,000 people and FedEx more than 300,000.

Ernst F. Schumacher. 1973. *Small is Beautiful: Economics as if People Mattered* (http://tinyco.re/3749799). New York, NY: HarperCollins.

7 FIRMS AND MARKETS FOR GOODS AND SERVICES

Most firms are much smaller than this, but in all high-income economies, most people work for large firms. For example, in 2015, 53% of US private-sector employees worked in firms with at least 500 employees. Firms grow because their owners can make more money if they expand, and people with money to invest get higher returns from owning stock in large firms. Employees in large firms are also paid more.

Figure 7.1 shows the growth measured by numbers of employees of some highly successful US firms during the twentieth century. (Note that Ford's employment in the US peaked before 1980, and more recent data shows that employment in the US by Walmart has fallen to 1.5 million in 2016, though it still employs 2.3 million globally.)

Why are some firms more successful than others? And why do some firms grow while others remain small or go out of business? Firms have many decisions to make: for example, how to choose, design, and advertise products that will attract customers; how to produce at lower cost and at a higher quality than their competitors; or how to recruit and retain employees who can make these things happen. In this unit, we look at one of the most important of these decisions: how to choose the price of a product, and therefore the quantity to produce. This depends on demand—that is, the willingness of potential consumers to pay for the product—and production costs. We also look at markets, in which the decisions of firms and consumers come together to determine the allocation of goods and services.

View this data at OWiD https://tinyco.re/ 8927352

Erzo G. J. Luttmer. 2011. 'On the Mechanics of Firm Growth'. *The Review of Economic Studies* 78 (3): pp. 1042–68.

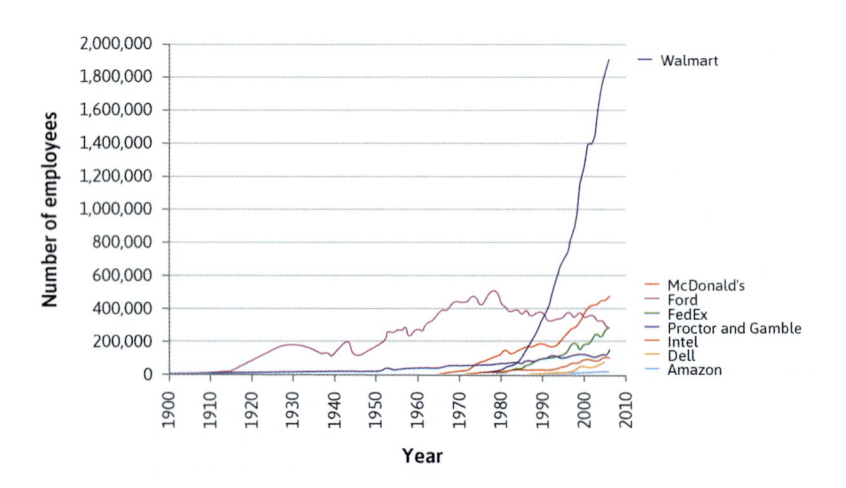

Figure 7.1 Firm size in the US: Number of employees (1900–2006).

7.2 ECONOMIES OF SCALE AND THE COST ADVANTAGES OF LARGE-SCALE PRODUCTION

Why have firms like Walmart, Intel, and FedEx grown so large? An important reason why a large firm may be more profitable than a small firm is that the large firm produces its output at lower cost per unit. This may be possible for two reasons:

- *Technological advantages:* Large-scale production often uses fewer inputs per unit of output.
- *Cost advantages:* In larger firms, costs that don't depend on number of units produced (such as advertising), have a smaller effect on the cost per unit. Larger firms may be able to purchase their inputs at a lower cost because they have more bargaining power.

Technological advantages

Economists use the term **economies of scale** or **increasing returns** to describe the technological advantages of large-scale production. For example, if doubling the amount of every input that the firm uses triples the firm's output, then the firm exhibits increasing returns.

Economies of scale may result from specialization within the firm, which allows employees to do the task they do best and minimizes training time by limiting the skill set that each worker needs. Economies of scale may also occur for purely engineering reasons. For example, transporting more of a liquid requires a larger pipe, but doubling the capacity of the pipe increases its diameter (and the material necessary to construct it) by much less than a factor of two.

> **economies of scale** These occur when doubling all of the inputs to a production process more than doubles the output. The shape of a firm's long-run average cost curve depends both on returns to scale in production and the effect of scale on the prices it pays for its inputs. *Also known as: increasing returns to scale. See also: diseconomies of scale.*
>
> **increasing returns to scale** These occur when doubling all of the inputs to a production process more than doubles the output. The shape of a firm's long-run average cost curve depends both on returns to scale in production and the effect of scale on the prices it pays for its inputs. *Also known as: economies of scale. See also: decreasing returns to scale, constant returns to scale.*

Cost advantages

There is usually a **fixed cost** of production to a firm. It does not depend on the number of units, and so would be the same whether the firm produced one unit or many. Examples of fixed costs include:

> **fixed costs** Costs of production that do not vary with the number of units produced.
>
> **research and development** Expenditures by a private or public entity to create new methods of production, products, or other economically relevant new knowledge.

- *Marketing expenses:* For example, advertising. The cost of a 30-second advertisement during the television coverage of the US Super Bowl football game in 2017 (https://tinyco.re/5012179) was $5.5 million, which would be justifiable only if a large number of units would be sold as a result.
- *Innovation:* For example, **research and development** (R&D), product design, acquiring a production licence, or obtaining a patent for a particular technique.
- *Lobbying:* The cost of trying to influence government bodies, or of contributions to election campaigns and public relations expenditures, are more or less independent of the level of the firm's output.

decreasing returns to scale These occur when doubling all of the inputs to a production process less than doubles the output. *Also known as:* diseconomies of scale. *See also:* increasing returns to scale.

network economies of scale These exist when an increase in the number of users of an output of a firm implies an increase in the value of the output to each of them, because they are connected to each other.

diseconomies of scale These occur when doubling all of the inputs to a production process less than doubles the output. *Also known as:* decreasing returns to scale. *See also:* economies of scale.

These fixed costs mean that, even if there were **decreasing returns** to scale (also known as diseconomies of scale), cost per unit may still fall if the firm increased its output.

Large firms have more bargaining power than small firms when negotiating with suppliers. This means they are also able to purchase their inputs on more favourable terms.

Demand advantages

Large size can also benefit a firm in selling its product, if people are more likely to buy a product or service that already has a lot of users. For example, a software application is more useful when everybody else uses a compatible version. These demand-side benefits of scale are called **network economies of scale**. There are many examples in technology-related markets.

Organizational disadvantages

Production by a small group of people is therefore often too costly to compete with larger firms. But while small firms typically either grow or die, there are limits to growth known as **diseconomies of scale**, or decreasing returns.

A larger firm needs more layers of management and supervision. Firms typically organize themselves as hierarchies in which employees are supervised by those at a higher level and, as the firm grows, the organizational costs will grow as a proportion of the firm's overall costs.

Outsourcing

Sometimes it is cheaper to outsource production of part of the product than to manufacture it within the firm. For example, Apple would be even more gigantic if its employees produced the touchscreens, chipsets, and other components that make up the iPhone and iPad, rather than purchasing these parts from Toshiba, Samsung, and other suppliers. Apple's outsourcing strategy limits the firm's size and increases the size of Toshiba, Samsung, and other firms that produce Apple's components. In our 'Economist in action' video (https://tinyco.re/0004374) Richard Freeman, an economist who specializes in labour markets, explains some of the consequences of outsourcing.

Richard Freeman: You can't outsource responsibility
http://tinyco.re/0004374

> **QUESTION 7.1 CHOOSE THE CORRECT ANSWER(S)**
> Which of the following are factors that contribute to a firm's diseconomies of scale?
>
> ☐ the firm needing to double the capacity of a pipe that transports its fuel when the production level is doubled
> ☐ fixed costs such as lobbying
> ☐ difficulty of monitoring workers' effort as the number of employees increases
> ☐ network effects of its output goods

7.3 THE DEMAND CURVE AND WILLINGNESS TO PAY

The story of the British retailer, Tesco, founded in 1919 by Jack Cohen, suggests one pricing strategy for firms.

Jack Cohen began as a street market trader in the East End of London. The traders would gather at dawn each day and, at a signal, race to their favourite stall site, known as a pitch. Cohen perfected the technique of throwing his cap to claim the most desirable pitch. He opened his first store in 1931. In the 1950s, Cohen began opening supermarkets on the US model, adapting quickly to this new style of operation. Tesco became the UK market leader in 1995, and now employs almost 500,000 people in Europe and Asia.

Today, Tesco's pricing strategy aims to appeal to all segments of the market, labelling some of its own-brand products as Finest and others as Value. The BBC Money Programme summarized the three Tesco commandments as 'be everywhere', 'sell everything', and 'sell to everyone'.

'Pile it high and sell it cheap,' was Jack Cohen's motto. In 2017, Tesco was ranked ninth by sales (https://tinyco.re/7943023) among the world's retailers. Keeping the price low, as Cohen recommended, is one possible strategy for a firm seeking to maximize its profits. Even though the profit on each item is small, the low price may attract so many customers that total profit is high.

Other firms adopt quite different strategies. Apple sets high prices for iPhones and iPads, increasing its profits by charging a price premium rather than lowering prices to reach more customers. For example, between April 2010 and March 2012, profit per unit on Apple iPhones was between 49% and 58% of the price. During the same period, Tesco's operating profit per unit was between 6.0% and 6.5%.

The demand curve and differentiated products

To decide what price to charge and how much to produce, a firm needs information about demand—how much potential consumers are willing to pay for its product. This information, as you know from the discussion of the effect of taxes on sales of sugary drinks (in Unit 3), is summarized in a **demand curve**.

Shoppers buying ready-to-eat breakfast cereals often face a bewildering choice of dozens of varieties each with distinct attributes. The table below gives some of the largest selling cereals in the US among brands targeted at 'families' (other categories are 'kids' and 'adults'). As you can see, the prices vary considerably. (Prices are stated per pound, and there are 2.2 pounds in 1 kg.)

In 1996, economist Jerry Hausman used data on weekly sales of breakfast cereals to estimate how the weekly quantity of cereal that customers in a typical city wished to buy would vary with its price per pound. Figure 7.3 shows the demand curve for Apple Cinnamon Cheerios.

The demand curve provides an answer to the hypothetical question: 'For each possible price that might be charged, how many pounds of cereal would be purchased?' From the figure, we could pick some hypothetical price, say $3 per pound and ask: 'If this price were charged, how many pounds would be purchased?' The answer is 25,000 pounds of Apple Cinnamon Cheerios. For most products, the lower the price, the more customers wish to buy.

> **demand curve** The curve that gives the quantity consumers will buy at each possible price.

differentiated product A product produced by a single firm that has some unique characteristics compared to similar products of other firms.

Breakfast cereals are **differentiated products**. Each brand is produced by just one firm and has some unique nutritional, taste, and other characteristics that distinguish it from the brands sold by other firms.

Many other consumer goods and services are also differentiated products. If you want to buy a car, a mobile phone, or a washing machine, it is not just the price that matters—you will want to find a brand and model with characteristics that match your own preferences. You might consider the design, the quality, or the service the manufacturer offers, rather than always choosing the cheapest.

What this means is that even if there are many firms selling similar products, each firm is alone as a seller of its particular type and brand. Only one firm sells General Mills Apple Cinnamon Cheerios: General Mills.

Jerry A. Hausman. 1996. 'Valuation of new goods under perfect and imperfect competition' (https://tinyco.re/595508). In *The Economics of New Goods*. pp. 207–48. Chicago: University of Chicago Press.

Brand	Company	Average price ($) per pound
Cheerios	General Mills	2.644
Honey-Nut Cheerios	General Mills	3.605
Apple-Cinnamon Cheerios	General Mills	3.480
Corn Flakes	Kellogg	1.866
Raisin Bran	Kellogg	3.214
Rice Krispies	Kellogg	2.475
Frosted Mini-Wheats	Kellogg	3.420
Frosted Wheat Squares	Nabisco	3.262
Raisin Bran	Post	3.046

Figure 7.2 Sales of major ready-to-eat breakfast cereals in the US (1992).

Adapted from Figure 5.2 in Jerry A. Hausman. 1996. 'Valuation of New Goods under Perfect and Imperfect Competition' (https://tinyco.re/595508). In *The Economics of New Goods*, pp. 207–48. Chicago, IL: University of Chicago Press.

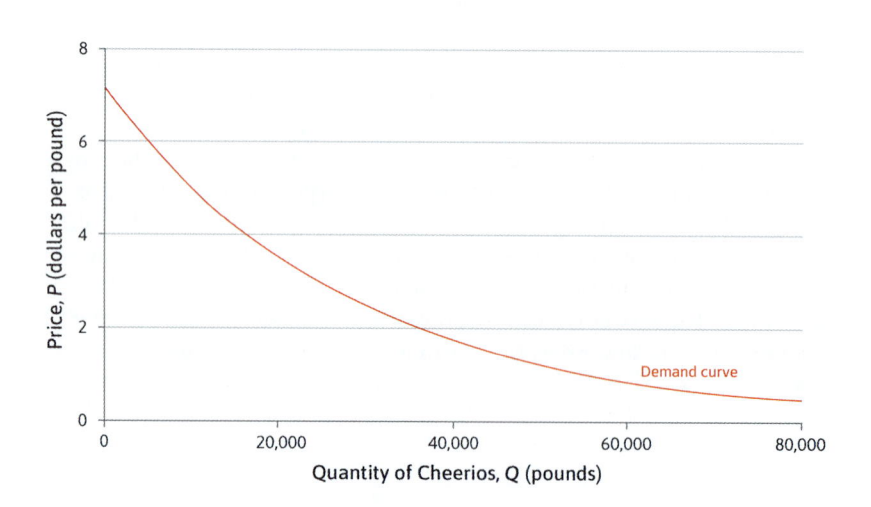

Figure 7.3 Estimated demand for Apple Cinnamon Cheerios.

280

7.3 THE DEMAND CURVE AND WILLINGNESS TO PAY

Willingness to pay and demand

From the point of view of the firm selling such a product, this means that it faces a downward-sloping demand curve like the one for Apple Cinnamon Cheerios. To see why the demand curve for a differentiated product slopes downward, think about an imaginary firm, called Language Perfection (LP), which offers lessons in English, Arabic, Mandarin, Spanish, and other languages. LP provides tutors offering one-on-one training at a public location of the learner's choice (a coffee shop, library, or park, for example). There are many other firms offering language lessons in LP's city, some of them in classroom settings, some online, and some, like LP, one-on-one.

The language lessons being offered by these firms differ in a great many ways. (To get some sense of how language lessons are a differentiated product, go online and search for lessons, and notice how many different choices you will have, even after you have chosen the language you want to learn.) Some will offer advanced courses, some accelerated teaching, others specialize in learning technical, business, or medical terms, while others are aimed at students or tourists. In some, you go to the tutor's location; in others, the tutor comes to you.

The potential language learners are even more different from one another than the firms offering the teaching. For some, the kind of course offered by LP might be exactly what they want, so they would buy the course even if the price was high. Others might be seeking something a little different from the LP course, and so would sign up with LP only at a low price.

Consumers differ not only in what they are looking for, but also in how much money they can afford to spend.

These differences are the basis of the demand curve. Think of all of the possible buyers and arrange them in order, starting with the person who would purchase LP's Spanish-language course at the highest price. Next in order is the person who would be willing to pay almost the highest price but not quite, and so on, ending with the person who would sign up for LP's course only if the price were very low. The highest price a person would be willing to pay for the course is called the individual's **willingness to pay (WTP)**.

A person will buy the course if the price is less than or equal to his or her WTP. Suppose we line up the consumers in order of WTP, with the highest first, and plot a graph to show how the WTP varies along the line (Figure 7.4). You can see from the figure, for example, that at a price of $700, nobody would buy the course; if the course were offered free, 100 people would sign up.

If we choose any price, say $P = \$255$, the graph shows the number of consumers whose WTP is greater than or equal to P. In this case, 60 consumers are willing to pay $255 or more, so the demand for LP's course at a price of $255 is 60.

The points on and under the demand curve in Figure 7.4, shaded and labelled as the 'feasible set', are all of the prices and quantities sold that are feasible for the firm. The feasible point that we picked out is labelled as A. But the firm could also set a price of $255 and admit just 50 students to their course, even if more than that would be willing to pay the price. The demand curve is the boundary of the feasible set and so it is another example of the feasible frontier.

willingness to pay (WTP) An indicator of how much a person values a good, measured by the maximum amount he or she would pay to acquire a unit of the good. *See also: willingness to accept.*

The law of demand dates back to the seventeenth century and is attributed to Gregory King (1648–1712) and Charles Davenant (1656–1714). King was a herald at the College of Arms in London, who produced detailed estimates of the population and wealth of England. Davenant, a politician, published the Davenant-King law of demand in 1699, using King's data. It described how the price of corn would change depending on the size of the harvest. For example, he calculated that a 'defect', or shortfall, of one-tenth (10%) would raise the price by 30%.

> **price discrimination** A selling strategy in which different prices for the same product are set for different buyers or groups of buyers, or per-unit prices vary depending on the number of units purchased.

Because we have arranged the potential buyers in order of their willingness to pay, it follows that if P is lower, there is a larger number of consumers willing to buy, so the demand is higher. Demand curves are often drawn as straight lines, as in this example, although there is no reason to expect them to be straight in reality—the demand curve for Apple Cinnamon Cheerios is not straight. But we do expect demand curves to slope downward—as the price rises, the quantity demanded falls. In other words, when the available quantity is low, the cereal can be sold at a high price. This relationship between price and quantity is sometimes known as the law of demand.

Price discrimination

If you were the owner of the firm, LP, how would you choose the price for the Spanish-language course?

The first thought the owner might have is that she should go to the person with the greatest willingness to pay and offer the course at a price slightly below that person's WTP, ensuring that the person would buy. Then she would move on to the person with the next greatest WTP and offer the course at a price just below that customer's WTP, and so on. This practice is called **price discrimination**. If the owner could do this, LP would make the most money possible from selling introductory Spanish instruction to this population.

But price discrimination—at least, the type that is finely tuned so that each individual pays a different price just below that customer's willingness to pay—is generally impossible. The seller has no way of determining the WTP of each potential buyer. The seller cannot find out by simply asking, because the potential buyer would often lie, so as to be able to buy the course at a lower price.

Another reason why price discrimination is not the rule is that a buyer who purchased the course (or any good) at a low price could then resell it to someone with a higher willingness to pay, ending up by making a profit.

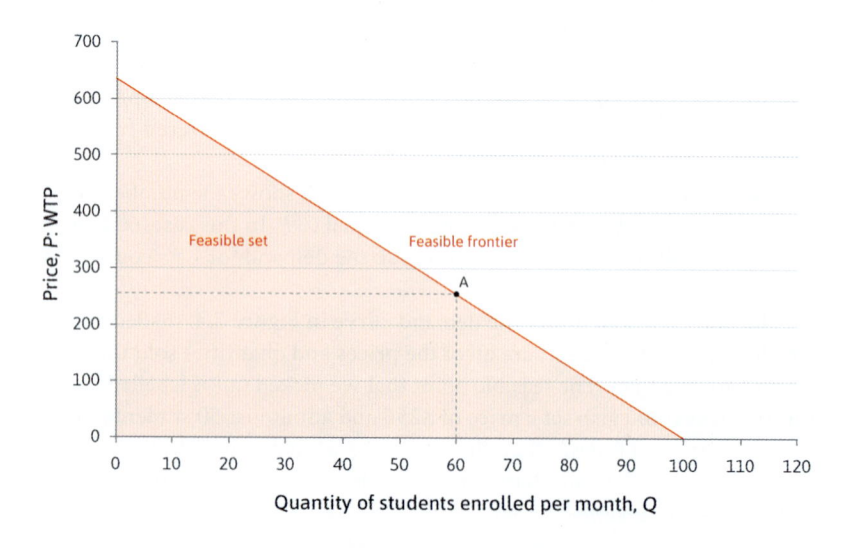

Figure 7.4 The demand for LP's Spanish-language courses.

Some firms are able to practice a less individualized form of price discrimination—lower prices for customers whose willingness to pay might be less due to lower income, for example. Lower prices charged for students or the elderly are examples of price discrimination of this type. But for the most part, the product is sold at a single price to all customers.

This price will be on the demand curve, because that maps out the feasible frontier facing the firm: it shows the maximum quantity that is demanded at any price the firm sets. The law of demand—the fact that the feasible frontier facing the firm slopes downward—means that the firm faces a trade-off. If it must sell its product at the same price to everyone, then selling more means a lower price, and a higher price means selling less. As in our other examples of feasible frontiers (page 159), the slope of the demand curve is a marginal rate of transformation (MRT), in this case of price into quantity.

Before finding out how the firm decides at which single price on the demand curve to sell the Spanish-language course, we need to introduce the concepts of costs and profits.

QUESTION 7.2 CHOOSE THE CORRECT ANSWER(S)
Figure 7.5 depicts two alternative demand curves, D and D', for a product. Based on this graph, which of the following are correct?

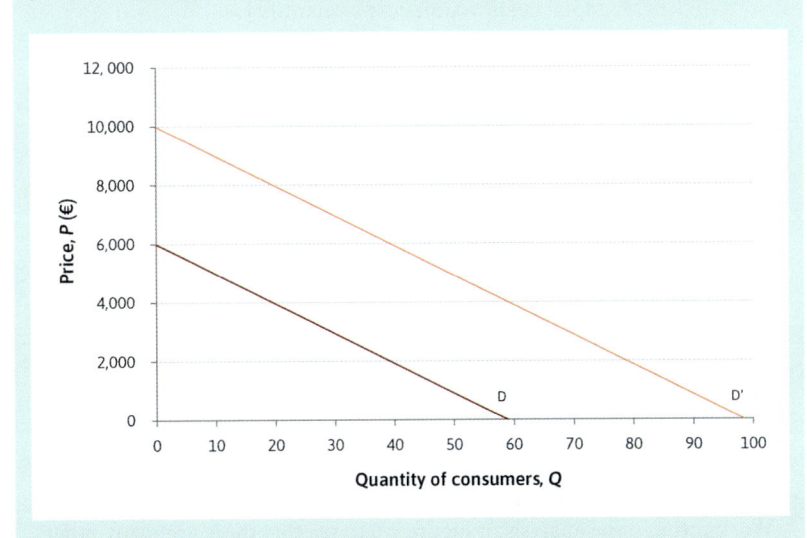

Figure 7.5 Two demand curves.

- ☐ On demand curve D, when the price is €5,000, the firm can sell 15 units of the product.
- ☐ On demand curve D', the firm can sell 70 units at a price of €3,000.
- ☐ At price €1,000, the firm can sell 40 more units of the product on D' than on D.
- ☐ With an output of 30 units, the firm can charge €2,000 more on D' than on D.

7.4 PROFITS, COSTS, AND THE ISOPROFIT CURVE

Imagining that you are the owner of a firm, your profits are the difference between sales revenue and production costs. So, before we can calculate profits, we need to know the production costs.

Let's assume that LP is a very simple firm with a single owner. The owner employs tutors to teach a ten-hour Spanish course, with one tutor for each student. Production costs to the owner, per student, would be:

- *Providing printed materials to the students:* These cost $30 per student.
- *The tutor's time:* The tutor costs $30 an hour, for ten hours.
- *The owner's time:* We value this at what she would earn if she were employed elsewhere. We know that she could close her firm and get a job as a manager of someone else's language school, making $60 an hour. She spends, on average, half an hour per student per course, so the opportunity cost of her time, per student, per course, would be $30.

Therefore, the cost to the owner, per student, per course, would be: $30 + (30 \times 10) + 30 = \$360$.

We assume that LP can simply hire more tutors and provide materials at the same costs, however many courses are offered (so the firm has **constant returns to scale**). **Unit costs** are constant at $360 for any level of the firm's output (number of courses actually offered).

To maximize profit, the owner should produce exactly the quantity she expects to sell, and no more. Then revenue, costs, and profit are given by:

$$\text{total costs} = \text{unit cost} \times \text{quantity}$$
$$= 360 \times Q$$
$$\text{total revenue} = \text{price} \times \text{quantity}$$
$$= P \times Q$$
$$\text{profit} = \text{total revenue} - \text{total costs}$$
$$= P \times Q - 360 \times Q$$

So we have a formula for profit:

$$\text{profit} = (P - 360) \times Q$$

Using this formula, the owner can calculate the profit for any hypothetical combination of price and quantity.

For example, if she sells 25 courses at $480, her profits are ($480 − $360) × 25 = $3,000. Similarly, selling 60 courses at $410 would give profits of ($410 − $360) × 60 = $3,000. And selling 100 courses at $390 would also give profits of ($390 − $360) × 100 = $3,000.

Work through the analysis of Figure 7.6 to see that there are many other combinations of price and number of courses sold per month that would give the owner profits of $3,000. The curve joining up all the combinations giving profits of $3,000 is called an **isoprofit curve**.

There will be an isoprofit curve where profits are zero—we have already seen that it is the average cost curve and it will be a horizontal line in Figure 7.6 at $P = C = \$360$.

Just as indifference curves join points in a diagram that give the same level of utility, isoprofit curves join points that give the same level of total profit. Because it is the owner who gets the profits, we can think of the isoprofit curves as the owner's indifference curves—the owner is

---

constant returns to scale These occur when doubling all of the inputs to a production process doubles the output. The shape of a firm's long-run average cost curve depends both on returns to scale in production and the effect of scale on the prices it pays for its inputs. See also: increasing returns to scale, decreasing returns to scale.

unit cost Total cost divided by number of units produced.

isoprofit curve A curve on which all points yield the same profit.

indifferent between the hypothetical combinations of price and quantity that would give her the same profit.

> **QUESTION 7.3 CHOOSE THE CORRECT ANSWER(S)**
> A firm's cost of production is €12 per unit of output. If P is the price of the output good and Q is the number of units produced, which of the following statements are correct?
>
> ☐ Point (Q, P) = (2,000, 20) is on the isoprofit curve representing the profit level €20,000.
> ☐ Point (Q, P) = (2,000, 20) is on a lower isoprofit curve than point (Q, P) = (1,200, 24).
> ☐ Points (Q, P) = (2,000, 20) and (4,000, 16) are on the same isoprofit curve.
> ☐ Point (Q, P) = (5,000, 12) is not on any isoprofit curve.

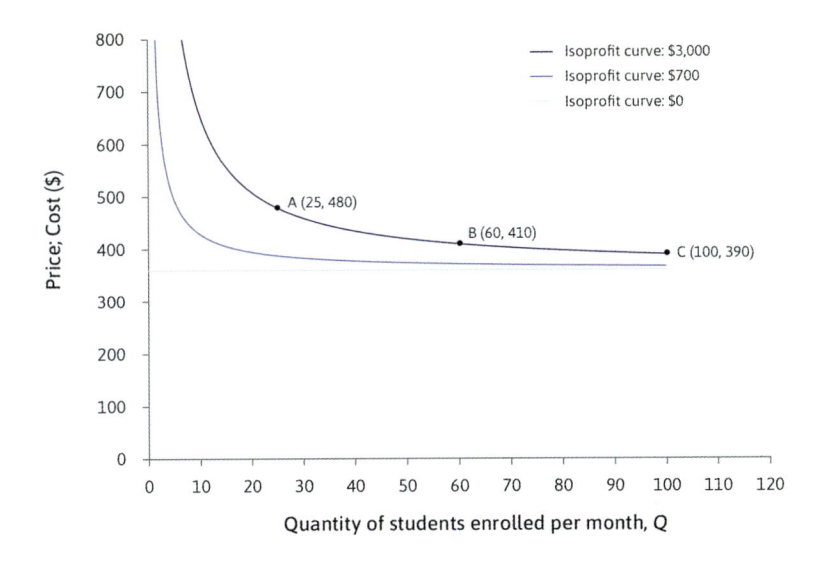

To explore all of the slides in this figure, see the online version at https://tinyco.re/8081383.

Figure 7.6 Isoprofit curves for the production of LP Spanish-language courses.

1. Profit of $3,000
If she could sell 25 courses at $480, her profits would be ($480 − 360) × 25 = $3,000 (point A).

2. Other ways to make the same profit
She could make $3,000 profit, not only by selling 25 courses at $480 (point A), but also by selling 60 courses at $410 (point B), or 100 courses at a price of $390 (point C).

3. Isoprofit curve—$3,000
There are many other ways to make a profit of $3,000. The isoprofit curve here shows all the possible ways of making a $3,000 profit.

4. Isoprofit curve—$700
The $700 isoprofit curve shows all the combinations of P and Q for which profit is equal to $700. The cost of each course is $360, so profit = (P − 360) × Q. This means that isoprofit curves slope downward. To make a profit of $700, P would have to be very high if Q was less than 5. But if Q = 80, the owner could make this profit with a low P.

5. Zero-profit isocost curve—the average cost curve
The horizontal line shows the choices of price and quantity where profit is zero; if she sets a price of $360, she would be selling each course for exactly what it cost.

6. Isoprofit curves
The graph shows a number of isoprofit curves for LP Spanish-language courses.

7.5 THE ISOPROFIT CURVES AND THE DEMAND CURVE

To achieve a high profit, the owner would like both price and quantity to be as high as possible. She prefers points on higher isoprofit curves, but she is constrained by the demand curve. If she chooses a high price, she will be able to sell only a small quantity; if she wants to sell a large quantity, she must choose a low price.

The demand curve determines what is feasible. Figure 7.7 shows the isoprofit curves and demand curve together. The owner faces a similar problem to Alexei, the student in Unit 4 (page 164), who wanted to choose the point in his feasible set at which his utility was maximized. The owner should choose a feasible price and quantity combination that will maximize her profit.

To explore all of the slides in this figure, see the online version at https://tinyco.re/6556856.

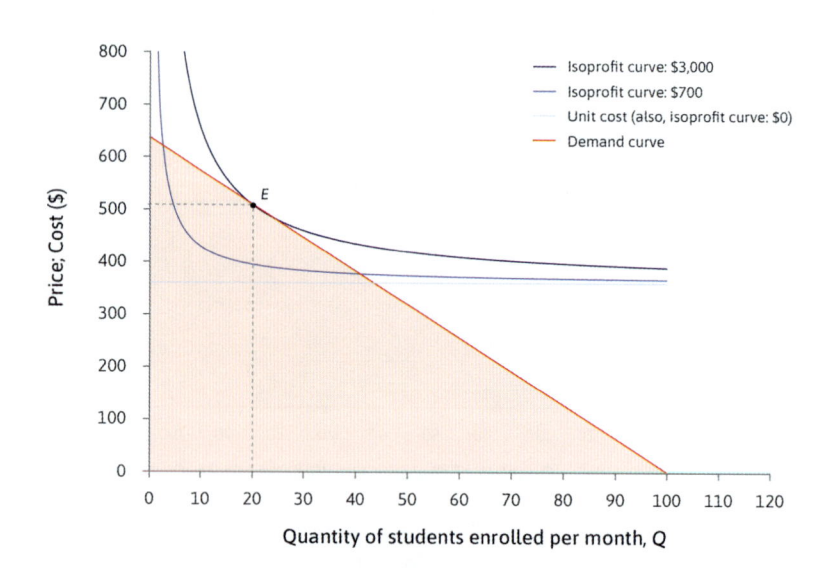

Figure 7.7 The profit-maximizing choice of price and quantity for LP Spanish-language courses.

1. The profit-maximizing choice
The owner would like to choose a combination of P and Q on the highest possible isoprofit curve in the feasible set.

2. Zero profits on the average cost curve
The horizontal line shows the choices of price and quantity at which profit is zero; if the owner sets a price of $360, she would be selling each course for exactly what it cost.

3. Profit-maximizing choices
The owner would choose a price and quantity corresponding to a point on the demand curve. Any point below the demand curve would be feasible, such as selling 30 courses at a price of $200, but she would make more profit if she raised the price.

4. Maximizing profit at E
The owner reaches the highest possible isoprofit curve while remaining in the feasible set by choosing point E, where the demand curve is tangent to an isoprofit curve. She should choose P = $510, selling Q = 20 courses.

286

The owner's best strategy is to choose point E in Figure 7.7—she should produce 20 courses and sell the course at a price of $510, making $3,000 profit. Just as in the case of Alexei in Unit 4 (page 164), the optimal combination of price and quantity involves balancing two trade-offs:

- *The isoprofit curve is the owner's indifference curve:* Its slope at any point represents the trade-off she is willing to make between P and Q—her **MRS**. She would be willing to substitute a high price for a lower quantity if she obtained the same profit.
- *The slope of the demand curve is the trade-off she is constrained to make:* It is her **MRT**, or the rate at which the demand curve allows her to 'transform' quantity into price. She cannot raise the price without lowering the quantity, because fewer consumers will buy a more expensive product.

These two trade-offs balance at the profit-maximizing choice of P and Q.

The owner of Language Perfection (LP) may not have thought about the decision in this way.

Perhaps she remembered past experience in setting prices too low or too high (trial and error), or did some market research. However she made the choice, we expect that a firm could discover a profit-maximizing price and quantity. The purpose of our economic analysis (page 172) is not to model the owner's thought process to get to this point, but to understand the outcome, and its relationship to the firm's cost and consumer's demand.

However, the owner may have conducted a thought experiment that we can relate to the model. Suppose she thinks first about how many courses she could sell if she were to charge only what it costs to produce them. This is where the demand curve intersects the cost curve, and she would make zero profits. If instead she charged a price just above the cost of production, she would now be making a profit. Imagine what happens as she continues moving leftwards along the demand curve. Initially, she will be crossing higher and higher isoprofit curves, due to the effect of a slightly higher price on her profits. But at a certain point, she will discover that if she increases the price further, her profits would begin to fall—in other words, she will start crossing ever-lower isoprofit curves. The point on the demand curve that touches the highest possible isoprofit curve is the combination of price and quantity on the demand curve at which profits are maximized. So, that is the price she will set. Graphically, it is where the isoprofit curve is tangent to the demand curve.

Like the cost curve, which is the isoprofit curve for zero profits, the other isoprofit curves are independent of the demand curve. A shift in the cost curve will shift the family of isoprofit curves with it. A shift in the demand curve will not.

> **marginal rate of substitution (MRS)** The trade-off that a person is willing to make between two goods. At any point, this is the slope of the indifference curve. See also: marginal rate of transformation.
>
> **marginal rate of transformation (MRT)** A measure of the trade-offs a person faces in what is feasible. Given the constraints (feasible frontier) a person faces, the MRT is the quantity of some good that must be sacrificed to acquire one additional unit of another good. At any point, it is the slope of the feasible frontier. See also: feasible frontier, marginal rate of substitution.

To see a different way of finding the profit-maximizing price using the concept of marginal revenue, go to Section 7.6 (https://tinyco.re/3081654) in *The Economy*.

7 FIRMS AND MARKETS FOR GOODS AND SERVICES

QUESTION 7.4 CHOOSE THE CORRECT ANSWER(S)
The table represents market demand Q for a good at different prices P.

Q	100	200	300	400	500	600	700	800	900	1,000
P	€270	€240	€210	€180	€150	€120	€90	€60	€30	€0

The firm's unit cost of production is €60. Based on this information, which of the following are correct?

- ☐ At Q = 100, the firm's profit is €20,000.
- ☐ The profit-maximizing output is Q = 400.
- ☐ The maximum profit that can be attained is €50,000.
- ☐ The firm will make a loss at all outputs above 800.

QUESTION 7.5 CHOOSE THE CORRECT ANSWER(S)
Which of the following statements regarding the marginal rate of substitution (MRS) and the marginal rate of transformation (MRT) of a profit-maximizing firm are correct?

- ☐ The MRT is how much in price the consumers are willing to give up for an incremental increase in the quantity consumed, keeping their utility constant.
- ☐ The MRS is how much in price the owner is willing to give up for an incremental increase in the quantity, holding profits constant.
- ☐ The MRT is the slope of the isoprofit curves.
- ☐ If MRT > MRS, then firms can increase their profit by increasing output.

EXERCISE 7.1 CHANGES IN THE MARKET
Draw diagrams to show how the curves in Figure 7.7 would change in each of the following cases:

1. A rival company producing a similar Spanish-language course slashes its prices.
2. The cost of hiring tutors for LP's course rises to $35 per hour (instead of $30).
3. LP introduces a local advertising campaign costing $20 per month.

In each case, explain what would happen to the price and the profit.

7.6 GAINS FROM TRADE

Remember from Unit 5 (page 185) that, when people engage voluntarily in an economic interaction, they do so because it makes them better off—they can obtain a surplus called **economic rent**, meaning the difference between how much they gain by this interaction compared to not engaging in the interaction. The **total surplus** for the parties involved is a measure of the **gains from exchange** (also known as **gains from trade**).

We can analyse the outcome of the economic interactions between consumers and a firm's owner—just as we did for Angela and Bruno in Unit 5 (page 185)—and calculate the total surplus and the way it is shared.

We have assumed that the rules of the game for allocating language courses to consumers are:

1. *A firm's owner decides how many items to produce:* The owner sets a single price at which admission to the course will be sold to all consumers.
2. *Then individual consumers decide whether to buy or not:* No consumer buys more than one course.

In the interactions between a firm like Language Perfection and its consumers, there are potential gains for both the owner and the students, as long as LP is able to hire tutors to teach the course at a cost less than its value to a consumer. (The tutors may also benefit from the pay they receive, but we will not consider their benefits or costs in this example.)

Recall that the demand curve shows the WTP of each of the potential consumers. A consumer whose WTP is greater than the price will buy the good and receive a surplus, since the value of the course to that customer is higher than the price.

And if the price paid by the customer is greater than what it costs the firm to offer the course, the owner receives a surplus too. This surplus is higher than the amount the owner would earn as a manager in another language company, which we have included in the cost of producing the course. Figure 7.8 shows how to find the total surplus for the firm and its consumers, when LP sets the price to maximize its profits.

In Figure 7.8, the shaded area above P^* measures the **consumer surplus**, and the shaded area below P^* is the **producer surplus**. We see from the relative size of the two areas in Figure 7.8 that, in this market, the firm obtains a greater share of the surplus.

As in the voluntary contracts between Angela and Bruno in Unit 5 (page 185), both parties gain in the market for learning Spanish. The division of the gains is determined by bargaining power. In this case, the firm is the only seller of this course, and can set a high price and obtain a high share of the gains, knowing that those who value the course highly have no alternative but to accept. The firm has many other potential customers, and so people have no power to bargain for a better deal.

---

economic rent A payment or other benefit received above and beyond what the individual would have received in his or her next best alternative (or reservation option). *See also: reservation option.*

total surplus The total gains from trade received by all parties involved in the exchange. It is measured as the sum of the consumer and producer surpluses. *See: joint surplus.*

gains from exchange The benefits that each party gains from a transaction compared to how they would have fared without the exchange. Also known as: *gains from trade.* See also: *economic rent.*

consumer surplus The consumer's willingness to pay for a good minus the price at which the consumer bought the good, summed across all units sold.

producer surplus The price at which a firm sells a good minus the minimum price at which it would have been willing to sell the good, summed across all units sold.

To explore all of the slides in this figure, see the online version at https://tinyco.re/8752968.

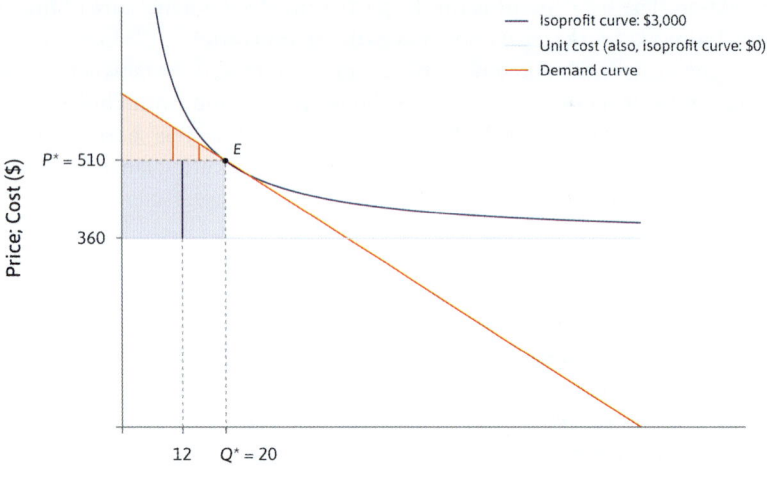

Figure 7.8 Gains from trade.

1. The firm set its profit-maximizing price
P^* = $510, and it sells Q^* = 20 courses per month, the 20th consumer, whose WTP is $510, is just indifferent between buying and not buying a course, so that particular buyer's surplus is equal to zero.

2. A higher WTP
Other buyers were willing to pay more. The tenth consumer, whose WTP is $574, makes a surplus of $64, shown by the vertical line at the quantity 10.

3. What would the fifteenth customer have been willing to pay?
This consumer has WTP of $542 and hence a surplus of $32.

4. The consumer surplus
To find the surplus obtained by consumers, we add together the surplus of each buyer. This is shown by the shaded triangle between the demand curve and the line where price is P^*. This measure of the consumer's gains from trade is the consumer surplus.

5. The producer surplus on a single lesson
Similarly, the firm makes a producer surplus of $150 on each course sold—the difference between the price ($510) and the unit cost ($360). The vertical line in the diagram shows the producer surplus on the twelfth course, but it is the same for every course sold—the distance between P^* and the unit cost line.

6. The total producer surplus
To find the producer surplus, we add together the surplus on each course offered—this is the purple-shaded rectangle.

CONSUMER SURPLUS, PRODUCER SURPLUS, AND PROFIT
- The consumer surplus is a measure of the benefits of participation in the market for consumers.
- The producer surplus is closely related to the firm's profit. In our example they are exactly the same thing, but that is because we have assumed that the firm doesn't have any fixed costs.
- In general, the profit is equal to the producer surplus minus the firm's fixed costs. The firm LP would have fixed costs if, for example, it paid for advertising for its courses.
- The total surplus arising from trade in this market, for the firm and consumers together, is the sum of consumer and producer surplus.

7.6 GAINS FROM TRADE

Evaluating the outcome using the Pareto efficiency criterion

Is the allocation of Spanish-language courses in this market **Pareto efficient**? To answer this question, we need to know all the technically feasible outcomes. These are combinations of price and quantity on the demand curve, where the price is no lower than the cost of production. If there is another technically feasible outcome in which at least one person (customer or owner) is better off and no one is worse off, then the outcome is not Pareto efficient.

Beginning at the allocation E in Figure 7.8, and considering the customers, it is clear that there are some consumers who do not purchase the course at the firm's chosen price, but who would nevertheless be willing to pay more than it would cost the firm to produce the course, namely $360.

But we also know that, at any price below $510 (the profit-maximizing price at point E), profits are lower (the owner would be on an isoprofit curve with lower profits). It appears that a **Pareto improvement** is not possible because, although consumers would be better off, the owner would be worse off.

But evaluating whether the outcome is Pareto efficient does not mean the rules of the game must be kept unchanged. If there is a technically feasible allocation in which at least one person is better off and nobody is worse off, then E is not Pareto efficient.

If LP could practise price discrimination, it could offer one more Spanish course and sell it to the 21st consumer at a price lower than $510 but higher than the production cost. (The other 20 customers would continue to pay $510.) This would be a Pareto improvement—both the firm and the 21st consumer would be better off; the other 20 would be no worse off. The firm's profit on the 21st course sold would be lower than on the 20th but total profits would rise. Remember that the isoprofit curve is drawn assuming that all customers pay the same price. We need to add the profit on the 21st course to $3,000 to calculate the firm's total profits.

The 21st consumer benefits from being able to buy the language course.

This example shows that the potential gains from trade in the market for this type of language course have not been exhausted at E.

The cost of producing one more unit of output is called the **marginal cost**. In practice, marginal costs may depend on the level of production. For example, if the firm had to pay overtime rates to achieve higher levels of output, the marginal cost of a course might be higher at high levels of production. But, in our simple model of LP Spanish courses, we have assumed that every course costs $360 to produce, irrespective of the total number of courses sold. In this case, the marginal cost of a course is the same as the unit cost—it is $360, however many courses are produced.

In Figure 7.9 we have drawn the demand curve again, as well as the marginal cost line, which is a horizontal line at $360. Look at point F, where the two lines cross. You can see that the forty-third consumer has a WTP that is equal to the marginal cost of a course. For the forty-second consumer, the willingness to pay exceeds the cost, so not offering the forty-second course would not be efficient. For the forty-fourth consumer, the willingness to pay is less than the cost, so offering more than 43 courses would also not be efficient.

> **Pareto efficient** An allocation with the property that there is no alternative technically feasible allocation in which at least one person would be better off, and nobody worse off.

> **Pareto improvement** A change that benefits at least one person without making anyone else worse off. See also: Pareto dominant.

> **marginal cost** The addition to total costs associated with producing one additional unit of output.

deadweight loss A loss of total surplus relative to a Pareto-efficient allocation.

Figure 7.9 shows that the total surplus, which we can think of as the pie to be shared between the owner and LP's customers, would be the highest possible if the firm produced 43 courses and sold them for $360.

Since the firm chooses E rather than F, there is a loss of potential surplus, known as the **deadweight loss**.

It might seem confusing that the firm chooses E when we said that, at this point, it would be possible for both the consumers and the owner to be better off. That is true, but only if LP could practise price discrimination—if courses could be sold to other consumers at a lower price than to the first 20 consumers. The owner chooses E because that is the best she can do given the rules of the game (setting one price for all consumers). To sell 43 courses without price discrimination, she would have to set a price of $360, so her profits would be zero.

To explore all of the slides in this figure, see the online version at https://tinyco.re/4878922.

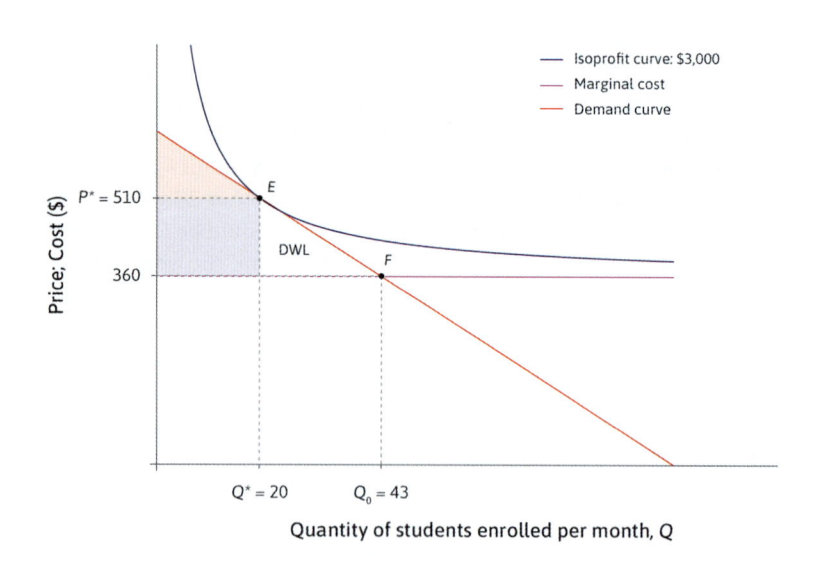

Figure 7.9 Deadweight loss.

1. The total surplus at F
If the firm offered 43 courses and sold them for $360, the shaded area shows the total surplus.

2. Producing at F would be Pareto efficient
If fewer than 43 courses were produced, there would be unexploited gains—some consumers would be willing to pay more for another course than it would cost to make. If more than 43 courses were produced, they could only be sold at a loss. Producing and selling 43 courses would be Pareto efficient.

3. The total surplus at E is smaller
The total surplus is smaller at E than F. The difference is called the deadweight loss. It is the white triangle between $Q = 20$, the demand curve and the marginal cost line.

4. The division of the surplus at E
At E, the surplus is divided between the consumers and the owner.

The allocation that results from price-setting by the producer of a differentiated product like Language Perfection's Spanish course is Pareto inefficient. The owner uses the firm's bargaining power to set a price that is higher than the marginal cost of a course. The firm keeps the price high by producing a quantity that is too low, relative to the Pareto-efficient allocation.

Exercise 7.2 below shows that, in an unlikely scenario in which the firm could engage in price discrimination and charge different prices for each buyer, it would be possible to achieve a Pareto-efficient allocation.

> **EXERCISE 7.2 CHANGING THE RULES OF THE GAME**
> 1. Suppose that Language Perfection had sufficient information and enough bargaining power to charge each individual consumer the maximum they would be willing to pay. Draw the demand curve and marginal cost line (as in Figure 7.9), and indicate on your diagram:
>   (a) the number of courses sold
>   (b) the highest price paid by any consumer
>   (c) the lowest price paid by any consumer
>   (d) the consumer and producer surplus.
> 2. Give examples of goods that are sold in this way.
> 3. Why is price discrimination not common practice? Explain your reasons.
> 4. Some firms charge different prices to different groups of consumers, for example, airlines may charge higher fares for last-minute travellers. Why would they do this, and what effect would it have on the consumer and producer surpluses?
> 5. Now suppose that price discrimination is impossible, and that it becomes very easy for language firms to set up in the city in which LP operates. How could this give consumers more bargaining power?
> 6. Under these rules, how many courses would be sold?
> 7. Under these rules, what would the producer and consumer surpluses be?

> **QUESTION 7.6 CHOOSE THE CORRECT ANSWER(S)**
> Which of the following statements are correct?
>
> ☐ Consumer surplus is the difference between the consumers' willingness to pay and what they actually pay.
> ☐ Producer surplus is always equal to the firm's profit.
> ☐ Deadweight loss is the loss that the producer incurs for not selling more courses.
> ☐ All possible gains from trade are achieved when the firm chooses its profit-maximizing output and price.

7.7 PRICE-SETTING, MARKET POWER, AND PUBLIC POLICY

Our analysis of pricing applies to any firm producing and selling a product that is in some way different from that of any other firm. In the nineteenth century, Augustin Cournot, carried out a similar analysis using the example of bottled water from 'a mineral spring which has just been found to possess salutary properties possessed by no other'. Cournot referred to this as a case of **monopoly**—in a monopolized market, there is only one seller. He showed, as we have done, that the firm would set a price greater than the marginal cost.

A more common market structure is called **monopolistic competition**. In this case each firm sells a unique product, like Cheerios, but there are other firms selling products that, while unique, are very similar in the minds (or tastes) of consumers, like Cornflakes.

Augustin Cournot and Irving Fischer. (1838) 1971. *Researches into the Mathematical Principles of the Theory of Wealth.* New York, NY: A. M. Kelley.

monopoly A firm that is the only seller of a product without close substitutes. Also refers to a market with only one seller. *See also: monopoly power, natural monopoly.*
monopolistic competition A market in which each seller has a unique product but there is competition among firms because firms sell products that are close substitutes for one another.
oligopoly A market with a small number of sellers of the same good, giving each seller some market power.
market failure When markets allocate resources in a Pareto-inefficient way.
profit margin The difference between the price and the marginal cost.
price markup The price minus the marginal cost, divided by the price. It is inversely proportional to the elasticity of demand for this good.

GREAT ECONOMISTS

Augustin Cournot

Augustin Cournot (1801–1877) was a French economist, now most famous for his model of **oligopoly** (a market with a small number of firms). Cournot's 1838 book, *Recherches sur les Principes Mathématiques de la Théorie des Richesses* (Research on the Mathematical Principles of the Theory of Wealth), introduced a new mathematical approach to economics, although he feared it would 'draw on me … the condemnation of theorists of repute'. Cournot's work influenced other nineteenth-century economists, such as Marshall and Walras, and established the basic principles we still use to think about the behaviour of firms. Although he used algebra rather than diagrams, Cournot's analysis of demand and profit maximization was very similar to ours.

We saw in Section 7.3 (page 279) that, when the producer of a differentiated good sets a price above the marginal cost of production, the market outcome is not Pareto efficient. When trade in a market results in a Pareto-inefficient allocation, we describe this as a case of **market failure**.

The deadweight loss gives us a measure of the unexploited gains from trade. The deadweight loss is high when the gap between the price and the marginal cost, which we call the firm's **profit margin**, is high. More precisely, what matters is the **markup**—the profit margin as a proportion of the price.

What determines the markup chosen by the firm? To answer this question, we need to think again about how consumers behave.

Markets with differentiated products reflect differences in the preferences of consumers as well as differences in their incomes. Like those wishing to learn a language, people who want to buy a car, for example, are looking for different combinations of characteristics. A consumer's willingness to pay for a particular model will depend not only on its characteristics, but also on the characteristics and prices of similar types of cars sold by other firms.

When consumers can choose between several similar cars, the demand for each of these cars is likely to be quite responsive to prices. If the price of the Ford Fiesta, for example, were to rise, demand would fall because people would choose to buy one of the other brands instead. Conversely, if the price of the Fiesta were to fall, demand would increase because consumers would be attracted away from the other cars.

The more similar the other cars are to the Fiesta, the more responsive consumers will be to price differences. Only those with the highest brand loyalty to Ford, and those with a strong preference for a characteristic of the Fiesta that other cars do not possess, would fail to respond. Therefore, the firm will not be able to raise the price much without losing consumers. To maximize its profits, it will choose a low markup.

Price elasticity of demand and market power

The responsiveness of consumers to price changes can be measured by calculating the **price elasticity of demand**, which, as we saw in Unit 3 (page 132), is defined as the percentage fall in the quantity demanded in response to a 1% rise in the price. If you think about the graph of a demand curve—with quantity as the horizontal axis variable and price as the vertical axis variable—you can see that the elasticity of demand for a good will be high when its demand curve is relatively flat, and low when it is slopes steeply downward.

In contrast, the manufacturer of a very specialized type of car, quite different from any other brand in the market, faces little competition and hence less elastic demand. It can set a price well above marginal cost without losing customers. Such a firm is earning **monopoly rents** (profits over and above its production costs), arising from its position as the only supplier of this type of car.

A firm will be in a strong position if there are few firms producing close **substitutes** for its own brand, because it faces little competition. Its elasticity of demand will be relatively low. We say that such a firm has **market power**. It will have sufficient bargaining power in its relationship with customers to set a high markup without losing them to competitors. This was the case with LP, because it was the only firm selling one-on-one Spanish-language courses in its city.

Thus, the main difference between monopoly and monopolistic competition is that the price elasticity of demand is low in the case of monopoly, because there are no competing firms selling close substitutes for the firm's product. By contrast, a monopolistically competitive firm faces a more elastic demand curve because, if it raises prices, consumers will switch to other firms selling close substitutes. Joan Robinson pioneered the economic theory of market competition among firms that were neither monopolies nor the price-taking firms that are the basis of the model of perfect competition.

> **price elasticity of demand** The percentage change in demand that would occur in response to a 1% increase in price. We express this as a positive number. Demand is elastic if this is greater than 1, and inelastic if less than 1.
> **monopoly rents** A form of profits, which arise due to restricted competition in selling a firm's product.
> **substitutes** Two goods for which an increase in the price of one leads to an increase in the quantity demanded of the other. *See also: complements.*
> **market power** An attribute of a firm that can sell its product at a range of feasible prices, so that it can benefit by acting as a price-setter (rather than a price-taker).

GREAT ECONOMISTS

Joan Robinson (1903–1983)

A letter to a female student in 1970, from Paul Samuelson, perhaps the most influential economist of the twentieth century, concluded: 'P.S. Do study economics. Perhaps the best economist in the world happens also to be a woman (Joan Robinson).'

Robinson earned respect and recognition in 1933 with her first major work, *The Economics of Imperfect Competition*. She challenged the conventional wisdom by developing an analysis of what we now call monopolistic competition. Facing a downward-sloping demand curve, firms act as price-setters, not price-takers.

She was a member of the small circle at the University of Cambridge that John Maynard Keynes drew upon to comment on and refine his *General Theory*, published in 1936. In 1937 she published *Introduction to the Theory of Employment*, which made Keynes' work accessible to students.

That Robinson's much-lauded intellectual achievements were not crowned with a Nobel prize has drawn much speculation. Was it because of her relentless critique of what she called 'mainstream' economics including, very pointedly, Samuelson's ideas?

Her advice to teachers of economics was to 'start from the beginning to discuss various types of economic system. Every society (except Robinson Crusoe) has to have some rules of the game for organizing production and the distribution of the product.' She also urged economists to 'displace the theory of the relative prices of commodities from the centre of the picture.'

Joan Robinson. 1933. *The Economics of Imperfect Competition* (https://tinyco.re/1766675). London: MacMillan & Co.

George R. Feiwel (ed.). 1989. *Joan Robinson and Modern Economic Theory*. New York: New York University Press: p. 4.

Competition policy

This discussion helps to explain why policymakers may be concerned about firms that have few competitors. Market power allows the firms to set high prices—and make high profits—at the expense of consumers. Potential consumer surplus is lost both because few consumers buy, and because those who buy pay a high price. The owners of the firm benefit, but overall there is a deadweight loss.

A firm selling a niche product catering for the preferences of a small number of consumers (such as a luxury car brand like a Lamborghini) is unlikely to attract the attention of policymakers, despite the loss of consumer surplus. But if one firm is becoming dominant in a large market, governments may intervene to promote competition. In 2000, the European Commission prevented the proposed merger of Volvo and Scania, on the grounds that the merged firm would have a dominant position in the heavy-trucks market in Ireland and the Nordic countries.

In Sweden the combined market share of the two firms was 90%. The merged firm would almost have been a monopoly—the extreme case of a firm that has no competitors at all.

When there are only a few firms in a market, they may form a **cartel**—a group of firms that colludes to keep the price high. By working together and behaving as a monopoly rather than competing, the firms can increase profits. A well-known example is OPEC, an association of oil-producing countries. OPEC members jointly agree to set production levels to control the global price of oil. Following sharp increase in oil prices in 1973 and again in 1979, the OPEC cartel played a major role in sustaining these high oil prices at a global level.

While cartels between private firms are illegal in many countries, firms often find ways to cooperate in the setting of prices so as to maximize profits. Policy to limit market power and prevent cartels is known as **competition policy**, or **antitrust policy** in the US.

Dominant firms may exploit their position by strategies other than high prices. In a famous antitrust case at the end of the twentieth century, the US Department of Justice accused Microsoft of behaving anticompetitively by 'bundling' its own web browser, Internet Explorer, with its Windows operating system. In the 1920s, an international group of companies making electric light bulbs—including Philips, Osram, and General Electric—formed a cartel that agreed to a policy of 'planned obsolescence' to reduce the lifetime of their bulbs to 1,000 hours, so that consumers would have to replace them more quickly.

> **cartel** A group of firms that collude in order to increase their joint profits.
> **competition policy** Government policy and laws to limit monopoly power and prevent cartels. *Also known as: antitrust policy.*
> **antitrust policy** Government policy and laws to limit monopoly power and prevent cartels. *Also known as: competition policy.*

Richard J. Gilbert and Michael L. Katz. 2001. 'An Economist's Guide to US v. Microsoft' (http://tinyco.re/7683758). *Journal of Economic Perspectives* 15 (2): pp. 25–44.

Markus Krajewski. 2014. 'The Great Lightbulb Conspiracy' (http://tinyco.re/3479245). *IEEE Spectrum.* Updated 25 September 2014.

> **EXERCISE 7.3 MULTINATIONALS OR INDEPENDENT RETAILERS?**
> Imagine that you are a politician in a town in which a multinational retailer is planning to build a new superstore. A local campaign is protesting that it will drive small independent retailers out of business, thereby reducing consumer choice and changing the character of the area. Supporters of the plan argue, in turn, that this will only happen if consumers prefer the supermarket.
> Which side are you on? Explain the reasons for your choice.

> **QUESTION 7.7 CHOOSE THE CORRECT ANSWER(S)**
> Which of the following statements regarding the film industry are correct?
>
> ☐ Industry regulators should cap the price of a DVD at its marginal cost.
> ☐ The marginal cost of producing additional copies of a film is high.
> ☐ The quantity sold in the film industry is inefficient.
> ☐ The price is above marginal cost due to lack of substitutes.

QUESTION 7.8 CHOOSE THE CORRECT ANSWER(S)

Suppose that a multinational retailer is planning to build a new superstore in a small town. Which of the following arguments could be correct?

☐ The local protesters argue that the close substitutability of some of the goods sold between the new retailer and existing ones means that the new retailer faces inelastic demand for those goods, giving it excessive market power.
☐ The new retailer argues that the close substitutability of some of the goods implies a high elasticity of demand, leading to healthy competition and lower prices for consumers.
☐ The local protesters argue that, once the local retailers are driven out, there will be no competition, giving the multinational retailer more market power and driving up prices.
☐ The new retailer argues that most of the goods sold by local retailers are sufficiently differentiated from its own goods that their elasticity of demand will be high enough to protect the local retailers' profits.

7.8 PRODUCT SELECTION, INNOVATION, AND ADVERTISING

The profits that the owners of a firm can achieve depend on the demand curve for its product, which in turn depends on the preferences of consumers and competition from other firms. But the firm may be able to move the demand curve to increase profits by changing its selection of products, or through advertising.

Parker Brothers first marketed a property-trading board game under the name *Monopoly* in 1935. In a series of court cases in the 1970s, Parker Brothers attempted to prevent Ralph Anspach, an economics professor, from selling a game called *Anti-Monopoly*. Anspach claimed that Parker Brothers did not have exclusive rights to sell *Monopoly*, since the company had not originally invented it.

After the court ruled in favour of Anspach, many competing versions of *Monopoly* appeared on the market. After a change in the law, Parker Brothers established the right to the *Monopoly* trademark in 1984, so *Monopoly* is now a monopoly again.

When deciding what goods to produce, the firm would ideally like to find a product that is both attractive to consumers and has different characteristics from the products sold by other firms. In this case, demand would be high (many consumers would wish to buy it at each price) and the elasticity low. Of course, this is not likely to be easy. A firm wishing to make a new type of sportswear, or type of car, knows that there are already many brands on the market. But technological innovation may provide opportunities to get ahead of competitors. In 1997, Toyota developed the first mass-produced hybrid car, the Prius. For many years afterwards, other manufacturers produced few similar cars, and Toyota effectively monopolized the hybrid market. By 2013, there were several competing brands, but the Prius remained the market leader, with more than 50% of hybrid sales.

John Kay. 'The Structure of Strategy' (reprinted from *Business Strategy Review* 1993) (http://tinyco.re/7663497).

7.8 PRODUCT SELECTION, INNOVATION, AND ADVERTISING

If a firm has invented or created a new product, it may be able to prevent competition altogether by claiming exclusive rights to produce it, using patent or copyright laws. For example, Parker Brothers spent years in court fighting to keep their monopoly of *Monopoly*. This kind of legal protection of monopoly may help to provide incentives for research and development of new products, but at the same time limits the gains from trade.

Advertising is another strategy that firms can use to influence demand. It is widely used by both car manufacturers and breakfast cereal producers. When products are differentiated, the firm can use advertising to inform consumers about the existence and characteristics of its product, attract them away from its competitors, and create brand loyalty.

According to Schonfeld and Associates, a firm of market analysts, advertising of breakfast cereals in the US is about 5.5% of total sales revenue—about 3.5 times higher than the average for manufactured products. The data in Figure 7.10 is for the highest-selling 35 breakfast cereal brands sold in the Chicago area in 1991 and 1992. The graph shows the relationship between market share and quarterly expenditure on advertising.

If you investigated the breakfast cereals market more closely, you would see that market share is not closely related to price. But it is clear from Figure 7.10 that the brands with the highest share are also the ones that spend the most on advertising. Matthew Shum, an economist, analysed cereal purchases in Chicago using this dataset, and showed that advertising was more effective than price discounts in stimulating demand for a brand. Since the best-known brands were also the ones spending most on advertising, he concluded that the main function of advertising was not to inform consumers about the product, but rather to increase brand loyalty and encourage consumers of other cereals to switch.

Matthew Shum. 2004. 'Does Advertising Overcome Brand Loyalty? Evidence from the Breakfast-Cereals Market' (http://tinyco.re/3909324). *Journal of Economics & Management Strategy* 13 (2): pp. 241–72.

Figure 1 in Matthew Shum. 2004. 'Does Advertising Overcome Brand Loyalty? Evidence from the Breakfast-Cereals Market' (http://tinyco.re/3909324). *Journal of Economics & Management Strategy* 13 (2): pp. 241–72.

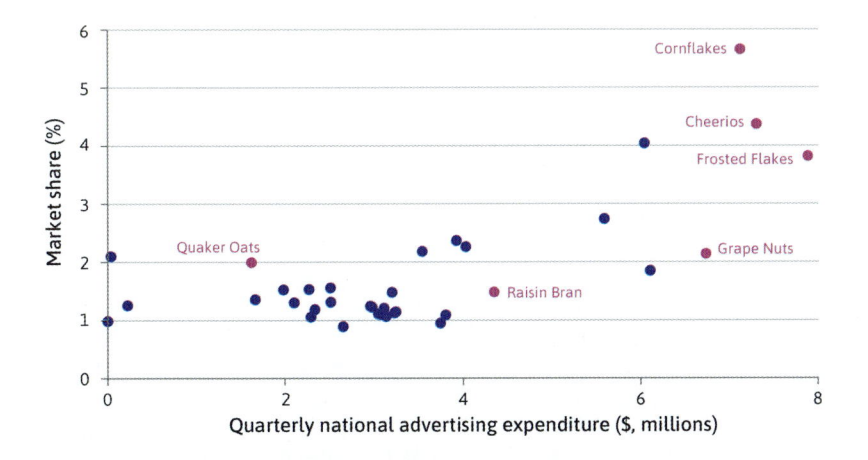

Figure 7.10 Advertising expenditure and market share of breakfast cereals in Chicago (1991–1992).

WTP is a useful concept for buyers in online auctions, such as eBay. If you want to bid for an item, one way to do it is to set a maximum bid equal to your WTP, which will be kept secret from other bidders. For how to do this on eBay, see their online customer service centre (http://tinyco.re/0107311). eBay will place bids automatically on your behalf until you are the highest bidder, or until your maximum is reached. You will win the auction if, and only if, the highest bid is less than or equal to your WTP.

willingness to accept (WTA) The reservation price of a potential seller, who will be willing to sell a unit only for a price at least this high. *See also: reservation price, willingness to pay.*

reservation price The lowest price at which someone is willing to sell a good (keeping the good is the potential seller's reservation option). *See also: reservation option.*

7.9 BUYING AND SELLING: DEMAND AND SUPPLY IN A COMPETITIVE MARKET

So far, we have considered the case of a differentiated product sold by just one firm. In the market for such a product there is one seller with many buyers. Now we look at markets in which many buyers and sellers interact, and show how the market price is determined by both the preferences of consumers and the costs of suppliers.

For a simple model of a market with many buyers and sellers, think about the potential for trade in second-hand copies of a recommended textbook for a university economics course. Demand for the book comes from students who are about to begin the course, and they will differ in their willingness to pay. No one will pay more than the price of a new copy in the campus bookshop. Below that, students' WTP may depend on how hard they work, how important they think the book is, and on their available resources for buying books.

Figure 7.11 shows the demand curve. As we did for Language Perfection, we line up all the consumers in order of willingness to pay, highest first. The first student is willing to pay $20, the 20th is willing to pay $10, and so on. For any price, P, the graph tells you how many students would be willing to buy—it is the number whose WTP is at or above P.

The demand curve represents the WTP of buyers. Similarly, supply depends on the sellers' **willingness to accept (WTA)** money in return for books.

The supply of second-hand books comes from students who have previously completed the course, who will differ in the amount they are willing to accept—that is, their **reservation price**. Recall from Unit 5 (page 209) that Angela was willing to enter into a contract with Bruno only if it gave her at least as much utility as her reservation option (no work and survival rations). Here, the reservation price of a potential seller represents the value to her of keeping the book, and she will only be willing to sell for a price at least that high. Poorer students (who are keen to sell so that they can afford other books) and those no longer studying economics may have lower reservation prices.

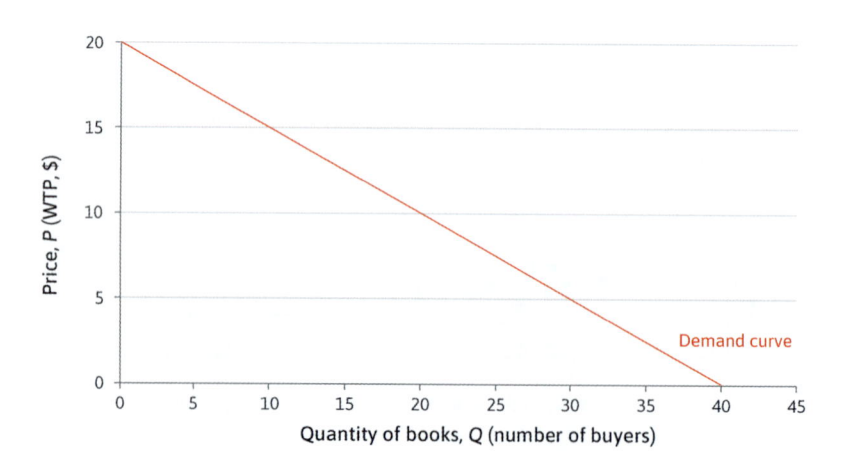

Figure 7.11 The market demand curve for books.

7.9 BUYING AND SELLING: DEMAND AND SUPPLY IN A COMPETITIVE MARKET

We can draw a **supply curve** by lining up the sellers in order of their reservation prices (their WTAs). Figure 7.12 is an example of a supply curve. To do this, we put the sellers who are most willing to sell—those who have the lowest reservation prices—first, so the graph of reservation prices slopes upward.

For any price, the supply curve shows the number of students willing to sell at that price—that is, the number of books that will be supplied to the market. We have drawn the supply and demand curves as straight lines for simplicity. In practice, they are more likely to be curves, with the exact shape depending on how valuations of the book vary among the students.

Online auctions like eBay allow sellers to specify their WTA. If you sell an item on eBay you can set a reserve price, which will not be disclosed to the bidders. See eBay's online customer service centre (http://tinyco.re/9324100) for how to set a reserve price on their platform. You are telling eBay that the item should not be sold unless there is a bid at (or above) that price. Therefore, the reserve price should correspond to your WTA. If no one bids your WTA, the item will not be sold.

supply curve The curve that shows the number of units of output that would be produced at any given price. For a market, it shows the total quantity that all firms together would produce at any given price.

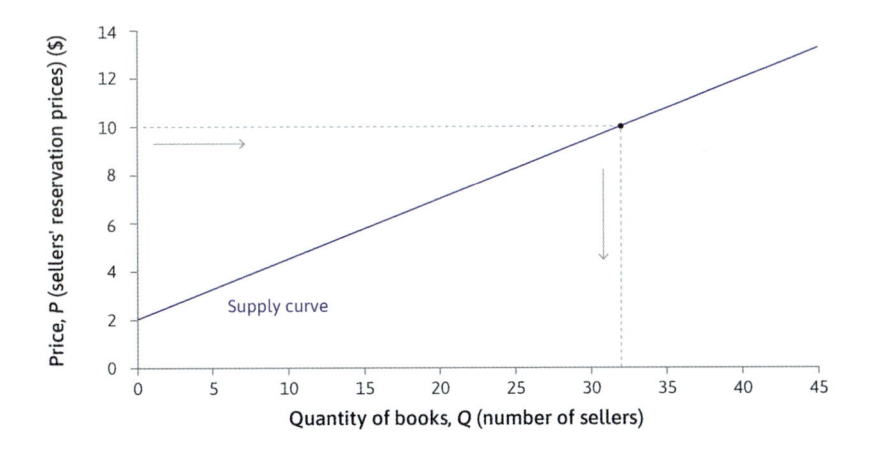

To explore all of the slides in this figure, see the online version at https://tinyco.re/1096561.

Figure 7.12 The supply curve for books.

1. Reservation price
The first seller has a reservation price of $2 and will sell at any price above that.

2. Seller 20
The 20th seller will accept $7.

3. Seller 40
The fortieth seller's reservation price is $12.

4. Supply curves slope upward
If you choose a particular price, say $10, the graph shows how many books would be supplied (Q) at that price—in this case, it is 32. The supply curve slopes upward: the higher the price, the more students will be willing to sell.

301

> **QUESTION 7.9 CHOOSE THE CORRECT ANSWER(S)**
> As a student representative, one of your roles is to organize a second-hand textbook market between the current and former first-year students. After a survey, you estimate the demand and supply curves. For example, you estimate that pricing the book at $7 would lead to a supply of 20 books and a demand of 26 books. Which of the following statements are correct?
>
> ☐ A rumour that the textbook may be required again in Year 2 would change the supply curve, shifting it upwards.
> ☐ Doubling the price to $14 would double the supply.
> ☐ A rumour that the textbook may no longer be on the reading list for the first-year students would change the demand curve, shifting it upwards.
> ☐ Demand would double if the price were reduced sufficiently.

> **EXERCISE 7.4 SELLING STRATEGIES AND RESERVATION PRICES**
> Consider three possible methods to sell a car that you own:
>
> - advertise it in the local newspaper
> - take it to a car auction
> - offer it to a second-hand car dealer.
>
> 1. Would your reservation price be the same in each case? Why?
> 2. If you used the first method, would you advertise it at your reservation price?
> 3. Which method do you think would result in the highest sale price?
> 4. Which method would you choose? Give reasons for your choice.

The equilibrium price

What will happen in the market for this textbook? That will depend on the market institutions that bring buyers and sellers together. If students need to rely on word of mouth, then when a buyer finds a seller they can try to negotiate a deal that suits both of them. But each buyer would like to be able to find a seller with a low reservation price, and each seller would like to find a buyer with a high willingness to pay. Before concluding a deal with one trading partner, both parties would like to know about other trading opportunities.

Traditional market institutions often brought many buyers and sellers together in one place. Many of the world's great cities grew up around marketplaces and bazaars along ancient trading routes such as the Silk Road between China and the Mediterranean. In the Grand Bazaar of Istanbul, one of the largest and oldest covered markets in the world, shops selling carpets, gold, leather, and textiles cluster together in different areas.

With modern communications and online marketplaces, sellers can advertise their goods and buyers can more easily find out what is available and where to buy it. But in some cases, it is still convenient for many buyers and sellers to meet. Large cities have markets for meat, fish, vegetables, or flowers, where buyers can inspect the produce and compare prices.

7.9 BUYING AND SELLING: DEMAND AND SUPPLY IN A COMPETITIVE MARKET

At the end of the nineteenth century, the economist Alfred Marshall introduced his model of supply and demand using a similar example to our case of second-hand books. Most English towns had a corn exchange—also known as a grain exchange—a building in which farmers met with merchants to sell their grain. In *Principles of Economics: Book Five: General Relations of Demand, Supply, and Value*, Marshall described how the supply curve of grain would be determined by the prices that farmers would be willing to accept, and the demand curve by the willingness to pay of merchants. Then he argued that, although the price 'may be tossed hither and thither like a shuttlecock' in the 'higgling and bargaining' of the market, it would never be very far from the particular price at which the quantity demanded by merchants was equal to the quantity the farmers would supply.

Marshall called the price that equated supply and demand the equilibrium price. If the price was above the equilibrium, farmers would want to sell large quantities of grain, but few merchants would want to buy—there would be **excess supply**. Then, even the merchants who were willing to pay that much would realize that farmers would soon have to lower their prices and would wait until they did. Similarly, if the price was below the equilibrium, sellers would prefer to wait rather than sell at that price. If, at the going price, the amount supplied did not equal the amount demanded, Marshall reasoned that some sellers or buyers could benefit by charging some other price. In modern terminology, we would say that the going price was not a **Nash equilibrium**. The price would tend to settle at an **equilibrium** level, where demand and supply were equated.

Marshall's supply and demand model can be applied to markets in which all sellers are selling identical (not differentiated) goods, so buyers are equally willing to buy from any seller.

Alfred Marshall. 1920. *Principles of Economics* (http://tinyco.re/0560708). 8th ed. London: MacMillan & Co.

excess supply A situation in which the quantity of a good supplied is greater than the quantity demanded at the current price. *See also: excess demand.*

Nash equilibrium A set of strategies, one for each player in the game, such that each player's strategy is a best response to the strategies chosen by everyone else.

equilibrium A model outcome that does not change unless an outside or external force is introduced that alters the model's description of the situation.

marginal utility The additional utility resulting from a one-unit increase of a given variable.

Alfred Marshall. 1920. *Principles of Economics* (http://tinyco.re/0560708). 8th ed. London: MacMillan & Co.

GREAT ECONOMISTS

Alfred Marshall

Alfred Marshall (1842–1924) was a founder—with Léon Walras—of what is termed the neoclassical school of economics. His *Principles of Economics*, first published in 1890, was the standard introductory textbook for English speaking students for 50 years. An excellent mathematician, Marshall provided new foundations for the analysis of supply and demand by using calculus to formulate the workings of markets and firms and to express key concepts such as marginal costs and **marginal utility**. The concepts of consumer and producer surplus are also attributed to Marshall. His conception of economics as an attempt to 'understand the influences exerted on the quality and tone of a man's life by the manner in which he earns his livelihood …' is close to our own definition of the field.

Sadly, much of the wisdom in Marshall's text has rarely been taught by his followers. Marshall paid attention to facts—and to ethics. His observation that large firms could produce at lower unit costs than small firms was integral to his thinking, but it never found a place in the neoclassical school. And he insisted that:

> Ethical forces are among those of which the economist must take account. Attempts have indeed been made to construct an abstract science with regard to the actions of an economic man who is under no ethical influences and who pursues pecuniary gain … selfishly. But they have not been successful. (*Principles of Economics*, 1890)

While advancing the use of mathematics in economics, he also cautioned against its misuse. In a letter to A. L. Bowley, a fellow mathematically inclined economist, he explained his own 'rules' as follows:

1. Use mathematics as a shorthand language, rather than as an engine of inquiry.
2. Keep to them [that is, stick to the maths] till you have done.
3. Translate into English.
4. Then illustrate by examples that are important in real life.
5. Burn the mathematics.
6. If you can't succeed in 4, burn 3. This last I did often.

A. C. Pigou (editor). 1966. *Memorials of Alfred Marshall*. New York, A. M. Kelley. pp. 427–28.

Marshall was Professor of Political Economy at the University of Cambridge between 1885 and 1908. In 1896, he circulated a pamphlet to the University Senate, objecting to a proposal to allow women to be granted degrees. Marshall prevailed, and women would wait until 1948 before being granted academic standing at Cambridge on a par with men.

Nevertheless, his work was motivated by a desire to improve the material conditions of working people:

> Now at last we are setting ourselves seriously to inquire whether it is necessary that there should be any so-called 'lower classes' at all: that is, whether there need be large numbers of people doomed from their birth to hard work in order to provide for others the requisites of a refined and cultured life, while they themselves are prevented by their poverty and toil from having any share or part in that life. … The answer depends in a great measure upon facts and inferences, which are within the province of economics; and this is it which gives to economic studies their chief and their highest interest. (*Principles of Economics*, 1890)

Would Marshall now be satisfied with the contribution that modern economics has made to creating a more just economy?

7.9 BUYING AND SELLING: DEMAND AND SUPPLY IN A COMPETITIVE MARKET

To apply the supply and demand model to the textbook market, we assume that all the books are identical (although in practice some may be in better condition than others) and that a potential seller can advertise a book for sale by announcing its price on a local website. We would expect most trades to occur at similar prices. Buyers and sellers could easily observe all the advertised prices, so if some books were advertised at $10 and others at $5, buyers would be queuing to pay $5; these sellers would quickly realize that they could charge more, while no one would want to pay $10, so these sellers would have to lower their prices.

We can find the equilibrium price by drawing the supply and demand curves on one diagram, as in Figure 7.13. At a price $P^* = \$8$, the supply of books is equal to demand—24 buyers are willing to pay $8 and 24 sellers are willing to sell. The equilibrium quantity is $Q^* = \$24$.

The **market-clearing price** is $8—that is, supply is equal to demand at this price—all buyers who want to buy, and all sellers who want to sell, can do so. The market is in equilibrium. In everyday language, something is in equilibrium if the forces acting on it are in balance, so that it remains still. We say that a market is in equilibrium if the actions of buyers and sellers have no tendency to change the price or the quantities bought and sold, until there is a change in market conditions. At the equilibrium price for textbooks, all those who wish to buy or sell are able to do so, so there is no tendency for change.

> **market-clearing price** At this price there is no excess supply or excess demand. *See also:* equilibrium.

> To explore all of the slides in this figure, see the online version at https://tinyco.re/8602647.

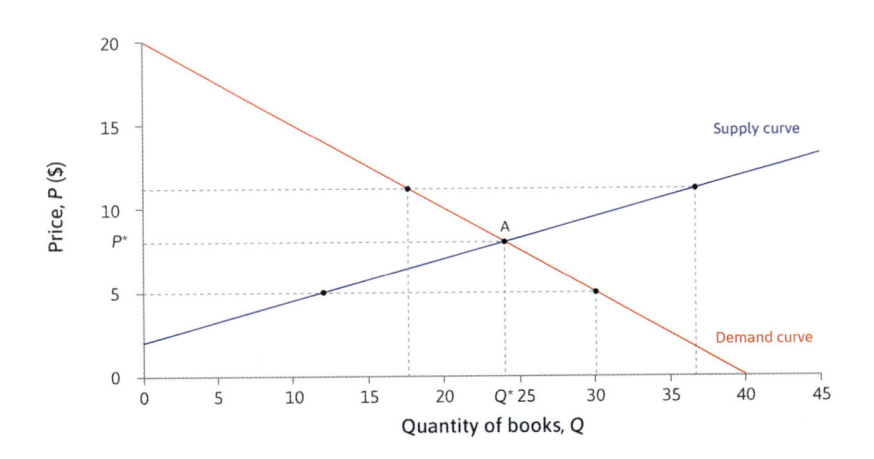

Figure 7.13 Equilibrium in the market for second-hand books.

1. Supply and demand
We find the equilibrium by drawing the supply and demand curves in the same diagram.

2. The market-clearing price
At a price $P^* = \$8$, the quantity supplied is equal to the quantity demanded: $Q^* = 24$. The market is in equilibrium. We say that the market clears at a price of $8.

3. A price above the equilibrium price—excess supply
At a price greater than $8 more students would wish to sell, but not all of them would find buyers. There would be excess supply, so these sellers would want to lower their price.

4. A price below the equilibrium price—excess demand
At a price less than $8, there would be more buyers than sellers—excess demand—so sellers could raise their prices. Only at $8 is there no tendency for change.

305

Not all online markets for books are in **competitive equilibrium**. Michael Eisen, a biologist, noticed that an out-of-print text, *The Making of a Fly*, was listed for sale on Amazon by two reputable sellers, with prices starting at $1,730,045.91 (+$3.99 shipping). Over the next week prices rose rapidly, peaking at $23,698,655.93, before dropping to $106.23. Eisen explains why in his blog (http://tinyco.re/0044329).

> **price-taker** Characteristic of producers and consumers who cannot benefit by offering or asking any price other than the market price in the equilibrium of a competitive market. They have no power to influence the market price.
> **excess demand** A situation in which the quantity of a good demanded is greater than the quantity supplied at the current price. *See also: excess supply.*
> **competitive equilibrium** A market outcome in which all buyers and sellers are price-takers, and at the prevailing market price, the quantity supplied is equal to the quantity demanded.

Price-taking

Will a market always be in equilibrium? No—when conditions change, it will take time for the market participants to adjust; while that happens, goods may be bought and sold at non-equilibrium prices. But, as Marshall argued, people would want to change their prices if there was excess supply or demand and would expect these changes to eventually move the economy toward a market equilibrium.

In the textbook market that we have described, individual students accept the prevailing equilibrium price determined by the supply and demand curves. This is because they could not benefit by offering to buy or sell at a price different from the equilibrium price. No one would trade with a seller asking a higher price or a buyer offering a lower one, because anyone could find an alternative seller or buyer with a better price.

The participants in this market equilibrium are **price-takers**, because there is sufficient competition from other buyers and sellers that the best they can do is to trade at the same price. They are free to choose other prices, but in contrast to the case when there is either excess supply or **excess demand**, when the market is in equilibrium they cannot benefit by doing so.

On both sides of the market, competition eliminates bargaining power. We describe the equilibrium in such a market as a competitive equilibrium. A competitive equilibrium is a Nash equilibrium because, given what all other actors are doing (trading at the equilibrium price), no actor can do better than to continue what they are doing (also trading at the equilibrium price).

In contrast, the seller of a differentiated product can set its price, because there are no close competitors. But the buyers are price-takers. In the example of Language Perfection, there are many consumers wanting to buy a Spanish-language course, so individual consumers have no power to negotiate a more advantageous deal—they have to accept the price that other consumers are paying.

> **EXERCISE 7.5 PRICE-TAKERS**
> Think about some of the goods you buy: perhaps different kinds of food, clothes, transport tickets, or electronic goods.
>
> 1. Are there many sellers of these goods?
> 2. Do you try to find the lowest price in each case?
> 3. If not, why not?
> 4. For which goods would price be your main criterion?
> 5. Use your answers to help you decide if the sellers of these goods are price-takers. Are there goods for which you, as a buyer, are not a price-taker?

QUESTION 7.10 CHOOSE THE CORRECT ANSWER(S)
Figure 7.14 shows the demand and the supply curves for a textbook. The curves intersect at $(Q, P) = (24, 8)$. Which of the following statements are correct?

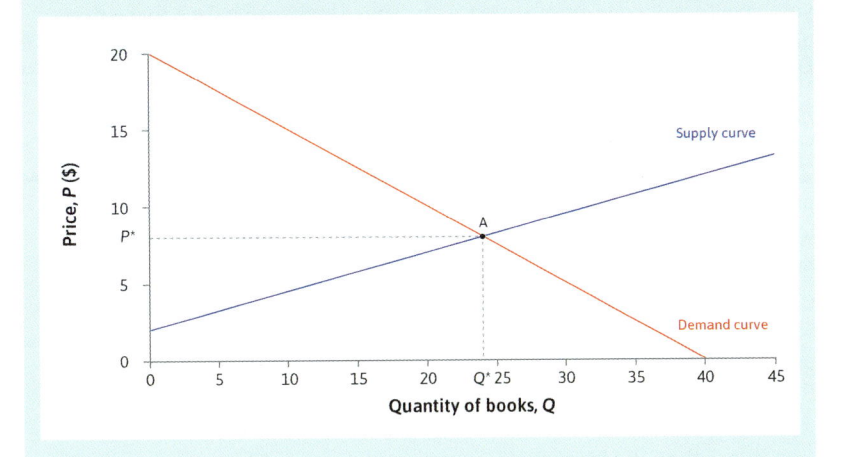

Figure 7.14 Supply and demand for textbooks.

☐ At price $10, there is an excess demand for the textbook.
☐ At $8, some of the sellers have an incentive to increase their selling price to $9.
☐ At $8, the market clears.
☐ Forty books will be sold in total.

7.10 DEMAND AND SUPPLY IN A COMPETITIVE MARKET: BAKERIES

In the second-hand textbook example, both buyers and sellers are individual consumers. Now we look at an example in which the sellers are firms producing output. We know how the firm sets the price and quantity of a differentiated product, and that the price depends on whether there is competition from firms selling quite similar products—if there is competition, demand will be elastic, and the firm will be unable to set a high price because that would cause consumers to switch to other similar brands.

If there are many firms producing identical products, and consumers can easily switch from one firm to another, then firms will be price-takers in equilibrium. They will be unable to benefit from attempting to trade at a price different from the prevailing price.

To understand how price-taking firms behave, consider a city in which many small bakeries produce bread and sell it directly to consumers. Figure 7.15 shows what the market demand curve (the total daily demand for bread of all consumers in the city) might look like. It is downward-sloping as usual because, at higher prices, fewer consumers will be willing to buy.

Suppose that you are the owner of one small bakery. You have to decide what price to charge and how many loaves to produce each morning. Suppose that neighbouring bakeries are selling loaves identical to yours at €2.35. The loaf is a large baguette. This is the prevailing market price; you will not be able to sell loaves at a higher price than other bakeries, because no one would buy—you are a price-taker.

What you should do depends on your costs of production—and, in particular, on your marginal costs. You may have some fixed costs, for example, the rent you pay on your premises—but you have to pay these irrespective of the number of loaves you produce. It is the additional costs of actually making each loaf of bread—the cost of the ingredients, and what you have to pay your employees for the time it takes to bake a loaf—that determine whether you should produce 30, 50 or 100 loaves per day. Having installed mixers, ovens, and other equipment, the marginal cost of each extra loaf may be relatively low, as long as you don't exceed the capacity of your equipment.

Figure 7.16 illustrates this situation. Your bakery has the capacity to produce up to 120 loaves per day. Below that level, the marginal cost of a loaf is €1.50. The horizontal line at $P^* = $ €2.35 represents the demand for bread from your bakery—because you are a price-taker, each loaf you produce can be sold for €2.35.

In this example, it is easy to find the profit-maximizing price and quantity without drawing isoprofit curves. Work through the analysis of Figure 7.16 to see how this is done.

Your optimal choice is $P^* = $ €2.35 and $Q^* = 120$; since your marginal cost is less than the market price, you maximize profit by making as many loaves as possible. Your profit will be the total surplus on 120 loaves minus your fixed costs.

What would you do if the market price changed? As long as it remains above €1.50, your profit-maximizing choice remains the same. But if the price fell below €1.50, you should immediately stop making bread. In that case, you would make a loss on any loaf produced.

Even if the market price were a little above €1.50, you might make a loss overall if your fixed costs were high. In this case, you still do the best you can by producing 120 loaves—at least the surplus will help you to cover part of the fixed costs. But in the longer term you would need to consider whether it is worth continuing in business. If you expect market conditions to remain bad, it might be best to sell up and leave the market—you could obtain a better return on your capital elsewhere.

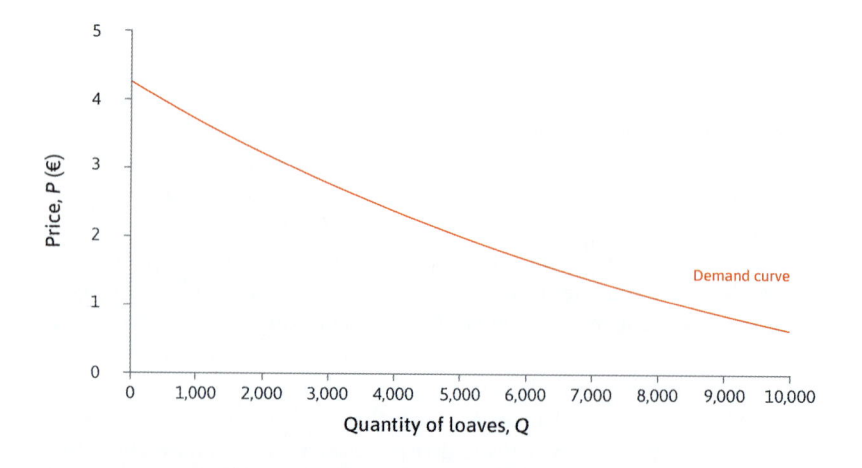

Figure 7.15 The market demand curve for bread.

7.10 DEMAND AND SUPPLY IN A COMPETITIVE MARKET: BAKERIES

The market supply curve

The market for bread in the city has many consumers and many bakeries. Let's suppose initially there are 20 bakeries, differing in their marginal costs and their production capacity. Costs differ across bakeries because they specialize in producing different kinds of bread. Those that specialize in making large baguettes have the lowest marginal costs; for other bakeries to supply this type of bread, they need to switch employees who are more skilled in other types of bread production to baguette baking and their costs are higher. Similarly, the equipment of the non-specialist bakeries is less suited to producing baguettes, which is another reason their marginal costs are higher. As bakeries less and less suited to produced large baguettes supply the market, marginal costs rise, as shown in Figure 7.17.

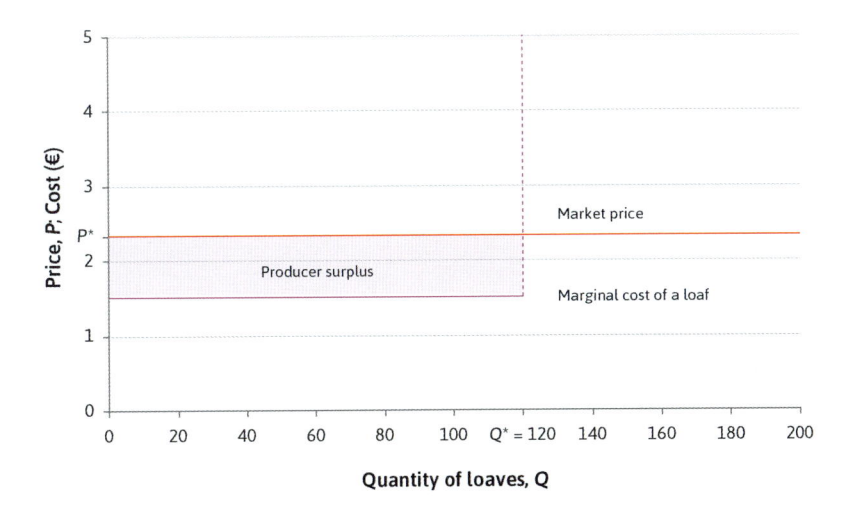

To explore all of the slides in this figure, see the online version at https://tinyco.re/2377985.

Figure 7.16 The profit-maximizing price and quantity.

1. The marginal cost of a loaf
Whatever quantity of loaves you decide to produce between 0 and 120, the cost of making one more loaf—that is, the marginal cost—is €1.50.

2. The maximum level of production
Given the capacity of your bakery, you cannot produce more than 120 loaves.

3. Price-taking
The bakery is a price-taker. The market price is $P^* = $ €2.35. If you choose a higher price, customers will go to other bakeries. Your feasible set of prices and quantities is the shaded area below the horizontal line at P^*, where the price is less than or equal to €2.35, and the quantity is less than or equal to 120.

4. The profit-maximizing price
However many loaves you produce, you should sell them at €2.35 each. A higher price is not feasible, and a lower price would bring less profit.

5. The profit-maximizing quantity
On every loaf you produce up to 120, you can make a surplus of €2.35 − €1.50=€0.85. You can increase your profit by making as many as possible. Your profit-maximizing quantity is $Q^* = $ 120.

6. Producer surplus
Your surplus is the shaded area below the line at P^* above the marginal cost. Surplus = (2.35 − 1.50) × 120 = €102.

Each bakery will decide how many loaves to produce in the same way:

- *When the market price is above its marginal cost:* It will produce and sell its maximum output.
- *When the market price is below its marginal cost:* It will make none of this kind of bread.

We can work out how much each bakery will supply at any given market price. To find the market supply curve, we just add up the total amount that all the bakeries will supply at each price.

We can do this in the same way as for second-hand textbooks. Figure 7.17 shows how to find the market supply by lining the 20 bakeries up in order of their marginal costs.

To explore all of the slides in this figure, see the online version at https://tinyco.re/5854244.

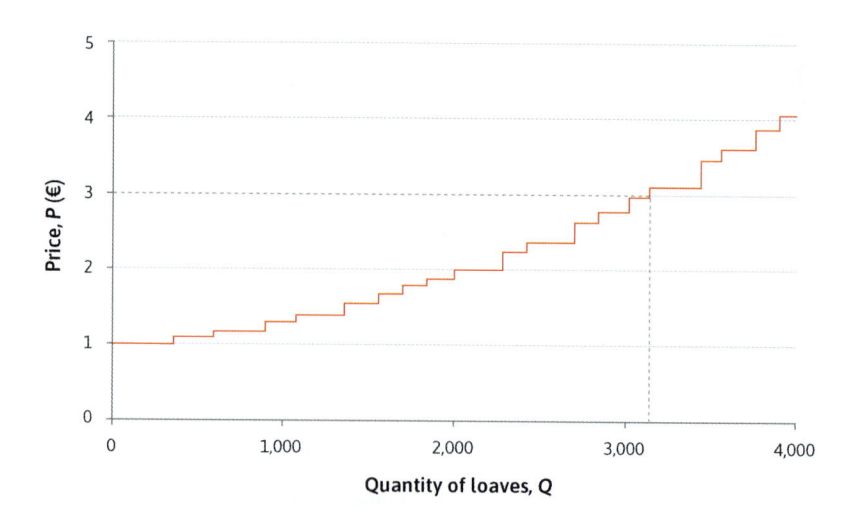

Figure 7.17 The market supply curve: 20 firms.

1. The market supply curve
To draw the market supply, we line up the 20 bakeries in order of their marginal costs—lowest first—and plot the marginal cost of each one, up to the maximum number of loaves it can produce.

2. The bakery with the lowest cost
The first bakery has marginal cost €1 and can make 360 loaves per day.

3. The next bakery
The next one has marginal cost €1.10 and can make 240 loaves per day.

4. The capacity of the market
If all the bakeries produce at full capacity, they can produce 4,000 loaves altogether.

5. Market supply when the price is P*
If the price is P*, only the bakeries with marginal cost less than or equal to P* will produce bread. If the price was €3, the graph shows that total market supply would be 3,140 loaves.

If there were many more bakeries in the city, more bread would be produced and there would be many more 'steps' on the supply curve. Rather than drawing them all, it is easier to approximate market supply with a smooth curve. Figure 7.18 shows an approximate market supply curve when there are many firms.

Notice that the supply curve tells us two different things. If we choose any price, it tells us how many loaves, in total, the bakeries would produce. But remember that, to construct it, we plotted the marginal cost of each loaf of bread in increasing order of marginal costs. So, if we choose a particular quantity (7,000, say) and use the curve to find the corresponding value on the vertical axis (€2.74), this tells us that the marginal cost of the 7,000th loaf is €2.74. In other words, the market supply curve is the marginal cost curve for all the bread produced in the city.

Competitive equilibrium

Now we know both the demand curve (Figure 7.15 (page 308)) and the supply curve (Figure 7.18) for the bread market as a whole. Figure 7.19 shows that the competitive equilibrium price is exactly €2.00. At this price, the market clears—consumers demand 5,000 loaves per day, and firms supply 5,000 loaves per day.

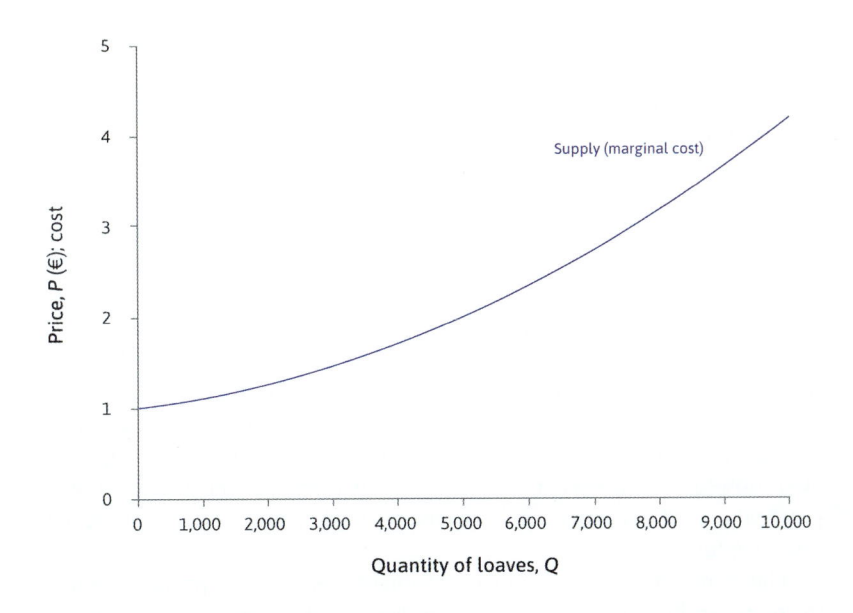

Figure 7.18 The market supply curve: Many bakeries.

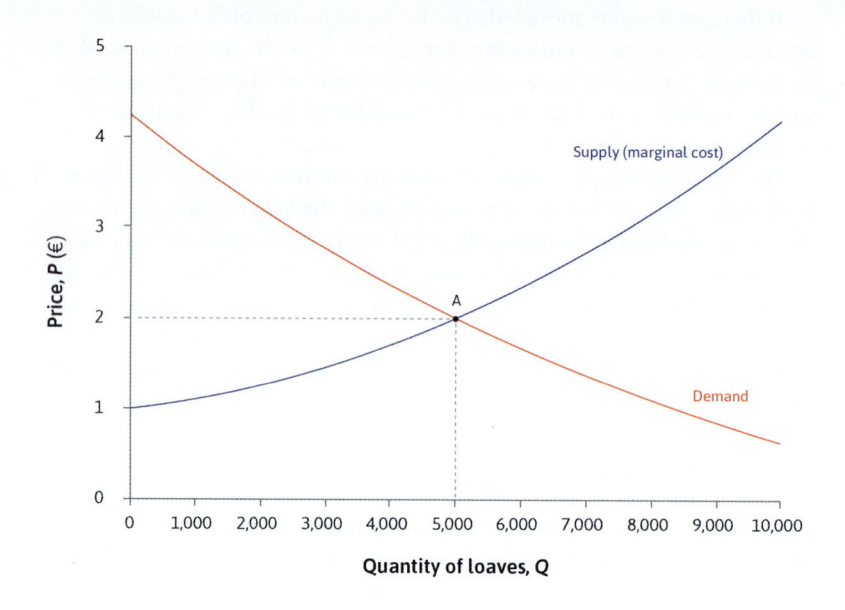

Figure 7.19 Equilibrium in the market for bread.

Since the equilibrium is the point where the demand curve crosses the marginal cost curve, we know that—in equilibrium—both the willingness to pay of the 5,000th consumer, and the marginal cost of the 5,000th loaf, are equal to the market price.

7.11 COMPETITIVE EQUILIBRIUM: GAINS FROM TRADE, ALLOCATION, AND DISTRIBUTION

Buyers and sellers of bread voluntarily engage in trade because both benefit. Their mutual benefits from the equilibrium allocation can be measured by the consumer and producer surpluses introduced in Section 7.7 (page 294). Any buyer whose willingness to pay for a good is higher than the market price, receives a surplus—the difference between the WTP and the price paid. Similarly, if the marginal cost of producing an item is below the market price, the producer receives a surplus. Figure 7.20 shows how to calculate the total surplus (the gains from trade) at the competitive equilibrium in the market for bread, in the same way as we did for the market for language courses (monopolistic competition).

When the market for bread is in equilibrium with the quantity of loaves supplied equal to the quantity demanded, the total surplus is the area below the demand curve and above the supply curve.

Notice how the equilibrium allocation in this market differs from the allocation of a differentiated product, such as LP's Spanish course. The equilibrium quantity of bread is at the point where the market supply curve (which is also the marginal cost curve) crosses the demand curve; the total surplus is the whole of the area between the two curves. Figure 7.16 (page 309) showed that the owner of LP chose to produce a quantity below the point where the marginal cost curve meets the demand curve, reducing the total surplus.

The competitive equilibrium allocation of bread has the property that the total surplus is maximized. The surplus would be smaller if fewer than 5,000 loaves were produced; if more than 5,000 loaves were produced, the surplus on the extra loaves would be negative—they would cost more to make than consumers were willing to pay.

At the equilibrium, all the potential gains from trade are exploited, which means there is no deadweight loss. This property—that the combined consumer and producer surplus is maximized at the point where supply equals demand—holds in general. If both buyers and sellers are price-takers, the competitive equilibrium allocation maximizes the sum of the gains achieved by trading in the market.

Pareto efficiency

At the competitive equilibrium allocation of bread, it is not possible to make any of the consumers or firms better off (that is, to increase the surplus of any individual) without making at least one of them worse off. Provided that what happens in this market does not affect anyone other than the participating buyers and sellers, we can say that the equilibrium allocation is Pareto efficient.

Pareto efficiency follows from three assumptions we have made about the bread market.

Joel Waldfogel, an economist, gave his chosen discipline a bad name by suggesting that gift-giving at Christmas may result in a deadweight loss (http://tinyco.re/7728778). If you receive a gift that is worth less to you than it cost the giver, he argued that the surplus from the transaction is negative (http://tinyco.re/0182759). Do you agree?

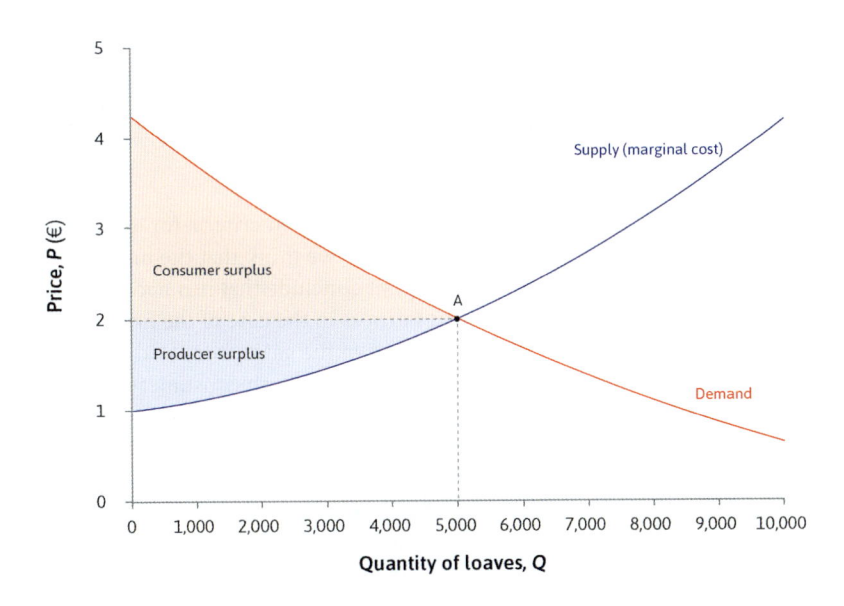

To explore all of the slides in this figure, see the online version at https://tinyco.re/4382391.

Figure 7.20 Equilibrium in the bread market: Gains from trade.

1. The consumer surplus
At the equilibrium price of €2.00 in the bread market, a consumer who is willing to pay €3.50 obtains a surplus of €1.50.

2. Total consumer surplus
The shaded area above €2.00 shows total consumer surplus—the sum of all the buyers' gains from trade.

3. The producer surplus
Remember that the producer's surplus on a unit of output is the difference between the price at which it is sold and the marginal cost of producing it. The marginal cost of the 2,000th loaf is €1.25; since it is sold for €2.00, the producer obtains a surplus of €0.75.

4. Total surplus
The shaded area below €2.00 is the sum of the bakeries' surpluses on every loaf that they produce. The whole shaded area shows the sum of all gains from trade in this market, known as the total surplus.

Price-taking

The participants are price-takers. They have no market power. When a particular buyer trades with a particular seller, each of them knows that the other can find an alternative trading partner willing to trade at the market price. Competition prevents sellers from raising the price in the way that the producer of a differentiated good would do.

A complete contract

The exchange of a loaf of bread for money is governed by a complete contract between buyer and seller. If you find there is no loaf of bread in the bag marked 'Bread' when you get home, you can get your money back. Compare this with the incomplete employment contract in Unit 6 (page 244), in which the firm can buy the worker's time, but cannot be sure how much effort the worker will put in. We will see in Unit 8 that this leads to a Pareto-inefficient allocation in the labour market.

No effects on others

We have implicitly assumed that what happens in this market affects no one except the buyers and sellers. To assess Pareto efficiency, we need to consider everyone affected by the allocation. If, for example, the early morning activities of bakeries disrupt the sleep of local residents, then there are additional costs of bread production and we ought to take the costs to the bakeries' neighbours into account too. Then, we may conclude that the equilibrium allocation is not Pareto efficient after all. We will investigate this type of problem in Unit 11.

Fairness and efficiency

Remember from Unit 5 (page 185) that there are two criteria for assessing an allocation—efficiency and fairness. Even if we think that the market allocation is Pareto efficient, we should not conclude that it is necessarily a desirable one. What can we say about fairness in the case of the bread market? We could examine the distribution of the gains from trade between producers and consumers. Figure 7.20 shows that both consumers and firms obtain a surplus; in this example consumer surplus is slightly higher than producer surplus. You can see that this happens because the demand curve is relatively steep (inelastic) compared with the supply curve.

We might also want to consider the market participants' standard of living. For example, if a poor student buys a book from a rich student, we might think that an outcome in which the buyer paid less than the market price (closer to the seller's reservation price) would be better, because it would be fairer. Or, if the consumers in the bread market were exceptionally poor, we might decide to pass a law setting a maximum bread price lower than €2.00 to achieve a fairer (although Pareto-inefficient) outcome.

The Pareto efficiency of a competitive equilibrium allocation is often interpreted as a powerful argument in favour of markets as a means of allocating resources. But we need to be careful not to exaggerate the value of this result:

- *The allocation may not be Pareto efficient:* We might not have taken everything into account.
- *There are other important considerations:* Fairness, for example.

Maurice Stucke, an antitrust lawyer, asks if competition in a market economy is always good (http://tinyco.re/8720076).

7.11 COMPETITIVE EQUILIBRIUM: GAINS FROM TRADE, ALLOCATION, AND DISTRIBUTION

- *Price-takers are hard to find in real life:* It is not as easy as you might think to find markets where all participants are price-takers. Goods (including bread) are rarely identical, and participants don't always know what prices are available.

Watch 'Economist in action', Kathryn Graddy explain how she collected data on the price of whiting from the Fulton Fish Market in New York and what she found out about the model of perfect competition.

EXERCISE 7.6 SURPLUS AND DEADWEIGHT LOSS
1. Sketch a diagram to illustrate the competitive market for bread, showing the equilibrium where 5,000 loaves are sold at a price of €2.00.
2. Suppose that the bakeries get together to form a cartel. They agree to raise the price to €2.70, and jointly cut production to supply the number of loaves that consumers demand at that price. Shade the areas on your diagram to show the consumer surplus, producer surplus, and deadweight loss caused by the cartel.
3. For what kinds of goods would you expect the supply curve to be highly elastic?
4. Draw diagrams to illustrate how the share of the gains from trade obtained by producers depends on the elasticity of the supply curve.

Kathryn Graddy: Fishing for perfect competition http://tinyco.re/7406838

QUESTION 7.11 CHOOSE THE CORRECT ANSWER(S)
Which of the following statements about a competitive equilibrium allocation are correct?

- ☐ It is the best possible allocation.
- ☐ No buyer's surplus or seller's surplus can be increased without reducing someone else's surplus.
- ☐ The allocation must be Pareto efficient.
- ☐ The total surplus from trade is maximized.

QUESTION 7.12 CHOOSE THE CORRECT ANSWER(S)
Figure 7.20 (page 313) shows the demand and supply curves in the bread market and the distribution of surplus in competitive equilibrium. *Ceteris paribus*, which of the following would affect the distribution of gains from trade between consumers and producers?

- ☐ legislation that sets the price above or below P^*
- ☐ relative elasticities of demand and supply
- ☐ total quantity traded
- ☐ the slope of the firms' marginal cost curve

315

7.12 CHANGES IN SUPPLY AND DEMAND

Quinoa is a cereal crop grown on the Altiplano, a high barren plateau in the Andes of South America. It is a traditional staple food in Peru and Bolivia. In recent years, as its nutritional properties have become known, there has been a huge increase in demand from richer, health-conscious consumers in Europe and North America. Figures 7.21a–c show how the market changed. You can see in Figures 7.21a and 7.21b that, between 2001 and 2011, the price of quinoa trebled and production almost doubled. Figure 7.21c indicates the strength of the increase in demand—in real terms, spending on imports of quinoa rose from just $2.4 million to over $40 million over 10 years. Note that the increase in spending on quinoa reflects the increase in the price shown in Figure 7.21b as well as the purchase of higher quantities of the grain.

For the producer countries, these changes are a mixed blessing. While their staple food has become expensive for poor consumers, farmers—who are amongst the poorest—are benefiting from the boom in export sales. Other countries are now investigating whether quinoa can be grown in different climates, and France and the US have become substantial producers.

How can we explain the rapid increase in the price of quinoa? In this section, we look at the effects of changes in demand and supply, illustrating our model by the real-world case of quinoa.

The supply of quinoa

At the beginning of the current century, there was ample land for growing quinoa on the Altiplano, and farmers producing other crops could easily switch to quinoa as the price rose. As a result, the initial increase in production between 2001 and 2007 to meet rising demand did not raise costs. This means that the supply curve was virtually flat. But in order to allow the continued output of quinoa after 2007, land less suited for the crop had to be brought into use, and the new farmers taking up the crop were giving up the production of other crops on which they had been making adequate incomes. As a result, costs rose. To represent this, we show the supply curve in Figure 7.23 (page 319) becoming increasingly steep as production rose.

Jose Daniel Reyes and Julia Oliver. 'Quinoa: The Little Cereal That Could' (http://tinyco.re/9266629). *The Trade Post*. 22 November 2013. Underlying data from Food and Agriculture Organization of the United Nations. FAOSTAT Database (http://tinyco.re/4368803).

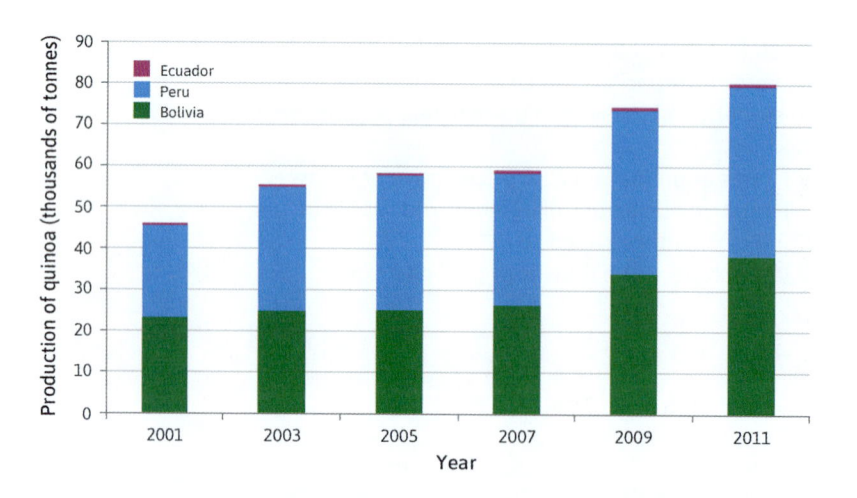

Figure 7.21a The production of quinoa.

7.12 CHANGES IN SUPPLY AND DEMAND

An increase in demand

As in the case of demand for language courses or Apple Cinnamon Cheerios, the demand curve for quinoa sloped downwards, as is shown by D_{2001} in Figure 7.23 (page 319). The original equilibrium was at point A.

The new fashion among North American and European consumers for eating quinoa meant that for any given price of the crop, the tonnes of quinoa purchased rose. In other words, the demand curve for quinoa shifted to the right. You could also say that it shifted up, meaning that the price that was sufficient to allow the sales of any given quantity of quinoa had now increased. This is shown in Figure 7.23 (see the new demand curve labelled '2008').

The increase in demand destroys the old equilibrium (the supply and demand curves no longer cross at A). With the new demand curve and initially with no change in sales of quinoa or in the price, there were a great many potential consumers whose willingness to pay for quinoa exceeded the price.

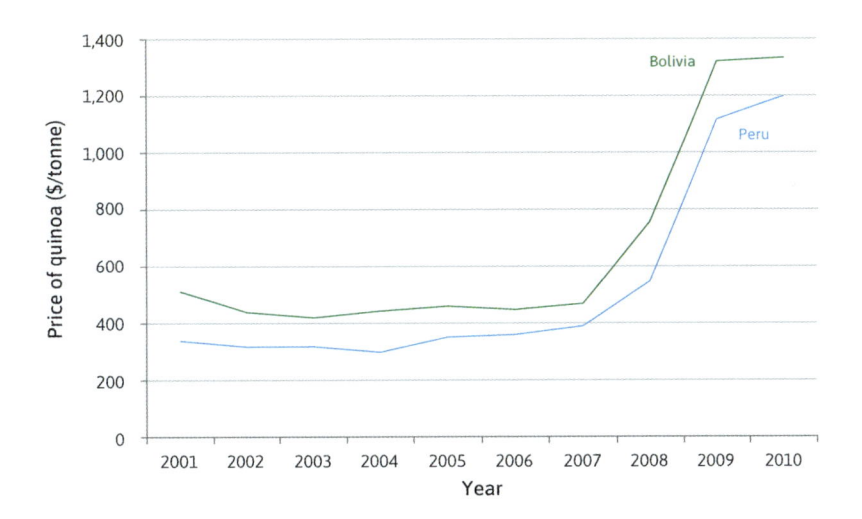

Jose Daniel Reyes and Julia Oliver. 'Quinoa: The Little Cereal That Could' (http://tinyco.re/9266629). *The Trade Post*. 22 November 2013. Underlying data from Food and Agriculture Organization of the United Nations. FAOSTAT Database (http://tinyco.re/4368803).

Figure 7.21b Quinoa real producer prices in Peru.

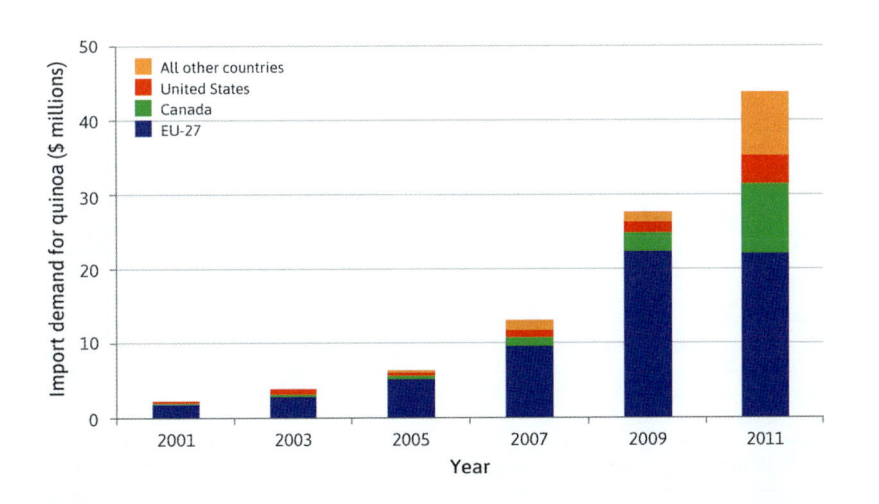

Jose Daniel Reyes and Julia Oliver. 'Quinoa: The Little Cereal That Could' (http://tinyco.re/9266629). *The Trade Post*. 22 November 2013. Underlying data from Food and Agriculture Organization of the United Nations. FAOSTAT Database (http://tinyco.re/4368803).

Figure 7.21c Global import demand for quinoa.

317

Market disequilibrium and adjustment to a new equilibrium

Thus, point A was no longer a Nash equilibrium because at least some of the producers would have realized that they could raise their prices without reducing their sales. The original price and quantity are termed a **disequilibrium** because, at point A, someone can benefit by changing the price. The reason is that at the initial price, there is excess demand. The increase in demand set off the sequence of events shown in Figure 7.22.

Figure 7.22 describes what economists call a disequilibrium adjustment process, which is simply how market actors react when the existing situation is not an equilibrium. How long will this process go on? It will continue until the combination of higher prices and greater production has eliminated the excess demand, shown in Figure 7.23 (page 319) as point C.

When we refer to 'increase in demand', it's important to be careful about what exactly we mean. Figure 7.24 uses the example of quinoa to explain.

This change is a movement along the supply curve. But the supply curve has not shifted! The amount supplied increased in response to the change in price. A shift in the supply curve would take place if, for example, an improved method of cultivating quinoa was invented so that for any given price, more would be supplied.

After an increase in demand, the equilibrium quantity rises. The price change depends on the steepness of the supply curve, which captures how responsive supply is to prices. We know that the price elasticity of demand measures how much demand falls when prices rise. Similarly, the **price elasticity of supply** is defined as the percentage increase in supply when prices rise by one percent.

You can see in Figure 7.23 that the steeper (more inelastic) the supply curve, the higher the price will rise and the less the quantity will increase. Initially, the supply curve was flat (elastic), so in the equilibrium at point B, the price was the same as at point A and the quantity sold was fully responsive to the demand **shock**.

---

disequilibrium A situation in which at least one of the actors can benefit by altering his or her actions and therefore changing the situation, given what everybody else is doing.

price elasticity of supply The percentage change in supply that would occur in response to a 1% increase in price. Supply is elastic if this is greater than 1, and inelastic if less than 1.

shock An exogenous change in some of the fundamental data or variables used in a model.

An increase in the willingness to pay for quinoa
⇩
The demand curve shifts out
⇩
The original price and quantity are now not a Nash equilibrium
⇩
Some producers raise their prices, increasing their profits
⇩   ⇩
New producers start quinoa production   Existing farmers produce more

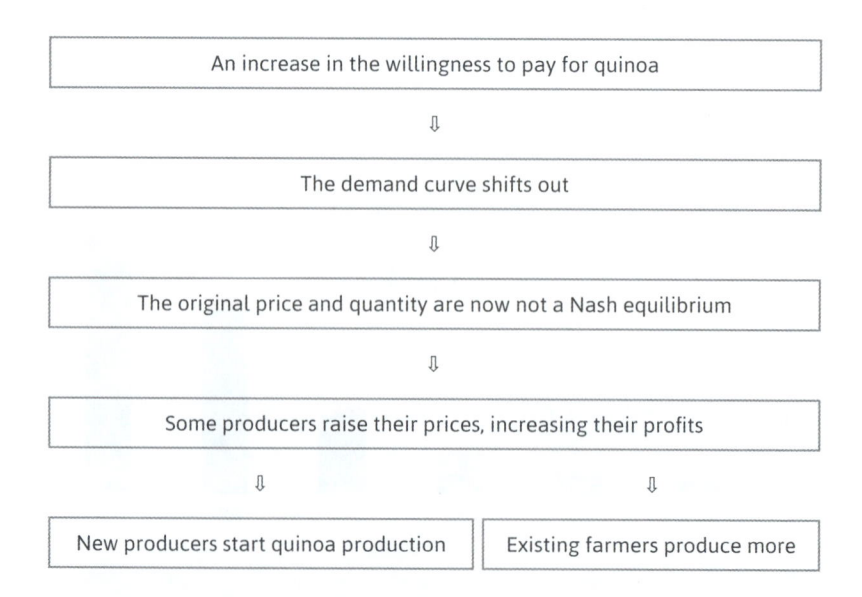

Figure 7.22 Disequilibrium in demand for quinoa.

7.12 CHANGES IN SUPPLY AND DEMAND

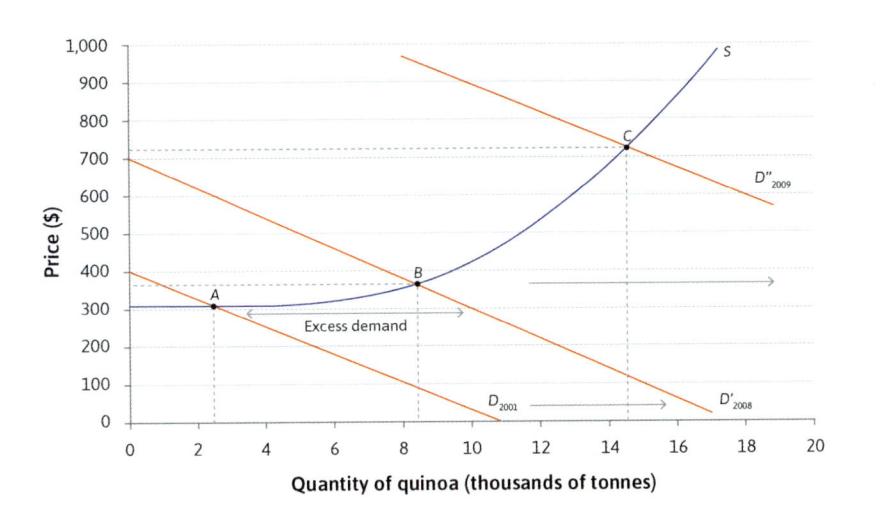

To explore all of the slides in this figure, see the online version at https://tinyco.re/3630822.

Figure 7.23 An increase in the demand for quinoa.

1. The initial equilibrium point
At the original levels of demand and supply, the equilibrium is at point A. The price is $340 per tonne, and $2.4 million tonnes of quinoa are sold.

2. An increase in demand
Demand for quinoa in Europe and North America increases between 2001 and 2008. There would be more consumers wanting to buy quinoa at each possible price. The demand curve shifts to the right.

3. Excess demand when the price is $340
If the price remained at $340, there would be excess demand for quinoa, that is, more buyers than sellers. Some producers raise the price and their profits increase. The market is in disequilibrium.

4. A new equilibrium point
The excess demand encourages more farmers to grow quinoa. The expansion of production eliminates the excess demand. There is a new equilibrium at point B with the price at $380 and a big increase in the quantity of quinoa sold.

5. A further increase in demand
Worldwide demand for quinoa continues to rise and the demand curve shifts out again to the one labelled 2009. There is excess demand. The land well suited to quinoa has all been used so the supply curve slopes upward.

6. A new equilibrium point with a higher price and larger quantity supplied
Some producers raise the price in response to the higher demand. Producers who have higher costs of production now find it profitable to switch to producing quinoa. At the new equilibrium at C, both price and quantity are higher.

Demand is higher at each possible price (the demand curve has shifted)

⇩

There is a change in the price

⇩

There is an increase in the quantity supplied

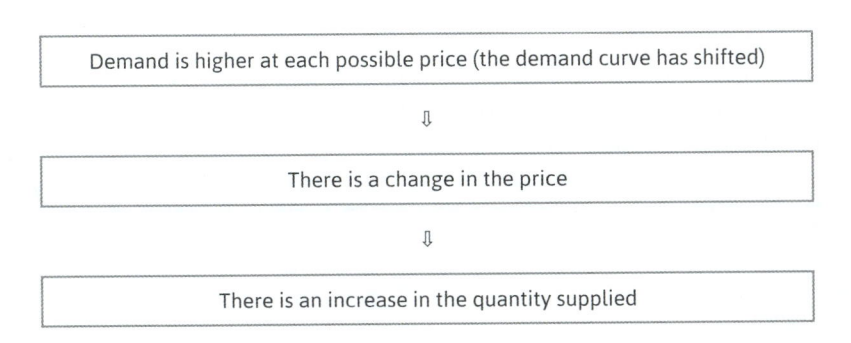

Figure 7.24 An increase in demand for quinoa.

319

exogenous Coming from outside the model rather than being produced by the workings of the model itself. *See also: endogenous.*

When either the supply curve or the demand curve shifts, an adjustment of prices is needed to bring the market into equilibrium. Such shifts in supply and demand are often referred to as shocks in economic analysis. We start by specifying an economic model and find the equilibrium. Then we look at how the equilibrium changes when something changes—the model receives a shock. The shock is called **exogenous** because the model doesn't explain why it happened—it shows the consequences of the shock, not the causes.

In the next section, we will examine another example in the world market for oil. Both the supply of and the demand for oil are more elastic in the long run, because producers can eventually build new oil wells and consumers can switch to different fuels for cars or heating. What we mean by the short run in this case is the period during which firms are limited by the capacity of existing wells, and consumers are limited by the cars and heating appliances they currently own.

> **EXERCISE 7.7 THE MARKET FOR QUINOA**
> Consider again the market for quinoa studied in Figures 7.21a–c (page 316).
>
> 1. Would you expect the price to fall eventually to its original level?
> 2. Use the same model to show the effects on price and quantity of a significant improvement in the methods for producing quinoa, resulting in lower costs for farmers.

Helge Berger and Mark Spoerer. 2001. 'Economic Crises and the European Revolutions of 1848'. *The Journal of Economic History* 61 (2): pp. 293–326.

> **EXERCISE 7.8 PRICES, SHOCKS, AND REVOLUTIONS**
> Historians usually attribute the wave of revolutions in Europe in 1848 to long-term socioeconomic factors and a surge of radical ideas. But a poor wheat harvest in 1845 lead to food shortages and sharp price rises, which may have contributed to these sudden changes.
>
> Figure 7.25 shows the average and peak prices of wheat from 1838 to 1845, relative to silver. There are three groups of countries: those in which violent revolutions took place; those in which constitutional change took place without widespread violence; and those in which no revolution occurred.
>
> 1. Explain, using supply and demand curves, how a poor wheat harvest could lead to price rises and food shortages.
> 2. Using Excel or other data analysis programs, find a way to present the data to show that the size of the price shock, rather than the price level, is associated with the likelihood of revolution.
> 3. Do you think this is a plausible explanation for the revolutions that occurred?
> 4. A journalist suggests that similar factors played a part in the Arab Spring in 2010 (http://tinyco.re/8936018). Read the post. What do you think of this hypothesis?

7.12 CHANGES IN SUPPLY AND DEMAND

Helge Berger and Mark Spoerer. 2001. 'Economic Crises and the European Revolutions of 1848.' *The Journal of Economic History* 61 (2): pp. 293–326.

		Average Price 1838–45	Maximum Price 1845–48
	Austria	52.9	104.0
	Baden	77.0	136.6
	Bavaria	70.0	127.3
	Bohemia	61.5	101.2
	France	93.8	149.2
	Hamburg	67.1	108.7
	Hesse-Darmstadt	76.7	119.7
Violent revolution 1848	Hungary	39.0	92.3
	Lombardy	88.3	119.1
	Mecklenburg-Schwerin	72.9	110.9
	Papal States	74.0	105.1
	Prussia	71.2	110.7
	Saxony	73.3	125.2
	Switzerland	87.9	146.7
	Württemberg	75.9	128.7

		Average Price 1838–45	Maximum Price 1845–48
	Belgium	93.8	140.1
	Bremen	76.1	109.5
Immediate constitutional change 1848	Brunswick	62.3	100.3
	Denmark	66.3	81.5
	Netherlands	82.6	136.0
	Oldenburg	52.1	79.3

		Average Price 1838–45	Average Price 1845–48
	England	115.3	134.7
	Finland	73.6	73.7
No revolution 1848	Norway	89.3	119.7
	Russia	50.7	44.1
	Spain	105.3	141.3
	Sweden	75.8	81.4

Figure 7.25 Average and peak prices of wheat in Europe, 1838–1845.

QUESTION 7.13 CHOOSE THE CORRECT ANSWER(S)
Look again at Figure 7.19 (page 312), which shows the equilibrium of the bread market to be 5,000 loaves per day at price €2. A year later, we find that the market equilibrium price has fallen to €1.50. What can we definitely conclude?

☐ The fall in the price must have been caused by a downward shift in the demand curve.
☐ The fall in the price must have been caused by a downward shift in the supply curve.
☐ The fall in price could have been caused by a shift in either curve.
☐ At a price of €1.50, there will be an excess demand for bread.

QUESTION 7.14 CHOOSE THE CORRECT ANSWER(S)
Which of the following statements are correct?

☐ A fall in the mortgage interest rate would shift up the demand curve for new houses.
☐ The launch of a new Sony smartphone would shift up the demand curve for existing iPhones.
☐ A fall in the oil price would shift up the demand curve for oil.
☐ A fall in the oil price would shift down the supply curve for plastics.

7.13 THE WORLD OIL MARKET
Figure 7.26 plots the real price of oil in world markets (in constant 2014 US dollars) and the total quantity consumed globally from 1865 to 2014. To understand what drives the large fluctuations in the oil price, we can use our supply and demand model, distinguishing between the short run and the long run.

BP. 2015. *BP Statistical Review of World Energy*, June 2015.

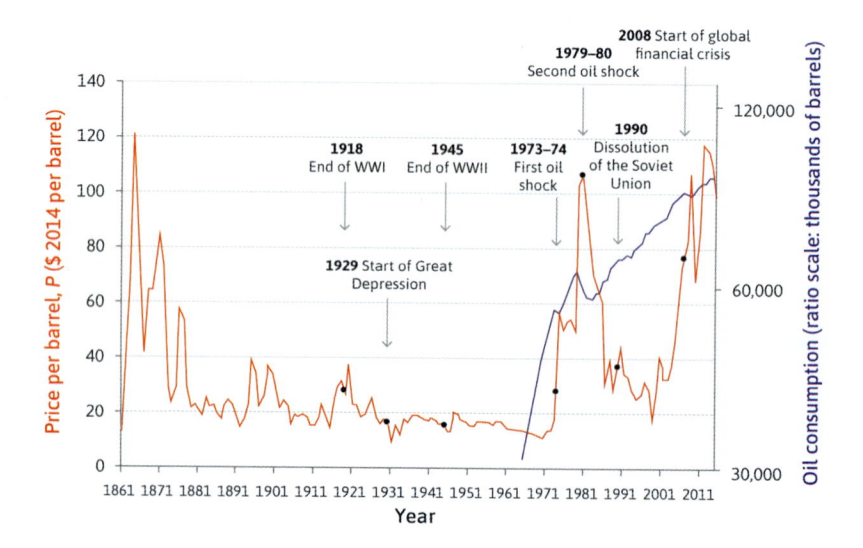

Figure 7.26 World oil prices in constant prices (1865–2014) and global oil consumption (1965–2014).

Prices reflect **scarcity**. If a good becomes scarcer or costlier to produce, then the supply will fall and the price will tend to rise. For more than 60 years, oil industry analysts have been predicting that demand would soon outstrip supply—production would reach a peak and prices would then rise as world reserves declined. 'Peak oil' is not evident in Figure 7.26. One reason is that rising prices provide incentives for further exploration. Between 1981 and 2014, more than 1,000 billion barrels were extracted and consumed, yet world reserves of oil more than doubled from roughly 680 billion barrels to 1,700 billion barrels.

Prices have risen strongly in the twenty-first century and an increasing number of analysts are predicting that conventional oil, at least, has reached a peak. But unconventional resources such as shale oil are now being exploited. Perhaps it will be climate change policies, rather than resource depletion, that eventually curb oil consumption.

The oil price data in Figure 7.26 is difficult to interpret because of the sharp swings from high to low and back again over short periods of time. These fluctuations cannot be explained by looking at oil reserves, because they reflect short-run scarcity. Both supply and demand are inelastic in the short run.

Short-run supply and demand

On the demand side, the main use of oil products is in transport services (air, road, and sea). Demand is inelastic in the short run because of the limited substitution possibilities. For example, even if petrol prices rise substantially, in the short run most commuters will continue to use their existing cars to travel to work because of the limited alternatives immediately available to them. Therefore, the short-run demand curve is steep.

Traditional oil extraction technology is characterized by a large up-front investment in expensive oil wells that can take many months or longer to construct, and once in place, can keep pumping until the well is depleted or oil can no longer be profitably extracted. Once the well is drilled, the cost of extracting the oil is relatively low, but the rate at which the oil is pumped faces capacity constraints—producers can get only so many barrels per day from a well. This means that, taking existing capacity as fixed in the short run, we should draw a short-run market supply curve that is initially low and flat, and then turns upwards very steeply as capacity constraints are hit. We also need to allow for the **oligopolistic** structure of the world market for crude oil. The Organization of Petroleum Exporting Countries (OPEC) is a cartel with a dozen member countries that currently accounts for about 40% of world oil production. OPEC sets output quotas for its members. We can represent this in our supply and demand diagram by a flat marginal cost line that stops at the total OPEC production quota. At that point, the line becomes vertical. This is not because of capacity constraints, but because OPEC producers will not sell any more oil.

> **scarcity** A good that is valued, and for which there is an opportunity cost of acquiring more.

> R. G. Miller and S. R. Sorrell. 2013. 'The Future of Oil Supply' (http://tinyco.re/6167443). *Philosophical Transactions of the Royal Society A: Mathematical, Physical and Engineering Sciences* 372 (2006) (December).

> Nick A. Owen, Oliver R. Inderwildi, and David A. King. 2010. 'The Status of Conventional World Oil Reserves—Hype or Cause for Concern?' (http://tinyco.re/8978100) *Energy Policy* 38 (8): pp. 4743–49.

> **oligopoly** A market with a small number of sellers of the same good, giving each seller some market power.

Figure 7.27 assembles the market supply curve by adding the OPEC production quota to the supply from non-OPEC countries (remember that we obtain market supply curves by adding the amounts supplied by each producer at each price) and combines it with the demand curve to determine the world oil price.

To explore all of the slides in this figure, see the online version at https://tinyco.re/5419253.

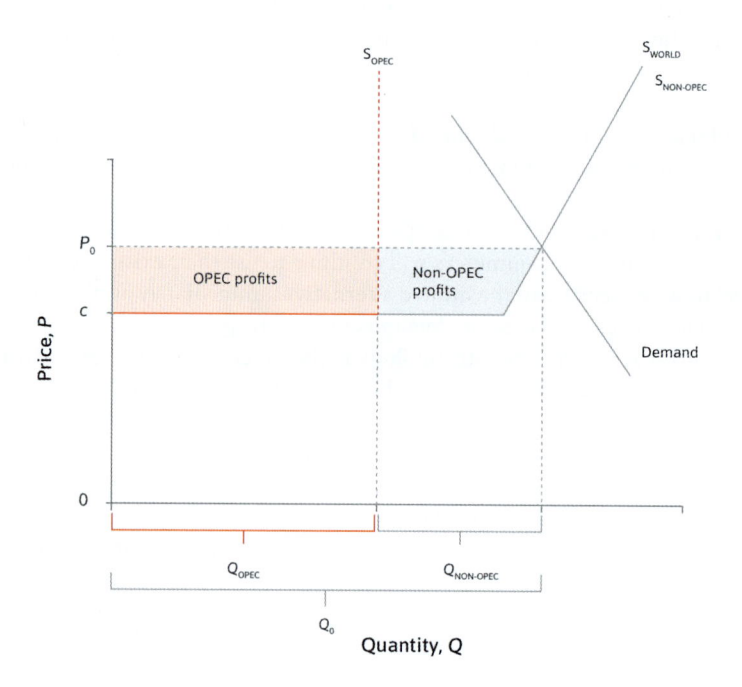

Figure 7.27 The world market for oil.

1. OPEC supply
OPEC's members can increase production easily within their current capacity, without increasing their marginal cost c. OPEC quotas limit their total production to Q_{OPEC}.

2. The non-OPEC supply
Non-OPEC countries can produce oil at the same marginal cost c until they get close to capacity, when their marginal costs rise steeply.

3. World supply curve
Total world supply is the sum of production by OPEC and other countries at each price.

4. The equilibrium oil price
The demand curve is steep—world demand is inelastic in the short run. In equilibrium, the price is P_0 and total oil consumption Q_0 is equal to Q_{OPEC} + $Q_{non-OPEC}$.

5. Profit
OPEC's profit is $(P_0 - c) \times Q_{OPEC}$, the area of the rectangle below P_0. Non-OPEC profit is the rest of the shaded area below P_0.

The 1970s oil price shocks

In 1973 and 1974, OPEC countries imposed a partial oil embargo in response to the Middle East war. In 1979 and 1980, oil production by Iran and Iraq fell because of the supply disruptions following the Iranian Revolution and the outbreak of the Iran–Iraq war. These are represented in Figure 7.28 by a leftward shift of the world supply curve S_{world}, driven by a reduction in the volume of OPEC production to Q'_{OPEC}. Total production and consumption falls, but because demand is very price inelastic, the percentage increase in price is much larger than the percentage decrease in quantity. This is what we see in the data in Figure 7.28. The oil price (in 2014 US dollars) goes from $18 per barrel in 1973 to $56 in 1974, and then to $106 in 1980, but the declines in world oil consumption after these price shocks are small by comparison (−2% between 1973 and 1975, and −10% between 1979 and 1983).

The 2000–2008 oil price shocks

The years 2000 to 2008 were a period of rapid economic growth in industrializing countries, especially China and India. The **income elasticity of demand** for oil and oil products is higher in these countries than in developed market economies, and demand for car ownership and tourist air travel is growing relatively rapidly as the countries become wealthier. This increase in income moves the demand curve to the right, as shown in Figure 7.28. In this case, it is the inelastic short-run supply curve for oil that accounts for the big increase in price and only a modest increase in world oil consumption. The sharp price decrease in 2009 has the same explanation, but in reverse—the financial crisis of 2008–2009 was a negative demand shock that moved the demand curve to the left, so world consumption fell by about 3%, and the price of crude fell from over $100 per barrel in the summer of 2008 to $40–50 in early 2009.

> **income elasticity of demand** The percentage change in demand that would occur in response to a 1% increase in the individual's income.

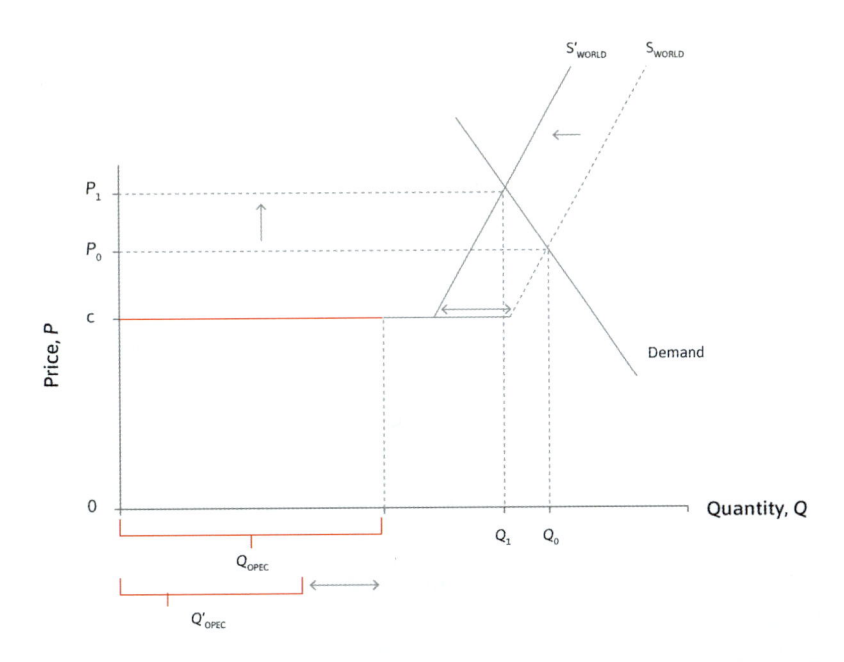

Figure 7.28 The OPEC oil price shocks of the 1970s: OPEC decreases output.

EXERCISE 7.9 THE WORLD MARKET FOR OIL

Using a supply and demand diagram:

1. Illustrate what happens when economic growth boosts world demand
   (a) in the short run
   (b) in the long run as producers invest in new oil wells
   (c) in the long run as consumers find substitutes for oil
2. Similarly, describe the short- and long-run consequences of a negative supply shock similar to the 1970s shock.
3. If you observed an oil price rise, how in principle could you tell whether it was driven by supply-side or demand-side developments?
4. How would the diagram, and the response to shocks, be different if there were:
   (a) a competitive market composed of many producers?
   (b) a single monopoly oil producer?
   (c) an OPEC cartel controlling 100% of world oil production and seeking to maximize the combined profits of its members?
5. Why would individual OPEC member countries have an incentive to produce more than the quota assigned to them?
6. Does this logic carry over to the situation in the real world where there are also non-OPEC producers?

EXERCISE 7.10 THE SHALE OIL REVOLUTION

An important development in the past 10 years has been the re-emergence of the US as a major oil producer via the 'shale oil revolution'. Shale oil is extracted using the technology of hydraulic fracturing or 'fracking'—injecting fluid into ground at high pressure to fracture the rock and allow extraction. In a speech called 'The New Economics of Oil' (https://tinyco.re/9345243) in October 2015, Spencer Dale, group chief economist at oil producer BP PLC, explained how shale oil production differs from traditional extraction.

1. According to Dale, how has the shale oil revolution affected the world market for oil?
2. How will the world oil market be different in future?
3. Explain how our supply and demand diagram should be changed if his analysis is correct.

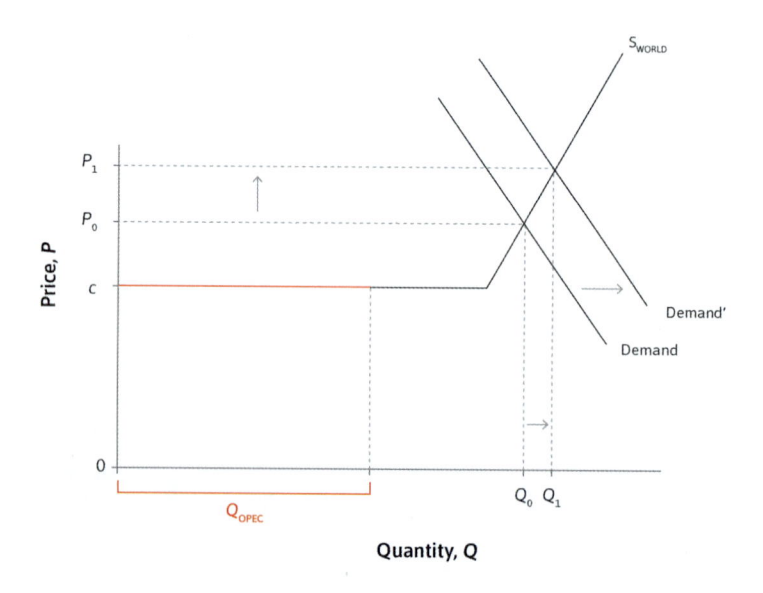

Figure 7.29 The oil price shocks of 2000–2008: Economic growth increases world demand.

7.14 CONCLUSION

This unit has looked at how the firm, as an actor in the economy, decides what prices to set and how much to produce. This decision depends on both the **willingness to pay (WTP)** of its customers (as summarized by the **demand curve** and the price elasticity), and on the firm's cost structure.

One advantage of large-scale production is lower **unit costs** due to increased bargaining power with suppliers, or a high initial **fixed cost**. But firms cannot benefit from **economies of scale** indefinitely.

To our economic toolkit we have added two models of firm behaviour, each relying on different assumptions regarding the nature of the product and the market structure.

	Price-setting firm (monopolistic competitor)	**Price-taking firm**
Setting and assumptions	The firm has few competitors as it produces a **differentiated product**. It faces a downward-sloping product demand curve. The firm sets price to maximize profits (price-setter). There is no **price discrimination**, so the chosen price is the same for all customers.	Competition from other firms producing identical products means that firms have no power to set their own prices. They each face a flat demand curve for their product. Given the market price, the firm chooses the quantity to produce to maximize profits (price-taker).
Economic toolkit	**Constrained optimization problem** The firm chooses the highest **isoprofit curve** possible, given the product demand curve as a constraint. The profit-maximizing choice is where the curves are tangent. This is where MRS (slope of isoprofit) equals MRT (slope of demand).	**Supply and demand analysis** The **supply curve** depends on suppliers' **willingness to accept** (their **reservation prices**). Its shape depends on the **marginal cost curve**. The **market-clearing price** is determined by the intersection of market supply and market demand curves.
Main result	Price is greater than marginal cost, and owners receive **economic rents**. There exist **deadweight losses**, meaning there are unexploited gains from trade. The outcome is **Pareto inefficient**.	Price is equal to marginal cost. In this **competitive equilibrium**, **total surplus** is maximized and the outcome is **Pareto efficient**, assuming only buyers and sellers are affected. Owners can only receive dynamic rents when markets are in **disequilibrium** following an **exogenous shock**.

A firm's **market power** determines the **markup** it can set, which is inversely related to the **price elasticity of demand**. **Competition policy** aims to prevent abuses of market power that may result from the formation of **cartels**. The model of perfect competition provides a useful benchmark against which to evaluate economic outcomes.

Price-setting firms face a multitude of decisions every day, and their success depends on more than just 'getting the price right'. As summarized in Figure 7.30, a firm can actively influence both consumer demand and costs in various ways, including innovation, advertising, wage-setting and influencing taxes and environmental regulation.

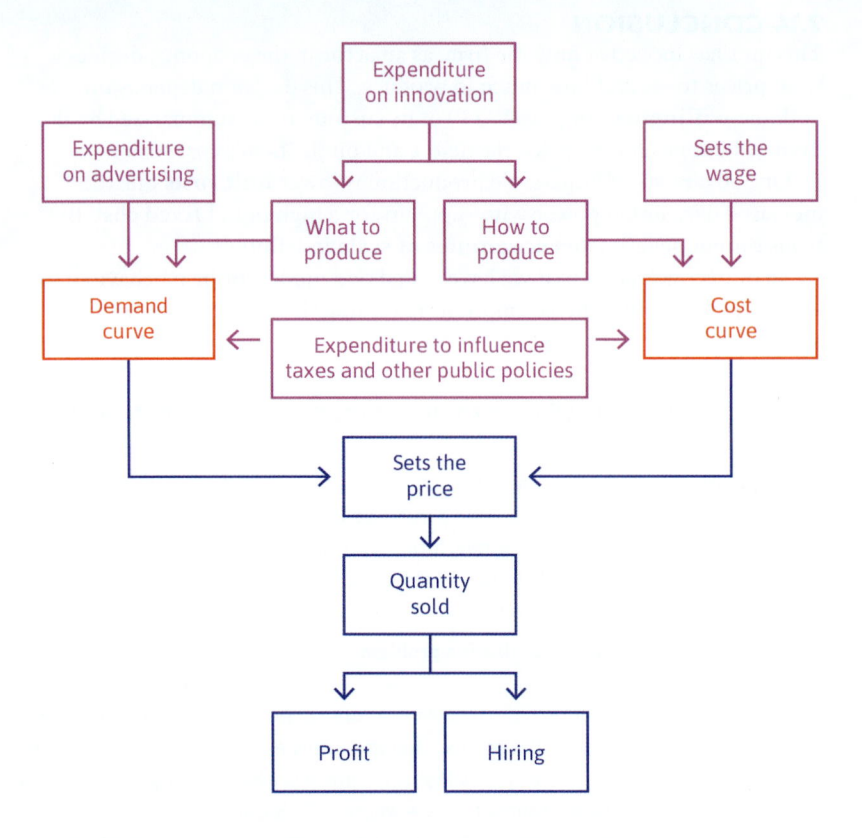

Figure 7.30 The price- and wage-setting firm's decisions.

7.15 DOING ECONOMICS: SUPPLY AND DEMAND

In this unit, we used demand and supply curves to find market equilibrium. But how do we know what the supply and demand curves look like in the real world? Unlike the models in this unit, we cannot ask consumers for their willingness to pay at different prices or ask firms to tell us their profit-maximizing decisions. Instead, usually the best data available are prices and quantities over a number of periods (both of the product we are interested in and of other products), and information about policies and other events that happened in those periods.

In *Doing Economics* Empirical Project 7 we will be using a 'real-world' example (the US market for watermelons in 1930–1951) to learn how to model demand and supply using available data and interpret the results.

> *Learning objectives*
> In this project you will:
>
> - convert values from natural logarithms to base 10 logarithms
> - draw graphs based on equations
> - give an economic interpretation of coefficients in supply and demand equations
> - distinguish between exogenous and endogenous shocks
> - explain how we can use exogenous supply/demand shocks to identify the demand/supply curve.

Go to *Doing Economics* Empirical Project 7 (http://tinyco.re/4242717) to work on this project.

7.16 REFERENCES

Berger, Helge, and Mark Spoerer. 2001. 'Economic Crises and the European Revolutions of 1848'. *The Journal of Economic History* 61 (2): pp. 293–326.

Cournot, Augustin, and Irving Fischer. (1838) 1971. *Researches into the Mathematical Principles of the Theory of Wealth*. New York, NY: A. M. Kelley.

Eisen, Michael. 2011. 'Amazon's $23,698,655.93 book about flies'. It is NOT junk. (https://tinyco.re/0044329). Updated 22 April 2011.

Feiwel, George R. (ed.). 1989. *Joan Robinson and Modern Economic Theory*. New York: New York University Press: p. 4.

Giberson, Michael. 2010. 'I Cringe When I See Hayek's Knowledge Problem Wielded as a Rhetorical Club' (https://tinyco.re/9189202). Knowledge Problem. Updated 5 April.

Gilbert, Richard J., and Michael L. Katz. 2001. 'An Economist's Guide to US v. Microsoft' (https://tinyco.re/7683758). *Journal of Economic Perspectives* 15 (2): pp. 25–44.

Hayek, Friedrich A. 1994. *The Road to Serfdom* (https://tinyco.re/0683881). Chicago, Il: University of Chicago Press.

Kay, John. 'The Structure of Strategy' (https://tinyco.re/7663497). Reprinted from *Business Strategy Review* 1993.

Krajewski, Markus. 2014. 'The Great Lightbulb Conspiracy' (https://tinyco.re/3479245). *IEEE Spectrum*. Updated 25 September 2014.

Marshall, Alfred. 1920. *Principles of Economics* (https://tinyco.re/0560708). 8th ed. London: MacMillan & Co.

Miller, R. G., and S. R. Sorrell. 2013. 'The Future of Oil Supply' (https://tinyco.re/6167443). *Philosophical Transactions of the Royal Society A: Mathematical, Physical and Engineering Sciences* 372 (2006) (December).

Owen, Nick A., Oliver R. Inderwildi, and David A. King. 2010. 'The Status of Conventional World Oil Reserves—Hype or Cause for Concern?' (https://tinyco.re/8978100) *Energy Policy* 38 (8): pp. 4743–49.

Pigou, A. C. (editor). 1966. *Memorials of Alfred Marshall*. New York, A. M. Kelley. pp.427–28.

Reyes, Jose Daniel, and Julia Oliver. 2013. 'Quinoa: The Little Cereal That Could' (https://tinyco.re/9266629). The Trade Post. 22 November 2013.

Robinson, Joan. 1933. *The Economics of Imperfect Competition* (https://tinyco.re/1766675). London: MacMillan & Co.

Schumacher, Ernst F. 1973. *Small is Beautiful: Economics as if People Mattered* (https://tinyco.re/3749799). New York, NY: HarperCollins.

Seabright, Paul. 2010. *The Company of Strangers: A Natural History of Economic Life* (Revised Edition). Princeton, NJ: Princeton University Press.

Shum, Matthew. 2004. 'Does Advertising Overcome Brand Loyalty? Evidence from the Breakfast-Cereals Market' (https://tinyco.re/3909324). *Journal of Economics & Management Strategy* 13 (2): pp. 241–72.

The Economist. 2001. 'Is Santa a Deadweight Loss?' (https://tinyco.re/7728778) Updated 20 December 2001.

The Economist. 2014. Keynes and Hayek: Prophets for Today (https://tinyco.re/0417474). Updated 14 March 2014.

Clothing workers in Huaibei, East China

8.1 INTRODUCTION

- By putting the labour market and the product market together in a single model, we have a way to understand how unemployment and inequality are determined in the economy as a whole.
- The labour market functions quite differently from the bread market, described in the previous unit, because firms cannot purchase the work of employees directly but only hire their time.
- In modern economies, most product markets—also unlike the bread market—are dominated by large firms that face downward-sloping demand curves. These so-called 'monopolistic competitors' can control the prices at which their goods sell, and they set prices to maximize their profits.
- The outcome of the wage-setting process across all firms in the economy is the wage-setting curve, which shows for each unemployment rate the lowest wage that will motivate employees to work.
- The outcome of the price-setting process across all firms is the price-setting curve, which gives the value of the real wage that is consistent with the level of productivity and the extent of competition in markets for goods and services.
- The wage-setting and price-setting curves together determine the structural unemployment in the economy.
- The level of structural unemployment can be altered by public policies that change the productivity of labour, the degree of competition facing firms in product markets, the extent and nature of labour unions and labour law, and the unemployment benefit.
- Changes in how the labour and product markets function alter the distribution of income as measured by the Lorenz curve and the Gini coefficient.
- The model of the whole economy—product and labour market together—helps to explain how the growing monopoly power of firms has contributed to rising inequality in the US economy.

Mining was not a job, it was a way of life for Doug Grey (https://tinyco.re/ 9964603), a rigger who operated giant cranes at mines in the Northern Territory, Australia. In the 1990s, he helped construct the MacArthur River zinc mine, one of the world's largest, where his son Rob got his first job. 'I ended up driving ore trucks,' Rob recalled, 'that was an awesome opportunity.'

Rob, it seemed then, had been born at the right time. He entered the labour market just as the worldwide natural resources boom was taking off, driven by the demand from China's rapidly growing economy. Rob lived in Thailand for a time, spending little. He would take a flight to his job in Borroloola, a round trip of 10,000 km.

At about the time that Rob started work, Doug, the elder Grey, took a job at the Pilbara iron ore mine in Western Australia, which paid about twice the average family income in Australia at the time. Both father and son were putting away substantial savings.

But by 2015, the natural resource boom was a distant memory, and the price of ore and zinc continued to plummet. Rob and his fellow miners were worried. 'Everybody knew the economic downturn and commodity prices were a problem. We had that in the back of our minds.' Their dream economy couldn't last. 'It was … obvious … that it was coming to an end,' Doug said.

And it did. In late 2015, Rob got the bad news: 'Two days into my break the general manager called and said, "Thanks for your service, we appreciate it, we have to let you go."' His father, too, was laid off.

Driving ore trucks is Rob's passion and he still hopes to get back behind the wheel. But that is not going to happen, at least not at the Pilbara mine where his dad once worked. Faced with collapsing demand, the mining company cut production, and also sought to drastically reduce costs. As part of this process, the company replaced human labour with machines wherever possible. In the Pilbara mine, *nobody* is behind the wheel of any of their giant robot ore trucks that are now being 'driven' by university graduates with joysticks 1,200 km away in Perth.

The rise and fall of the Grey family's economic fortunes is an example of the workings of the labour market in the mining and construction industries in Western Australia and the Northern Territory. Figure 8.1 shows that their experience was far from unusual. The boom in ore prices (in the top figure) made mining highly profitable, leading to strong demand for labour, which eventually dried up the pool of unemployed riggers and truck drivers. Mining companies had no choice but to pay extraordinarily high salaries, and while the mining boom lasted, the companies remained highly profitable.

The downturn in commodity prices began in mid-2011 and unemployment began to rise. Born-at-the-right-time Rob Grey's luck had run out.

We learn from the patterns in the Australian labour market that wages increase when unemployment falls. From Unit 6 (page 258), we know that firms have to set higher wages to ensure that employees work hard and well when unemployment in the economy is low. And from Unit 6 (page 257), we also know that there will always be more people seeking jobs than the number of jobs offered. These are the involuntarily unemployed.

The model we develop in this unit helps to explain why, over very long periods, unemployment rates differ between countries. Take, for example, two large European countries, Germany and Spain. These countries share many characteristics. As well as belonging to the European Union, which provides conditions for borderless trade, firms based in both countries compete in global markets on the same terms. They share access to the same robot technologies and other labour-saving innovations.

8.1 INTRODUCTION

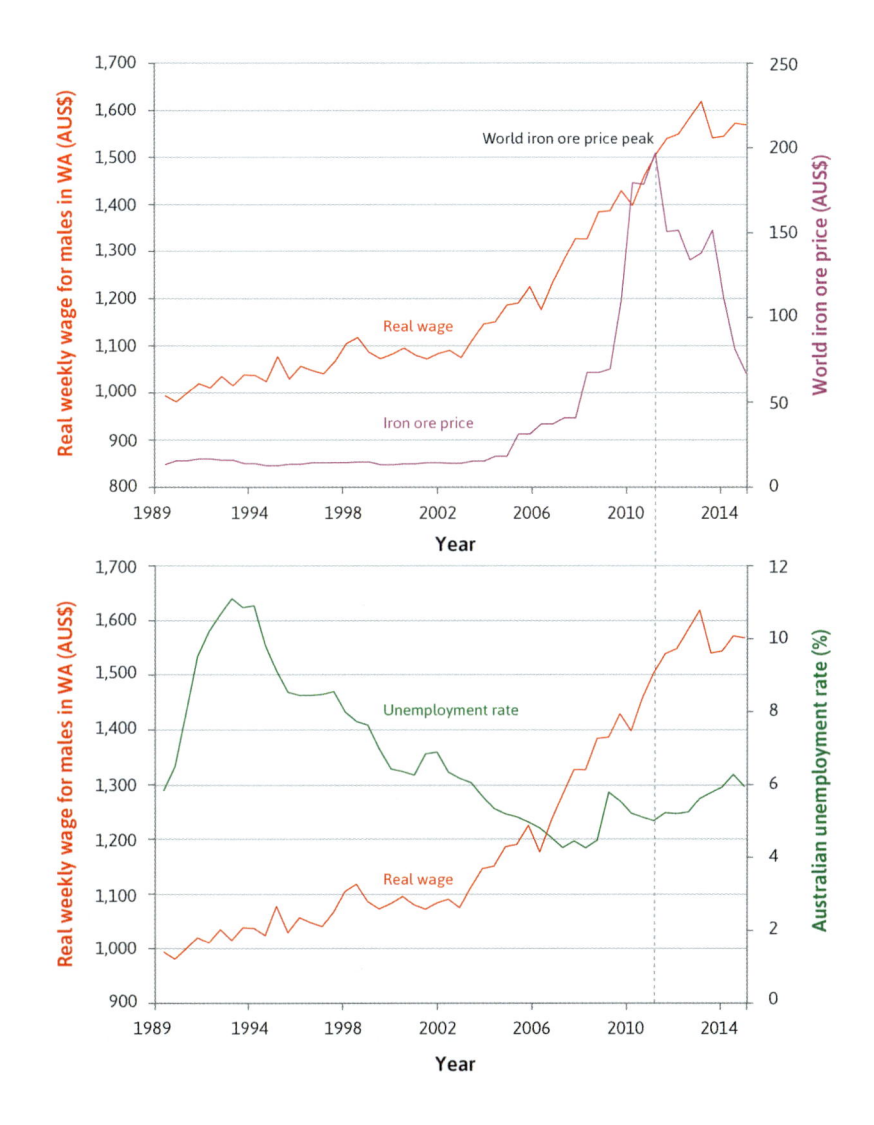

Figure 8.1 Real weekly earnings for males in Western Australia (left-hand axis), world price of iron ore and unemployment rate in Australia (right-hand axis), (1989–2015).

To explore all of the slides in this figure, see the online version at https://tinyco.re/7230123.

Australian Bureau of Statistics (https://tinyco.re/1648810) and International Monetary Fund (https://tinyco.re/8213274). *Note*: Unemployment rates are seasonally adjusted.

1. Weekly earnings
The chart shows real weekly earnings for males in Western Australia, together with the world price of iron ore in the top panel and the unemployment rate in Australia in the bottom panel. As the unemployment rate dropped from 1994, real wages began to grow rapidly.

2. Growth slows, unemployment rises
Following the peak in iron ore prices, unemployment began to rise and real wage growth slowed.

333

The two countries appear to be equally vulnerable to what are generally considered to be the two potential 'job killers' for the high-income countries in the early twenty-first century—automation and globalization. Yet, for the period from 1960 to 2018, the unemployment rate in Germany averaged 5.5%, compared with a rate more than double this in Spain (13.8%).

The comparison of Spain and Germany directs attention to the contrasting ways in which both labour and product markets work in different countries. The model of the economy as a whole we develop in this unit helps to explain these differences, and how they can lead to different outcomes for unemployment and inequality. This information in turn can be the basis of more effective policies to sustain high wages and employment, and to limit the extent of inequality.

8.2 MEASURING THE ECONOMY: EMPLOYMENT AND UNEMPLOYMENT

What does it mean to say that the unemployment rate was 13.8% in Spain and 5.5% in Germany? What exactly is '**unemployment**'?

According to the standardized definition of the International Labour Organization (ILO) (https://tinyco.re/8208329), the unemployed are the people who:

- were without work during a reference period (usually four weeks); in other words, they were not in paid employment or self-employment
- were available for work
- were seeking work; in other words, they had taken specific steps in that period to seek paid employment or self-employment.

Figure 8.2 provides an overview of the labour market and shows how these components fit together. We begin on the left-hand side, with the population. The next box shows the **population of working age**. This is the total population, minus children and those over 64. It is divided into two parts: the **labour force** and those out of the labour force (known as the **inactive population**). People out of the labour force are not employed or actively looking for work, for example, people unable to work due to sickness or disability, students, or parents who stay at home to raise children. Only members of the labour force can be considered as employed or unemployed.

There are a number of statistics that are useful for evaluating labour market performance in a country and for comparing labour markets between countries. The statistics depend on the relative sizes of the boxes shown in Figure 8.2.

Participation rate

The first is the **participation rate**, which shows the proportion of the working-age population that is in the labour force. It is calculated as follows:

$$\text{participation rate} = \frac{\text{labour force}}{\text{population of working age}}$$

$$= \frac{\text{employed} + \text{unemployed}}{\text{population of working age}}$$

---

unemployment A situation in which a person who is able and willing to work is not employed.

population of working age A statistical convention, which in many countries is all people aged between 15 and 64 years.

labour force The number of people in the population of working age who are, or wish to be, in work outside the household. They are either employed (including self-employed) or unemployed. See also: unemployment rate, employment rate, participation rate.

inactive population People in the population of working age who are neither employed nor actively looking for paid work. Those working in the home raising children, for example, are not considered as being in the labour force and therefore are classified this way.

participation rate The ratio of the number of people in the labour force to the population of working age. See also: labour force, population of working age.

Unemployment rate

Next is the most commonly cited labour market statistic—the **unemployment rate**. This shows the proportion of the labour force that is unemployed. It is calculated as follows:

$$\text{unemployment rate} = \frac{\text{unemployed}}{\text{labour force}}$$

Employment rate

Lastly, we come to the **employment rate**, which shows the proportion of the population of working age that are in paid work or self-employed. It is calculated as follows:

$$\text{employment rate} = \frac{\text{employed}}{\text{population of working age}}$$

It is important to note that the denominator (the statistic on the bottom of the fraction) is different for the unemployment and the employment rate. Hence, two countries with the same unemployment rate can differ in their employment rates if one has a high participation rate and the other has a low one.

Comparing labour markets

The table in Figure 8.3 provides a picture of the labour markets in four countries—Australia, Germany, Norway, and Spain—between 2000 and 2016, and shows how the labour market statistics relate to each other.

It also shows that the structure of the labour market differs widely among different countries. We can see that the Norwegian labour market worked better than the Spanish labour market in the last 17 years—Norway had a much higher employment rate and a much lower unemployment rate. Norway also had a higher participation rate, which is a reflection of the higher proportion of women in the labour force.

Norway and Spain are illustrations of two common cases. Norway is a low-unemployment, high-employment economy (the other Scandinavian countries—Sweden, Denmark, and Finland—are similar; and in the table, Australia is the country most similar to Norway). Spain is a high-unemployment, low-employment economy (the other southern European economies—Portugal, Italy and Greece—are other examples). Other combinations are possible, however—Germany's participation rate is low like Spain's but its unemployment and employment rate performance are much better.

> **unemployment rate** The ratio of the number of the unemployed to the total labour force. (Note that the employment rate and unemployment rate do not sum to 100%, as they have different denominators.) See also: *labour force, employment rate*.
>
> **employment rate** The ratio of the number of employed to the population of working age. See also: *population of working age*.

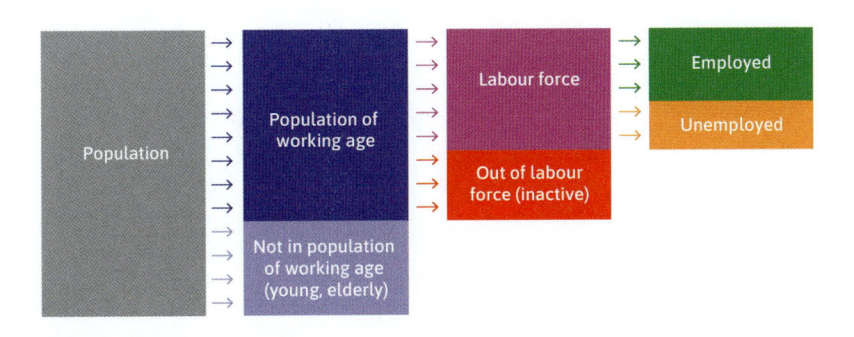

Figure 8.2 The labour market.

EXERCISE 8.1 USING EXCEL: EMPLOYMENT, UNEMPLOYMENT, AND PARTICIPATION

1. Visit the ILO's website and use the ILOSTAT Database (https://tinyco.re/2173706) to calculate the average employment, unemployment, and participation rates over the period 2000–2016, for two economies of your choice.
2. Create appropriate chart(s) to display these statistics for the countries in Figure 8.3 and your chosen countries. Using your chart(s), describe the similarities and differences in these statistics.
3. After studying this unit, use the model of the labour market to suggest possible reasons for the differences in unemployment rates in these countries. You may need to find out more about the labour markets in your chosen countries.

QUESTION 8.1 CHOOSE THE CORRECT ANSWER(S)
Which of the following statements are correct?

☐ participation rate = employed ÷ labour force
☐ unemployment rate = unemployed ÷ population of working age
☐ employment rate = employed ÷ population of working age
☐ employment rate + unemployment rate = 1

International Labour Organization. 2018. ILOSTAT Database (https://tinyco.re/2173706).

	Australia	Germany	Norway	Spain
Number of persons, millions				
Population of working age	17.2	69.6	3.5	37.6
Labour force	11.1	41.0	2.5	21.6
Out of labour force (inactive)	6.1	28.5	1.0	16.0
Employed	10.5	38.0	2.4	18.1
Unemployed	0.6	3.1	0.1	3.5
Rates (%)				
Participation rate	11.1/17.2 = 65%	41.0/69.6 = 59%	2.5/3.5 = 71%	21.6/37.6 = 58%
Employment rate	10.5/17.2 = 61%	38.0/69.6 = 55%	2.4/3.5 = 69%	18.1/37.6 = 48%
Unemployment rate	0.6/11.1 = 6%	3.1/41.0 = 7%	0.1/2.5 = 4%	3.5/21.6 = 16%

Figure 8.3 Labour market statistics for Australia, Germany, Norway, and Spain (averages over 2000–2016).

8.3 THE LABOUR MARKET, THE PRODUCT MARKET AND THE AGGREGATE ECONOMY: THE WS/PS MODEL

To see why, over the long run, some countries (like Spain) have had much higher unemployment rates than others (like Germany), we will set out a model for an entire economy. This is referred to as a model of the aggregate economy or the macroeconomy. Economists use the term *aggregate* (meaning 'whole') to describe economy-wide facts or variables, like the labour market statistics in the previous section.

The same model will be used in Section 8.9 (page 359) to show what happens when there is a change in the monopoly power of firms over time. This has happened in the past 30 years, for example, with the growth in market power of large firms in the technology sector.

The actors in the labour market include the employees, and the owners or managers of each firm. But within the management of the firm, there are two distinct actors: the human resources department ('HR') is in charge of setting wages to ensure that employees 'work', while the marketing department is tasked with setting a price that will maximize the firm's profits.

The model of the aggregate economy has two parts:

- *The labour market*: In which the focus is the relationship between employers and workers and on how wages are set by HR.
- *The product market*: In which the focus is the relationship between firms and their customers and on how prices are set by the marketing department.

> We give the actors in our model these names, and imagine them in different departments, because this clarifies two different decisions taken in the operation of a firm. In reality, HR and marketing departments influence these decisions, but do not make them.

Putting them together for all firms gives us a model of the aggregate economy.

- *From the labour market, we get the wage-setting (WS) curve*: For every level of employment it gives the real wage that HR would like to pay.
- *From the product market, we get the price-setting (PS) curve*: It tells us the real wage that results from the price-setting decisions of Marketing.

Where the two curves intersect shows the level of employment (and unemployment) and the real wage for which the decisions of the two departments are consistent. This is the equilibrium of the whole economy; you can think of it as a situation in which both Marketing and HR in all firms are satisfied.

> **WS/PS model** Model of the aggregate economy that combines wage-setting (WS) and price-setting (PS) decisions. Where the WS and PS curves intersect is the Nash equilibrium and determines structural unemployment and the real wage. *See also, wage-setting curve, price-setting curve, structural unemployment.*

We call the two curves—the wage-setting (WS) curve and the price-setting (PS) curve—including the reasoning behind them, the model of the aggregate economy. And we refer to it by its nickname, the **WS/PS model**.

8.4 THE LABOUR MARKET AND THE WAGE-SETTING CURVE (FIRMS AND WORKERS)

We started with the labour market and the fact that Rob Grey and his father—the Australian miners—did well while the economy was booming, earning high wages and having little fear of unemployment, and not so well when the economy hit the doldrums.

We generalize their experience in Figure 8.4, where the horizontal axis represents the proportion of the working-age population and goes up to a value of 1. The vertical axis is the economy-wide real wage.

- *The labour force is the vertical line furthest to the right:* It has a value less than 1, depending on the participation rate.
- *Inactive workers* are to the right of the labour force line.
- *The employment rate* is the vertical line to the left of the labour force, indicating the share of the population who are actually working.
- *The unemployment rate is the proportion of those in the labour force who are not employed:* that is, those workers in between the employment rate line and the labour force line.

> **wage-setting (WS) curve** The curve—arising from the wage-setting decisions of firms in the labour market—that gives the real wage necessary at each level of economy-wide employment to provide workers with incentives to work hard and well.
>
> **worker's best response function (to wage)** The amount of work that a worker chooses to perform as her best response to each wage that the employer may offer. *Also known as: best response curve.*

The upward-sloping line is called the **wage-setting (WS) curve**. The wage-setting curve for the whole economy is based directly on the employer's wage-setting decision and the employee's effort decision in an economy that is composed of many firms, like the economy we modelled in Unit 6 (page 244).

Follow the analysis in Figure 8.4 to understand the upward-sloping wage-setting curve. We focus on two specific rates of unemployment—5% and 12%—but there is nothing special about these numbers. They are purely illustrative.

Figure 8.5 brings together Figure 8.4 (the economy-wide wage-setting curve) and Figure 6.7 (page 256) (how the firm sets the wage). The top panel of Figure 8.5 shows the employee's **best response curve** at the two unemployment rates of 12% and 5%. The same analysis applies to any other unemployment rate you wish to choose.

As we saw in Unit 6, a higher unemployment rate reduces the reservation wage, because a worker faces a longer expected period of unemployment if they lose a job. This weakens the bargaining power of the employee and shifts the best response curve to the left. With an unemployment rate of 12%, the reservation wage is shown by point F. The employer's profit-maximizing choice is point A with the low wage (w_L).

In the lower panel, we plot point A on the wage-setting curve. The dashed line from an unemployment rate of 12% indicates that the wage is set at w_L. We assume a fixed size for the labour force and the horizontal axis gives the number of workers employed, N. As employment increases to the right, the unemployment rate falls.

Using exactly the same reasoning, we find the profit-maximizing wage set when unemployment is 5%. Both the reservation wage and the wage set by the employer are higher, as shown by point B. This gives the second point on the wage-setting curve in the lower panel.

When Rob and Doug Grey write their biography, they will label point B as a Golden Age, early in this century, when Rob was living in Thailand and flying to his job at Borroloola, and his father was operating giant cranes at the Pilbara mine. Point A is Paradise Lost, after the minerals boom ended.

8.4 THE LABOUR MARKET AND THE WAGE-SETTING CURVE (FIRMS AND WORKERS)

We derived the wage-setting curve as part of the **labour discipline model**, which was designed to illustrate how employees and employers interact when setting wages and determining the level of work effort. We will use the same model when we describe government policies to alter the level of unemployment in the entire economy. Later in this unit, we will look at the ways in which labour unions can affect the wage-setting process and so alter the workings of the labour market.

labour discipline model A model that explains how employers set wages so that employees receive an economic rent (called employment rent), which provides workers an incentive to work hard in order to avoid job termination. *See also: employment rent, efficiency wages.*

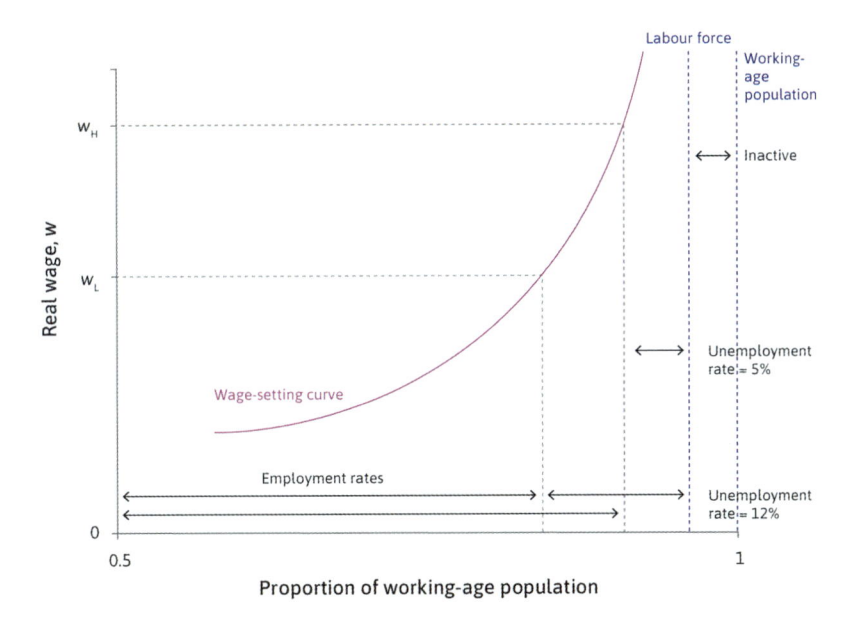

To explore all of the slides in this figure, see the online version at https://tinyco.re/2197400.

Figure 8.4 The wage-setting (WS) curve: Labour discipline and unemployment in the economy as a whole.

1. The wage-setting (WS) curve
The upward-sloping line is called the wage-setting curve.

2. The wage set by firms when unemployment is high
At a relatively high unemployment rate (we chose 12%) in the economy, the employee's reservation wage is low and they will put in high effort for a relatively low wage. Therefore, the firm's chosen wage is low.

3. The wage set by firms when unemployment is low
At a relatively low unemployment rate (in this case, 5%) in the economy, the employee's reservation wage is high and they will not put in adequate effort unless the wage is high. Therefore, the firm's chosen wage is higher.

4. Employment, unemployment, and out of the labour force
The right-most dotted blue line shows the total working-age population, which is divided into the employed, the unemployed, and those not participating in the labour force.

339

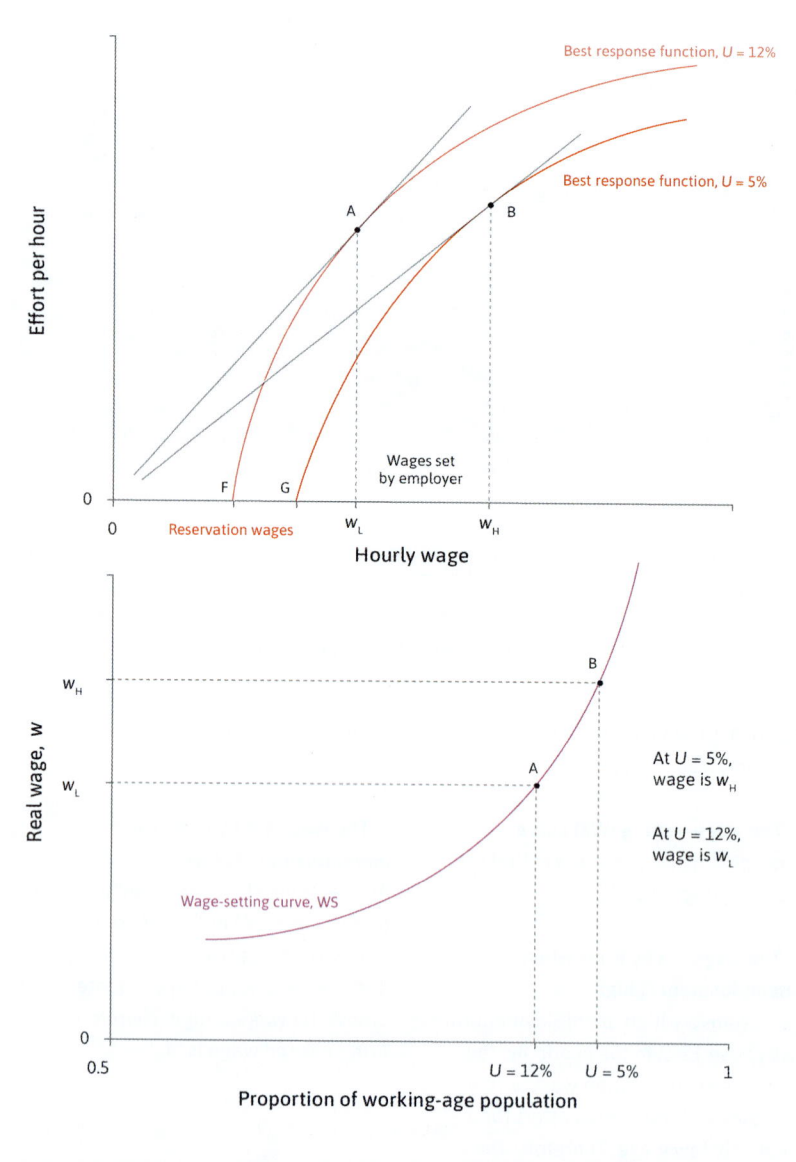

Figure 8.5 Deriving the wage-setting curve: Varying the unemployment rate in the economy.

8.4 THE LABOUR MARKET AND THE WAGE-SETTING CURVE (FIRMS AND WORKERS)

Real wages and nominal wages

When the employer sets the wage, it is set in nominal terms, that is in euros, dollars, or pesos, for example. But workers care about what they can buy with their wages. They care about the **real wage**, which is written as $w = W/P$, where P is the price level in the economy. The price level is constructed by combining the prices of the goods and services in a typical basket of goods consumed by the worker. An example of a price level is the **consumer price index (CPI)**. Throughout the analysis of the interaction between the employee and employer in wage-setting, we use the real wage, w, because it is the real wage that motivates the worker to work hard.

The wage-setting curve for the US economy

Figure 8.6 is a wage-setting curve estimated from data for the US. Note that, in Figure 8.6, the horizontal axis shows the unemployment rate explicitly, falling from left to right. On the vertical axis is the real wage, measured by real annual earnings. By using data on unemployment rates and wages in local areas, economists can estimate and plot the wage-setting curve for an economy.

Wage-setting curves have been estimated for many economies. David Blanchflower and Andrew Oswald explain how it is done in their paper 'The Wage Curve' (https://tinyco.re/9574365).

Simplifying the model

We can simplify the worker motivation problem and the wage curve by letting there be just two levels of effort:

- 'working': providing the level of effort that the firm's owners and managers have set as sufficient
- 'shirking': providing no effort at all.

This will be useful later because it will allow us to take the level of effort as given with wages being set to ensure this.

> **real wage** The nominal wage, adjusted to take account of changes in prices between different time periods. It measures the amount of goods and services the worker can buy. *See also:* nominal wage.
>
> **consumer price index (CPI)** A measure of the general level of prices that consumers have to pay for goods and services, including consumption taxes.

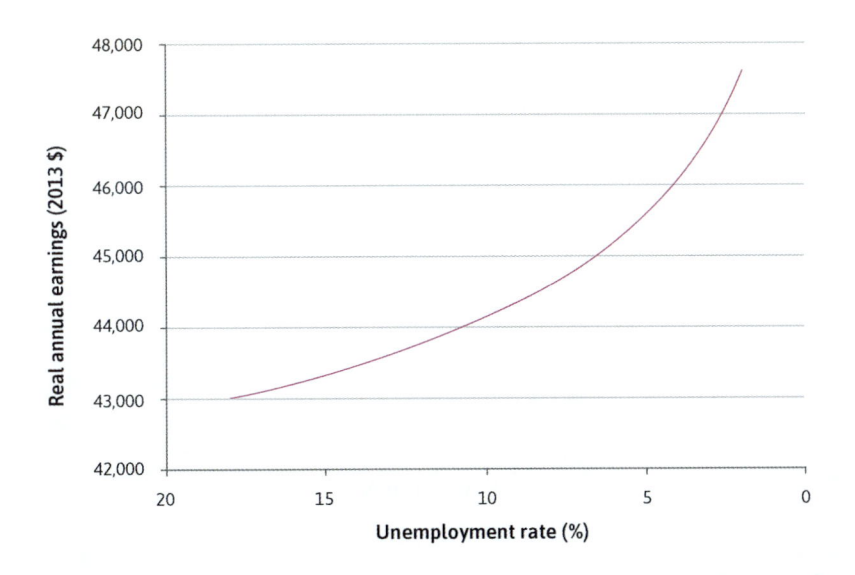

Figure 8.6 A wage-setting curve estimated for the US economy (1979–2013).

Estimated by Stephen Machin (UCL, 2015) from Current Population Survey (https://tinyco.re/5638236) microdata from the Outgoing Rotation Groups for 1979 to 2013.

In this case, the worker is represented as similar to a machine with just one speed, and it is either 'on' or 'off'. As shown in Figure 8.7, the wage curve is the boundary between two 'regions': on and above the wage curve are all the combinations of the real wage and employment level for which employees work, and below it the combinations for which employees shirk.

We will use this 'work or shirk' simplification in the model from now on.

What shifts the wage-setting curve?

What determines the height of the wage-setting curve? In Unit 6, we studied the determinants of the cost of job loss. For any unemployment rate, a change in any of the elements raising the **employment rent** a worker gets from their job shifts the wage-setting curve downwards, as shown in the table in Figure 8.8.

For example, because a lower unemployment benefit makes it more costly if you lose your job, your employment rent is higher and the firm can set a lower wage and you will work, rather than shirk. Another example is an increase in the labour force. If there are more people searching for jobs, then you can expect to remain without work for longer if you lose your job. This increases the rents you get from your current job and shifts the wage-setting curve downwards.

A new technology that allows easier monitoring of shirking (such as the use of GPS trackers in trucks, monitoring their location at any time) makes detection of shirking less costly; the firm can set a lower wage and the worker will work rather than shirk. The wage-setting curve shifts downwards.

employment rent The economic rent a worker receives when the net value of her job exceeds the net value of her next best alternative (that is, being unemployed). *Also known as: cost of job loss.*

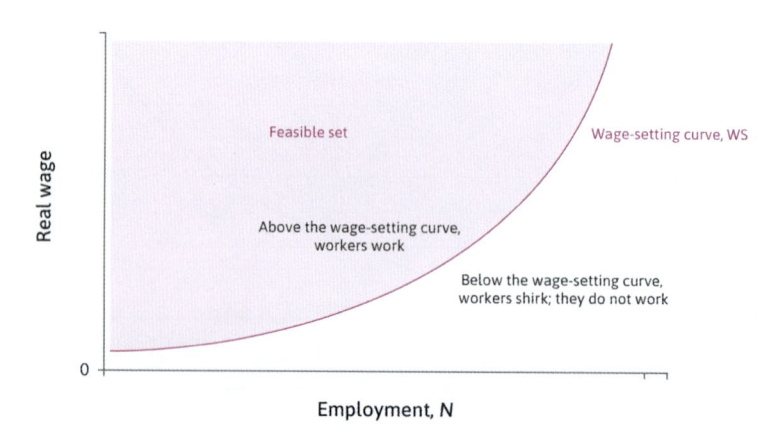

Figure 8.7 The wage-setting curve: The wage level required to make employees work rather than shirk.

8.4 THE LABOUR MARKET AND THE WAGE-SETTING CURVE (FIRMS AND WORKERS)

EXERCISE 8.2 SHIFTS IN THE WAGE-SETTING CURVE
1. Referring back to Unit 6 (page 229), provide a brief explanation of the shift in the wage-setting curve for each row in Figure 8.8, using a diagram to show the best response function and the wage-setting curve. For the second and third rows, give an example from a real-world workplace.
2. Explain why a rise in the unemployment rate shifts the best response function but not the wage-setting curve.

Change	Shifts the wage-setting curve
Decrease in unemployment benefit	Down
Increase in social stigma attached to being unemployed	Down
A decrease in the disutility of working	Down

Figure 8.8 Shifts in the wage-setting curve.

QUESTION 8.2 CHOOSE THE CORRECT ANSWER(S)
Figure 8.5 (page 340) depicts the wage-setting curve and how it is derived using the best response function of the employees and the iso-cost lines for effort of the employers.

Based on this figure:

- ☐ A cut in the unemployment benefit would shift the best response function to the left and raise the wage-setting curve.
- ☐ If the expected period of unemployment increased, it would shift the best response function to the right, raising the wage-setting curve.
- ☐ In a country in which the stigma attached to unemployment is high, the wage-setting curve would be lower.
- ☐ A sudden drop in the working-age population (due, for example, to the retirement of the baby-boomer generation) would shift the wage-setting curve lower.

8.5 THE PRODUCT MARKET AND THE PRICE-SETTING CURVE (FIRMS AND CUSTOMERS)

The wage-setting curve alone does not fix the level of employment in the model—the economy could be at any combination of employment and the real wage along it. To pin this down, we need to bring in the market for goods and services, the product market, and another curve, the **price-setting (PS) curve**.

It gets its name because it gives the real wage that is the outcome of the choice by the firm's marketing department of a profit-maximizing *price* for their products. We will see how this price-setting curve is determined just below; but first we explain how bringing together the labour market and the product market in the WS and PS curves provides the information we need to determine the wage and employment level in the economy.

The two curves intersect at the real wage and level of employment (and the associated rate of unemployment) the economy can sustain. It is an equilibrium in the labour market and in the product market because:

- *If the economy is on the wage-setting curve, workers won't shirk:* At this rate of unemployment, this is the real wage at which workers will provide adequate effort and production can take place.
- *If the economy is on the price-setting curve, then given their costs and the markup, firms are setting their profit-maximizing price:* The result of that decision is a real wage shown by the price-setting curve.

When the economy is at the intersection of the wage- and price-setting curves, employees provide adequate effort *and* firms are willing to employ that number of workers because, given the demand they face for their output and their costs, the firms are setting their profit-maximizing price.

This is what is called the **structural unemployment**, because it is the equilibrium level of unemployment determined by the two curves, representing the structure of the economy: profit-maximizing price-setting by firms in product markets, and profit-maximizing wage-setting by firms in labour markets. Structural unemployment is affected by shifts in the wage- and price-setting curves. What is called cyclical unemployment varies over the business cycle (we address this at the end of this unit).

> **price-setting (PS) curve** The curve—arising from the price-setting decisions of firms in markets for goods and services (the product market)—that gives the real wage paid when firms choose their profit-maximizing price.

> **structural unemployment** The level of unemployment at the Nash equilibrium of the labour and product market model.

Price-setting and the price-setting real wage: A numerical example

To understand the key idea on which the price-setting real wage is based, think first of an economy composed of just a single firm.

- *It employs many workers, paying them a nominal wage, W:* This is set by the firm as described in the previous section, and in Unit 6.
- *It sells its product at a price P:* This is also set by the firm and described in Unit 7 (page 286).

The real wage that the workers receive will be W/P. In our very simple model, the price set by the firm is also the price level for the economy. This tells us how many units of output they can buy with what they are paid for one hour of their labour.

Think about how the owners of the firm will set the price at which they sell the product. Their reasoning was explained in Unit 7 (page 286) and is depicted in Figure 8.9. Given their costs, including the wage they pay their workers, and the demand curve for their product they will pick the point on the demand curve that is on the highest isoprofit curve, that is, point A, with price P_A.

Given the wage the firm is paying, W, this price will then determine the real wage. So W/P_A is the real wage that is on the price-setting curve. Notice, from the figure that had the firm chosen a higher price P_B, their profits would have been lower (shown by the lower isoprofit curve), and the real wage would have been lower too (with a constant W and a higher P, the real wage is lower). Had they chosen point C and price P_C, profits also would have been lower, but in this case the real wage would have been higher.

The price-setting real wage is the real wage that results when the firm sets a price to maximize its profits.

At its profit maximizing price—where the isoprofit curve is tangent to the demand curve—the price is above the firm's **marginal cost**. Remember that in the case where the average cost (or unit cost) is constant, the average and marginal cost curves coincide. This gap is called the **profit margin**, which the firm receives on each unit of output sold.

The size of the profit margin depends on the extent of competition in the market for the firm's product, which is measured by the **elasticity of demand**. If demand is more elastic, the demand curve is flatter and, as we saw in Unit 7 (page 294), this means there are more close competitors to the firm and its profit margin is lower.

By dividing the profit margin (a dollar amount) by the price (in dollars), we get the **markup**, μ (a number between zero and one), chosen by the firm when it sets its price. This summarizes the competitive conditions in the economy (a lower markup indicates more competitive conditions).

Deriving the price-setting real wage: A numerical example

To derive the price-setting real wage, we use three pieces of information about the economy. The nominal wage per hour divided by hourly productivity is the firm's average (or per unit) cost of production. The third element is the markup, which, as we saw in Unit 7 (page 294), reflects the competitive conditions in the economy. Even in our model of a single firm economy, there are two sources of competitive pressure on the firm. The first is the threat from

> **marginal cost** The addition to total costs associated with producing one additional unit of output.
> **profit margin** The difference between the price and the marginal cost.
> **price elasticity of demand** The percentage change in demand that would occur in response to a 1% increase in price. We express this as a positive number. Demand is elastic if this is greater than 1, and inelastic if less than 1.
> **price markup** The price minus the marginal cost, divided by the price. It is inversely proportional to the elasticity of demand for this good.

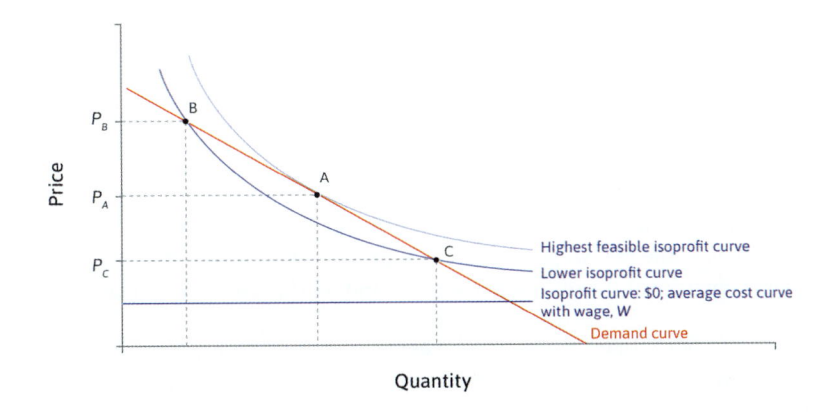

Figure 8.9 The firm sets the profit-maximizing price, P; given the nominal wage, W, this gives the real wage on the price-setting curve, W/P.

new start-ups and the second is from goods and services produced abroad and consumed by households in the home economy.

Given this information, and before drawing a diagram, we can do a simple calculation to work out the value of the real wage that results from price-setting in the product market.

In our numerical example, the wage is $15 per hour. Hourly **labour productivity** is 2—that is, a worker produces 2 units of output per hour—and we assume that this does not vary with the quantity produced. This is the **average product** of labour, λ (lambda). Dividing the hourly wage by hourly productivity, implies that the marginal (and average) cost of production, also called unit cost is $15/2 = $7.50.

The markup, called mu (μ), is 0.25, or equivalently, 25%. See the 'Find out more' box (page 352) to see that the elasticity of demand in this case is 4, meaning a 1% rise in the price would be associated with a 4% fall in the quantity demanded.

Given this information, profit maximization (when the isoprofit curve is tangential to the demand curve) means that:

$$\mu = \frac{\text{profit margin}}{P} = \frac{P - MC}{P}$$

where MC is the firm's marginal cost. (To see the underlying algebra, read the 'Find out more' box at the end of this section.)

Applying the equation to our example, we have $0.25 = (P - 7.50)/P$ and from this, we can calculate that the firm sets the price at $10. Working back the other way, when the price is $10 and the marginal cost is $7.50, we can confirm that the markup is 0.25, or 25%.

Using this information, we can calculate the real wage in the economy, implied by the firm setting its price to maximize profits:

$$\frac{W}{P} = \frac{15}{10} = 1.5$$

Notice that the real wage is in units of output, not dollars. It shows how much output workers can buy with their hourly wage. This number is the price-setting real wage.

The price-setting real wage can be written as:

$$\frac{W}{P} = \lambda(1 - \mu)$$

Using the numbers in our example, the price-setting real wage is:

$$\frac{W}{P} = 2(1 - 0.25) = 1.5$$

The output per worker per hour (2 units) is split up as 1.5, which goes to the employees in the real wage, and 0.5 that goes to owners as profit. Owners get one-quarter of the output per worker and workers get three-quarters.

output per worker per hour	=	real wage per hour	+	real profits per worker per hour
2	=	1.5	+	(0.25 × 2)

labour productivity Total output divided by the number of hours or some other measure of labour input.

average product Total output divided by a particular input, for example per worker (divided by the number of workers) or per worker per hour (total output divided by the total number of hours of labour put in).

8.5 THE PRODUCT MARKET AND THE PRICE-SETTING CURVE (FIRMS AND CUSTOMERS)

Hence:

$$\frac{\text{real}}{\text{wage}} = \frac{\text{output}}{\text{(per worker)}} - \frac{\text{profits in real}}{\text{terms (per worker)}}$$

This equation shows that, as a consequence of firms setting prices to get a markup, μ, the output produced per worker in the economy is divided into the share that goes to workers as wages (1 − μ) and the share that goes to owners as profits (μ).

Price-setting and the price-setting real wage, in diagrams

In Figure 8.5 (page 340), we showed how to derive the economy-wide wage-setting curve from the game between the worker and the employer, when we vary the economy-wide unemployment rate.

In this section, we do the parallel analysis to derive the economy-wide price-setting curve from the price-setting firm's profit-maximizing behaviour, when we vary the economy-wide demand for output.

For the simple model, we continue to assume that there is just a single firm in the economy with labour as its only input.

We now show how to derive the price-setting curve diagrammatically using the same numerical example.

Figure 8.10 shows how the inputs (nominal wage, unit cost, markup) and outputs (price and quantity) of the firm's profit-maximization problem are illustrated in the diagram.

Next, we show in a diagram with employment on the horizontal axis and the real wage on the vertical axis, the combination of real wage and employment associated with point A in Figure 8.10. To translate the quantity produced (60 million) into the number of workers employed, we assume a working day of 7 hours. So in a day, given the per-hour productivity we have assumed (2 units per worker per hour shown in the dashed line in the lower panel of Figure 8.11), each worker produces 14 units. To produce 60 million units, 4.3 million workers are needed. This is shown on the horizontal axis of the lower panel.

The price-setting real wage at point A is 1.5 as we calculated above, and is shown in the lower panel. A characteristic of this model is that whatever the level of output and employment, the profit margin is 0.5. This implies

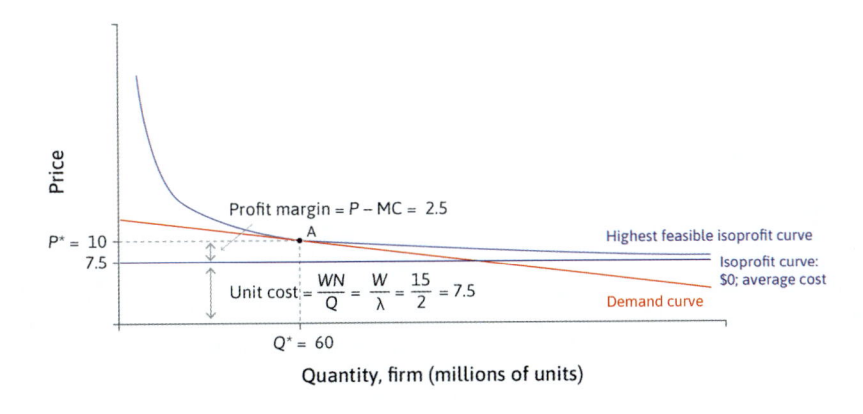

Figure 8.10 shows: Price on vertical axis, Quantity, firm (millions of units) on horizontal axis. $P^* = 10$, 7.5, $Q^* = 60$. Profit margin = P − MC = 2.5 at point A. Unit cost = $\frac{WN}{Q} = \frac{W}{\lambda} = \frac{15}{2} = 7.5$. Highest feasible isoprofit curve; Isoprofit curve: $0; average cost; Demand curve.

Figure 8.10 The firm sets the profit-maximizing price at A.

that the price-determined real wage does not vary with employment and we therefore label the horizontal line at $W/P = 1.5$ in the lower panel of Figure 8.11 the price-setting real wage (the price-setting curve). We work out an example to illustrate this.

Different points on the price-setting (PS) curve: Effects of an increase in economy-wide demand for goods and services

Figure 8.12 shows the outcome for the real wage of the price-setting decisions of firms when there is an increase in economy-wide demand for goods and services. To make the example as simple as possible, we continue to assume there is a single firm in the economy. However, the lessons of this model can be applied to the real-world case where there are large numbers of firms, each of which faces a downward-sloping demand curve for its differentiated product. Then, instead of a single price, P, as the denominator in the real wage, W/P, each firm will set its price using the same method to maximize its profits. But the overall price level in the economy will be the outcome of the decisions by all firms.

An increase in demand for goods and services in the economy shifts the demand curve to the right. We assume that demand increases by a constant factor at every price. This means that the demand curve rotates around the point where it intercepts the vertical axis (as shown in Figure 8.12). When the demand curve shifts like this, there is no change in the markup at the

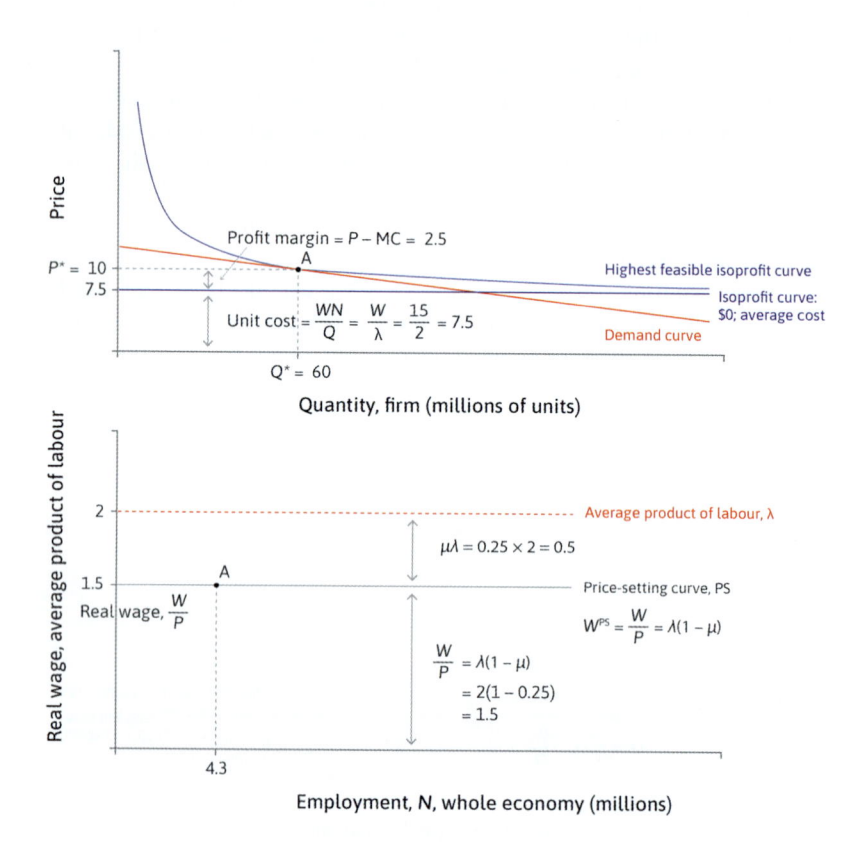

Figure 8.11 The price-setting real wage at point A.

given price. So this means that the firm will be setting the same profit-maximizing price whenever the demand curve shifts in this way.

In the example, the demand curve shifts by a factor of 1.05. This means that at the given price, the quantity is 5% higher. So the quantity produced rises by 5%, from 60 to 63 million units.

The new profit-maximizing outcome is at point D in Figure 8.12. Employment has also risen by 5% from 4.3 to 4.5 million workers.

By varying economy-wide demand we can derive more points like A and D, and so confirm that the price-setting real wage curve is a horizontal line.

So what we call the price-setting 'curve' is not really much of a curve—it is just a single number that gives the value of the real wage that is consistent with the markup, when all firms set their price to maximize their profits. In our numerical example, this number is 1.5.

To sum up, using our assumptions that neither productivity nor the markup vary with the level of employment, the value of the price-setting real wage is constant and is therefore shown, as in Figure 8.12, as a horizontal line.

What shifts the price-setting curve up or down?

Both from the diagram and the equation, we can see that the price-setting real wage will increase if productivity increases or if the markup falls. But what mechanisms bring this about?

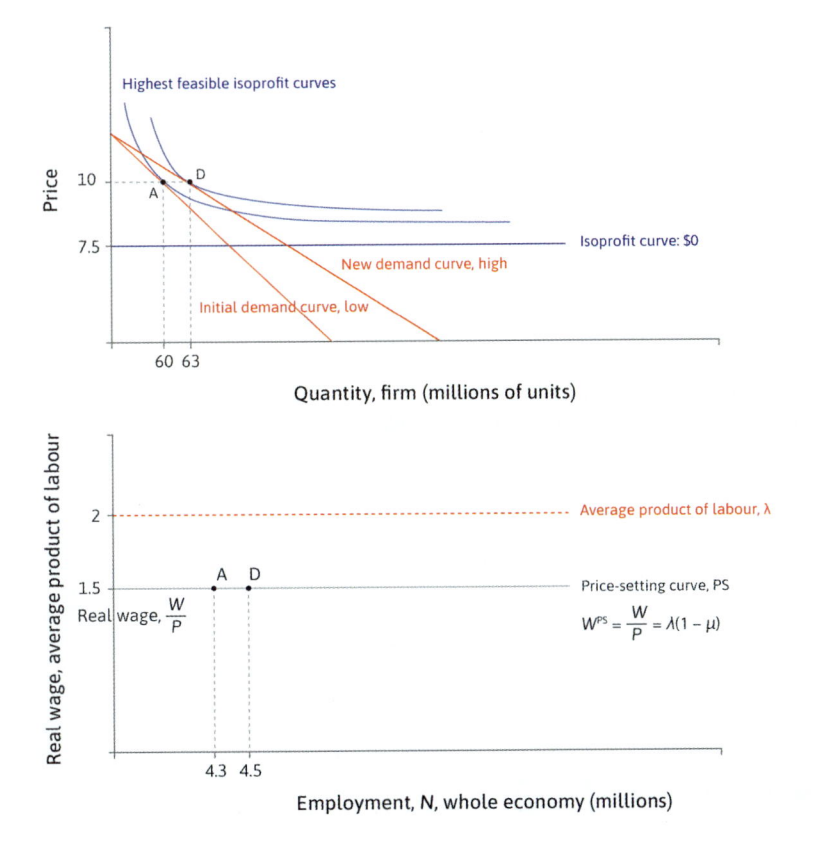

Figure 8.12 The price-setting curve: The effect of an increase in economy-wide demand for goods and services.

In the lower panel: $W^{PS} = \frac{W}{P} = \lambda(1 - \mu)$

Higher labour productivity
Returning to our example, if productivity doubles from 2 to 4 units produced per hour, then:

$$\frac{W}{P} = 4(1 - 0.25) = 3$$

So the price-setting real wage doubles from 1.5 to 3.

Digging a bit deeper, we can see that the increase in productivity has halved the firm's marginal cost (to $3.75). To keep its markup unchanged at 25% (since competitive conditions are assumed to be unchanged), the firm reduces its price to $5—it halves its price. The **nominal wage** is unchanged at $15 per hour, so the real wage has doubled to 3.

The mechanism by which higher productivity raises the price-setting real wage is summarized as follows. Higher productivity reduces costs and firms cut their prices. The result is a higher real wage.

$$\uparrow \text{productivity} \rightarrow \downarrow \text{MC} \rightarrow \downarrow P \rightarrow \uparrow \frac{W}{P}$$

> **nominal wage** The actual amount received in payment for work, in a particular currency. Also known as: money wage. See also: real wage.

More competition resulting in a lower markup
The price-setting real wage will increase if the demand curve becomes more elastic, that is if the markup in the economy falls as a result of more intense competition. This makes sense because, with fiercer competition, the share of profits will be lower and real wages will rise.

Suppose the markup falls from 0.25 to 0.2. Then:

$$\frac{W}{P} = 2(1 - 0.2) = 1.6$$

In words, the real wage rises from 1.5 to 1.6.

The mechanism by which a lower markup raises the price-setting real wage is as follows—a lower markup reduces the price the firm can set because of the more intense competition. The result is a higher real wage.

$$\downarrow \text{markup} \rightarrow \downarrow P \rightarrow \uparrow \frac{W}{P}$$

What if the nominal wage rises?
What happens to the price-setting real wage if the *nominal* wage increases? Suppose the hourly wage increases from $15 to $16. This increases the marginal cost from $7.50 to $8.00. Hence:

$$\mu = \frac{P - \text{MC}}{P}$$

$$0.25 = \frac{P - 8}{P}$$

$$P = \frac{8}{0.75} = 0.17$$

So the real wage is:

$$\frac{W}{P} = \frac{16}{8/0.75} = 1.5$$

8.5 THE PRODUCT MARKET AND THE PRICE-SETTING CURVE (FIRMS AND CUSTOMERS)

The answer is that nothing happens to the real wage on the price-setting curve when the nominal wage increases. The reason is that, to maximize their profits, firms raise their prices to keep the markup (the profit margin divided by the price) unchanged, which means that prices increase by the same proportionate amount as wages.

$$\uparrow W \;\to\; \uparrow P \;\to\; \text{no change in } \frac{W}{P}$$

Summary

We now summarize what determines the height of the price-setting curve. Later in the unit, we will look at how government policy can affect this.

- *Labour productivity:* For any given markup, the level of labour productivity—how much a worker produces in an hour—determines the real wage on the price-setting curve. The greater the level of labour productivity (or equivalently, the average product of labour, called lambda, λ), the higher the real wage that is consistent with a given markup. In Figure 8.12, higher labour productivity shifts the dashed line upwards, and, keeping the markup unchanged, the price-setting curve will shift upwards, raising the real wage.

Higher productivity pushes the price-setting curve upwards. Shares stay the same; the price-setting real wage is higher.

- *Competition:* You know from the previous unit that the intensity of competition facing firms determines the extent to which they can profit by charging a price that exceeds their costs, that is, their markup. The more intense the competition, the lower the markup. Since this leads to lower prices across the whole economy, it implies higher real wages, pushing the price-setting curve upwards.

More competition in markets for goods and services pushes the price-setting curve upwards. Workers get a bigger share; the price-setting real wage is higher.

We summarize the influences on the price-setting curve in Figure 8.13.

Price-setting real wage = λ (output per hour worked) − $\mu\lambda$ (profits per hour worked)

Technology, knowledge, skills → λ (output per hour worked)

Extent of competition in relevant market → Firms' profit-maximizing markup, μ → $\mu\lambda$ (profits per hour worked)

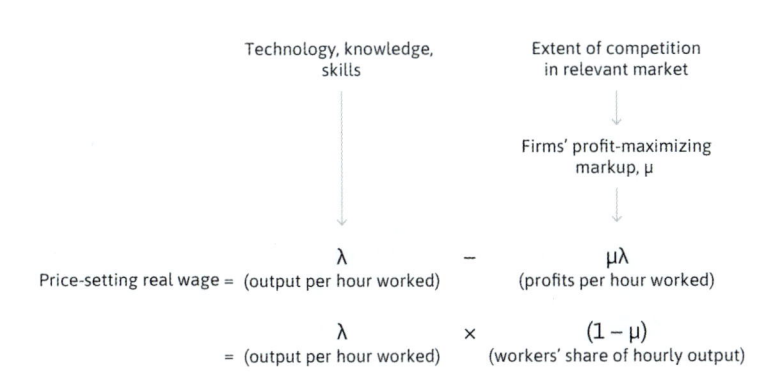

= λ (output per hour worked) × $(1 - \mu)$ (workers' share of hourly output)

Figure 8.13 Determinants of the price-setting curve.

price elasticity of demand The percentage change in demand that would occur in response to a 1% increase in price. We express this as a positive number. Demand is elastic if this is greater than 1, and inelastic if less than 1.

FIND OUT MORE

The size of the markup chosen by the firm

We can find a formula that shows that the markup is high when the elasticity of demand is low.

The firm maximizes its profits by setting its price where the slope of the isoprofit curve is equal to the slope of the demand curve, and we know that the slope of the demand curve is related to the **price elasticity of demand**:

$$\varepsilon = -\frac{P}{Q} \times \frac{1}{\text{slope of demand curve}}$$

Rearranging this formula:

$$\text{slope of demand curve} = -\frac{P}{Q} \times \frac{1}{\text{elasticity}}$$

We also know from Section 7.5 (page 286):

$$\text{slope of isoprofit curve} = -\frac{(P - MC)}{Q}$$

When the two slopes are equal:

$$\frac{(P - MC)}{Q} = \frac{P}{Q} \times \frac{1}{\text{elasticity}}$$

Rearranging this gives us:

$$\frac{(P - MC)}{P} = \frac{1}{\text{elasticity}}$$

The left-hand side is the profit margin as a proportion of the price, which is called the markup. Therefore:

The firm's markup is inversely proportional to the elasticity of demand.

Hence:

$$\mu = \frac{P - MC}{P} = \frac{1}{\text{elasticity}}$$

In the example, if $\mu = 0.25$ (the elasticity is 4) and MC = $7.50, then we can calculate the price:

$$\frac{P - MC}{P} = 0.25$$
$$0.25P = P - 7.5$$
$$P(1 - 0.25) = 7.5$$
$$P = \$10$$

QUESTION 8.3 CHOOSE THE CORRECT ANSWER(S)
Suppose the nominal wage W = $10, the markup μ = 0.5, and the marginal cost is $5. Based on this information and the discussion in this section, which of the following statements are true?

☐ The elasticity of demand is 4.
☐ The marginal cost is equal to the price.
☐ The real wage (W/P) is 1.
☐ Average productivity (λ) is 2.

QUESTION 8.4 CHOOSE THE CORRECT ANSWER(S)
Suppose the nominal wage W = $20, the markup μ = 0.4, the marginal cost is $15, and the firm's profit-maximising quantity is Q = 50. Assume there are no fixed costs. Based on this information and the discussion in this section, which of the following statements are true?

☐ The real wage (W/P) is $1.25.
☐ For the marginal cost given, the point (Q, P) = (100, 20) is on the same isoprofit curve as the firm's profit-maximising point (at Q = 50).
☐ Average productivity (λ) is 0.75.
☐ Profits per hour worked, μλ, is 8/15 (0.533).

8.6 WAGES, PROFITS, AND UNEMPLOYMENT IN THE AGGREGATE ECONOMY

Putting the wage-setting and the price-setting curves together, we have a model for the macroeconomy from which we can directly determine the real wage and the level of structural employment.

We ask what the equilibrium of an economy will be, as depicted by the two curves. Remember, a **Nash equilibrium** is a situation in which none of the actors would like to change what they are doing, given what the others are doing.

Who are the actors? Recall that the firm has two departments: Marketing and human resources (HR), both of course operating under the direction of the owners of the firm or their top managers. HR knows, for any level of unemployment, the real wage that is the least cost way to get workers to work. Marketing knows, given the demand curve facing the firm, what the price of the goods sold should be to maximize the firm's profits.

When we say that in the Nash equilibrium, 'none of the actors would like to change what they are doing, given what the others are doing', we are referring to the actions taken by Marketing and HR in respectively setting the price and the nominal wage.

Their interaction is summarized in Figure 8.14.

Can anybody do better? Is the intersection of the two curves a Nash equilibrium?
To determine the equilibrium of this economy, we need to ask the question: 'Can anybody do better?' In the left-hand panel of Figure 8.15, we ask if HR can do better. We see that, for any combination of wage and employment below the wage-setting curve, they are sounding the alarm—nobody is working, we need to raise wages. Above the wage-setting curve, they are sounding a different alarm—the firm is throwing away money by paying too much.

> **Nash equilibrium** A set of strategies, one for each player in the game, such that each player's strategy is a best response to the strategies chosen by everyone else.

In the right-hand panel, we ask if Marketing can do better. We see that, for any combination of wage and employment above the price-setting wage, the firm can charge a higher price and make more profits. Below the price-setting curve, the marketing department is alarmed because the firm is losing customers and should lower the price.

The Nash equilibrium of the economy

By superimposing the wage-setting curve on the price-setting curve in the right-hand panel of Figure 8.15, we have a picture of the macroeconomy, illustrated in Figure 8.16.

Department	… knows	… and on this basis sets the firm's
HR	Prices and wages in other firms, and the unemployment rate in the economy	Nominal wage, W
Marketing	All of the above, and firm's demand function	Price of output, P

Figure 8.14 The two departments in each firm determine the wage and price set by the firm.

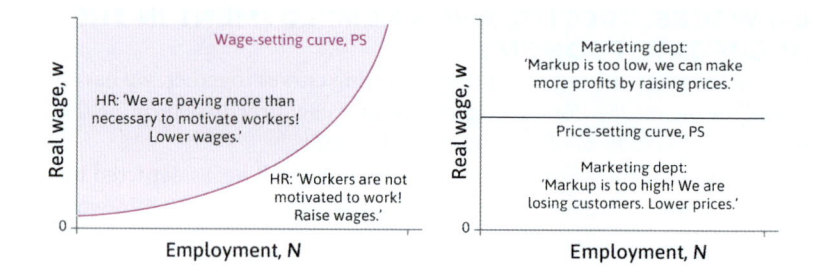

Figure 8.15 Can anybody do better? The HR and marketing departments of the firm.

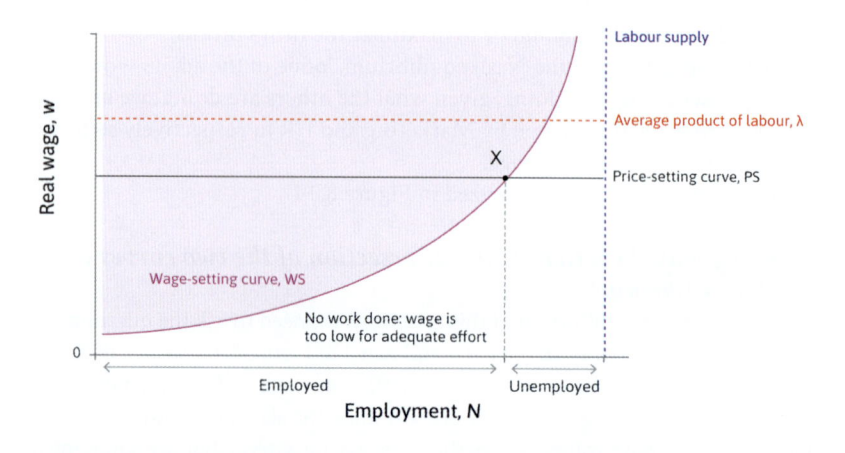

Figure 8.16 Equilibrium in the economy: Structural unemployment at X.

8.6 WAGES, PROFITS, AND UNEMPLOYMENT IN THE AGGREGATE ECONOMY

The equilibrium of the economy is the point at which the wage- and price-setting curves intersect, shown by X in the figure.

- *Workers are working:* They have no **incentive** to shirk. If they demanded higher pay, their employer would refuse, or replace them.
- *HR does not want to change the wage:* The workers are motivated, at the lowest possible cost.
- *Marketing is satisfied:* Prices have been set at the profit-maximizing level.

What about the unemployed, who, apart from not having a job, are identical to the employed? They are surely unhappy in this situation. Those who fail to get jobs would rather have a job, but in this situation there is no way for them to get one—not even if they offer to work at a lower wage than others. The unemployment at the equilibrium of the labour and product market in the economy—**equilibrium unemployment**—is **involuntary unemployment**; also known as **structural unemployment**.

This is a Nash equilibrium because all parties are doing the best they can (even the unfortunate unemployed), given what everyone else is doing.

> **QUESTION 8.5 CHOOSE THE CORRECT ANSWER(S)**
> Which of the following statements about outcome X in Figure 8.16 (page 354) are correct?
>
> ☐ Once they are employed, employees are better off not exerting any effort in their work.
> ☐ The firms' wage offered is at the point of tangency between their isocost line and the workers' best response function curve for effort.
> ☐ The unemployed can get jobs by offering to work for a wage lower than the equilibrium wage.
> ☐ Above the price-setting curve, the marketing department can do better by raising prices.

> **QUESTION 8.6 CHOOSE THE CORRECT ANSWER(S)**
> Figure 8.16 (page 354) depicts the model of the aggregate economy. Consider a reduction in the degree of competition faced by the firms. Which of the following statements regarding the effects of reduced competition are correct?
>
> ☐ The price-setting curve shifts upwards.
> ☐ The wage-setting curve shifts downwards.
> ☐ The equilibrium real wage falls.
> ☐ The unemployment level falls.

---

incentive Economic reward or punishment, which influences the benefits and costs of alternative courses of action.

equilibrium unemployment The number of people seeking work but without jobs, which is determined by the intersection of the wage-setting and price-setting curves. This is the Nash equilibrium of the labour market and product market where neither employers nor workers could do better by changing their behaviour. *See also: involuntary unemployment, structural unemployment, wage-setting curve, price-setting curve, WS/PS model, inflation-stabilizing rate of unemployment.*

involuntary unemployment A person who is seeking work, and willing to accept a job at the going wage for people of their level of skill and experience, but unable to secure employment is involuntarily employed.

structural unemployment The level of unemployment at the Nash equilibrium of the labour and product market model.

8.7 UNEMPLOYMENT AS A CHARACTERISTIC OF EQUILIBRIUM

We now show why there will *always* be structural unemployment in the equilibrium of the aggregate economy.

Unemployment means that there are people seeking work but not finding it. This is also called **excess supply** in the labour market, meaning that demand for labour at the given wage is lower than the number of workers willing to work for that wage. Those unable to get a job are involuntarily unemployed. To understand why there will always be unemployment in equilibrium (where the wage- and price-setting curves intersect), we contrast the wage-setting curve with the labour supply curve. We shall see that the wage-setting curve is always to the left of the labour supply curve: for any real wage, the gap between the level of employment on the wage curve and on the labour supply curve measures involuntary unemployment.

In our model, we assume that higher wages do not—in the economy as a whole—lead more people to offer more hours at work. At higher wages some people seek (and find) more hours of work, and others seek (and find) shorter hours. The first is the **substitution effect** of a wage increase, and the second is the **income effect**. We introduced these effects in Section 4.9 (page 169). For simplicity, we draw a vertical labour supply curve such that these two effects cancel out. But this is not important. The model would not be different if higher wages led to either more or fewer people seeking work. To see this, you can experiment with labour supply curves with different shapes in Figure 8.16.

Why will there always be some involuntary unemployment in equilibrium?

- *If there was no unemployment:* The cost of job loss would be zero (no employment rent) because a worker who loses her job can immediately get another one at the same pay.
- *Therefore, some unemployment is necessary:* It means the employer can motivate workers to provide effort on the job, which is essential to production.
- *Therefore, the wage-setting curve is always to the left of the labour supply curve.*
- *It follows that in any equilibrium, where the wage- and price-setting curves intersect, there must be unemployed people.*

> **EXERCISE 8.3 IS THIS REALLY A NASH EQUILIBRIUM?**
> In this model, the unemployed are no different from the employed (except for their bad luck). Imagine you are an employer, and one of the unemployed comes to you and promises to work at the same effort level as your current workers, but for a slightly lower wage.
>
> 1. How would you reply?
> 2. Does your reply help explain why unemployment must exist in a Nash equilibrium?

---

excess supply A situation in which the quantity of a good supplied is greater than the quantity demanded at the current price. *See also*: excess demand.

substitution effect The effect for example, on the choice of consumption of a good that is only due to changes in the price or opportunity cost, given the new level of utility.

income effect The effect, for example, on the choice of consumption of a good that a change in income would have if there were no change in the price or opportunity cost.

QUESTION 8.7 CHOOSE THE CORRECT ANSWER(S)

Suppose the real wage increases. Which of the following statements about the labour supply of a worker are correct?

☐ The income effect means that the worker will increase his labour supply.
☐ The substitution effect means that the worker will increase his consumption of leisure.
☐ The income and substitution effects always enhance each other, leading to higher labour supply.
☐ At high wages, the income effect dominates the substitution effect, leading to lower labour supply.

8.8 WHY WAS UNEMPLOYMENT HIGHER IN SPAIN THAN IN GERMANY?

Recall that at the beginning of this unit (page 334) we contrasted the unemployment rates of Germany and Spain. Figure 8.17 provides more details, comparing unemployment in Germany and Spain from 1960 to 2018. We can use the WS/PS model developed in this unit to propose some explanations for the wide gap between the unemployment rates in these two large European countries.

The model directs our attentions to the position of the wage- and price-setting curves. The point at which they cross pins down unemployment at the Nash equilibrium. The differences in the average unemployment rates over many decades between Germany and Spain suggests that structural unemployment in the two countries must be different.

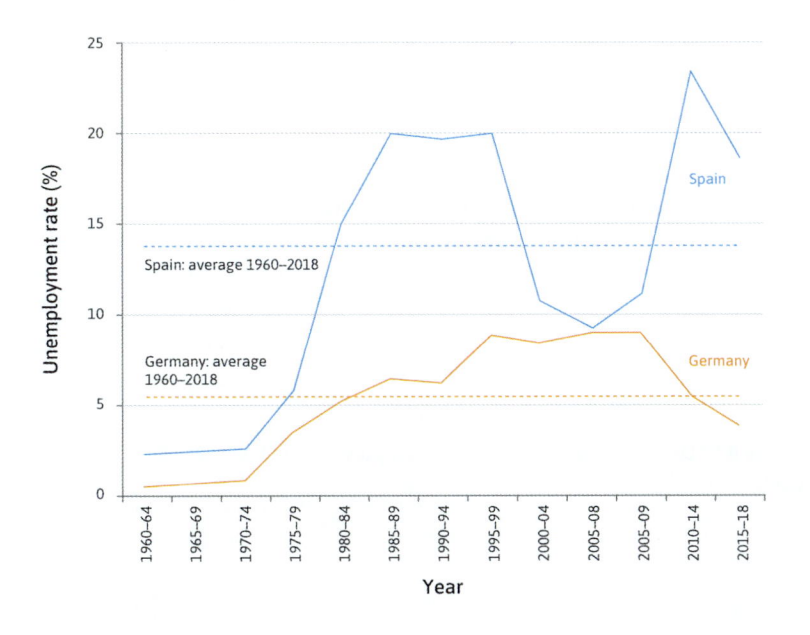

Data from 1960–2004: David R. Howell, Dean Baker, Andrew Glyn, and John Schmitt. 2007. 'Are Protective Labor Market Institutions at the Root of Unemployment? A Critical Review of the Evidence' (https://tinyco.re/2000761). *Capitalism and Society* 2 (1) (January). Data from 2005 to 2018: OECD. 2019. *OECD Statistics* (https://tinyco.re/9377362).

Figure 8.17 Unemployment in Spain and Germany (1960–2018).

The table in Figure 8.18 brings together summary data that helps to explain the Germany–Spain comparison.

In the model, the structural unemployment rate (unemployment at the Nash equilibrium) is increased by factors that shift the wage-setting curve upwards and reduced by factors that shift the price-setting curve downwards.

Comparing these two countries, we can see that Spain has a more generous unemployment benefit regime. *Ceteris paribus*, the higher unemployment benefits in Spain shift the wage-setting curve upwards relative to the case of Germany.

We shall see the importance of the *ceteris paribus* assumption later in this unit. There are countries with more generous unemployment benefits than Spain with much lower structural unemployment. In those countries, generous unemployment benefits were not simply generous but were designed to help the unemployed re-enter employment quickly. This was not the case in Spain.

Turning to the price-setting curve, from the model we know that, if there is stronger competitive pressure on firms, the price-setting curve will shift upwards. In Figure 8.18, using data from 1976 to 2011, we use the measure of the openness of the economy to international trade, calculated as the sum of its exports plus its imports divided by GDP as a proxy for the pressure of competition. According to this indicator, the German economy is much more open to competition than is the Spanish economy. *Ceteris paribus*, this shifts the price-setting curve upwards in Germany relative to Spain.

The data in the final column of the table highlights the difference in output per worker hour between the two economies. The measure we use is hourly productivity in manufacturing because it is likely that productivity is better measured there than elsewhere in the economy. By this measure, productivity in Germany is 60% higher than in Spain. *Ceteris paribus*, this shifts the price-setting curve upwards in Germany relative to that in Spain.

Data from 1976–2004: David R. Howell, Dean Baker, Andrew Glyn, and John Schmitt. 2007. 'Are Protective Labor Market Institutions at the Root of Unemployment? A Critical Review of the Evidence' (https://tinyco.re/2000761). *Capitalism and Society* 2 (1) (January). Data from 2005 to 2011: OECD. 2015. *OECD Statistics* (https://tinyco.re/9377362).

Note: Generosity of unemployment benefits is measured as Gross Unemployment Benefit Replacement Rates. Openness of the economy to global competition is exports plus imports as a share of GDP. Labour productivity is gross value added per hour worked, in manufacturing sector, measured in 2005 US$. All data is averaged over the period 1976–2011.

	Unemployment rate (%)	Generosity of unemployment benefits (%)	Openness of the economy to global competition (% of GDP)	Labour productivity in manufacturing (2005 US$)
Germany	6.8	26.9	71.0	43.3
Spain	15.4	31.9	65.1	30.6

Figure 8.18 Determinants of structural unemployment in Spain and Germany (1976–2011).

Figure 8.19 illustrates how these differences can be shown in the model. Spain's structural unemployment at point X is higher than Germany's at Y, as a result of a higher wage-setting and a lower price-setting curve. The model predicts that Germany's real wage is higher than Spain's.

8.9 DECLINING COMPETITION AND INCREASING INEQUALITY IN THE US

Firms have become more powerful in relation to their customers since the 1980s. And we shall use the model of the labour market and product market to see how this phenomenon increases economic inequality. A fall in the degree of competition in markets for goods and services, *ceteris paribus*, entails higher structural unemployment and a higher share of profits. Both raise inequality among households.

Recent research shows the rise in the markup in the US, and in many other countries. Figure 8.20 for the US, shows a falling average markup from the mid-1960s to 1980, a rapid increase until 2000, and then, after a decade of stability, a renewed rise since the global financial crisis. The average markup is more than twice now what it was in 1980.

Over the same period, the share of the economy's income going in **economic profits** to the owners of firms has been increasing, as illustrated also for the US in Figure 8.21.

The research on trends in both markups and the share of profits points to the central role of declining competition in markets for goods and services. This development suggests that there has been a long-term shift in the balance of power in the US economy (and in some other countries) toward the owners of firms and away from their customers.

Figure 8.22 shows the increase in inequality among US households in their market income (before the payment of taxes and receipt of transfers) from 1970 to 2015.

economic profit A firm's revenue minus its total costs (including the opportunity cost of capital).

Listen to John Van Reenen (https://tinyco.re/6674199), an economist, talking about the rise of superstar firms and the challenges they pose for policy-makers seeking to sustain or restore a competitive economy.

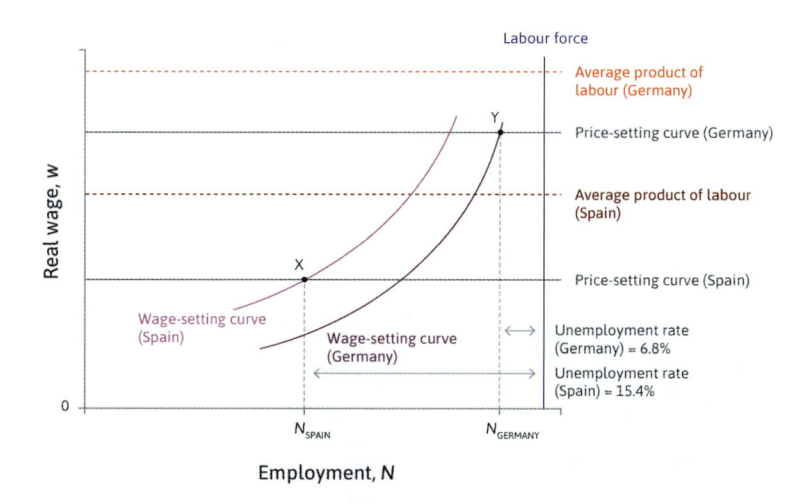

Figure 8.19 Using the model to compare structural unemployment in Spain and Germany.

The upward trend in inequality among US households from 1980 measured by the Gini coefficient is clear. As we shall see in the next section, the model of the labour and product market predicts that a decline in competition in product markets leads to a rise in inequality measured by the Gini coefficient. We return in Section 8.12 (page 370) to US economic performance.

Jan De Loecker, Jan Eeckhout, and Gabriel Unger. 2018. The Rise of Market Power and the Macroeconomic Implications (https://tinyco.re/2379411). NBER Working Paper.

Note: Our measure of the markup is 1 minus the inverse of the measure used in the source data.

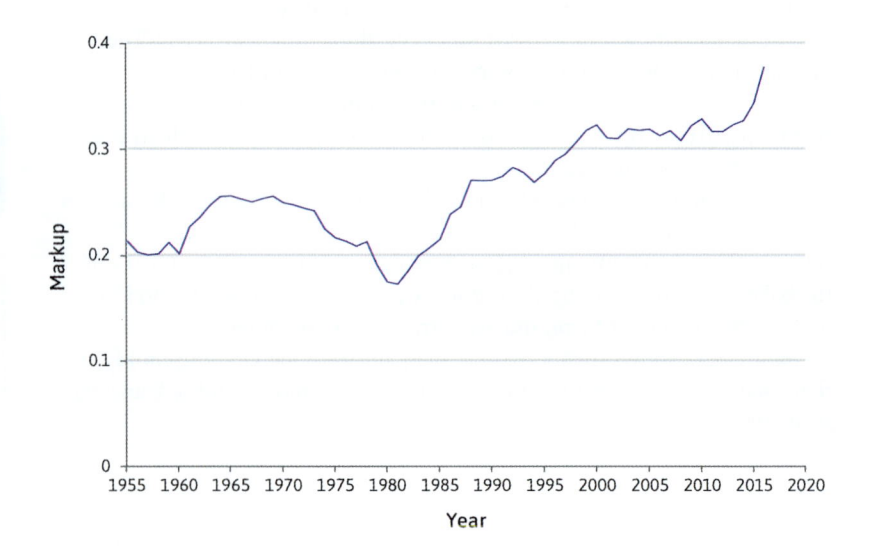

Figure 8.20 The estimated average markup for firms in the US (1955–2016).

Simcha Barkai 2016. Declining Labor and Capital Shares (https://tinyco.re/8914061). Stigler Center for the Study of the Economy and the State, New Working Paper Series No. 2.

Note: In estimating the profit share for the US economy the author divides income into three parts. One is the labour share. The rest is 'profits', which are split into the other two shares. The 'capital share is the opportunity cost of capital as a share of income; the remainder is what is labelled in the chart 'Profit share' and is the share of economic profits in income.

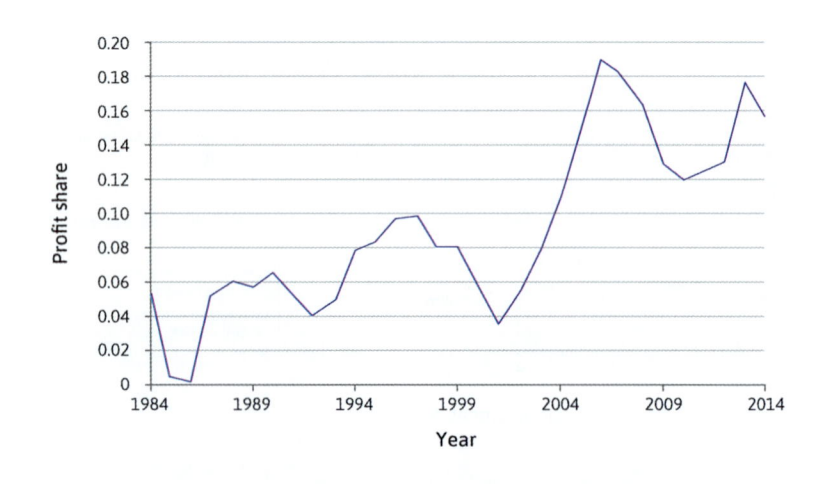

Figure 8.21 The share of economic profits in income in the US (1984–2014).

8.10 THE LABOUR AND PRODUCT MARKET MODEL AND INEQUALITY: USING THE LORENZ CURVE AND GINI COEFFICIENT

As we have seen, the model for the aggregate economy determines not only the level of employment, unemployment, and the wage rate, but also the division of the economy's output between workers (both employed and unemployed) and employers. It is therefore also a model of the distribution of income in a simple economy in which labour is the only input and there are just these two classes. The classes are employers—who are the owners of the firms—and workers—some of whom are without work.

The distribution of income at the Nash equilibrium

As we did in Unit 5, we can construct the **Lorenz curve** and calculate the **Gini coefficient** for the economy in this model. Refer back to Unit 5 (page 214) to recall how to construct the Lorenz curve and calculate the Gini coefficient.

In the left-hand panel of Figure 8.23, we show an economy with 80 identical employees of 10 identical firms. As you can see, there are 10 unemployed people. Each firm has a single owner. The economy is in equilibrium at point A, at which the real wage is both sufficient to motivate workers to work and consistent with the firm's profit-maximizing price markup over costs.

The right-hand panel shows the Lorenz curve for income in this economy. Because there are no unemployment benefits, the unemployed people receive no income, the Lorenz curve (the solid blue line) begins on the horizontal axis to the right of the left-hand corner. The price-setting curve in the left-hand panel indicates that total output is divided up so that workers receive a 60% share and their employers receive the rest. In the right-hand panel, this is shown by the second 'kink' in the Lorenz curve, where we see that the poorest 90 people in the population (the 10 unemployed workers and the 80 employees, shown on the horizontal axis) receive 60% of the total output (on the vertical axis). The size of the shaded area measures the extent of inequality, and the Gini coefficient is 0.36.

Lorenz curve A graphical representation of inequality of some quantity such as wealth or income. Individuals are arranged in ascending order by how much of this quantity they have, and the cumulative share of the total is then plotted against the cumulative share of the population. For complete equality of income, for example, it would be a straight line with a slope of one. The extent to which the curve falls below this perfect equality line is a measure of inequality. See also: Gini coefficient.

Gini coefficient A measure of inequality of any quantity such as income or wealth, varying from a value of zero (if there is no inequality) to one (if a single individual receives all of it).

Anthony Atkinson, Joe Hasell, Salvatore Morelli, and Max Roser. 2017. *The Chartbook of Economic Inequality* (https://tinyco.re/8272861).

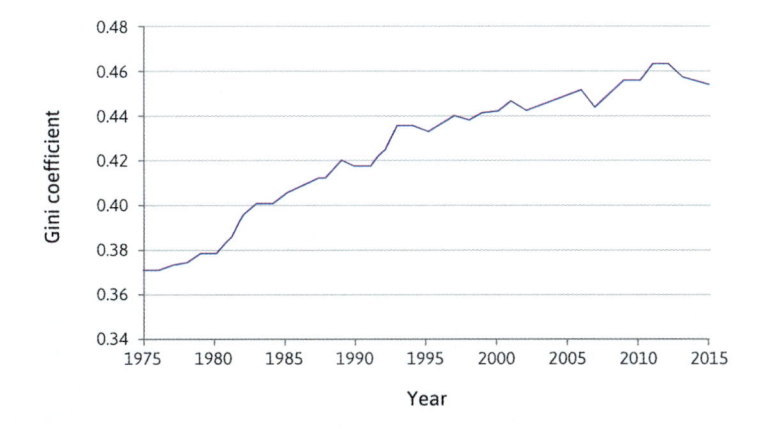

Figure 8.22 The Gini coefficient for market income in the US (1970-2015).

The Lorenz curve is made up of three line segments, with the beginning point having coordinates of (0, 0) and the endpoint (1, 1). The first kink in the curve occurs when we have counted all the unemployed people.

The second is the interior point, whose coordinates are (fraction of total number of economically active population, fraction of total output received in wages). The fraction of output received in wages, called the wage share in total income, s, is:

$$s = \text{wage share}$$
$$= \frac{\text{real wage per worker day}}{\text{output per worker day}}$$
$$= \frac{w}{\lambda}$$

When does inequality increase?

The shaded area in the figure—and hence inequality measured by the Gini coefficient—will increase if:

- *A larger fraction of the employees is without work (higher unemployment rate):* The first kink shifts to the right.
- *The real wage falls (or equivalently, the markup rises) and nothing else changes:* The second kink shifts downwards.
- *Productivity rises and nothing else changes (real wages do not rise):* This implies that the markup rises, so again the second kink shifts downwards.

More competition in markets for goods and services, lower inequality

What can change the level of employment and the distribution of income between profits and wages in equilibrium? Follow the analysis in Figure 8.24 to see what would happen if there were an increase in the degree of competition faced by firms, perhaps as a result of a fall in the barriers preventing firms from other countries competing in this economy's markets.

The markup would decrease, and as a result the real wage shown by the price-setting curve would increase, leading to a new equilibrium at point B with a higher wage and a higher level of employment. The share of output going to profits falls, and the share going to wages rises—inequality falls.

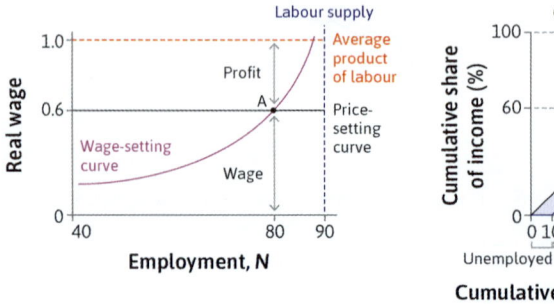

Figure 8.23 The distribution of income at labour and product market equilibrium.

8.10 THE LABOUR AND PRODUCT MARKET MODEL AND INEQUALITY

> **QUESTION 8.8 CHOOSE THE CORRECT ANSWER(S)**
>
> Figure 8.23 is the Lorenz curve associated with a particular labour market equilibrium. In a population of 100, there are 10 firms, each with a single owner, 80 employed workers, and 10 unemployed workers. The employed workers receive 60% of the total income as wages. The Gini coefficient is 0.36. In which of the following cases would the Gini coefficient increase, keeping all other factors unchanged?
>
> ☐ a rise in the unemployment rate
> ☐ a rise in the real wage
> ☐ a rise in the workers' productivity while the real wage is unchanged
> ☐ a rise in the degree of competition faced by the firms

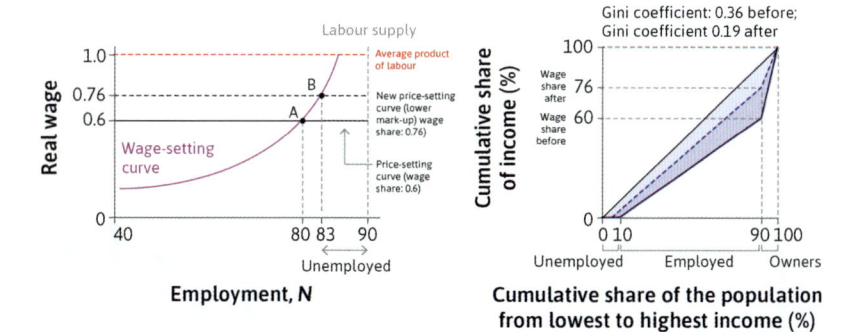

Figure 8.24 The effect of an increase in the extent of competition faced by firms: The price-setting curve shifts upwards and inequality falls.

1. The initial equilibrium
We start from the equilibrium at A with a Gini coefficient of 0.36. Suppose that the degree of competition faced by firms is increased.

2. A new equilibrium
The markup charged by firms in the market will decrease, and so the price-setting curve will be higher. The new equilibrium is at B.

3. A new, lower Gini coefficient
At the new equilibrium there is a higher wage and a higher level of employment. Stronger competition means that firms have weaker market power—the share going to profits falls, and the share going to wages rises. Inequality falls: the new Gini coefficient is 0.19.

8.11 LABOUR UNIONS: BARGAINED WAGES AND THE UNION VOICE EFFECT

The model of the aggregate economy presented so far is about firms and individual workers. But, in many countries, labour unions play a big part in how the labour market works. A **trade union** (or labour union) is an organization that can represent the interests of a group of workers in negotiations with employers over issues such as pay, working conditions, and working hours. The resulting contract is between the firm or organization representing employers and the labour union.

As you can see from Figure 8.25, the fraction of the workforce employed under collective bargaining agreements negotiated by labour unions varies greatly between countries, from virtually all workers in France and some northern European economies, to hardly any in the US and South Korea.

trade union An organization consisting predominantly of employees, the principal activities of which include the negotiation of rates of pay and conditions of employment for its members.

Sunny Freeman. 2015. 'What Canada can learn from Sweden's unionized retail workers' (https://tinyco.re/0808135). *Huffington Post Canada Business*. Updated 19 March 2015.

Barry T. Hirsch. 2008. 'Sluggish institutions in a dynamic world: Can unions and industrial competition coexist?' *Journal of Economic Perspectives* 22 (1) (February): pp. 153–76.

Labour unions and the bargained wage-setting curve
Where workers are organized into trade unions, the wage is not set by the HR department but instead is determined through a process of negotiation between a union representing workers and the firm's HR department. Although the wage must always be at least as high as the wage indicated by the wage-setting curve for the given level of unemployment, the bargained wage can be above the wage-setting curve.

The threat of going on strike
The reason is that the employer's threat to dismiss the worker is now not the only exercise of power that is possible. The union can threaten to 'dismiss' the employer (at least temporarily) by going on strike, that is, withdrawing the employees' labour from the firm.

View this data at OWiD https://tinyco.re/8246237

Jelle Visser. 2015. 'ICTWSS Data base. version 5.0' (https://tinyco.re/3654275). Amsterdam: Amsterdam Institute for Advanced Labour Studies AIAS. Updated October 2015.

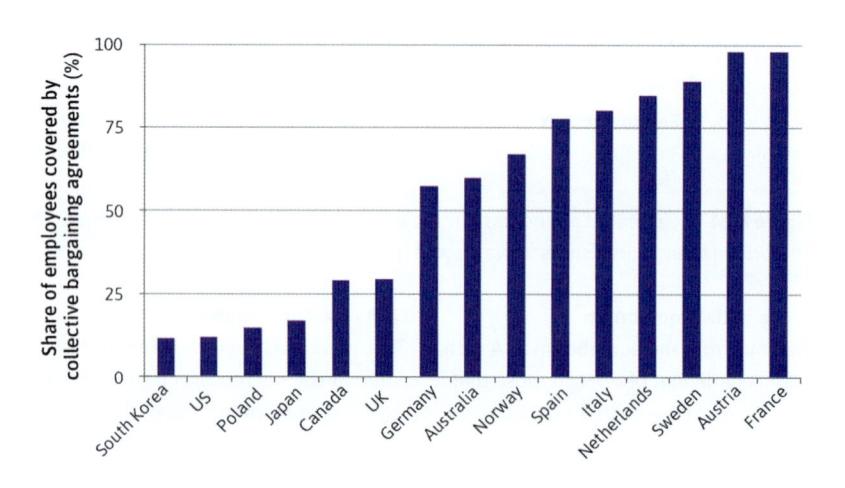

Figure 8.25 Share of employees whose wages are covered by collective bargaining agreements (early 2010s).

8.11 LABOUR UNIONS: BARGAINED WAGES AND THE UNION VOICE EFFECT

Therefore, the firm must agree to a wage that ensures that it will have the required work done to produce the goods or services on which its profits depend. This requires both that:

- *The workers will provide sufficient effort when they come to work:* The wage-setting curve determines this.
- *The workers will come to work rather than go on strike:* A bargained wage-setting curve will determine this.

We can think of a 'bargaining curve' lying above the wage-setting curve, which indicates the wage that the union–employer bargaining process will produce for every level of employment.

The relative bargaining power of the union and the employer determines how far this bargaining curve lies above the wage-setting curve. The union's power depends on the ability to withhold labour from the firm, so its bargaining strength will be greater if it can ensure that during a strike, no other workers will offer their services to the firm.

This and the other determinants of bargaining power depend on the laws and social norms in force in an economy. In many countries, for example, it is a serious violation of a social norm among workers to seek employment in a firm whose workers are on strike.

To see the difference that a labour union can make, let's see how the labour market would work if, instead of the employer setting the wage and the employees individually responding, the process would now be as shown in Figure 8.26.

In this case, the employer no longer sets the wage that maximizes profits (the point of tangency of the isocost line for effort and the best response curve at point A in Figure 8.27). Use the analysis in Figure 8.27 to see what happens when the union, rather than the firm, sets the wage. To see the outcome for structural unemployment in the economy, see Figure 8.28.

As shown in Figure 8.27, the wage will be higher than that preferred by the employer. Workers will now be working harder, but wages increase by more than productivity, so firms receive less effort for each dollar spent on wages. It follows that profits will be lower than without the union, that is, on the flatter isocost line passing through C.

By translating Figure 8.27 to the model of the labour market and product market in Figure 8.28, we see that the bargained wage-setting curve lies above the wage-setting curve. Looking at the equilibrium where the bargained wage-setting curve intersects with the price-setting curve, the wage is unaffected, but the level of employment is lower.

| The union sets the wage | ⇒ | The employer informs workers that insufficient work will result in job termination | ⇒ | Employees respond to the wage and the prospect of dismissal by choosing how hard to work |

Figure 8.26 If the union sets the wage.

To explore all of the slides in this figure, see the online version at https://tinyco.re/3711562.

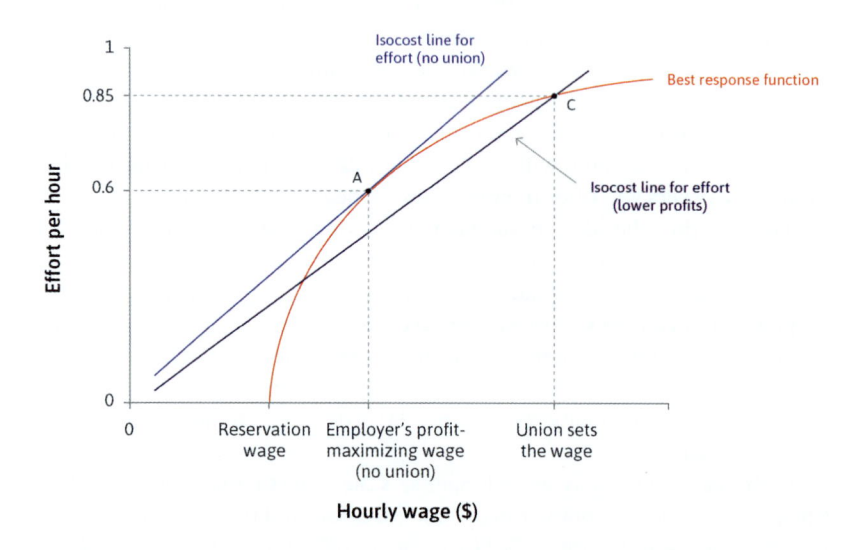

Figure 8.27 If the union sets the firm's wage instead of the employer.

1. The employer sets the wage
At point A, the employer sets the wage that maximizes profits at the point of tangency of the isocost line and the best response function.

2. The union sets the wage instead
If the union sets the wage, it will be higher than that preferred by the employer, and effort levels correspondingly higher …

3. Higher effort but lower profits
… but profits would be lower (indicated by the flatter isocost line passing through C).

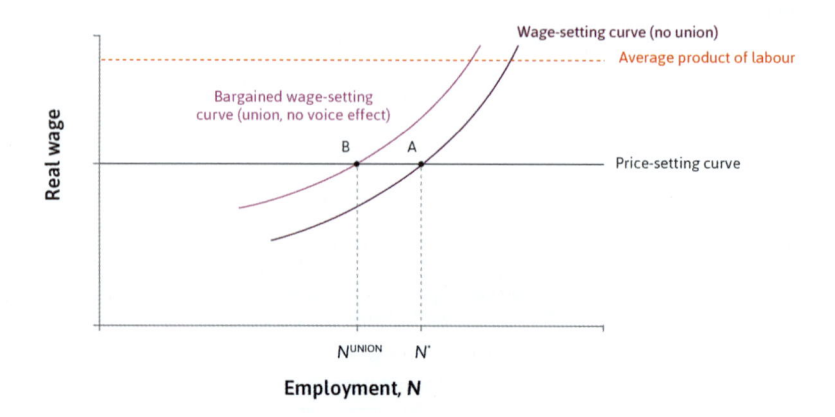

Figure 8.28 The bargained wage-setting curve when there is union wage-setting.

8.11 LABOUR UNIONS: BARGAINED WAGES AND THE UNION VOICE EFFECT

Unions in the model and in the data
Paradoxically, it seems from the model that the union's success in bargaining would harm workers, since the real wage is unchanged and more people are out of work. But if we look at the data on union bargaining coverage and unemployment in Figure 8.29, unemployment does not seem to be higher in countries where union bargains are important in wage-setting.

Austria, with almost all employees covered by union wage bargains, has a lower unemployment rate (averaged over 2000–2014) than the US, where fewer than one in five workers is covered by union contracts. Spain and Poland both had massive unemployment over this period, but union coverage was very high in Spain and very low in Poland.

Therefore, the fact that unions can push the wage-setting curve upwards to the new 'bargained wage-setting curve' must not be the entire story.

A powerful union may choose restraint
One possible explanation is that a powerful union may choose not to raise the wage, even if it has the power to do so. This is because even a very powerful union can only set the wage, and it cannot determine how many people the firm hires. Too high a wage may squeeze profits sufficiently to lead the firm to close down or cut back on employment.

Unions may choose to restrain their use of bargaining power. If their wage-setting covers a substantial part of the economy, they will take into account the effect of their wage decision on the wages and employment of workers in the economy as a whole.

The union voice effect
Unions differ in other ways.

Suppose that, over time, the employer and the trade union develop a constructive working relationship—for example, solving problems that arise in ways that benefit both employees and the owners. The employees may interpret the employer's recognition of the trade union, and its willingness to compromise over a higher wage, as a sign of goodwill.

View this data at OWiD https://tinyco.re/2742500

Jelle Visser. 2015. 'ICTWSS Data base. version 5.0' (https://tinyco.re/3654275). Amsterdam: Amsterdam Institute for Advanced Labour Studies AIAS. Updated October 2015.

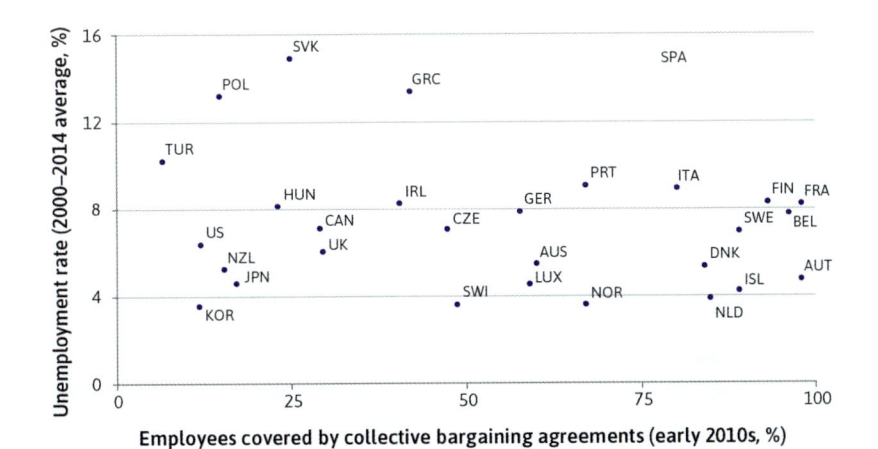

Figure 8.29 Collective wage bargaining coverage and unemployment across the OECD.

As a result, the employees might identify more strongly with their firm and experience effort as less of a burden than before, shifting their best response curve upwards in Figure 8.30.

The result of the greater bargaining power of the workers, and their reciprocation of the company's worker-friendly policy, is shown as point D in the Figure 8.30. The wage is the same as in the previous case but, because worker effort is higher, the firm's profits are higher. Note that in the example shown, the firm is still worse off than it was in the absence of the union.

With the new best response function, there is of course an outcome for a wage-setting firm that is even better than D—where the isocost curve is tangent to it (not shown). However, this is not feasible. The workers will not exert the higher effort in the absence of the negotiations about wages and conditions opened up by the union's role in wage-setting.

To explore all of the slides in this figure, see the online version at https://tinyco.re/2117126.

Figure 8.30 The union sets the firm's wage, and employees reciprocate.

1. The employer sets the wage
At point A, the employer sets the wage that maximizes profits at the point of tangency of the isocost line and the best response curve.

2. The employer recognizes a trade union
If the employees interpret the employer's recognition of the trade union, and its willingness to compromise over a higher wage, as a sign of goodwill, the best response curve shifts upwards.

3. The effect of a worker-friendly policy
The result of the greater bargaining power of the workers, and their reciprocation of the company's worker-friendly policy, is shown as point D.

8.11 LABOUR UNIONS: BARGAINED WAGES AND THE UNION VOICE EFFECT

Unions may raise or lower structural unemployment
We have shown two effects of the presence of a labour union, which we can now represent in the WS/PS diagram:

- *The union forces the firm to pay a wage greater than the minimum necessary to induce the employees to work:* The bargaining curve is always above the wage-setting curve.
- *The union provides employees with a voice in how decisions are made:* This may lower the disutility of effort and therefore reduce the lowest wage necessary to motivate employees to work effectively.

The two effects are illustrated in Figure 8.31. In this figure, we show the case in which the equilibrium level of employment is higher and unemployment lower with the union (point Y) than without (point X). This is because the second effect (called the **union voice effect**) that shifts the wage-setting curve downwards was greater than the bargaining effect that shifts the wage-setting curve upwards.

But it could have worked out the other way around. The bargained wage effect could have been greater than the union voice effect, in which case the effect of unions would have been to raise structural unemployment.

This provides a reason why the data in Figure 8.29 (page 367) does not show any clear correlation (either positive or negative) between the extent of union contracts and the amount of unemployment.

Unions may also affect the average productivity of labour, which will shift the price-setting curve. If unions foster cooperation with management in solving production problems, the average product and the price-setting curve will rise (leading to higher wages and less unemployment). If unions resist productivity improvements, such as the introduction of new machinery or changes in work rules, then the effect will go in the opposite direction.

> **union voice effect** The positive effect on labour effort (and hence labour productivity) of trade union members' sense that they have a say (a voice) in how the firm is run.

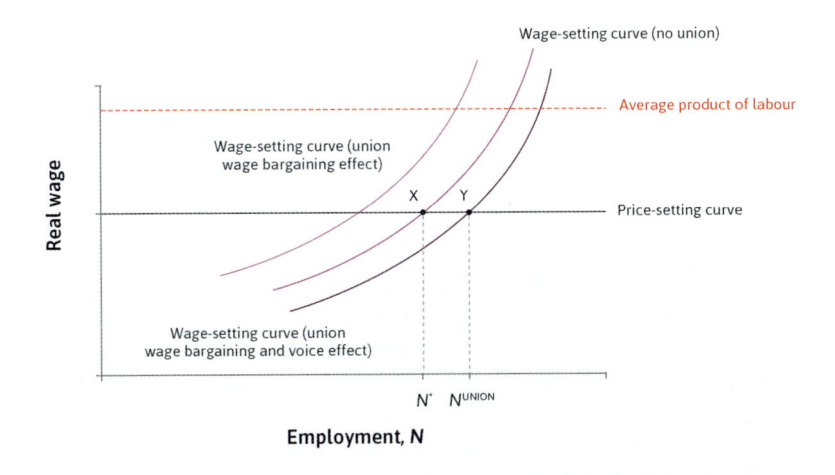

Figure 8.31 The bargained wage-setting curve and equilibrium when there is a union voice effect.

QUESTION 8.9 CHOOSE THE CORRECT ANSWER(S)
Figure 8.27 (page 366) depicts the effect of union wage-setting. What can we conclude from this figure?

☐ Compared to A, at C the effort per hour is higher and therefore the firm's profit is higher.
☐ The resulting bargained wage-setting curve will be above the wage-setting curve with no union.
☐ The effect of a strong union is always to increase unemployment.
☐ Under union wage-setting, the firm is still setting the wage that maximizes its profits.

QUESTION 8.10 CHOOSE THE CORRECT ANSWER(S)
Which of the following statements regarding labour unions and wage bargaining are correct?

☐ A labour union can set both the wage level and the employment level.
☐ The bargaining curve can be above or below the wage-setting curve.
☐ Unions may choose to restrain their use of bargaining power.
☐ The unions' bargaining power comes from their ability to shut down firms.

8.12 RISING MARKUPS AND PROFIT SHARE, WEAKER TRADE UNIONS, AND RISING INEQUALITY

The data on rising markups and profit share in the US since 1980 in Section 8.9 (page 359) suggest that the extent of competition faced by firms has declined. In the WS/PS model, this is represented by a downward shift in the price-setting curve. The new equilibrium is at point B in Figure 8.32. The model predicts that a decline in the degree of competition and the resulting downward shift in the price-setting curve will bring about a rise in inequality for two reasons:

- *A higher markup means a higher profit share*: In the model with only labour costs, the markup *is* the profit share. See the new lower price-setting curve in Figure 8.32 and the fall in the wage share from 0.76 to 0.60.
- *Unemployment in equilibrium is higher*: In the figure for an economy of 100 people, the number of unemployed people rises from 7 to 10.

But the predicted rise in unemployment at point B did not occur in the US economy. That employment, if anything, rose, may be explained by the fact that trade unions became weaker in the US over this period in ways that shifted the wage-setting curve downward.

The union density rate, which measures the share of employees who belong to a union, fell from 20.1% in 1983 to 10.5% in 2018. As a result, it became easier (less costly) for employers to fire workers whose work they find unsatisfactory. This would increase the probability that a worker would be terminated if they were not working up to speed. From the previous section, this can be represented by a downward shift in the wage-setting curve (Figure 8.23). Over the same period, other changes in the

8.12 RISING MARKUPS AND PROFIT SHARE, WEAKER TRADE UNIONS, AND RISING INEQUALITY

labour market including the emergence of the gig economy, discussed in Section 6.14 (page 267), have reduced the reservation wage of workers and contributed to the downward shift of the wage-setting curve.

Work through the analysis in Figure 8.32 to see how the combination of growing monopoly power, with a weaker bargaining position for workers, can realize the model's prediction that inequality rises, without a rise in unemployment. Indeed, the example shown in the figure (point C) has lower unemployment than the initial situation at point A.

Using Section 8.10 (page 361), we can now illustrate the implications for inequality of the rise in monopoly power combined with the weakening of trade unions and emergence of the gig economy (Figure 8.33).

In this example, the impact of the rise in the profit share in pushing the Lorenz curve away from the line of equality outweighs the impact of the fall in unemployment in reducing inequality.

The combination of the model (Figures 8.32 and 8.33), with the data on markups, and the profit share in Figures 8.20 (page 360) and 8.21 (page 360) in Section 8.8, support the hypothesis that falling competition in markets for goods and services in the US is part of the reason for rising inequality among households, as shown by the Gini coefficient in Figure 8.22 (page 361). The trends in these charts are similar, but other factors may still be at work.

Two other important factors affecting the inequality of household market incomes are automation (https://tinyco.re/1875368) and the China shock (https://tinyco.re/4027605). People in particular occupations have been the losers from the development of new technologies that replace

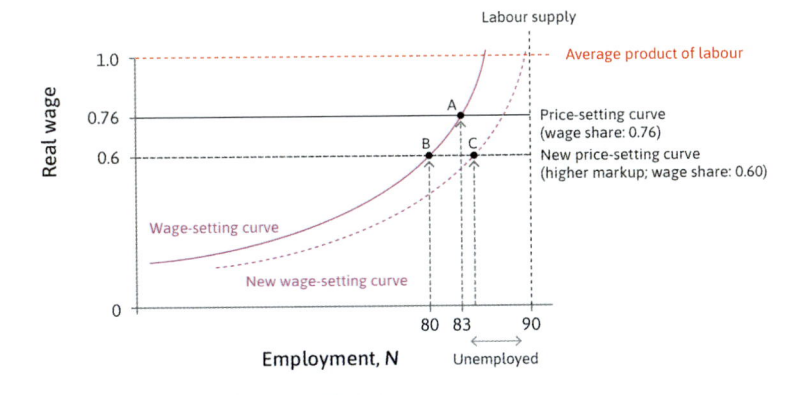

To explore all of the slides in this figure, see the online version at https://tinyco.re/9485514.

Figure 8.32 Rising monopoly power (the product market) and declining worker power (the labour market)—a new equilibrium.

1. The initial situation
The economy is at point A, with a wage share of 0.76 and an unemployment rate of 7%.

2. The new price-setting curve
Due to the decrease in the level of competition, the price-setting curve shifts down. The wage share falls to 0.6 and the unemployment rate increases to 10% (point B).

3. The new wage-setting curve
Due to the weaker bargaining position of workers, the wage-setting curve also shifts down. Depending on how far the wage-setting curve shifts, unemployment can decrease compared to the initial situation, as shown by point C.

routine work. Other losers have been those working in particular industries subject to competition from imports from China, as it rapidly industrialized and became a large supplier of manufactured goods, such as furniture and toys.

8.13 LABOUR MARKET POLICIES TO ADDRESS UNEMPLOYMENT AND INEQUALITY

The objectives of labour market policies typically include reducing structural unemployment and raising wages (particularly of the least well off). Policies that shift the price-setting curve upwards reduce structural unemployment and raise the real wage. As we saw in Section 8.10 (page 361), both of these outcomes reduce inequality.

Education and training

Consider an improvement in the quality of education and training that future employees receive, which increases the productivity of labour. What is the effect of this productivity increase on real wages and equilibrium employment?

To explore all of the slides in this figure, see the online version at https://tinyco.re/8579443.

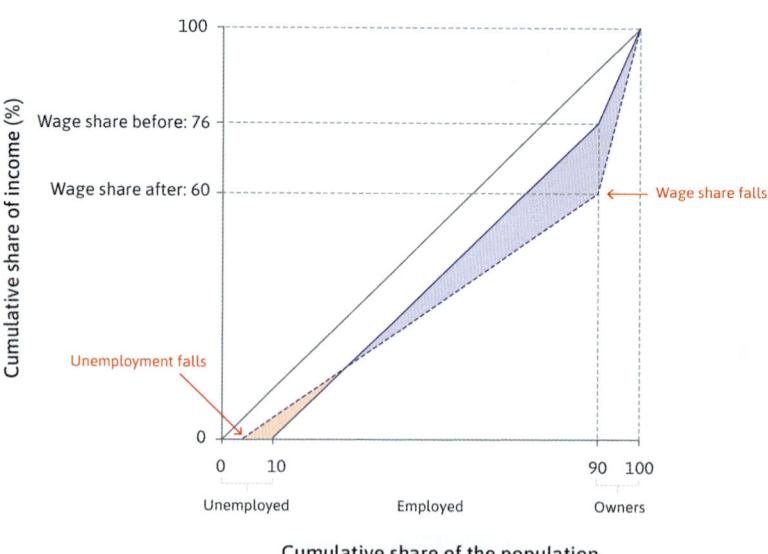

Figure 8.33 Rising monopoly power (the product market) and declining worker power (the labour market)—higher inequality in the new equilibrium.

1. Lorenz curves in the initial and new equilibrium
The dotted line shows the Lorenz curve in the initial equilibrium, and the solid line shows the Lorenz curve in the new equilibrium.

2. The decline in the wage share
The fall in the wage share increased inequality, as shown by the shaded blue area.

3. The fall in unemployment
The increase in employment (relative to the new equilibrium) decreased inequality, as shown by the shaded red area. However, the blue area is larger so the net effect is an increase in inequality.

The markup chosen by the firm when it sets its price to maximize its profits is determined by the amount of competition that the firm faces, so it is unaffected by the increase in productivity.

This markup determines the distribution of the firm's revenue between the employees and the owners, and has not changed either—wages remain the same fraction of revenue. Therefore, since the firm's output per worker has risen, real wages and the price-setting curve must also rise.

The outcome of an improvement in education and training is a fall in structural unemployment and a rise in the real wage.

A wage subsidy

A policy that has been advocated to increase employment is a subsidy paid to firms in proportion to the wages it pays its workers. For example, suppose that hiring a worker for an hour would cost the firm $40 in wages, but it would receive a 10% subsidy of that amount from the government, or $4. Therefore, the net wage cost to the firm would now be $36.

How would this affect the price-setting curve? The costs of the firm have now fallen, but as above, the markup that the firm will use to determine its price has not changed, so the firm will lower its price to restore the old markup. When all firms do this, the prices of goods that the worker consumes fall, and real wages rise. The effect, as above, is to shift the price-setting curve upwards.

The outcome of a **wage subsidy** policy is a fall in structural unemployment and a rise in the real wage.

> **wage subsidy** A government payment either to firms or employees, to raise the wage received by workers or lower the wage costs paid by firms, with the objective of increasing hiring and workers' incomes.

Paying for labour market policies

Assessing the full effect of each of these policies should take account of how the education and training or the wage subsidy were financed, but to allow a simple illustration of how the model works, we assume that the funds necessary for these programs could be raised without affecting the labour or product markets.

8.14 LABOUR MARKET POLICIES: SHIFTING THE NASH EQUILIBRIUM

In Unit 3 (page 124) you learned that many important economic actions cannot be simply enforced by the government. When the government decided to raise the tax rate to raise additional revenue for programs that improve the life chances of less well-off children, it did not take account of the incentives it created for tax avoidance.

Two examples of important but 'difficult to command' economic activities are investing and working hard. Governments do not have the information or the legal authority to command wealthy individuals to use their financial resources to invest in new buildings, research, and equipment (other than in exceptional circumstances, such as wartime). Nor can governments command workers to work hard and well.

To understand why this can constrain policymakers, consider the case of the proposal to introduce an unemployment benefit. The aim of the policy is to improve the standard of living of the unemployed without increasing the unemployment rate. We assume that the government shifts its spending priorities in order to be able to finance the unemployment benefits.

Unintended consequences

We begin by identifying the Nash equilibrium in the initial situation before the policy is introduced. In Figure 8.34, the economy is at the point marked N, where the wage- and price-setting curves intersect. This is a Nash equilibrium because neither a worker (employed or unemployed) nor a firm could be better off by setting a different wage or price, offering to work at a different wage, or hiring a different number of workers.

First, we look at the short-run impact of the policy using Figure 8.34.

- *Initial equilibrium with no unemployment benefit:* With no unemployment benefits, the Nash equilibrium is at point N.
- *Voters successfully demand an unemployment benefit:* The workers—employed and unemployed—vote to elect a government that offers a new policy. Workers will receive it when they are out of work.
- *The benefit raises the reservation option of employed workers:* In the short run, this shifts the wage-setting curve upwards, so that employers now have to pay more to induce workers to work hard and well. This is shown by point C.

The policy has its intended effect—the unemployed receive a higher income. Moreover, employed workers' wages have risen too, seemingly an unexpected feature of the policy. However, this unintended effect—raising wages—takes the economy away from its initial Nash equilibrium. We will see how the long-run effects can differ from the short-run effects.

Using the analysis in Figure 8.34, follow the logic of the model as the actors respond to the policy.

We can summarize the impact of the policy:

- *Short-run impact shifts the wage-setting curve upwards:* The unemployed receive higher benefits and the employed receive higher wages (point C).
- *Long-run impact is higher structural unemployment:* There is a new Nash equilibrium in the long run. The economy is at point N'. As intended, the unemployed now receive higher income when out of work. But fewer workers are employed, which was not intended.

Unemployment benefits in the model and in the data

Surprisingly, when we look at the data, we find that countries with more generous unemployment benefits do not, on average, have higher unemployment rates. In Figure 8.35, for example, Sweden has quite generous unemployment benefits and a relatively low level of unemployment. This is even more the case for Norway, Denmark, and the Netherlands.

Unemployment benefits, unions, and wage-setting in Sweden

This suggests that these countries were able to achieve a Nash equilibrium outcome different from either N or N'. Figure 8.36 shows how this may have happened—there is a third Nash equilibrium at N", where a new higher price-setting curve intersects the post reform wage-setting curve.

The Swedish approach had its origins in the 'solidarity wage policy', devised in 1951 by Gösta Rehn and Rudolph Meidner, two economists who worked at the research institute of the Trade Union Confederation in Sweden.

They reasoned that workers and employers have a common interest in rapid productivity growth, and that workers could enjoy higher wages without the profits of firms being reduced if more of the economy's output was produced by high-productivity firms rather than by firms with low productivity.

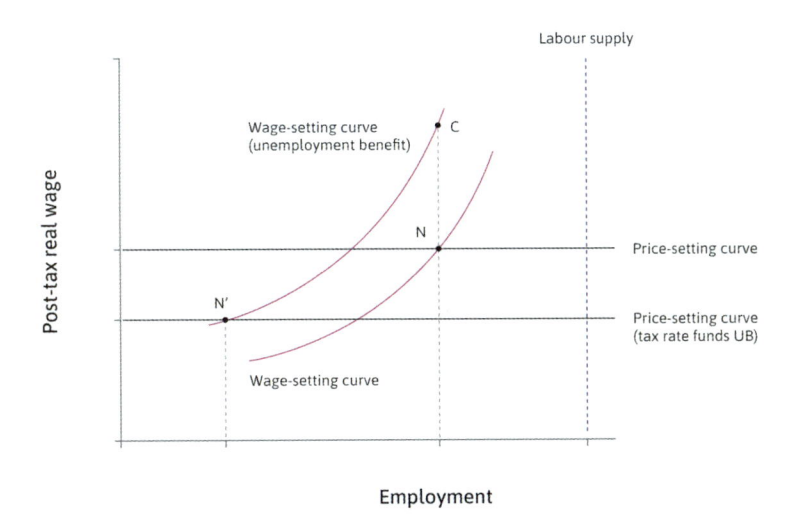

To explore all of the slides in this figure, see the online version at https://tinyco.re/5859631.

Figure 8.34 Short- and long-run effects of introducing an unemployment benefit.

1. The status quo
The Nash equilibrium is at point N. The new government introduces an unemployment benefit that workers will receive when out of work.

2. The unintended consequence
This raises the reservation option of employed workers, so that employers now have to pay more to induce workers to work hard and well. This is shown by point C.

3. The result
The new Nash equilibrium is at N′, with higher unemployment.

View this data at OWiD https://tinyco.re/2762873

OECD (2019). *OECD Statistics* (https://tinyco.re/4359913).

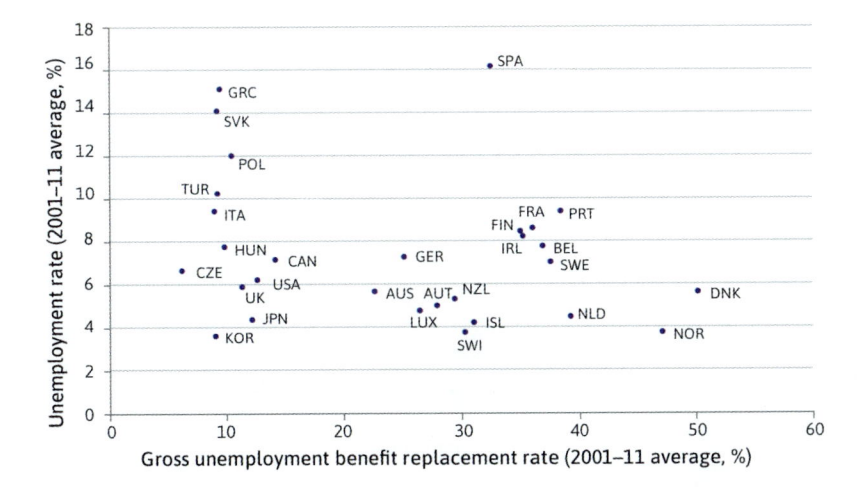

Figure 8.35 Unemployment benefit generosity and unemployment rates across the OECD (2001–2017).

In our 'Economist in action' video, John Van Reenen uses the game of cricket to explain how the economy's average productivity is affected by the survival of low productivity firms.

The solidarity wage policy in Sweden was actually three linked policies:

- *Equal wages for equal work:* This means that the wage for each job was set at the national level by negotiations between the employers' association and the union. This had the effect of reducing wage differences among workers doing similar jobs. The lowest-productivity firms had survived by paying lower wages than other firms paid to equivalent workers. Under the new policy, these firms could not pay the negotiated wage and still remain profitable, so they had to exit the industry. Higher-productivity firms survived and took over the market share of the failed firms.
- *Unemployment benefits:* These were generous but were only available for a relatively short time.
- *Active labour market policy:* Retraining and mobility allowances helped displaced workers find new jobs.

The solidarity wage policy forced low-productivity firms out of the market. The remaining firms had higher productivity and could, therefore, maintain their profit margins at lower prices, pushing the price-setting curve upwards. Retraining and mobility allowances ensured that these high-productivity firms had access to a well-trained workforce, allowing them to cut costs and prices even further.

Figure 8.36 shows how this combination of policies results in a new equilibrium with higher real wages at N", and without the rise in unemployment at N'.

Van Reenen: What determines productivity? https://tinyco.re/4455896

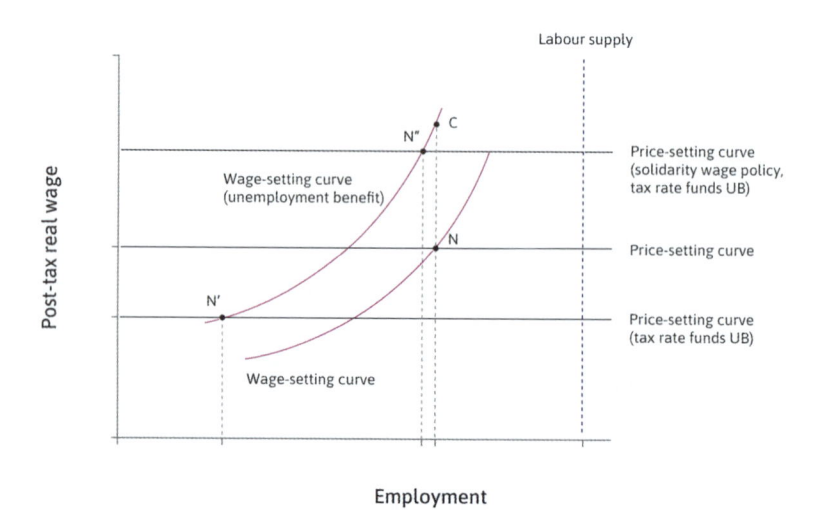

Figure 8.36 Combining the introduction of an unemployment benefit with a solidarity wage policy to raise productivity in the economy.

> **QUESTION 8.11 CHOOSE THE CORRECT ANSWER(S)**
> Referring to Figure 8.36 (page 376), which of the following statements are true?
>
> ☐ The upward shift in the wage-setting curve would have caused real wages to increase.
> ☐ Policies that shift the wage-setting curve without also changing the price-setting curve cannot increase real wages in equilibrium.
> ☐ The solidarity wage policy raises wages because it forces low productivity firms out of business.
> ☐ Increasing unemployment benefits (without a solidarity wage policy) made all workers worse off.

8.15 LOOKING BACKWARD: BARISTAS AND BREAD MARKETS

We have devoted much of this unit to the labour market for two reasons:

- *It is important to society:* If the labour market works well, the economy better serves our interests.
- *It does not function like a price-taking market:* It is essential to know the differences to understand how the economy as a whole works.

A good way to review these differences is to contrast the market for bread—used in the previous unit to illustrate the model of a competitive equilibrium of price-takers—with the market for, say, baristas (who, for readers unfamiliar with Italian-inspired coffee shops, are those who make espresso-based coffee drinks).

Taking a price, setting a price

Recall that, in the equilibrium of the bread market, neither bread consumers nor bakeries selling bread could benefit by offering to pay a different price or setting a different price from the one that prevailed in other transactions throughout the market. Buyers and sellers were price-takers in equilibrium:

- *No (bread) buyer could benefit from offering to pay less than the prevailing price:* No bakery would agree to the sale.
- *No buyer could benefit by offering to pay more than the going price:* This would just be throwing away money. Buyers in the bread market are price-takers because they wish to purchase bread at the lowest possible price.
- *No seller (bakery) could benefit from setting a higher price:* There would be no customers.
- *No seller could benefit by offering a lower price:* This would be throwing away money. Sellers can have as many customers as they like, at the existing price.

Now think about a buyer in the labour market. This is an employer who buys the employee's time. The price is the wage. An employer who acts like a bread buyer would offer the employee the lowest wage that the individual would accept to take the job. This lowest possible wage is the reservation wage.

We know from Unit 6 (page 258) that an employer who did this would be disappointed. The worker who is paid just a reservation wage does not worry about losing the job, and so would have little incentive to work hard. Instead, we saw that employers choose a wage to balance their wage costs against the positive effects of a higher wage on the employee's motivation to work.

Complete and incomplete contracts

In the bread market, the sales contract between buyer and seller is for bread; if you buy bread you get what you want. It's a complete contract (remember, a contract need not be in writing and it need not be signed to be enforceable—your receipt is enough to get a refund if the bag labelled 'fresh bread' turned out to contain a week-old loaf when you got home).

In contrast, in the labour market, the employment contract is usually for the employee's work time and not for the work itself. Because it is the employee's work that produces the firm's goods and is essential to the firm's profits, this means the contract is an **incomplete contract**: something that matters to one of the parties to the exchange is not covered in the contract.

The implication is that, in contrast to the bread market, a buyer in the labour market is not throwing money away by paying more than is necessary to buy the employee's time; it is the way that employers get what they want (work) and how they make profits. And because employers are deciding on the wage that they will offer the worker, they are wage-setters and not price-takers. This is why Unit 7's model of the competitive equilibrium of price-takers (page 300) does not work in the labour market.

> **incomplete contract** A contract that does not specify, in an enforceable way, every aspect of the exchange that affects the interests of parties to the exchange (or of any others affected by the exchange).

Pareto efficiency and unexploited opportunities for mutual gains

In Unit 3, you encountered many situations in which the Nash equilibrium of some social interaction is not **Pareto efficient**. Examples include the **prisoners' dilemma** and the **public goods games**.

- *We use the Nash equilibrium:* This concept helps us predict what outcomes we will observe when people interact.
- *We use Pareto efficiency:* This concept evaluates whether there is some other outcome in which all parties might have done better (or at least as well).

> **Pareto efficient** An allocation with the property that there is no alternative technically feasible allocation in which at least one person would be better off, and nobody worse off.
> **prisoners' dilemma** A game in which the payoffs in the dominant strategy equilibrium are lower for each player, and also lower in total, than if neither player played the dominant strategy.
> **public goods game** Similar to a prisoners' dilemma game with more than two people; the dominant strategy is not to contribute to the public good.

Recall from the model used to illustrate the bread market in Unit 7 that there were no unexploited opportunities for mutual gain at the competitive equilibrium (where the demand and supply curves intersect). In this situation, it is not possible to make one of the buyers or sellers better off without making at least one of them worse off. Therefore, the outcome was Pareto efficient.

This is not the case in the labour market. Competition among many buyers (firms hiring employees) and sellers (people seeking work) results in an equilibrium outcome—the wage w^* and the level of employment N^*—that is not Pareto efficient. What this means is that there is some *other* outcome—a different wage and level of employment that is feasible from the standpoint of the available resources and technology—that both employers and employees would prefer.

To see this, imagine that we are at the equilibrium of the labour market and product market (intersection of the wage-setting and price-setting curves at w^* and N^*), and one of the unemployed workers (identical to those employed) goes to an employer and says: 'Give me a break. I'll work as hard as the rest of your workforce, but you can pay me a little less.'

The employer thinks: 'If I pay him a slightly lower wage, and if he works as hard as the rest, then my profits will go up.'

For the unemployed worker, getting a job makes a big difference. She now receives an employment rent, which measures how much better it is for her to have a job than not. The deal is a good one for her despite the fact that the employment rent she receives is slightly lower than that received by other workers (because her wage is slightly lower).

This example shows that there is some other technically feasible outcome—employ $N^* + 1$ workers at the wage w^* for N^* of them and w^* minus a little bit for the last worker hired—that would be an improvement for both the unemployed worker and the employer. Therefore, the outcome (N^*, w^*) is Pareto inefficient.

Why not hire a worker who is prepared to take a lower wage?

But if that is the case, why doesn't the employer hire the unemployed person?

The answer is that the deal, while technically feasible, is not economically possible. This is because there is no way to enforce the unemployed person's promise to work as hard as the rest in return for a slightly lower wage. Remember the w^* on the wage-setting curve is the *minimum* the firm can pay to identical workers to ensure they work rather than shirk.

The problem, therefore, goes back to a fundamental fact about the relationship between the firm and its employees—the contract is incomplete in that it cannot ensure a given level of effort from the worker. The Nash equilibrium in the labour market is Pareto inefficient.

The politics and sociology of markets

Here is another difference between the bread market and the barista market. The baker probably does not know the name of the person buying the bread, or anything about the buyer other than that he is offering the right price for the loaf. The buyer most likely cares equally little about the baker, other than the taste of the bread.

Now think about the barista. What are the chances that he does not know the name of his immediate supervisor? And vice versa?

Why the difference? The bread market tends to be a one-off interaction among virtual strangers, while the labour market is an ongoing interaction among people who not only know each other's names, but also care about what the other person is like. We call it the **employment relationship**.

The barista's supervisor cares about what the barista is like because his personality, loyalty to the brand, and his respect for social norms—such as honesty and hard work—influence the quality and quantity of effort that he puts into the job. The buyer of the bread does not care about these aspects of the baker because what matters is the quality of the loaf—which can be easily determined—and a new bakery readily found if the taste is not right.

Another major difference is that the supervisor directs what the barista does—to dress a certain way, to show up at work at a certain time, and to not waste time on the job—with the expectation that he will comply with her orders. Because the barista receives an employment rent that he would lose if the supervisor were to dismiss him, the supervisor can exercise power over him, getting him to do things that he might not do without the threat of dismissal.

employment relationship The interaction between an employee and an employer in which the employer sets the hours and other conditions of work and the wage, directs the employee's activities and may terminate her employment, and the employee chooses how hard to work and whether to quit her job. The employee's level of effort, or her decision to remain in the firm, are determined by the choices made by the two parties—and are affected by the exercise of power by the employer and the social norms of both parties.

This is not the case in the bread market. If the buyer complains about the baker's attire, he would be invited to shop elsewhere. The difference is that neither the buyer nor the seller in the bread market is receiving a rent. For each of them, the transaction yields benefits virtually identical to the next best alternative. When both can walk away (selling to another customer; buying from another vendor) at virtually no cost, neither can exercise power over the other.

These are some of the differences—both economic and also political and sociological—between the bread market and the barista market. These are also the reasons why the model of the bread market with price-taking buyers and sellers and market clearing in equilibrium, does not work for the labour market. The table in Figure 8.37 summarizes the differences.

QUESTION 8.12 CHOOSE THE CORRECT ANSWER(S)
Which of the following statements are correct?

☐ Contracts are complete in both competitive goods markets and labour markets.

☐ In a competitive goods market, the buyers are price-takers, while in a labour market the buyers of employment (the firms) are price-setters.

☐ There is no economic rent for either the buyers or the sellers in competitive goods markets. In contrast, in labour markets the sellers receive economic rents.

☐ Social norms do not affect the outcomes in either goods markets or in labour markets.

Market	Bread: A market clearing equilibrium of price-takers	Baristas: Wage-setting by employers and equilibrium unemployment
Buyers	Individual consumers	Firms (employers)
Sellers	Firms (shops)	Individual workers
What is sold?	A loaf of bread	The worker's time
What does the buyer want?	A loaf of bread	The employee's effort on the job; not the worker's time
Competition among sellers?	Yes: There are many bakeries competing to sell bread.	Yes: There are many actual or would-be baristas competing to sell their time.
Is the contract complete?	Yes: If the bag labelled bread did not contain bread, you get your money back.	No: The firm's profits depend on the worker's effort per hour/week/month worked, which is not in the contract.
Price-taking buyers?	Yes: Individual buyers cannot bargain for a lower price than others are willing to pay (and would not want to pay more).	No: The buyer (the firm) sets the wage to minimize the cost of getting the worker to work; it cannot benefit by offering the lowest wage at which the worker (the seller) would accept the job.
Is there excess supply or demand in equilibrium?	No: The market clears. Sales take place at the lowest price the seller would accept.	Yes: Firms offer a wage higher than the worker's reservation wage (minimum price the seller would accept) to maximize their profits.

Figure 8.37 Differences between the labour market and competitive (price-taking) product markets.

8.16 STRUCTURAL AND CYCLICAL UNEMPLOYMENT: THE ROLE OF DEMAND

Look back at Figure 8.17 (page 357). There are large changes in the rate of unemployment relative to its long-term average (much more so in Spain than in Germany). It seems unlikely that the Nash equilibrium rate of unemployment in our model for Spain would drop precipitously from the late 1990s to the first five years of this century, and then jump back up five years later. It looks like more is going on in the unemployment data than is captured in our model.

Another case in point. At the beginning of this unit, you read about the father and son working in the Australian minerals sector (Doug and Rob Grey). The boom and bust in their lives reflected changes in economic conditions in the Australian economy as a whole. The minerals boom had produced the large-scale construction of mining facilities in Western Australia, Queensland, and the Northern Territory. As construction was coming to an end on existing projects, global iron ore prices collapsed, with the result that work was not started on new mines, ports, and processing facilities. In Figure 8.1 (page 333), unemployment began to rise as the global price of iron ore plummeted.

Demand fluctuates and causes cyclical unemployment

Unemployment increased because the demand for labour in mining and in the related service activities shrank. Not only did the demand for minerals fall, but demand also declined for the goods and services that the Grey family and others like them would have purchased if they had kept their jobs. As a result, demand for goods and services fell across the economy, and with it the derived demand for labour. The term 'derived demand for labour' is used to highlight the fact that the firms' demand for labour depends on the demand for their goods and services.

Aggregate demand is the sum of the demand for all of the goods and services produced in the economy, whether from consumers, firms, the government, or buyers in other countries. The increase in unemployment caused by a fall in aggregate demand is called 'demand-deficient' unemployment—or, **cyclical unemployment**.

Observed unemployment is the sum of the cyclical unemployment and the level of unemployment at the Nash equilibrium of the labour market and product market, where the wage-setting and price-setting curves intersect (the structural unemployment):

Observed unemployment = cyclical unemployment + structural unemployment

Because the observed unemployment may fall below the equilibrium level—as it did during the mineral resources boom in Australia that underpinned the 'good times' for the Grey family—cyclical unemployment may be a negative number.

Cyclical and structural unemployment

How does this cyclical unemployment appear in our model of the economy, and how does it relate to structural unemployment?

Follow the analysis in Figure 8.38 to compare unemployment at the Nash equilibrium (at X) with the unemployment caused by a low level of aggregate demand (at B).

> **cyclical unemployment** The increase in unemployment above equilibrium unemployment caused by a fall in aggregate demand associated with the business cycle. *Also known as: demand-deficient unemployment. See also: equilibrium unemployment.*

An unemployed person at X is involuntarily unemployed because that person would accept a job at the real wage shown by the intersection of the wage- and price-setting curves.

Notice that an unemployed person at point B is also involuntarily unemployed. In fact, such a person would accept a job with a wage below the wage shown at B, and would still be willing to work hard on the job.

To find out more about using the WS/PS model to understand business cycles, inflation and unemployment, see Units 13-17 in the CORE team's *The Economy* (https://tinyco.re/6612325), and *Macroeconomics: Institutions, Instability and the Financial System* by Wendy Carlin and David Soskice.

> **QUESTION 8.13 CHOOSE THE CORRECT ANSWER(S)**
> Look again at Figure 8.38. Denote employment at point B as N_B, employment at X as N_X, and the total labour supply as N_L. Which of the following statements about Figure 8.38 are correct?
>
> ☐ The demand-deficient unemployment at B is $N_L - N_B$.
> ☐ The firms' demand for labour is N_X at X, and is N_B at B.
> ☐ $N_L - N_X$ and $N_L - N_B$ are the levels of involuntary unemployment at X and B, respectively.
> ☐ The equilibrium level of unemployment is $N_L - N_B$.

To explore all of the slides in this figure, see the online version at https://tinyco.re/4516968.

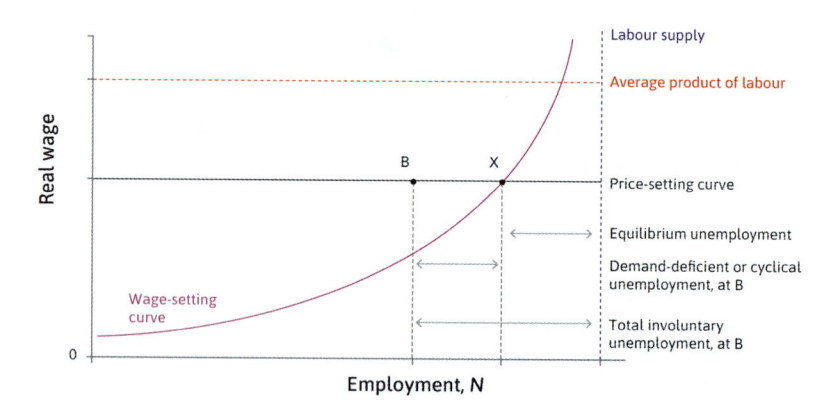

Figure 8.38 Equilibrium (structural) and demand-deficient (cyclical) unemployment.

1. Point X
At X, unemployment is at its labour market equilibrium level. Someone losing a job at X is not indifferent between being employed and unemployed because that person experiences a cost of losing the job.

2. Point B
At B, there are additional people looking for work who are also involuntarily unemployed. The additional unemployment at B is due to low aggregate demand and is called demand-deficient, or cyclical, unemployment. They would be prepared to accept a lower wage, as long as it is not lower than the wage shown by the wage-setting curve. But without higher demand for their output, firms will not offer such jobs.

3. The Nash equilibrium
At point B, total involuntary unemployment is given by the sum of cyclical and structural unemployment.

8.17 CONCLUSION

The model of the aggregate economy presented here the (**WS/PS model**) brings together four decisions:

- workers deciding how hard to work
- owners of firms, through their HR department, deciding what wages to pay
- owners of firms, through their marketing department, deciding what prices to charge for their goods
- customers deciding how much to buy.

The relationships among the four actors and their four decisions are depicted in Figure 8.39.

Though the marketing and HR departments of the firm make decisions independently, they are unified under the direction of the firm's owner who directs each to make decisions that will maximize his profits. Similarly, the customers and the employees may be the same people, or be members of the same family unified under their desire to have what they consider to be a good life.

The WS/PS model places all four decisions under a single lens and asks how the economy works as a result of their interactions. It identifies levels of **real wages** and **structural unemployment** that are consistent with the decisions taken independently by each of these decision-makers, that is the **Nash equilibrium** of the model.

The WS curve shifts downwards if:

- unemployment benefits decrease
- disutility of working decreases
- social stigma of unemployment increases
- technology lowers the cost of monitoring the worker's effort.

The PS curve shifts downwards if:

- labour productivity decreases
- the markup increases as the result of markets being less competitive.

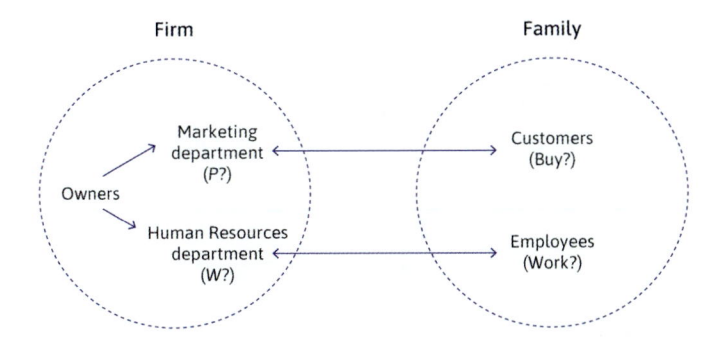

Figure 8.39 The WS/PS model: Actors and their decisions.

Trade unions can have different effects depending on size, bargaining power and behaviour:

- *Bargained wage effect:* How far the bargained WS curve lies above the employer-set curve depends on unions' relative bargaining power, which is also influenced by laws and social norms.
- *Union voice effect:* The reciprocation of worker-friendly policies that reduce the disutility of effort shifts the best response curve as workers exert more effort.
- *Labour productivity effect:* By fostering a cooperative culture with management and encouraging productivity improvements unions can shift the PS curve.

The model of the aggregate economy allows us to chart the effect of changes in labour productivity, the extent of competition and the institutions governing the relationship between employers and employees not only on wages and employment but also on the degree of inequality in the economy as a whole using the **Lorenz curve** and **Gini coefficient**.

8.18 *DOING ECONOMICS:* MEASURING THE NON-MONETARY COST OF UNEMPLOYMENT

In Section 8.7 (page 356), we explained why there will always be involuntary unemployment in labour market equilibrium, in order to create an employment rent that motivates employed workers. The employment rent takes into account both monetary and non-monetary costs and benefits, such as social status from being employed. On the other hand, being unemployed may be psychologically as well as financially detrimental because of the stress of looking for a new job, as well as social norms and expectations regarding work.

In *Doing Economics* Empirical Project 8, we will use self-reported wellbeing to measure the disutility from unemployment, and see whether social norms can explain any differences in wellbeing between the employed and unemployed in European countries.

Go to *Doing Economics* Empirical Project 8 (https://tinyco.re/7135249) to work on this project.

> *Learning objectives*
> In this project you will:
>
> - practise working with fairly large datasets
> - detect and correct entries in a dataset
> - re-code variables to make them easier to analyse
> - calculate percentiles for subsets of the data
> - calculate confidence intervals for the difference in means between groups.

8.19 REFERENCES

Carlin, Wendy, and David Soskice. 2015. *Macroeconomics: Institutions, Instability, and the Financial System*. New York, NY: Oxford University Press.

Freeman, Sunny. 2015. 'What Canada can learn from Sweden's unionized retail workers' (https://tinyco.re/0808135). *Huffington Post Canada Business*. Updated 19 March 2015.

Hirsch, Barry T. 2008. 'Sluggish institutions in a dynamic world: Can unions and industrial competition coexist?' *Journal of Economic Perspectives* 22 (1) (February): pp. 153–76.

The CORE team. *The Economy* (https://tinyco.re/6612325). New York, NY: Oxford University Press.

9

THE CREDIT MARKET: BORROWERS, LENDERS, AND THE RATE OF INTEREST

Payday loan shop, Soho, London

9.1 INTRODUCTION

- People with wealth are able to borrow substantial amounts, and they often lend money to less-wealthy people.
- People can rearrange the timing of their spending by borrowing, lending, investing, and saving.
- While mutual gains for both borrowers and lenders motivate credit market transactions, there is a conflict of interest between them over the rate of interest, the prudent use of loaned funds, and the repayment of loans.
- Borrowing and lending is a principal-agent relationship in which there is no enforceable contract that can guarantee for the lender (the principal) that the loan will be repaid by the borrower (the agent).
- To solve this problem, lenders often require borrowers to contribute some of their own funds to a project as collateral or equity.
- People with limited wealth are unable to contribute collateral or equity, and as a result are often unable to secure loans or can only do so at higher interest rates.

The market town of Chambar in southeastern Pakistan serves as the financial centre for 2,400 farmers in surrounding villages. At the beginning of the kharif planting season in April, when the farmers sow cotton and other cash crops, they buy fertilizer and other inputs. Months have passed since they sold the last harvest, and so the only way they can buy inputs is to borrow money, promising to repay at the next harvest. Others borrow to pay for medicines or doctors.

But few farmers have ever walked through the shiny glass and steel doors of the JS Bank on Hyderabad Road. Instead, they visit one of approximately 60 moneylenders.

Irfan Aleem. 1990. 'Imperfect information, screening, and the costs of informal lending: A study of a rural credit market in Pakistan'. *The World Bank Economic Review* 4 (3): pp. 329–49.

Jessica Silver-Greenberg. 2014. 'New York prosecutors charge payday loan firms with usury'. *DealBook*. Updated 11 August 2014.

Those seeking loans to purchase a car are often required to allow a device to be installed in the vehicle that is controlled by the bank, which will disable the ignition of the car if the loan payments are not made as required, as this *New York Times* video shows. The practice has not made lenders very popular. http://tinyco.re/2009482

If they are seeking a first-time loan, they will be questioned intensively by the moneylender, asked for references from other farmers known to the lender, and in most cases given a small trial loan as a test of creditworthiness. The lender will probably visit to investigate the condition of a farmer's land, animals, and equipment.

The lenders are right to be wary. If the farmer's crop fails due to drought or lack of attention, the lender will make a loss. Unlike many financial institutions, lenders do not usually require that the farmer set aside some property or belongings—for example, some gold jewelry—that would become the lender's property if the farmer does not repay the loan.

If the would-be first-time borrower looks reliable or trustworthy enough, the farmer is offered a loan. In Chambar, this is at an average interest rate of 78% per annum. If the borrower pays the loan back in four months (the growing period of the crop prior to harvest), 100 rupees borrowed before planting is paid back as 126 rupees. But, knowing that more than half the loan applications are refused, the borrower would feel fortunate.

And indeed, the borrower in Chambar would be, at least compared to some people 12,000 km away in New York, who take out short-term loans to be repaid when their next paycheck comes in. These payday loans bear interest rates ranging from 350% to 650% per annum, much higher than the legal maximum interest rate in New York (25%). In 2014, the 'payday syndicate' offering these loans was charged with criminal usury in the first degree.

Given the interest rates charged, is the business of lending in Chambar or of payday loans in New York likely to be exceptionally profitable? The evidence from Chambar suggests it is not. Some of the funds lent to farmers are borrowed from commercial banks, like the JS Bank, at interest rates averaging 32% per annum, representing a cost to the moneylenders. And the costs of the extensive screening of borrowers and collection of the debts further reduces the profits made by the moneylenders.

Partly as a result of the careful choices made by the moneylenders in Chambar, default is rare—fewer than one in 30 borrowers fail to repay. By contrast, default rates on loans made by commercial banks are much higher—one in three. The moneylenders' success in avoiding default is based on their accurate assessment of the likely trustworthiness of their clients.

Not everyone passes the trustworthiness tests set by the moneylenders and the payday lenders—some would-be borrowers find it impossible to get a loan. And, in Chambar and New York, some of those who do, pay much higher interest rates than others.

Long before there were the employers, employees, and the unemployed that we studied in the previous unit, there were lenders and borrowers. Some of the first written records of any kind were records of debts. Differences in income between those who borrow—like the farmers in Chambar and those seeking payday loans in New York—and those who lend—like the money lenders in Chambar and the payday lenders in New York—remain an important source of economic inequality today.

In this unit, we study borrowers and lenders and the workings of the market for credit. We examine the nature of the benefits that arise from lending and borrowing; we also show how the nature of credit markets can limit those benefits. Like the labour market, the credit market is essential to the functioning of a capitalist economy, and also like the labour market the credit market differs in important ways from the markets for bread, language courses, and the other goods and services studied in Unit 7 (page 279).

9.2 INCOME, CONSUMPTION, AND WEALTH

In everyday language, terms like 'money', 'wealth', and 'investment' are often used loosely. We hear people say: 'I want a job that pays good money,' or: 'I want to invest some money for when I retire,' or: 'I need to borrow some money to see me through to the end of the month.'

To understand the credit market, we need to clarify how these terms are used in economics.

It turns out that, for economists, one of the trickiest things to define precisely is money. Economists like to define money in terms of what it *does*. They point to a number of functions that money fulfils. Some of these functions are also fulfilled by other things, but only money fulfils *all* these functions. We shall delve deeper into these functions in Unit 10 (page 437).

But at this stage, we only need to think about one function of money—money is a 'store of value'. In simple terms, this means that anyone who *has* money can turn it into goods and services. When people say they want more money, what they really want is more of the goods and services that money will buy.

Thus:

- *'I want a job that pays good money,'* means: 'I want a job that enables me to have more stuff.'
- *'I want to invest some money for when I retire,'* means: 'I want to *postpone* some of my **consumption** of goods and services until I retire.'
- *'I need to borrow some money to see me through to the end of the month,'* means: 'I want to bring *forward* some spending so that I can maintain my desired level of consumption until the end of the month.' (It is, crucially, a bringing forward, since borrowing means that higher consumption this month must imply *lower* consumption at a later date).

Why are our paraphrases more precise than the original sentences? In each case, they focus on the person's motivation. One way to show this is to note that money itself does *not* play a unique role in the original sentences. Thus:

- *'I want a job with good fringe benefits,'* still means: 'I want a job that enables me to have more stuff.'
- *'I want to invest in the stock market for when I retire,'* still means: 'I want to *postpone* some of my consumption of goods and services until I retire.'
- *'I need to increase my overdraft to see me through to the end of the month,'* still means: 'I want to bring *forward* some spending so that I can maintain my desired level of consumption until the end of the month.'

In this unit, we shall postpone any further discussion of money. We first focus on consumption and **investment** directly in terms of goods and services, and on **wealth** as *potential* spending power. We then analyse the role of borrowing and lending in allowing us to shift spending across time. We return to the topic of what money is and does in Unit 10.

Wealth

One way to think about the amount of wealth that you have as a household is that it is the largest amount that you could spend without borrowing, after having paid off your debts and collected any debts owed to you—for example, if you sold your house, car, and everything you owned.

---

consumption (C) Expenditure on both short-lived goods and services and long-lived goods, which are called consumer durables. *See also: consumer durables.*

investment (I) Expenditure on newly produced capital goods (machinery and equipment) and buildings, including new housing.

wealth Stock of things owned or value of that stock. It includes the market value of a home, car, any land, buildings, machinery, or other capital goods that a person may own, and any financial assets, such as bank deposits, shares, bonds, or loans made to others. Debts to others are subtracted from wealth—for example, the mortgage owed to the bank.

income The amount of labour earnings, dividends, interest, rent, and other payments (including transfers from the government) received by an economic actor, net of taxes paid, measured over a period of time, such as a year. The maximum amount that you could consume and leave your wealth unchanged. *Also known as: disposable income. See also: gross income.*

human capital The stock of knowledge, skills, behavioural attributes, and personal characteristics that determine the labour productivity or labour earnings of an individual. It is part of an individual's endowments. Investment in this through education, training, and socialization can increase the stock, and such investment is one of the sources of economic growth. *See also: endowment, labour productivity.*

earnings Wages, salaries, and other income from labour.

flow variable A quantity measured per unit of time, such as annual income or hourly wage. *See also: stock variable.*

stock variable A quantity measured at a point in time. Its units do not depend on time. *See also: flow variable.*

disposable income Income available after paying taxes and receiving transfers from the government.

depreciation The loss in value of a form of wealth that occurs either through use (wear and tear) or the passage of time (obsolescence).

The term wealth is also sometimes used in a broader sense to include immaterial or intangible aspects, such as your health, skills, and ability to earn an **income** (your **human capital**). But we will use the narrower definition of material wealth in this unit since we focus on forms of wealth that can potentially be turned into spending on goods and services.

Income

Income is the amount of money you receive over some period of time, whether from market **earnings**, assets that you own, or as transfers from the government.

Since it is measured over a period of time (such as weekly or yearly), it is a **flow variable** illustrated below in Figure 9.1. Wealth is a **stock variable**, meaning that it has no time dimension. At any moment of time it is just there. In this unit, we only consider after-tax income, also known as **disposable income**.

To highlight the difference between wealth and income, think of filling a bathtub, as in Figure 9.1. Wealth is the amount (stock) of water in the tub, while income is the flow of water into the tub. The inflow is measured by litres (or gallons) per minute; the stock of water is measured by litres (or gallons) at a particular moment in time.

As we have seen, some wealth takes physical forms, such as a house, or car, or office, or factory. The value of physical wealth tends to decline, either due to use or simply the passage of time. This reduction in the value of a stock of wealth over time is called **depreciation**. Using the bathtub analogy, depreciation is the amount of evaporation of the water. In economics, an example of depreciation is the fall in the value of a car with mileage and with

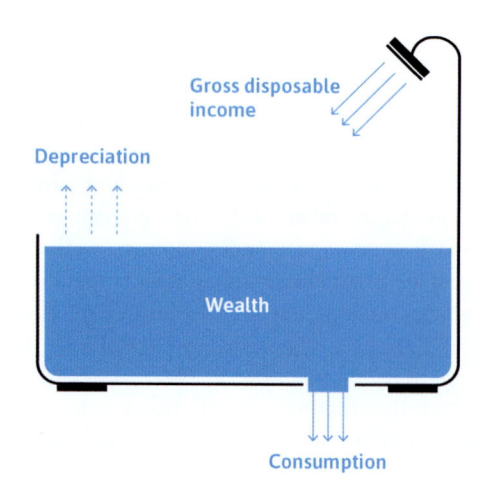

Figure 9.1 Wealth, income, depreciation, and consumption: The bathtub analogy.

age. Like income, depreciation is a flow (for example, you could measure it in dollars per year for a car or computer), but a negative one.

When we take account of depreciation, we must distinguish between net income and gross income. Gross income is the flow of disposable income into the bathtub. It either adds to wealth, is used for consumption spending or is lost as depreciation. Before the income enters the bathtub, taxes are subtracted and transfers are added, such as pension payments from the government. Net interest receipts are part of the flow into the bathtub, and so are net receipts of transfers from others (such as gifts).

Income net of depreciation is the maximum amount that you could consume and leave your wealth unchanged.

Consumption, saving, and investment

Water also flows out of the tub. The flow through the drain is called consumption, and it reduces wealth just as net income increases it.

Measured consumption includes spending on goods that provide services over long periods of time, like screens, bicycles and cars. Where the services are provided over a very long period as for new housing, the spending is classified as investment.

An individual (or household) saves when consumption is less than net income, so wealth increases. Wealth is the accumulation of past and current **saving**. Saving can take a number of forms, for example, in bank deposits, or in financial assets, such as shares (also known as stocks) in a company or a government bond. These are often held indirectly by investing in a pension fund. In everyday language these purchases are sometimes referred to as 'investment', but in economics investment means spending on capital goods that provide services over long periods of time, such as equipment or buildings.

The distinction between investment and purchasing shares or bonds (sometimes called financial investment) is illustrated by a sole proprietor business. At the end of the year, the owner decides what to do with her net income. Out of the net income, she decides on her consumption expenditure for the year ahead and saves the remainder, so her wealth rises.

With her savings, she could buy financial assets that provide funds to businesses or the government, such as shares or bonds. Contributions to a personal pension fund are an example of the use of savings to buy financial assets. Or, instead, she could spend on new assets such as computers to expand her business, which would be investment expenditure.

To summarize: in this example, the wealth of the owner of the small business has increased. The form that the increase in wealth takes is a combination of money (bank deposits), financial assets (bonds, shares, and pension fund assets), and physical assets (computer equipment for her business).

Lending and borrowing

Households borrow from banks, finance companies, payday lenders, or from other individuals to spend on consumer durables and nondurables and for the purchase of housing. Businesses and governments also borrow; when a household buys bonds with their savings, they are making a loan to the government (a government bond) or to a business (a corporate bond).

> **income net of depreciation** Disposable income minus depreciation. *See also: disposable income, gross income, depreciation.*
> **saving** When consumption expenditure is less than net income, saving takes place and wealth rises. *See also: wealth.*

QUESTION 9.1 CHOOSE THE CORRECT ANSWER(S)
Which of the following statements are correct?

☐ Your material wealth is the largest amount that you can consume without borrowing; it includes the value of your house, car, financial savings, and human capital.
☐ Income net of depreciation is the maximum amount that you can consume and leave your wealth unchanged.
☐ In economics, investment means saving in financial assets, such as shares and bonds.
☐ Depreciation is the loss in your financial savings due to unfavourable movements in the market.

QUESTION 9.2 CHOOSE THE CORRECT ANSWER(S)
Mr Bond has wealth of £500,000. He has a market income of £40,000 per year, on which he is taxed 30%. Mr Bond's wealth includes some equipment, which depreciates by £5,000 every year. Based on this information, which of the following statements are correct?

☐ Mr Bond's disposable income is £40,000.
☐ Mr Bond's net income is £28,000.
☐ The maximum amount of consumption expenditure possible for Mr Bond is £23,000.
☐ If Mr Bond decides to spend 60% of his net income on consumption and the rest on investment, then his investment is £9,200.

9.3 BORROWING: BRINGING CONSUMPTION FORWARD IN TIME

Borrowing and lending are about shifting consumption and production over time. The moneylender offers funds to the farmer to purchase fertilizer now, to pay back after the crop matures, as long as the harvest is good. The payday borrower will be paid at the end of the month but needs to buy food now. The borrower brings some future buying power to the present.

To understand borrowing and lending, we will use feasible sets and **indifference curves**. In Unit 4 (page 161) and Unit 5 (page 194), you studied how Alexei and Angela make choices between conflicting objectives, such as free time and grades or grain. They made choices from the feasible set, based on **preferences** described by indifference curves that represented how much they valued one objective relative to the other.

Here, you will see that the same feasible set and indifference curve analysis apply to choosing between having something now and having something later. In earlier units we saw that giving up free time is a way of getting more goods, or grades, or grain. We shall see that giving up some goods to be enjoyed now will sometimes allow us to have more goods later. The **opportunity cost** of having more goods now is having fewer goods later.

Borrowing and lending allow us to rearrange our capacity to buy goods and services across time. Borrowing allows us to buy more now but constrains us to buy less later.

To see how this works, think about Julia. She can count on her family (now and in the future) to provide the bare necessities. But she would like to consume more now. She may be a payday borrower in New York City or a

---

indifference curve A curve of the points which indicate the combinations of goods that provide a given level of utility to the individual.

preference Pro-and-con evaluations of the possible outcomes of the actions we may take that form the basis by which we decide on a course of action.

opportunity cost The opportunity cost of some action A is the foregone benefit that you would have enjoyed if instead you had taken some other action B. This is called an *opportunity* cost because by choosing A you give up the opportunity of choosing B. It is called a *cost* because the choice of A costs you the benefit you would have experienced had you chosen B.

farmer in Chambar at planting time, or perhaps she has just graduated and needs to finance a period before her first job begins.

Julia knows that, in the next period ('later'), she will have $100 when she is paid or when the crop is sold. Julia's situation is shown in Figure 9.2. Each point in the figure shows a given combination of Julia's consumption beyond the bare necessities provided by her family—both now (measured on the horizontal axis) and later (measured on the vertical axis).

We will use a figure like this throughout the unit, and often refer to the 'slope' of lines and curves that we draw. You may remember from studying geometry that, when a line slopes downwards from left to right, the slope is negative. This is logical—to get more income now (a positive change), Julia accepts less income later (a negative change).

When economists talk about the 'slope' of the trade-off between now and later, they usually simplify things in the description by using the positive value of this number. This is called taking the absolute value of the slope. When we refer to the 'slope' of a line or curve in this unit, we will refer to the absolute value, and so the slope is always a positive number. You will find this is easier when you are describing the trade-off that borrowers make.

Julia is not free to simply pick any combination of consumption now and later. She has to buy what she consumes over and above what her family provides.

A closer look at borrowing

In Figure 9.2, Julia is at the point labelled 'Julia's endowment'. To consume at least something now, Julia considers taking out a loan, as shown.

If the **interest rate** were 10%, Julia could, for example, borrow a bit less than $91 now and promise to pay the lender the whole $100 that she will have later. Her total repayment of $100 would include the principal (how much she borrowed, namely $91) plus the interest charge ($9) at the rate r, or:

$$\begin{aligned}\text{repayment} &= \text{principal} + \text{interest} \\ &= 91 + 91r \\ &= 91(1+r) \\ &= \$100\end{aligned}$$

And if 'later' means in one year from now, then the annual interest rate, r, is:

$$\begin{aligned}\text{interest rate} &= \frac{\text{repayment}}{\text{principal}} - 1 \\ &= \frac{100}{91} - 1 \\ &= 0.1 = 10\end{aligned}$$

You can think of the interest rate as the price of bringing some spending power forward in time.

At the same interest rate (10%), Julia could also borrow $70 to spend now, and repay $77 at the end of the year, that is:

$$\begin{aligned}\text{repayment} &= 70 + 70r \\ &= 70(1+r) \\ &= \$77\end{aligned}$$

interest rate The price of bringing some spending power forward in time. See also: nominal interest rate, real interest rate.

9 THE CREDIT MARKET: BORROWERS, LENDERS, AND THE RATE OF INTEREST

feasible frontier The curve made of points that defines the maximum feasible quantity of one good for a given quantity of the other. *See also: feasible set.*

In this case, she would have $23 to spend next year. Another possible combination is to borrow and spend just $30 now, which would leave Julia with $67 to spend next year, after repaying her loan.

All of her possible combinations of consumption now and consumption later, for example ($91, $0), ($70, $23) ($30, $67), are the points that make up the **feasible frontier** shown in Figure 9.2. This is the boundary of the feasible set when the interest rate is 10%.

To explore all of the slides in this figure, see the online version at https://tinyco.re/2723214.

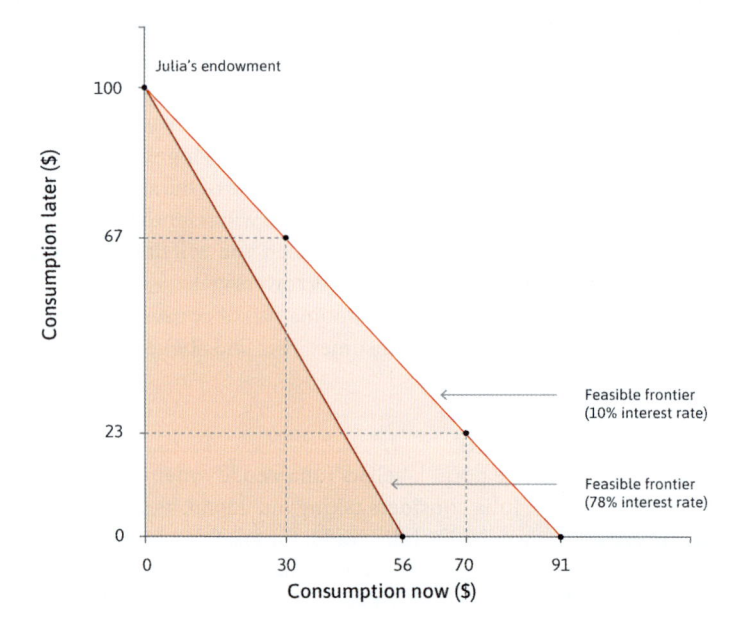

Figure 9.2 Borrowing, the interest rate, and the feasible set.

1. Julia has nothing
Julia has no money now but she knows that, in the next period, she will have $100. Given this state of affairs, her consumption now is $0 and $100 later. This point is labelled as her endowment. It is what she has now or expects to get before any other interaction, such as borrowing.

2. Bringing future income to the present
Assuming an interest rate of 10%, Julia could, for example, borrow $91 now and promise to pay the lender the $100 that she will have later, assuming an interest rate of 10%.

3. Borrowing less
At the same interest rate (10%), she could also borrow $70 to spend now, and repay $77 at the end of the year. In that case, she would have $23 to spend next year.

4. Borrowing even less
At the same interest rate (10%), she could also borrow $30 to spend now, and repay $33 at the end of the year. In that case she would have $67 to spend next year.

5. Julia's feasible set
By repeating these hypothetical borrowing and repayment combinations, the boundary of Julia's feasible set—called her feasible frontier—is formed. This is shown for the assumed interest rate of 10%.

6. Julia's feasible frontier
If Julia can borrow at 10%, she can move from her endowment by borrowing now and choose any combination on her feasible frontier.

7. A higher interest rate
If, instead of 10%, the interest rate is 78%, Julia can only borrow a maximum of $56 now.

8. The feasible set
The feasible set with the interest rate of 78% is the dark shaded area, while the feasible set with an interest rate of 10% is the dark shaded area plus the light shaded area.

9.3 BORROWING: BRINGING CONSUMPTION FORWARD IN TIME

The fact that Julia can borrow means that she does not have to consume only in the later period. She can borrow now and choose any combination on her feasible frontier. But the more she consumes now, the less she can consume later. With an interest rate of $r = 10\%$, the opportunity cost of spending one dollar now is that Julia will have to spend $1.10 = 1 + r$ dollars less later.

One plus the interest rate $(1 + r)$ is the **marginal rate of transformation** of goods from the future to the present, because to have one unit of the good now, you have to give up $1 + r$ goods in the future. This is the same concept as the marginal rate of transformation of goods, grain, or grades into free time that you encountered in Units 4 and 5 (page 158).

A higher interest rate raises the price of bringing buying power forward

Suppose that, instead of 10%, the interest rate is 78%, the average rate paid by the farmers in Chambar. At this interest rate, Julia can now only borrow a maximum of $56, because the interest on a loan of $56 is $44, using up all $100 of her future income. Her feasible frontier therefore pivots inward and the feasible set becomes smaller. Because the price of bringing buying power forward in time has increased, the capacity to consume in the present has fallen, just as your capacity to consume grain would fall if the price of grain went up (unless you are a producer of grain).

Of course, the lender will benefit from a higher interest rate (as long as the loan is repaid) so there is a **conflict of interest** between the borrower and the lender.

> **marginal rate of transformation (MRT)** A measure of the trade-offs a person faces in what is feasible. Given the constraints (feasible frontier) a person faces, the MRT is the quantity of some good that must be sacrificed to acquire one additional unit of another good. At any point, it is the slope of the feasible frontier. See also: feasible frontier, marginal rate of substitution.

> **conflict of interest** The situation which arises if in order for one party to gain more from the interaction, another party must do less well.

EXERCISE 9.1 JULIA'S FEASIBLE FRONTIER

We construct Julia's feasible frontier by finding all the combinations of consumption now and next period, given her endowment and the interest rate.

1. Complete the table below, using the information given. Round your answers to the nearest dollar.
2. Using your completed table, draw a diagram similar to Figure 9.2 (page 394), showing the feasible frontier, consumption amounts and the amount of repayment.

	Point on the feasible frontier	Consumption now	Consumption later	Repayment
Calculation		= amount borrowed	= income later − repayment = income later − $(1 + r)$ × amount borrowed	= income later − consumption later
Endowment point				
	(0, 100)	0	100	0
Interest rate = 10%				
	(91, 0)	91	100 − (1.1)91 = 0	100
	(70, 23)			
	(30, 67)	30		33
Interest rate = 78%				
	(56, 0)	56	100 − (1.78)56 = 0	100
		30		
				33

395

9.4 REASONS TO BORROW: SMOOTHING AND IMPATIENCE

Given the opportunities for bringing forward consumption shown by the feasible set, what will Julia choose to do? How much consumption she will bring forward depends on how impatient she is. She could be impatient for two reasons:

- She prefers to **smooth out her consumption** instead of consuming everything later and nothing now.
- She may be an impatient type of person.

Smoothing

The first reason is that she would like to smooth her consumption because she enjoys an additional unit of something more when she has not already consumed a lot of it. Think about food—the first few bites of a dish are likely to be much more pleasurable than bites from your third serving. This is a fundamental psychological reality, sometimes termed the law of satiation of wants.

More generally, the value to the individual of an additional unit of consumption in a given period declines the more that is consumed. This is called **diminishing marginal returns to consumption**. You have already encountered something similar in Unit 4 (page 151), when Alexei experienced diminishing marginal returns to free time. Holding his grade constant, the more free time he had, the less each additional unit was worth to him, relative to how important the grade would be. We can apply this to consumption in general. Diminishing marginal returns imply that we prefer to smooth our consumption. We would optimally choose to consume similar amounts now and later, as Figure 9.3 shows.

Pure impatience, or how impatient you are as a person

If Julia knows she can have two meals tomorrow but she has none today, then diminishing marginal returns to consumption could explain why she might prefer to have one meal today and one tomorrow. Note that Julia would opt for the meal now, not because she is an impatient person, but because she does not expect to be hungry in the future. She prefers to smooth her consumption of food.

But there is a different reason for preferring the good now, called **pure impatience**. To see whether someone is impatient as a person, we ask whether, if she initially had the same amount of the good in both periods, she would value having more of the good now more highly than more of the good later? Two reasons for pure impatience are:

- *Myopia (short-sightedness):* People experience the present satisfaction of hunger or some other desire more strongly than they imagine the same satisfaction at a future date.
- *Prudence:* People know that they may not be around in the future, and so choosing present consumption may be a good idea.

---

consumption smoothing Actions taken by an individual, family, or other group in order to sustain their customary level of consumption. Actions include borrowing or reducing savings to offset negative shocks, such as unemployment or illness; and increasing saving or reducing debt in response to positive shocks, such as promotion or inheritance.

diminishing marginal returns to consumption The value to the individual of an additional unit of consumption declines, the more consumption the individual has. *Also known as: diminishing marginal utility.*

pure impatience In a situation in which a person's endowment is the same amount of consumption this period and later, she would have this characteristic if she values an additional unit of consumption now over an additional unit later. It arises when a person is impatient to consume more now because she places less value on consumption in the future for reasons of myopia, weakness of will, or for other reasons. *See also: weakness of will.*

9.4 REASONS TO BORROW: SMOOTHING AND IMPATIENCE

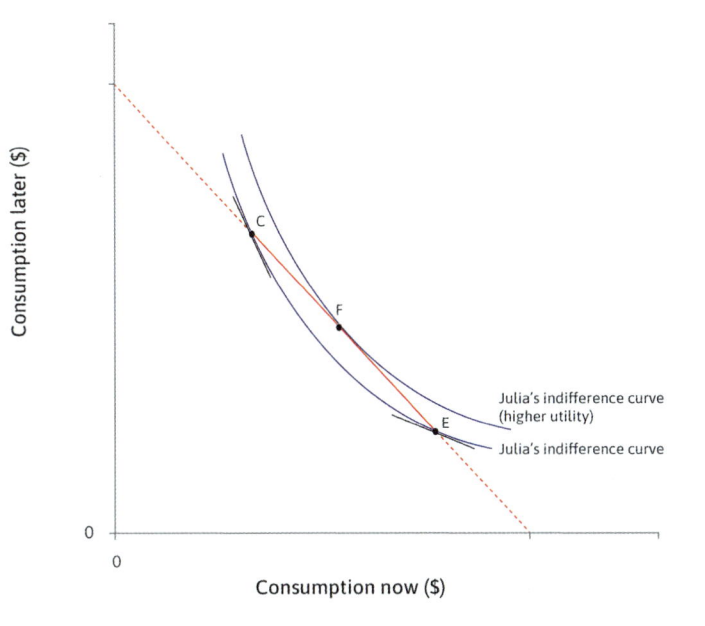

To explore all of the slides in this figure, see the online version at https://tinyco.re/5494139.

Figure 9.3 Consumption smoothing: Diminishing marginal returns to consumption.

1. Julia's choices
The dashed line shows the combinations of consumption now and consumption later from which Julia can choose.

2. Diminishing marginal returns to consumption
Julia's indifference curve is bowed toward the origin as a consequence of diminishing marginal returns to consumption in each period. The more goods she has in the present, the less she values an additional one now relative to more in the future. The slope of the indifference curve is the marginal rate of substitution (MRS) between consumption now and consumption later.

3. What choices would Julia make?
The MRS at C is high (the slope of her indifference curve is steep)—Julia has little consumption now and a lot later, so diminishing marginal returns mean that she would like to move some consumption to the present. The MRS at E is low. She has a lot of consumption now and less later, so diminishing marginal returns mean that she would like to move some consumption to the future. So she will choose a point between C and E.

4. MRS falls
We can see that the MRS is falling as we move along the indifference curve from C to E. The slope is steeper at C than at E.

5. Julia's optimal choice
Given the choice shown by the line CE, Julia will choose point F. It is on the highest attainable indifference curve. She prefers to smooth consumption between now and later.

We saw that Julia, who will earn $100 in the future, wants to borrow. The situation that she is in gives her a strong desire to smooth by borrowing. Think about what Julia's indifference curve, passing through her endowment point, might look like. As shown in Figure 9.4, she has a strong preference for increasing consumption now.

This is called Julia's **reservation indifference curve**, because it is made of all the points at which Julia would be just as well off as at her reservation position, which is her endowment with no borrowing or lending. Julia's endowment and reservation indifference curves are similar to those of Angela, the farmer, in Unit 5 (page 201). At point A, with no expenditure at all on consumption now, we assume Julia has some way of maintaining herself.

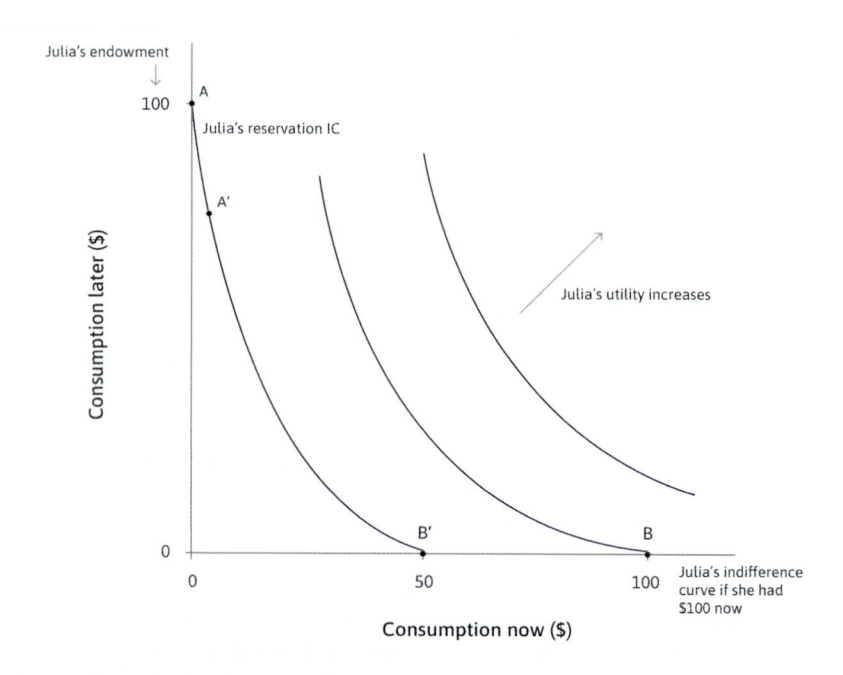

Figure 9.4 shows Julia's indifference curves:

- *Her reservation indifference curve:* The curve closest to the origin.
- *Her reservation indifference curve if she had the $100 now:* The next-highest curve assumes that she has already earned $100.
- *A higher indifference curve.*

> **reservation indifference curve** A curve that indicates allocations (combinations) that are as highly valued as one's reservation option. See also: reservation option.

Figure 9.4 Julia's indifference curves.

9.4 REASONS TO BORROW: SMOOTHING AND IMPATIENCE

For any particular point in the figure, the individual's **impatience** can be seen from the steepness of the indifference curve. At her endowment point—$100 later, nothing now—shown by point A, her indifference curve is very steep. Because she has nothing now, she is very impatient. It means she would be willing to give up a substantial amount of consumption later to gain a little bit of consumption now. This could be illustrated by a move from point A to A'.

We define a person's **discount rate**, ρ (economists use the Greek letter *rho*, as the slope (remember, we take the absolute—positive—value) of the indifference curve minus one. It is a measure of impatience, namely how much Julia values an extra unit of consumption now, relative to an extra unit of consumption later.

> **impatience** Any preference to move consumption from the future to the present. This preference may be derived either from pure impatience or diminishing marginal returns to consumption.
>
> **discount rate** A measure of a person's impatience: how much that person values an additional unit of consumption now relative to an additional unit of consumption later. It is the absolute value of the slope of a person's indifference curve for consumption now and consumption later, minus one. Also known as: subjective discount rate.
>
> **utility** A numerical indicator of the value that one places on an outcome, such that higher-valued outcomes will be chosen over lower-valued ones when both are feasible.

Her discount rate ρ, which measures her impatience, depends both on her desire to smooth consumption and on her degree of *pure* impatience. A high discount rate means a high degree of impatience.

Notice in Figure 9.4 that if Julia hypothetically had the $100 now (point B), she would be much less impatient; at B, her indifference curve is very flat, which means that she would like to have more consumption in the future and less now and would be willing to give up a dollar now, even if she got less than a dollar in return later.

Not only would Julia be less impatient at point B (with $100 now) than at point A (in her initial situation of having $100 later), but she would also be better off. In Figure 9.4, the indifference curve through B is above the indifference curve through A. This is because, as a person, she has a degree of pure impatience.

To see this, notice that when Julia's **utility** is at the same level as when she has the $100 in the future, she must be on the same indifference curve, that is, the one going through A. You can see that on that indifference curve at B', her consumption is much lower than $100. For the indifference curves shown in Figure 9.4, she values $100 later the same as she values half that amount now (B' is one half of B).

> **QUESTION 9.3 CHOOSE THE CORRECT ANSWER(S)**
> Figure 9.3 (page 397) depicts Julia's indifference curves for consumption in periods 1 (now) and 2 (later). Based on this information, which of the following statements are correct?
>
> ☐ The slope of the indifference curve is the marginal rate of substitution between the consumption in the two periods.
> ☐ The marginal return to consumption in period 1 is higher at E than at C.
> ☐ Julia's consumption is more equal across the two periods at C than at E. Therefore, she prefers consumption choice C to E.
> ☐ Consuming exactly the same amount in the two periods is Julia's most preferred choice.

399

9.5 BORROWING ALLOWS SMOOTHING BY BRINGING CONSUMPTION TO THE PRESENT

How much will Julia borrow? If we combine Figures 9.2 and 9.3, we will have the answer. As in the other examples of a feasible set and indifference curves, Julia wishes to get to the highest possible indifference curve but is limited by her feasible frontier. The highest feasible indifference curve when the interest rate is 10% will be the one that is tangent to the feasible frontier, shown as point E in Figure 9.5. This means that Julia borrows just enough so that:

slope of the indifference curve (MRS) = slope of the feasible frontier (MRT)

We know that:

$$MRS = 1 + \rho$$
$$MRT = 1 + r$$

Therefore:

$$MRS = MRT$$
$$1 + \rho = 1 + r$$

If we subtract 1 from both sides of this equation, we have:

$$\rho = r$$
discount rate = rate of interest

Here, Julia chooses to borrow and consume $56 and repay $62 later, leaving her $38 to consume later.

Now consider how much she would borrow if she had to pay not 10%, but the 78% that was the average among the Chambar farmers. Figure 9.5 shows that, as before, finding the point of tangency between the new feasible frontier given by the 78% interest rate and one of Julia's indifference curves, she will choose point G, meaning that she will borrow much less—$35—to consume now, paying $62 with interest, and having $38 to consume later.

The higher 'price' of moving consumption forward in time means two things:

- *She is less well off than with the lower interest rate:* Compare her two indifference curves (one through E, the other through G).
- *She will borrow less and consume less now:* $35 rather than $56.

In the example we considered above, her consumption later does not change. But, depending on the shape of her indifference curves, it could be lower or higher. With the higher interest rate, she is less well off, so this would tend to push down her consumption later. But the higher interest rate makes it costlier to bring consumption forward, which would tend to push up her consumption later.

Use the analysis in Figure 9.5 to see how Julia will choose consumption when the interest rate is 10% and when it is 78%.

9.5 BORROWING ALLOWS SMOOTHING BY BRINGING CONSUMPTION TO THE PRESENT

QUESTION 9.4 CHOOSE THE CORRECT ANSWER(S)

Figure 9.5 depicts Julia's choice of consumptions in periods 1 and 2. She has no income in period 1 (now) and an income of $100 in period 2 (later). The current interest rate is 10%. Based on this information, which of the following statements are correct?

☐ At F, the interest rate exceeds Julia's discount rate (degree of impatience).
☐ At E, Julia is on the highest possible indifference curve, given her feasible set.
☐ E is Julia's optimal choice, as she is able to completely smooth out her consumption over the two periods and consume the same amount.
☐ G is not a feasible choice for Julia.

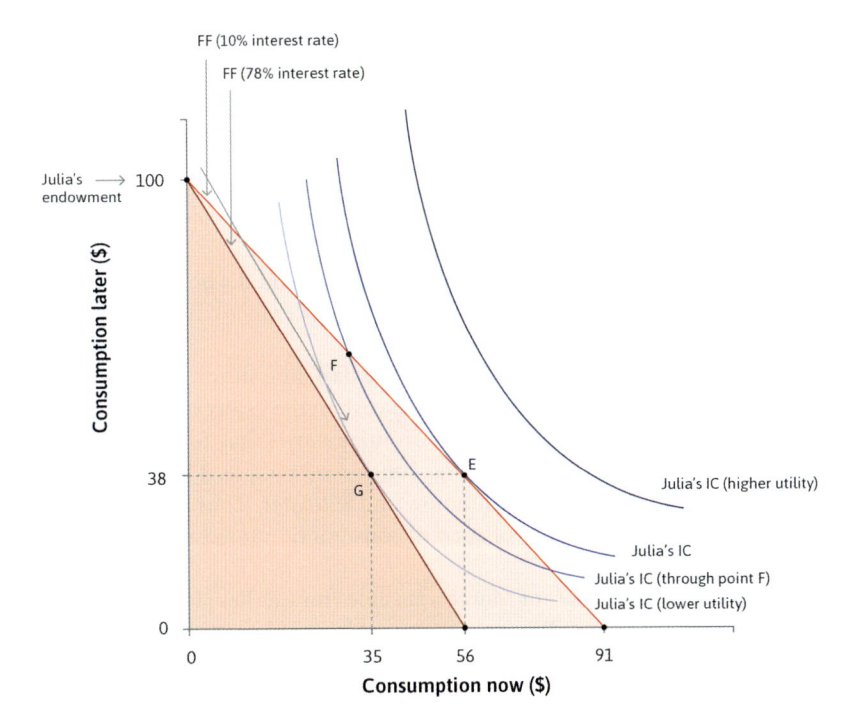

To explore all of the slides in this figure, see the online version at https://tinyco.re/9291848.

Figure 9.5 Moving consumption over time by borrowing.

1. Julia's feasible frontier
Julia wishes to get to the highest indifference curve but is limited by her feasible frontier.

2. Julia's best option
When the interest rate is 10%, the highest attainable indifference curve is the one that is tangent to the feasible frontier shown as point E.

3. MRS and MRT
At this point, MRS = MRT.

4. The decision to borrow
At point F, her discount rate, ρ, exceeds r, the interest rate, so she would like to bring consumption forward in time. This means that the benefits to her of bringing some consumption forward to the present (ρ) are greater than the costs (r), so she will borrow more to finance current consumption. Similar reasoning eliminates all points except E on the feasible frontier.

5. An increase in the interest rate
If the interest rate at which she can borrow increases, the feasible set gets smaller.

6. The effect of a higher interest rate
The best Julia can do now is to borrow less ($35 instead of $56), as shown by point G.

9.6 STORING OR LENDING ALLOWS SMOOTHING AND MOVING CONSUMPTION TO THE FUTURE

Now think about Marco, an individual otherwise identical to Julia, but facing a very different situation. Marco has wealth of $100 but does not (yet) anticipate receiving any income later.

By identical, we mean that Marco's preferences between consumption now and later are the same as Julia's. For example, in Figure 9.4 we showed a hypothetical indifference curve for Julia if she had $100 now. This is Marco's reservation indifference curve in Figure 9.6.

Marco and Julia have the same degree of pure impatience but are in very different situations. Julia wishes to bring forward some consumption; Marco could use all of his $100 to buy goods to consume now, but as we have seen, this would probably not be the best he could do given the circumstances. In order to smooth his consumption over time, he wishes to move some consumption to the future.

Marco's options for smoothing: Storing

Marco could do this by just putting some of his wealth in cash in a drawer, not spending it now, and having it later. We assume that his $100 will not be stolen and that $100 will purchase the same amount of goods now and later because there is no inflation (that is, the price level in the economy doesn't rise).

In Figure 9.6, we see that Marco's endowment is on the horizontal axis, as he has $100 available now. His reservation indifference curve includes the point $100 on the horizontal axis.

Figure 9.6 analyses Marco's decision. The dark line shows Marco's feasible frontier if he just 'stores' his wealth in cash in the drawer, and the dark shaded area shows his feasible set. The frontier shows that, for every dollar that Marco stores, he will have a dollar later—for example, if he stored $50 he could consume $50 of his wealth now and $50 later. Thus, the marginal rate of transformation (MRT) of current consumption into future consumption is just 1.

In Figure 9.6, some part of Marco's feasible frontier lies above and to the right of his reservation indifference curve, so he can do better by storing. If storing were the only option, he would definitely store some of his $100.

In the figure we see that he stores less than half, so he ends up consuming more now than later. This means that Marco, like Julia, has some degree of pure impatience. If this were not the case, he would store half of his endowment and have the same levels of consumption now and later.

Marco's options for smoothing: Lending

A better plan, if Marco could find a trustworthy borrower who would repay for sure, would be to lend some of his wealth. If he did this and could be assured of repayment of $(1 + r)$ for every $1 lent, then he could have feasible consumption of $100 \times (1 + r)$ later, or any of the combinations along his new feasible frontier. The light line in Figure 9.7 shows the feasible frontier when Marco lends at 20%. By lending, Marco has raised the marginal rate of transformation of current spending into future spending. With storing it was just 1. Now it is 1.2.

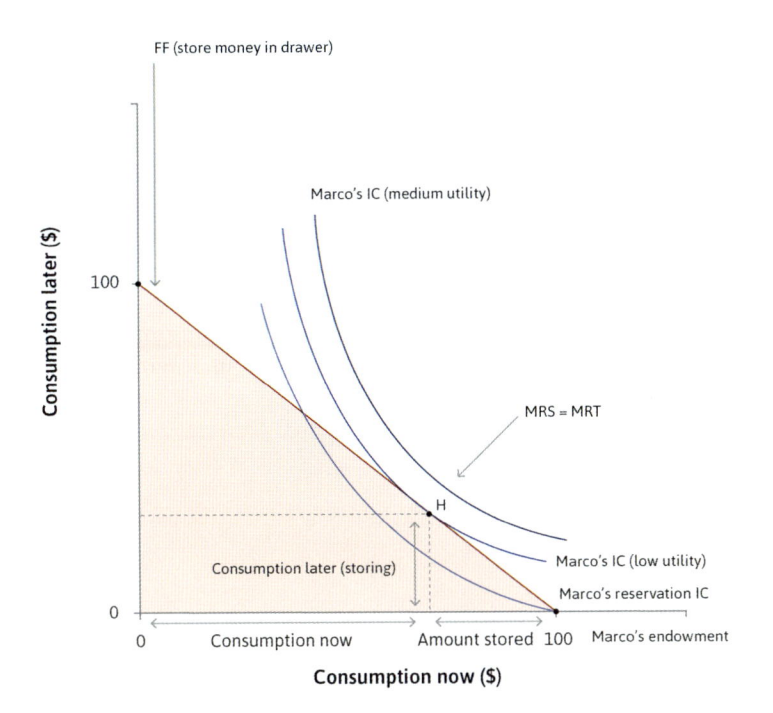

9.6 STORING OR LENDING ALLOWS SMOOTHING AND MOVING CONSUMPTION TO THE FUTURE

Figure 9.6 Smoothing consumption by storing.

1. Marco's preferences
Marco's reservation indifference curve goes through his endowment.

2. Marco's preferences
Indifference curves to the right of Marco's reservation curve indicate higher levels of utility.

3. Marco's feasible frontier
With storage, there is a one-to-one trade-off between consumption now and consumption later.

4. Marco's decision to store
Point H on Marco's indifference curve denotes the amount of storage that he will choose.

As you can see from Figure 9.7, Marco's feasible set is now expanded by the opportunity to lend money at interest, compared to storing the cash (putting it in his drawer). Anything that expands a person's feasible set so that the old feasible set is entirely inside the new one must allow that person to be better off. Marco is able to reach a higher indifference curve by lending rather than storing.

As we shall see in Unit 10 (page 436), there are a variety of financial instruments in a contemporary economy that Marco can use to shift consumption to the future by lending—such as term deposits or bonds issued by companies or by the government. Note that, in recent years, returns of 20%, as in Figure 9.7, have been very unusual indeed.

But how much will Marco lend? Like Julia, he will seek the highest feasible indifference curve by finding the point of tangency between the indifference curve and the feasible frontier. This is point J, at which Marco has equated his MRS between consumption now and in the future to the MRT, which is the cost of moving goods from the present to the future.

In the example, the amount Marco lends does not change. But it could be lower or higher. When he lends, he is better off, so this would tend to push up his consumption now and push down his lending. But when he can earn interest, this increases his return from postponing consumption. This would tend to push up his lending and raise his consumption later. The case in the diagram assumes that these cancel out, leaving lending and consumption now unchanged.

To explore all of the slides in this figure, see the online version at https://tinyco.re/3512996.

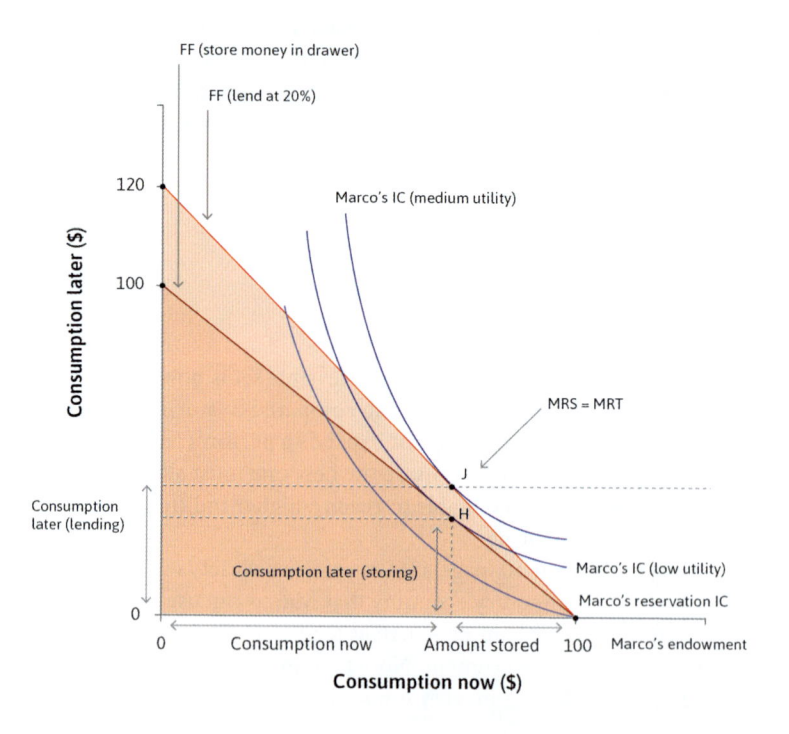

Figure 9.7 Smoothing consumption by storing and lending.

1. Marco's decision to lend
The light line shows the feasible frontier when Marco lends at 20%.

2. The effect of the decision to lend
Marco is now able to reach a higher indifference curve.

9.6 STORING OR LENDING ALLOWS SMOOTHING AND MOVING CONSUMPTION TO THE FUTURE

EXERCISE 9.2 MARCO'S FEASIBLE FRONTIER

As we did with Julia, we construct Marco's feasible frontier under storing or lending by finding all the combinations of consumption now and in the next period, given his endowment and the interest rate.

1. Complete the table below, using the information given. Round your answers to the nearest dollar.
2. Using your completed table, draw a diagram similar to Figure 9.7, showing the feasible frontier, consumption, and lending options.

	Point on the feasible frontier	Consumption now	Consumption later	Amount stored or lent (excluding interest)
Calculation		= Income now – Amount stored or lent	= Amount stored or = Amount lent including interest on the loan or = (1 + r) × Amount lent	
Endowment point				
	(100, 0)	100	0	0
Store money in a drawer				
		91	9	9
			50	
		30		
Lend at an interest rate of 20%				
	(56, 53)	56	(1 + 0.2)(100 – 56) = 53	44
		30		
				33

QUESTION 9.5 CHOOSE THE CORRECT ANSWER(S)

Figure 9.7 (page 404) depicts Marco's choice of consumption in periods 1 (now) and 2 (later). He has $100 in period 1 and no income in period 2. Marco has two choices: he can store the money that he does not spend in period 1, or he can lend the money he does not consume at an interest rate of 20%. Based on this information, which of the following statements are correct?

☐ With storage, if Marco consumes $68 in period 1, he can consume $32 in period 2.
☐ With lending, if Marco consumes $68 in period 1, he can consume $35 in period 2.
☐ The marginal rate of transformation is higher when storing than when lending.
☐ Marco will always be on a higher indifference curve when lending than when storing.

9.7 MUTUAL GAINS AND CONFLICTS OVER THEIR DISTRIBUTION IN THE CREDIT MARKET

In the initial situation, Julia and Marco would both get $100 eventually, but time creates a difference. In the present, Marco's wealth, narrowly defined, is $100. Julia's wealth is zero.

Marco and Julia's indifference curves, and hence their pure impatience, are identical. They differ according to their situation, not their preferences. Marco's reservation indifference curve is superior to Julia's (farther away from the origin) because he has wealth now, and she has the same amount, but later. Julia borrows because she is poor in the present, unlike Marco, which is why she is more impatient than him. She wants to smooth her consumption by bringing some buying power to the present.

Julia and Marco are on opposite sides of the credit market

The fact that Marco is in exactly the opposite situation—he is looking for ways to move some consumption to the future—explains why they can mutually benefit, Marco by lending and Julia by borrowing. We are not assuming that they are borrowing and lending directly to each other. Rather, they are borrowing and lending on the same market.

The solid lines in Figure 9.8 show the borrowing opportunities for Julia and lending opportunities for Marco, both measured by their feasible frontiers.

The feasible frontiers of the two both have a slope of $(1 + r)$. For Julia, the cost of moving $1 from the future to the present by borrowing is $1 + r$, while for Marco the gain from moving $1 from the present to the future by lending is also $1 + r$. They face the same 'price' of moving consumption in time, but they are moving their buying power in different directions.

> Remember, in this unit what we call the 'slope' will always be a positive number, even though the line slopes downwards.

This is why Marco's feasible frontier is uniformly outside Julia's; he has more choices open to him than she does. Because they have identical indifference curves, we know that he will be able to enjoy a higher level of utility than Julia.

Figure 9.8 also shows the effect of an increase in the rate of interest from $r = 0.20$ to $r = 0.78$. The increase in the rate of interest makes both feasible frontiers steeper, but this:

- *Moves Marco's feasible frontier outwards:* Expanding his set of choices.
- *Moves Julia's feasible frontier inwards:* Shrinking her set of choices.

Let's return to how Marco differs from Julia. They have identical preferences, but:

- *Marco starts with wealth while Julia starts with nothing:* Julia has the guarantee of a similar asset later, but this puts the two on opposite sides of the credit market.
- *Because of this difference in their situation, they can both benefit by participating in the credit market, Julia by borrowing and Marco by lending.*
- *Because Marco's feasible frontier is entirely outside Julia's, he can end up on a higher indifference curve than can Julia.*
- *Because the cost of moving consumption forward in time by borrowing (the rate of interest) is the same as the gain to Marco by postponing his consumption (by lending), they have a conflict of interest over how the mutual gains from exchange are shared.*

9.7 MUTUAL GAINS AND CONFLICTS OVER THEIR DISTRIBUTION IN THE CREDIT MARKET

Real and nominal interest rates: who benefits from inflation?
We have thus far referred simply to 'the interest rate'. But in relating it so explicitly to the price of future consumption, we have implicitly been using what economists call the ***real* interest rate**—since what Julia cares about is her loss of real spending power, that is, what she can buy in the future taking account of inflation.

> **real interest rate** The price of bringing some real spending power forward in time. *See also:* nominal interest rate.

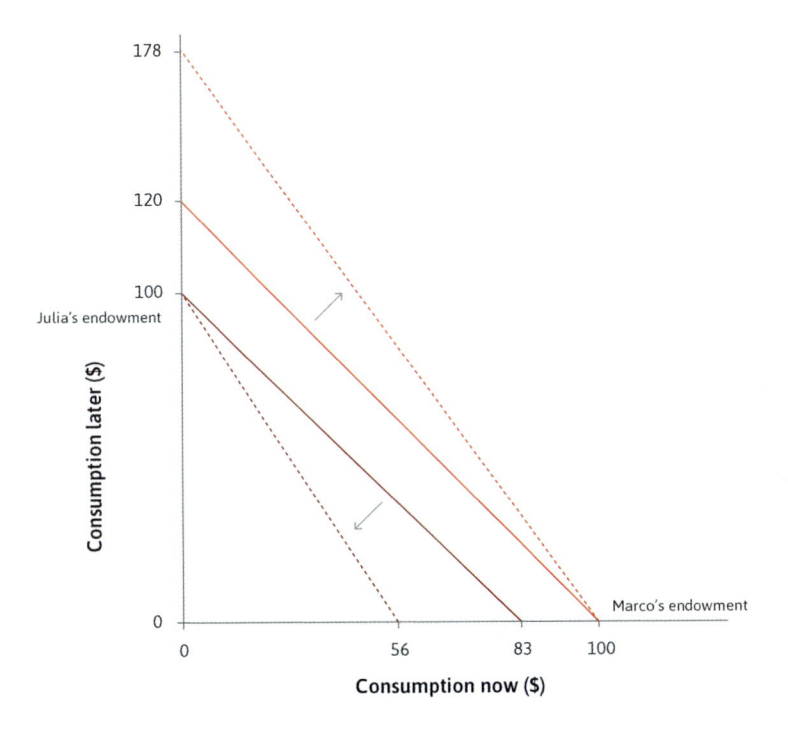

To explore all of the slides in this figure, see the online version at https://tinyco.re/5799675.

Figure 9.8 On opposite sides of the market: An increase in the interest rate improves Marco's welfare and reduces Julia's.

1. Julia's feasible frontier
The dark red line shows Julia's feasible frontier when the interest rate is 20%.

2. Marco's feasible frontier
The bright red line shows Marco's feasible frontier when the interest rate is 20%.

3. Effect of an interest rate rise on Julia's frontier
When the interest rate rises to 78%, Julia's feasible set shrinks.

4. Effect of an interest rate rise on Marco's frontier
When the interest rate rises to 78%, Marco's feasible set expands.

nominal interest rate The price of bringing some spending power (in dollars or other nominal terms) forward in time. The policy rate and the lending rate quoted by commercial banks are examples of nominal interest rates. See also: real interest rate, interest rate, Fisher equation.

Fisher equation The relation that gives the real interest rate as the difference between the nominal interest rate and expected inflation: real interest rate = nominal interest rate − expected inflation.

Economists contrast this to the **nominal interest rate**, which is the rate that is typically actually paid on loans. When the price of goods and services is rising—that is, if there is a positive inflation rate—the nominal interest rate overstates the real interest rate.

To take account of inflation when analysing borrowing and lending, we must use the real interest rate because it represents how many goods in the future one gets for the goods not consumed now. The **Fisher equation**, named after Irving Fisher (1867–1947), summarizes the relationship between the real and nominal interest rates, and inflation:

real interest rate (% per annum) = nominal interest rate (% per annum) − the inflation rate (% per annum)

Whether you lose or benefit from inflation depends on which side of the credit market you are on. As we have seen, Julia the borrower and Marco the lender have a conflict about the real interest rate: she benefits from a fall in the interest rate and he benefits from a rise. So they also have differing perspectives on inflation, because if prices rise before Julia repays her loan, a lender like Marco would find that he can buy less with the repayment than would have been the case if there were zero inflation. She benefits from a fall in the real interest rate because of inflation; he loses out.

More precisely, the real interest rate measures the buying power of the repayment of a loan at the stipulated nominal interest rate, taking account of the prices that exist when the loan is repaid. To see what this means, let's consider a situation in which Julia were to borrow $50 directly from Marco with a repayment of $55 next year. The nominal interest rate for this loan contract between them is 10%. But if next year's prices were 6% higher than this year's (6% inflation rate), then what Marco could buy with the repayment is not 10% more than he could have bought with the sum he loaned to Julia, but instead only 4%. The real interest rate is 4%.

QUESTION 9.6 CHOOSE THE CORRECT ANSWER(S)
The following table shows the nominal interest rate and the annual inflation rate (the GDP deflator) of Japan in the period 1996–2015 (Source: World Bank).

	1996–2000	2001–2005	2006–2010	2011–2015
Interest rate	1.5%	1.4%	1.3%	1.2%
Inflation rate	−1.9%	−0.9%	−0.5%	1.6%

Based on this information, which of the following statements are correct?

☐ The real interest rate in 1996–2000 was −0.4%.
☐ Japan's real interest rate has been rising consistently over this period.
☐ Japan's real interest rate turned from being positive to negative during the period.
☐ The real interest rate has been falling faster than the nominal interest rate.

> **EXERCISE 9.3 LIFETIME INCOME**
> Consider an individual's income over his or her lifetime, from leaving school to retirement. Using the concepts in this unit, explain in words how an individual may move from a situation like Julia's to one like Marco's over the course of their lifetime (assume that their pure impatience remains unchanged over their lifetime).

9.8 BORROWING MAY ALLOW INVESTING: JULIA'S BEST HOPE

Like Julia in our model, payday borrowers in New York often buy groceries or clothes for their children with their borrowed funds; farmers in Chambar also often borrow for purposes of consumption, for example, to pay for a wedding. But both the Chambar farmers and New York payday borrowers sometimes use the borrowed funds for an investment. For the Pakistani farmers, this could be the purchase of equipment that would improve the crop yield.

Now suppose that Julia is considering becoming a Lyft (https://tinyco.re/1408840) driver and to qualify needs to make some cosmetic repairs on her brother's car that she will drive. She cannot use the car as **collateral** (it is not hers), so she finds it difficult to get a conventional loan. She goes to a payday lender, who, as in the example above, will charge her an interest rate of 78%. Figure 9.9 shows Julia's feasible set and frontier based on borrowing at this rate.

Julia has a new option—she can borrow and then split how much she has borrowed between consuming some now and investing the rest. This is how she does her planning:

- Take some of the $56 that she can borrow and invest this in fixing up the car.
- The more she spends fixing up the car, the more money she will make as a driver, so she now has a new feasible frontier.

Suppose it is the case that every dollar Julia spends on the car will result in $3 more in income next year (that is, a rate of return of 200%). With this investment, she can move along the new dashed feasible frontier.

To see the full range of her new options, if she invested the entire $56 (so that she would have no consumption now), she would have $168 (3 × 56) next year. All the points on the dashed feasible frontier with investment are now open to her. The slope of the feasible frontier with investment is 3, which is the ratio of income later to amount invested. The steeper the slope is, the better for Julia. This slope is the marginal rate of transformation of current investment into future income.

The investment opportunity has greatly increased Julia's wellbeing. She consumes the same amount now that she did when only the borrowing opportunity was available—$35—but she can now consume $63 later, rather than only $38. Note that she will only invest if she has an investment project with a rate of return higher than 78%—the rate of return has to be higher than the borrowing rate in order to expand her feasible set.

> **collateral** An asset that a borrower pledges to a lender as a security for a loan. If the borrower is not able to make the loan payments as promised, the lender becomes the owner of the asset.

To explore all of the slides in this figure, see the online version at https://tinyco.re/4380507.

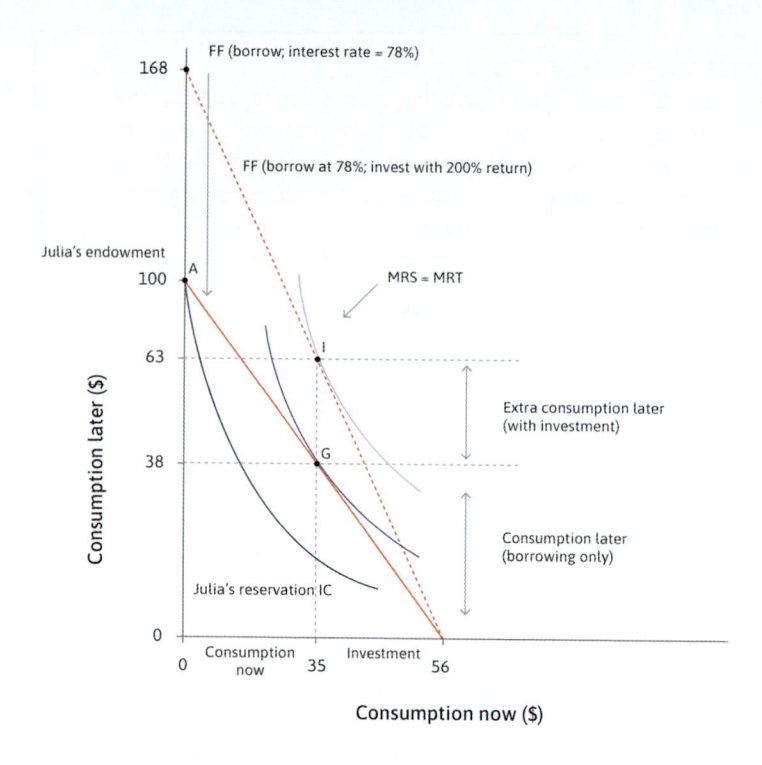

Figure 9.9 Options for the individual (Julia) who starts without assets but can borrow and invest.

1. Julia's options
She can borrow at an interest rate of 78% and can also choose to invest some of her income with a return of 200%. The dotted line shows her feasible frontier when she chooses to borrow and invest.

2. How much will Julia invest?
She will use the same rule that she used in deciding how much to borrow when there was no option to invest. She will find the highest feasible indifference curve by finding the tangency of an indifference curve and the feasible frontier, or what is the same thing, equating the MRT (slope of the feasible frontier) with the MRS (slope of the indifference curve.)

3. Julia's optimal choice
Doing this, Julia chooses point I in the figure. How does this work out for her? Having borrowed the maximum—$56—she invests $21 and consumes $35 now. The investment of $21 will yield her an income of $63 later.

410

9.8 BORROWING MAY ALLOW INVESTING: JULIA'S BEST HOPE

In our example, Julia consumes the same amount now under the borrowing only and borrowing and investment options; her current consumption could be either greater than or less than in the case without the investment opportunity. What is certain is that she is better off with the investment opportunity because her feasible set is expanded.

We can thus contrast three situations in which Julia might have found herself:

- *Exclusion from the credit market:* She is unable to get a loan of any kind. Her feasible set is just a single point (A) in Figure 9.9. Many would-be borrowers—those without collateral, for example—are simply excluded from borrowing at any rate of interest. Her reservation indifference curve indicates her wellbeing in that situation.
- *Borrowing:* Now she has a larger feasible set, including point A, but also all the other points in the solid line in Figure 9.9, including point G—her choice when she can borrow but not invest.
- *Borrowing and investing:* She now has the opportunity to bring buying power forward in time to the present (by borrowing) and then shifting some of it back in time while tripling its value (by investing), enabling her to achieve point I.

QUESTION 9.7 CHOOSE THE CORRECT ANSWER(S)

Figure 9.9 (page 410) depicts two possible feasible frontiers for Julia, who has no income in period 1 (now) and $100 in period 2 (later). The solid line (option 1) shows her feasible frontier if she borrows at an interest rate of 78%. The dotted line shows her feasible frontier if she borrows at an interest rate of 78% and can invest for a return of 200% (option 2). Based on this information, which of the following statements are correct?

- ☐ When borrowing only, Julia is worse off than at her initial endowment (point A) because of the high interest rate.
- ☐ The consumption choice G can only be attained under option 1.
- ☐ If the interest rate for borrowing increases to 100%, *ceteris paribus* the feasible frontiers become steeper and the vertical axis intercept under option 2 is now $150.
- ☐ If the return on investment increases to 250%, *ceteris paribus* the vertical axis intercept under option 2 is now $200.

9.9 BALANCE SHEETS: ASSETS AND LIABILITIES

A balance sheet summarizes what the household, bank, or firm owns and what it owes to others. The things you own (including what you are owed by others) are called your **assets**, and the debts you owe others are called your **liabilities** (to be liable means to be responsible for something, in this case to repay your debts to others). The difference between your assets and your liabilities is called your **net worth**. The relationship between assets, liabilities, and net worth is shown in Figure 9.10.

If the value of assets is below that of liabilities, the net worth of the entity (household, firm, or bank) is negative and it is **insolvent**.

When the components of an equation are such that by definition, the left-hand side is equal to the right-hand side, it is called an accounting identity, or identity for short. The balance sheet identity states:

$$\text{assets} \equiv \text{liabilities} + \text{net worth}$$

To understand the concept of net worth, which is what makes the left- and right-hand sides balance by definition, we can turn the identity around by subtracting liabilities from both sides so that:

$$\begin{aligned}\text{net worth} &\equiv \text{assets} - \text{liabilities} \\ &\equiv \text{what the household owns or is owed} \\ &\quad - \text{what the household owes to others}\end{aligned}$$

The composition of the balance sheets of banks and non-financial companies look very different. Figure 9.11 illustrates the relationship between liabilities and net worth in the case of a bank—Barclays—and a motor vehicle company, Honda. It is immediately evident that the bank is a very debt-heavy entity compared to the non-financial firm.

> **asset** Anything of value that is owned. *See also: balance sheet, liability.*
> **liability** Anything of value that is owed. *See also: balance sheet, asset.*
> **net worth** Assets less liabilities. *See also: balance sheet, equity.*
> **insolvent** An entity is this if the value of its assets is less than the value of its liabilities. *See also: solvent.*

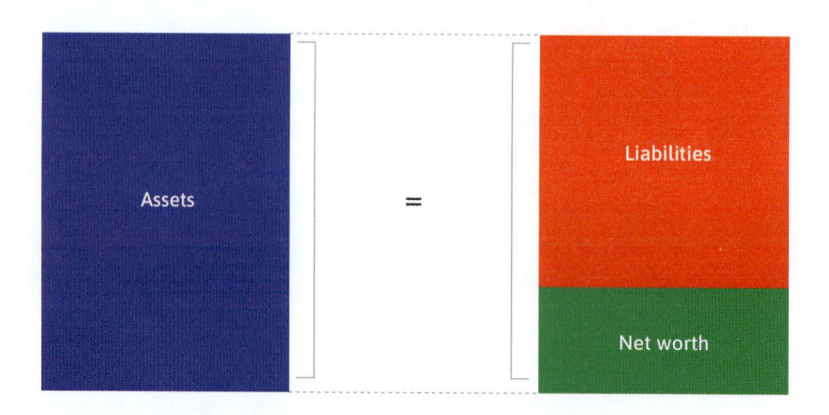

Figure 9.10 A balance sheet.

Balance sheets help us to understand the relationships between households and banks in the economy. Bank deposits make up part of the typical household's assets and they appear on the liability side of the balance sheet of banks in the economy. Another typical asset of a household is its house. Unless the household owns the house outright, the household has a liability as well as an asset—the liability is the mortgage. The mortgage, in turn, is an asset of the bank.

In Unit 10, we return to the balance sheets of households and banks in the **global financial crisis**. For some households, when house prices fell, their assets were worth less than the mortgage (that is, their liability—what they owed on the house). Households defaulted on their mortgage payments.

Many banks—with a balance sheet similar in structure to that of Barclays in Figure 9.11—were vulnerable to their net worth being 'wiped out' by a fall in the value of their assets. When net worth is a tiny fraction of the size of the balance sheet, a small percentage change in the value of the bank's assets can reduce it below the unchanged value of its debts (its liabilities). Given that mortgages and other assets based on mortgages accounted for a substantial part of banks' assets, when house prices fell and households defaulted on their mortgages, this reduced the banks' assets and threatened to reduce the individual bank's net worth below zero.

Banks were insolvent and as we shall see, governments stepped in to bail them out.

Borrowing, lending, and net worth

In the bathtub analogy in Figure 9.1 (page 390), the water in the bathtub represents wealth as accumulated savings and is the same as net worth. As we saw, net worth or wealth increases with income (inflow to the bathtub), and declines with consumption and depreciation (outflow).

But your wealth or net worth does not change when you lend or borrow. This is because a loan creates both an asset and a liability on your balance sheet; if you borrow money, you receive a bank deposit or cash as an asset, while the debt is an equal liability.

> **global financial crisis** This began in 2007 with the collapse of house prices in the US, leading to the fall in prices of assets based on subprime mortgages and to widespread uncertainty about the solvency of banks in the US and Europe, which had borrowed to purchase such assets. The ramifications were felt around the world, as global trade was cut back sharply. Goverments and central banks responded aggressively with stabilization policies.

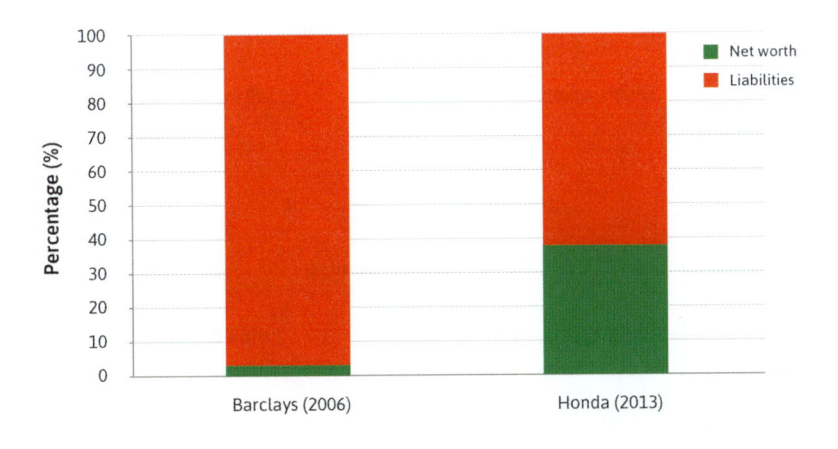

Barclays Bank. 2017. *Barclays PLC Annual Report 2017* (http://tinyco.re/1302456). Honda Motor Co. 2013. *Annual Report* (http://tinyco.re/0428289).

Figure 9.11 Liabilities and net worth (Barclays and Honda).

In our example, Julia starts off with neither assets nor liabilities and a net worth of zero, but on the basis of her expected future income a bank lends her $56 at an interest rate of 10% (point E in Figure 9.5 (page 401)). At this time, her asset is the $56 in the bank deposit that she is holding, while her liability is the loan that she must pay back later. We record the value of the loan as $56 now, since that is what she received for getting into debt (her liability rises to $62 later only once interest has been added). This is why taking out the loan has no effect on her current net worth—the liability and the asset are equal to one another, so her net worth remains unchanged at zero. In Figure 9.12, this is recorded in her balance sheet under the heading 'Now (before consuming)'.

She then consumes the $56—it flows out through the bathtub drain, to use our earlier analogy. Since she still has the $56 liability, her net worth falls to –$56. This is recorded in Figure 9.12 in her balance sheet under the heading 'Now (after consuming)'.

Later, she receives income of $100 deposited in her bank account (an inflow to the bathtub). Also, because of the accumulated interest due, the value of her loan has risen to $62. So her net worth becomes $100 – $62 = $38. Again, we suppose that she then consumes the $38, leaving her with $62 to pay off her debt of $62. At this point, her net worth falls back to zero. The corresponding balance sheets are also shown in Figure 9.12.

Now—before consuming

Julia's assets		Julia's liabilities	
Bank deposit	$56	Loan	$56

Net worth = $56 – $56 = $0

Now—after consuming

Julia's assets		Julia's liabilities	
Bank deposit	0	Loan	$56

Net worth = –$56

Later—before consuming

Julia's assets		Julia's liabilities	
Bank deposit	$100	Loan	$62

Net worth = $100 – $62 = $38

Later—after consuming

Julia's assets		Julia's liabilities	
Bank deposit	$62	Loan	$62

Net worth = 0

Figure 9.12 Julia's balance sheets.

QUESTION 9.8 CHOOSE THE CORRECT ANSWER(S)

The following diagram depicts Julia's choice of consumption in periods 1 (now) and 2 (later) when the interest rate is 78%. She has no income in period 1 and an income of $100 in period 2. Her consumption choice is shown by G. Based on this information, which of the following statements regarding Julia's balance sheet are correct?

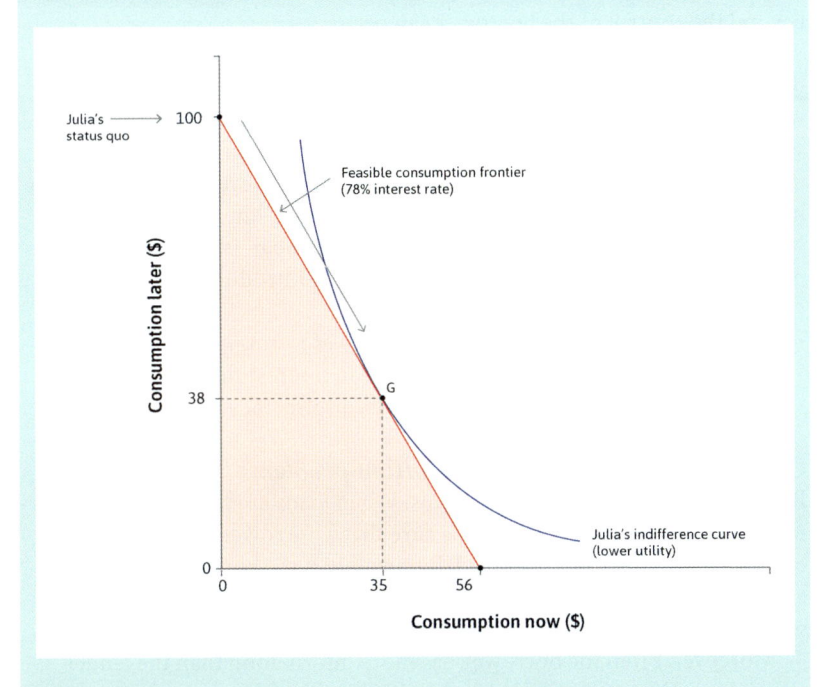

Figure 9.13 Julia's consumption choices.

- ☐ The asset after borrowing but before consumption in period 1 is $56.
- ☐ The net worth after consumption in period 1 is $0.
- ☐ The liability before consumption in period 2 is $35.
- ☐ The asset after consumption but before repaying the loan in period 2 is $62.

9.10 CREDIT MARKET CONSTRAINTS: ANOTHER PRINCIPAL–AGENT PROBLEM

Lending is risky

Up until now, we have said little about the elephant in the room—lending is a risky activity for a bank or money lender. A loan is made now and must be repaid in the future. Between now and then, unanticipated events beyond the control of the borrower can occur.

If the crops in Chambar, Pakistan were destroyed by bad weather or disease, the moneylenders would not be repaid, even though the farmers worked hard. The obsolescence of the skill you have invested in using your student loan is an unavoidable risk and will mean the loan may not be repaid.

The greater the risk of default due to unavoidable events, the greater the interest rate set by a bank or a moneylender. This is one explanation for why an interest rate of 78%, as is the case in Chambar, is not highly profitable. Two other reasons were noted in the introduction:

- *The moneylenders themselves face a high cost of borrowing:* The JS Bank lends them money to lend to farmers at an interest rate of 32%.
- *The moneylenders compete:* This limits the profits they are able to make.

Conflicts of interest, and information problems

But lenders face two further problems. When loans are taken out for investment projects, the lender cannot be sure that a borrower will exert enough effort to make the project succeed. Remember, if the borrower has not put any of her own money into the project, it is the lender, not the borrower, who loses money if the project fails and the loan is not repaid.

Moreover, often the borrower has more information than the lender about the quality of the project and its likelihood of success.

These problems arise in turn from a difference (or conflict) of interest between the borrower and lender, and from the difference between the information the borrower and the lender have about the borrower's project and actions. The problems impose costs of monitoring and loan enforcement that will push up the interest rate on loans.

If the project doesn't succeed because the borrower made too little effort or because it just wasn't a good project, the lender loses money. If the borrower were using only her own money, it is likely that she would have been more conscientious or maybe not engaged in the project at all.

The borrower may decide to use the borrowed funds for a much riskier project than the one that she told the lender she would use it for. To illustrate this (with an extreme example), she could simply buy lottery tickets with the money she has borrowed—if one of them pays off, she is rich; if not, the lender does not get repaid.

The relationship between the lender and the borrower is a **principal–agent problem** similar in many ways to the relationship between the employer and employee studied in the previous unit. The lender is the 'principal' and the borrower is the 'agent'.

The principal–agent problem between borrower and lender is also similar to the 'somebody else's money' problem discussed in Unit 6 (page 238). In that case, the manager of a firm (the agent) makes decisions about the use of the funds supplied by the firm's owners (the principals), but they cannot contractually require the manager to act in a way that maximizes their wealth, rather than pursuing her own objectives.

---

principal–agent relationship This is an asymmetrical relationship in which one party (the principal) benefits from some action or attribute of the other party (the agent) about which the principal's information is not sufficient to enforce in a complete contract. *See also: incomplete contract. Also known as: principal–agent problem.*

9.10 CREDIT MARKET CONSTRAINTS: ANOTHER PRINCIPAL-AGENT PROBLEM

Incomplete contracts

In the case of borrowing and lending, it is often not possible for the lender (the principal) to write a contract that ensures a loan will be repaid by the borrower (the agent). The reason is that it is impossible for the lender to ensure *by contract* that the borrower will use the funds in a prudent way and repay according to the terms of the loan.

The table in Figure 9.14 compares two principal–agent problems.

Lenders will attempt to secure repayment of a loan through legal measures but this will often be difficult if the borrower is poor or declares bankruptcy because they are insolvent. In the introduction to this unit, we reported an example of a method of improving compliance (http://tinyco.re/2009482) in car loan repayments—companies install devices that disable the ignition of the car if the repayments are not made as required.

If legal methods fail, lenders may use illegal ones, such as threatening physical violence.

The role of collateral in lending

One response of the lender to the conflict of interest in the credit market is to require the borrower to put some of her wealth into the project (this is called **equity**). The more of the borrower's own money that is invested in the project, the more closely aligned her interests are with those of the lender. Another common response is to require the borrower to set aside property that will be transferred to the lender if the loan is not repaid (this is called collateral).

Collateral is used in loans for houses (called mortgages) and for cars. For many people, these are the only large loans they can get, and that is because of the collateral—the house, or the car reverts to the lender if repayments are not made.

The pawnbroker is a common example of collateral in small-scale lending and borrowing that has existed for thousands of years. The pawnbroker, found today on shopping streets under the slogan 'Cash converter' or similar, extends a loan to the borrower with a date and amount of repayment specified. And the borrower turns over some item of his or her property to the pawnbroker, which will be returned to the borrower when the loan is repaid. Items commonly lodged with a pawnbroker because they can easily be sold include jewelry, computers and other electronic equipment, cameras, or valuable household items.

> **equity** An individual's own investment in a project. This is recorded in an individual's or firm's balance sheet as net worth. See also: net worth. An entirely different use of the term is synonymous with fairness.

	Actors	Conflict of interest over	Enforceable contract covers	Left out of contract (or unenforceable)	Result
Labour market (Unit 6)	Employer Employee	Wages, work (quality and amount)	Wages, time, conditions	Work (quality and amount), duration of employment	Effort under-provided; unemployment
Credit market (Unit 9)	Lender Borrower	Interest rate, conduct of project (effort, prudence)	Interest rate	Effort, prudence, repayment	Too much risk, credit constraints

Figure 9.14 Principal–agent problems: The credit market and the labour market.

417

A loan with collateral is called a secured loan because, as long as the collateral (the house or the pawned item) can readily be sold for more than the amount of money owed, the lender is secure. With a secured loan, the lender does not run any risk.

Equity or collateral reduces the conflict of interest between the borrower and the lender. The reason is that, when the borrower has some of her money (either equity or collateral) at stake:

- *She has a greater interest in working hard:* She will try harder to make prudent business decisions to ensure the project's success.
- *It is a signal to the lender:* It signals that the borrower thinks that the project is of sufficient quality to succeed.

Credit rationing and inequality

But there is a hitch. If the borrower had been wealthy, she could either have used her wealth as collateral and as equity in the project, or she could have been on the other side of the market, lending money. Often the reason why the borrower needs a loan is that, like Julia, she is not wealthy. As a result, she may be unable to provide enough equity or collateral to sufficiently reduce the conflict of interest and hence the risk faced by the lender, and the lender refuses to offer a loan.

This is called **credit rationing**—those with less wealth borrow on unfavourable terms compared with those with more wealth or are refused loans entirely.

Borrowers whose limited wealth makes it impossible to get a loan at any interest rate are termed **credit-excluded**. Those who borrow, but only on unfavourable terms, are termed **credit-constrained**. Both are sometimes said to be wealth-constrained, meaning that their lack of wealth limits their credit market opportunities.

The relationship between wealth and credit is summarized in Figure 9.15.

The exclusion of those without wealth from credit markets or their borrowing on unfavourable terms is evident in these facts:

- *In a survey, one in eight US families had their request for credit rejected by a financial institution:* The assets of these credit-constrained families were 63% lower than the unconstrained families. 'Discouraged borrowers' (those who did not apply for a loan because they expected to be rejected) had even lower wealth than the rejected applicants.
- *Credit card borrowing limits are often increased automatically:* If borrowing increases in response to an automatic change in the borrowing limit, we can conclude that the individual was credit-constrained. The authors of this study suggested that approximately two-thirds of US families may be credit-constrained or excluded.
- *Inheritance leads the self-employed to considerably increase the scale of their operations:* An inheritance of £5,000 in 1981 (around $24,000 today) doubled a typical British youth's likelihood of setting up a business.
- *Owning a house can be used as collateral:* A 10% rise in value of housing assets that could be used as collateral to secure loans in the UK increases the number of startup businesses by 5%.

---

credit rationing The process by which those with less wealth borrow on unfavourable terms, compared to those with more wealth.

credit-excluded A description of individuals who are unable to borrow on any terms. See also: *credit-constrained*.

credit-constrained A description of individuals who are able to borrow only on unfavourable terms. See also: *credit-excluded*.

Adam Smith had credit rationing in mind when he wrote: 'Money, says the proverb, makes money. When you have got a little it is often easy to get more. The great difficulty is to get that little.' Adam Smith. 1776. 'Of the profits of stock' (http://tinyco.re/9527891). In *An Inquiry into the Nature and Causes of the Wealth of Nations*.

David Gross and Nicholas Souleles. 2002. 'Do liquidity constraints and interest rates matter for consumer behavior? Evidence from credit card data'. *The Quarterly Journal of Economics* 117 (1) (February): pp. 149–85.

9.10 CREDIT MARKET CONSTRAINTS: ANOTHER PRINCIPAL–AGENT PROBLEM

- *Asset-poor people in the US frequently take out short-term 'payday loans':* In the state of Illinois, the typical short-term borrower is a low-income ($24,104 annual income) woman in her mid-thirties, living in rental housing, borrowing between $100 and $200, and paying an average annual rate of interest of 486%.
- *Poor and middle-income Indian farmers could substantially raise their incomes if they did not face credit constraints:* Not only do they generally underinvest in productive assets, but the assets they hold are biased towards those they can sell in times of need (bullocks) and against highly profitable equipment (irrigation pumps), which have little resale value.

Samuel Bowles. 2006. *Microeconomics: Behavior, Institutions, and Evolution (The Roundtable Series in Behavioral Economics)*. Princeton, NJ: Princeton University Press.

> **QUESTION 9.9 CHOOSE THE CORRECT ANSWER(S)**
> Which of the following statements regarding the principal–agent problem are correct?
>
> ☐ A principal–agent problem exists in the credit market due to a positive possibility of the principal not being repaid.
> ☐ The principal–agent problem can be resolved by writing a binding contract for the borrower to exert full effort.
> ☐ One solution for the principal–agent problem in the credit market is for the borrower to provide equity.
> ☐ The principal–agent problem leads to credit rationing in the credit market.

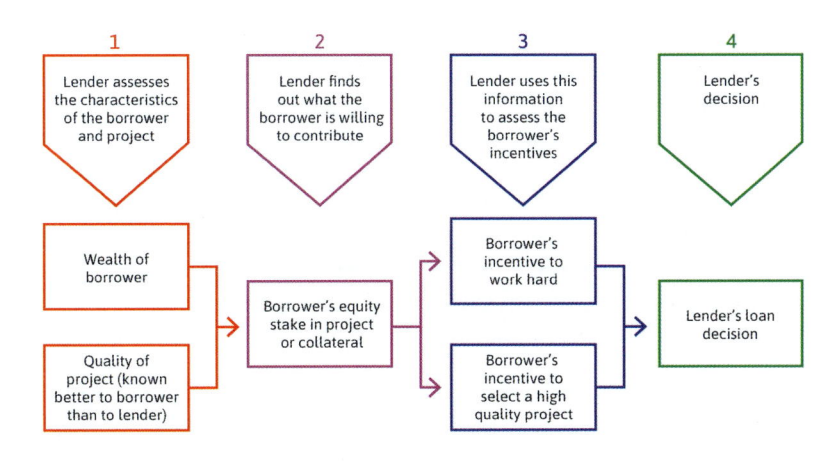

Figure 9.15 Wealth, project quality, and credit.

EXERCISE 9.4 HOW JULIA PAID FOR HER CHRISTMAS PRESENTS

On Christmas Day in 2014, the *New York Times* published an article entitled 'Rise in Loans Linked to Cars is Hurting the Poor' (https://tinyco.re/9099517). Read the article and watch the video in the article with the title: 'No credit, no problem'.

Here are two quotes from the article:

'The lenders argue that they are providing a source of credit for people who cannot obtain less-expensive loans from banks. The high interest rates, the lenders say, are necessary to offset the risk that borrowers will stop paying their bills.'

'And because many lenders make the loan based on an assessment of a used car's resale value, not on a borrower's ability to repay that money, many people find that they are struggling to keep up almost as soon as they drive off with the cash.'

Based on the information in the article and the video:

1. What are the loans discussed in this article used for, and are they secured (i.e. with collateral) or unsecured (i.e. without collateral)? What role, if any, is played by collateral?
2. Does the interest rate charged depend on the wealth of the borrower? Illustrate your argument using a diagram with consumption now on the horizontal axis and consumption later on the vertical axis.
3. In the video, Marcelina Mojica mentions that she went bankrupt (a legal procedure that can follow when a person or a business is insolvent). Using information in the article, provide a plausible explanation of why she went bankrupt, referring to the assets and liabilities in her balance sheet.

Jonathan Morduch. 1999. 'The Microfinance Promise'. *Journal of Economic Literature* 37 (4) (December): pp. 1569–1614.

EXERCISE 9.5 MICROFINANCE AND LENDING TO THE POOR

Read the paper 'The Microfinance Promise' (http://tinyco.re/2004502).

The Grameen Bank in Bangladesh makes loans available to groups of individuals who together apply for individual loans, under the condition that the loans to the group members will be renewed in the future if (but only if) each member has repaid the loan on schedule.

1. Explain how you think such an arrangement would affect the borrower's decision about what to spend the money on, and how hard she will work to make sure that repayment is possible.
2. Use the concepts in this section to explain how the Grameen Bank's lending method could affect credit rationing and credit exclusion.
3. Find evidence about whether or not microfinance has been effective in increasing investment by groups who would normally be excluded from the credit market.

9.10 CREDIT MARKET CONSTRAINTS: ANOTHER PRINCIPAL–AGENT PROBLEM

EXERCISE 9.6 PAWN SHOPS AS A SOURCE OF CREDIT

Pawn broking is one of the oldest sources of credit in the world. A pawn shop offers loans in exchange for items such as jewelry which are held by the shop until the loan is repaid. Such shops are mainly used by people on low incomes. In Texas, the maximum interest rate that can be charged is 20% per month. According to a study of pawn shops in Texas, default rates are lower when items of sentimental value such as rings rather than items of equivalent resale value such as TV screens are held by the shop.

In this exercise, we will provide an economic explanation for the phenomenon of pawn broking.

1. Draw a diagram with 'Consumption now' on the horizontal axis and 'Consumption later' on the vertical axis. Draw a feasible set, endowment, and indifference curves on this diagram, and use the diagram to explain why someone might choose to use a pawn shop.
2. Define the term that is used for the items held by the shop (such as jewelry), and explain its role in the pawn broking business.
3. Comment on the statement that pawn shops are 'one of the oldest sources of credit in the world'.
4. Suggest an explanation for the differential default rates on the type of item held by the pawn shops (You may find it useful to refer to the discussion of 'My diet begins tomorrow' in Unit 13 of *The Economy* (https://tinyco.re/7954936).)

If you want to find out more about pawn broking, this quote is taken from Susan Payne Carter and Paige Marta Skiba. 2012. 'Pawnshops, Behavioral Economics, and Self-Regulation'. *Review of Banking and Financial Law* 32 (1): pp. 193-220.

9.11 INEQUALITY: LENDERS, BORROWERS, AND THOSE EXCLUDED FROM CREDIT MARKETS

We can analyse inequalities between borrowers and lenders (and among borrowers) using the same Lorenz curve and Gini coefficient model that we used to study inequality among employers and employees in Unit 8, and farmers and landowners in Unit 5.

Lenders and borrowers in the Lorenz curve diagram

Here is an illustration. An economy is composed of 90 farmers who borrow from 10 lenders and use the funds to finance the planting and tending of their crops. The harvest (on average) is sold for an amount greater than the farmer's loan, so that for every euro borrowed and invested, the farmer receives $1 + R$ when the crop is sold after the harvest. This is the farmer's revenue.

Following the harvest, the farmers repay the loans with interest, at rate i. To focus on the Lorenz curve model, we simplify in this section by assuming that all of the loans are repaid and that all lenders lend the same amount to the farmers at the same interest rate. The main message would not be altered if we included the probability that loans were not repaid (as in the Chambar case study), but the mathematics would be a lot more complicated.

- *What is the total income?* Since each euro invested produces total revenue of $1 + R$, each farmer generates income (revenue less costs) of R.
- *How is the income divided?* The lender receives an income of i for every euro lent, and so the borrower (the farmer) receives the remainder, $R - i$. So the lender receives a share of i/R of total output, which means that the borrower (farmer) receives what remains, which is $1 - (i/R)$.

Thus, if $i = 0.10$ and $R = 0.15$, then the lender's share of total income is two-thirds and the borrower's is one-third.

Inequality in this economy is shown by the dark-shaded area bordered by a solid line in Figure 9.16. The Gini coefficient is 0.57.

Excluded borrowers raise the Gini coefficient

In the previous sections, we showed why some would-be borrowers (those unable to post collateral or lacking their own funds to finance a project) might be excluded entirely from borrowing even if they would be willing to pay the interest rate. How does this affect the Lorenz curve and the Gini coefficient?

To explore this, imagine that 40 of the prospective borrowers are now excluded. Since they cannot borrow, they receive no income at all. For the other farmers, i and R remain unchanged.

The dashed line in Figure 9.16 shows the new situation. The new Gini coefficient is 0.70, showing an increase in inequality when the poor are excluded from the credit market.

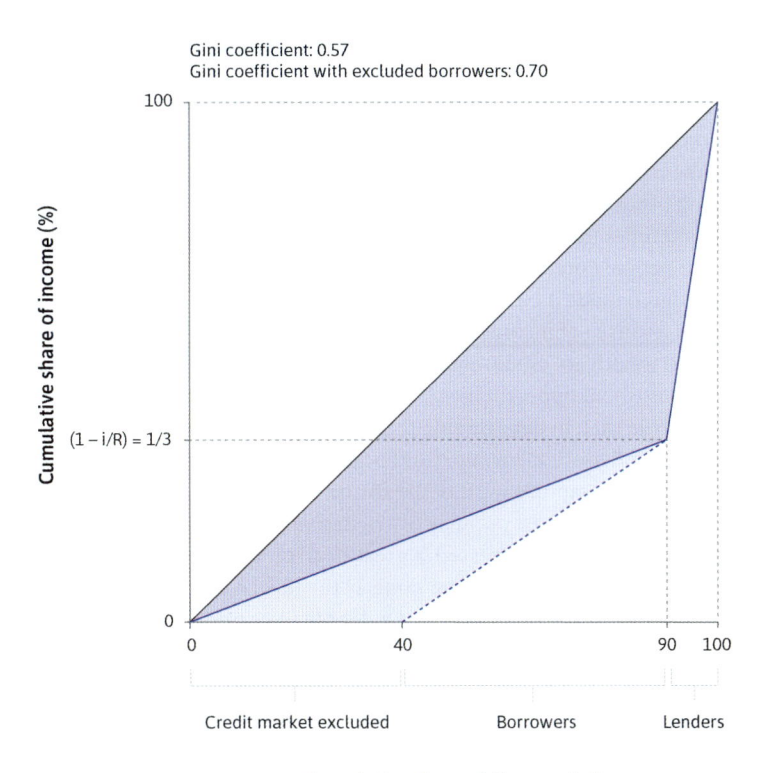

9.11 INEQUALITY: LENDERS, BORROWERS, AND THOSE EXCLUDED FROM CREDIT MARKETS

Gini coefficient: 0.57
Gini coefficient with excluded borrowers: 0.70

To explore all of the slides in this figure, see the online version at https://tinyco.re/1481822.

Figure 9.16 Inequality in a borrowing and lending economy. The Gini coefficient when everyone in the population can borrow is 0.57. When 40% of would-be borrowers are excluded from the credit market, it is 0.70.

1. A model economy of lenders and borrowers
An economy is composed of 90 farmers who borrow from 10 lenders. Since $i = 0.10$ and $R = 0.15$, the lenders' share of total income is two-thirds and the borrowers' is one-third. The Gini coefficient is 0.57.

2. Some borrowers are credit market excluded
Suppose that 40 of the prospective borrowers are excluded. Since they cannot borrow, they receive no income at all.

3. Inequality increases
When some prospective borrowers are excluded, the Gini coefficient increases to 0.70.

QUESTION 9.10 CHOOSE THE CORRECT ANSWER(S)

In an economy with a population of 100, there are 80 farmers and 20 lenders. The farmers use the funds to finance the planting and tending of their crops. The rate of profit for the harvest is 12.5%, while the interest rate charged is 10%. Compare the following two cases:

Case A: All farmers are able to borrow.

Case B: Only 50 farmers are able to borrow.

Based on this information, which of the following statements are correct?

☐ The share of total output received by the farmers who can borrow is 25%.
☐ The Gini coefficient for case A is 0.5.
☐ The Gini coefficient for case B is 0.6.
☐ There is a 10% increase in the Gini coefficient in case B compared to case A.

423

The credit market can provide mutual gains but perpetuates inequalities

This example illustrates the fact that one cause of inequality in an economy is that some people (like Marco) are in a position to profit by lending, just as others, like Bruno in Unit 5 (page 213), are in a position to profit by employing others.

It is sometimes said that rich people lend on terms that make them rich, while poor people borrow on terms that make them poor. Our example of Julia and Marco made it clear that one's view of the interest rate—as a cost for Julia and as a source of income for Marco—depends on one's wealth. People with limited wealth are credit-constrained, which limits their ability to profit from the investment opportunities that are open to those with more assets.

It is also true that, in determining the rate of interest at which an individual borrows, the lender often has superior bargaining power, and so can set a rate that enables him to capture most of the **mutual gains** from the transaction.

Banks are not the most popular or trusted institutions. In the US, for example, 73% of people expressed 'a great deal' or 'quite a lot' of confidence in the military in 2016, exactly the same as the level a decade earlier. In contrast, in 2016, only 27% expressed a degree of confidence in banks, down from 49% a decade earlier. Surveys show that the public in Germany, Spain and many other countries hold their banks in low esteem. This has particularly been the case since the financial crisis of 2008. In Unit 10, we look at banks as economic actors in a modern economy.

Like other profit-making firms, banks are owned by wealthy people and they often transact on terms (rates of interest, wages) that perpetuate the lack of wealth of borrowers and employees. But as we saw in the Chambar case, the profitability of the lending also depends on the extent of competition among lenders. The interest rate charged by the moneylenders in Chambar would have been even higher if—as in many villages—there is only a single moneylender.

mutual gains An outcome of an interaction among two or more people, in which all parties are better off as a result than they would have been without the interaction (or at least some parties are better off and none are worse off).

Like the labour market, the credit market provides opportunities for mutual gains

But even those who dislike banks do not think that the less wealthy would be better off in their absence, any more than that the less wealthy would benefit if firms ceased to employ workers. Access to credit is essential to a modern economy—including access of the less well off to economic opportunities—because it provides opportunities for mutual gains that occur when people can benefit by moving their buying power from one time period to another, either borrowing (moving it to the present) or lending (the opposite).

EXERCISE 9.7 UNPOPULAR BANKS
Why do you think that banks tend to be more unpopular than other profit-making firms (Honda or Microsoft, for example)?

EXERCISE 9.8 LIMITS ON LENDING
Many countries have policies that limit how much interest a moneylender can charge on a loan.

1. Do you think these limits are a good idea?
2. Who benefits from the laws and who loses?
3. What are the likely long-term effects of such laws?
4. Contrast this approach to helping the poor gain access to loans with the Grameen Bank in Exercise 9.5 (page 420).

9.12 THE CREDIT MARKET AND THE LABOUR MARKET

The credit and labour markets share similarities. We use a principal–agent model to describe both.

- *Principals (employers, lenders) and agents (employees, borrowers) can both benefit from transacting with each other:* But they have conflicting interests over the terms of the exchange (wages and effort, interest rate and repayment).
- *Some would-be agents are unable to make a transaction:* The unemployed, or those who are refused credit.

The two markets are not only similar, they are related to each other, the credit market providing the funds allowing some (but not others) to become employers in the labour market. This is shown in Figure 9.17.

Starting at the upper left of Figure 9.17, wealthy individuals can use their wealth to purchase the capital goods to become employers and they can also lend to others. Among the less wealthy, there will be some successful borrowers who can, as a result, also become employers. Those with even less wealth cannot borrow (they are the credit market excluded or can only borrow where the house provides the collateral for the mortgage), and must seek work as employees. Employers then hire employees from among the less wealthy, with some remaining unemployed (due to the workings of the labour market that you studied in Unit 8).

To explore all of the slides in this figure, see the online version at https://tinyco.re/7178169.

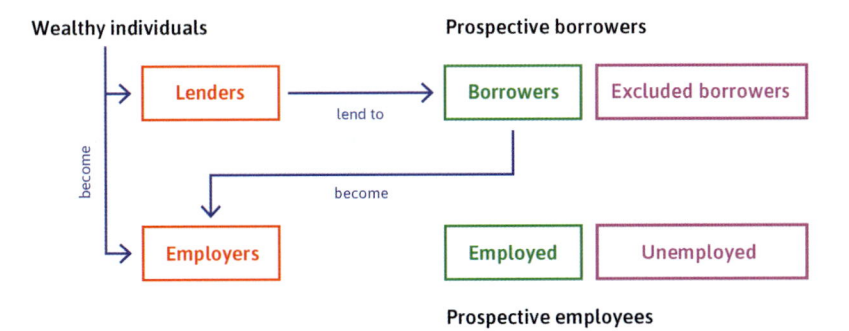

Figure 9.17 The credit and labour markets shape the relationships between groups with different endowments.

1. A model economy
Consider an economy with wealthy individuals and employees.

2. Credit market excluded
Those without wealth (collateral) or insufficient wealth are excluded from the credit market.

3. Wealthy individuals and successful borrowers
These people can purchase capital goods so as to become employers.

4. Those who are not wealthy
These are employees or unemployed.

5. Employers hire employees on the labour market
This excludes the unemployed.

425

Horizontal arrows ('lend to' and 'hire') indicate a principal–agent relationship. Lenders and employers are the principals in Figure 9.17; their common orange colour indicates this similarity. Agents—successful borrowers, and employees—are coloured green to distinguish them from would-be agents (credit market excluded and unemployed), who are coloured purple. You definitely do not want to be in the purple boxes. But even if you are an agent lucky enough to be in one of the green boxes, the principal can put you back in the purple box just by refusing to deal with you. This is why lenders and employers have power over borrowers and employees.

Figure 9.17 helps us understand why some people end up as principals (employers, for example), while others end up as agents (employees). If one is wealthy, one can be both a lender and an employer. There is some truth to the saying that 'people are born into their position in the economic order'. This was literally true in some economies of the past, for example, when the position of the slave was perpetuated in the slave's children as a matter of law.

Something similar can occur in places where wealth is inherited from parent to child. The children of employees (who inherit little wealth) are also more likely to become the next generation's workers than are the children of employers. The children of well-off parents in the US also tend to have high incomes when they become adults.

If you want to study this topic in more detail, you can read about it in Unit 19 of *The Economy* (https://tinyco.re/7407436), which is all about the causes and effects of economic inequality.

9.13 CONCLUSION

We have explained how credit markets, like labour markets, shape the relationship between groups with different levels of wealth. To do so, we began by differentiating between **wealth** (a **stock** of accumulated **savings**) and **income** (a **flow** affected by direct taxes and transfers). Wealth can include money, financial assets, and physical assets. A broader definition of wealth includes **human capital**, seen as an asset contributing to higher labour earnings.

Using the feasible set and indifference curves of our constrained choice toolkit, we have developed a model of borrowing and lending to analyse how individuals decide to allocate their consumption across time periods.

Constraint	Preferences
The **feasible frontier**—consumption now and in the future cannot exceed one's present and future income.	**Indifference curves** join together all combinations of present and future consumption that provide the same level of **utility**.
The slope of the feasible frontier is determined by the **interest rate** r, which affects the opportunity cost of consuming today. The marginal rate of transformation (MRT) is $(1 + r)$, indicating that one must forgo $(1 + r)$ units of consumption in the future in order to consume one more unit today.	The slope of the indifference curves is determined by the **discount rate** ρ, which reflects both a preference to **smooth consumption** (there are **diminishing marginal returns to consumption** in a given period) and **pure impatience** (be it due to myopia or prudence). The MRS is given by $(1 + \rho)$.

Optimal choice: MRT = MRS
$$(1 + r) = (1 + \rho)$$
$$r = \rho$$

While the different situations of borrowers and lenders give rise to the possibility of **mutual gains** from interacting in the credit market, there is a **conflict of interest** over how these gains are distributed. An increased interest rate expands a lender's feasible set but shrinks that of a borrower. The lender benefits from the repayment of the loan, which is a cost to the borrower.

These conflicts of interest, along with the fact that repayment cannot be guaranteed by an enforceable contract, motivate us to model this as a **principal–agent relationship** in which the credit contract is incomplete: It cannot enforce a prudent use of funds and the repayment of the loan.

Putting some of one's own wealth at stake (be it as **equity** in a project or **collateral** on a loan) means that the borrower has less incentive to misuse the funds (by taking extraordinary risks, for example) and more incentive to work to make the project succeed. Individuals with limited wealth, however, may not have access to loans because they cannot provide equity or collateral, or they can only borrow at high interest rates. This **credit rationing** can perpetuate inequalities as it limits the ability of less wealthy people to profit from the investment opportunities that are open to those with more assets.

9.14 *DOING ECONOMICS:* CREDIT-EXCLUDED HOUSEHOLDS IN A DEVELOPING COUNTRY

In Sections 9.10 (page 416) and 9.11 (page 422), we outlined the principal–agent problem in credit markets, which leads to some households being credit-constrained or credit-excluded.

In *Doing Economics* Empirical Project 9, we will use survey data from a developing country (Ethiopia) to identify households that face credit constraints and look at how borrowing conditions vary with household characteristics.

Go to *Doing Economics* Empirical Project 9 (http://tinyco.re/6719860) to work on this project.

> *Learning objectives*
> In this project you will:
>
> - identify credit-constrained and credit-excluded households using survey information
> - create dummy (indicator) variables
> - explain why selection bias is an important issue.

9.15 REFERENCES

Aleem, Irfan. 1990. 'Imperfect information, screening, and the costs of informal lending: A study of a rural credit market in Pakistan' (https://tinyco.re/4382174). *The World Bank Economic Review* 4 (3): pp. 329–49.

Bowles, Samuel. 2006. *Microeconomics: Behavior, Institutions, and Evolution (The Roundtable Series in Behavioral Economics)*. Princeton, NJ: Princeton University Press.

Carter, Susan Payne, and Paige Marta Skiba. 2012. 'Pawnshops, Behavioral Economics, and Self-Regulation' (https://tinyco.re/3000562). *Review of Banking and Financial Law* 32 (1): pp.193–220

Gross, David, and Nicholas Souleles. 2002. 'Do liquidity constraints and interest rates matter for consumer behavior? Evidence from credit card data'. *The Quarterly Journal of Economics* 117 (1) (February): pp. 149–85.

Morduch, Jonathan. 1999. 'The Microfinance Promise' (https://tinyco.re/2004502). *Journal of Economic Literature* 37 (4) (December): pp. 1569–1614.

Silver-Greenberg, Jessica. 2014. 'New York prosecutors charge payday loan firms with usury' (https://tinyco.re/8917188). *DealBook*.

Smith, Adam. 1776. 'Of the profits of stock' (https://tinyco.re/9527891). In *An Inquiry into the Nature and Causes of the Wealth of Nations*.

10
BANKS, MONEY, HOUSING, AND FINANCIAL ASSETS

Abandoned housing development, Keshcarrigan, Ireland, 2012

10.1 INTRODUCTION

- Money is a medium of exchange consisting of bank notes and bank deposits, or anything else that can be used to purchase goods and services. It is accepted as payment because others can use it for the same purpose.
- Commercial banks are firms that provide financial services including both short-term financial investment opportunities (interest on savings accounts for example) and long-term loans (mortgages for home purchases).
- These banks create money in the form of bank deposits when they make loans.
- A nation's central bank lends to commercial banks at what is called the policy interest rate, which plays a critical role in how a central bank regulates the amount of spending in the economy as a whole.
- This works because the policy interest rate chosen by the central bank affects the interest rate charged by commercial banks on loans to firms and households, which in turn affects the demand for housing, cars and other durable goods.
- Housing and financial assets differ from other goods and services because they are valued not only for the services they provide (for example, a place to live), but also because their value may increase in the future.
- The price of an asset depends on the return expected from holding it, its riskiness, and how much people value a 'sure thing' over taking risks.
- Asset prices may be subject to bubbles when a price increase motivates people to purchase more of the asset in anticipation of future price increases, causing the price to rise further.

- Because governments sometimes bail out failed banks (generally citing the need to avoid a financial system collapse), banks often engage in overly risky practices, knowing that some of the downside of their risk-taking will be borne by taxpayers.
- The trust and social norms on which many transactions in financial markets depend cannot be guaranteed either by enforceable contracts, or by relying on competition to weed out 'bad actors'.

On 4 May 1970, a notice titled 'Closure of banks' appeared in the *Irish Independent* newspaper in the Republic of Ireland. It read:

> As a result of industrial action by the Irish Bank Officials' Association … it is with regret that these banks must announce the closure of all their offices in the Republic of Ireland … until further notice.

Banks in Ireland did not open again until 18 November, six-and-a-half months later.

Did Ireland fall off a financial cliff? To everyone's surprise, instead of collapsing, the Irish economy continued to grow much as before. A two-word answer has been given to explain how this was possible—Irish pubs. Andrew Graham, an economist, visited Ireland during the bank strike and was fascinated by what he saw:

> Because everyone in the village used the pub, and the pub owner knew them, they agreed to accept deferred payments in the form of cheques that would not be cleared by a bank in the near future. Soon they swapped one person's deferred payment with another thus becoming the financial intermediary. But there were some bad calls and some pubs took a hit as a result. My second experience is that I made a payment with a cheque drawn on an English bank and, out of curiosity, on my return to England, I rang the bank (in those days you could speak to someone you knew in a bank) and they told me my cheque had duly been paid in but that on the back were several signatures. In other words, it had been passed on from one person to another exactly as if it were money.

Andrew Graham, in an email message to author.

The closure of the Irish banks is a vivid illustration of the definition of money—it is anything accepted in payment. At that time, notes and coins made up about one-third of the money in the Irish economy, with the remaining two-thirds in bank deposits. The majority of transactions used cheques, but paying by cheque requires banks to ensure that people have the funds to back up their paper payments.

In a functioning banking system, the cheque is cashed at the end of the day, and the bank credits the current account of the shop. If the writer of the cheque does not have enough money to cover the amount, the bank bounces the cheque, and the shop owner knows immediately that he must collect in some other way. People generally avoid writing bad cheques as a result.

Credit or debit cards were not yet widely used. Today, a debit card works by instantly verifying the balance of your bank account and debiting from it. If you get a loan to buy a car, the bank credits your current account and you then write a cheque, use a debit card, or initiate a bank transfer to the car dealer to buy the car. This is money in a modern economy.

So what happens when the banks close their doors and everyone knows that cheques will not bounce, even if the cheque writer has no money? Will anyone accept your cheques? Why not just write a cheque to buy the car when there is not enough money in your current account or in your approved overdraft? If you start thinking like this, you would not trust someone offering you a cheque in exchange for goods or services. You would insist on being paid in cash. But there is not enough cash in circulation to finance all of the transactions that people need to make. Everyone would have to cut back, and the economy would suffer.

How did Ireland avoid this fate? As we have seen, it happened at the pub. Cheques were accepted in payment as money, because of the trust generated by the pub owners. Publicans (owners of the pubs) spend hours talking and listening to their patrons. They were prepared to accept cheques, which could not be cleared in the banking system, as payment from those judged to be trustworthy. During the six-month period that the banks were closed, individuals and businesses wrote cheques to the value of about £5 billion, which were not processed by banks. It helped that Ireland had one pub for every 190 adults at the time. With the assistance of pub and shop owners who knew their customers, cheques could circulate as money. With money in bank accounts inaccessible, the citizens of Ireland created the amount of new money needed to keep the economy growing during the bank closure.

Neither Irish publicans, nor the moneylenders in the market town of Chambar that we introduced in Unit 9 (page 387), would recognize that, by lending in this way, they were creating money. They would also not know that, in doing so, they were providing a service essential for the functioning of their respective economies.

10.2 ASSETS, MONEY, BANKS, AND THE FINANCIAL SYSTEM

In the bathtub model of Unit 9 (page 390), the amount of water in the tub represents a household's wealth. But wealth is not a homogeneous substance like water. Wealth is held in many forms, as both financial and non-financial assets. Money, shares, and bonds are financial assets. Non-financial assets include housing, cars, intellectual property (such as a **trademark** or a **patent**), and works of art.

In the sections that follow, we introduce the main actors and markets in which assets are traded, which are part of a model of the financial system.

Actors

The main actors in the financial system are commercial banks (called **banks** from here on), the central bank, pension funds, and other financial institutions. Households and non-bank firms are also part of the financial system when they buy, sell, borrow, lend, save, invest, and interact in other ways with banks and the central bank.

Like other firms, banks are predominantly privately owned and seek to make profits. Unlike other firms, they make profits by supplying loans; through this process, they create money, known as **bank money**. Banks set the lending rate. This is the interest rate—the **nominal interest rate**—that borrowers must pay on a loan (page 406). The way banks operate in a modern economy is explained in the next three sections.

Felix Martin. 2013. *Money: The Unauthorised Biography*. London: The Bodley Head.

Antoin E. Murphy. 1978. 'Money in an economy without banks: The case of Ireland'. *The Manchester School* 46 (1) (March): pp. 41–50.

---

trademark A logo, a name, or a registered design typically associated with the right to exclude others from using it to identify their products.

patent A right of exclusive ownership of an idea or invention, which lasts for a specified length of time. During this time it effectively allows the owner to be a monopolist or exclusive user.

bank A firm that creates money in the form of bank deposits in the process of supplying credit.

bank money Money in the form of bank deposits created by commercial banks when they extend credit to firms and households.

nominal interest rate The price of bringing some spending power (in dollars or other nominal terms) forward in time. The policy rate and the lending rate quoted by commercial banks are examples of nominal interest rates. *See also: real interest rate, interest rate, Fisher equation.*

> **base money** Cash held by households, firms, and banks, and the balances held by commercial banks in their accounts at the central bank, known as reserves. *Also known as: high-powered money.*
>
> **policy (interest) rate** The interest rate set by the central bank, which applies to banks that borrow base money from each other, and from the central bank. *Also known as: base rate, official rate. See also: real interest rate, nominal interest rate.*

To see how secondary trading on the stock market works and how prices of shares are set through a continuous double auction, see Section 11.6 in *The Economy* (https://tinyco.re/9929540).

As we shall see, banks need a different kind of money, called **base money**, in order to carry out transactions with other banks. The only supplier of base money is the central bank. This allows the central bank to set the 'price' for borrowing base money, which is the **policy interest rate**, and like the lending rate, this is a nominal interest rate.

Pension funds manage the contributions of employees and employers, purchase financial assets using those contributions, and pay out pension benefits at retirement.

Other financial institutions include insurance companies, investment banks, payday lenders, and specialist lenders, such as mortgage providers in the housing market.

Markets

Asset markets are the money market, the stock market, the housing market, and other financial markets.

The central bank and commercial banks lend to each other and other financial institutions in the money markets.

Companies make what are called initial public offerings (IPOs), using the stock market. In an IPO, shares in a company are sold to the general public for the first time. After that, the shares are traded on the stock exchange. This is called secondary trading.

The housing market plays an important role in the economy. Houses are the main form of wealth of households (except for the very rich). Households borrow long term from banks or specialist mortgage lenders to buy houses.

There are many other financial markets: for government and corporate bonds, derivatives, and other financial assets.

Financial assets

Money is a financial asset and is the subject of the next section.

By selling bonds, a government or a firm can borrow money. The bond issuer promises to pay a given amount to the bondholder on a fixed schedule. Selling a bond is equivalent to borrowing, because the bond issuer receives cash today and promises to repay in the future. Conversely, a bond buyer is a lender or saver, because the buyer gives up cash today, expecting to be repaid in the future. Both governments and firms borrow by issuing bonds. Households buy bonds as a form of saving, both directly, and indirectly through pension funds. Although a bond is a way a firm can borrow, it is different from a bank loan because it can be bought and sold in secondary trading in the bond market. To learn more about bonds and how assets are priced, read the two 'Find out more' boxes at the end of this section.

Shares (stocks) are a part of the assets of a firm that may be traded on the stock market. The owner of a share has a right to receive a proportion of a firm's profit (when dividends are paid out) and to benefit when and if the firm's assets become more valuable.

As we saw in Unit 9 (page 402), people whose incomes fluctuate want to smooth their consumption and they do so, in part, by saving. One factor that affects whether a household saves by holding money in a savings account, or by buying bonds or shares, is its attitude to risk. Holding shares, as we shall see, offers the potential for a higher return on savings, but because the price of shares goes up and down, there is a risk that the value of the asset itself will fall. We explain the trade-offs facing households choosing which assets to hold in Section 10.8; in Sections 10.9 and 10.11, we show why holding shares and other financial assets other than bonds may be risky.

> **FIND OUT MORE**
>
> *Present value (PV) and the price of an asset*
> Assets, like shares in companies or bonds, typically provide a stream of income in the future. Since these assets are bought and sold, we must ask the question: 'How do we value a stream of future payments?' The answer is the present value (PV) of the expected future income.
>
> To make this calculation, we must assume that people participating in the market to buy and sell assets have the capability to save and borrow at a certain interest rate. Imagine that you face an interest rate of 6% and are offered a financial contract that says you will be paid €100 in one year's time. That contract is an asset. How much would you be willing to pay for it today?
>
> You would not pay €100 today for the contract, because if you had €100 today, you could put it in the bank and get €106 in a year's time, which would be better than buying the asset.
>
> Imagine you are offered the asset for €90 today. Now you will want to buy it, because you could borrow €90 today from the bank at 6%, and in a year's time you would pay back €95.40, while you receive €100 from the asset, making a profit of €4.60.
>
> The break-even price or present value (PV) for this contract would make you indifferent between buying the contract and not buying it. It must be equal to whatever amount of money would give you €100 in a year's time if you put it in the bank today. With an interest rate of 6%, that amount is:
>
> $$PV = \frac{100}{1 + 0.06} = \frac{100}{1.06} = €94.34$$
>
> We say that the income next year is discounted by the interest rate; a positive interest rate makes it worth less than income today.
>
> The same logic applies further in the future, when we allow for interest compounding over time. If you receive €100 in t years' time, then today its value to you is:
>
> $$PV = \frac{100}{1.06^t}$$
>
> $$PV = \frac{X_1}{(1+i)^1} + \frac{X_2}{(1+i)^2} + \ldots + \frac{X_T}{(1+i)^T}$$
>
> The present value of these payments obviously depends on the amounts of the payments themselves. But it also depends on the interest rate; if the interest rate increases, then the PV will decline, because future payments are discounted (their PV reduced) by more. Note that it is easy to adjust the present value formula to take into account different interest rates for years 1, 2, and so on.

Net present value (NPV)

This logic applies to any asset that provides income in the future. If a firm is considering whether or not to make an investment, it must compare the cost of making the investment with the present value of the future profits it expects from the investment. In this context, we consider the net present value (NPV), which takes into account the cost of making the investment as well as the expected profits. If the cost is c and the present value of the expected profits is PV, then the NPV of making the investment is:

$$\text{NPV} = \text{PV} - c$$

If NPV is positive, then the investment is worth making, because the expected profits are worth more than the cost (and vice versa).

QUESTION 10.1 CHOOSE THE CORRECT ANSWER(S)

Which of the following statements are correct?

- ☐ If the annually compounding interest rate is 5%, then the present value of £100 in two years' time is £90.91.
- ☐ If you pay £96 for an investment that pays £100 in one year's time when the interest rate is 5%, then your net present value is £0.76.
- ☐ If the annually compounding interest rate is 5%, then the present value of receiving £100 at the end of each year for two years is £185.94.
- ☐ £95 today is worth the same as £100 in one year's time if the interest rate is 5%.

FIND OUT MORE

Bond prices and yields

Recall that a bond is a financial asset:

- Issuing or selling a bond is equivalent to borrowing.
- A bond buyer is a lender or saver.
- Governments and firms borrow by issuing bonds.
- Households buy bonds as a form of saving.

What do the holders of bonds receive? Bonds typically last a predetermined amount of time, called the maturity of the bond, and provide two forms of payment: the face value F, which is an amount paid when the bond matures, and a fixed payment every period until maturity (for example, every year or every three months). In the past, bonds were physical pieces of paper and when one of the fixed payments was redeemed, a coupon was clipped from the bond. For this reason, the fixed payments are called coupons and we label them C.

As we saw in the calculation of PV, the amount that a lender is willing to pay for a bond is its present value, which depends on the bond's face value, the series of coupon payments, and also on the interest rate. No one will buy a bond for more than its present value because they would be better off putting the money in the bank. No one will sell a bond for less than its present value, because they would be better off borrowing from the bank. So:

price of bond = discounted present value of coupons
      + discounted present value of face value when it matures

Or, for a bond with a maturity of T years:

$$P = \underbrace{\frac{C}{(1+i)^1} + \frac{C}{(1+i)^2} + \ldots + \frac{C}{(1+i)^T}}_{\text{coupons}} + \underbrace{\frac{F}{(1+i)^T}}_{\text{face value}}$$

An important characteristic of a bond is its yield. This is the implied rate of return that the buyer gets on their money when they buy the bond at its market price. We calculate the yield using an equation just like the PV equation. The yield y solves the following:

$$P = \underbrace{\frac{C}{(1+y)^1} + \frac{C}{(1+y)^2} + \ldots + \frac{C}{(1+y)^T}}_{\text{coupons}} + \underbrace{\frac{F}{(1+y)^T}}_{\text{face value}}$$

If the interest rate stays constant, as we have assumed, then the yield will be the same as that interest rate. But in reality, we cannot be sure how interest rates are going to change over time. In contrast, we know the price of a bond, its coupon payments, and its face value, so we can always calculate a bond's yield. Buying a bond with yield y is equivalent to saving your money at the guaranteed constant interest rate of $i = y$.

Since a saver (a lender) can choose between buying a government bond, lending the money in the money market, or putting it into a bank account, the yield on the government bond is very close to the rate of interest in the money market (set by the central bank's policy interest rate). If it weren't, money would be switched very quickly from one asset to the other by traders until the rates of return were equalized, a strategy called **arbitrage**.

Let's take a numerical example: a government bond with a face value of €100, yearly coupon of €5, and a maturity of 4 years. The nominal interest rate in the money market is 3%, and we use this to discount the cash flows we receive.

So the price of this bond is given by:

$$P = \frac{5}{(1.03)^1} + \frac{5}{(1.03)^2} + \frac{5}{(1.03)^3} + \frac{5}{(1.03)^4} + \frac{100}{(1.03)^4}$$
$$= 4.85 + 4.71 + 4.58 + 4.44 + 88.85$$
$$= 107.43$$

We would be willing to pay, at most, €107.43 for this bond today, even though it generates €120 of revenue over four years. The yield is equal to the interest rate of 3%. If the central bank raises the policy interest rate, then this will reduce the market price of the bond, increasing the yield in line with the interest rate.

> **arbitrage** The practice of buying a good at a low price in one market to sell it at a higher price in another. Traders engaging in arbitrage take advantage of the price difference for the same good between two countries or regions. As long as the trade costs are lower than the price gap, they make a profit. See also: price gap.

QUESTION 10.2 CHOOSE THE CORRECT ANSWER(S)

Which of the following statements regarding a bond are correct?

- ☐ The face value of a bond is how much you pay for the bond.
- ☐ The coupon is the certificate that you receive when you buy a bond.
- ☐ If the price of a bond with a face value of £100, yearly coupon of £4, and a maturity of 1 year is £100.97, then the bond's yield is 4%.
- ☐ When the nominal interest rate is 3%, then the price of a bond with a face value of £100, yearly coupon of £5, and a maturity of 2 years is £103.83.

10.3 MONEY AND BANKS

For money to do its work, almost everyone must believe that, if they accept money from you in return for handing over goods or services, then they will be able to use the money to buy something else in turn. In other words, they must trust that others will accept your money as payment. Governments and banks usually provide this trust. As an indication of the centrality of trust to banking, the origin of the word 'credit' is the Latin *credere*—to believe, to trust.

The Irish bank closure shows that, when there is sufficient trust between households and businesses, money can function in the absence of banks. The publicans and shops accepted a cheque as payment, even though they knew it could not be cleared by a bank in the foreseeable future. As the bank dispute went on, the cheque presented to the pub or shop relied on a lengthening chain of uncleared cheques received by the person or business presenting the cheque. Some cheques circulated many times, endorsed on the back by the pub or shop owner, just like a bank note.

Money

Money is used for transactions—buying and selling—in the economy. When you pay for a train ticket on your smartphone linked to your bank account, by a cardless transfer, or by your debit card, the payment is made to the train company from deposits in your bank. There are many ways to activate the transfer between you and the vendor, but the money itself is the bank deposit. You can also pay by cash. Cash and bank deposits are the main forms of money in contemporary economies.

In a barter economy, I might exchange my apples for your oranges because I want some oranges, not because I intend to use the oranges to pay my rent. Money makes more exchanges possible because it's not hard to find someone who is happy to have your money (in exchange for something), whereas unloading a large quantity of apples could be a problem. This is why barter plays a limited role in virtually all modern economies.

Money allows purchasing power to be transferred among people so that they can exchange goods and services, even when payment takes place at a later date (for example, through the clearing of a cheque or settlement of credit card or trade credit balances). Therefore, money requires trust to function.

---

money Money is something that facilitates exchange (called a medium of exchange) consisting of bank notes and bank deposits, or anything else that can be used to purchase goods and services, and is generally accepted by others as payment because others can use it for the same purpose. The 'because' is important and it distinguishes exchange facilitated by money from barter exchange, in which goods are directly exchanged without money changing hands.

David Graeber. 2012. 'The myth of barter' (https://tinyco.re/6552964). *Debt: The First 5,000 years*. Brooklyn, NY: Melville House Publishing.

What does money do?

Some of the functions that money fulfils are also fulfilled by other things. But only money clearly fulfils *all* these functions (although even money may not fulfil them equally well in all times and places).

These functions are:

1. *A medium of exchange:* We can use money to pay for things. Note that, to be a true medium of exchange, money must be *divisible*, ideally into sufficiently small units that even the smallest value purchases are possible.
2. *A store of value:* We can hold money as a means of storing up future consumption of goods and services.
3. *A unit of account:* A more subtle (but nonetheless important) distinction, whereby we use money as a yardstick by which we can measure the value of anything we own or want to buy.

One reason for confusion around the use of the term 'money' is that what people have used to fulfil these functions has changed over the course of time.

If we look back far enough, to an era well before the Industrial Revolution, most people in most countries would have recognized only one form, namely *commodity money*. The commodity chosen was often (but by no means always) a precious metal—most commonly gold or silver—which had some kind of *intrinsic value* (because it could in principle be used for other purposes, like jewelry or gold teeth).

But commodity money did not fulfil the three functions very well and understanding its limitations helps explain the emergence of banks.

Someone attempting to pay for a loaf of bread with a gold coin would have severe problems getting change, thus failing the test of divisibility. The risk of theft detracted from commodity money as a store of value (gold was much easier to steal than houses or cattle, for example). And there have always been significant fluctuations in the value of gold and silver in terms of what people really cared about—consumption of goods and services—thus detracting from its usefulness both as a store of value *and* as a unit of account.

As a result, even in periods when commodity money was widely used, alternatives that could fulfil at least some of the functions of money were available. In due course, these alternatives evolved into forms that eventually supplanted commodity money (almost) entirely.

Money in the modern economy is an IOU

These new forms of money share with commodity money the defining characteristic that they are accepted by other people as a means of payment. They differ from commodity money and share the feature, whether bank deposits or currency, that they are created when a bank or the central bank as part of the government creates a liability.

A liability is just an IOU ('I owe you'). To understand how money works based on IOUs rather than on a commodity like gold, recall the Irish bank strike. The cheques that circulated as money and were used for payments—endorsed on the back by the publicans—were the way in which IOUs were passed around in exchange for goods and services.

IOU-based money is nothing new. A famous example originated hundreds of years ago on the remote island of Yap, in the Pacific Ocean. As you can read in the article 'The Island of Stone Money' (https://tinyco.re/7295970), even when the giant stone 'coins' were lost overboard and remained on the bottom of the sea, the transfer of purchasing power in exchange for goods and services among different people went on. Find out more about the Yap stones and their use as money in a video by the Federal Reserve Bank of Atlanta:

Money: An Economist's Perspective—The Curious Case of the Yap Stones https://tinyco.re/5134829

balance sheet A record of the assets, liabilities, and net worth of an economic actor such as a household, bank, firm, or government.

Paul Krugman compares cryptocurrencies like Bitcoin to commodity money and fiat money, and asks what problems cryptocurrencies solve (https://tinyco.re/6892456).

What we call money today *is* IOU or liability-based money. To be more precise, if I own some form of liability money, it is because either a commercial bank or the central bank owes me that amount, *and someone else will accept a transfer of all or part of that debt via electronic transfer or currency as a means of payment.*

Even in the era of commodity money, the fear of theft often led wealthy individuals to deposit their gold coins with goldsmiths. The goldsmiths in turn would issue 'promissory notes', which were open commitments to return the gold whenever required. These IOUs in due course evolved into the first prototype banknotes, which were the liabilities of the goldsmith. If the depositor wanted to make a purchase, they did not need to retrieve the gold, but could make payments directly using the promissory notes, that is, the goldsmith's liabilities. In due course, these forms of arrangements evolved into the modern banking system.

Money in bank accounts: IOUs of commercial banks

Today, in most countries, virtually all forms of money are liability-based money. But whose liabilities are they? Mostly, they are the liabilities of banks. If you have $1,000 in your current account, this means that the bank owes you $1,000. In your **balance sheet** as we saw in Section 9.9 (page 412), your bank deposit would appear as an asset; in the bank's balance sheet, it appears as a liability.

Money as coins and notes: IOUs of central banks

The other institution that issues liabilities that we call money is the government. While banknotes and coins are officially the liability of the central bank, in almost all countries the central bank is owned by the government, so the central bank is issuing liabilities on the government's behalf.

In earlier times, banknotes and coins issued by the central bank were exchangeable for gold, just like the promissory notes of the goldsmiths. In modern monetary systems, there is no gold-backing for currency and it is called 'fiat currency'. The central bank promises to honour the debt printed on the bank note with the words: 'I promise to pay the bearer on demand the sum of twenty pounds' (signed by the Chief Cashier on behalf of the Governor of the Bank of England). On US dollar bills, it says the equivalent: 'This note is legal tender for all debts, public and private' and is signed by the Treasurer of the United States. Euro notes are signed by the President of the European Central Bank. If the design changes, for example, the central bank will swap the old note for a new one. Trust in fiat currency originates partly from the government's commitment to accept it in payment of taxes.

EXERCISE 10.1 MONEY AND ITS ROLE IN THE ECONOMY

Using the following references, write a 400-word explanation of how economists can learn from anthropologists about what money is and does, in the style of 'How economists learn from data'.

- the note above on the Yap stones
- William Henry Furness. 1910. Chapter 7 'Money and currency'. *The Island of Stone Money, Uap of the Carolines* (https://tinyco.re/6247026).
- Felix Martin. 2013. 'Chapter 1'. *Money: the Unauthorised Biography*. Bodley Head.

> **QUESTION 10.3 CHOOSE THE CORRECT ANSWER(S)**
> Which of the following statements about money are correct?
>
> ☐ Money allows purchasing power to be transferred between consumers.
> ☐ In economics, money refers to the coins and notes in circulation.
> ☐ If I can exchange my apples for your oranges, then apples can be classified as money.
> ☐ Banks must exist for money to do its work.

Looking for Questions 10.1 and 10.2? They are in the optional sections 'Present value and the price of an asset' (page 433) and 'Bond prices and yields' (page 434), and if you skipped those sections you don't need to attempt them.

10.4 BANKS, PROFITS, AND THE CREATION OF MONEY

Among the moneylenders in Chambar, Pakistan and payday lenders in New York (in Unit 9 (page 387)), the profitability of their lending businesses depend on:

- the cost of their borrowing
- the default rate on the loans they extended
- the interest rate they set.

This provides the starting point for analysing banks as businesses.

Banks create money when providing payment services and making loans

A bank is a firm that makes profits through its lending and borrowing activities. The terms on which banks lend to households and firms differ from their borrowing terms. The interest they pay on deposits is lower than the interest they charge when they make loans, and this spread or margin allows banks to make profits.

To explain this process, we must first explore the concept of money in more detail.

We saw that anything that is accepted as payment can be counted as money. Unlike bank deposits or cheques, base money or high-powered money is cash plus the balances held by commercial banks at the **central bank**, called commercial bank reserves.

Reserves are equivalent to cash because a commercial bank can always take out reserves as cash from the central bank, and the central bank can always print any cash it needs to provide. As we will see, this is not the case with accounts held by households or businesses at commercial banks; commercial banks do not necessarily have the cash available to satisfy all their customers' needs.

> **central bank** The only bank that can create base money. Usually part of the government. Commercial banks have accounts at this bank, holding base money. See also: base money.

> **TYPES OF MONEY**
> **Money** can take the form of bank notes, bank deposits, or whatever else one purchases things with.
> - *Base money:* Cash held by households, firms, and banks, and the balances held by commercial banks in their accounts at the central bank, known as reserves. Base money is the liability of the central bank.
> - *Bank money:* Money in the form of bank deposits created by commercial banks when they extend credit to firms and households. Bank money is the liability of commercial banks.
> - *Broad money:* The amount of broad money in the economy is measured by the stock of money in circulation. This is defined as the sum of bank money and the base money that is in the hands of the non-bank public.

Most of what we count as money is not base money issued by the central bank, but instead is created by commercial banks when they make loans. In the UK, 97% of money is bank money; 3% is base money. We explain how money is created using bank balance sheets.

Payment services

Unlike our balance sheet example in Unit 9 (page 412) in which a bank deposit arises from a loan to Julia, let us suppose that Marco has $100 in cash that he puts in a bank account with Abacus Bank. Abacus Bank puts the cash in a vault or deposits the cash in its account at the central bank. Abacus Bank's balance sheet gains $100 of base money as an asset, and a liability of $100 that is payable on demand to Marco, as shown in Figure 10.1a.

Marco wants to pay $20 to his local grocer, Gino, in return for groceries, so he instructs Abacus Bank to transfer the money to Gino's account in Bonus Bank (he could do this by using a debit card to pay Gino). What happens immediately is that Abacus Bank transfers a liability to Bonus Bank, saying it owes Bonus Bank $20. However, it must only transfer what it owes at the close of business that day—so in the short term, no base money needs to be transferred.

This is shown on the balance sheets of the two banks in Figure 10.1b. Abacus Bank now owes $80 to Marco and $20 to Bonus Bank. Bonus Bank's assets are increased by this promise of $20 owed by Abacus Bank, and its liabilities increase by $20 payable on demand to Gino. For both banks, net worth (assets minus liabilities) stays the same, although the net worth of their customers, Marco and Gino, changes.

To complete the story, at the close of business that day, Abacus Bank must transfer the base money it owes Bonus Bank. The balance sheets are shown in Figure 10.1c.

Note that both banks may make many other transactions in the same day, and the base money that must be transferred at close of business is the net value of those transactions. So suppose Marco pays $20 to Gino, but then another Bonus Bank customer transfers $5 to another Abacus Bank customer. Then at the end of the day Abacus Bank need only transfer $20 − $5 = $15 to Bonus Bank.

Our hypothetical Abacus Bank is not linked to the real-life Abacus Federal Savings Bank, which had an interesting role in the financial crisis of 2008 (https://tinyco.re/7436450).

Abacus Bank's assets		Abacus Bank's liabilities	
Base money	$100	Payable on demand to Marco	$100

Figure 10.1a Marco deposits $100 in Abacus Bank.

Abacus Bank's assets		Abacus Bank's liabilities	
Base money	$100	Payable on demand to Marco	$80
		Liability owed to Bonus Bank	$20

Bonus Bank's assets		Bonus Bank's liabilities	
Owed by Abacus Bank	$20	Payable on demand to Gino	$20

Figure 10.1b Marco pays $20 to Gino.

10.4 BANKS, PROFITS, AND THE CREATION OF MONEY

This illustrates the **payment services** provided by banks. You may have noticed in Figure 10.1b that the total amount of assets and liabilities of the two banks increased from $100 to $120; however, at close of business it was back down to $100 again (Figure 10.1c). The increase occurred because Abacus Bank created a new liability by effectively borrowing from Bonus Bank for the duration of the day. As long as it owed $20, that $20 was a new liability in the banking system and represented new bank money. When Abacus redeemed the loan at the end of the day by transferring base money, the loan disappeared. But this mechanism also applies for longer-term term loans; when a bank lends money to a firm or a household, it increases the money supply. In this way, banks create money in the process of making loans, as we now show.

> **payment service** Any service provided by a financial institution to allow one person or organization to pay another for a product or service.

Making a loan

Suppose that Gino borrows $100 from Bonus Bank. Bonus Bank lends him the money by crediting his bank account with $100, so he is now owed $120 (taking into account the $20 Gino paid him earlier). But he owes a debt of $100 to the bank. So Bonus Bank's balance sheet has expanded. Its assets have grown by the $100 owed by Gino, and its liabilities have grown by the $100 it has credited to his bank account, shown in Figure 10.1d.

Bonus Bank has now expanded the money supply. Gino can make payments up to $120, so in this sense the money supply has grown by $100—even though base money has not grown. The money created by his bank is called **bank money**.

Because of the loan, the total 'money' in the banking system has grown, as Figure 10.1e shows.

> **bank money** Money in the form of bank deposits created by commercial banks when they extend credit to firms and households.

Abacus Bank's assets		Abacus Bank's liabilities	
Base money	$80	Payable on demand to Marco	$80

Bonus Bank's assets		Bonus Bank's liabilities	
Base money	$20	Payable on demand to Gino	$20

Figure 10.1c Marco pays $20 to Gino (end of transaction).

Bonus Bank's assets		Bonus Bank's liabilities	
Base money	$20	Payable on demand to Gino	$120
Bank loan	$100		
Total	$120		

Figure 10.1d Bonus Bank gives Gino a loan of $100.

Assets of Abacus Bank and Bonus Bank		Liabilities of Abacus Bank and Bonus Bank	
Base money	$100	Payable on demand	$200
Bank loan	$100		
Total	$200		

Figure 10.1e The total money in the banking system has grown.

441

While banks are free to create bank money when they make loans, they need base money to settle transactions at the end of each business day, as we saw above. In practice, banks perform many transactions among each other on any given day, most cancelling each other out. This means that the net that must be transferred at the end of each day is small compared with the amount of money flowing around in transactions. This means banks do not need to have sufficient base money available to cover all transactions.

The ratio of base money to broad money varies across countries and over time. For example, before the financial crisis, base money comprised about 3–4% of broad money in the UK, 6–8% in South Africa, and 8–10% in China.

Banks provide maturity transformation services, borrowing short term and lending long term

Creating money may sound like an easy way to make profits, but as we have seen, the money banks create is a liability, not an asset, because it must be paid on demand to the borrower. It is the corresponding loan that is an asset for the bank. Banks make profits out of the process that allows people to shift consumption from the future to the present by charging interest on the loans. So if Bonus Bank lends Gino $100 at an interest rate of 10%, then next year the bank's liabilities have fallen by $10 (the interest paid on the loan, which is a fall in Gino's deposits). This income for the bank increases its accumulated profits and therefore its net worth by $10. Since net worth is equal to the value of assets minus the value of liabilities, this allows banks to create positive net worth.

By taking deposits and making loans, banks provide the economy with the service called **maturity transformation**. Bank depositors (individuals or firms) can withdraw their money from the bank without notice. But when banks lend, they give a fixed date on which the loan will be repaid, which in the case of a **mortgage** loan for a house purchase, may be 30 years in the future. They cannot require the borrower to repay sooner, which allows those receiving bank loans to engage in long-term planning. This is called maturity transformation because the length of a loan is termed its maturity, so the bank is engaging in short-term borrowing and long-term lending. It is also called liquidity transformation—the lenders' deposits are liquid (free to flow out of the bank on demand), whereas bank loans to borrowers are illiquid.

> **maturity transformation** The practice of borrowing money short term and lending it long term. For example, a bank accepts deposits, which it promises to repay at short notice or no notice, and makes long-term loans (which can be repaid over many years). *Also known as:* liquidity transformation.
> **mortgage (or mortgage loan)** A loan contracted by households and businesses to purchase a property without paying the total value at one time. Over a period of many years, the borrower repays the loan, plus interest. The debt is secured by the property itself, referred to as collateral. *See also:* collateral.
> **liquidity risk** The risk that an asset cannot be exchanged for cash rapidly enough to prevent a financial loss.
> **default risk** The risk that credit given as loans will not be repaid.

Maturity transformation, liquidity risk, and bank runs

While maturity transformation is an essential service in any economy, it also exposes the bank to a new form of risk (called **liquidity risk**), aside from the possibility that its loans will not be repaid (called **default risk**).

10.4 BANKS, PROFITS, AND THE CREATION OF MONEY

Banks make money by lending much more than they hold in base money, because they count on depositors not to need their funds all at the same time. The risk they face—liquidity risk—is that depositors can all decide they want to withdraw money instantaneously, but the money won't be there. In Figure 10.1e, the banking system owed $200 but only held $100 of base money. If all customers demanded their money at once, the banks would not be able to repay. This is called a **bank run**. If there's a run, the bank is in trouble. Liquidity risk is a cause of bank failures and explains why many governments provide automatic insurance for depositors against the risk that their banks will fail to meet payments. Protection limits and the extent to which banks contribute to the insurance fund vary across countries.

If people become frightened that a bank is experiencing a shortage of liquidity, there will be a rush to be the first to withdraw deposits. If everyone tries to withdraw their deposits at once, the bank will be unable to meet their demands because it has made long-term loans that cannot be called in at short notice.

> **bank run** A situation in which depositors withdraw funds from a bank because they fear that it may go bankrupt and not honour its liabilities (that is, not repay the funds owed to depositors).

QUESTION 10.4 CHOOSE THE CORRECT ANSWER(S)
Which of the following statements are correct?

- ☐ Money is the cash (coins and notes) used as the medium of exchange to purchase goods and services.
- ☐ Bank money is the money deposited by savers in bank accounts.
- ☐ Base money in circulation is broad money minus bank money.
- ☐ Liquidity transformation occurs when the banks transform illiquid deposits into liquid loans.

QUESTION 10.5 CHOOSE THE CORRECT ANSWER(S)
Figure 10.2 shows a balance sheet of a bank.

Assets		Liabilities	
Cash	£10 million	Deposits	£110 million
Loans	£100 million		

Figure 10.2 A bank's balance sheet.

The interest rate charged on loans is 10%. Based on this information, which of the following statements are correct?

- ☐ The possibility that the loans will not be repaid is called the liquidity risk.
- ☐ The bank holds £10 million of base money.
- ☐ In one year's time, both assets and liabilities grow by £10 million.
- ☐ There is a bank run if depositors ask to withdraw more than £10 million of their deposits at the same time and the bank is unable to raise the difference.

10.5 THE CENTRAL BANK, BANKS, AND INTEREST RATES

Commercial banks make profits from providing banking services and loans. To run the business, they need to be able to make transactions, for which they need base money. There is no automatic relationship between the amount of base money they require and the amount of lending they do. Rather, they need whatever amount of base money that covers the net transactions they make on a daily basis. The price of borrowing base money is the **short-term interest rate**.

> **interest rate (short-term)** The price of borrowing base money. This is a nominal interest rate.

Suppose, in the example of Gino and Marco, that Gino wants to pay $50 to Marco after borrowing $100. Also assume there are no other transactions that day. At close of business that day, Gino's bank, Bonus Bank, doesn't have enough base money to make the transfer to Abacus Bank, as we can see from its balance sheet in Figure 10.1f.

Bonus Bank's assets		Bonus Bank's liabilities	
Base money	$20	Payable on demand to Gino	$120
Bank loan	$100		
Total	$120		

Figure 10.1f Bonus Bank does not have enough base money to pay $50 to Abacus Bank.

So Bonus Bank must borrow $30 of base money to make the payment. Banks borrow from each other in the money markets since, at any moment, some banks will have excess money in their bank accounts, and others not enough. They could try to induce a household or firm to deposit additional money, but deposits also have costs, due to interest payments, marketing, and maintaining bank branches. Thus, cash deposits are only one part of bank financing.

But what determines the price of borrowing in the money market (the interest rate)? We can think in terms of supply and demand:

- The demand for base money depends on the volume of transactions commercial banks must make.
- The central bank supplies base money.

Since the central bank controls the supply of base money, it can decide the interest rate. The central bank intervenes in the money market by saying it will lend (i.e. supply) whatever quantity of base money is demanded at the interest rate (i) that it chooses.

The technicalities of how the central bank implements its chosen policy interest rate vary among central banks around the world. The details can be found on each central bank's website.

Banks in the money market respect that price; no bank borrows at a higher rate or lends at a lower rate, since they can borrow at rate i from the central bank. This i is also called the base rate, official rate or **policy (interest) rate** (often shortened to 'policy rate').

> **policy (interest) rate** The interest rate set by the central bank, which applies to banks that borrow base money from each other, and from the central bank. *Also known as: base rate, official rate. See also: real interest rate, nominal interest rate.*

10.5 THE CENTRAL BANK, BANKS, AND INTEREST RATES

The base rate applies to banks that borrow base money from each other and from the central bank. The base rate matters in the rest of the economy because of its knock-on effect on other interest rates. The average interest rate charged by commercial banks to firms and households is called the **bank lending rate**. This rate is typically above the policy interest rate, ensuring that banks make profits (it is also higher for borrowers perceived as risky by the bank, as we saw earlier). The difference between the bank lending rate and the base rate at which they can borrow is the markup, or spread on commercial lending.

In the UK, for example, the policy interest rate set by the Bank of England was 0.75% in 2019, but few banks would lend at less than 3%. In emerging economies, this gap can be quite large, owing to the uncertain economic environment. In Brazil, for instance, the central bank policy rate in 2018 was 6.5% but the average bank lending rate was 53%.

The central bank does not control this markup, but generally the bank lending rate goes up and down with the base rate, in the same way that other firms adjust their prices as their costs rise and fall.

Figure 10.3 greatly simplifies the financial system. It does not include all the actors, financial assets, or markets introduced in Section 10.2 (page 431). In this simplified model, we show household savers facing just two choices: to deposit money in a bank current account, which (for simplicity) we assume pays no interest, or buy **government bonds** in the money market. The interest rate on government bonds is called the **yield**.

Go back to the 'Find out more' box (page 434) at the end of Section 10.2 for an explanation of these bonds, and why the yield on government bonds is close to the policy interest rate. We also give an explanation of what are called **present value** calculations, which are essential for you to understand how assets like bonds are priced.

> **lending rate (bank)** The average interest rate charged by commercial banks to firms and households. This rate will typically be above the policy interest rate: the difference is known as the markup or spread on commercial lending. This is a nominal interest rate. *Also known as:* market interest rate. *See also:* interest rate, policy (interest) rate.

> **government bond** A financial instrument issued by governments that promises to pay flows of money at specific intervals.
> **yield** The implied rate of return that the buyer gets on their money when they buy a bond at its market price.
> **present value** The value today of a stream of future income or other benefits, when these are discounted using an interest rate or the person's own discount rate. *See also:* net present value.

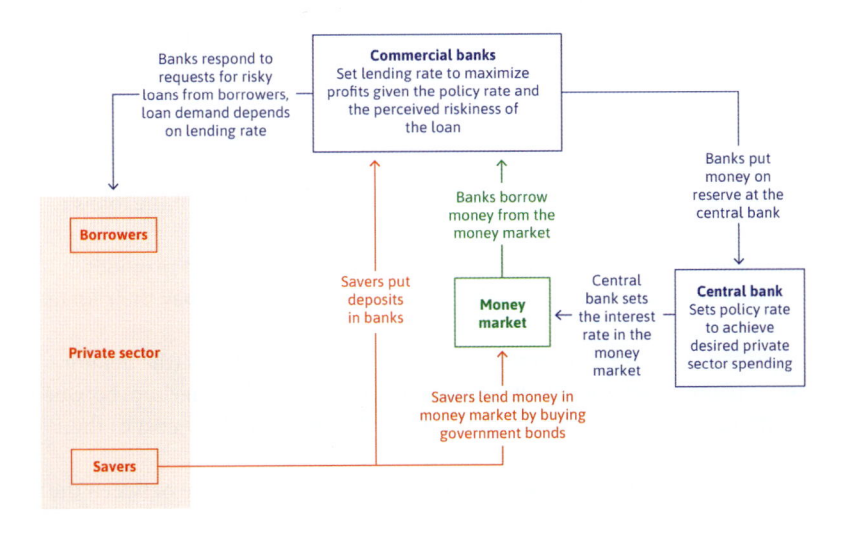

Adapted from Figure 5.12 in Chapter 5 of Wendy Carlin and David Soskice. 2015. *Macroeconomics: Institutions, Instability, and the Financial System*. Oxford: Oxford University Press.

Figure 10.3 Banks, the central bank, borrowers, and savers.

> **EXERCISE 10.2 INTEREST RATE MARKUPS**
> Use the websites of two central banks of your choice to collect data on the monthly policy interest rate and the mortgage interest rate between 2000 and the most recent year available.
>
> 1. Plot the data for both countries on a single line chart, with the date on the horizontal axis and the interest rate on the vertical axis.
> 2. How does the banking markup (difference between the mortgage interest rate and the monthly policy interest rate) compare between the two countries? Suggest possible reasons for what you observe. You may find it helpful to research characteristics of the economies of your chosen countries.
> 3. Do banking markups change over time? Suggest possible reasons for what you observe.

> **QUESTION 10.6 CHOOSE THE CORRECT ANSWER(S)**
> Which of the following statements are correct?
>
> ☐ The supply of base money depends on how many transactions commercial banks must make.
> ☐ The central bank chooses the interest rate to charge on loans to banks, but not the lending rate.
> ☐ When savers buy bonds, they are lending money in the money market.
> ☐ The central bank sets the policy rate in order to maximize its profits.

10.6 THE BUSINESS OF BANKING AND BANK BALANCE SHEETS

Having introduced the banks and the central bank as actors in the economy, we can understand the business of banking better if we can look at a commercial bank's costs and revenues:

- *The bank's operational costs:* These include the administration costs of making loans. For example, the salaries of loan officers who evaluate loan applications, the costs of renting and maintaining a network of branches and call centres used to supply banking services.
- *The bank's interest costs:* Banks must pay interest on their liabilities, including deposits and other borrowing.
- *The bank's revenue:* This is the interest on and repayment of the loans it has extended to its customers.
- *The bank's expected return:* This is the return on the loans it provides, taking into account the fact that not all customers will repay their loans.

As was the case for moneylenders, if the risk of making loans (the default rate) is higher, then there will be a larger gap (or spread or markup) between the interest rate banks charge on the loans they make and the cost of their borrowing.

The profitability of the business depends on the difference between the cost of borrowing and the return to lending, taking account of the default rate and the operational costs of screening the loans and running the bank.

10.6 THE BUSINESS OF BANKING AND BANK BALANCE SHEETS

A good way to understand a bank is to look at its entire balance sheet (Figure 10.4), which summarizes its core business of lending and borrowing.

- *Bank borrowing is on the liabilities side:* Deposits and borrowing are recorded as liabilities. Loans can be either secured (the borrower has provided **collateral**) or unsecured (the borrower has not provided collateral). See Section 9.10 (page 416) for more on the role of collateral in lending.
- *Bank lending is on the assets side.*

As we saw in the example of Abacus and Bonus Bank in Section 10.4:

$$\text{net worth} \equiv \text{assets} - \text{liabilities}$$

collateral An asset that a borrower pledges to a lender as a security for a loan. If the borrower is not able to make the loan payments as promised, the lender becomes the owner of the asset.

Assets (owned by the bank or owed to it)		% of balance sheet	Liabilities (what the bank owes households, firms and other banks)		% of balance sheet
Cash reserve balances at the central bank (A1)	Owned by the bank: immediately accessible funds	2	Deposits (L1)	Owned by households and firms	50
Financial assets, some of which (government bonds) may be used as collateral for borrowing (A2)	Owned by the bank	30	Secured borrowing (collateral provided) (L2)	Includes borrowing from other banks via the money market	30
Loans to other banks (A3)	Via the money market	11	Unsecured borrowing (no collateral provided) (L3)		16
Loans to households (A4)		55			
Fixed assets such as buildings and equipment (A5)	Owned by the bank	2			
Total assets		100	Total liabilities		96
Net worth = total assets − total liabilities = equity (L4)					4

Adapted from Figure 5.9 in Chapter 5 of Wendy Carlin and David Soskice. 2015. *Macroeconomics: Institutions, Instability, and the Financial System*. Oxford: Oxford University Press.

Figure 10.4 A simplified bank balance sheet.

insolvent An entity is this if the value of its assets is less than the value of its liabilities. *See also: solvent.*

Another way of saying this is that the net worth of a firm, like a bank, is equal to what is owed to the shareholders or owners. This explains why net worth is on the liabilities side of the balance sheet. If the value of the bank's assets is less than the value of what the bank owes others, then its net worth is negative, and the bank is **insolvent**.

Like any other firm in a capitalist economy, banks can fail by making bad investments, such as by giving loans that do not get paid back. But in some cases, banks are so large or so deeply involved throughout the financial system that governments decide to rescue them if they are at risk of going bankrupt. This is because, unlike the failure of a firm, a banking crisis can bring down the financial system as a whole and threaten the livelihoods of people throughout the economy. Bank failures and the threat of bank failures played a major role in the global financial crisis of 2008.

Let's examine the asset side of the bank balance sheet:

liquidity Ease of buying or selling a financial asset at a predictable price.

- (A1) *Cash and central bank reserves:* Item 1 on the balance sheet is the cash it holds, plus the bank's balance in its reserve account at the central bank. Cash and reserves at the central bank are the bank's readily accessible, or **liquid**, funds. This is base money and amounts to a tiny fraction of the bank's balance sheet—just 2% in this example of a typical contemporary bank.
- (A2) *Bank's own financial assets:* These assets can be used as collateral for the bank's borrowing in the money market. As we have discussed, they borrow to replenish their cash balances (item 1, Figure 10.4) when depositors withdraw (or transfer) more funds than the bank has available.
- (A3) *Loans to other banks:* A bank also has loans to other banks on its balance sheet.
- (A4) *Loans to households and firms:* The bank's lending activities are the largest item on the asset side. The loans made by the bank to households and firms make up 55% of the balance sheet in Figure 10.4. This is the bank's core business.
- (A5) *Bank assets* such as buildings and equipment will be recorded on the asset side of the balance sheet.

On the liability side of the bank balance sheet, there are three forms of bank borrowing, shown in Figure 10.4:

- (L1) The most important one is *bank deposits*, making up 50% of the bank's balance sheet in this example. The bank owes these to households and firms. As part of its profit-maximization decision, the bank makes a judgement about the likely demand by depositors to withdraw their deposits. Across the banking system withdrawals and deposits occur continuously, and when the cross-bank transactions are cleared, most cancel each other out. Any bank must ensure that it has cash and reserves at the central bank to meet the demand by depositors for funds, and the net transfers they have made that day. Holding cash and reserves for this purpose has an opportunity cost, because those funds could instead be lent out in the money market in order to earn interest, so banks aim to hold the minimum prudent balances of cash and reserves.

- (L2) and (L3) on the liabilities side of the balance sheet are what the bank has borrowed from households, firms, and other banks in the money market.
- Item (L4) on the balance sheet is the bank's net worth. This is the bank's **equity**. It comprises the shares issued by the bank and the accumulated profits, which have not been paid out as dividends to shareholders over the years. For a typical bank, its equity is only a few per cent of its balance sheet. The bank is a very debt-heavy company.

Equity is the difference between the value of an asset owned and the value of liabilities associated with that asset. (The term 'equity' is also used in an entirely different sense to mean the quality of being fair or impartial.)

We can see this from real-world examples illustrated in Figures 10.5 and 10.6.

Figure 10.5 shows the simplified balance sheet of Barclays Bank (just before the financial crisis) and Figure 10.6 shows the simplified balance sheet of a company from the non-financial sector, Honda.

Current assets refer to cash, inventories, and other short-term assets. Current liabilities refer to short-term debts and other pending payments.

A way of describing the reliance of a company on debt is to refer to its **leverage ratio**, also known as gearing.

Unfortunately the term *leverage ratio* is defined differently for financial and non-financial companies (both definitions are shown in Figures 10.5 and 10.6). Here, we calculate the leverage for Barclays and Honda, using the definition used for banks (total assets divided by net worth). Barclays' total assets are 36 times their net worth. This means that, given the size of its liabilities (its debt), a very small change in the value of its assets (1/36 ≈ 3%) would be enough to wipe out its net worth and make the bank insolvent. By contrast, using the same definition we see that Honda's leverage is less than three. Compared to Barclays, Honda's equity is far higher in relation to its assets. Another way to say this is that Honda finances its assets by a mixture of debt (62%) and equity (38%), whereas Barclays finances its assets with 97% debt and 3% equity.

> **equity** An individual's own investment in a project. This is recorded in an individual's or firm's balance sheet as net worth. *See also: net worth. An entirely different use of the term is synonymous with fairness.*
>
> **leverage ratio (for banks or households)** The value of assets divided by the equity stake in those assets.

> Leverage for non-banks is defined differently from leverage for banks. For companies, the leverage ratio is defined as the value of total liabilities divided by total assets. For an example of the use of the leverage definition for non-banks, see: Marina-Eliza Spaliara. 2009. 'Do Financial Factors Affect the Capital–labour Ratio? Evidence from UK Firm-Level Data' (http://tinyco.re/1270501). *Journal of Banking & Finance* 33 (10) (October): pp. 1932–47.

Barclays Bank. 2006. *Barclays Bank PLC Annual Report* (https://tinyco.re/6435688). Also presented as Figure 5.10 in Chapter 5 of Wendy Carlin and David Soskice. 2015. *Macroeconomics: Institutions, Instability, and the Financial System*. Oxford: Oxford University Press.

Assets		Liabilities	
Cash reserve balances at the central bank	7,345	Deposits	336,316
Wholesale reserve repo lending	174,090	Wholesale repo borrowing secured with collateral	136,956
Loans (for example mortgages)	313,226	Unsecured borrowing	111,137
Fixed assets (for example buildings, equipment)	2,492	Trading portfolio liabilities	71,874
Trading portfolio assets	177,867	Derivative financial instruments	140,697
Derivative financial instruments	138,353	Other liabilities	172,417
Other assets	183,414		
Total assets	996,787	Total liabilities	969,397
		Net worth	
		Equity	27,390

Memorandum item: Leverage ratio (total assets/net worth)   996,787/27,390 = 36.4

Figure 10.5 Barclays Bank's balance sheet in 2006 (£m).

Honda Motor Co. 2013. *Annual Report* (https://tinyco.re/0428289).

Assets		Liabilities	
Current assets	5,323,053	Current liabilities	4,096,685
Finance subsidiaries-receivables, net	2,788,135	Long-term debt	2,710,845
Investments	668,790	Other liabilities	1,630,085
Property on operating leases	1,843,132		
Property, plant and equipment	2,399,530		
Other assets	612,717		
Total assets	13,635,357	Total liabilities	8,437,615
		Net worth	
		Equity	5,197,742

Memorandum item: Leverage ratio as defined for banks (total assets/net worth)	13,635,357/ 5,197,742 = 2.62
Memorandum item: Leverage ratio as defined for non-banks (total liabilities/total assets)	8,437,615/ 13,635,357 = 61.9%

Figure 10.6 Honda Motor Company's balance sheet in 2013 (¥m).

QUESTION 10.7 CHOOSE THE CORRECT ANSWER(S)

The following example is a simplified balance sheet of a commercial bank. Based on this information, which of the following statements are correct?

Assets		Liabilities	
Cash and reserves	£2m	Deposits	£45m
Financial assets	£27m	Secured borrowing	£32m
Loans to other banks	£10m	Unsecured borrowing	£20m
Loans to households and firms	£55m		
Fixed assets	£6m		
Total assets	£100m	Total liabilities	£97m

Figure 10.7 A commercial bank's balance sheet.

- ☐ The bank's base money consists of cash and reserves and financial assets.
- ☐ Secured borrowing is borrowing with zero default risk.
- ☐ The bank's net worth is its cash and reserves of £2 million.
- ☐ The bank's leverage is 33.3.

QUESTION 10.8 CHOOSE THE CORRECT ANSWER(S)

Which of the following statements are correct?

- ☐ The net worth of a bank belongs to its employees.
- ☐ A bank is insolvent if the value of its liabilities exceeds the value of its assets.
- ☐ The more a bank holds in cash and reserves, the higher its profits.
- ☐ A loan is secured if it is default-free.

10.7 HOW KEY ECONOMIC ACTORS USE AND CREATE MONEY: A SUMMARY SO FAR

Here is a summary of how key economic actors use and create money in a modern economy.

Households

- *Use money for transactions:* Using deposit accounts and currency.
- *Borrow short term:* Often from a bank, using an overdraft or credit card debt.
- *Borrow long term:* Also often from a bank, to purchase durable goods such as a house or car, or from a specialized institution for a student loan.

Their income is wages, salaries, interest, rent, profits, government transfers, and gifts. From this, they:

- *Pay taxes.*
- *Pay interest:* On loans.
- *Purchase goods and services:* This is consumption.
- *Save to add to their net worth:* To do this, they:
    - use deposit or savings accounts
    - purchase assets (financial and non-financial)
    - repay debt.

Firms (other than banks)

- *Use money for transactions.*
- *Borrow short term:* Often from a bank, to allow payments ahead of sales.
- *Borrow long term:* Also often from a bank, to purchase new machinery and equipment and fund other investment projects. This is called bank debt financing of investment.
- *Sell financial assets:* To purchase new machinery and equipment and fund other investment projects. These are:
    - shares, called equity financing of investment
    - bonds, called market debt financing of investment.

Their revenue is the money taken in through sales of goods and services. From this, they:

- *Pay taxes.*
- *Pay interest:* On loans, coupons to corporate bondholders.
- *Purchase inputs:* These include wages and salaries.
- *Replace depreciated machinery, equipment, and buildings.*

They make profits. After paying tax, interest and depreciation, they:

- *Make purchases:* New machinery, equipment and buildings.
- *Fund other investment projects:* These include R&D. This is called financing investment from retained earnings.
- *Pay dividends:* To shareholders.
- *Purchase assets:* These can be financial or non-financial.
- *Repay debt.*

Banks

- *Create bank money:* By making loans.
- *Lend money:* To households and other firms.
- *Borrow reserves (base money) from the money market:* They pay the central bank's policy interest rate. Borrowed funds are used to cover lending in excess of the expected level.

They have reserves accounts at the central bank. They use these to:

- *Settle payments:* With other banks.
- *Convert into cash:* To pay out to depositors.

Central bank

- *Chooses the policy interest rate:* It does this to influence:
  - the demand for loans
  - the level of borrowing and hence spending by households and firms in the economy.
- *Meets the demand from banks for base money (that is, currency and reserves).* The money supply is endogenous.

Government

- *Uses money:* For transactions.
- *Sells financial assets:* To cover its spending in excess of tax revenues. These assets are government bonds, which may, for example, promise to pay a fixed amount per year, called a coupon.

It also has revenues, primarily from taxes. From these, a government:

- *Pays interest (for example, coupons) to bondholders.*
- *Purchases inputs:* These include wages and salaries.
- *Replaces depreciated machinery and equipment.*
- *Purchases new machinery, equipment, and buildings.*
- *Funds other investment projects:* These include R&D and infrastructure.
- *Repays debt.*

Having explained the major actors in financial markets, we turn now to how individuals value financial assets.

10.8 THE VALUE OF AN ASSET: EXPECTED RETURN AND RISK

People buy fresh fish or clothes for their consumption value—to eat or to wear. But when people buy an asset—a house, a car, a work of art, a bond, or a share (a piece of ownership in a company)—they often have a second motive. Their objective is not only to benefit in some way while owning the asset (for example, living in the house), but also to be able to sell it later for more than they paid for it. Assets are distinguished from other goods because they are long-lasting in a particular sense; unlike fish or used clothes, asset owners care about the resale value of their assets in the future.

In Unit 7 (page 307), we studied the factors that determine the price of ordinary goods and services. As in those cases, the interaction of supply and demand determines the price for assets, but the demand for an asset is not based only on how much the buyer wishes to have it, but also on the buyer's estimation of how valuable it will be to other potential buyers in future years.

The fact that the value of an asset today depends on how much it will be worth to others in the future introduces an important new consideration: the uncertainty caused by the fact that an asset's value may increase or decrease. As a result, unlike the clothes or the fish—where what you buy is what you get—buying an asset in most cases means taking a risk about its future value.

To study how risk affects the price of an asset, we will contrast how a person might value a government bond, which is as close to a riskless asset as you can get, and shares in a company. A government bond is considered to be a riskless asset because it is a promise from the government to pay some *fixed amount* to the holder of the bond on a given schedule over a fixed period of time and because it is assumed that the government will not default on the payments.[*]

[*] This assumption was brought into question in the Eurozone crisis that followed the global financial crisis. To find out about the Eurozone crisis, read this article (https://tinyco.re/7835092).

Shares are literally a share in the ownership of a company. The holder owns some fraction of the company's buildings, equipment, intellectual property, and other assets. As a part owner of the firm, the shareholder also owns a share of the profits of the firm. The value of a share depends on how profitable the firm is and is expected to be in the future. Shares thus differ from bonds in two important respects: there is no promised payment to the holder (it depends on how profitable the firm is), and there is no fixed maturity period for the ownership of a share (it may be held for a lifetime).

Safe bonds and risky shares

Now think about Ayesha, who is deciding whether to buy a government bond or a share in one of a large number of companies with publicly listed shares. What does she care about? Two things. The first is her best guess about what her wealth will be at some future date depending on what she buys, called the expected value of her wealth. The second thing she cares about is how much risk she is taking when she buys a particular bond or share. The expected value is her best guess but what actually happens could be very different, either much better or much worse.

In the case of the bond, there is no risk attached to holding the bond—the promise to pay a certain amount over a certain period can be counted on. But the value of the share that she purchases may go up or down. We will use a model to explain how Ayesha could decide what kind of asset to purchase, taking account of both expected value and risk.

10.8 THE VALUE OF AN ASSET: EXPECTED RETURN AND RISK

To simplify things, suppose that in the future there are just two possible states of the world affecting the value of the share she has purchased. There is a 'good' state in which the price is higher than her expected value, and a 'bad' state in which the price is lower than her expected value. Ayesha does not know which will occur, and that is why purchasing shares is risky.

Some shares are much riskier than others. For some shares the difference in the good and the bad state is very small. Something close to the expected value (a bit higher or a bit lower) will definitely occur. But for other shares, the difference is substantial: the share may double in value or be reduced to a worthless piece of paper. The difference in the share's value between the good and the bad state is the degree of risk that Ayesha will face, depending on which share she purchases, or if she purchases the bond.

To summarize so far: Ayesha prefers shares with a greater expected value and a lower degree of risk.

The trade-off between a higher expected return and higher risk

Ayesha would like, of course, to buy an asset that has a high expected value and a low degree of risk. But there is a hitch—low-risk assets typically have low expected values, and assets with high expected value are often associated with high levels of risk. In other words, Ayesha faces a trade-off, similar to the trade-offs faced by the student and the farmer in Unit 4, who wanted both more free time and also more of the other thing they valued—success in the exam and grain produced on the farm.

Facing this trade-off between expected value and risk, what will she buy? We have the two pieces of information necessary to describe the choice that will make her the best off—give her the maximum utility—of all the choices open to her, that is, we know her:

- feasible set and its boundary, the **feasible frontier**
- **indifference curves**, representing how Ayesha dislikes risk and values expected return.

Figure 10.8a explains how the combinations of risk and return associated with different assets are represented by a feasible set and feasible frontier.

- The level of risk associated with different assets is measured along the horizontal axis, and called Δ, the Greek letter, delta, denoting a difference, in this case between the good and the bad states.
- The expected value of the asset next year is measured on the vertical axis, denoted by w (for 'wealth').

Each point in the figure represents some combination of these two aspects of an asset—risk and expected return.

From Figure 10.8a, we can see that not all the conceivable combinations of risk and return are possible by buying an asset. If Ayesha has $1,000 to purchase an asset, the ones that are available to her—the feasible set of combinations of risk and expected return—make up the shaded area in Figure 10.8a. The red curve is the familiar feasible frontier, which in this case is called the risk–return schedule (a 'schedule' is just a curve or function, and return refers to the expected value).

> **feasible frontier** The curve made of points that defines the maximum feasible quantity of one good for a given quantity of the other. See also: feasible set.

> **indifference curve** A curve of the points which indicate the combinations of goods that provide a given level of utility to the individual.

The risk-free bond is shown by point A where the feasible frontier intersects the vertical axis—the level of risk, Δ, is equal to zero. If Ayesha wishes to entirely avoid risk, she can purchase bonds. But the risk–return frontier shows that she can achieve a higher expected return (measured on the vertical axis, by w) if she purchases a risky asset such as the one shown by point C.

As highlighted in the figure, the feasible frontier is very steep near the vertical axis when risk is very low. By moving to a riskier asset, Ayesha can achieve large gains in expected return. As the frontier gets flatter, the riskier the assets become.

To explore all of the slides in this figure, see the online version at https://tinyco.re/1966129.

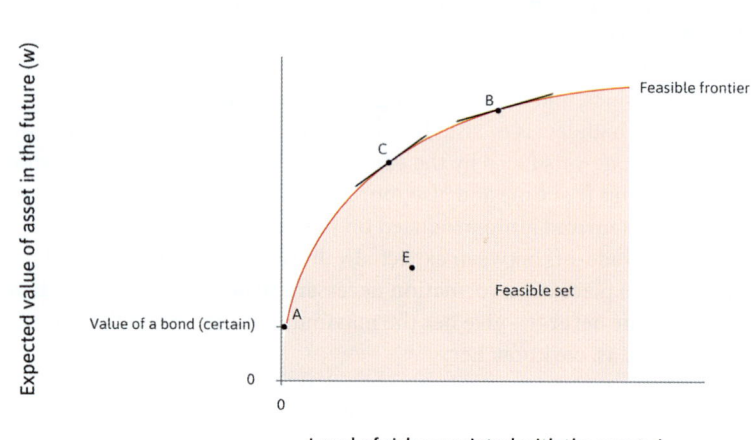

Figure 10.8a The trade-off between risk and return: The feasible set.

1. The feasible set
Points A, B, C, and E represent combinations of risk and expected return associated with different assets that Ayesha can buy. The shaded area represents the feasible set of combinations of risk and expected return.

2. The risk–return schedule
The only points of interest to Ayesha are those on the feasible frontier, called the risk–return schedule. Asset A is the risk-free bond. An asset like E inside the feasible frontier, is not worth considering, because there will always be some other asset (like C) which has both a higher expected return and a lower risk.

3. Upward-sloping risk–return schedule
Ayesha can entirely opt out of risk-taking by purchasing the bond (point A). But she also has a large choice of shares with more or less risk. Notice that the risk–return schedule is upward sloping. Higher returns (greater expected values) are possible only by taking greater risk, for example, by purchasing the share indicated by point C, or—even more risky—point B.

4. Marginal rate of transformation
The slope of the risk–return schedule is called the marginal rate of transformation of risk into return. For low levels of risk (near the vertical axis), the slope of the feasible frontier is steep, meaning that taking a little more risk yields large gains in expected return. However, the curve gets flatter (and may even slope downwards) when the level of risk is greater.

The slope of the risk–return schedule is called the **marginal rate of transformation** of risk into return.

Ayesha's preferences about risk and return

To determine what choice would give Ayesha the greatest utility, we need a second piece of information—how much she values each of the outcomes (combinations of w and Δ). To do this, we introduce Ayesha's preferences, which we represent by her indifference curves. Figure 10.8b explains the shape of Ayesha's indifference curves. Two of these are shown in Figure 10.8b as the blue curves. To see what these mean, notice that point A (no risk, low expected value) is on the same indifference curve as point B (high risk, high expected return), meaning that, as far as Ayesha is concerned, these two outcomes are equally valued by her.

> **marginal rate of transformation (MRT)** A measure of the trade-offs a person faces in what is feasible. Given the constraints (feasible frontier) a person faces, the MRT is the quantity of some good that must be sacrificed to acquire one additional unit of another good. At any point, it is the slope of the feasible frontier. *See also: feasible frontier, marginal rate of substitution.*

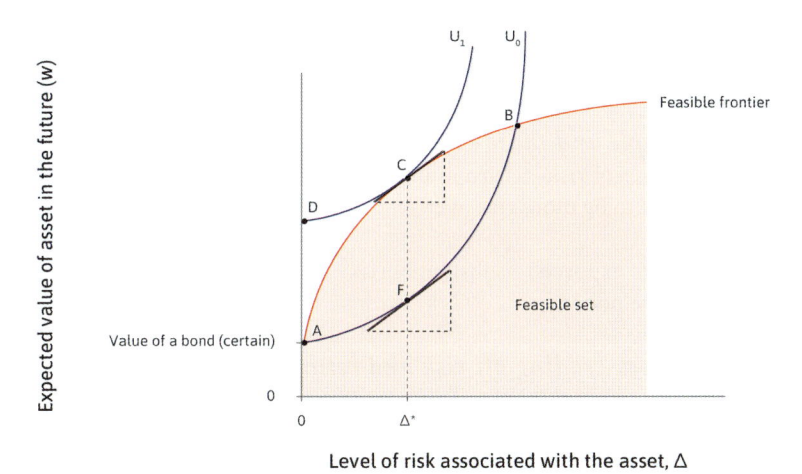

To explore all of the slides in this figure, see the online version at https://tinyco.re/3180786.

Figure 10.8b The trade-off between risk and return: Ayesha's preferences.

1. Ayesha's preferences
The blue curves show combinations of w and Δ) that give Ayesha the same level of utility. They are upward sloping, meaning that Ayesha needs to be compensated for risk-taking through a higher expected return.

2. Marginal rate of substitution
The slope of Ayesha's indifference curves is called the marginal rate of substitution between risk and expected value. A steep indifference curve means that taking on a given increase in risk would have to be compensated by a large increase in return. When comparing Ayesha's indifference curves, notice that at a given level of risk such as Δ^*, she is less risk averse when her expected wealth is higher: the slope is flatter at C than at F.

Notice about these risk–return indifference curves:

- *They slope upwards:* This reflects Ayesha's trade-off. She values a high-risk, high-return share as much as some other low-risk, low-return share.
- *The curves are flatter when the level of risk is low:* This means that, when Ayesha is exposed to very little risk, taking a little more risk is not very costly to her; only a small increase in the expected value is required to offset the increased risk. But for higher levels of risk (further to the right), the curves are steeper, indicating that Ayesha will be willing to take on yet more risk only if compensated by a substantial gain in expected value.

The slope of Ayesha's indifference curves is called the **marginal rate of substitution** between risk and expected value. The steepness of the indifference curve measures how much of a 'bad' risk is, compared to how much of a 'good' the expected value is. This is termed **risk aversion**, meaning how much the individual is averse to (does not like) risk.

Now notice a third thing about the indifference curves:

- *For any given level of risk Δ, the higher-up curves are flatter than those lower down:* This means that people who can expect greater wealth in the future are also less risk averse.

Wealthier people and those exposed to less risk are less risk averse

The three features of risk–return indifference curves discussed above mean that people tend to be more risk averse:

- when they are exposed to substantial risk
- when they are poor.

Ayesha's choice: Trading off risk and return

In Figure 10.8c, we combine the indifference curves with the risk–return schedule to see how Ayesha makes her asset choice.

Putting together the indifference curves and the risk–return schedule, we see that the best Ayesha can do is to select point C, that is, a share with an expected value of w^* and a risk level of Δ^*.

We can compare Ayesha's choice of this share with what she would have gained had she purchased the bond. Point D and point C (the point she chose) are on the same indifference curve, so they are equally good from Ayesha's standpoint. Point D indicates the expected value with no risk that would have been just as good as point C (higher return, some risk).

Point D is called the certainty equivalent of point C, meaning it is the outcome with no risk that would be just as good as the risky point she chose. We can compare point D with point A because both are outcomes with no risk. Notice that point D, and hence also point C (on the same indifference curve), are preferred to point A, the purchase of a bond. Hence, taking on some risk can give Ayesha higher utility than buying a bond.

---

marginal rate of substitution (MRS) The trade-off that a person is willing to make between two goods. At any point, this is the slope of the indifference curve. See also: marginal rate of transformation.

risk aversion A preference for certain over uncertain outcomes.

10.8 THE VALUE OF AN ASSET: EXPECTED RETURN AND RISK

> **EXERCISE 10.3 UNDERSTANDING AYESHA'S RISK–RETURN TRADE-OFFS**
> 1. Using Figure 10.8b, show how high the value of the bond would have to be for Ayesha to choose to purchase it rather than the share C, whose expected value and risk level remains unchanged. Hint: look at the indifference curve through point C and recall that its vertical axis intercept is the certainty equivalent of C.
> 2. Redraw Figure 10.8b to illustrate the following situations:
>   (a) Draw a new indifference curve through point C to show that, if Ayesha were less risk averse, she would choose a riskier share than C. Hint: draw a less risk averse indifference curve through point C.
>   (b) Draw a set of indifference curves according to which Ayesha would choose to purchase share B.
>   (c) If all shares became riskier without affecting their expected value this would displace points C, F and B horizontally to the right. Show this in your figure by introducing new points C′, F′ and B′ to the right of the initial points.
>   (d) Show that though she initially preferred share C to share B (you showed this above) she now would choose share B over share C.

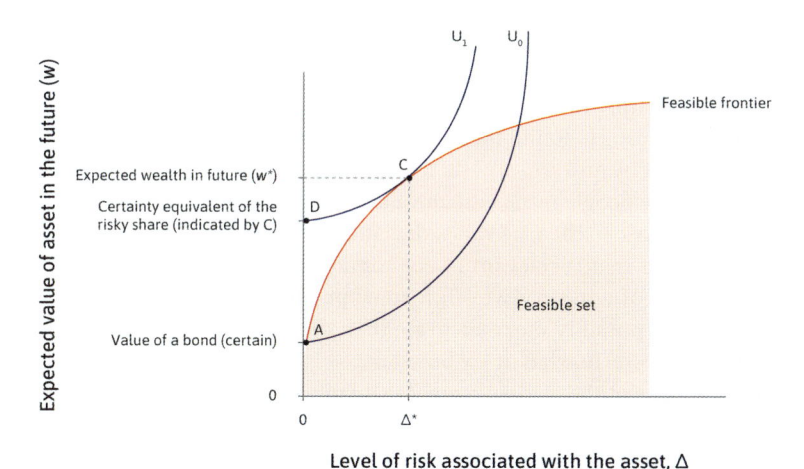

Figure 10.8c Ayesha's choice: MRS = MRT.

1. MRS = MRT
We see that the best Ayesha can do is to select point C, that is, a share with an expected value of w^* and a risk level of Δ^*.

2. Ayesha does better by buying a share
Point D is called the 'certainty equivalent' of point C, meaning it is the outcome with zero risk that would be just as good as the risky asset she chooses. But D is not feasible. This explains Ayesha's choice of a risky share at C rather than the safe bond at A.

QUESTION 10.9 CHOOSE THE CORRECT ANSWER(S)
Which of the following statements about assets and risk are true?

☐ All assets have a high level of risk involved.
☐ Risk aversion occurs because the value of an asset is determined in the future and people are impatient.
☐ The value of shares in a company varies according to the profits that people expect the firm to make in the future.
☐ Exposure to greater risk makes people more risk averse.

HOW ECONOMISTS LEARN FROM DATA

The wisdom of crowds: The weight of (live)stock and the value of shares

What is the right price for, say, a share in Facebook? Would it be better for the price to be set by economic experts, rather than determined in the market by the actions of millions of people, few of whom have expert knowledge about the economy or the company's prospects?

Economists are far from understanding the details of how this mechanism actually works. But an important insight comes from an unusual source—a guessing game played in 1907 at an agricultural fair in Plymouth, England. Attendees at the fair were presented with a live ox. For sixpence (2.5p), they could guess the ox's 'dressed' weight, meaning how much saleable beef could be obtained. The entrant whose answer, written on a ticket, came closest to the correct weight would win the prize.

The polymath, Francis Galton, later obtained the tickets associated with that contest. He found that a player, chosen at random, missed the correct weight by an *average* of 40 lbs. But what he called the '*vox populi*' or 'voice of the people'—the *median* value of all the guesses—was remarkably close to the true value, deviating by only 9 lbs (less than 1%).

The insight that is relevant to economics is that the average of a large number of not-very-well-informed people is often extremely accurate. It is possibly more accurate than the estimate of an experienced veterinarian or ox breeder.

Galton's use of the median to aggregate the guesses meant that *vox populi* was the voice of the (assumed) most informed player, but it was the guesses of all the others that picked out this most informed player. *Vox populi* was obtained by taking all of the information available, including the hunches and fancies that drove outliers high or low.

Galton's result is an example of the 'wisdom of the crowd'. This concept is particularly interesting for economists because it contains, in a stylized format, many of the ingredients that go into a good price mechanism.

As Galton himself noted, the guessing game had a number of features contributing to the success of *vox populi*. The entry fee was small, but not zero, allowing many to participate but also deterring practical jokers. Guesses were written and entered privately, and judgements were uninfluenced 'by oratory and passion'. The promise of a reward focused the participants' attention.

Although many participants were well informed, many were less so and, as Galton noted, were guided by others at the fair and their imaginations. Galton's choice of the median value would reduce (but not eliminate) the influence of these less-informed guessers, preventing individual wild guesses (say, those 10 times the true value) from pulling the *vox populi* away from the views of the group as a whole.

The stock market represents another expression of *vox populi*, which sees people guessing at the value of a company, often (but not always) quite accurately tracking changes in the quality of management, technology, or market opportunities.

The wisdom of crowds also explains the success of prediction markets. The Iowa Electronic Markets (https://tinyco.re/0124936), run by the University of Iowa, allows individuals to buy and sell contracts that pay off, depending on who wins an upcoming election. The prices of these assets pool the information, hunches, and guesses of large numbers of participants. Such prediction markets—often called political stock markets—can provide uncannily accurate forecasts of election results months in advance, sometimes better than polls and even poll-aggregation sites. Other prediction markets allow thousands of people to bet on events, such as who will win the Oscar for best female lead. It was even proposed to create a prediction market for the next occurrence of a major terrorist attack in the US.

10.9 CHANGING SUPPLY AND DEMAND FOR A FINANCIAL ASSET

Prices in financial markets are constantly changing. The graph in Figure 10.9 shows how News Corp's (NWS) share price on the Nasdaq **stock exchange** fluctuated over one day in May 2014 and, in the lower panel, the number of shares traded at each point. Soon after the market opened at 9.30 a.m., the price was $16.66 per share. As investors bought and sold shares through the day, the price reached a low point of $16.45 at both 10 a.m. and 2 p.m. By the time the market closed, with the share price at $16.54, nearly 556,000 shares had been traded.

The flexibility demonstrated by News Corp share prices is common in markets for other financial assets, such as government bonds, currencies under floating exchange rates, **commodities**, such as gold, crude oil and corn, and tangible assets such as houses and works of art.

But share prices are not only volatile hour-by-hour and day-by-day. Figure 10.10 shows the value of the Nasdaq Composite Index between 1995 and 1999. This index is an average of prices for a set of shares, with companies weighted in proportion to their market capitalization. The Nasdaq Composite Index at this time included many fast-growing and hard-to-value companies in technology sectors.

The index began the period at less than 750, and rose to 2,300 over four years, reflecting strong demand for these shares, arising from the view that there were new profitable opportunities for firms in the technology sector.

> **stock exchange** A financial marketplace where shares (also known as stocks) and other financial assets are traded. It has a list of companies whose shares are traded there. *See also: share.*
>
> **commodities** Physical goods traded in a manner similar to shares. They include metals such as gold and silver, and agricultural products such as coffee and sugar, oil and gas. Sometimes more generally used to mean anything produced for sale. *See also: share.*

Data from *Bloomberg L.P.*
(https://tinyco.re/9335006), accessed 28 May 2014.

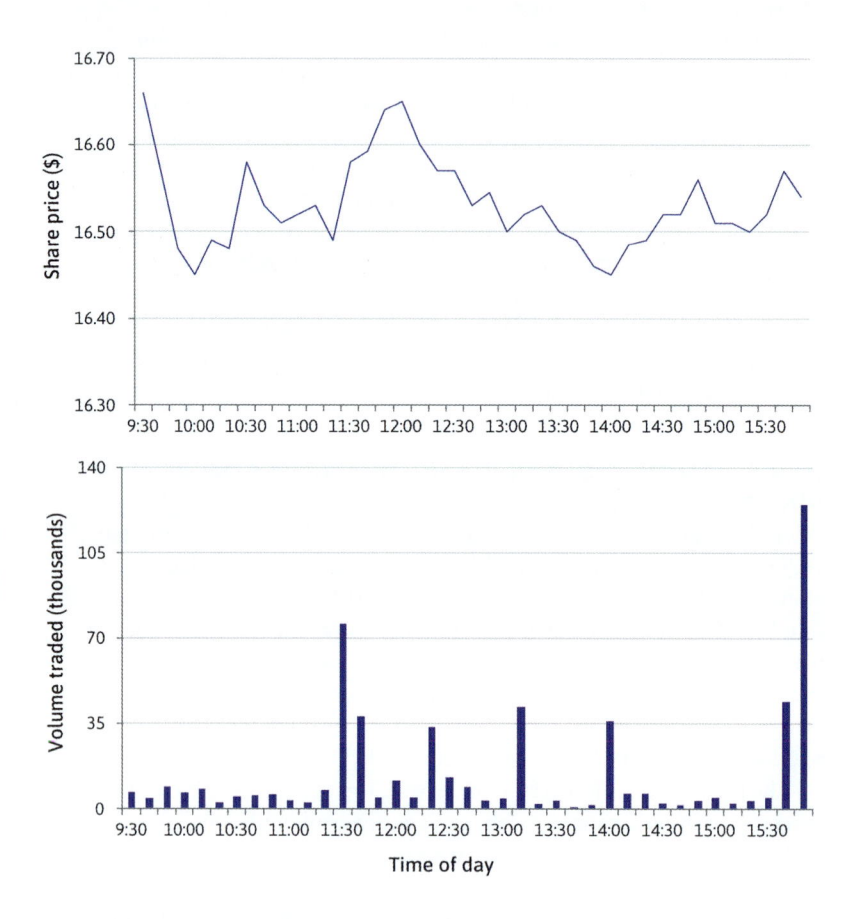

Figure 10.9 News Corp's share price and volume traded (7 May 2014).

Data from *Yahoo Finance*
(https://tinyco.re/6764389), accessed 14 January 2014.

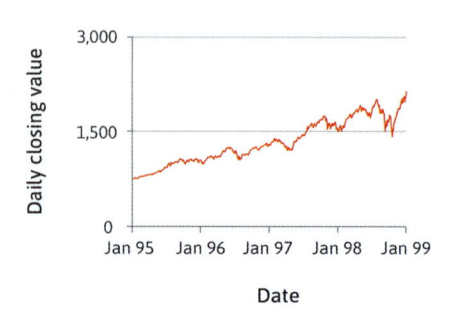

Figure 10.10 Information technology and rising prices for tech shares: Nasdaq Composite Index (1995–1999).

10.10 ASSET MARKET BUBBLES

The logic of market stability and bubbles

As well as reflecting long-term technology trends, share prices can also display large swings, often referred to as **bubbles**.

To see how this happens, we should distinguish between the so-called **fundamental value of a share** (based on the expectations of the firm's profitability in the future), and the *changes in value* associated with beliefs about how much *others* would be willing to pay for the share in the future and therefore its future price trends.

To model markets for assets like shares, paintings, or houses, we need to allow for the effects of beliefs about future prices. Figure 10.11 contrasts two alternative scenarios following an exogenous shock of good news about future profits of a fictitious firm, Flying Car Company (FCC), that raises the share price from $50 to $60.

In the left-hand panel, beliefs dampen price rises; some market participants respond to the initial price rise with scepticism about whether the fundamental value of FCC is really $60, so they sell shares, taking a profit from the higher price. This behaviour reduces the price and it stabilizes—the news has been incorporated into a price between $50 and $60, reflecting the aggregate of beliefs in the market about the new fundamental value of FCC.

By contrast, in the right-hand panel beliefs amplify price rises. When demand rises, others believe that the initial rise in price signals a further rise in future. These beliefs produce an increase in the demand for FCC shares. Other traders see that those who bought more shares in FCC benefited as its price rose, so they follow suit. A self-reinforcing cycle of higher prices and rising demand takes hold.

> **asset price bubble** A sustained and significant rise in the price of an asset, fuelled by expectations of future price increases.
> **fundamental value of a share** The share price based on anticipated future earnings and the level of risk.

Beliefs dampen price rises

Beliefs amplify price rises: a bubble

Figure 10.11 Positive vs negative feedback.

> **QUESTION 10.10 CHOOSE THE CORRECT ANSWER(S)**
> Which of the following statements about asset prices are correct?
>
> ☐ A bubble occurs when beliefs about future prices amplify a price rise.
> ☐ When positive feedback occurs, the market is quickly restored to equilibrium.
> ☐ Negative feedback occurs when prices give traders the wrong information about the fundamental value.
> ☐ When beliefs dampen price rises, the market equilibrium is stable.

Example: The tech bubble

Figure 10.12 extends the series in Figure 10.10 through to 2004. The rise in the index—from less than 750 to more than 5,000 in less than five years at its peak—implied a remarkable annualized rate of return of around 45%. It then lost two-thirds of its value in less than a year, and eventually bottomed out at around 1,100, almost 80% below its peak. The episode has come to be called the *tech bubble*.

Bubbles, information, and beliefs

The term 'bubble' refers to a sustained and significant departure of the price of any asset (financial or otherwise) from its fundamental value.

Sometimes, new information about the fundamental value of an asset is quickly and reliably expressed in markets. Changes in beliefs about a firm's future earnings growth result in virtually instantaneous adjustments in its share price. Both good and bad news, (such as information about patents or lawsuits, the illness or departure of important personnel, earnings surprises, or mergers and acquisitions) can all result in active trading—and swift price movements.

Data from *Yahoo Finance* (https://tinyco.re/6764389), accessed 14 January 2014.

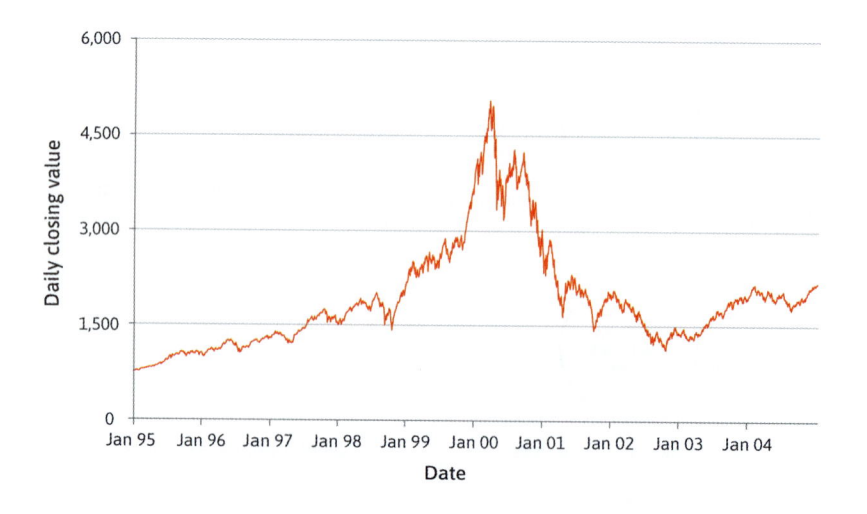

Figure 10.12 The tech bubble: Nasdaq Composite Index (1995–2004).

Three distinctive and related features of markets may give rise to bubbles:

- *Resale value:* The demand for the asset arises both from the benefit to its owner and because it offers the opportunity for speculation on a change in its price. A landlord may buy a house, both for the rental income and also to create a capital gain by holding the asset for a period of time and then selling it. People's beliefs about what will happen to asset prices differ and change as they receive new information or believe others are responding to new information.
- *Ease of trading:* In financial markets, the ease of trading means that you can switch between being a buyer and being a seller if you change your mind about whether you think the price will rise or fall. Switching between buying and selling is not possible in markets for ordinary goods and services, where sellers are firms with specialized capital goods and skilled workers, and buyers are other types of firms or households.
- *Ease of borrowing to finance purchases:* If market participants can borrow to increase their demand for an asset that they believe will increase in price, this allows an upward movement of prices to continue, creating the possibility of a bubble and subsequent crash.

WHEN ECONOMISTS DISAGREE

Do bubbles exist?

The price movements in Figure 10.12 give the impression that asset prices can swing wildly, bearing little relation to the stream of income that might reasonably be expected from holding them.

But do bubbles really exist, or are they an illusion based only on hindsight? In other words, is it possible to know that a market is experiencing a bubble before it crashes? Perhaps surprisingly, some prominent economists working with financial market data disagree on this question. They include Eugene Fama and Robert Shiller, two of the three recipients of the 2013 Nobel Prize.

Fama denies that the term 'bubble' has any useful meaning at all:

> These words have become popular. I don't think they have any meaning … It's easy to say prices went down, it must have been a bubble, after the fact. I think most bubbles are twenty-twenty hindsight. Now after the fact you always find people who said before the fact that prices are too high. People are always saying that prices are too high. When they turn out to be right, we anoint them. When they turn out to be wrong, we ignore them. They are typically right and wrong about half the time.

John Cassidy. 'Interview with Eugene Fama' (https://tinyco.re/0438887). *The New Yorker.* 13 January 2010.

Tim Harford. 2012. 'Still think you can beat the market?' (https://tinyco.re/7063932) *The Undercover Economist*. Updated 24 November 2012.

Burton G. Malkiel. 2003. 'The efficient market hypothesis and its critics' (https://tinyco.re/4628706). *Journal of Economic Perspectives* 17 (1) (March): pp. 59–82.

Robert Lucas. 2009. 'In defence of the dismal science' (https://tinyco.re/6052194). *The Economist*. Updated 6 August 2009.

Markus Brunnermeier. 2009. 'Lucas roundtable: Mind the frictions' (https://tinyco.re/0136751). *The Economist*. Updated 6 August 2009.

Robert J. Shiller. 2003. 'From efficient markets theory to behavioral finance' (https://tinyco.re/3989503). *Journal of Economic Perspectives* 17 (1) (March): pp. 83–104.

This is an expression of what economists call the *efficient market hypothesis*, which claims that all generally available information about fundamental values is incorporated into prices virtually instantaneously.

Robert Lucas—another Nobel laureate, firmly in Fama's camp—explained the logic of this argument in 2009, in the middle of the financial crisis:

> One thing we are not going to have, now or ever, is a set of models that forecasts sudden falls in the value of financial assets, like the declines that followed the failure of Lehman Brothers in September. This is nothing new. It has been known for more than 40 years and is one of the main implications of Eugene Fama's efficient-market hypothesis … If an economist had a formula that could reliably forecast crises a week in advance, say, then that formula would become part of generally available information and prices would fall a week earlier.

Responding to Lucas, Markus Brunnermeier explains that this argument is not watertight. Brunnermeier argues Lucas was right to emphasize that financial market frictions are a counter-argument to the efficient market hypothesis:

> Of course, as Bob Lucas points out, when it is commonly known among all investors that a bubble will burst next week, then they will prick it already today. However, in practice each individual investor does not know when other investors will start trading against the bubble. This uncertainty makes each individual investor nervous about whether he can be out of (or short) the market sufficiently long until the bubble finally bursts. Consequently, each investor is reluctant to lean against the wind. Indeed, investors may in fact prefer to ride a bubble for a long time such that price corrections only occur after a long delay, and often abruptly. Empirical research on [share] price predictability supports this view. Furthermore, since funding frictions limit arbitrage activity, the fact that you can't make money does not imply that the 'price is right'.

This way of thinking suggests a radically different approach for the future financial architecture. Central banks and financial regulators have to be vigilant and look out for bubbles, and should help investors to synchronize their effort to lean against asset price bubbles. As the current episode has shown, it is not sufficient to clean up after the bubble bursts, but essential to lean against the formation of the bubble in the first place.

Shiller has argued that relatively simple and publicly observable statistics, such as the ratio of share prices to earnings per share, can be used to identify bubbles as they form. Leaning against the wind by buying assets that are cheap based on this criterion, and selling those that are dear, can result in losses in the short run, but long-term gains that, in Shiller's view, exceed the returns to be made by simply investing in a diversified basket of securities with similar risk attributes.

In collaboration with Barclays Bank, Shiller has launched a product called an exchange-traded note (ETN) that can be used to invest in accordance with his theory. This asset is linked to the value of the cyclically adjusted price-to-earnings (CAPE) ratio, which Shiller believes is predictive of future prices over long periods. So this is one economist who has put his money where his mouth is! You can follow the fluctuation of Shiller's index on Barclays Bank's website (https://tinyco.re/7309155).

So there are two quite different interpretations of the 'tech bubble' episode in Figure 10.12:

- *Fama's view:* Asset prices throughout the episode were based on the best information available at the time, and fluctuated because information about the prospects of the companies was changing sharply. In John Cassidy's 2010 interview with Fama in *The New Yorker*, Fama describes many of the arguments for the existence of bubbles as 'entirely sloppy'.
- *Shiller's view:* Prices in the late 1990s had been driven up simply by expectations that the price would still rise further. He called this '**irrational exuberance**' among investors. The first chapter of his book, *Irrational Exuberance*, explains the idea.

irrational exuberance A process by which assets become overvalued. The expression was first used by Alan Greenspan, then chairman of the US Federal Reserve Board, in 1996. It was popularized as an economic concept by the economist Robert Shiller.

John Cassidy. 2010. 'Interview with Eugene Fama' (https://tinyco.re/0438887). *The New Yorker*. Updated 13 January 2010.

Robert J. Shiller. 2015. *Irrational Exuberance*, Chapter 1 (https://tinyco.re/4263463). Princeton, NJ: Princeton University Press.

EXERCISE 10.4 MARKETS FOR GEMS
A *New York Times* article (https://tinyco.re/6343875) describes how the worldwide markets for opals, sapphires, and emeralds are affected by discoveries of new sources of gems.

1. Explain, using supply and demand analysis, why Australian dealers were unhappy about the discovery of opals in Ethiopia.
2. What determines the willingness to pay for gems? Why do Madagascan sapphires command lower prices than Asian ones?
3. Explain why the reputation of gems from particular sources might matter to a consumer. Shouldn't you judge how much you are willing to pay for a stone according to how much you like it yourself?
4. Do you think that the high reputation of gems from particular origins necessarily reflects true differences in quality?
5. Could we see bubbles in the markets for gems?

Charles P. Kindleberger. 2005. *Manias, Panics, and Crashes: A History of Financial Crises* (https://tinyco.re/9848004). Hoboken, NJ: Wiley, John & Sons.

> **EXERCISE 10.5 THE BIG TEN ASSET PRICE BUBBLES OF THE LAST 400 YEARS**
>
> According to Charles Kindleberger, an economic historian, asset price bubbles have occurred across a wide variety of countries and time periods. The bubbles of the last 100 years have predominantly been focused on real estate, shares, and foreign investment.
>
> - 1636: The Dutch tulip bubble
> - 1720: The South Sea Company
> - 1720: The Mississippi Scheme
> - 1927–29: The 1920s share price bubble
> - 1970s: The surge in loans to Mexico and other developing economies
> - 1985–89: The Japanese bubble in real estate and shares
> - 1985–89: The bubble in real estate and shares in Finland, Norway, and Sweden
> - 1990s: The bubble in real estate and shares in Thailand, Malaysia, Indonesia, and several other Asian countries between 1992 and 1997, and the surge in foreign investment in Mexico 1990–99
> - 1995–2000: The bubble in over-the-counter shares in the US
> - 2002–07: The bubble in real estate in the US, Britain, Spain, Ireland, and Iceland
>
> Pick one of these asset price bubbles, find out more about it, and then:
>
> 1. Tell the story of this bubble, referring to Figure 10.11 (page 463) to illustrate the events.
> 2. Explain the relevance to your story, if any, of the arguments about the existence of bubbles (refer to the 'When economists disagree' box (page 465) in this section).

> **QUESTION 10.11 CHOOSE THE CORRECT ANSWER(S)**
> Which of the following statements about bubbles are correct?
>
> ☐ A bubble occurs when the fundamental value of a share rises too quickly.
> ☐ A bubble is less likely to occur in a market in which people can easily switch from buying to selling.
> ☐ Permitting the use of housing equity as collateral for new housing loans makes house price bubbles more likely.
> ☐ Bubbles can only occur in financial markets.

10.11 HOUSING AS AN ASSET, COLLATERAL, AND HOUSE PRICE BUBBLES

When households borrow to buy a house, this is a secured or **collateralized** loan. As part of the mortgage agreement, the bank can take possession of the house if the borrower does not keep up repayments. Collateral plays an important role in sustaining a house price boom. When the house price goes up—driven, for example, by beliefs that a further price rise will occur—this increases the value of the household's collateral (see the left-hand diagram in Figure 10.13). Using this higher collateral, households can increase their borrowing and move up the housing ladder to a better property. This, in turn, pushes up house prices further and sustains the bubble, because the banks extend more credit based on the higher collateral. Increased borrowing, made possible by the rise in the value of the collateral, is spent on goods and services as well as on housing.

When house prices are expected to rise, it is attractive to households to increase their borrowing. Suppose a house costs $200,000 and the household makes a down payment of 10% ($20,000). This means it borrows $180,000. Its initial leverage ratio, in this case the value of its assets divided by its equity stake in the house, is 200/20 = 10. Suppose the house price rises by 10% to $220,000. The return to the equity the household has invested in the house is 100% (since the value of the equity stake has risen from $20,000 to $40,000, it has doubled). Households who are convinced that house prices will rise further will want to increase their leverage—that is how they get a high return. The increase in collateral, due to the rise in the price of their house, means they can satisfy their desire to borrow more.

On the right-hand side, we see what happens when house prices decline. The value of collateral falls and the household's spending declines, pushing house prices down.

The assets and liabilities of a household can be represented in its balance sheet. The house is on the asset side of the household's balance sheet. The mortgage owed to the bank is on the liabilities side. When the market value of the house falls below what is owed on the mortgage, the household has negative net worth. This condition is sometimes referred to as the household being 'underwater'. Using the example above, if the leverage ratio is 10, a fall in the house price by 10% wipes out the household's equity. A fall of more than 10% would place the household 'underwater'.

> **collateral** An asset that a borrower pledges to a lender as a security for a loan. If the borrower is not able to make the loan payments as promised, the lender becomes the owner of the asset.

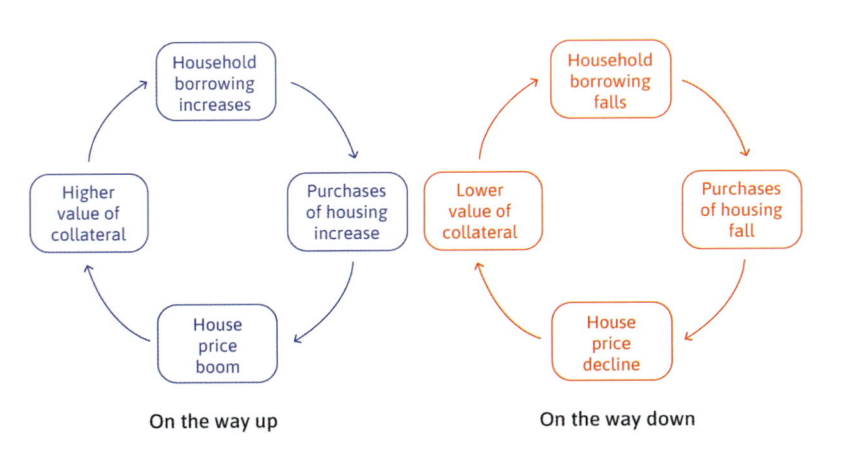

Figure 10.13 The housing market on the way up and on the way down.

Adapted from a figure in Hyun Song Shin. 2009. 'Discussion of "The Leverage Cycle" by John Geanakoplos' (https://tinyco.re/7184580).

10.12 BANKS, HOUSING, AND THE GLOBAL FINANCIAL CRISIS

Before the 1980s, financial institutions had been restricted in the kinds of loans they could make and in the interest rates they could charge. **Financial deregulation** generated aggressive competition for customers, and gave those customers much easier access to credit.

Financial deregulation and subprime borrowers

Moreover, in the boom period before the global financial crisis, house prices were expected to rise, and the riskiness of home loans to the banks fell. As a result, banks extended more loans. The opportunities for poor people to borrow for a home loan expanded as lenders asked for lower deposits, or even no deposit at all. This new class of homeowners were called **subprime borrowers**, and the effect of this deregulation in the US is shown in Figure 10.14.

Financial deregulation and bank leverage

In the context of the deregulated financial system, banks increased their borrowing. This enabled them:

- to extend more loans for housing
- to extend more loans for consumer durables, like cars and furnishings
- to buy more financial assets based on bundles of home loans.

Just as households took on more mortgage debt, banks also became more leveraged.

---

financial deregulation Policies allowing banks and other financial institutions greater freedom in the types of financial assets they can sell, as well as other practices.

subprime borrower An individual with a low credit rating and a high risk of default. *See also: default risk, subprime mortgage.*

View this data at OWiD https://tinyco.re/3924753

US Federal Reserve. 2016. *Financial Accounts of the United States, Historical* (https://tinyco.re/7453711). December; US Bureau of Economic Analysis (https://tinyco.re/9376977); Federal Reserve Bank of St Louis (FRED).

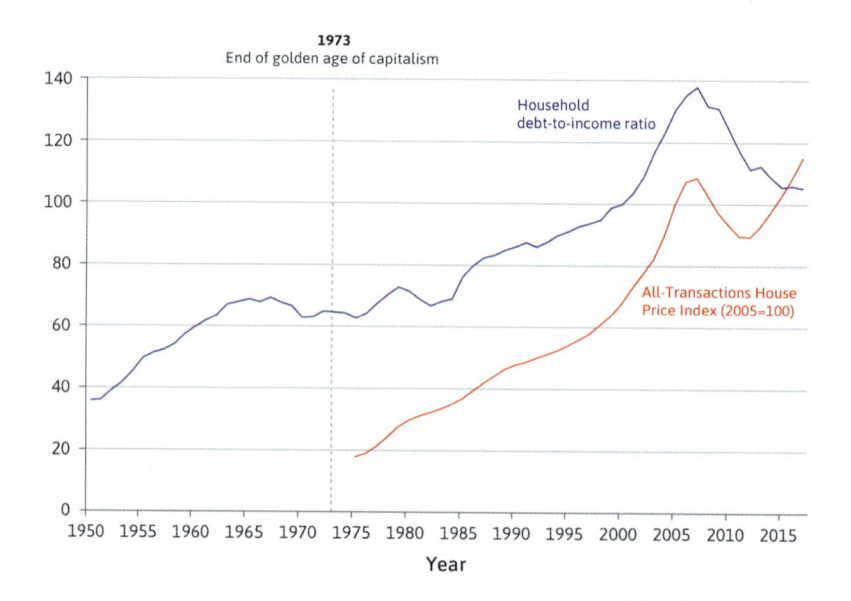

Figure 10.14 The household debt-to-income ratio and house prices in the US (1950–2017).

10.12 BANKS, HOUSING, AND THE GLOBAL FINANCIAL CRISIS

Figure 10.15 shows the leverage of US investment banks and all UK banks. In the US, the leverage ratio of investment banks was between 12 and 14 in the late 1970s, rising to more than 30 in the early 1990s. It hit 40 in 1996 and peaked at 43 just before the financial crisis. By contrast, the leverage of the median UK bank remained at the level of around 20 until 2000. Leverage then increased very rapidly to a peak of 48 in 2007.

The subprime housing crisis of 2007

The interrelated growth of the indebtedness of poor households in the US and global banks meant that, when homeowners began to default on their repayments in 2006, the effects could not be contained within the local or even the national economy. The crisis caused by the problems of **subprime mortgages** in the US spread to other countries. Financial markets were frightened on 9 August 2007 when French bank BNP Paribas halted withdrawals from three investment funds because it could not 'fairly' value financial products (https://tinyco.re/5697732) based on US mortgage-based securities—it simply did not know how much they were worth.

The recession that swept across the world in 2008–09 was the worst contraction of the global economy since the Great Depression. The financial crisis took the world by surprise. The world's economic policymakers were unprepared. To find out more about the global financial crisis, read Sections 17.10 (https://tinyco.re/8229057) and 17.11 (https://tinyco.re/1299563) of *The Economy*.

> **subprime mortgage** A residential mortgage issued to a high-risk borrower, for example, a borrower with a history of bankruptcy and delayed repayments. *See also:* subprime borrower.

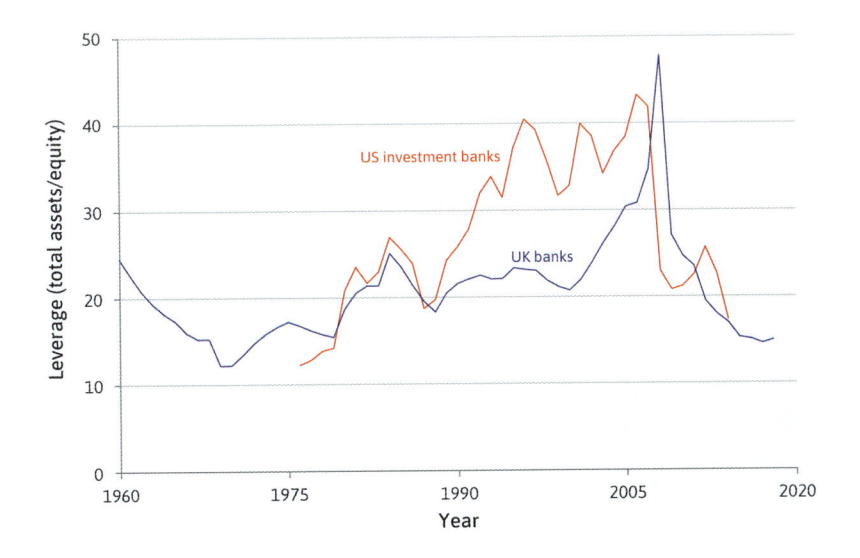

Figure 10.15 Leverage ratio of banks in the UK and US (1960–2018).

View this data at OWiD https://tinyco.re/8394378

US Federal Reserve. 2016. *Financial Accounts of the United States, Historical* (https://tinyco.re/7453711). 9 June; Bank of England. 2012. *Financial Stability Report*, Issue 31. Most recent UK data received directly from the Bank of England.

QUESTION 10.12 CHOOSE THE CORRECT ANSWER(S)
Figure 10.14 shows the household debt-to-income ratio and the house prices in the US between 1950 and 2017. Based on this information, which of the following statements are correct?

☐ The real value of household debt more than doubled from the end of the golden age to the peak on the eve of the financial crisis.
☐ The causality is from the house price to household debt, that is, higher house prices encourage higher debt, but not the other way around.
☐ A household debt-to-income ratio of over 100 means that the household is bankrupt.
☐ Subprime mortgages partly explain the rise in debt in the US prior to the financial crisis.

QUESTION 10.13 CHOOSE THE CORRECT ANSWER(S)
Figure 10.15 is the graph of leverage of banks in the UK and the US between 1960 and 2018.

The leverage ratio is defined as the ratio of the banks' total assets to their equity. Which of the following statements are correct?

☐ A leverage ratio of 40 means that only 2.5% of the asset is funded by equity.
☐ The total asset value of US banks doubled between 1980 and the late 1990s.
☐ A leverage ratio of 25 means that a fall of 4% in the asset value would make a bank insolvent.
☐ UK banks increased their leverage rapidly in the 2000s in order to make more loans to UK house buyers.

10.13 THE ROLE OF BANKS IN THE CRISIS

House prices and bank solvency
The financial crisis was a banking crisis. The banks were in trouble because they had become highly leveraged and were vulnerable to a fall in the value of the financial assets that they had accumulated on their balance sheets (refer back to Figure 10.15 for the leverage of US and UK banks). The values of the financial assets were in turn based on house prices.

With a ratio of net worth to assets of 4%, as in the example of the bank in Figure 10.5 (page 450), a fall in the value of its assets of an amount greater than this will render a bank insolvent. House prices fell by much more than 4% in many countries in the 2008–09 financial crisis. In fact, the peak-to-trough fall in house price indices for Ireland, Spain, and the US were 50.3%, 31.6%, and 34.6% respectively. This created a problem of solvency for the banks. Just as with the underwater households, banks were in danger of their net worth being wiped out.

Governments rescue banks

Across the advanced economies, banks failed and were rescued by governments.

In Section 10.6 (page 446), we highlighted the fact that banks do not bear all the costs of bankruptcy. The bank owners know that others (taxpayers or other banks) will bear some of the costs of the banks' risk-taking activity. So the banks take more risks than they would take if they bore all the costs of their actions. As we shall see in the following unit, excess risk-taking by banks is an example of a negative **external effect** leading to a **market failure**.

It arises because of the **principal–agent problem** between the government (the principal) and the agent (the bank). The government is the principal because it has a direct interest in (and is held responsible for) maintaining a healthy economy, and will bear the cost of bank bailout as a consequence of excessive risk-taking by banks. Governments cannot write a complete set of rules that would align the interests of the banks with those of the government or the taxpayer.

The first row in Figure 10.16 summarizes the principal–agent problem between the government and the banks; the second and third rows review the similar principal–agent problems introduced in Units 6 and 9.

To find out more about how they did this, and for more background on how the financial system failed during the crisis, we suggest reading *The Baseline Scenario* (https://tinyco.re/4748992).

external effect When a person's action confers a benefit or cost on some other individual, and this effect is not taken account of by the person in deciding to take the action. It is external because it is not included in the decision-making process of the person taking the action. Positive effects refer to benefits, and negative effects to costs, that are experienced by others. A person breathing second-hand smoke from someone else's cigarette is a negative external effect. Enjoying your neighbour's beautiful garden is a positive external effect. Also known as: externality. See also: incomplete contract, market failure, external benefit, external cost.

market failure When markets allocate resources in a Pareto-inefficient way.

principal–agent relationship This is an asymmetrical relationship in which one party (the principal) benefits from some action or attribute of the other party (the agent) about which the principal's information is not sufficient to enforce in a complete contract. See also: incomplete contract. Also known as: principal–agent problem.

	Actors: Principal Agent	Conflict of interest over	Enforceable contract covers	Left out of contract (or unenforceable)	Result
Government and Banks	Government Banks	Risk by banks	Taxes, other bank regulations	Risk level chosen by banks	Banks adopt too much risk
Labour market (Units 6 and 8)	Employer Employee	Wages, work (quality and amount)	Wages, time, conditions	Work (quality and amount), duration of employment	Effort under-provided; unemployment
Credit market (Unit 9)	Lender Borrower	Interest rate, conduct of project (effort, prudence)	Interest rate	Effort, prudence, repayment	Too much risk, credit constraints

Figure 10.16 Principal–agent problems: The credit market and the labour market.

Banks expend substantial resources lobbying governments to bail them out when they fail. But there are reasons beyond the self-interest of banks to think that the failure of a bank is different from the failure of a typical firm or household and more dangerous to the stability of a capitalist economy. Banks play a central role in the payments system of the economy and in providing loans to households and firms. Chains of assets and liabilities link banks, and those chains had extended across the world in the years before the financial crisis.

Thus, the banking system, like an electricity grid, is a network. The failure of one of the elements in this connected network creates pressure on every other element. Just as happens in an electricity grid, the network effects in a banking system may create a cascade of subsequent failures, as occurred between 2006 and 2008.

> **EXERCISE 10.6 BEHAVIOUR IN THE FINANCIAL CRISIS**
> 'The crisis of credit visualized' is an animated explanation of the behaviour of households and banks in the financial crisis.
> Use the models and concepts discussed in this unit to explain the story told in the video.

The crisis of credit visualized
https://tinyco.re/3866047

> **QUESTION 10.14 CHOOSE THE CORRECT ANSWER(S)**
> Which of the following statements about the principal–agent problem in the banking system are correct?
>
> ☐ The government is the principal and the banks are the agents.
> ☐ The principal–agent problem arises because of the interconnectedness of the banking system.
> ☐ The result of the principal–agent problem is that banks take on more risk than they otherwise would have.
> ☐ The government can solve the principal–agent problem by enforcing stricter banking regulations.

10.14 BANKING, MARKETS, AND MORALS

The deregulation of financial markets during the three decades prior to the financial crisis of 2008 not only created an institutional environment vulnerable to instability, it also altered the culture of the banking industry in many countries, changing the social norms and informal rules of moral behaviour that governed the business. In many occupations, such as medicine, professional bodies uphold an expectation of pro-social behaviour and truth-telling among their members. Members are expected to take account of the effects of their actions on others. Banking in the main financial centres of the world was no different.

But support for financial deregulation included the argument that the pursuit of profits on substantially unregulated financial markets alone was sufficient to produce socially beneficial outcomes. And if this is really the case, why not dispense with the traditional social norms among bankers, auditors, and accountants that they should take account of the interests of the debtors, investors, savers, shareholders, customers, and others with whom they interact?

Many accepted the logic that a deregulated market would punish 'bad' firms and individuals. 'Greed is good', a slogan from a 1987 film, *Wall Street*, expressed the idea that we can count on markets, not morals to get rid of the 'bad actors'. This seemed to give bankers license to take advantage of their expertise and access to private information to profit in ways that ultimately contributed to the destabilization of the entire financial system, for example, taking on too much risk, and engaging in misleading if not illegal sales pitches. As a result, deregulation of financial markets contributed to the financial crisis, not only by changing the rules of the game in ways that made bubbles and busts more likely, but it also changed how bankers and others acted, and in ways that exacerbated the crisis.

The transformation of the culture of The City (of London), the hub of the UK financial system and the largest financial centre in the world, illustrates this process.

Deregulation and 'unethical behaviour' in the City of London

Prior to deregulation in the so-called 'Big Bang' of 1986, The City had a highly developed ethical culture where participants were vetted to ensure they were deemed 'fit and proper' to carry out their functions. The system led to the groundless exclusion of many women and ethnic minorities. But individuals, firms, and partnerships that, in the eyes of the leading firms and individuals, didn't display pro-social preferences could not join the professional networks of The City. Investment bankers depended very much on their reputation, which was developed through long-term relationships with clients and other counterparties within The City. Most banks had centralized, and demanding, inspection regimes which ensured that rules and procedures were strictly followed and clients were served well.

The City was deregulated progressively over the closing decades of the twentieth century, and by the eve of the global financial crisis, it had embraced the prevailing global banking culture, based on the idea that making profits is not only the bottom line, it is all that matters, as long as markets are competitive. A junior policy advisor to Prime Minister Margaret Thatcher expressed concern about the likely resulting 'unethical behaviour' and that financial deregulation could lead to 'increased risk-taking' and 'boom and bust'. Events in The City and around the world proved him correct.

In the run-up to the financial crisis, a violation of their responsibilities to both customers and shareholders, US issuers and underwriters of mortgage-backed securities (MBSs) bet against them even as they sold them to trusted clients and lied to shareholders about their own MBS holdings. (See the video (page 474) in Exercise 10.6 for further details). Most of the largest mortgage originators and MBS issuers and underwriters have been implicated in regulatory settlements and have since paid multibillion-dollar penalties. In the UK, Barclays and four former executives have been charged with fraud dating back to 2008.

To see why trusting the deregulated market to produce socially beneficial effects might have failed, think about a particular firm, hiring staff to sell MBSs to the public. Initially, the firm instils a code of conduct that the sales pitch should inform the potential buyer fully and honestly about the product being sold. But the idea that market competition would be sufficient to discipline sellers led to the adoption of new ways of compensating those selling financial products—pay was closely linked to how much they sold. Because these incentive-based compensation plans

---

S. Jaffer, N. Morris, E. Sawbridge, and D. Vines. 2014. 'How changes to the financial services industry eroded trust'. In *Capital Failure: Rebuilding Trust in Financial Services,* ed. N. Morris and D. Vines. 2014. Oxford: Oxford University Press.

J. Pickard and B. Thompson. 2014. 'Archives 1985 & 1986: Thatcher policy fight over "Big Bang" laid bare' (https://tinyco.re/3866414). *Financial Times*. Accessed 7 August 2018.

N. Fligstein and A. Roehrkasse. 2016. 'The causes of fraud in the financial crisis of 2007 to 2009'. *American Sociological Review* 81(4): 617–643. 'Barclays and four former executives are charged with fraud'. *The Economist*, 22 June 2017.

rewarded sales without monitoring the pitch or other sales techniques, they could be easily gamed by sellers who cut corners to make the products look safer than they were.

A vicious circle

The problem is a very general one in economics. Just like in an employment contract, these compensation plans for sellers typically cover some aspects of a transaction, like the amounts sold, but cannot cover more subtle aspects, like the degree of honesty in the sales pitch that results in the sale. Even if the firm wishes all customers to be fully informed, the use of such an incentive plan will lead at least some sellers to misinform buyers so as to increase their pay. Ethical traders were disadvantaged under these schemes, as the corner-cutters were able to bring in more sales. The result would be the advancement of the unethical employees within the firm, and perhaps the conversion of some of the ethical traders to less scrupulous methods.

Banks also increasingly took risks, for which the costs of failure would be paid by the owners of other banks (who would become insolvent if one of the banks that owed them money failed), or by tax payers, if governments bailed out 'too big to fail' banks.

Why morals as well as markets?

Why is it important that bankers and others in financial markets be guided by morals as well as markets? A headline from a previous financial crisis is a place to start. In the aftermath of the stock market crash of 1987 (the same year that the 'greed is good' film was released), the *New York Times* headlined an editorial, 'Ban Greed? No: Harness It', which continued:

'Ban greed? No: Harness it' (https://tinyco.re/9781012). 1988. *New York Times*. 20 January: editorial page.

> Perhaps the most important idea here is the need to distinguish between motive and consequence. Derivative securities attract the greedy the way raw meat attracts piranhas. But so what? Private greed can lead to public good. The sensible goal for securities regulation is to channel selfish behaviour, not thwart it.

As the housing bubble burst in 2008 and the financial crisis unfolded, many US homeowners found that their properties were worth less than their mortgage obligations to the bank. Some of these 'underwater owners' did the maths and strategically defaulted on their loans, sending the bank the keys and walking away. Unlike the *New York Times* two decades earlier, in 2010 Don Bisenius, then the executive vice president of Freddie Mac, the US Federal Home Loan Mortgage Corporation, made a plea for moral behaviour by homeowners in the economy on the organization's website. He suggested that, although it might be individually advantageous to default, if default is widespread, communities and future home buyers would be harmed:

Don Bisenius. 2010. 'A perspective on strategic defaults'. Cited in Bowles, Samuel. 2016. *The Moral Economy: Why Good Incentives Are No Substitute for Good Citizens.* Yale University Press.

> While a personal financial strategy might argue for a strategic default, entire communities and future home buyers can be harmed as a result. And that is why our broader social and policy interests will be best served by discouraging strategic defaults.

Rather than trusting that by getting the prices right the market would induce people to internalize the external effects of their actions, Freddie Mac urged that borrowers considering a strategic default should recognize the damaging impact their actions could have on others. In short, the hope was that morals would do the work of prices.

There was no shortage of moral reasoning on the question. Large majorities of those surveyed held that strategic default is immoral. Yet most defaults were not strategic at all—they were impelled by job loss or other misfortunes. And Freddie Mac's plea for morality from underwater debtors could not have been very persuasive for those who accused the financial institutions of having double standards. After having pursued their own interests single-mindedly for decades, they now implored home owners to act otherwise when their own house of cards tumbled. Although the main determinant of strategic default was economic—how far underwater the property was—defaulters were supported by others who gave moral reasons, such as predatory and unfair banking practices.

EXERCISE 10.7 MORALS AND MARKET FAILURE

Read Section 3.10 (page 128) (on how monetary incentives backfired at the Haifa daycare centres) and the *NY Times* editorial 'Ban Greed? No Harness it' (https://tinyco.re/9781012). Consider what Kenneth Arrow, the economist, wrote:

> In the absence of trust ... opportunities for mutually beneficial cooperation [through market exchange] would have to be forgone ... norms of social behavior, including ethical and moral codes (may be) ... reactions of society to compensate for market failures.

Explain how the messages of these three cases differ and describe how the *NY Times* editors might have modified their editorial had they known about the Haifa experiment or had been convinced by Arrow's statement above.

Kenneth J. Arrow. 1971. 'Political and economic evaluation of social effects and externalities' in M. D. Intriligator, ed. *Frontiers of Quantitative Economics*. Amsterdam: North-Holland: pp. 3–23.

QUESTION 10.15 CHOOSE THE CORRECT ANSWER(S)

Which of the following statements about morals, markets, and money are correct?

- ☐ If markets are competitive, then the economy can function efficiently whatever the preferences of people are, including entirely selfish.
- ☐ Monetary incentives (like bonuses or fines) can motivate people to work harder and do a good job; they can also have the opposite effect.
- ☐ Moral and ethical preferences, like telling the truth and a strong work ethic, are especially important when contracts are incomplete.
- ☐ The heightened competition associated with the deregulation of financial markets make The City and other financial centres operate more efficiently.

10.15 CONCLUSION

This unit has explored the workings of a modern-day financial system, explaining how its main actors (commercial banks, the central bank, governments, pension funds, households, and non-bank firms) interact on various stages (including money markets, credit markets, stock exchanges, and bond markets) to buy and sell different types of financial assets. Banks play a key role in the economy, as they create **bank money** by extending new loans and provide **maturity transformation** services. These functions, however, expose them to both **default risk** and **liquidity risk**, the latter making **bank runs** possible in the event that many depositors attempt to withdraw their funds at the same time.

As the sole supplier of **base money** (which banks require for net daily transfers with other banks and to meet demand from depositors), the **central bank** can set the price of borrowing by choosing the **policy interest rate**. While the short-term interest rate at which banks borrow and lend in the money market is typically close to the policy rate, the **bank lending rate** is ordinarily substantially higher. The difference is called the markup or spread on commercial lending and is the basis of the commercial banks' profits.

Using **balance sheets**, we have characterized banks as debt-heavy, profit-oriented firms whose interconnectedness, systemic importance to the economy, and political influence sometimes motivate governments to bail them out in the case of **insolvency**. We have also seen how a high **leverage ratio** implies that a small change in the value of a bank's assets will wipe out its **equity** base. A **principal–agent problem** arises as the central bank (the principal) would like commercial banks (the agents) to avoid overly risky practices that they may find profitable, given that taxpayers are likely to bear much of the costs of a bailout should insolvency result.

The concept of **present value** has helped us value assets that provide a stream of income in the future. Furthermore, based on the feasible set and indifference curves of our constrained choice toolkit, we have analysed the trade-off between risk and return, and the important role that the degree of **risk aversion** (reflected in the slope of the indifference curves) plays in an individual's choice between risk-free bonds and riskier shares. Wealthier people and those exposed to less risk are less risk averse.

We also showed why share prices can depart substantially from their **fundamental value**, resulting in **bubbles**.

A precursor to the global financial crisis was a house-price boom that enabled households to borrow more, based on the increasing value of their **collateral** (their house). At the same time, **financial deregulation** allowed banks to increase their leverage, exposing them to greater risk, and generated aggressive competition for customers, including **subprime borrowers**, many of whom would later default on their mortgages as the housing bubble burst. Overall, the financial crisis has re-emphasized the importance of government regulation of financial markets as well as moral and ethical behaviour as essential preconditions for market mechanisms to produce acceptable outcomes, especially in cases of incomplete contracts.

10.16 *DOING ECONOMICS*: CHARACTERISTICS OF BANKING SYSTEMS AROUND THE WORLD

In Sections 10.13 and 10.14, we discussed the role of banks in the 2008 global financial crisis. Aside from emphasizing the need for moral and ethical behaviour in the banking system to produce acceptable outcomes, the crisis also highlighted important issues in data collection and measurement, as policymakers lacked good quality, cross-country, and cross-time (so-called 'time series') data on financial systems.

In *Doing Economics* Empirical Project 10, we will use the World Bank's Global Financial Development Database to explore the following questions:

- How do banking systems around the world differ in size and in the access that they provide to financial services?
- Have banking systems become more stable since the 2008 global financial crisis?

Go to *Doing Economics* Empirical Project 10 (https://tinyco.re/2953288) to work on this project.

> *Learning objectives*
> In this project you will:
>
> - compare characteristics of banking systems around the world and across time
> - use box and whisker plots to identify outliers
> - calculate weighted averages and explain the differences between weighted and simple averages
> - use confidence intervals to assess changes in the stability of financial institutions before and after the 2008 global financial crisis.

10.17 REFERENCES

Bowles, Samuel. 2016. *The Moral Economy: Why Good Incentives Are No Substitute for Good Citizens*. New Haven, CT: Yale University Press.

Brunnermeier, Markus. 2009. 'Lucas roundtable: Mind the frictions' (https://tinyco.re/0136751). *The Economist*. Updated 6 August 2009.

Cassidy, John. 2010. 'Interview with Eugene Fama' (https://tinyco.re/0438887). *The New Yorker*. Updated 13 January 2010.

Fligstein, N., and A. Roehrkasse. 2016. 'The causes of fraud in the financial crisis of 2007 to 2009'. *American Sociological Review* 81 (4): pp. 617–43.

Graeber, David. 2012. 'The Myth of Barter' (https://tinyco.re/6552964). *Debt: The First 5,000 years*. Brooklyn, NY: Melville House Publishing.

Harford, Tim. 2012. 'Still think you can beat the market?' (https://tinyco.re/7063932). *The Undercover Economist*. Updated 24 November 2012.

Jaffer, S., N. Morris, E. Sawbridge, and D. Vines. 2014. 'How changes to the financial services industry eroded trust'. In *Capital Failure: Rebuilding Trust in Financial Services*, ed. N. Morris and D. Vines. Oxford: Oxford University Press.

Kindleberger, Charles P. 2005. *Manias, Panics, and Crashes: A History of Financial Crises* (https://tinyco.re/6810098). Hoboken, NJ: Wiley, John & Sons.

Lucas, Robert. 2009. 'In defence of the dismal science' (https://tinyco.re/6052194). *The Economist*. Updated 6 August 2009.

Malkiel, Burton G. 2003. 'The efficient market hypothesis and its critics' (https://tinyco.re/4628706). *Journal of Economic Perspectives* 17 (1) (March): pp. 59–82.

Martin, Felix. 2013. *Money: The Unauthorised Biography*. London: The Bodley Head.

New York Times. 1988. 'Ban greed? No: Harness it' (https://tinyco.re/9781012). 20 January: editorial page.

Pickard, J., and B Thompson. 2014. 'Archives 1985 & 1986: Thatcher policy fight over "Big Bang" laid bare' (https://tinyco.re/3866414). *Financial Times*. Accessed 7 August 2018.

Shiller, Robert J. 2003. 'From Efficient Markets Theory to Behavioral Finance' (https://tinyco.re/3989503). *Journal of Economic Perspectives* 17 (1) (March): pp. 83–104.

Shiller, Robert J. 2015. *Irrational Exuberance*, Chapter 1 (https://tinyco.re/4263463). Princeton, NJ: Princeton University Press.

The Economist. 2017. 'Barclays and four former executives are charged with fraud'. 22 June: Finance and Economics section.

11
MARKET SUCCESSES AND FAILURES

Air pollution

11.1 INTRODUCTION

- Governments and markets, along with firms and families, are the major economic institutions today. Their organization and interactions affect the extent to which economic outcomes are efficient and fair.
- Some economic activities are better organized primarily in markets, others by firms, families, or governments.
- Market competition allows large numbers of people to interact in mutually beneficial ways.
- This is because market-determined prices convey important economic information that would be difficult, if not impossible, for a government to obtain and use in any other way.
- If market-determined prices consistently induced people to fully account for the effects of their actions on others, outcomes would be efficient. When prices do not capture these external effects, markets fail, and public policy remedies may improve economic outcomes.
- External effects arise when property rights and legal contracts are either entirely absent, or do not cover some of the external effects of the decision-maker's actions. For example, one cannot sue the smoker for the damages experienced from second-hand smoke.
- Policies can address market failures if they can induce actors to internalize these external effects.
- Other policies can directly regulate the actions of firms and households, for example, by banning smoking or the use of chemicals (such as pesticides) that impose costs on others.
- Private bargaining can sometimes internalize the effect of one party's actions on others, for example, a merger between a firm emitting pollutants and a firm suffering damage as a result.

The pesticide chlordecone was used on banana plantations in the Caribbean islands of Guadeloupe and Martinique (both part of France) to kill the banana weevil. It was perfectly legal, and to the plantation owners it was an effective way of reducing costs and boosting the plantations' profits.

As the chemical was washed off the land into rivers that flowed to the coast, it contaminated freshwater prawn farms, the mangrove swamps where crabs were caught, and what had been rich coastal spiny lobster fisheries. The livelihoods of fishing communities were destroyed and those who ate contaminated fish fell ill.

The fact that this pesticide was a grave danger to humans had been known since the time it was introduced, when workers in the US producing the chemical reported symptoms of neurological damage, leading to its prohibition in 1976. The French government received reports on contamination in Guadeloupe a few years later, but waited until 1990 to ban the substance, and were pressured by banana plantation owners to give them a special exemption until 1993.

Twenty years later, fishermen protesting the slow pace of French government assistance in addressing the fallout from the contamination demonstrated in the streets of Fort de France (the largest town in Martinique) and barricaded the port. Franck Nétri, a Gaudeloupean fisherman, worried: 'I've been eating pesticide for 30 years. But what will happen to my grandchildren?'

He was right to worry. By 2012, the fraction of Martiniquean men suffering from prostate cancer was the highest in the world and almost twice that of the second-highest country, and the mortality rate was well over four times the world average. Neurological damage in children, including cognitive performance, had also been documented.

Let's think of the chlordecone problem as a doctor would.

First, we diagnose the problem. The problem is that the actions of the banana plantation owners endanger the fishermen's livelihood and health, but these costs of using the pesticide do not show up anywhere in the profit and loss calculations of the plantation owners. The price of pesticides—their cost as seen by the plantation owners—does not include the downstream costs imposed on the fishermen.

- *Our diagnosis:* Actors do not take account of the costs their decisions impose on others. This is the origin of the chlordecone **social dilemma**.

Next, we aim to devise a treatment. In some cases, the treatment is obvious. Chlordecone was simply banned in France and the US, and its use could have been vastly reduced if the plantation owners had been required (by law or by private agreement with those affected) to pay damages to the fishing communities for the harm inflicted by their pesticide.

- *Our suggested treatment:* Either directly regulate the actions that impose costs on others (for example, by banning or limiting the use of the chemical), or adopt taxes or other policies that force the decision-maker to bear these costs.

The social dilemma associated with the use of chlordecone is termed a **market failure** as it arises from the buying and selling of pesticides and bananas on markets.

---

social dilemma A situation in which actions, taken independently by individuals in pursuit of their own private objectives, may result in an outcome that is inferior to some other feasible outcome that could have occurred if people had acted together, rather than as individuals.

market failure When markets allocate resources in a Pareto-inefficient way.

But notice that our suggested treatment of the problem was not simply to abandon using markets as a way of distributing bananas, pesticides, fish, and the other products making up the sad story of Martinique's experience in this case. Our treatment was to harness the market through targeted policies to better serve social ends, not to abandon its use. The very fact that bananas—a crop that originated half the world away in the islands of the western Pacific Ocean—are grown in the Caribbean for consumption around the world is itself an example of a market success.

To understand why markets fail in cases like that of chlordecone, it is helpful to remember the conditions that are needed for markets to work well.

11.2 THE MARKET AND OTHER INSTITUTIONS

Markets are one way of organizing the production and distribution of goods and services. For example, you may hire a person on the labour market to take care of your child while you are at work. But your child's caregiver could also be a relative who is not paid a wage. Or the infant could be cared for in a government daycare centre that is free as a matter of right to any citizen, or by the firm you work for, as part of your compensation package. Each of these are examples of different economic institutions—markets, families, governments, and firms—organizing some particular activity.

In Unit 2 (page 55) you learned that our interactions with others can be represented as games; for this reason, the institutions that organize these interactions can be described as the rules of the game. In Unit 5 (page 186) you saw that the way pirates interacted at sea was determined by the rules of the game laid out in the constitution of *The Royal Rover*.

In Section 11.1, we contrasted markets with firms, families, and governments. As economists, we can think of each situation as a different game with its own particular rules. In this sense, markets are just one of the ways that we organize our societies—you pay for what you get. But what about the others?

- *In firms:* Your interaction with other members of the firm you work for is organized, in part using a contract that you (or your trade union) negotiated with the owners, and in part according to your position in the firm's organizational structure.
- *In families:* you get what you get as a matter of love, reciprocity and obligation among family members.
- *In governments:* What you give to and get from the government depends on your rights and responsibilities. A country's constitution is typically a written document that lays out the formal structure of a government, that is, the rules of the game for our interactions with the government.

Just like a country's constitution, we can take all the rules of the game that apply to us in our roles as parents, voters, employees, shoppers, and so on, and consider them to also have constitutions. The rules of the game of markets can be seen as a 'constitution', with firms, families, and governments making up the institutions that jointly organize how we interact with each other in producing and distributing our livelihoods.

Markets are essential economic institutions, not because they work perfectly (as we shall see in this unit), but because there are a great many aspects of production and distribution for which markets do better than the alternative institutions—governments, families, and firms.

11.3 MARKETS, SPECIALIZATION, AND THE DIVISION OF LABOUR

When you hear the word 'market' what word do you think of? 'Competition' probably comes to mind, and you would be right to associate the two words.

But 'cooperation' applies too. Why?

Because markets allow each of us, pursuing our private objectives, to work together, producing and distributing goods and services in a way that, while far from perfect, is in many cases better than the alternatives. Markets allow us to interact with people (for the most part complete strangers to us) in ways that we can mutually benefit from, specializing in the things we are relatively good at doing.

This is a more amazing accomplishment than it might at first seem.

Look around at the objects in your workspace. Do you know the people who made them? What about your clothing? Or anything else in sight from where you are sitting?

Now imagine that it is 1776, the year that Adam Smith (page 17) wrote *The Wealth of Nations*. The same questions, asked anywhere in the world at that date, would have had different answers.

At that time, many families produced a wide array of goods for their own use, including crops, meat, clothing, even tools. Many of the things that you might have spotted in Adam Smith's day would have been made by a member of the family or someone in the village. You would have made some objects yourself; others would have been made locally and purchased from the village market.

One of the changes that was underway during Adam Smith's life, but has greatly accelerated since, is specialization in the production of goods and services. As Smith explained, we become better at producing things when we each focus on a limited range of activities. This is true for three reasons:

- *Learning by doing:* We acquire skills as we produce things.
- *Some people are better at producing some things than others:* This might be because they have more skill, or because of natural surroundings, such as the quality of the soil.
- *Economies of scale:* Producing a large number of units of some good is often more cost effective than producing a smaller number. (We studied **economies of scale** in Unit 7 (page 277).)

These are the advantages of working on a limited number of tasks or products. People do not typically produce the full range of goods and services that they use or consume in their daily lives. Instead, we specialize, some producing one good, others producing other goods, some working as welders, others as teachers or farmers. This is called the division of labour.

Adam Smith begins *The Wealth of Nations* with the following sentence:

> The greatest improvement in the productive powers of labour, and the greater part of the skill, dexterity, and judgment with which it is anywhere directed, or applied, seem to have been the effects of the division of labour.

But people do not specialize unless they have a way to acquire the other goods they need. For this reason, specialization and the resulting division

---

economies of scale These occur when doubling all of the inputs to a production process more than doubles the output. The shape of a firm's long-run average cost curve depends both on returns to scale in production and the effect of scale on the prices it pays for its inputs. *Also known as: increasing returns to scale. See also: diseconomies of scale.*

Adam Smith. (1776) 2003. *An Inquiry into the Nature and Causes of the Wealth of Nations* (http://tinyco.re/9804148). New York, NY: Random House Publishing Group.

of labour pose a problem for society: how are the goods and services to be distributed from the producer to the final user?

This result—the coordination of the division of labour—is accomplished in different ways, depending on a society's institutions. In the course of history, the division of labour has been coordinated by means of direct government requisitioning and distribution, as was done in the US and many economies during the Second World War, or by gifts and voluntary sharing as we do in families today; it was even practised among unrelated members of a community by our hunter-gatherer ancestors. Today, in most countries, markets play an essential role in coordinating the division of labour.

Chapter 3 in Smith's *Wealth of Nations* is titled 'That the Division of Labour is Limited by the Extent of the Market', in which he explains:

> When the market is very small, no person can have any encouragement to dedicate himself entirely to one employment, for want of the power to exchange all that surplus part of the produce of his own labour, which is over and above his own consumption, for such parts of the produce of other men's labour as he has occasion for.

Markets accomplish an extraordinary result: they create unintended cooperation on a global scale. The people who produced the phone in your pocket did not know or care about you. They produced it because they are better at producing phones than you are, or were willing to work for lower wages than you are. You ended up with the phone because you paid the producers, allowing them to buy goods, also produced by total strangers to them.

11.4 THE 'MAGIC OF THE MARKET': PRICES ARE MESSAGES PLUS MOTIVATION

The key to how this process works can be expressed in a single sentence. When markets work well, prices send messages about the real scarcity of goods and services. The messages provide information that motivates people to take account of what is scarce and what is abundant, and as a result to produce, consume, invest, and innovate in ways that make the best use of an economy's productive potential.

Prices coordinate specialization among complete strangers

If drought in the American Great Plains means that there is less wheat on the world market, the resulting increase in the price of bread sends a message to the shopper: 'Consider putting potatoes or rice on the table tonight instead of bread.' The shopper may know nothing about weather conditions in America and need not be the slightest bit concerned about consuming less of a good that has become scarcer. To respond to the message of the higher price in a way that makes the best use of a society's available resources, the shopper needs to be concerned about just one thing: saving money. The shopper not only gets the message, but has a good reason to act on it.

It is this—the fact that prices combine information and a reason to act on the information—that allows the market system (many markets interlinked) to coordinate the division of labour through the exchange of goods among entire strangers, without centralized direction. Friedrich Hayek, who was part economist and part philosopher, suggested we think of the market as a giant information-processing machine that produces prices; the prices provide information that guides the economy, usually in desirable directions. The remarkable thing about this massive computational device is that it's not really a machine at all. Nobody designed it, and nobody is at the controls. When it works well, we use phrases like 'the magic' of the market.

Are the prices sending the right messages?

But for this to be the case, the messages that prices send must convey the right information—how scarce a good really is. Think about what this means—the scarcity of a good is measured by its social marginal cost, that is, the total cost of having one more unit of it, including not only the cost of those producing and distributing it, but also the external effects imposed on others (for example, environmental damages).

You have seen many cases in the previous units in which the price of a good is not equal to its social marginal cost. The price of bananas in Martinique, for example, did not include the loss of life and livelihood inflicted on the downstream fishing community by the pesticides used on the plantations.

The price may fail to reflect the social marginal cost due to either:

- *A lack of competition:* Price is greater than the private marginal cost to the producer.
- *External effects that are costs:* For example, the negative environmental effects just mentioned.
- *External effects that are benefits:* For example, the positive external effect for others if your scientific research created a valuable piece of knowledge that was a public good.

When prices send the wrong messages, we ask whether some modification of how markets work could be introduced by public policies to improve economic outcomes, for example, taxing production processes that emit greenhouse gases or subsidizing basic research.

We now illustrate how prices can send the right message, and sometimes not, by two real world cases.

Joseph A. Schumpeter. (1943) 2003. *Capitalism, Socialism and Democracy* (https://tinyco.re/4138375). pp. 167–72. Routledge.

GREAT ECONOMISTS

Friedrich Hayek

The Great Depression of the 1930s ravaged the capitalist economies of Europe and North America, throwing a quarter of the workforce out of work in the US. During the same period, the centrally planned economy of the Soviet Union continued to grow rapidly under a succession of five-year plans. Even the arch-opponent of socialism, Joseph Schumpeter, had conceded: 'Can socialism work? Of course it can. … There is nothing wrong with the pure logic of socialism.'

11.4 THE 'MAGIC OF THE MARKET': PRICES ARE MESSAGES PLUS MOTIVATION

Friedrich Hayek (1899–1992) disagreed. Born in Vienna, he was an Austrian (later British) economist and philosopher who believed that the government should play a minimal role in the running of society. He was against any efforts to redistribute income in the name of social justice. He was also an opponent of the policies advocated by John Maynard Keynes, designed to moderate the instability of the economy and the insecurity of employment.

Hayek's book, *The Road to Serfdom*, was written against the backdrop of the Second World War, when economic planning was being used both by German and Japanese fascist governments, by the Soviet communist authorities, and by the British and American governments. He argued that well-intentioned planning would inevitably lead to a totalitarian outcome.

His key idea about economics—that prices are messages—revolutionized how economists think about markets. Messages convey valuable information about how scarce a good is, information that is available only if prices are free to be determined by supply and demand, rather than by the decisions of planners. Hayek even wrote a comic book (http://tinyco.re/9802258), which was distributed by General Motors, to explain how this mechanism was superior to planning.

But Hayek did not think much of the theory of competitive equilibrium, in which all buyers and sellers are price-takers. 'The modern theory of competitive equilibrium,' he wrote, 'assumes the situation to exist which a true explanation ought to account for as the effect of the competitive process.'

In Hayek's view, assuming a state of equilibrium (as Walras, one of the founders of the neoclassical school of economics, had done in developing general equilibrium theory) prevents us from analysing competition seriously. He defined competition as 'the action of endeavouring to gain what another endeavours to gain at the same time.' Hayek explained:

> Now, how many of the devices adopted in ordinary life to that end would still be open to a seller in a market in which so-called 'perfect competition' prevails? I believe that the answer is exactly none. Advertising, undercutting, and improving ('differentiating') the goods or services produced are all excluded by definition—'perfect' competition means indeed the absence of all competitive activities.

The advantage of capitalism, to Hayek, is that it provides the right information to the right people. In 1945, he wrote:

> Which of these systems [central planning or competition] is likely to be more efficient depends mainly on the question under which of them we can expect [to make fuller use] of the existing knowledge. This, in turn, depends on whether we are more likely to succeed in putting at the disposal of a single central authority all the knowledge which ought to be used but which is initially dispersed among many different individuals, or in conveying to the individuals such additional knowledge as they need in order to enable them to dovetail their plans with those of others.

Friedrich A. Hayek. 1944. *The Road to Serfdom* (http://tinyco.re/0683881). Chicago, Il: University of Chicago Press.

Hayek, Friedrich A. 1948. 'The Meaning of Competition', in *Individualism and Economic Order* (http://tinyco.re/3958172). Chicago, Il: University of Chicago Press.

Hayek, Friedrich A. 1948. 'The Meaning of Competition', in *Individualism and Economic Order* (http://tinyco.re/3958172). Chicago, Il: University of Chicago Press.

Hayek, Friedrich A. 1945. 'The Use of Knowledge in Society', reprinted in Friedrich A. Hayek. 1948. *Individualism and Economic Order* (http://tinyco.re/3958172). Chicago, Il: University of Chicago Press.

11.5 PRICES AS MESSAGES

Prices worked as messages on a global scale even before the transatlantic telegraph was introduced. Students of American history learn that the defeat of the southern Confederate states in the American Civil War ended the use of slaves in the production of cotton and other crops in that region. There is also an economics lesson in this story.

At the war's outbreak on 12 April 1861, President Abraham Lincoln ordered the US Navy to blockade the ports of the Confederate states. To preserve the institution of slavery, these states had declared themselves independent of the US.

Lincoln's blockade halts the export of cotton

As a result of the naval blockade, the export of US-grown raw cotton to the textile mills of Lancashire in England came to a virtual halt, eliminating three-quarters of the supply of this critical raw material. Sailing at night, a few blockade-running ships evaded Lincoln's patrols, but 1,500 ships were destroyed or captured.

We have seen in Unit 7 (page 300) that the market price of a good, such as cotton, is determined by the interaction of supply and demand. In the case of raw cotton, the tiny quantities reaching England through the blockade were a dramatic reduction in supply. There was large **excess demand**—at the prevailing price, the quantity of raw cotton demanded exceeded the available supply. As a result, some sellers realized they could profit by raising the price. Eventually, cotton was sold at prices six times higher than before the war, keeping the lucky blockade runners in business. Consumption of cotton fell to half the prewar level, throwing hundreds of thousands of people who worked in cotton mills out of work.

> **excess demand** A situation in which the quantity of a good demanded is greater than the quantity supplied at the current price. *See also: excess supply.*

British textile mill owners increase demand

Mill owners responded. For them, the price rise was an increase in their costs. Some firms failed and left the industry due to the reduction in their profits. Mill owners looked to India to find an alternative to US cotton, greatly increasing the demand for cotton there. The excess demand in the markets for Indian cotton gave some sellers an opportunity to profit by raising prices, resulting in increases in the prices of Indian cotton, which quickly rose to almost match the price of US cotton.

Farmers in India and Egypt switch to cotton

Responding to the higher income now obtainable from growing cotton, Indian farmers abandoned other crops and grew cotton instead. The same occurred wherever cotton could be grown, including Brazil. In Egypt, farmers who rushed to expand the production of cotton in response to the higher prices began employing slaves, captured (like the American slaves that Lincoln was fighting to free) in sub-Saharan Africa.

There was a problem. The only source of cotton that could come close to making up the shortfall from the US was in India. But Indian cotton differed from American cotton and required an entirely different kind of processing. Within months of the shift to Indian cotton, new machinery was developed to process it.

Mill owners introduce new machinery

As the demand for this new equipment soared, firms that made textile machinery, like Dobson and Barlow, saw profits take off. We know about this firm, because detailed sales records have survived. Dobson and Barlow responded by increasing production of these new machines and other equipment. No mill could afford to be left behind in the rush to retool, because if it didn't, it could not use the new raw materials. The result was, in the words of Douglas Farnie, a historian who specialized in the history of cotton production: 'such an extensive investment of capital that it amounted almost to the creation of a new industry.'

Douglas A. Farnie. 1979. *The English Cotton Industry and the World Market: 1815–1896*. Oxford: Oxford University Press.

A change in price was the message and the motivation

The lesson for economists—Lincoln ordered the blockade, but in what followed, the farmers and sellers who increased the price of cotton were not responding to orders. Neither were the mill owners, who cut back the output of textiles and laid off the mill workers, nor were the mill owners desperately searching for new sources of raw material. By ordering new machinery, the mill owners set off a boom in investment and new jobs.

All these decisions took place over a matter of months, made by millions of people, most of whom were total strangers to one another, each seeking to make the best of a totally new economic situation. American cotton was now scarcer, and people responded, from the cotton fields of Maharashtra in India, to the Nile delta, to Brazil, to the Lancashire mills.

To understand how the change in the price of cotton transformed the world cotton and textile production system, think about the prices determined by markets as messages. The increase in the price of US cotton shouted: 'Find other sources, and find new technologies appropriate for their use.' Similarly, when the price of petrol rises, the message to the car driver is: 'Take the train', which is passed on to the railway operator: 'There are profits to be made by running more train services.' When the price of electricity goes up, the firm or the family is being told: 'Think about installing photovoltaic cells on the roof.'

In many cases (like the chain of events that began at Lincoln's desk on 12 April 1861) the messages make sense, not only for individual firms and families, but also for society; if something has become more expensive, then it is likely that more people are demanding it, or the cost of producing it has risen, or both. By finding an alternative, the individual is saving money and conserving society's resources. This is because, in some conditions, prices provide an accurate measure of the scarcity of a good or service.

Centrally planned economies (or firms)

In Unit 1 (page 29) we discussed planned economies, which operated in the Soviet Union and other central and eastern European countries before the 1990s. In these economies, messages about how things are produced are sent deliberately by government experts. They decide what is produced and at what price it is sold. The same is true, as we saw in Unit 6 (page 231), in large firms like General Motors, where managers (and not prices) determine who does what.

The amazing thing about prices determined by markets is that individuals do not send the messages, but rather the anonymous interaction of sometimes millions of people. And when conditions change—a cheaper way of producing bread, for example—nobody has to change the message ('put

See 'Who's in Charge?' (http://tinyco.re/9867111), Chapter 1 of Paul Seabright's book, for more detail on how market economies manage to organize complex trades among strangers.

Paul Seabright. 2010. *The Company of Strangers: A Natural History of Economic Life* (Revised Edition). Princeton, NJ: Princeton University Press.

bread instead of potatoes on the table tonight'). A price change results from a change in firms' costs. The reduced price of bread says it all.

11.6 PUTTING MOTIVATION BEHIND THE PRICE MESSAGE

Fish and fishing are a major part of the life of the people of Kerala in India. Most of them eat fish at least once a day, and more than a million people are involved in the fishing industry. But before 1997, prices were high and fishing profits were limited due to a combination of waste and the bargaining power of fish merchants, who purchased the fishermen's catch and sold it to consumers.

The importance of timing

When returning to port to sell their daily catch of sardines to the fish merchants, many fishermen found that the merchants already had as much fish as they needed that day. They refused to buy any more fish at any price. The price was effectively zero! Fishermen at these markets just dumped their worthless catch back into the sea.

A lucky few returned to the right port at the right time when demand exceeded supply, and they were rewarded by extraordinarily high prices.

On 14 January 1997, for example, 11 boatloads of fish were brought to the market at Badagara, which was found to be oversupplied; the catch was jettisoned. There was excess supply of 11 boatloads. But at fish markets within 15 km of Badagara, there was excess demand—15 buyers left the Chombala market unable to purchase fish at any price. The luck, or lack of it, of fishermen returning to the ports along the Kerala coast is illustrated in Figure 11.1.

Only seven of the 15 markets did not suffer either from over- or undersupply. In these seven villages (on the vertical line), prices ranged from Rs4 per kg in the market at Aarikkadi to more than Rs7 per kg in Kanhangad.

Robert Jensen. 2007. 'The Digital Provide: Information (Technology), Market Performance, and Welfare in the South Indian Fisheries Sector.' *The Quarterly Journal of Economics 122* (3) (August): pp. 879–924.

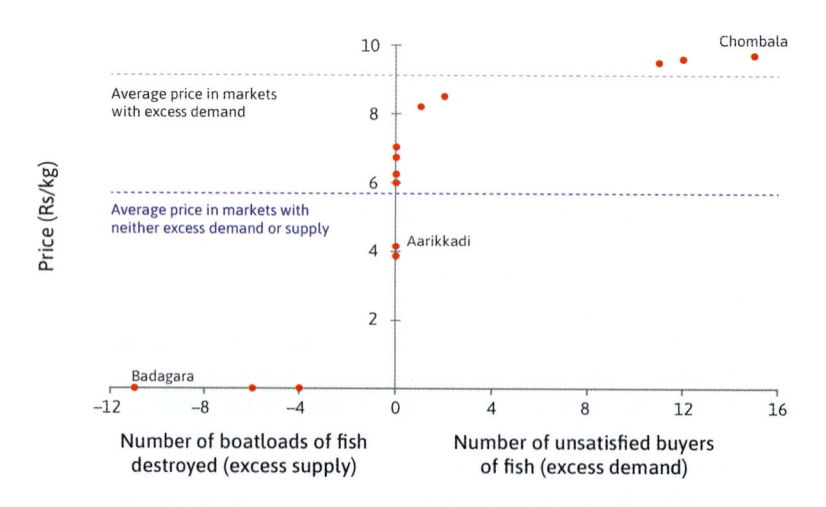

Figure 11.1 Bargaining power and prices in the Kerala wholesale fish market (14 January 1997). (Note: Two markets had the same outcome, with a price of Rs6.2 per kg.)

When the fishermen had bargaining power because there was excess demand, they got much higher prices. In markets with neither excess demand nor excess supply, the average price was Rs5.9 per kg, shown by the horizontal dashed line. In markets with excess demand, the average was Rs9.3 per kg. The fishermen fortunate enough to put in at these markets obtained extraordinary profits, if we assume that the price in markets with neither excess demand nor supply was high enough to yield economic profits. Of course, on the following day they may have been the unlucky ones who found no buyers at all and would have to dump their catch into the sea.

Prices contained important messages: 'Fish are scarce in Chombala, but not in Badagara', but the fisherman did not receive them in time to motivate them to change what they did so as to adjust to surpluses in one market and excess demand in others.

Cell phones deliver the message on time

This all changed when the fishermen got cell phones. While still at sea, the returning fishermen phoned the beach fish markets and picked the one where the prices were highest that day. If they returned to a high-priced market, they would earn an economic rent (that is, income in excess of their next best alternative—returning to a market with no excess demand or, even worse, one with excess supply).

By gaining access to real-time market information on relative prices for fish, the fishermen could adjust their pattern of production (fishing) and distribution (the market they visit) to secure the highest returns.

A study of 15 beach markets along 225 km of the northern Kerala coast found that, once the fishermen had cell phones, differences in daily prices among the beach markets were cut to a quarter of their previous levels. No boats jettisoned their catches. Reduced waste and the elimination of the dealers' bargaining power raised the profits of fishermen by 8%, at the same time as consumer prices fell by 4%.

Cell phones allowed the fishermen to become very effective rent seekers. Their rent-seeking activities changed how Kerala's fish markets worked—virtually eliminating the periodic excess demand and supply—to the benefit of fishermen and consumers, but not of the fish dealers who had acted as middlemen.

This happened because the Kerala sardine fishermen could respond to price messages. The information given by the prices at different beach markets came at the right time, so they were motivated to land at the markets where fish was needed most.

> **QUESTION 11.1 CHOOSE THE CORRECT ANSWER(S)**
>
> Figure 11.1 shows how bargaining power affected prices in Kerala beach markets on 14 January 1997. Based on this information, what can we conclude?
>
> ☐ The higher the excess supply, the lower the price of fish.
> ☐ The price of fish in all markets with excess demand is Rs9.3 per kg.
> ☐ In cases of demand being equal to supply, the price that fishermen faced was the same in all markets.
> ☐ The data demonstrates that buyers have bargaining power when there is excess supply.

11.7 MARKET FAILURE: EXTERNAL EFFECTS OF POLLUTION

But markets do not always work well. We return to take a closer look at the diagnosis and treatment of a case like the one in Section 11.1 (page 481), of pesticides in Martinique and Guadeloupe. As we saw in Unit 1 (page 23), private property is a key requirement for a market system. For something to be bought and sold, someone must claim the right to own it. You would not pay for something unless you believed that others would acknowledge (and if necessary protect) your right to keep it.

For a market to work effectively (or even to exist), other social institutions and social norms are required. Governments provide a system of laws and law enforcement that guarantees **property rights** and enforces contracts.

Many of the problems with markets that we investigate in this unit arise because of difficulties of guaranteeing property rights or writing appropriate contracts. There are goods—like clean rivers—that matter to people but cannot easily be bought and sold. There are 'bads' like second-hand smoke that a person can impose on others without paying the damages, as he might, for example, if the damage was to the other person's car.

> **property rights** Legal protection of ownership, including the right to exclude others and to benefit from or sell the thing owned.

Marcel Fafchamps and Bart Minten. 1999. 'Relationships and Traders in Madagascar'. *Journal of Development Studies* 35 (6) (August): pp. 1–35.

EXERCISE 11.1 PROPERTY RIGHTS AND CONTRACTS IN MADAGASCAR

Marcel Fafchamps and Bart Minten, two economists, studied grain markets in Madagascar in 1997, where the legal institutions for enforcing property rights and contracts were weak. Despite this, they found that theft and breach of contract were rare. The grain traders avoided theft by keeping their stocks very low, and if necessary, sleeping in the grain stores. They refrained from employing additional workers for fear of employee-related theft. When transporting their goods, they paid protection money and travelled in convoy. Most transactions were paid in cash. Trust was established through repeated interaction with the same traders.

1. Do these findings suggest that strong legal institutions are not necessary for markets to work?
2. Consider some market transactions in which you have been involved. Could these markets work in the absence of a legal framework, and how would they be different if they did?
3. Can you think of any examples in which repeated interaction helps to facilitate market transactions?
4. Why might repeated interaction be important even when a legal framework is present?

> **market failure** When markets allocate resources in a Pareto-inefficient way.

When markets allocate resources in a Pareto-inefficient way, we describe this as a **market failure**. We encountered one cause of market failure in Unit 7 (page 286)—a firm producing a differentiated good chooses its price and output level such that the price is greater than the marginal cost. In contrast, we know from later in Unit 7 (page 289) that a competitive market allocation maximizes the total surplus of the producers and consumers and is Pareto efficient, as long as no one else is affected by the production and consumption of the good.

11.7 MARKET FAILURE: EXTERNAL EFFECTS OF POLLUTION

But others are often affected by the production or consumption of the good. The market allocation of the good will not be Pareto efficient if the decisions of producers and consumers affect others in ways that they do not adequately consider. This is a social dilemma, and in this case, a cause of market failure. Recall the social dilemmas we studied in Unit 2 (page 49) such as the overuse of antibiotics. When we analyse gains from trade in such cases, we must consider, not only the consumer and producer surplus, but also the costs or benefits experienced by parties who are neither buyers nor sellers. For example, the superbug that emerges because of the sale and overuse of an antibiotic may kill someone who had no part in its sale or purchase.

In this unit, we focus on social dilemmas in markets, and hence, on market failure.

We will analyse the gains from trade in a case in which the production of a good creates an **external cost**—pollution. Our example is based on the real-world case of the plantations' use of the pesticide chlordecone to control the banana weevil in Guadeloupe and Martinique. To simplify the analysis, we are focusing solely on the adverse effects of the pesticide on the fishing industry, and are setting aside the health impact on the fishing community.

A thought experiment

To see why this is called an **external effect** (you will also see this called an 'externality' in some economics books), imagine that the same company owned the banana plantations and fisheries; the company hired fishermen and sold what they caught for profit. The owners of the company would decide on the level of banana pesticide to use, taking account of its downstream effects. They would trade-off the profits from the banana part of their business against the losses from the fisheries.

But this was not the case in Martinique and Guadeloupe, the islands we described in Section 11.1 (page 481). The plantations owned the profits from banana production, which were increased by using a pesticide. The fisherman 'owned' the losses from fishing. The pollution effect of the pesticide was external to the people making the decision on its use. Joint ownership of the plantations and fisheries would have internalized this effect, but the plantations and fisheries were under separate ownership.

Separate ownership and external effects

To model the implications of this kind of external effect, Figure 11.2 shows the marginal costs of growing bananas on an imaginary Caribbean island where a fictional pesticide called Weevokil is used. The marginal cost of producing bananas for the growers is labelled as the **marginal private cost (MPC)**. It slopes upward because the cost of an additional tonne of bananas increases as the land is more intensively used, requiring more Weevokil. By contrast, the marginal private cost curve in the case of the production of Spanish language courses in Unit 7 (page 279) was flat.

Use the analysis in Figure 11.2 to compare the MPC of producing bananas with the **marginal social cost (MSC)**, which includes the costs borne by fishermen whose waters are contaminated by Weevokil.

---

external cost A negative external effect: that is, the negative effect of production, consumption, or other economic decisions on another person or party, which is not specified as a liability in a contract. *Also known as: external diseconomy. See also: external effect.*

external effect When a person's action confers a benefit or cost on some other individual, and this effect is not taken account of by the person in deciding to take the action. It is external because it is not included in the decision-making process of the person taking the action. Positive effects refer to benefits, and negative effects to costs, that are experienced by others. A person breathing second-hand smoke from someone else's cigarette is a negative external effect. Enjoying your neighbour's beautiful garden is a positive external effect. *Also known as: externality. See also: incomplete contract, market failure, external benefit, external cost.*

marginal private cost (MPC) The cost for the producer of producing an additional unit of a good, not taking into account any costs its production imposes on others. *See also: marginal external cost (MEC), marginal social cost (MSC).*

marginal social cost (MSC) The cost of producing an additional unit of a good, taking into account both the cost for the producer and the costs incurred by others affected by the good's production. Marginal social cost is the sum of the marginal private cost and the marginal external cost.

A Pareto-inefficient outcome

You can see in Figure 11.2 that the marginal social cost of banana production is higher than the marginal private cost. To focus on the essentials, we will consider a case in which the wholesale market for bananas is competitive, and the market price is $400 per tonne. If the banana plantation owners wish to maximize their profit, we know that they will choose their output so that price is equal to their marginal cost—that is, the marginal private cost. Figure 11.3 shows that their total output is 80,000 tonnes of bananas (point A). Although 80,000 tonnes maximizes profits for banana producers, this does not include the cost imposed on the fishing industry, so it is not a Pareto-efficient outcome.

To see this, think about what would happen if the plantations were to produce less. The fishermen would benefit but the plantation owners would lose. Therefore, it appears that producing 80,000 tonnes must be Pareto efficient. But let's imagine that the fishermen could persuade the plantation owners to produce one tonne less.

To explore all of the slides in this figure, see the online version at https://tinyco.re/3746495.

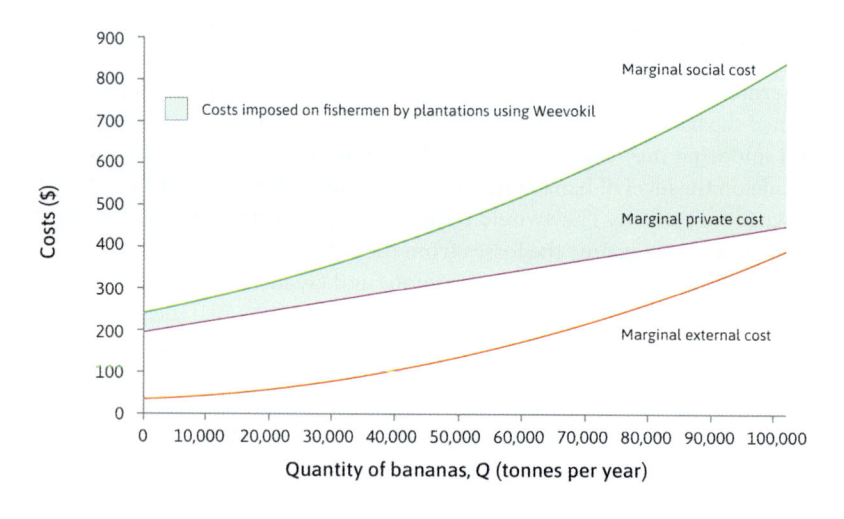

Figure 11.2 Marginal costs of banana production using Weevokil.

1. The marginal private cost
The purple line is the marginal cost for the growers—the marginal private cost (MPC) of banana production. It slopes upward because the cost of producing an additional tonne increases as the land is more intensively used, requiring more Weevokil.

2. The marginal external cost (MEC)
The orange line shows the marginal cost imposed by the banana growers on fishermen—the marginal external cost. This is the cost of the reduction in quantity and quality of fish caused by each additional tonne of bananas.

3. The marginal social cost
Adding together the MPC and the MEC, we get the full marginal cost of banana production—the marginal social cost (MSC). This is the green line in the diagram.

4. The total external cost
The shaded area in the figure shows the total costs imposed on fishermen by plantations using Weevokil. It is the sum of the differences between the marginal social cost and the marginal private cost at each level of production.

- *The fishermen would gain $270:* They would no longer suffer the loss of revenue from the damage to their fishing that is caused by the production of the 80,000th tonne of bananas.
- *The plantation owners would lose very little:* Their revenues would fall by $400, but their costs would fall by almost exactly this amount because, when producing 80,000 tonnes, the marginal private cost is equal to the price ($400).

The fishermen pay the plantation owners to reduce production

If the fishermen paid the plantation owners any amount between just greater than zero and just less than $270, *both groups would be better off* with 79,999 tonnes of bananas.

What about another payment to get the plantation owners to produce 79,998 tonnes instead? You can see that, because the **marginal external cost** imposed on the fishermen is still much higher than the surplus received by the plantation owners on the next tonne (the difference between the price and the MPC), such a payment would also make both parties better off.

By how much could the fishermen persuade the plantations to reduce production? Look at the point in Figure 11.3 at which the price of bananas is equal to the marginal social cost. At this point, 38,000 tonnes of bananas are produced. If the payments by the fishermen to the plantation owners resulted in them producing just 38,000 tonnes, then the fishermen could no longer benefit by making further payments in return for reduced output. If production were lowered further, the loss to the plantation owners (the difference between price and marginal cost) would be greater than the gain to the fishermen (the difference between private and social cost, shaded). At this point, the maximum payment the fishermen would be willing to make would not be enough to induce the plantations to cut production further. The Pareto-efficient level of banana output is, therefore, 38,000 tonnes.

> **marginal external cost (MEC)** The cost of producing an additional unit of a good that is incurred by anyone other than the producer of the good. *See also:* marginal private cost, marginal social cost.

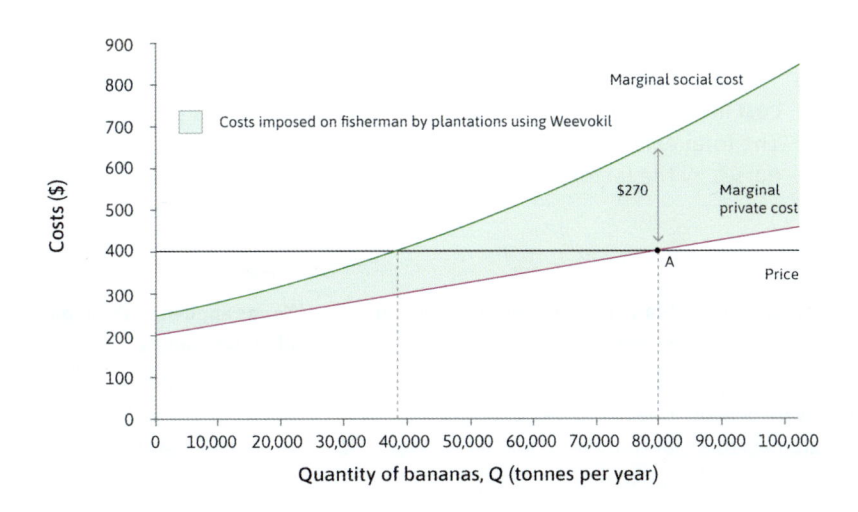

Figure 11.3 The plantations' choice of banana output.

The possibility of a Pareto-efficient outcome without government intervention

To summarize:

- *The plantations produce 80,000 tons of bananas:* At this point price equals MPC.
- *The Pareto-efficient level of output is 38,000 tonnes of bananas:* Price equals MSC.
- *When production is 38,000 tonnes, it is not possible for the plantation owners and fishermen to both be made better off.*
- *What if a single company owned both the banana plantations and fisheries?* This company would choose to produce 38,000 tonnes because, for the single owner, price would be equal to MPC at 38,000 tonnes.

In general, pollutants like Weevokil have negative external effects, sometimes called *environmental spillovers*. They bring *private benefits* to those who decide to use them, but by damaging the environment—water resources, in this case—they impose *external costs* on other firms or on households that rely on environmental resources. For society as a whole, this is a market failure; compared with the Pareto-efficient allocation, the pollutant is overused, and too much of the associated good (bananas, in our example) is produced.

The features of this case of market failure are summarized in Figure 11.4. In the following sections, we summarize other examples of market failure in a similar table. At the end of this unit, we bring all the examples together in Figure 11.15 (page 523) so that you can compare them.

> **QUESTION 11.2 CHOOSE THE CORRECT ANSWER(S)**
> A factory is situated next to a dormitory for nurses who work night shifts. The factory produces 120 humanoid robots a day. The production process is rather noisy, and the nurses often complain that their sleep is disturbed. Based on this information, which of the following statements are correct?
>
> ☐ The marginal private cost is the factory's total cost of producing 120 robots a day.
> ☐ The marginal social cost is the noise cost incurred by the nurses from production of an additional robot.
> ☐ The marginal external cost is the cost to the factory, plus the noise cost incurred by the nurses, when an additional robot is produced.
> ☐ The total external cost is the total costs per day imposed on the nurses by the factory's production.

Decision	How it affects others	Cost or benefit	Market failure (misallocation of resources)	Terms applied to this type of market failure
A firm uses a pesticide that runs off into waterways	Downstream damage	Private benefit, external cost	Overuse of pesticide and overproduction of the crop for which it is used	Negative external effect, environmental spillover

Figure 11.4 Market failure: Water pollution.

11.8 EXTERNAL EFFECTS AND PRIVATE BARGAINING

To demonstrate that the market allocation of bananas (producing 80,000 tonnes, using Weevokil) is not Pareto efficient, we showed that the fishermen could pay the plantation owners to produce fewer bananas, and both would be better off.

Does this suggest a remedy for this market failure that might be implemented in the real world?

It does. The fishermen and the plantation owners could negotiate a private bargain. Solutions of this type are often called *Coasean* bargaining, after Ronald Coase who pioneered the idea that private bargaining might be preferable to dealing with external effects by governmental intervention. He argued that the two parties to the exchange often have more of the information necessary to implement an efficient outcome than does the government.

> More real-world cases of external effects and remedies can be found in Unit 20 of *The Economy*. See, for example, Section 20.3 (https://tinyco.re/6032279) on cost-benefit analysis of climate change abatement policies and Section 20.5 (https://tinyco.re/2504209) on cap and trade environmental policies. Unit 21 of *The Economy*, Section 21.7 (https://tinyco.re/6391691) covers the design of patent policy.

GREAT ECONOMISTS

Ronald Coase

You have already met Ronald Coase (1910–2013). He was featured in Unit 6 (page 236) for his representation of the firm as a political organization. He is also known for his idea that private bargaining could address market failures, in some cases doing this more effectively than government policies.

He explained that, when one party is engaged in an activity that has the incidental effect of causing damage to another, a negotiated settlement between the two may result in a Pareto-efficient allocation of resources. He used the 1879 legal case of Sturges v Bridgman (http://tinyco.re/2709868) in the UK to illustrate his argument. The case concerned Bridgman, a confectioner (candy-maker) who for many years had been using machinery that generated noise and vibration. This caused no external effects until his neighbour Sturges built a consulting room on the boundary of his property, close to the confectioner's kitchen. The courts granted the doctor an injunction that prevented Bridgman from using his machinery.

Coase pointed out that, once the doctor's right to prevent the use of the machinery had been established, the two sides could modify the outcome. The doctor would be willing to waive his right to stop the noise in return for a compensation payment. And the confectioner would be willing to pay if the value of his annoying activities exceeded the costs that they imposed on the doctor.

Also, the court's decision in favour of Sturges rather than Bridgman would make no difference to whether Bridgman continued to use his machinery. If the confectioner had been granted the right to use it, the doctor could have paid him to stop. But he would have been willing to do this if, and only if, the costs to him were greater than the confectioner's profits gained by using the machinery.

In other words, private bargaining would ensure that the machinery was used if, and only if, its use, along with a compensation payment, made both better off. Private bargaining would ensure Pareto efficiency. Bargaining gives the confectioner an incentive to take into account not only the marginal private costs of using the machine to produce candy, but also the external costs imposed on the doctor. That is, the confectioner takes account of the entire social cost. To the confectioner, the cost of using the annoying machinery during the doctor's visiting hours would now send the right message. Private bargaining could be a substitute for legal liability. It ensures that those harmed are compensated, and that those who could inflict harm would make efforts to avoid harmful behaviour.

Whether the courts decided in favour of Sturges (the doctor) or Bridgman (the confectioner) made no difference from the standpoint of Pareto efficiency. As long as the court clearly established who had the right to do what, so that the two could bargain, the result would be efficient. But the legal decision did matter for the distribution of income between the two. Because the court decided in favour of Sturges, Bridgeman would have to pay Sturges for the right to use the machinery. Had it gone the other way, Sturges might have paid Bridgeman to stop using the machinery.

To summarize:

- *The court establishes the initial property rights:* In this case, Bridgman's right to make a noise or Sturges' right to quiet.
- *This leads to a Pareto-efficient outcome:* As long as private bargaining exhausts all the potential mutual gains, the result would (by definition) be Pareto efficient, regardless of which party owned the initial rights.
- *Is this fair?* We might object that the court's decision resulted in an unfair distribution of profits, but however one evaluates this concern (or if, like Coase, one puts 'questions of equity aside'), the outcome would be Pareto efficient.

Coase emphasized that his model could not be directly applied to most situations because of the costs of bargaining and other impediments that prevent the parties from exploiting all possible mutual gains. Costs of bargaining, sometimes called **transaction costs**, may prevent Pareto efficiency. If the confectioner cannot find out how badly the noise affects the doctor, the doctor has an incentive to overstate the costs to get a better deal. Establishing each party's actual costs and benefits is part of the cost of the transaction, and this cost might be too high to make a bargain possible.

However difficult it might be for the doctor and the confectioner to acquire this information, it is often even more difficult for a government to gather the information necessary to directly impose an efficient and fair solution, beyond simply clarifying the property rights in question.

Coase's analysis suggests that a lack of clear property rights, and other impediments leading to high transaction costs, may stand in the way of using bargaining to resolve external effects. But with a clear legal framework in which one side initially owned the rights to produce (or to prevent production of) the external effect, there might be no need for government policies to address the market failure.

> **transaction costs** Costs that impede the bargaining process or the agreement of a contract. They include costs of acquiring information about the good to be traded, and costs of enforcing a contract.

Until now you have probably thought about property rights as referring to goods and services that are typically bought and sold in markets, like food, flights, or houses. Coase's approach suggests that we could think of other rights—in his example, the right to make a noise or to have a quiet work environment—as goods that can be bargained over and traded in return for money.

Could private bargaining solve the pesticide problem?

Let's see how a private bargain might solve the pesticide problem. Initially, it is not illegal to use Weevokil; the allocation of property rights is such that the plantation owners have the right to use it, and choose to produce 80,000 tonnes of bananas. This allocation and the associated incomes and environmental effects represent the **reservation options** of the plantation owners and fishermen. This is what they will get if they do not come to some agreement.

For the fishermen and the plantation owners to negotiate effectively, they would each have to be organized so that a single person (or body) could make agreements on behalf of the entire group. Let's imagine that a representative of an association of fishermen sits down to bargain with a representative of an association of banana growers. To keep things simple, we assume that there are no feasible alternatives to Weevokil, so they bargain only over the output of bananas.

Both sides should recognize that they could gain from an agreement to reduce output to the Pareto-efficient level. In Figure 11.5, the situation before bargaining begins is point A, and the Pareto-efficient quantity is 38,000 tonnes. The total shaded area shows the gain for the fishermen (from cleaner water) if output is reduced from 80,000 to 38,000. But reducing banana production leads to lower profits for the plantation owners. Use the analysis in Figure 11.5 to see that the fall in profit is smaller than the gain for the fishermen, so there is a net social gain that they could agree to share.

Since the gain to the fishermen would be greater than the loss to the plantation owners, the fishermen would be willing to pay the banana growers to reduce output to 38,000 tonnes if they had the funds to do so.

The **minimum acceptable offer** from the fishermen depends on what the plantations get in the existing situation, which is their reservation profit (shown by the blue area labelled 'loss of profit'). If plantation owners agreed to this minimum payment to compensate them for their loss of profit, the fishing industry would achieve a net gain equal to the net social gain, while plantations would be no better (and no worse) off.

The maximum the fishing industry would pay is determined by their reservation option (also known as their fallback option), as in the case of the plantation owners. It is the sum of the blue and green areas. In this case, the plantation owners would get all the net social gain, while the fishermen would be no better off. As in the examples of bargaining in Unit 5 (page 209), the compensation the plantation owners and fishermen agree on between these maximum and minimum levels is determined by the bargaining power of the two groups.

> **reservation option** A person's next best alternative among all options in a particular transaction. *Also known as: fallback option. See also: reservation price.*

> **minimum acceptable offer** In the ultimatum game, the smallest offer by the Proposer that will not be rejected by the Responder. Generally applied in bargaining situations to mean the least favourable offer that would be accepted.

11 MARKET SUCCESSES AND FAILURES

The legal framework affects who benefits from solving the market failure

You may think it unfair that the fishermen need to pay for a reduction in pollution. At the Pareto-efficient level of banana production, the fishing industry is still suffering from pollution (shown by the fact that the MSC is above the MPC), and it must pay to stop the pollution getting worse. This happens because we have assumed that the plantation owners have a legal right to use Weevokil.

An alternative legal framework could give the fishermen a right to clean water. If that were the case, the plantation owners wishing to use Weevokil could propose a bargain in which they paid the fishermen to give up some of their right to clean water to allow the Pareto-efficient level of banana production. This would be a much more favourable outcome for the fishermen. In principle, the bargaining process would result in a Pareto-efficient allocation independently of whether the initial rights were granted to the plantations (right to pollute) or to the fishermen (right to unpolluted water). But the two cases differ dramatically in who gains and who loses when the market failure is solved. This limitation, among others pointed out in a UMassEconomics video (http://tinyco.re/9289964) and discussed below, make Coase's proposal difficult to implement in practice.

To explore all of the slides in this figure, see the online version at https://tinyco.re/2799537.

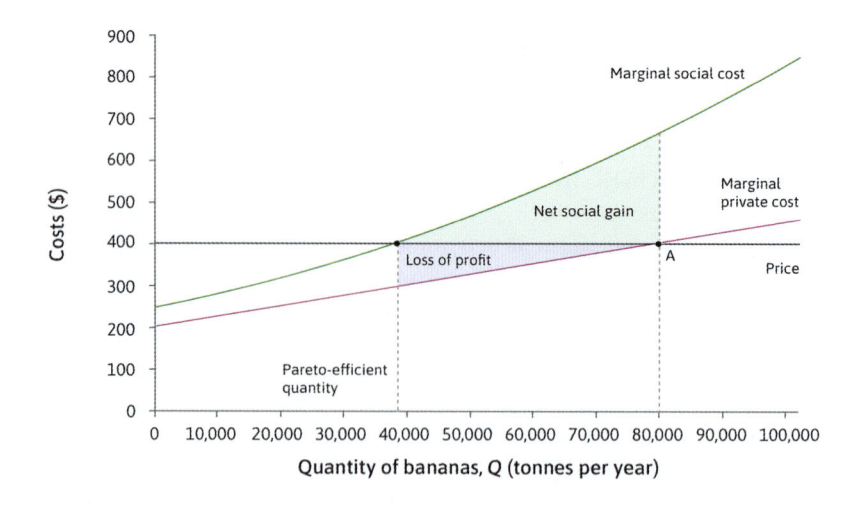

Figure 11.5 The gains from bargaining.

1. The status quo at point A
The situation before bargaining is represented by point A, and the Pareto-efficient quantity of bananas is 38,000 tonnes. The total shaded area shows the gain for fishermen if output is reduced from 80,000 to 38,000 (that is, the reduction in the fishermen's costs).

2. Lost profit
Reducing output from 80,000 to 38,000 tonnes reduces the profits of plantations. The lost profit is equal to the loss of producer surplus, shown by the blue area.

3. The net social gain
The net social gain is the gain for the fishermen minus the loss for the plantation owners, shown by the remaining green area.

Why private bargains may not work

As Coase acknowledged, practical obstacles to bargaining may prevent the achievement of Pareto efficiency:

- *Impediments to collective action:* Private bargaining may be impossible if there are many parties on both sides of the external effect, for example, many fishermen and many plantation owners. Each side needs to find someone they trust to bargain for them, and agree how payments will be shared within each industry. The individuals representing the two groups would be performing a public service that might be difficult to secure.
- *Missing information:* Devising the payment scheme makes it necessary to measure the costs of Weevokil, not just in aggregate, but to each fisherman. We also need to establish the exact origin of the pollutant, plantation by plantation. Only when we have this information can we calculate the size of the payment that each fisherman must pay, and how much each plantation should receive. It's easy to see that it is far harder to make a polluting industry accountable for the damage it does than to calculate the liability for damage done, for example, by a single reckless driver.
- *Tradability and legal enforcement:* The bargain involves the trading of property rights, and the contract governing the trade must be enforceable. Having agreed to pay thousands of dollars, the fishermen must be able to rely on the legal system if a plantation owner does not reduce output as agreed. This may require the fishermen and the courts to discover information about the plantation's operations that are not publicly known or available.
- *Limited funds:* The fishermen may not have enough money to pay the plantation owners to reduce output to 38,000 tonnes (we saw in Unit 9 (page 416) why they would probably not be able to borrow large sums).

In his famous article published in 1960, Coase examined market failure caused by externalities.

James K. Boyce discusses the assumptions and limitations of the Coase theorem. http://tinyco.re/9289964

The pesticide example illustrates that, although correcting market failures through bargaining may not require direct government intervention, it does require a legal framework for enforcing contracts to ensure that all parties stick to the bargains they make. Even with this framework, the problems of collective action, missing information, and enforcement of what are inevitably complex contracts make it unlikely that Coasean bargaining alone can address market failures.

The polluter pays principle

According to the Rio Declaration on Environment and Development (https://tinyco.re/365442), issued in 1992 by the United Nations:

> National authorities should endeavour to promote the internalization of environmental costs and the use of economic instruments, taking into account the approach that the polluter should, in principle, bear the cost of pollution, with due regard to the public interest and without distorting international trade and investment.

> **polluter pays principle** A guide to environmental policy according to which those who impose negative environmental effects on others should be made to pay for the damages they impose, through taxation or other means. *See also: external cost.*

Several of the approaches we describe in this unit are consistent with this principle, called the **polluter pays principle**. Either option—giving the fisherman a right to clean water or enforcing compensation—means that the plantations will have to pay at least as much as the costs incurred by the fishing industry. A tax also means that the polluter pays, although the payment goes to the government rather than the fishing industry. The same abatement could be accomplished by providing the plantation owners with a subsidy for the use of an alternative technology that resulted in a lower level of pollution.

The firm's view of these two policies may be that the tax is the 'stick' and the subsidy the 'carrot'. The tax, which reflects the polluter pays principle, lowers the profits of the firm. A subsidy raises the firm's profits. Whether the carrot or the stick is the right policy depends on the feasibility and cost of implementing the subsidy compared to the tax, and whether raising or lowering the income of the target of the policy is desired on fairness grounds.

Seen in this light, the polluter pays principle is not always a good guide to the best policy. Think of a large city in a low-income country in which much of the cooking is still done over wood fires, generating high levels of airborne particulate matter and causing asthma and other respiratory illnesses:

- *Fairness:* It is mostly poor families who lack the income or access to electricity that would allow them to cook and heat their homes with fewer external environmental effects. In this case, many would object to making the polluters pay on the grounds of fairness, and instead favour subsidizing kerosene or providing a better electricity supply.
- *Effectiveness:* Subsidizing kerosene is likely to be cost effective in reducing smog, compared to tracking down and extracting payments from hundreds of thousands of people who are polluting the city's air with wood fires.

> **EXERCISE 11.2 BARGAINING POWER**
> In the example of plantation owners and fishermen, explain some factors that might affect the bargaining power of these parties.

> **EXERCISE 11.3 A POSITIVE EXTERNAL EFFECT**
> Imagine a beekeeper, who produces honey and sells it at a constant price per kilogram.
>
> 1. Draw a diagram with the quantity of honey on the horizontal axis, showing the marginal cost of honey production as an upward-sloping line, and the price of honey as a horizontal line. Show the amount of honey that the profit-maximizing beekeeper produces.
> 2. For the beekeeper, the **marginal private benefit (MPB)** of producing a kilogram of honey is equal to the price. But since the bees benefit a neighbouring farmer by helping to pollinate her crops, honey production has a positive external effect. Draw a line on your diagram to represent the **marginal social benefit (MSB)** of honey production. Show the quantity of honey that would be Pareto efficient. How does it compare with the quantity chosen by the beekeeper?
> 3. Explain how the farmer and beekeeper could both be made better off through bargaining.

> **marginal private benefit (MPB)** The benefit (in terms of profit, or utility) of producing or consuming an additional unit of a good for the individual who decides to produce or consume it, not taking into account any benefit received by others.
> **marginal social benefit (MSB)** The benefit (in terms of utility) of producing or consuming an additional unit of a good, taking into account both the benefit to the individual who decides to produce or consume it, and the benefit to anyone else affected by the decision.

QUESTION 11.3 CHOOSE THE CORRECT ANSWER(S)

The graph depicts the MPC and MSC of production by the robot factory introduced in Question 11.2 (page 496).

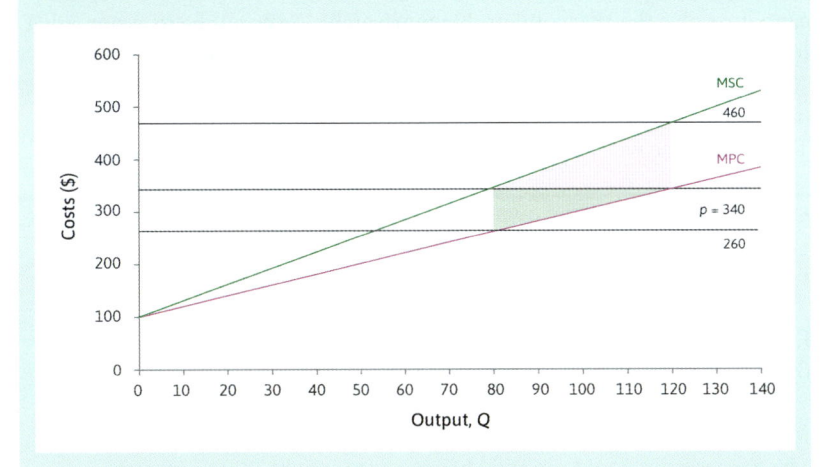

Figure 11.6 Robot factory production.

The robot market is competitive and the market price is $340. Currently, the factory is producing an output of 120, but 80 would be Pareto efficient. Which of the following statements are correct?

- ☐ To reduce output to 80, the factory's minimum acceptable payment would be $1,600.
- ☐ The maximum that the nurses are willing to pay to induce the factory to reduce the output to 80 is $2,400.
- ☐ The factory would not reduce its output to 80 unless it received at least $4,000.
- ☐ The net social gain from the output reduction to 80 depends on the amount paid by the nurses to the factory.

QUESTION 11.4 CHOOSE THE CORRECT ANSWER(S)

Consider the situation in which the noise of a factory's production affects nurses in the dormitory next door. If there are no transaction costs to impede Coasean bargaining, which of the following statements are correct?

- ☐ Whether the final output level is Pareto efficient depends on who has the initial property rights.
- ☐ The nurses would be better off in the bargained allocation if they initially had a right to undisturbed sleep than they would if the factory has the right to make noise.
- ☐ If the factory has the right to make noise, it will prefer not to bargain with the nurses.
- ☐ If the nurses have the initial rights, they will obtain all the net social gain from robot production.

11.9 EXTERNAL EFFECTS: GOVERNMENT POLICIES AND INCOME DISTRIBUTION

Suppose in the case of our Weevokil example that Coasean bargaining proves to be impractical, and that the fisherman and plantation owners cannot resolve the Weevokil problem privately. We continue to assume that it is not possible to grow bananas without using Weevokil.

What can the government do to achieve a reduction in the output of bananas to the level that takes into account the costs for the fishermen? There are three ways this might be done:

- *regulation:* capping the quantity of bananas produced
- *taxation:* charged on the production or sale of bananas
- *compensation:* for the costs imposed on the fishermen.

Each of these policies has different distributional implications for the fisherman and plantation owners.

Regulation

The government could cap total banana output at 38,000 tonnes, the Pareto-efficient amount. This looks like a straightforward solution. On the other hand, if the plantations differ in size and output, it may be difficult to determine and enforce the right quota for each one.

This policy would reduce the costs of pollution for the fishermen, but it would lower the plantation owners' profits. They would lose their surplus on each tonne of bananas between 38,000 and 80,000.

The distributional effect of this policy is to shift income from the plantations to the fishermen.

Taxation

Figure 11.7 shows the MPC and MSC curves again. At the Pareto-efficient quantity (38,000 tonnes), the MSC is $400 and the MPC is $295. The price is $400. If the government puts a tax on each tonne of bananas produced, equal to $400 − $295 = $105 (the marginal external cost), then the after-tax price received by plantations is $295. Now, if plantation owners maximize their profit, they will choose the point where the after-tax price equals the marginal private cost and produce 38,000 tonnes, the Pareto-efficient quantity. Use the analysis in Figure 11.7 to see how this policy works.

The tax corrects the message conveyed by the price of bananas, so that the plantations face the full marginal social cost of their decisions and choose to produce less. When the plantations are producing 38,000 tonnes of bananas, the tax is exactly equal to the cost imposed on the fishermen. This approach is known as a **Pigouvian tax**, after the economist Arthur Pigou who advocated it. It also works in the case of a positive external effect; the marginal social benefit of a decision is greater than the marginal private benefit (MPB), this becomes a Pigouvian subsidy, which can ensure that the decision-maker takes this **external benefit** into account.

The distributional effects of taxation are different from those of regulation. The costs of pollution for fishermen are reduced by the same amount, but the reduction in banana profits is greater, since the plantation owners pay taxes as well as reducing output, and the government receives tax revenue.

Pigouvian tax A tax levied on activities that generate negative external effects so as to correct an inefficient market outcome. *See also: external effect, Pigouvian subsidy.*

external benefit A positive external effect: that is, a positive effect of a production, consumption, or other economic decision on another person or people that is not specified as a benefit in a contract. *Also known as: external economy. See also: external effect.*

11.9 EXTERNAL EFFECTS: GOVERNMENT POLICIES AND INCOME DISTRIBUTION

Compensation
The government could require the plantation owners to pay compensation for costs imposed on the fishermen. The compensation required for each tonne of bananas is equal to the difference between the MSC and the MPC, which is the distance between the green and purple lines in Figure 11.8. Once compensation is included, the marginal cost of each tonne of bananas is the MPC plus the compensation, which is equal to the MSC. Now the plantation owners will maximize profit by choosing point P_2 in Figure 11.8 and produce 38,000 tonnes. The shaded area shows the total compensation paid. The fishermen are fully compensated for pollution, and the plantation owners' profits are equal to the true social surplus of banana production.

The effect of this policy on the plantation owners' profits is similar to the effect of the tax, but the fishermen do better because they, rather than the government, receive payment from the plantations.

Diagnosis and treatment in the case of chlordecone
When we identified 38,000 tonnes as the Pareto-efficient level of output in our model, we assumed that growing bananas inevitably involves Weevokil pollution. Our diagnosis was that too many bananas were being produced, and we looked at policies for reducing production.

The correct diagnosis
In real life, in Guadeloupe and Martinique, there were alternatives to chlordecone. Therefore the problem was caused by the *use* of chlordecone, not the *production* of bananas.

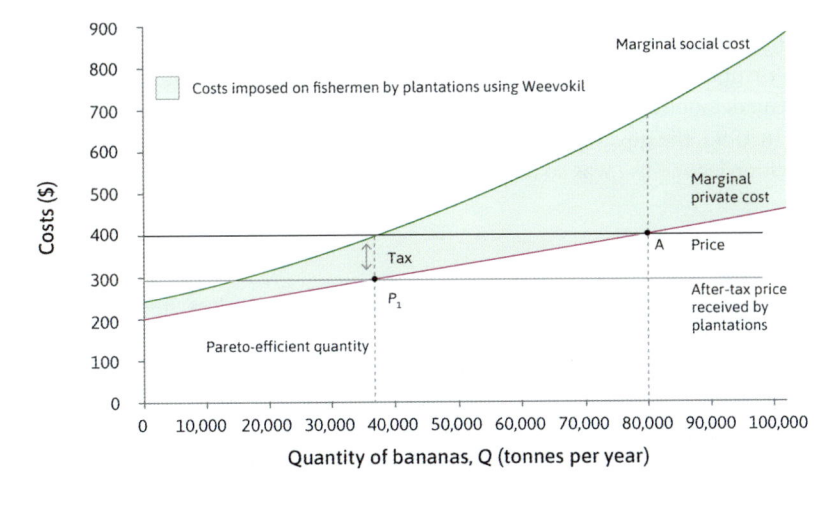

Figure 11.7 Using a tax to achieve Pareto efficiency.

To explore all of the slides in this figure, see the online version at https://tinyco.re/1933000.

1. The marginal external cost
At the Pareto-efficient quantity, 38,000 tonnes, the MPC is $295. The MSC is $400. Therefore, the marginal external cost is MSC − MPC = $105.

2. Tax = MSC − MPC
If the government puts a tax on each tonne of bananas produced equal to $105, the marginal external cost, then the after-tax price received by plantations is $295.

3. The after-tax price is $295
To maximize profit, the plantation owners will choose their output so that the MPC is equal to the after-tax price. They will choose point P_1 and produce 38,000 tonnes.

505

The market failure occurred because the price of chlordecone did not incorporate the costs that its use inflicted on the fishermen, and so it sent the wrong message to the firm. Its low price said: 'Use this chemical, it will save you money and raise profits. However, if its price had included the full external costs of its use, it might have been high enough to have said: 'Think about the downstream damage and look for an alternative way to grow bananas.'

The best treatment

In this situation, a policy of requiring the plantation owners to compensate the fishermen would have given them the incentive to find production methods that caused less pollution and could, in principle, have achieved an efficient outcome.

But the other two policies would not do so. Rather than taxing or regulating *banana* production, it would be better to regulate or tax the sale or the use of *chlordecone*, to motivate plantations to find the best alternative to intensive chlordecone use.

In theory, if the tax on a unit of chlordecone was equal to its marginal external cost, the price of chlordecone for the plantations would be equal to its marginal social cost, which would send the right message about the choice of pest control method. The plantation owners could then choose the best production method, taking into account the high cost of chlordecone. This would involve reducing the use of chlordecone or switching to a different pesticide, and would determine their profit-maximizing output. As with the banana tax, the profits of the plantation owners and the pollution costs for the fishermen would fall, but the outcome would be better for the plantations, and possibly the fishermen also, if chlordecone were taxed instead of bananas.

What actually happened?

Unfortunately, none of these remedies was used for 20 years, and the people of Guadeloupe and Martinique are still living with the consequences.

In 1993, the government finally recognized that the marginal social cost of chlordecone use was so high that it should be banned altogether.

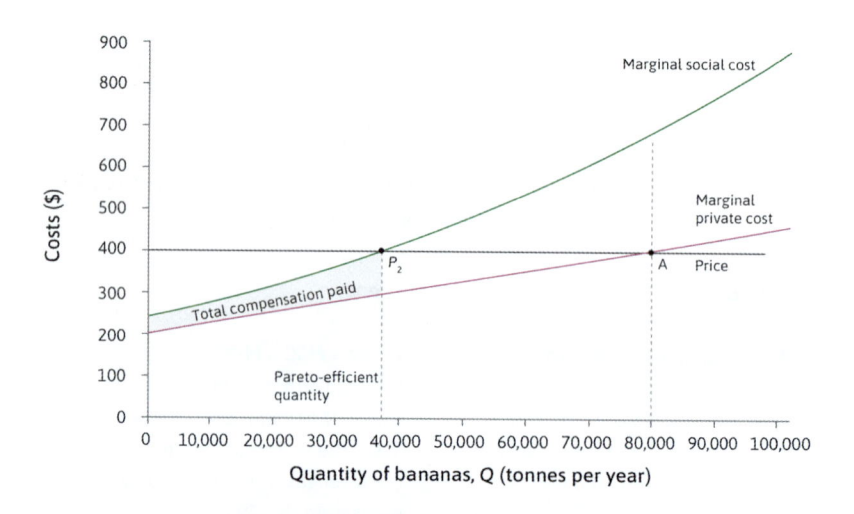

Figure 11.8 The plantation owners compensate the fishermen.

11.9 EXTERNAL EFFECTS: GOVERNMENT POLICIES AND INCOME DISTRIBUTION

Chlordecone was first listed as carcinogenic in 1979. It was obvious that the external costs were much higher than in our case of Weevokil, damaging the health of islanders as well as the livelihood of fishermen. In fact, the marginal social cost of any bananas produced with the aid of chlordecone was higher than their market price, justifying an outright ban on its use.

The pollution turned out to be much worse than anyone realized at the time, and is likely to persist in the soil for 700 years. In 2013, fishermen in Martinique barricaded the port of Fort de France with their boats until the French government agreed to allocate $2.6 million in aid.

Limits to the success of tax, regulation, and compensation remedies

There are limits to how well governments can implement Pigouvian taxes, regulation and compensation—often for the same reasons as for Coasean bargaining:

- *The government may not know the degree of harm suffered by each fisherman:* As a result, it can't create the best compensation policy.
- *Marginal social costs are difficult to measure:* While the plantations' marginal private costs are probably well known, it is harder to determine marginal social costs, such as the pollution costs, to individuals or to society as a whole. Furthermore, it matters who owns the rights in the first place as the willingness-to-pay for clean air may be significantly different than the willingness to accept air pollution as shown in a UMassEconomics video featuring James K. Boyce (http://tinyco.re/2507039).
- *The government may favour the more powerful group:* In this case, it could impose a Pareto-efficient outcome that is also unfair, such as having the fishermen compensate the plantations for reducing production of bananas.

James K. Boyce discusses the difficulties in ensuring efficiency and fairness when addressing negative externalities. http://tinyco.re/2507039

GREAT ECONOMISTS

Arthur Pigou

Arthur Pigou (1877–1959) was a pioneer in using economics for the good of society, which is why he is sometimes seen as the founder of welfare economics. He won awards in history, languages, and moral sciences (there was no dedicated economics degree at the time) during his studies at the University of Cambridge. He became a protégé of Alfred Marshall. Pigou was an outgoing and lively person when young, but his experiences as a conscientious objector and ambulance driver during the First World War, as well as anxieties over his own health, turned him into a recluse who hid in his office except for lectures and walks.

Arthur Pigou. 1912. *Wealth and Welfare* (https://tinyco.re/2519065). London: Macmillan & Co.

Arthur Pigou. 1920. *The Economics of Welfare* (http://tinyco.re/2042156). London: Macmillan & Co.

His book *Wealth and Welfare* was described by Joseph Schumpeter as 'the greatest venture in labour economics ever undertaken by a man who was primarily a theorist', and provided the foundation for his later work, *The Economics of Welfare*. Together, these works built up a relationship between a nation's economy and the welfare of its people. Pigou focused on happiness and wellbeing. He recognized that concepts such as political freedom and relative status were important.

Pigou believed that the reallocation of resources was necessary when the interests of a private firm or individual diverged from the interests of society, causing what we would today call external effects. He suggested that taxation could solve the problem; Pigouvian taxes are intended to ensure that producers face the true social costs of their decisions.

Pigouvian taxes were largely unrecognized until the 1960s, but they have become a major policy tool for reducing pollution and environmental damage.

Now we can extend the table we started creating in Section 11.7 (Figure 11.4 (page 496)). Look at the fifth column in Figure 11.9—it adds the possible remedies for the problem of negative external effects.

EXERCISE 11.4 PIGOUVIAN SUBSIDY
Consider the beekeeper and neighbouring farmer in Exercise 11.3 (page 502).

1. Why might they be unable to bargain successfully to achieve a Pareto-efficient outcome in practice? Use the diagram you drew to show how the government might improve the situation by subsidizing honey production.
2. Describe the distributional effects of this subsidy, and compare it to the Pareto-efficient bargaining outcome.

EXERCISE 11.5 COMPARING POLICIES
Consider the three policies of regulation, taxation, and compensation arrangements discussed above. Evaluate the strengths and weaknesses of each policy from the standpoint of Pareto efficiency and fairness.

Decision	How it affects others	Cost or benefit	Market failure (misallocation of resources)	Possible remedies	Terms applied to this type of market failure
A firm uses a pesticide that runs off into waterways	Downstream damage	Private benefit, external cost	Overuse of pesticide and overproduction of the crop for which it is used	Taxes, quotas, bans, bargaining, common ownership of all affected assets	Negative external effect, environmental spillover

Figure 11.9 Water pollution market failure, with remedies.

QUESTION 11.5 CHOOSE THE CORRECT ANSWER(S)

Look back at Figure 11.6 (page 503), which showed the MPC and MSC of robot production for the factory situated next to a dormitory for nurses who work nightshifts.

The market for robots is competitive and the market price is $340. The initial output is 120, but the government uses a Pigouvian tax to reduce this to the efficient level of 80. Which of the following statements are correct?

- ☐ Under the Pigouvian tax, the factory's surplus is $6,400.
- ☐ The required Pigouvian tax is $120 per robot.
- ☐ The nurses are at least as well off as they would be under Coasean bargaining.
- ☐ The nurses obtain no benefit from the imposition of the Pigouvian tax.

11.10 PROPERTY RIGHTS, CONTRACTS, AND MARKET FAILURES

In taking an action to maximize profits (choosing the level of banana production or the choice of pesticide), the plantation owners did not take account of the external costs they imposed on the fishermen. And they had no reason to take account of them—they had the right to pollute the fisheries and it cost them nothing to do so.

The same is true for the overuse of antibiotics analysed in Unit 2 (page 49). A self-interested person has no reason to use antibiotics sparingly, because the superbug that may be created will probably infect someone else.

If the prices of chlordecone and the antibiotic were high enough, there would be no overuse. But the prices of these goods were based on the costs of production and excluded costs that their use would inflict on others. As you have seen, the private cost to the user (how much he paid to acquire the good) fell short of the social cost for this reason.

Another example: when automobile fuel costs are low, more people decide to drive to work rather than taking the train. The message conveyed by the low price ('It's not very costly to use your car') does not include the environmental costs of deciding to drive. The effects on the decision-maker are termed private costs and benefits, while the total effects, including those inflicted or enjoyed by others, are social costs and benefits.

Costs inflicted on others (such as pollution and congestion that are worse because you drive to work) are termed **external diseconomies** or **negative external effects**, while uncompensated benefits conferred on others are **external economies** or **positive external effects**.

We can understand why market failures are common by thinking about how they could be avoided.

How could the cost of driving to work accurately reflect all the costs incurred by anyone, not just the private costs made by the decision-maker? The most obvious (if impractical) way would be to require the driver to pay everyone affected by the resultant environmental damage (or traffic congestion) an amount exactly equal to the damage inflicted. This is, of course, impossible to do, but it sets a standard of what should be done or approximated if the 'price of driving to work' is to send the correct message to the decision-maker.

external diseconomy A negative effect of a production, consumption, or other economic decision, that is not specified as a liability in a contract. Also known as: *external cost, negative externality*. See also: *external effect*.

external economy A positive effect of a production, consumption, or other economic decision, that is not specified as a benefit in a contract. Also known as: *external benefit, positive externality*. See also: *external effect*.

Something like this approach applies if you drive recklessly on the way to work, skid off the road, and crash into somebody's house. Tort law (the law of damages) in most countries would require you to pay for repairing the damage to the house. You are held liable for the damages so that you would pay the cost you had inflicted on another. Knowing this, you might think twice about driving to work (or at least slow down a bit when you are late). It will change your behaviour and the allocation of resources.

But while tort law in most countries covers some kinds of harm inflicted on others (reckless driving), other important external effects of driving your car (such as adding to air pollution or congestion) are not necessarily covered. Here are two further examples:

- *A firm operates an incinerator that produces fumes:* The fumes lower the surrounding air quality. Those being polluted do not have a right to clean air, which is the right that would be the basis for a claim for compensation from the firm. Therefore, the firm does not have to pay these costs.
- *You play music loudly at night and disturb the sleep of the people next door:* Sleeping neighbours do not have an enforceable right not to be woken by your music. There is no way that your neighbours can make you pay them compensation for the inconvenience you cause.

Legal systems also fail to provide compensation for the benefits that one's actions confer on others:

- *A firm trains a worker who quits for a better job:* The skills of the trained worker go with them to the new job. Therefore, even though a different firm receives the benefit, the firm that paid for the training cannot collect compensation from the new firm.
- *Kim, the farmer in Section 2.7 (page 66), contributes to the cost of an irrigation project while other farmers free ride on Kim's contribution:* Kim has no way of claiming payment for this public-spirited act. The free riders do not compensate Kim.
- *A country invests in reducing carbon emissions that lower the risks of climate change for other countries:* As we saw in Section 2.13 (page 86), unless a treaty guarantees compensation for the costs of reduced emissions, other countries do not need to pay for this. The environmental improvement for the other countries is an uncompensated benefit.

External effects arise because of incomplete contracts and missing markets

Market failures occur in these examples because the external benefits and costs of a person's actions are not owned by anyone. Think about waste. If you redecorate your house and you tear up the floor or knock down a wall, you own the debris and have to dispose of it, even if you need to pay someone to take it away. But this is not the case with fumes from the incinerator or loud music at night. You do not have a contract with the incinerator company specifying at what price you are willing to accept fumes, or with your neighbour about the price of the right to play music after 10 p.m. In these cases, economists say that we have 'incomplete, missing, or unenforceable property rights'—or, simply, **incomplete contracts**.

incomplete contract A contract that does not specify, in an enforceable way, every aspect of the exchange that affects the interests of parties to the exchange (or of any others affected by the exchange).

11.10 PROPERTY RIGHTS, CONTRACTS, AND MARKET FAILURES

We saw an important example of an incomplete contract in Unit 6 (page 268). In the employment relationship, the employer can pay for the worker's time, but the contract cannot specify how much effort the worker must make. Likewise, the external effects of a person's actions are effects that are not governed by contracts. Another way to express the problem is to say that there is no market within which these external effects can be compensated. Economists also use the term **missing markets** to describe problems like this.

In the case of Weevokil pollution:

- *The fishermen's property rights were incomplete:* They did not own a right to clean water in their fisheries, which would enable them to receive compensation for pollution, and they could not purchase such a right.
- *There was no market for clean water.*

Why don't countries just rewrite their laws to reward people for the benefits they confer on others, and make economic actors pay for the costs they inflict on others?

In Unit 6, we reviewed the reasons why the kinds of contracts that would enforce these objectives are incomplete or unenforceable. These are that:

- necessary information is either not available or not **verifiable**
- the external effects are too complex or difficult to measure to be written into an enforceable contract
- there may be no legal system to enforce the contract (as in pollution, which crosses national borders).

You can see in our example that it would not be possible to write a complete set of contracts in which each individual fisherman could receive compensation from each plantation for the effects of its individual decisions.

For these and other reasons, it is impractical in most cases to use tort law to make people liable for the costs they inflict on others. And it is equally infeasible to use the legal system to compensate people for the beneficial effects they have on others, for example, to pay those who keep beautiful gardens an amount equal to the pleasure this confers on those who pass their house. A court would have to know how much that pleasure was worth to each passerby.

In each of the examples in this section (incinerator, loud music, training, irrigation, and climate change), uncompensated external costs and benefits occur for the same reason, as shown in Figure 11.10.

> **missing market** A market in which there is some kind of exchange that, if implemented, would be mutually beneficial. This does not occur due to asymmetric or non-verifiable information.

> **verifiable information** Information that can be used to enforce a contract.

> **EXERCISE 11.6 INCOMPLETE CONTRACTS**
> In each of the five cases above (incinerator, loud music, training, irrigation, and climate change):
>
> 1. Explain why the external effects are not (and possibly cannot be) covered by a complete contract.
> 2. What critical piece(s) of information required for a complete contract are asymmetric or non-verifiable?

11.11 PUBLIC GOODS, COMMON POOL RESOURCES, AND MARKET FAILURE

Public goods and non-rivalry

An extreme form of external effect occurs in the case of public goods. Recall from the experiments described in Unit 2 (page 66) that the defining characteristic of a public good is that, if it is available to one person, it can be available to everyone at no additional cost. An example is a view of the setting sun; your enjoyment of the sunset does not deprive anyone else of their enjoyment. Another is weather forecasting (if I can go online to find out if it's likely to rain today, so can you and everybody else, at no additional cost).

The knowledge assembled in CORE's *Economy, Society, and Public Policy* (and other works) is a public good: access to it by another user does not diminish the availability of it to other users. And because we wanted it to be available to everyone at its marginal cost (which is zero) we have made the material open access online using a Creative Commons licence (https://tinyco.re/5453318).

A weather forecast is a public good, or the online version of the book you are reading, but so is knowledge more generally. You can use your knowledge of a recipe for a cake or the rules of multiplication without affecting the ability of others to use the same knowledge.

In these cases, once the good is available at all, the marginal cost of making it available to additional people is zero. Goods with this characteristic are also called **non-rival goods** because potential users are not in competition with each other (rivals) for the good.

Of course, this is a good thing, but it results in a market failure. Think about a firm considering investing in research. If other firms can freely access and use the knowledge that the research of another firm produces, then the firm's research is providing an external benefit to all other firms. In this case the benefits of the research (including the positive external effects) may far exceed the costs to the particular firm. But because the firm does not capture these benefits (as profits) it will invest less in research than would make sense if all of the benefits were considered.

Sometimes economists refer to '**public bads**', which are just a negative kind of public good: something that people dislike, which, if it is experi-

> **non-rival good** A good that, if available to anyone, is available to everyone at no additional cost. *See also: rival good, non-excludable public good.*
>
> **public bad** The negative equivalent of a public good. It is non-rival in the sense that a given individual's consumption of the public bad does not diminish others' consumption of it.
>
> **asymmetric information** Information that is relevant to all the parties in an economic interaction, but is known by some and not by others. *See also: adverse selection, moral hazard.*

| Information that is of concern to someone other than the decision-maker is non-verifiable or **asymmetric** |

⇩

| There can be no contract or property rights ensuring that external effects are compensated. |

⇩

| Some of the social costs or benefits of the decision-maker's actions are not included (or are not sufficiently important) in the decision-making process. |

Figure 11.10 How external costs and benefits occur.

enced by anyone it is 'available' to all. Exposure to an adverse climate change falls under this heading.

Artificial scarcity: Excluding users from a non-rival good
For some public goods, it is possible to exclude additional users, even though the additional cost of using it is zero. Examples are satellite TV, the information in a **copyrighted** book, or a film shown in an uncrowded cinema; it costs no more if an additional viewer is there, but the owner can nonetheless require that anyone who wants to see the film must pay. The same goes for an uncrowded road on which toll gates have been erected. Drivers can be excluded (unless they pay the toll) even though the marginal cost of an additional traveller is zero.

Public goods for which it is feasible to exclude others are sometimes called **artificially scarce goods** or **club goods**, because they function like joining a private club—when the golf course is not crowded, adding one more member costs the golf club nothing, but the club will still charge a membership fee. (Some economists exclude club goods from the category of public goods, defining a public good as not only non-rival, but also non-excludable).

> **copyright** Ownership rights over the use and distribution of an original work.
> **artificially scarce good** A public good for which it is possible to exclude some people from enjoying. *Also known as:* club good. *See also:* public good.
> **common-pool resource** A rival good that one cannot prevent others from enjoying. *Also known as:* common property resource. *See also:* rival good.

Common-pool resources: Rival but non-excludable goods
The opposite of artificially scarce or club goods (that are non-rival but excludable) are **common pool resources** which are rival, but not excludable. An example is fisheries that are open to all. What one fisherman catches cannot be caught by anyone else, but anyone who wants to fish can do so. We can also think of busy public roads as a common-pool resource. Anyone who chooses to use them may do so, but each user makes the road more congested and slows down the journeys of others.

Non-rivalry, non-excludability and market failures
Figure 11.11 shows four distinct categories of goods, including private goods. These are both rival and excludable, things like portions of a cake, plots of land, flights to your dream vacation spot, and many of the products we have already studied like one-on-one language tutorials, and Cheerios.

Both the extent of rivalry or excludability in goods is a matter of degree. For some kinds of goods, the cost of additional users is not literally zero (which is what pure non-rivalry would require), but instead very small. An example is a medical drug that cost millions in research funds to create the first pill, but only cents per application to make treatments available to additional users once created. The knowledge that makes the drug possible is the major cost, and it is a public good; the pill in which the knowledge is embodied and delivered to the patient is both rival and excludable, and hence private.

	Rival	Non-rival
Excludable	Private goods (food, clothes, houses, most forms of medical care)	Public goods that are artificially scarce (subscription TV, uncongested toll roads, knowledge subject to intellectual property rights)
Non-excludable	Common-pool resources (fish stocks in a lake, common grazing land)	Non-excludable public goods and bads (view of a lunar eclipse, public broadcasts, rules of arithmetic or calculus, national defence, noise and air pollution)

Figure 11.11 Private goods and public goods.

As can be seen from the examples, whether a good is private or public depends not only on the nature of the good itself, but also on legal and other institutions:

- Knowledge that is not subject to copyright or other intellectual property rights would be classified as a non-excludable public good (like the CORE textbooks).
- But when the author uses copyright law to create a monopoly on the right to reproduce that knowledge, it is a public good that is artificially scarce (like most textbooks).
- Common grazing land is a common-pool resource.
- But if the same land is fenced to exclude other users, it becomes a private good.

As you can see from the example in Figure 11.11, governments play an important role in the provision of public goods. Some important private goods, too, are produced and allocated by governments, for example, in many countries, medical care.

Most private goods are allocated in markets. Where external effects are absent or minor, the results may be Pareto efficient.

But for the other three kinds of good, markets are either not possible or very likely to fail. There are two reasons:

- *When goods are non-rival, the marginal cost of an additional user is zero:* Setting a price equal to marginal cost (as is necessary for a Pareto-efficient market transaction) would bankrupt the seller, and hence is not possible unless the provider is subsidized.
- *When goods are not excludable, there is no way to charge a price for them:* The provider cannot exclude people who haven't paid.

Market failure in the case of public goods is closely related to the problems discussed earlier in this unit—external effects, absent property rights, and incomplete contracts. We analysed Weevokil pollution as a problem in which the decisions of banana plantation owners imposed a negative external effect on fisherman. The private cost of using Weevokil was below the social cost, so the pesticide was overused. But we can also interpret the plantations as contributing to a public bad, suffered by all the fishermen.

The user of a common-pool resource imposes an external cost on other users. By driving your car on a busy road, for example, you contribute to the congestion experienced by other drivers.

Thus, any of the examples of non-private goods introduced in this section can be described using the framework we set up in Section 11.9 (page 504) to summarize cases of market failure. See the table in Figure 11.12.

11.11 PUBLIC GOODS, COMMON POOL RESOURCES, AND MARKET FAILURE

EXERCISE 11.7 RIVALRY AND EXCLUDABILITY
For each of the following goods or bads, decide whether they are rival and whether they are excludable, and explain your answer. If you think the answer depends on factors not specified here, explain how.

1. a free public lecture held at a university lecture theatre
2. noise produced by aircraft around an international airport
3. a public park
4. a forest used by local people to collect firewood
5. seats in a theatre to watch a musical
6. this e-text, *Economy, Society, and Public Policy*
7. bicycles available to the public to hire to travel around a city.

QUESTION 11.6 CHOOSE THE CORRECT ANSWER(S)
Which of the following statements are correct?

☐ Some public goods are rival.
☐ A public good must be non-excludable.
☐ A good cannot be rival and non-excludable.
☐ If a good is non-rival, then the cost of an additional person consuming it is zero.

Decision	How it affects others	Cost or benefit	Market failure (misallocation of resources)	Possible policy remedies	Terms applied to this type of market failure
You take an international flight	Increase in global carbon emissions	Private benefit, external cost	Overuse of air travel	Taxes, quotas	Public bad, negative external effect
You travel to work by car	Congestion for other road users	Private cost, external cost	Overuse of cars	Tolls, quotas, subsidized public transport, tax on petrol	Common-pool resource, negative external effect
A firm invests in R&D	Other firms can exploit the innovation	Private cost, external benefit	Too little R&D	Publicly funded research, subsidies for R&D, patents	Public good, positive external effect

Figure 11.12 Examples of market failure, with remedies.

515

11.12 MISSING MARKETS: INSURANCE AND LEMONS

> **asymmetric information** Information that is relevant to all the parties in an economic interaction, but is known by some and not by others. *See also: adverse selection, moral hazard.*

We know that a common reason for contracts to be incomplete is that information about an important aspect of the interaction is unavailable, or unverifiable. Information is often **asymmetric**—that is, one party knows something relevant to the transaction that the other doesn't know.

One form of asymmetric information is a **hidden action**. In Unit 6 (page 249) we studied the case of the employee whose choice of how hard to work is hidden from the employer. This causes a problem known as **moral hazard**. There is a conflict of interest because the employee would prefer not to work as hard as the employer would like, and work effort cannot be specified in the contract. We also saw in Unit 6 (page 257) how the employer's response (paying a wage above the reservation level) led to involuntary unemployment, which is a Pareto-inefficient outcome in the labour market.

In this section, we introduce a second form of asymmetric information, that of **hidden attributes**. When you want to purchase a used car, for example, the seller knows the quality of the vehicle. You do not. This attribute of the car is hidden from the prospective buyer. Hidden attributes can cause a problem known as **adverse selection**.

Hidden attributes and adverse selection

George Akerlof, an economist, was the first to analyse what came to be called the 'lemons problem' in 1970. (In addition to being a fruit, a 'lemon' is something which after being purchased turns out to be faulty.) Initially his paper on the subject was rejected by two economics journals for being trivial. Another returned it, saying that it was incorrect. Thirty-one years later, he was awarded the Nobel Prize for this work.

Hidden actions and moral hazard

The problem of hidden action occurs when some action taken by one party to an exchange is not known or cannot be verified by the other. For example, the employer cannot know (or cannot verify) how hard the worker is actually working.

The term moral hazard originated in the insurance industry to express the problem that insurers face, namely, the person with home insurance may take less care to avoid fires or other damages to his home, thereby increasing the risk above what it would be in absence of insurance. This term now refers to any situation in which one party to an interaction is deciding on an action that affects the profits or wellbeing of the other but which the affected party cannot control by means of a contract, often because the affected party does not have adequate information on the action. It is also referred to as the hidden actions problem.

Hidden attributes and adverse selection

The problem of hidden attributes occurs when some attribute of the person engaging in an exchange (or the product or service being provided) is not known to the other parties. An example is that the individual purchasing health insurance knows her own health status, but the insurance company does not.

The term adverse selection refers to the problem faced by parties to an exchange in which the terms offered by one party will cause some exchange partners to drop out. An example is the problem of asymmetric information in insurance: if the price is sufficiently high, the only people who seek to purchase medical insurance are people who know they are ill (but the insurer does not). This will lead to further price increases to cover costs. Also referred to as the 'hidden attributes' problem (the state of already being ill is the hidden attribute), to distinguish it from the 'hidden actions' problem of moral hazard.

A famous example of how hidden attributes may result in a market failure is known as the *market for lemons*. The model describes a used-car market:

- Every day, ten owners of ten used cars consider selling.
- The cars differ in quality, which we measure by the true value of the car to its owner. Quality ranges from zero to $9,000 in equal steps—there is one worthless car, one worth $1,000, another worth $2,000, and so on. The average value of the cars is thus $4,500.
- There are many prospective buyers and each would happily buy a car for a price equal to its true value, but not more.
- Sellers do not expect to receive the full value of their vehicle, but they are willing to sell if they can get more than half the true value. So the total surplus on each car—the gain from trading it—is half the price of the car.

If prospective buyers were able to observe the quality of every car, then buyers would approach each seller and bargain over the price, and by the end of the day all the cars (except for the entirely worthless one) would be sold at a price somewhere between their true value and half the true value. The market would have assured that all mutually beneficial trades would take place.

But, on any day, there is a problem—potential buyers have no information about the quality of any car that is for sale. All they know is the price at which cars sold the previous day. The most that prospective buyers are willing to pay for a car is the average value of the cars sold the day before.

Now suppose that ten cars had been offered on the market the day before. We use a proof by contradiction to show that one by one, the sellers of the highest quality cars will drop out of the market, until there is no market for used cars. Consider the market today, as shown in Figure 11.13:

Economists call processes like this adverse selection because the prevailing price selects which cars are left in the market. If any cars are traded, they will be the lower quality ones. The selection of cars is adverse for buyers. In the example above, there are no cars left at all—the market disappears altogether.

Adverse selection in the market for health insurance

The market for lemons is a well-known term in economics, but the lemons problem—that is, the problem of hidden attributes—is not restricted to the used-car market.

Another important example is health insurance. Imagine that you were born into a population in which you do not know whether you would have a serious health problem or develop such a problem later in life, or perhaps be entirely healthy until old age. There is a health insurance policy available covering any medical services you may need, and the premium is the same for everyone; it is set according to the average expected medical costs of people in the population. For the insurance company, the premiums will cover the total expected payout, assuming everyone signs up. Would you buy this health insurance policy?

Akerlof and co-author Robert Shiller give a simple explanation of the so-called market for lemons in this book: George A. Akerlof and Robert J. Shiller. 2015. *Phishing for Phools: The Economics of Manipulation and Deception.* Princeton, NJ: Princeton University Press. Watch Robert Shiller's TED talk on the book (https://tinyco.re/8503899).

Yesterday, all the cars (as we assumed at the start) were put on the market and sold. The average value of these cars was $4,500, so the most a buyer is willing to pay today is $4,500.

⇩

At the beginning of the day, each prospective seller considers selling their car, expecting a price of $4,500 at the most. Most of the owners are happy, because it is more than half the true value of their cars. But one owner isn't pleased. The owner of the best car will not sell unless the price exceeds half the value of his car—more than $4,500.

⇩

Prospective buyers will not pay this price. Therefore, the owner of the best car will not offer it for sale today. No one with a car worth $9,000 is willing to participate in this market.

⇩

The rest of the cars will sell today; their value averages $4,000.

⇩

Tomorrow, buyers will know the average value of the cars sold today. Therefore, buyers will decide they are willing to pay at most $4,000 for a car tomorrow.

⇩

The owner of tomorrow's highest-quality car (the one worth $8,000) will know this, and know that she will not get her minimum price, which is greater than $4,000. Tomorrow, she will not offer her car for sale.

⇩

As a result, the average quality of cars sold on the market tomorrow will be $3,500, which means the owner of the third-best car will not put his car up for sale the day after tomorrow.

⇩

And so it goes on, until, at some point next week, only the owner of a lemon worth $1,000 and a totally worthless car will remain in that day's market.

⇩

If cars of these two values had sold the previous day, then, the next day, buyers would be willing to pay at most $500 for a car.

⇩

Knowing this, the owner of the car worth $1,000 will decide she would rather keep her car.

⇩

The only car on the market will be worth nothing. Cars that remain in this market are lemons, because only the owner of a worthless car would be prepared to offer that car for sale.

Figure 11.13 The market for lemons.

In this situation, most people would be happy to purchase the policy, because serious illness imposes high costs that are often impossible for an average family to pay. The costs of protecting you and your family from a financial catastrophe (or the possibility that you can't afford healthcare when you need it) are worth the insurance premium.

The assumption that you do not know anything about your health status in this thought experiment is unrealistic. It is another use of John Rawls' veil of ignorance, discussed in Unit 3 (page 115). Thinking about this problem as an impartial observer highlights the importance of the veil of ignorance assumption.

Though everyone would have bought insurance if they did not know about their future health status, the situation changes dramatically if we can choose whether to buy health insurance without the veil of ignorance, that is, knowing our health status. In this situation, information is asymmetric. Look at the situation from the standpoint of the insurance company:

- *People are more likely to purchase insurance if they know that they are ill:* Therefore, the average health of people buying insurance is poorer than the average health of the population.
- *This information is asymmetric:* The person buying the insurance knows how healthy they are, but the insurance company does not.
- *Insurance companies will only be profitable if they charge higher prices:* These prices would be higher than they would charge if all members of the population were forced to purchase the same insurance.
- *This leads to adverse selection:* In which case, the price is high enough that only people who know they are ill would wish to purchase insurance.
- *This leads to even higher prices for insurance:* To remain in business, the insurance companies now have to raise prices again. Eventually, the vast majority of the people purchasing insurance are those who already know that they have a serious health problem.
- *Healthy people are priced out of the market:* Those who want to buy insurance in case they fall ill in the future will not do so.

This is another example of a missing market: many people will be uninsured. It is a market that could exist, but only if health information were symmetrical and verifiable (ignoring for the moment the problem of whether everyone would want to share their health data). It could provide benefits to both insurance company owners and people who wanted to insure themselves. Not having such a market is Pareto inefficient.

To address the problem of adverse selection due to asymmetric information, and the resulting missing markets for health insurance, many countries have adopted policies of compulsory enrolment in private insurance programs or universal tax-financed coverage, so that the healthy and the lucky pay the medical costs of the unhealthy and the unlucky.

Moral hazard in the insurance market
Hidden attributes are not the only problem facing insurers, whether private or governmental. There is also a problem of hidden actions. Buying an insurance policy may make the buyer more likely to take exactly the risks that are now insured. For example, a person who has purchased full coverage against damage or theft of his car may take less care in driving or locking the car than someone who has not purchased insurance.

Insurers typically place limits on the insurance they sell. For example, coverage may not apply (or may be more expensive) if someone other than the insured is driving, or if the car is usually parked in a place where a lot of cars are stolen. These provisions can be written into an insurance contract.

But the insurer cannot enforce a contract about how fast you drive or whether you drive after having had a drink. These are the actions that are hidden from the insurer because of the asymmetric information—you know these facts, but the insurance company does not.

This is a problem of moral hazard, similar to the one of labour effort. They are both **principal–agent problems**—the agent (an insured person, or employee) chooses an action (how careful to be, or how hard to work) that matters to the principal (the insurance company, or the employer), but the action cannot be included in the contract because it is not verifiable.

Though seemingly very different from the problem of chlordecone pollution or from public goods and common-pool resources described in the previous section, these moral hazard problems are similar in an important respect. In every case, someone makes a decision that has external costs or benefits for someone else. In other words, costs or benefits that are uncompensated. For example, in the moral hazard case, the insured person (the agent) decides how much care to take. Taking care has an external benefit for the insurer (principal) but is costly for the agent; consequently we have a market failure—the level of care chosen is too low.

Therefore, these problems of moral hazard (and also the adverse selection problems described earlier in this section) can be placed within the framework of external effects and market failure we are using throughout this unit. The problems arising from asymmetric information are summarized in the table in Figure 11.14.

> **principal–agent relationship** This is an asymmetrical relationship in which one party (the principal) benefits from some action or attribute of the other party (the agent) about which the principal's information is not sufficient to enforce in a complete contract. *See also: incomplete contract. Also known as: principal–agent problem.*

Decision	How it affects others	Cost or benefit	Market failure (misallocation of resources)	Possible remedies	Terms applied to this type of market failure
An employee on a fixed wage decides how hard to work	Hard work raises employer's profits	Private cost, external benefit	Too little effort, wage above reservation wage, unemployment	More effective monitoring, performance-related pay, reduced conflict of interest between employer and employee	Incomplete labour contract, hidden action, moral hazard
Someone who knows he has a serious health problem buys insurance	Loss for insurance company	Private benefit, external cost	Too little insurance offered, insurance premiums too high	Mandatory purchase of health insurance, public provision, mandatory health information sharing	Missing markets, adverse selection
Someone who has purchased car insurance decides how carefully to drive	Prudent driving contributes to insurance company's profits	Private cost, external benefit	Too little insurance offered, insurance premiums too high	Installing driver-monitoring devices	Missing markets, moral hazard

Figure 11.14 Asymmetric information, market failures, with remedies.

EXERCISE 11.8 HIDDEN ATTRIBUTES

1. Identify the hidden attributes in the following markets and how they may impede market participants from exploiting all the possible mutual gains from exchange:
   (a) a second-hand good being sold on eBay (http://tinyco.re/2913411)
   (b) Craigslist (http://tinyco.re/2392254) or a similar online platform
   (c) renting apartments through Airbnb (http://tinyco.re/2409089)
   (d) restaurants of varying quality.
2. Explain how the following may facilitate mutually beneficial exchanges, even in the presence of hidden attributes:
   (a) electronic ratings shared among past and prospective buyers and sellers
   (b) exchanges among friends, and friends of friends
   (c) trust and social preferences
   (d) intermediate buyers and sellers, such as used-car dealers.

QUESTION 11.7 CHOOSE THE CORRECT ANSWER(S)

There are ten cars on the market, of which six are good quality cars worth $9,000 to buyers, and the others are lemons, worth zero. There are many potential buyers who do not know the quality of each car, but they know the proportion of good quality cars, and are willing to pay the average value. All sellers are happy to accept a price at least half the value of their car. Based on this information, which of the following statements are correct?

☐ The buyers are willing to pay at most $4,500.
☐ Only the lemons will be sold in this market.
☐ All cars will be sold at a price of $5,400.
☐ All cars will be sold at a price of $4,500.

QUESTION 11.8 CHOOSE THE CORRECT ANSWER(S)

In which of the following cases is there an adverse selection problem?

☐ a motor insurance market, in which the insurers do not know how carefully the insured people drive
☐ a health insurance market, in which the insurers do not know whether or not the applicants for insurance are habitual smokers
☐ online sales of nutritional supplements, when consumers cannot tell whether their contents are as claimed by sellers
☐ a firm that employs home-workers, but cannot observe how hard they are working

11.13 MARKET FAILURE AND GOVERNMENT POLICY

Figure 11.15 brings together the examples we have seen in which markets fail to allocate resources efficiently. At first sight they seem different from each other, but in each one, we can identify an external benefit or cost that a decision-maker does not consider. The table in Figure 11.16 (page 524) shows that the fundamental source of market failure is an information problem—some important aspect of an interaction that cannot be observed by one of the parties, or cannot be verified by a court.

Possible remedies for market failures

The table in Figure 11.15 also shows some possible remedies. Governments play an important role in the economy in their attempts to diminish the inefficiencies associated with many kinds of market failure. However, the same information problems can hamper a government seeking to use taxes, subsidies, or prohibitions to improve on the market outcome. For example, the French government eventually decided to ban the use of chlordecone rather than collect the information necessary to devise a tax on banana production or provide compensation to the fisheries.

Sometimes, a combination of remedies is the best way to cope with these information problems and resulting market failures. An example is car insurance. In many countries, third-party insurance (covering damage to others) is compulsory to avoid the adverse selection problem that would occur if only the accident-prone drivers purchased insurance. To address the moral hazard problem of hidden actions, insurers sometimes require the installation of on-board monitoring devices so that prudent driving habits can be an enforceable part of the insurance contract.

Implementing the remedies

In this unit, we have diagnosed market failures and used economic models to propose remedies. Although in some cases private bargaining may resolve the market failure, in many cases it is the government that must implement the remedy. This raises the question of the conditions under which governments actually implement policies to rectify market failures.

This is the subject of Unit 12, in which we consider the way both markets and hierarchies—including governments—resolve problems of resource allocation. And we also explain why, even in democratic societies, governments often fail to adopt policies that will make economic outcomes more efficient and fair.

EXERCISE 11.9 MARKET FAILURE

Construct a table like the one in Figure 11.15 to analyse the possible market failures associated with the decisions below. In each case, identify which markets or contracts are missing or incomplete.

1. You inoculate your child with a costly vaccination against an infectious disease.
2. You use money that you borrow from the bank to invest in a highly risky project.
3. A fishing fleet moves from the overfished coastal waters of its own country to international waters.
4. A city airport increases its number of passenger flights by allowing nighttime departures.
5. You contribute to a Wikipedia page.
6. A government invests in research in nuclear fusion.

11.13 MARKET FAILURE AND GOVERNMENT POLICY

Decision	How it affects others	Cost or benefit	Market failure (misallocation of resources)	Possible remedies	Terms applied to this type of market failure
A firm uses a pesticide that runs off into waterways	Downstream damage	Private benefit, external cost	Overuse of pesticide and overproduction of the crop for which it is used	Taxes, quotas, bans, bargaining, common ownership of all affected assets	Negative external effect, environmental spillover
You take an international flight	Increase in global carbon emissions	Private benefit, external cost	Overuse of air travel	Taxes, quotas	Public bad, negative external effect
You travel to work by car	Congestion for other road users	Private cost, external cost	Overuse of cars	Tolls, quotas, subsidized public transport	Common-pool resource, negative external effect
An employee on a fixed wage decides how hard to work	Hard work raises employer's profits	Private cost, external benefit	Too little effort, wage above reservation wage, unemployment	More effective monitoring, performance-related pay, reduced conflict of interest between employer and employee	Incomplete labour contract, hidden action, moral hazard
Someone who knows he has a serious health problem buys insurance	Loss for insurance company	Private benefit, external cost	Too little insurance offered, insurance premiums too high	Mandatory purchase of health insurance, public provision, mandatory health information sharing	Missing markets, adverse selection
Someone who has purchased car insurance decides how carefully to drive	Prudent driving contributes to insurance company's profits	Private cost, external benefit	Too little insurance offered, insurance premiums too high	Installing driver-monitoring devices	Missing markets, moral hazard
Borrower devotes insufficient prudence or effort to the project in which the loan is invested	Project more likely to fail, resulting in non-repayment of loan	Private benefit, external cost	Excessive risk, too few loans issued to poor borrowers	Redistribute wealth, common responsibility for repayment of loans (Grameen Bank (page 420))	Moral hazard, credit market exclusion
Bank that is 'too big to fail' makes risky loans	Taxpayers bear costs if bank fails	Private benefit, external cost	Excessively risky lending	Regulation of banking practices	Moral hazard
A firm producing a differentiated good	Price is too high for some potential buyers	Private benefit, external cost	Too low a quantity sold	Competition policy	Imperfect competition

Figure 11.15 Market failures with remedies.

11.14 CONCLUSION

Markets facilitate the division of labour by providing a means for people who are specialized in one type of production to acquire the full range of goods and services that make up their livelihood. Ideally, market prices provide information about how scarce a good or service is. The message that this information sends motivates people to produce goods that are scarce because others value them. It also motivates people to limit their use of scarce goods. The combination of the message and the motivation provided by prices can sometimes produce efficient economic outcomes.

But markets often do not match this ideal, and as a result outcomes that are Pareto inefficient (that is, **market failures**) may occur. In some cases, a thing that is scarce—like clean air or water—does not have a price, and so it is treated by users as if it were not scarce. In other cases, prices fail to reflect the entire social costs of the good (such as the environmental damage resulting from the use of fossil fuels).

Where prices are either entirely missing or fail to reflect true social costs, the decision-maker does not fully account for the costs or benefits of their actions for others (**external effects**). Where external effects are present, we say that the contract governing the transaction is incomplete (or even entirely absent). Contracts are incomplete because the information that would be necessary to write and enforce a contract is either not known by at least one of the parties (**asymmetric information**) or cannot be used in court (for example, non-verifiable information).

Asymmetric information comes in two forms: **hidden actions** (such as how hard an employee is working, considered in Units 6 and 8), which causes a problem known as **moral hazard**, and **hidden attributes** (such as whether the person seeking to buy health insurance is already ill), which causes a problem called adverse selection. In the case of **adverse selection**, a mutually beneficial market for the good (namely the insurance) could exist if information were symmetrical and verifiable, but otherwise there is a **missing markets** problem.

Question	Answer
Why do market failures happen?	People, guided only by market prices, do not take account of the full effect of their actions on others
Why is the full effect of their actions on others not taken into account?	There are external benefits and costs that are not compensated by payments
Why are some benefits or costs not compensated?	No markets exist in which they can be traded
Why not? And why can't private bargaining and payments solve the problem?	The required property rights and contracts cannot be enforced by courts of law
What prevents property rights and contracts from being enforceable?	Asymmetric or non-verifiable information

Figure 11.16 Market failures and information problems.

Where market failures exist, private Coasean bargaining between parties involved or public policies such as a **Pigouvian tax** (or subsidy) can improve outcomes. When seeking to use taxes, subsidies, or prohibitions to improve market outcomes governments face many of the same asymmetric information problems that confront private economic actors. Governments may fail to address market failures for another reason: powerful groups may benefit from the status quo. We address these limits to governmental policies in the next unit.

11.15 *DOING ECONOMICS:* MEASURING WILLINGNESS TO PAY FOR CLIMATE CHANGE MITIGATION

In this unit, we discussed external effects and how they arise, along with ways to mitigate them. When designing policies to reduce carbon emissions or air pollution, or to save an endangered species or preserve biodiversity, economists face the problem that markets for environmental amenities are missing. How can the value to people of the abatement of environmental damage be calculated and set against the cost of implementing any abatement? The issue of how to measure willingness to pay (WTP) of non-market goods is important for policymaking, since governments use the economic value of these goods as a major factor in deciding what quantity of these goods to provide (or whether to provide the good at all). Incorrectly estimating the WTP may result in inefficiencies, such as providing too much or too little of the good in question.

In *Doing Economics* Empirical Project 11, we will look at climate change mitigation as an example. Since tackling climate change may entail short-term costs such as decreased production, governments may want to know how much their citizens are willing to pay to reduce carbon emissions as a method of mitigating climate change. Using survey data, we will compare WTP (mean and median) under each method and assess whether WTP responses differ according to question type.

Go to *Doing Economics* Empirical Project 11 (https://tinyco.re/5541771) to work on this project.

> ### *Learning objectives*
> In this project you will:
>
> - compare survey measures of willingness to pay
> - construct indices to measure attitudes or opinions
> - use Cronbach's alpha to assess indices for internal consistency
> - practise re-coding and creating new variables.

11.16 REFERENCES

Fafchamps, Marcel, and Bart Minten. 1999. 'Relationships and Traders in Madagascar'. *Journal of Development Studies* 35 (6) (August): pp. 1–35.

Farnie, Douglas A. 1979. *The English Cotton Industry and the World Market 1815–1896*. Oxford: Clarendon Press.

Hayek, Friedrich A. 1948. *Individualism and Economic Order* (https://tinyco.re/3958172). University of Chicago Press.

Hayek, Friedrich A. 1994. *The Road to Serfdom* (https://tinyco.re/0683881). Chicago, Il: University of Chicago Press.

Jensen, Robert. 2007. 'The Digital Provide: Information (Technology), Market Performance, and Welfare in the South Indian Fisheries Sector.' *The Quarterly Journal of Economics* 122 (3) (August): pp. 879–924.

Pigou, Arthur. 1912. *Wealth and Welfare* (https://tinyco.re/2519065). London: Macmillan & Co.

Pigou, Arthur. (1920) 1932. *The Economics of Welfare* (https://tinyco.re/2042156). London: Macmillan & Co.

Schumpeter, Joseph. (1943) 2003. *Capitalism, Socialism and Democracy* (https://tinyco.re/4138375). pp. 167—72. Routledge.

Seabright, Paul. 2010. *The Company of Strangers: A Natural History of Economic Life* (Revised Edition). Princeton, NJ: Princeton University Press.

Smith, Adam. 1776. *An Inquiry into the Nature and Causes of the Wealth of Nations* (https://tinyco.re/9804148). New York: NY: Random House Publishing Group.

12 GOVERNMENTS AND MARKETS IN A DEMOCRATIC SOCIETY

Seat of government, the Michigan State Capitol

12.1 INTRODUCTION

- A government is distinct from other actors in society, but not because public officials are less self-interested than other people. It is because it has the capacity to act on behalf of all the people and to require citizens to abide by its decisions, using force if necessary.
- Governments also use tax funds to provide goods and services (such as the courts or schooling and, in some countries, healthcare), that are usually free of charge.
- Because of the unique powers held by governments, political elites can sometimes act like monopolists and enjoy substantial rents based on taxes paid by citizens.
- Ideally, democracy empowers citizens by extending voting rights in competitive elections to everyone, and limits what governments and other powerful bodies can do by ensuring individual rights of speech and association.
- Even in cases in which public policies to address unfairness or market failures are economically feasible, they may still not be carried out because powerful groups, including the wealthy or government elites, pursue other objectives, or because governments do not have the capacity to implement them.
- The effects on fairness and efficiency of policies concerning early childhood education, university tuition and rent control can be analyzed using the concepts you have learned thus far.

The Social Science 125 course at Harvard University was oversubscribed; more students had signed up for it than could be enrolled, given the 95-student limit placed on class size. Students who crowded into the lecture hall on the first day of the semester were surprised when the professor announced that admission to the course would go to the 95 highest bidders. The sums collected, he explained, would help to pay for the cost of extra materials to be circulated to students. He then asked students to write down their student ID numbers and the amount of US dollars they were willing to pay for admission to the course.

Who was this professor? Samuel Bowles (https://tinyco.re/7818700), one of our authors.

'Why should I pay to get into a class?' one of the students asked politely. The professor replied that limiting the class size was regrettable but necessary. In the circumstances, he said, the best way to allocate the scarce places was to identify the students most willing to pay for a place.

What other methods could he have considered?

- *Randomly selecting students to be admitted by lot:* This would mean that some students who really wanted to take the class would be excluded, while others who were barely interested would be enrolled.
- *Asking students how interested they were:* This would not work, he explained to his students, because there would be no reason to tell the truth if it meant you might not win a place. Each student would have an incentive to exaggerate.

As an economist, the professor proposed to allocate places in the class in a similar manner to the way in which access to most goods and services is allocated in a capitalist economy, that is, by means of a market. Students could bid for their places. Imagine that you had been there, hoping to enrol in the class that day. Would you have accepted his logic? Most of the students did not. And when he tried the same thing in another class, some students shouted insults at him and walked out!

The professor wasn't really going to auction places in his class to the highest bidders; his experiment was simply a first lesson in economics for the students. Nevertheless, every day school administrators, healthcare providers, managers of food banks, and many others face the problem of allocating scarce resources among individuals with differing needs. Their decisions are real.

How to allocate kidneys for transplant

Here is one of those real-life dilemmas. You must decide who will receive an organ transplant, say, a kidney:

- *Buying and selling kidneys is illegal in most places:* An illegal (black) market exists, in which the huge differences between the price received by organ donors (many of them very poor) and price paid by organ recipients (mostly rich) deliver profits to the criminals who organize the transactions.
- *Some generous people choose to donate a kidney:* This is legal, and they are allocated according to medical professionals' determination of medical need; possible beneficiaries are under the care of well-connected physicians.

Kidneys can be allocated using a combination of medical need and generosity. We know that many people waiting for kidney transplants die every day, because there are too few donors to save everyone who needs a transplant. So, might it be feasible to let people buy a kidney instead? If so, we can add a third option:

- *Create a legal market for kidneys:* Some people would prefer to be able to buy and sell kidneys, if there were strict regulations to ensure the safety of donor and recipient.

But letting kidneys be allocated by markets like any other good that is sold—like clothes or cars—has been criticized on the grounds that, under this arrangement, only rich people would get transplants. You might object to this system, reasoning: 'The difference between the people who get replacement kidneys and the people who don't, is not that one group values life more than the other; it is that only one group can afford it.' In this case, 'willingness to pay' is simply 'ability to pay'.

There is yet another way to improve the way in which kidney transplants can be organized:

- *Create a matching platform for kidneys:* This would use a digital technology like Airbnb or Uber. The platform would connect potential donors and recipients, but with a twist. Suppose your brother needed a replacement kidney, and you were willing to donate one of yours. But you are very unlikely to be able to donate your kidney to your brother because matching between donors and recipients is complicated (blood and tissue type must match). So, under this proposal, you would contribute your kidney to the overall supply of available kidneys, and in return be entitled to a properly matched kidney for your brother.

A network of exactly this kind is providing replacement kidneys in the US under the New England Program for Kidney Exchange (NEPKE), which you can hear more about in our 'Economist in action' video featuring Alvin Roth, a Nobel Laureate in economics and former president of the American Economic Association. NEPKE is like a market in that it allows exchanges to take place among total strangers who are matched by what they need or can provide. But unlike a market, who gets what is not based on the willingness to pay. The key to getting a replacement kidney is not being wealthy enough to afford one, but instead having some friend or family member (or even a stranger) who is willing to contribute a kidney to the pool so that the person needing the replacement gets a kidney matching his type.

Markets sometimes seem to be everywhere in the economy, but this is not so.

- *Firms are not markets:* Recall Herbert Simon's image from Unit 6 (page 232) of a Martian viewing the economy. The Martian mainly sees green fields, which are firms. They are connected by red lines representing buying and selling in markets, but many resource allocation decisions are made within the firms.
- *Families are not markets:* They do not allocate resources among members of the household by buying and selling.
- *Governments are not markets:* They use the political process rather than market competition to determine where, and by whom, schools are built and roads maintained.

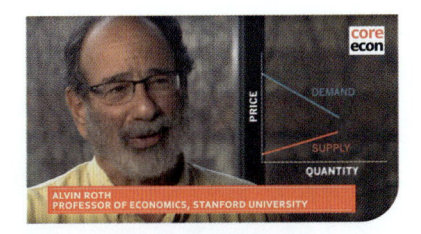

Alvin Roth explains how matching markets work. https://tinyco.re/ 8435358

Why are some goods and services allocated in markets, while firms, families, and governments allocate others? This is an old question, and one that is hotly debated. But the main reason is that some kinds of activities are better organized if they are regulated by the rules of the game that characterize families, or governments, or firms, instead of by markets. It is hard to see, for example, how conceiving and raising children could be effectively carried out by firms or markets. A combination of families and governments (schooling) does the job in most societies.

People disagree about the appropriate extent of the market. Some think that things that are now to some extent for sale—like sex, or influence over political decisions—should be allocated by other means. Others think that markets should take a larger role in the economy. These disagreements are about matters of fact (for example, do public schools or home schooling do a better job?) and matters of value (is the sale of sexual services or bodily organs immoral, even if these transactions are well regulated?).

In this unit, we consider why some economic activities are organized primarily by markets and some are organized in other ways, by firms, families and governments. Family is the main institution that organizes how we give birth to children and raise them in their first few years of life. In the rules of the game characteristic of families, parents teach and set limits for children, and these rules differ from the way markets determine outcomes. Similarly, as you learned in Unit 6, firms organize the process of production through a top–down structure of command, from owners to managers at various levels, down to production workers. Here, we explore how governments work, and how they interact with firms, families, markets and other institutions.

We have seen in the previous units that markets often fail to implement efficient and fair outcomes, and we have shown how governments can address market failures and unfairness. In this unit, we will also explain why governments often fail to address the problems of market failures and unfairness, and how these government failures can themselves be addressed.

In the previous unit, we explained that market failures—large and small—are the rule, not the exception, and result in Pareto-inefficient outcomes. So why do we use markets at all?

Firms, governments, and the extent of the market

In many cases, we do not use markets. The structure of our economy, taken as a whole, shows that markets are not the chosen way to organize many aspects of the production and distribution of goods and services.

If you think of the economy as a territory, as Herbert Simon's imaginary Martians did in Unit 6 (page 232), then even setting aside families, vast areas are not organized by markets.

- *Firms are centrally planned economies:* Firms are organized this way because it costs more for privately owned firms to buy some of the components of the product they sell than to make the components in-house. As a result, in-house production is more profitable than acquiring the same thing by purchase.

Ronald Coase (page 497) explained that, as a result, the boundaries of this divide between the firm and the market are set by the relative costs of the 'make it' and 'buy it' options. Thus, the extent of the market is determined by the firm's decision about which components of a product to produce and which ones to buy.

His explanation underlines an important fact that is often lost in heated debates about the merits of decentralized systems of organization-like markets, as opposed to more centralized ones like governments. There are some things that centralized systems (like the firm) are better at, and others that are better handled by the market.

The beauty of this demonstration is that it is not a judgement by some, possibly biased, observer; *it is the verdict of the market itself*. Competition among firms ultimately punishes firms that overdo the 'make it' option by overextending the boundaries of the centralized system through internal expansion. And market competition equally punishes the firms that fail to take advantage of centralized decision making by overly opting for the 'buy it' option.

- *Governments are top–down organizations:* We will see that they organize very substantial portions of the economic life in most societies today. Given the prevalence of market failures, why is the whole of the economy not organized by some combination of firms and governments?

The answer is that, just as there are market failures, there are also failures of centralized and top–down organization. And there are limits too, to what families can do. Markets are important parts of all modern economies and have been important in most economies in human history.

12.2 THE LIMITS OF MARKETS: REPUGNANT MARKETS AND MERIT GOODS

Seeing prices as both message and motivation teaches us the following: markets work well when prices are informative about the real scarcity of goods and services, and when people can change their behaviour to take account of changes in this information. When this is the case, we have 'the magic of the market'; when it is not the case, we have market failures.

But even when markets work well in this sense, many (probably most) people think that there are reasons to organize the production and distribution of some particular goods and services by other means.

- *Repugnant markets*: Marketing some goods and services—vital organs, votes, prizes, or human beings—may violate an ethical norm, or undermines human dignity.
- *Merit goods*: It is widely held that some goods and services (called merit goods) should be available to all, independently of a person's ability or willingness to pay. Access to personal security, basic and emergency healthcare, and fair judicial proceedings are examples.

> **repugnant market** Buying or selling something that people believe ought not to be exchanged on a market.
> **merit goods** Goods and services that should be available to everyone, independently of their ability to pay.

Repugnant markets

In most countries, there are well-established institutions that allow parents to voluntarily give up a baby for adoption, but laws typically prevent parents from selling their infants.

Alvin E. Roth. 2007. *'Repugnance as a Constraint on Markets'* (https://tinyco.re/2118641). *Journal of Economic Perspectives* 21 (3): pp. 37–58.

Michael Walzer and Michael Sandel, two philosophers, have discussed the moral limits of markets. Some market transactions conflict with the way we value humanity, such as buying and selling people as slaves; others conflict with principles of democracy, such as allowing people to sell their votes.

Michael Sandel. 2009. *Justice*. London: Penguin.

Michael Walzer. 1983. *Spheres of Justice: A Defense of Pluralism and Equality*. New York, NY: Basic Books.

Sandel investigates the moral limits of his audience (students around the world) in a talk called 'Why we shouldn't trust markets with our civic life' (https://tinyco.re/2385666) and in a series of videos called 'What money can't buy' (https://tinyco.re/7062034).

democracy A political system, that ideally gives equal political power to all citizens, defined by individual rights such as freedom of speech, assembly, and the press; fair elections in which virtually all adults are eligible to vote; and in which the government leaves office if it loses.

The research done by Alvin Roth, the economist whose video you watched when we discussed kidney transplants, has identified many of these repugnant markets.

Why do most countries ban the buying and selling of babies? Is it not true that a market for infants would provide opportunities for mutual gains from exchange between parents wishing to sell and would-be parents wishing to buy?

A common response is that some goods and services are different from the shirts, haircuts, and other goods that we routinely buy and sell on markets. Virtually all countries ban the sale of human organs for transplant. Commercial surrogacy—a woman becoming pregnant and giving birth to a baby for another couple for pay—is not legal in most countries (although it is legal in some states in the US, Thailand, and Russia).

Some economists might reason that it is wrong to prevent these transactions if both parties engage in them voluntarily—preventing those exchanges would be Pareto inefficient. But economic reasoning of this kind does not apply to just any transaction, and most economists now recognize that not everything should be put up for sale.

- *The sale may not be truly voluntary:* For example, poverty might force people to enter into a transaction that they might later regret, and the baby put up for sale is surely not doing this voluntarily.
- *Can you put a value on dignity?* Putting a price on a baby, or a body part, or sex may violate the principle of human dignity.
- *It undermines institutions:* Putting votes or human beings up for sale undermines the workings of valued social institutions or principles, such as **democracy** and freedom of movement.
- *It might not be fair:* Allocating goods according to the willingness to pay (which depends on an individual's income), as is done in markets, may seem less fair than other ways of determining who gets what, such as 'first come first served' or universal access to the good.
- *It encourages self-interest:* Markets, and the monetary incentives on which they are based, may lead people to act in a more self-interested and a less public-spirited way than they would under other institutions.

Regarding the final bullet point, recall (from Section 3.10 (page 128)) that this seems to have occurred when parents were fined for coming late to pick up their children at daycare centres in Israel (more parents picked their kids up later after the fine was imposed).

Merit goods

Economists recognize that there are some goods and services that are considered special in that they should be made available to all people, even those who lack the ability or willingness to pay for them. These are called merit goods; they are provided by governments rather than allocated by a market governed by the willingness to pay.

In most countries, primary education is provided free to all children and financed by taxation. Basic healthcare—at least emergency care—is also often available to all, irrespective of the ability to pay. The same holds for legal representation at trial in many countries—a person unable to pay for a lawyer should be assigned legal representation without charge. Personal security—protection from criminal assault or home fires, for example—is typically ensured in part by publicly provided police protection and fire-fighting services.

Why should merit goods be provided to people free of charge? People of limited income do not have access to a great many things. They typically live in substandard and often unhealthy housing and have very limited opportunities for recreational travel. Why are basic healthcare and schooling, legal representation, and police and fire protection different? The answer is that in many countries, these goods and services are considered the right of every citizen.

> **EXERCISE 12.1 CAPITALISM AMONG CONSENTING ADULTS**
> Should all voluntary contractual exchanges be allowed among consenting adults?
>
> State what you think about the following (hypothetical) exchanges. You may assume in each case that the people involved are sane, rational adults who have thought about the alternatives and consequences of what they are doing. In each case, decide whether you approve, and if you do not approve, whether you think the transaction should be prohibited. In each case explain why the transaction described produces mutual benefits (that is, it is a Pareto improvement over not allowing the exchange).
>
> 1. A complicated medical procedure has been discovered that cures a rare form of cancer in patients who will otherwise certainly die. Staff shortages make it impossible to treat all those who could benefit, and the hospital has established a policy of first come, first served. Ben, a wealthy patient who is at the bottom of the list, offers to pay Aisha, a poor person on the top of the list, $1 million to exchange places. If Aisha dies (which is very likely), then her children will inherit the money. Aisha agrees.
> 2. Melissa is 18. She has been admitted to a good university but does not have any financial aid, and cannot get any. She signs a four-year contract to be a stripper on the Internet and will begin work when she is 19. The company will pay her tuition fees.
> 3. You are waiting in line to buy tickets for a movie that is almost sold out. Someone from the back of the line approaches the woman in front of you and offers her $25 to exchange positions in the line (he takes her position in front of you and she takes his at the back of the line).
> 4. A politically apathetic person, who never votes, agrees to vote in an election for the candidate who pays him the highest amount.
> 5. William and Elizabeth are a wealthy couple who give birth to a baby with a minor birth defect. They sell this baby to their (equally wealthy) neighbours and buy a child without any birth defects from a family that needs the money.
> 6. An individual with an adequate income decides that he would like to sell himself to become the slave of another person. He finds a buyer willing to pay his asking price. The aspiring slave will use the money to further his children's education.

12.3 THE GOVERNMENT AS AN ECONOMIC ACTOR

The reasons why institutions other than markets play an important part in production and distribution include market failures, the status of some goods or services as merit goods, and the morally repugnant nature of some exchanges. This helps to explain why governments are major economic actors. Government spending, taxation, laws, wars, and other activities are as much a part of economic life as the working, investment, saving, buying, and selling activities of families and firms.

When we say that governments are economic actors (as we did in calling firms economic actors), we refer to those making the key decisions—policy-makers, military leaders, and top judicial authorities in a government.

In earlier units, especially the previous one, we identified many cases in which government policies could be introduced to address problems of either inefficiency or unfairness. But in Unit 3 (page 124), we also showed how governments (like firms and individuals) are limited in what they can do, not only because they have limited resources to accomplish their objectives, but also because, in most economic matters, even a powerful government cannot dictate what citizens do.

The government can require that a minimum wage be paid to all workers, but it cannot require workers to work hard instead of shirking on the job. The government can require the owners of a business to pay taxes, but it cannot require them to invest in building new productive capacity instead of purchasing a second home. In many cases, the most it can do is to alter the circumstances under which people decide what to do. Here we return to the question of government policies, stressing not what governments might do to address market failures, unfairness, and other problems, but instead what they actually do and why that sometimes falls short of what we would like.

A government allows people to do things together that they could not do individually. An example is going to war. Governments also engage in activities that vastly improve living standards and the quality of life of their citizens. Examples include:

- *Reduced poverty:* Fifty years ago, even in rich countries, many retired or elderly people were trapped in poverty. For example, in 1966, 28.5% of US citizens aged 65 and over were classed as 'poor'. Government transfers in many countries have greatly reduced serious economic deprivation among the elderly. In 2017, just 9.2% of elderly people in the US were poor.
- *Increased life expectancy and the dramatic reduction in child mortality in many countries:* When these improvements occurred in the late nineteenth and early twentieth century, they were not primarily the result of advances in medicine, most of which came later. They followed government policies that improved sanitation and water supply.
- *Economic security:* The increased size of government spending has reduced economic insecurity by dampening the extent of booms and busts. This is referred to as reducing the volatility of the business cycle.

More about the economics of poverty reduction: Angus Deaton. 2013. *The Great Escape: health, wealth, and the origins of inequality* (https://tinyco.re/5750302). Princeton: Princeton University Press.

Coercion and providing public services

Governments are actors on a scale unparalleled by families and most firms. The US government—federal, state and local—employs almost 10 times as many people as the country's largest firm, Walmart. However, governments were not always economic actors on this large a scale. In Figure 12.1 we show the total tax revenues collected by the government of the UK as a fraction of gross domestic product—a measure of the size of the government relative to the size of the economy—over more than 500 years. The figure rises from about 3% in the period prior to 1650 to 10 times that amount after the Second World War.

Even when tax revenues were only 3% of gross domestic product, the government of the UK was an immensely important actor. It is not the size of governments that make them unique, or uniquely important as actors.

Within a given territory, only a government has the authority to use force and restraints on an individual's freedom to achieve its objectives. Because citizens generally see the use of the government's coercive powers to maintain order, regulate the economy and deliver services as legitimate—meaning that they accept the government's authority—most citizens comply with government-made laws. One application of government's coercive power is the collection of taxes, which can be used to fund its operations.

To distinguish governments from private economic actors like firms, families, individuals, trade unions, and professional organizations, we define the **government** as the only body in a geographical territory (the nation) that can legitimately use force and the threat of force to pursue its ends. Governments routinely do things—locking people up, for example—which, if done by a private individual, are considered wrong and illegal.

Beyond its legitimate use of coercive powers, a second feature of the government is that it has obligations to its citizens based on civil and human rights; this feature also distinguishes the government from firms and other private economic entities. To advance and protect these rights, governments use tax funds to provide services such as national defence, police protection, and schooling. These services are often available to citizens without restrictions to those who use them, and without charging a price.

People differ greatly in their income and wealth and, therefore, in the taxes they pay; however, as citizens, they are equally entitled to many government-provided services. This simple fact is at the root of many debates about the appropriate 'size' of the government; people with less income and wealth benefit from many government services, but people with more wealth and income pay more (in absolute terms) of the taxes that finance these services. The tax, transfer, and expenditure systems of democratic governments typically redistribute income from those with higher incomes to those with lower incomes (See Figures 5.20 (page 221) and 5.21 (page 222) in Unit 5).

Peter Lindert. 2004. *Growing Public: Social Spending and Economic Growth since the Eighteenth Century*. Cambridge: Cambridge University Press.

Jon Bakija, Lane Kenworthy, Peter Lindert, and Jeff Madrick. 2016. *How Big Should Our Government Be?* Berkeley: University of California Press.

government Within a given territory, the only body that can dictate what people must do or not do, and can legitimately use force and restraints on an individual's freedom to achieve that end. *Also known as: state.*

12 GOVERNMENTS AND MARKETS IN A DEMOCRATIC SOCIETY

Part of the solution

Jean Tirole, an economist who specializes in the role of intervention and regulation, describes the way that governments can intervene in his Nobel prize lecture (https://tinyco.re/2393310).

Governments may adopt the twin objectives that we have used in this course:

- *Maximizing the surplus:* They may try to ensure that the mutual gains possible through our economic interactions are as large as possible and are fully realized.
- *Ensuring fairness:* They can influence how these gains are shared.

Examples of policies commonly adopted by governments to address market failures and unfairness include:

- *Competition policies:* To reduce the price-setting powers of monopolies.
- *Environmental policies:* To reduce emissions of pollutants.
- *Subsidies:* For Research and Development (R&D).
- *Policies that establish the expectation that the economy is relatively stable:* So that firms invest.
- *Public provision of health care or compulsory insurance.*
- *Providing information:* To allow people to make better decisions, such as the risks associated with financial products, children's toys, and foods.
- *Central bank policies:* That require commercial banks to minimize their risk exposure by restricting the leverage of their balance sheets.
- *Minimum wage laws:* That prohibit contracts that pay below a stated minimum.

UK Public Revenue (https://tinyco.re/2111182); Patrick K. O'Brien and Philip A. Hunt. 1993. 'The rise of a fiscal state in England, 1485–1815'. *Historical Research* 66 (160): pp.129–76. Note: *Pax Britannica* refers to the century between the end of the Napoleonic Wars and the beginning of the First World War, in which (compared to earlier or subsequent periods) Europe and most of the world was relatively peaceful, with the UK the militarily dominant nation. The Glorious Revolution deposed King James II in 1688 and increased the independent power of parliament.

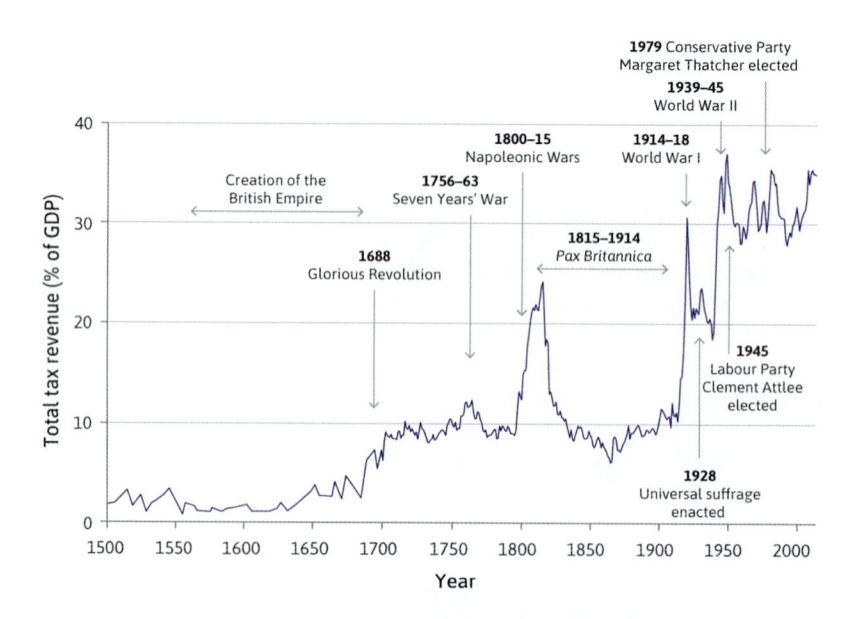

Figure 12.1 The growth of government in the UK (1500–2015).

Governments pursue these objectives by some combination of four means:

- *Incentives:* Taxes, subsidies, and other expenditures alter the costs and benefits of activities that have external effects that would lead to market failures or unfair outcomes if left unaccounted for.
- *Regulation:* Direct regulation of economic activities, such as the degree of competition, including mandatory universal participation in social and medical insurance, and regulation of aggregate demand.
- *Persuasion or information:* Altering available information and people's expectations about what others will do (for example, their belief that their property is secure or that other firms will invest) so as to allow people to coordinate their actions in a desirable way.
- *Public provision:* In-kind provision or through monetary transfers, including merit goods such as basic education, legal representation in court proceedings, and income transfers to alter the distribution of living standards.

Part of the problem

To accomplish these valuable objectives, governments must have extraordinary powers to acquire information and to compel compliance. This creates a dilemma. For the government to be a successful problem solver, it must also be powerful enough to potentially be a problem itself. Examples from history, and today's news, show governments using their monopoly on the use of force to silence opposition and to acquire huge personal wealth for their officials and leaders.

- *Ivory Coast:* As president from 1960 to 1993, Felix Houphouet Boigny accumulated a fortune estimated to be between $7 billion and $11 billion, much of it held in Swiss bank accounts. He once asked, 'Is there any serious man on earth not stocking parts of his fortune in Switzerland?'
- *Romania:* Nicolae Ceausescu, the head of state under Communist Party rule 1965–1989, amassed extraordinary wealth, the most visible parts of which were more than a dozen palaces that had bathrooms with gold-tiled baths and solid-gold toilet paper holders.
- *Russia:* Since the turn of the 21st century, personal connections with President Vladimir Putin have allowed a class of business people called *oligarchs* to obtain hundreds of millions of roubles' worth of assets.

Before the French Revolution, Louis XIV of France constructed a luxurious palace and grounds for himself at the Palace of Versailles, which is now one of the top tourist attractions in the world. He was called the Sun King by his subjects and claimed, '*L'etat, c'est moi*' ('I am the state'). The word 'state' is sometimes used—as the Sun King did here—to mean 'government in general', distinguishing it from any particular body, such as the government of France. In neighbouring Britain, at almost the same time, William Pitt had a different view of his King, declaring that 'The poorest man may in his cottage bid defiance to all the forces of the Crown,' as we saw in Unit 1, Exercise 1.5 (page 25).

Well-governed societies have devised ways to limit the damage that the use of government powers can inflict, without undermining the government's capacity to solve society's problems. These have generally included a combination of:

- *Democratic elections:* To allow citizens to dismiss a government that is using its powers for its own benefit or for the interests of some other small group.
- *Institutional checks and balances and constitutional restrictions on what the government can do:* These entirely prohibit some actions by a government, such as imposing a particular religion on a population.

The second point is why Pitt could observe that, while the farmer may have difficulty keeping rain out of his cottage, he could confidently exclude the King of England.

In a capitalist economy, aside from the obligation to pay taxes, other than in exceptional circumstances, the government cannot seize what you own. This limits the government's capacity to enrich itself at your expense. This is an essential limit on arbitrary government powers.

An example of an exceptional case would be if you owned a piece of land that was the only possible site for a bridge needed to solve a traffic problem. Most governments have the right to acquire the land at what is independently judged to be a fair price, even if you are unwilling to sell. This power to take private property for public use has many names. For example, it is known as the 'right of eminent domain' in the US or a 'compulsory purchase order' in the UK. Even with well-designed limits on government powers and provision for exceptions allowing governments to better serve the public, we will see that governments, like markets, sometimes fail.

> **QUESTION 12.1 CHOOSE THE CORRECT ANSWER(S)**
> Which of the following statements are correct?
>
> ☐ A government should not be able to seize private property.
> ☐ A government should not be the monopoly supplier of a service.
> ☐ A government should not be allowed to use force against its citizens.
> ☐ A government should not collect information about its citizens.

Government failure

To understand why neither markets nor governments may provide ideal solutions to economic problems (https://tinyco.re/8993136), think about the case of a **natural monopoly**. An example would be the provision of tap water in a city, or electricity transmission over a national network. In these cases, as a result of economies of scale, the most efficient solution is to have a single entity provide the service. This could be a private firm, an economic monopoly, or the government, which is a political monopoly.

If the firm were privately owned as a monopoly, we know from Unit 7 (page 286) that it would face a downward-sloping demand curve, which would limit the price at which it could sell its goods. In order to maximize the profits of the firm, and hence the value of the owners' assets, the monopoly firm would both seek to reduce costs and restrict output so that

natural monopoly A production process in which the long-run average cost curve is sufficiently downward-sloping to make it impossible to sustain competition among firms in this market.

it could charge a higher price. The result would be a price above the marginal cost of production, which would mean that some consumers who value the service at more than its marginal cost would not consume it. Private ownership of the monopoly would result in a market failure.

Would the government do a better job?

Ideally, a government-owned natural monopoly would set the price equal to the marginal cost and finance the fixed costs through taxation. But the government may have little incentive to reduce costs. The publicly owned water- or electricity-supply company may be under pressure to overstaff the company with well-paying jobs for politically connected individuals. As a result, the costs may be higher. Wealthy individuals or firms may lobby the government-owned monopoly to provide its services on favourable terms to special-interest groups. These outcomes of public ownership would be a **government failure**.

This case illustrates both the similarities and differences between the **economic accountability** provided by the market and the **political accountability** provided by a democratic form of government. Both the owners of the monopoly firm and the government decision-makers may act to further their own interests at the expense of the consumer or citizen, but they would both operate within constraints. The monopoly firm would not be free to charge whatever price it wished; its profits are limited by the demand curve. The government would not be entirely free to inflate the costs of provision by hiring or catering only to 'friends of the government', because it may suffer an election defeat.

These two cases—private or government ownership of a natural monopoly—illustrate the problem of **market failure** (the monopoly charging more than the marginal cost) and what is sometimes called government failure (the failure to minimize the cost of providing the service).

Which works better? There is no general answer to this question. And there are many choices besides private ownership or government ownership, including private ownership under public regulation, or public ownership with competition among private firms for the time-limited right to produce and price the service.

Viewing the government as an economic actor that pursues its objectives but is constrained by what is feasible, helps us clarify which factors can influence a government to be more of a problem solver, and less of a problem.

> **government failure** A failure of political accountability. (This term is widely used in a variety of ways, none of them strictly analogous to market failure, for which the criterion is simply Pareto inefficiency). See also: political accountability.
>
> **economic accountability** Accountability achieved by economic processes, notably competition among firms or other entities in which failure to take account of those affected will result in losses in profits or in business failure. See also: accountability, political accountability.
>
> **political accountability** Accountability achieved by political processes such as elections, oversight by an elected government, or consultation with affected citizens. See also: accountability, economic accountability.
>
> **market failure** When markets allocate resources in a Pareto-inefficient way.

Andrei Shleifer. 1998. 'State versus private ownership' (https://tinyco.re/4317440). *Journal of Economic Perspectives* 12 (4): pp. 133–50.

Alexander Hamilton, James Madison, and John Jay (1961). *The Federalist*. Middletown, Ct., Wesleyan University Press.

EXERCISE 12.2 BUILDING SELF-CONTROL INTO GOVERNMENT

James Madison, a leading figure in the debates about the US Constitution after the formerly British colonies in the United States of America won its war of independence, wrote in 1788:

> In framing a government which is to be administered by men over men, the great difficulty lies in this: you must first enable the government to control the governed; and in the next place oblige it to control itself.

How does democracy (including the rule of law) address Madison's concerns to oblige the government to 'control itself'?

EXERCISE 12.3 THE RELATIONSHIP BETWEEN ECONOMIC DEVELOPMENT AND SIZE OF GOVERNMENT
Use Figure 12.1 (page 536) to help you answer the following questions:

1. Why was *Pax Britannica* a period of smaller government?
2. Compare Figure 12.1 with Figure 1.6 (page 14). Why do you think the growth of the size of government coincides with both the emergence of capitalism as an economic system in the seventeenth and eighteenth centuries, and the increase in output per capita?
3. Compare two 'peacetime' periods—*Pax Britannica* and the period since the end of the Second World War. Why do you think the size of government was so much larger in the second period?

QUESTION 12.2 CHOOSE THE CORRECT ANSWER(S)
In order to be able to deal effectively with cases of market failure and unfairness, and to discharge its other obligations, the state needs to be sufficiently large and powerful. This means that the problem solver is also big enough to be a potential problem. How is this paradox usually resolved?

- ☐ the rule of law
- ☐ constitutional restrictions
- ☐ international pressure
- ☐ democratic elections that give citizens the power to dismiss the government

12.4 THE GOVERNMENT AS A RENT-SEEKING MONOPOLIST

Governments, as we have seen, have the power to solve problems, but also to cause them. Heads of governments and their associates often misuse their power for personal gain. Other governments, even undemocratic ones like those just mentioned, sometimes provide valuable public services and rule without extravagant personal gain.

Political rents

Our analogy between firms and governments suggests a similarity between a dictator and a monopolist—neither faces much competition. But there are other similarities. Think about what a dictator can do. The examples above (page 537) from Russia, Ivory Coast, France and Romania show that the lack of competition allows the ruler to gain substantial income that would not be possible were it not for his political position.

This income is called a **political rent**. It is political because it is associated with a political position or connections. It is a rent in the sense already used many times in this course—a payment above and beyond what the actor can get from their next best alternative.

This is similar, for example, to the employment rents received by an employed worker. In the case of the worker, the next best alternative is considered to be unemployment; for a member of the political elite, the next best alternative is what the person would receive without a political position or connections. In the case of Russian oligarchs, their political

political rent A payment or other benefit in excess of the individual's next best alternative (reservation position) that exists as a result of the individual's political position. The reservation position in this case refers to the individual's situation were they to lack a privileged political position. See also: economic rent.

rents are the income they have received above and beyond what they would have had in the absence of any privileged connection to the Russian government.

Unlike the stationary rents that encourage workers to work hard and well, or the dynamic rents received by successful innovators, these rents do not play a useful role in the economy. They are simply a reward for having power.

Objectives and constraints

To understand why governments do what they do, we begin by modelling the government as a single individual, and use the usual concepts:

- his preferences
- the constraints that determine which actions and outcomes are feasible for him.

To begin, we model the government as a 'political monopolist', which means there is no competition from elections that could remove it from power. We call this the 'government as monopolist' model, and we would usually call a government like this a dictatorship. Even in the absence of elections, the dictator faces a feasibility constraint: his powers are not unlimited, because if he takes too much from the population, he may be removed from office by an uprising of citizens.

Depending on his preferences and the constraints he faces, the dictator (that is the political monopolist) may use the tax revenues the government collects for purposes that may include:

- *The provision of services to virtually all citizens*: These include schooling and health.
- *The delivery of government services or other benefits to a narrowly targeted group*: These might be well-paying jobs, or special reductions in tax obligations.
- *Granting substantial incomes to themselves*: Or other economic benefits, to themselves or their families.

A rent-seeking dictator

As with all models, we simplify greatly so we can focus on the most important aspects of the problem. We assume that:

- The dictator is entirely selfish.
- He decides on a tax that he will collect from the citizens.
- He keeps the tax revenue that is left over after spending on public services (such as a basic health service and schools).
- He provides these services to citizens because, if he keeps too much, he risks a popular uprising that would remove him from office.

While simple, this model captures some key realities:

- The Romanian people revolted against Nicolae Ceausescu in 1989 after he had been in office for 29 years. The armed forces joined the revolt, and he and his wife were executed.
- Louis XVI of France was removed from power in a revolution in 1789, during which thousands of armed men and women besieged the Palace of Versailles. He was executed by guillotine in 1793.

Rent-seeking by the dictator (activities to enlarge or to perpetuate these high incomes) often involves using the economy's resources to police the population. This is to keep the dictator in power, rather than to produce goods and services. These are similar to some of the rent-seeking activities of a profit-maximizing firm—advertising or lobbying the government to gain a tax break, for example—but are different from rent-seeking activities such as innovation that create substantial economic benefits.

To simplify the dictator's decision-making problem, we assume that the dictator does not choose the public service to supply—the public service is taken as given. The dictator only chooses how much to collect in taxes.

Even a dictator faces constraints on what he can do

As in Unit 5 (page 194), when Bruno was using his coercive powers to exploit Angela, the dictator will not want to collect so much in taxes that the citizens would lack the strength and ability to produce. But the dictator will face the possibility of a revolution, an additional constraint.

We assume there are two reasons for removing the dictator:

- *Performance-related reasons*: He collects too much tax, for example.
- *Reasons unrelated to performance*: He has no control over these.

The dictator wants to maximize the total political rent that he can expect to get over his period in office, not the rent he can get in any particular year. So, he has to think about how long he is likely to last. Of course, this is impossible to predict, but he will reasonably expect that if he is providing a given amount of the public service, then the lower the taxes he imposes, the longer his duration in office will be.

Figure 12.2 illustrates how a forward-looking dictator would evaluate two possible levels of taxation. With the higher tax, the dictator gets a larger rent per year, but for a shorter time in office (the likelihood of being removed is greater).

Assuming the private sector does not also provide this service to the public, you can think about the government as a monopolist providing the public service at a price (the tax) that citizens are legally obliged to pay. The dictator faces a constraint similar to a demand curve. Just as the amount a monopolistic firm is able to sell is inversely related to the price that it sets, the duration of the government's time in office is inversely related to the tax rate it sets.

Figure 12.3 shows how the tax rate imposed by the dictator affects the expected duration of the government, defined as the number of years he may expect to stay in office following this year.

What is the longest time (D^{max}) that the dictator could expect to remain in office? To figure this out, imagine that our dictator suddenly lost interest in money and simply wanted to remain in office as long as possible. What would he do?

He cannot reduce the probability that he will be removed for reasons unrelated to his performance. But he can reduce the 'performance-related' probability of being removed by only collecting enough taxes to meet the production costs of the public service. In Figure 12.3, D^{max} is therefore where the duration curve meets the cost line. It is the expected duration when only considering factors unrelated to the dictator's performance. Any tax rate above the cost of production will reduce the expected duration below D^{max}, as shown by the downward slope of the duration curve.

12.4 THE GOVERNMENT AS A RENT-SEEKING MONOPOLIST

The duration curve goes through points X and Y in Figure 12.2 and does not go below the cost line because if it did, the dictator would be paying out of his own pocket toward the cost of the public service. A dictator in a country with a stronger rule of law—and therefore a lower likelihood of a

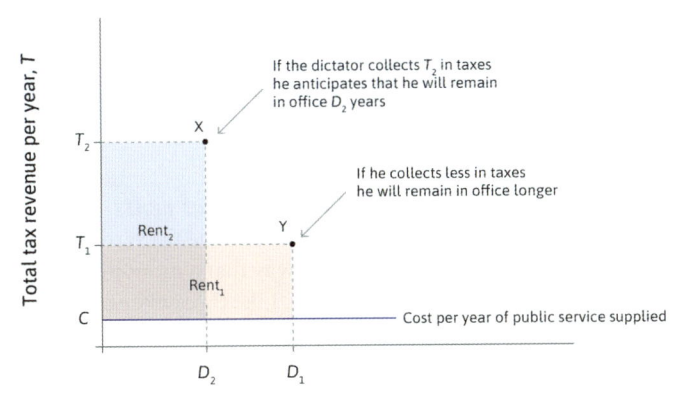

To explore all of the slides in this figure, see the online version at https://tinyco.re/2199748.

Figure 12.2 The forward-looking dictator contemplates the total political rent he will get with two different levels of annual taxation.

1. Higher tax
If the dictator collects T_2 in taxes, he anticipates that he will remain in office for D_2. His total political rent is $(T_2 - C)D_2$, where C is the cost of supplying the public good.

2. Lower tax
If he collects less in taxes, he will expect to remain in office longer. His total political rent is $(T_1 - C)D_1$. You can see from the figure that he does better by imposing a higher tax (the light blue rectangle, Rent₂, is larger than the light red rectangle, Rent₁).

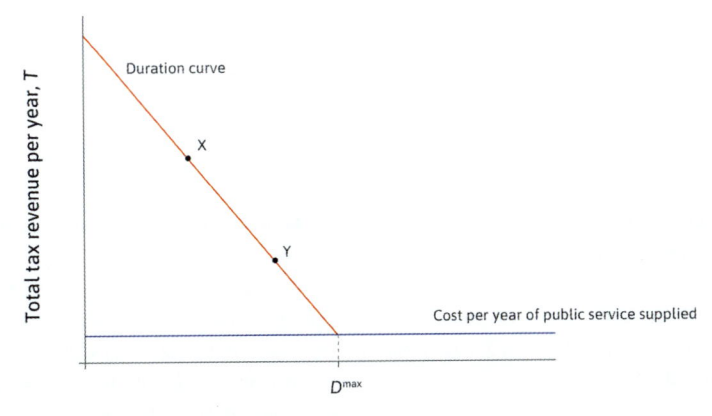

Figure 12.3 The duration curve: The dictator sets the tax given the cost of the public service.

543

coup unrelated to performance—would face a duration curve that meets the cost line to the right of the one shown.

The duration curve is the feasible frontier for the dictator. Points in the feasible set above the cost curve result in positive rents for him. The curve represents a familiar trade-off:

- *Higher taxes*: More rents in the short run at the cost of a greater likelihood of an early dismissal from office. A shorter duration in office is the opportunity cost of higher rents per year.
- *Lower taxes*: The dictator earns rents for longer, but at a lower level per year. Lower rents per year is the opportunity cost of a longer duration in office.

The dictator chooses a tax to maximize his total rents

How does a dictator facing a duration curve decide the tax rate to impose on the citizens? The answer is similar to the way that a monopolistic firm decides on the price to charge for its product. Like the owner of a monopoly, the dictator faces a trade-off: he would like to extract a large amount of total taxes from the citizenry, and remain in office for a long time. But the duration curve tells him that he cannot have both. So, he has to evaluate differing combinations of tax revenue (T) and duration (D).

He does this using a set of isorent curves (similar to the monopolist's iso-profit curves), shown in Figure 12.4. Points V and Z on Isorent$_2$ in the

To explore all of the slides in this figure, see the online version at https://tinyco.re/6719400.

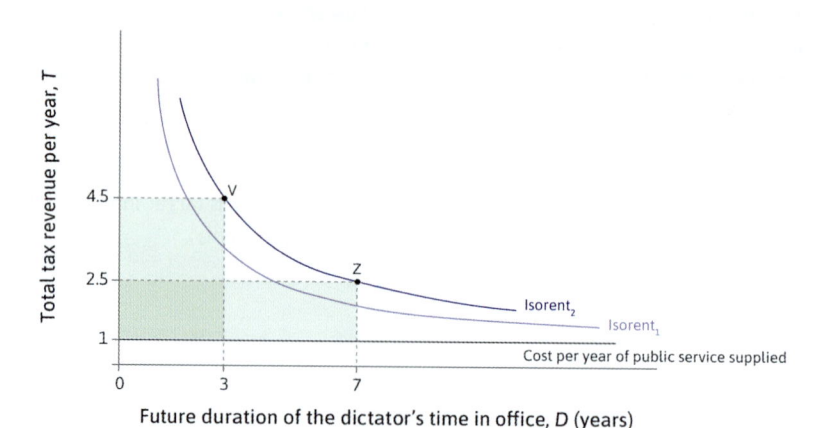

Figure 12.4 The dictator's isorent curves.

1. Isorent curves
Some of the dictator's isorent curves are shown, with Isorent$_2$ indicating a higher political rent than Isorent$_1$. Here we assume the cost per year of supplying public services is 1.

2. Relatively high tax revenue, relatively short duration
Point V corresponds to a duration of 3 years, and a yearly tax revenue of 4.5. The rent at V is (4.5 − 1) × 3 = 10.5 (the green shaded area).

3. Another point on the same isorent curve
Point Z corresponds to a duration of 7 years, and a yearly tax revenue of 2.5, giving a rent of (2.5 − 1) × 7 = 10.5 (an identically-sized area to that enclosed by point V). Note that rents are calculated by subtracting the cost per year of supplying the public service from the yearly tax revenue.

figure, are two different combinations of total taxes per year and duration in office that yield the dictator the same level of rent. High taxes and a short duration in office (point V) yield him the same total rent as lower taxes and a longer term in office (point Z). The points on the blue curve (Isorent$_2$) all yield the same level of total rent, and this is greater than the total rent possible by the points on Isorent$_1$.

The shape of the isorent curves is similar to the isoprofit curves of a monopolist:

- Higher isorent curves are further from the origin.
- They are 'bowed inward' towards the origin, as shown in the figure.
- The 'no rent' isorent curve is the horizontal cost line.

Using these isorent curves, the monopolist can determine which point on the duration curve—the frontier of his feasible set—yields him the highest total rent. This can be seen in Figure 12.5.

The dictator will find the tax that maximizes his total expected political rent, which is the quantity $(T - C)D$. The dictator reasons in a way that is analogous to the profit-maximizing firm that chooses the price to get the highest expected profits equal to $(P - C)Q$, where P is the price charged by the firm and Q is the quantity sold.

Just as we used the firm's isoprofit curves to determine the price it would charge in order to maximize profits, we can now use the dictator's isorent curves to determine the tax rate it will impose on the citizens.

Suppose the dictator is considering setting a modest tax and expecting a long tenure in office, indicated by point A. Because the isorent curve is flatter than the duration curve at this point, we can see that he would do better by raising the tax and bearing the opportunity cost associated with doing so (a shorter expected stay in office).

Continuing this reasoning, we can see that the tax rate indicated by point F on the duration curve earns the dictator a large surplus per year, but not enough to offset the short duration of his government. A lower tax rate would increase his expected rent.

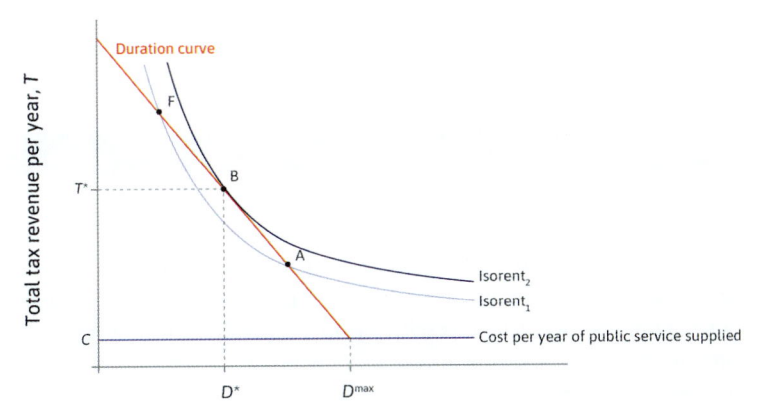

Figure 12.5 The dictator chooses a tax level to maximize his political rents.

To maximize his political rent, the dictator will select point B, imposing the tax T^* and expecting to stay in office for D^* years, making a total rent of $(T^* - C)D^*$. At this point, the slope of the highest isorent curve is equal to the slope of the feasible frontier (the duration curve):

Slope of the duration curve = MRT
= MRS
= slope of the highest feasible isorent curve

> **QUESTION 12.3 CHOOSE THE CORRECT ANSWER(S)**
> Consider Figure 12.5. Which of the following statements is true?
>
> ☐ A self-interested dictator will maximize the annual tax revenue they collect.
> ☐ Moving from A to B in the diagram is a Pareto improvement, improving outcomes for both citizens and the dictator.
> ☐ At T^*, an increase in the tax rate will increase total expected rent.
> ☐ Dictators use some tax revenues to provide essential public services.

12.5 COMPETITION CAN LIMIT POLITICAL RENT-SEEKING

Competition disciplines firms in the economy by limiting the profits they can get by setting too high a price, or producing goods of low quality. Competition to win elections is the way that a democracy disciplines its politicians to provide the services desired by the public at a reasonable cost (in terms of taxes). Below we give some evidence of this from the US.

There is also evidence from other countries that the prospect of being removed from office affects how politicians act.

Even in undemocratic settings, the threat of losing office can discipline politicians. In China, provincial governors and Communist Party secretaries are not subject to review by voters but instead by higher officials in the central government. Governors and party secretaries are frequently promoted and almost as frequently fired. The records of all terminations between 1975 and 1998 (https://tinyco.re/2714104) show that those whose provinces experienced rapid economic growth were promoted, while those whose provinces lagged behind were dismissed. The introduction of village-level elections in China led to increased provision of local public services such as health services and schooling, and arguably a reduction in corruption.

Monica Martinez-Bravo, Gerard P. I. Miquel, Nancy Qian, and Yang Yao. 2014. 'Political reform in China: The effect of local elections' (https://tinyco.re/6544486). NBER working paper 18101.

> **HOW ECONOMISTS LEARN FROM DATA**
>
> *Does electoral competition affect policy?*
> Think of a politician as wanting to stay in office and knowing that she must satisfy a majority of voters when seeking re-election. But she also has her own objectives: to advance a particular project that she favours, or to maintain good relations with wealthy individuals who would support her political campaigns or employ her when her political career was over. Does the threat of 'give the voters what they want or get thrown out' lead her to emphasize the public's interests, instead of her own?
>
> Comparing the policies adopted by politicians in districts that are non-competitive (for example, there will be no other candidate for the

seat) with those who face electoral competition will not answer the question. The reason is that competitive and non-competitive political districts, and the politicians who represent them, are different in so many ways that the comparison would mix the effects of political competition with the effects of other differences.

Economists Tim Besley and Anne Case devised an ingenious way to answer the question (https://tinyco.re/2599264). Some state governors in the US are limited to two four-year terms of office. This means that at the end of their first term they will face electoral competition when they ask voters to re-elect them. During their second term, the prospect of political competition does not affect them, because they are not allowed to stand for re-election.

This is a **natural experiment**. The 'treatment' is the prospect of electoral competition, and so governors in the first term are the 'treatment group'. The same governors in the second term are the 'control group'. As in any good experiment, other important influences are held constant. We are measuring the same individuals, in the same districts, under a treatment and a control condition.

They found that during their first terms (the treatment period), Republican and Democratic governors implemented virtually identical levels of total taxation per capita. But during their second terms (the control period), Democratic Party governors, who tend to favour more public expenditures and taxation, implemented much higher levels of taxation than Republicans did. And Republican governors, when not facing political competition, implemented much lower levels of the state minimum wage.

Whether Democrat or Republican, governors faced with electoral competition in their first term implemented very similar policies to those favoured by 'swing' voters. These are voters who tend to change who they vote for, and so tend to decide many elections. The common policies were lower taxes and higher minimum wages. But they diverged according to their own political preferences or economic interests when electoral competition was removed.

natural experiment An empirical study exploiting naturally occurring statistical controls in which researchers do not have the ability to assign participants to treatment and control groups, as is the case in conventional experiments. Instead, differences in law, policy, weather, or other events can offer the opportunity to analyse populations as if they had been part of an experiment. The validity of such studies depends on the premise that the assignment of subjects to the naturally occurring treatment and control groups can be plausibly argued to be random.

Political competition as a constraint

Because it affects what governments do, now we introduce political competition to the model to see how it affects the government's choice of tax level. The government leadership is no longer represented by a dictator, but instead by what we call a **governing elite**, that is the top government officials and legislative leaders, unified by a common interest such as membership in a particular party. Unlike a dictator, the elite can only be removed from office by losing an election, and not by a citizen uprising or some other non-electoral means.

When we speak of the elite's 'removal from power' or the duration of its 'time in office', we do not mean the removal or duration in office of an individual (as might have been the case with a dictator), but rather the removal from power of the entire group and its affiliation with a political party. In the US, for example, the Republican Party governing elite was removed from office in 2008, when President Obama was elected. The Democratic Party governing elite associated with President Obama was removed from office when President Trump was elected eight years later.

governing elite Top government officials such as the president, cabinet officials, and legislative leaders, unified by a common interest such as membership in a particular party.

Figure 12.6 illustrates a few of examples of governing elites' duration in office and the reasons that they eventually left office. The longest continuous rule by a governing elite was the government of the Mexican Institutional Revolutionary Party (PRI). It governed Mexico from the time of the Mexican revolution in the early twentieth century right into the twenty-first century. The longest rule by an individual at the head of a governing elite was by Fidel Castro (49 years) in Cuba, who was then succeeded by his brother Raul. The shortest period in office in this table is the elected government of Gough Whitlam in Australia, which was removed by the Governor General (not an elected official) following a parliamentary impasse over the budget.

The key idea in our model is that political competition makes the likelihood of losing an election more dependent on the government's performance. This means that it makes the duration curve flatter. In other words, an increase in taxes by the government will have a larger effect on the elite's expected duration in office than it would if there was no political competition.

The flatter, more competitive, duration curve that you see in Figure 12.7 shows a situation in which raising taxes above the cost of providing the public services is associated with a reduction in the current governing elite's period in power.

Governing elite	Country	Rule	Came to power by	Left power by
Congress Party	India	1947–1977	Election (end of colonial rule)	Election
Communist Party	Cuba	1959–	Revolution	Still in power as of 2019
Social Democratic Party	Sweden	1932–1976	Election	Election
Second Republic	Spain	1931–1939	Election	Military coup civil war
Francisco Franco	Spain	1939–1975	Military coup, civil war	Natural death; return to democracy
Institutional Revolutionary Party	Mexico	1929–2000	Election	Election
Democratic Party	US	1933–1953	Election	Election
Sandinista Party	Nicaragua	1979–1990	Armed revolution	Election
African National Congress	South Africa	1994–	Non-violent revolution & election	Still in power as of 2019
Australian Labor Party	Australia	1972–1975	Election	Dismissed by (unelected) executive

Figure 12.6 Examples of governing elites, their period of rule, and reasons for their end (where applicable).

The model helps show why governing elites, and the wealthy and powerful members of society who are allied to these elites, have so often resisted democracy, and attempted to limit the political rights of the less well off. In Figure 12.8, voting is initially restricted to the wealthy and as a result, the elite faces little political competition (the duration curve is steep), and maximizes its rents at point B. But now suppose that everyone has the right to vote and that opposition political parties are allowed to challenge the elite. This increase in political competition is represented by the flatter duration curve, indicating that the feasible set of the elite has shrunk. It now chooses point G, and collects lower taxes per year.

Notice that, in the figure, the governing elite in a more competitive political system implements lower taxes but has the same expected duration as the elite in the less competitive system (with higher taxes). But this need not be the case. Generally, the duration could be longer or shorter if conditions become more competitive. But the tax rate will definitely be lower.

12.6 POLITICAL MONOPOLY AND COMPETITION COMPARED

In the model the 'government' is a single person—the dictator—or a 'political elite' which we have treated as if it were a single person. In both cases their actions are constrained by nothing other than the fact that if they collect too much in taxation, this may result in them being removed from office. But governments are large bodies of people, regulated by complex rules of the game.

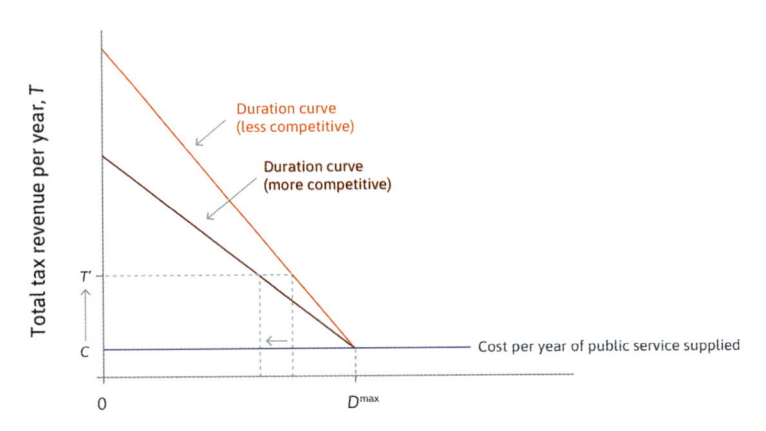

To explore all of the slides in this figure, see the online version at https://tinyco.re/8131174.

Figure 12.7 The feasible set for taxes and government duration in a relatively uncompetitive and competitive political system.

1. A dictatorship
In a dictatorship, the duration curve is steep.

2. A flatter curve
The more competitive duration curve (darker) is flatter.

3. A rise in taxes
Raising taxes to T' above the cost of providing the public services is associated with a more substantial reduction in the current government's expected lifetime when political competition is stronger.

political institution The rules of the game that determine who has power and how it is exercised in a society.

In Unit 6 (page 231) we explained that the firm is not only an actor, it is also a stage on which the various groups making up the firm also act, sometimes in conflict, sometimes in cooperation. The same can be said of governments. On the stage of government, politicians, political parties, soldiers, judges, citizens, and bureaucrats interact according to their particular preferences and the informal and formal rules that make up **political institutions**.

The political institutions of a country are the rules of the game that determine who has power and how it is exercised in a society. Democracy is a political institution, which means it is a set of rules that determine

- who makes up the government
- the powers they can use when governing.

Political institutions differ from country to country and over time. Major categories of political institutions include democracy and dictatorship. Recall that in Unit 1 we defined democracy as 'A political system, that ideally gives equal political power to all citizens, defined by individual rights such as freedom of speech, assembly, and the press; fair elections in which virtually all adults are eligible to vote; and in which the government leaves office if it loses.'

The key value motivating democracy is political equality. Citizens should have substantially equal opportunities to be able to express their views in ways that can shape the policies and other activities of the government. Recall that in Unit 1 (page 37) we explained that we use the term 'democracy' to refer to a form of government characterized by the rule of law, civil liberties, and inclusive, fair, and decisive elections. Inclusive means that no major group—for example, women, ethnic minorities, those without property—can be excluded from the right to vote.

In Figure 12.9 we illustrate political institutions by contrasting the effects of competition and the lack of competition in the economy and in government.

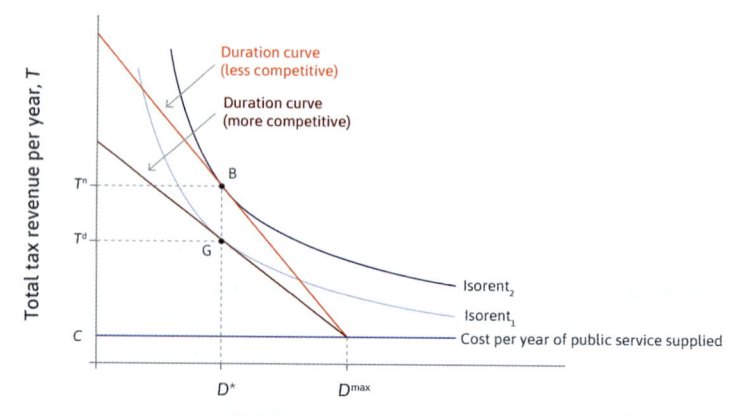

Figure 12.8 Choice of taxes under less and more competitive conditions.

12.6 POLITICAL MONOPOLY AND COMPETITION COMPARED

QUESTION 12.4 CHOOSE THE CORRECT ANSWER(S)
Why is the term 'political rent' used to describe the increases in personal wealth often enjoyed by dictators?

☐ The income is derived from hiring out public property to private individuals.
☐ These are 'excessive' earnings resulting from the dictator's political position.
☐ Political rent is income that dictators earn from confiscating private property and letting it to friends at preferable rates.
☐ 'Rent' is a term used to describe any excessive level of income.

QUESTION 12.5 CHOOSE THE CORRECT ANSWER(S)
The magnificent chateaux in France's Loire Valley, built between 1550 and 1780, are a major tourist attraction. Many of them were commissioned and built by finance ministers serving French kings of the period. How might this be explained in the context of this unit?

☐ There was a lack of accountability.
☐ The king's ministers were drawn from aristocratic French families who were generally very wealthy.
☐ Building a magnificent chateau was a way of confirming one's status.
☐ The Loire valley was well provided with the essential materials for building.

Varieties of political and economic competition	Source of rents or reasons for their absence	Controls on political elites and firm owners	Power of the non-elite (citizens and consumers)	Profits/rents
The extreme case of limited political competition (a dictator)	The dictator uses tax and other government revenues as a source of personal income above what he would receive as an ordinary citizen.	Limited threat of removal from office, e.g. revolutionary overthrow	Little	Political rents > 0
The extreme case of limited economic competition (a monopolist)	The monopolist restricts sales, charges prices above the average cost of production and receives a profit greater than the opportunity cost of capital.	Limited threat of market entry by competing firms	Little	Economic profits > 0
'Ideal democracy'	Rents are eliminated by competition among political parties and other freedoms such as a free press	Electoral loss is certain if significant political rents are extracted.	Exercised mainly through 'Voice'—vote for someone else	Political rents = 0
'Perfect competition' among firms	Rents are eliminated by competition among firms	Zero sales (and firm failure) if sets a price higher than average cost.	Exercised mainly through 'Exit'—buy from someone else	Economic profits = 0

Figure 12.9 Political and economic rents under competition and monopoly.

> **QUESTION 12.6 CHOOSE THE CORRECT ANSWER(S)**
>
> The role of the dictator can perhaps be compared to that of the monopolist, in that both earn rents that they try to protect, either by spending on police and security services (dictator) or by creating barriers to entry (monopolist). In what important respects do these rent seekers differ?
>
> ☐ The dictator is looking to maximize benefits for himself, and possibly for his family and various interest groups.
> ☐ The monopolist is a private firm and subject to government regulation, whereas the dictator *is* the government. The state is always more powerful than an individual firm.
> ☐ Unlike the monopolist, the dictator seeks to maximize long-run rents by staying in office for as long as possible.
> ☐ Some of the barriers to entry used to protect monopoly rents (for example, economies of scale, innovation) yield some economic benefits. This not true for the dictatorship.

12.7 SPENDING BY DEMOCRATIC GOVERNMENTS: PRIORITIES OF A NATION

Joseph Schumpeter (page 28) once wrote that the public budget is the 'skeleton of the state stripped of all misleading ideologies'. He argued that the way in which a government spends its money reveals its true priorities, much in the way that an individual's spending pattern is a lens through which to study their preferences.

As we have seen, before the twentieth century a major activity of governments was defence (in some cases, predation on other nations), and raising the taxation to support it. But well before that time, some ruling institutions came to understand that they would benefit from providing conditions for the growth of the economy—building canals, roads and schools in the nineteenth century, for example. Economic development could be an asset by creating a larger tax base, educating a more scientifically oriented cadre of citizens, or by building financial institutions that could loan money to the government.

During the twentieth century, large-scale production in firms was easy for the government to see and it happened in one place. This made taxation and regulation of firms easier, and governments could also use the accounting books and payroll records of firms to find out who was paid what. This meant that taxing individuals became easier, too. Governments in many countries deducted tax directly from the pay of their citizens, and many workers were taxed explicitly for 'social security', that is, to fund pensions and sometimes healthcare.

Many governments are currently investigating whether their systems of taxation are efficient and fair. An example is the 2010 *Mirrlees Review* (https://tinyco.re/6726989), which offered proposals for a comprehensive reform of the UK's tax and transfer system, establishing the scope for better addressing market failures and unfairness.

Changes in the structure of the economy also made it easier for governments to levy taxes, not only on a specific good, such as salt or imports, but also on consumption in general and ultimately on value added in production. These broad-based taxes play an important role in the public finances of advanced economies. With the extension of voting

Joseph Schumpeter. 1918. 'The crisis of the tax state.' Reproduced in Swedberg R. (ed.) 1991. *Joseph A. Schumpeter, The Economics and Sociology of Capitalism*. Princeton University Press.

12.7 SPENDING BY DEMOCRATIC GOVERNMENTS: PRIORITIES OF A NATION

rights to virtually all adults, governments became accountable to their citizens for delivering services.

The historical processes of transition from political monopoly to political competition have produced most of the modern governments in the world, with their distinctive patterns of spending.

Figure 12.10 shows how the democratic governments of the US, South Korea, and Finland spent their money in 2016.

The size of the government spending in Finland is 55.9% of its GDP, which is the largest of the three countries. For the US, it is 38.2%. Note: this does not mean that the US spends less than Finland in absolute terms, just that government expenditure is a smaller fraction of the country's GDP. Expenditure by South Korea's government is 32.3% of its GDP.

This is what the categories mean:

- *Public services:* These include funds for running parliament, congress, local councils, also foreign aid and public debt transactions.
- *Military:* As previously stated, one of the motivations for government has been for protection or to wage war.
- *Economic affairs:* This includes expenditures on infrastructure such as roads, bridges, and the Internet.
- *Public order and safety:* This includes police, fire, prison services, and law courts.
- *Social protection:* **Social insurance** spending that a government might make, such as unemployment benefits and pensions is labelled 'Social protection' in the figure.
- *Schooling:* All governments are responsible for at least some education provision.
- *Health:* This includes medical equipment, hospital and outpatient services, and public health.

social insurance Expenditure by the government, financed by taxation, which provides protection against various economic risks (for example, loss of income due to sickness, or unemployment) and enables people to smooth incomes throughout their lifetime. See also: co-insurance.

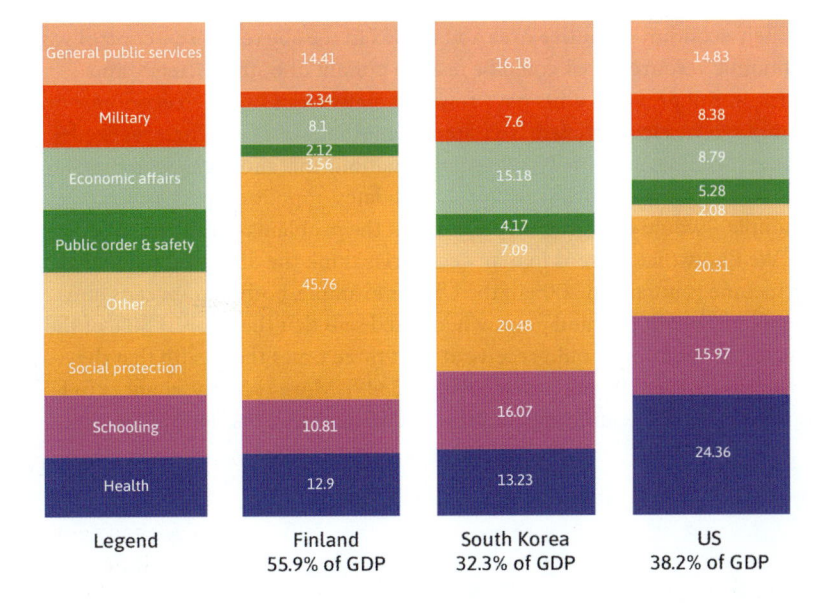

Figure 12.10 Patterns of public expenditure in Finland, the US, and South Korea (2016) measured as a percentage of total spending by government.

OECD. 2017. 'Government at a Glance' (https://tinyco.re/2331814). This dataset takes data from OECD National Accounts Statistics (https://tinyco.re/9200122) and from Eurostat government finance statistics (https://tinyco.re/4616738).

Category	Finland	South Korea	US
General public services	14.41	16.18	14.83
Military	2.34	7.6	8.38
Economic affairs	8.1	15.18	8.79
Public order & safety	2.12	4.17	5.28
Other	3.56	7.09	2.08
Social protection	45.76	20.48	20.31
Schooling	10.81	16.07	15.97
Health	12.9	13.23	24.36
Total % of GDP	55.9%	32.3%	38.2%

553

There are many reasons why governments differ in their spending patterns. One reason is that political institutions differ, even among democracies.

> **EXERCISE 12.4 PAST INFLUENCES ON CURRENT GOVERNMENT SPENDING PATTERNS**
> 1. Looking at Figure 12.10, how would you characterize the two biggest differences in the spending patterns among the three pairs of countries (the US vs South Korea, the US vs Finland, and Finland vs South Korea)?
> 2. Can you think of factors in the countries and their histories that might account for these differences? You need to do some research to support your claims.

> **EXERCISE 12.5 USING EXCEL: COMPARING GOVERNMENT EXPENDITURES**
> Go to the source of Figure 12.10, OECD statistics (http://tinyco.re/2331814), and see if you can find different countries for each of the criteria below (for the year 2016, or the most recent year available). For each of your chosen countries, plot a stacked column chart similar to Figure 12.10.
>
> - General government expenditure (as a percentage of GDP) is greater than South Korea's, but less than Finland's.
> - Government expenditure on health (as a percentage of GDP) is greater than the US's.
> - Government expenditure on social protection (as a percentage of GDP) is greater than Finland's.
> - Government expenditure on defence (as a percentage of GDP) is greater than South Korea's.

A puzzle: Persistence of unfairness and market failures

It is clear that even governments considered to be 'small' in spending relative to their economy—South Korea and the US in the above figure—control vast economic resources that could be used in pursuit of both efficiency and fairness. But previous units have revealed many cases in which economic outcomes are Pareto inefficient, so potential mutual gains remain unrealized. These seem like potentially 'win–win' situations that those engaged in political competition—aspiring electoral candidates or political parties, for example—would energetically exploit. Yet the problems persist.

We know that citizens in many countries think the distribution of wealth or income is unfair. In 2005 in the US, for example, both Republicans and Democrats, both rich and poor, when asked said that the poorest 80% of the wealth distribution should receive at least three times the wealth that they then had received (https://tinyco.re/5232349). More recently, changes in US tax policy have favoured the wealthy, not the bottom 80%. This is a puzzle.

12.8 THE FEASIBILITY OF ECONOMIC POLICIES

To make sense of this puzzle, we must think about the feasibility of the policies that a government might adopt. Fixing some problem of Pareto inefficiency or perceived unfairness will happen only if:

- It is **economically feasible**: The policy to fix the problem, if implemented, must work.
- It is **administratively feasible**: The government must have the capacity to implement the policy.
- It is **politically feasible**: Those who determine which policies are implemented—both officials and private interests—must want to see the policy implemented and, if they do implement the policies, they or others supporting the policy must remain in office.

We take up these three problems in turn, starting with economic feasibility.

Given people's preferences and the information available to private economic actors, there may not be a feasible set of policies that would sustain an efficient and fair outcome. For a policy to have economic feasibility, it must be a Nash equilibrium, which means no actor can improve its position by changing its behaviour.

In Section 3.9 (page 124) we showed that a government's policy to raise the tax rate for the rich to be able better to provide needed services to low-income families might be less effective than expected if the high tax rates make it cost effective for the wealthy to engage in tax evasion.

To take another example, a government that tries to enforce perfect competition in every industry will fail. Since firms are free to advertise, and to differentiate their products, it is impossible for the policymaker to legislate that demand curves be horizontal.

We have also seen that no macroeconomic policy can entirely eliminate unemployment, given that the threat of unemployment motivates people to work hard and well.

> **economically feasible** Policies for which the desired outcomes are a Nash equilibrium, so that once implemented private economic actors will not undo the desired effects.
> **politically feasible** Capable of being implemented given the existing political institutions.
> **administratively feasible** Policies for which the government has sufficient information and staff for implementation.

Economic feasibility: An example from Chile

The model of tax evasion in Unit 3 is a simplification, but it helps us understand real economic forces operating in the world. The experience of Chile provides such an example.

In 1970, the socialist Salvador Allende was democratically elected president of Chile in a surprise victory, on a platform promising greater public services and nationalization of many of the privately held firms in the country.

To interpret the data in Figure 12.11, notice the vertical line that marks the day before the election. The series for share prices dropped dramatically the next day. The fall in share prices indicates a major sell-off of shares in Chilean companies as soon as the news arrived. This tells us that the victory of Allende was a surprise. Had his victory been anticipated, the stock market would have fallen *before* the election.

A stock (or share) is a share in the ownership of a company; its price measures how much it is worth to own part of that company and as a result receive a share of its profits, and benefit in the future from selling it to another person.

Share prices rise when, taking everything into account, owners or potential buyers of shares think that the company will be more profitable in the future. When a socialist president was elected in Chile, wealthy people were worried about:

- higher taxes
- policies favouring employees that would mean paying them higher wages
- the possibility that the government or even workers might expropriate (take over the ownership of) the assets of private firms.

In turn, these worries created a limit to the policies that would prove economically feasible for the Allende government. If the wealthy thought that the firms they owned would be less profitable in the future, they would have no incentive to invest in increasing the assets of the firm. Rather than invest in these firms, these people might instead invest in another country (known as capital flight), in housing, or in other Chilean assets more likely to be valuable in the future.

The result was poor economic performance of the Chilean economy. We will return to the Chile story a bit later, when we will see that political interests, as well as economic infeasibility, can limit what a democratically elected government can do.

> **QUESTION 12.7 CHOOSE THE CORRECT ANSWER(S)**
> What is meant by economic feasibility?
>
> ☐ Policies that solve the problem must be possible to implement in practice.
> ☐ For a policy to have economic feasibility, it must produce a Nash equilibrium and sustain a fair and efficient outcome.
> ☐ Policies that would solve the problem and are politically acceptable.
> ☐ Must be able to make someone better off without making anyone else worse off.

Proprietary data from the Santiago stock market. Time zero is the first trading day on the Santiago stock market following the election. Daniele Girardi and Samuel Bowles. 2017. 'Institutional Shocks and Economic Outcomes: Allende's Election, Pinochet's Coup and the Santiago Stock Market', *Journal of Development Economics*.

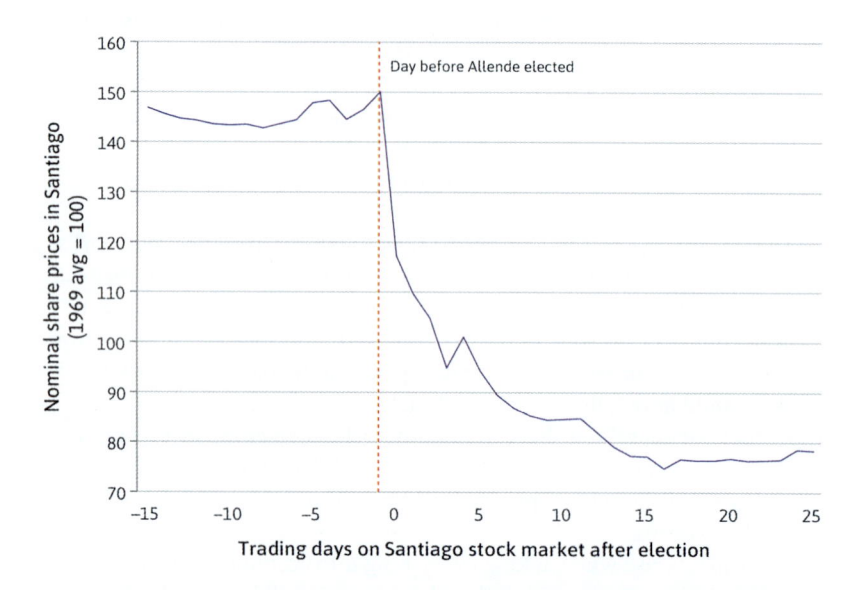

Figure 12.11 Stock market prices in Chile: The election of a socialist president, 1970.

556

12.9 ADMINISTRATIVE FEASIBILITY: INFORMATION AND CAPACITIES

Even if there exists an economically feasible set of policies that would address market failures, in order to design and implement these policies, the government needs:

- information about the nature of the uncompensated external effects that account for the market failure
- the administrative and **fiscal capacity** to design and implement effective policies.

As we have seen, the magic of the market means that, as long as prices reflect social marginal costs, the information required to direct resources to more highly valued rather than less highly valued uses arises as a by-product of people's everyday transactions.

Contrast this with the case of a citizen attempting to get a remedy through the courts for an environmental market failure. If the citizen suffering from a respiratory illness could bring a lawsuit against the polluting firm that caused it, and secure compensation for the costs of his illness, then this might 'internalize' the external costs of the polluter's actions, leading to more effective abatement efforts. But in most cases, this cannot be done because the citizen does not have the necessary information about who is polluting, or cannot afford the legal and other costs of pursuing the case.

fiscal capacity The ability of a government to impose and collect substantial taxes from a population at low administrative and other costs. One measure of this is the amount collected divided by the cost of administering the tax system.

Governments have limited information

Market failures arise because essential information is not available to buyers, sellers, and other private economic actors. But this information is not likely to be available to the government either, limiting its ability to design policies that address environmental market failures. Governments often do not know how much citizens value environmental quality, or how effective environmental policies will be in ensuring a sustainable environment. If prices are sending the wrong messages, and if the government is to correct them through the implementation of taxes, subsidies, or regulation, it must find ways of collecting the necessary information to design those interventions.

Limited information is not the only factor limiting the **administrative feasibility** of policies to remedy market failures.

administratively feasible Policies for which the government has sufficient information and staff for implementation.

Limited fiscal capacities

To levy taxes effectively and collect the revenue, governments need revenue officers who are competent, not corrupt, with sufficient resources to find and punish tax evaders, and with enough legitimacy to ensure that most people pay their taxes.

Administrative capacity is required for many different kinds of taxes, from trade tariffs enforced at the border, to payroll taxes levied on wages, and to corporate income taxes charged on legally incorporated economic entities. The use of accounting books in large firms makes it easier to audit firms and accurately assess their tax bill. But this also depends on the technology and institutions available. International flows of difficult-to-track financial obligations make illegal tax evasion, and legal tax avoidance (for example, by moving profits to international tax havens), a problem for governments who want to collect tax. This lowers their fiscal capacity.

Timothy Besley and Torsten Persson. 2014. 'Why do developing countries tax so little?' (https://tinyco.re/3513621) *The Journal of Economic Perspectives* 28 (4): pp. 99–120.

Lack of administrative capacity affects all aspects of government, not just taxes. An educational reform, for example, requiring teachers to abandon rote-learning methods and engage in more active student-centred learning may simply be impossible to implement, given the skills of the current teaching force.

> ### HOW ECONOMISTS LEARN FROM DATA
>
> #### Administrative infeasibility: An application from Nigeria
> A lack of information about the progress of infrastructure projects funded by the government, and a poorly functioning and corrupt administration, resulted in poor outcomes in Nigeria.
>
> In 2006–2007, the public sector was given funding and made responsible for implementing 4,700 small-scale infrastructure projects like installing water wells, constructing dams, and building health centres. Just 31% of the projects were completed and 38% were not even started. For example, the funding was paid for 1,348 water wells, but 846 were never completed, leaving hundreds of thousands of people without improved access to water.
>
> Economists Imran Rasul and Daniel Rogger wanted to find out why some organizations succeeded in completing projects on schedule and budget, while others did not. They could do their research because the Nigerian government had collected information from independent teams of engineers about the quantity and quality of completed projects. Accurate information of this kind from independent observers is very rare for a low-income country.
>
> Rasul and Rogger found that 'getting things done' by public sector organizations is affected by how the organizations are managed. They were surprised to discover that using performance incentives, with which managers were rewarded for good performance as measured by the organization (not by independent assessors), was correlated with lower completion rates. In organizations where officials had greater autonomy in making decisions—not in response to performance incentives—outcomes were better.
>
> While financial incentives can play a positive role in motivating government officials, the Nigerian case shows that, if it is difficult to collect and verify information, trying to attach simple performance incentives to complex tasks may backfire. If there is poor information, then it may be better to give organizations greater autonomy. In this case, officials given autonomy observed social norms of responsibility, and completion rates were higher.

Imran Rasul and Daniel Rogger. 2016. 'Management of bureaucrats and public service delivery: Evidence from the Nigerian civil service' (https://tinyco.re/1535739). *The Economic Journal* 128 (608): pp. 413–46.

12.10 POLITICAL FEASIBILITY

In a democracy, it is often said that ideally the government is the servant of the people. In economic terms, government officials are the agents and the citizens are the principals. But this immediately raises two questions:

- *Why would the agent (the elected official) do what the principals (the citizens) desire?* As in any **principal–agent relationship**, the agent has their own objectives, and they differ from the principal's objectives. We saw that, although political competition can help, the problem does not disappear in a democracy.
- *Who are 'the people'?* In economic terms, who is (or are) the principal(s)? Until now the principal has been the lender or the employer, which we could simplify by representing as a single individual. But there are many citizen-principals and they have differing priorities for what the government should do, for example, abatement of pollution, school improvement, policies to boost innovation, tax-funded transfers to the poor, and so on.

> **principal–agent relationship** This is an asymmetrical relationship in which one party (the principal) benefits from some action or attribute of the other party (the agent) about which the principal's information is not sufficient to enforce in a complete contract. *See also: incomplete contract. Also known as: principal–agent problem.*

Think about the first problem—motivating the elected official to do what the citizens prefer—as a principal–agent problem, like the employer trying to motivate a worker to contribute to the profits of the firm. What are the possible solutions when the manager tries to motivate workers? The manager could:

- *Pay the agent an economic rent:* She will fear losing it if she does an unsatisfactory job.
- *Monitor the work activity of the employee:* To detect signs of inadequate work.
- *Replace the worker with another worker:* If the work is found to be unsatisfactory.

In a democracy, elected officials are held accountable to the electorate by a similar set of strategies:

- *Give the official a sufficient salary, prestige, and other amenities of office:* The official would then like to keep the job.
- *Monitor the activities of the government:* Determine the quality of the government's performance using legal principles of transparency and judicial review, along with a free press and free speech.
- *Hold periodic elections:* A government that has not performed well in the citizens' eyes is replaced by a different set of political leaders.

But these methods—while essential components of a democratic society—sometimes work imperfectly, if at all. There are many reasons. But one is that citizens or groups that can amass substantial wealth for the purposes of influencing the government have extraordinary political influence even in a democracy.

12 GOVERNMENTS AND MARKETS IN A DEMOCRATIC SOCIETY

Elites and organized groups seem to have much more influence on policy than average citizens: Martin Gilens and Benjamin I. Page. 2014. 'Testing theories of American politics: Elites, interest groups, and average citizens' (https://tinyco.re/7911085). *Perspectives on Politics* 12 (03): pp. 564–81.

Joshua L. Kalla and David E. Broockman. (2015). 'Campaign contributions facilitate access to congressional officials: A randomized field experiment' (https://tinyco.re/6564191). *American Journal of Political Science* 60 (3): pp. 1–14.

It seems that democracy alone cannot reverse rising inequality: Adam Bonica, Nolan McCarty, Keith T. Poole, and Howard Rosenthal. 2013. 'Why hasn't democracy slowed rising inequality?' (https://tinyco.re/5838764) *The Journal of Economic Perspectives* 27 (3): pp. 103–23.

HOW ECONOMISTS (AND POLITICAL SCIENTISTS) LEARN FROM DATA

Does money talk?

In the US, people often say 'money talks'. Many are concerned that it talks particularly loudly when it comes to politics.

To some, it is obvious that, when a candidate for political office receives a large contribution for his electoral campaign from a business or a trade union, the candidate is more likely to use political power to influence policy in favour of the contributor.

Research by Joshua Kalla and David Broockman, two political scientists, shows that election campaigns for the US congress in 2012 spent on average $8.5 million per congressional seat. But did the winners provide favours for the donors that would not have occurred without the donors' contributions? We might ask if the members of congress who received contributions from those with investments in the oil industry tended to favour the interests of those firms afterwards. Or did those receiving funds from trade union members support an agenda that favoured the union's interests? The answer in both cases would be that they did.

But this does not demonstrate that donor contributions purchased influence over the legislator. Remember, causation can work both ways; those with oil wealth are likely to donate to candidates who already favour that industry's interests; trade union members will donate money to those who already support the interests of trade unions. Simply showing a correlation between the source of the funding and the policies supported by the legislator does not show that the contributions *caused* the legislator to act differently.

Kalla and Broockman designed a clever experiment to see if the donation caused the congress member to behave in the donor's interest. They reasoned that citizens could influence legislators by meeting with them and expressing their views. Members of congress are busy people, so gaining access to them for a meeting is something that groups compete for.

Kalla and Broockman wanted to find out if those who gave money to a congress member were more likely to be granted a meeting. With the cooperation of a (real) interest group Credo Action (https://tinyco.re/3459944), they contacted 191 members of congress to ask for a meeting. All the constituents making this request had contributed some funds to the member's campaign. The control group, randomly chosen, and half of the total sample, said only that they were residents of the member's district. The treatment group also identified themselves as donors. All callers in both groups read from a script, so the requests for a meeting were otherwise identical.

Among those not identified as donors, 2.4% gained a meeting with either the congress member or the chief of staff. For those identified as donors, 12.5% got a meeting.

The authors concluded: 'The vast majority of Americans who cannot afford to contribute to campaigns in meaningful amounts are at a disadvantage when attempting to express their concerns to policy makers.'

Political feasibility: The story of Chile continued

What happened after the election of Allende in Chile in 1970 tells a story not only of economic limits to feasible policies, but also of political limits.

Amid faltering economic performance, due in part to potential investors holding back on investment in Chile, opposition to President Allende's government mounted, some of it supported in secret by the US government. In 1973, the Chilean armed forces attacked the presidential palace, defeating troops loyal to Allende. They took over the government, ending democracy and replacing Allende with General Augusto Pinochet, who ruled as a dictator—without the democratic constraints of elections and individual political rights—for the next 17 years.

The wealthy anticipated that Pinochet would introduce pro-business policies, so stock prices rose again (Figure 12.12). The Pinochet dictatorship would remain until a constitutional referendum in 1988 demanded a return to democracy, which the armed forces respected.

Allende's economic program was infeasible for two reasons:

- *It was economically infeasible:* He could not force private firms to invest in Chile, and without their investment the economy would stagnate or even shrink.
- *It was politically infeasible:* Though democratically elected, he did not control the Chilean armed forces that, with the support of businesses and the US Central Intelligence Agency, turned against him.

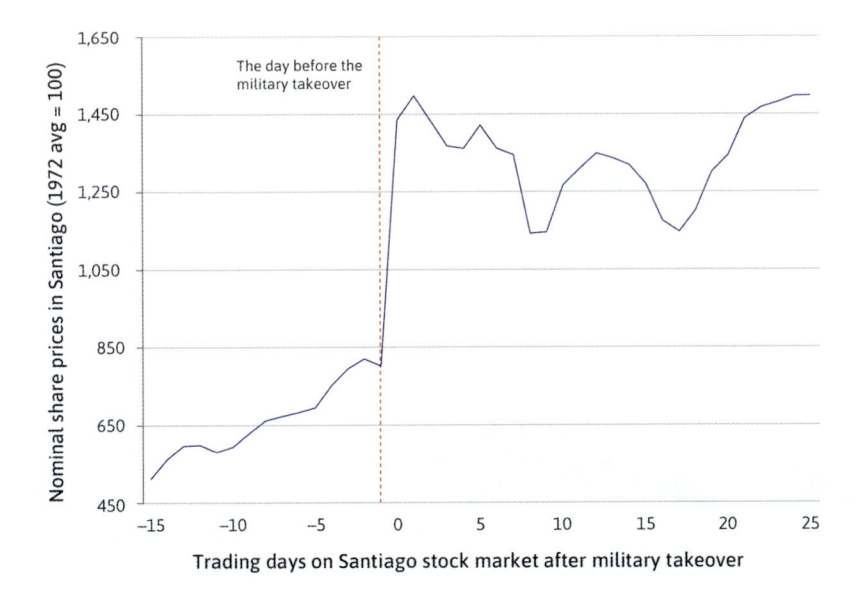

Figure 12.12 Stock market prices in Chile: The military overthrow of the socialist government, 1973.

Proprietary data from the Santiago stock market. Time zero is the first trading day on the Santiago stock market following the election. Daniele Girardi and Samuel Bowles. 2017. 'Institutional Shocks and Economic Outcomes: Allende's Election, Pinochet's Coup and the Santiago Stock Market'. *Journal of Development Economics*.

12.11 POLICY MATTERS

In this unit, you have learned that for a policy to improve an outcome, it must change the current Nash equilibrium to a different and preferable one (economic feasibility). And it also must be favoured by a governing elite with the authority and capacity to implement it (political and administrative feasibility).

The limits posed by special interests, as well as economic and administrative feasibility, explain why governments often do not successfully address the problems of market failure and unfairness that we have encountered throughout this course. Looking at the different economies of the world, however, you see substantial differences in the extent to which these problems are effectively addressed. As a result, the limits posed by economic, political, and administrative feasibility differ substantially among countries.

Policies differ across countries

To see this, we return to the problem of climate change introduced in Section 2.13 (page 86). In Figure 12.13 we can see that Germany, Australia and the US have roughly the same per capita income. If they all faced similar constraints of economic, administrative, and political feasibility in adopting policies to limit greenhouse gas impacts on climate, then we might expect to see their similarity in income matched by similarity in CO_2 emissions per capita.

But this is not at all what we see in the figure. The US and Australia emit about two times as much per capita as Germany. It seems likely that what is economically feasible may not differ very much in these three countries, as all share the same knowledge about technologies, and their citizens are likely to respond in similar ways to incentives to adopt cleaner energy sources. The government information and capacities in the three countries are also similar—all have well-informed and capable governments.

Although carbon dioxide emissions are affected by industrial structure and trade specialization, they are also affected by what is desired by the elites, who have political influence. Policies to address climate change are more likely to have political support in Germany than in Australia and the US. One reason for this difference is the importance in US and Australian

View this data at OWiD https://tinyco.re/3443425

The World Bank. 2018. 'World Development Indicators.' (https://tinyco.re/2105434); Maddison Project Database, version 2018. Bolt, Jutta, Robert Inklaar, Herman de Jong, and Jan Luiten van Zanden (2018), "Rebasing 'Maddison': new income comparisons and the shape of long-run economic development", Maddison Project Working paper 10 (https://tinyco.re/8062169).

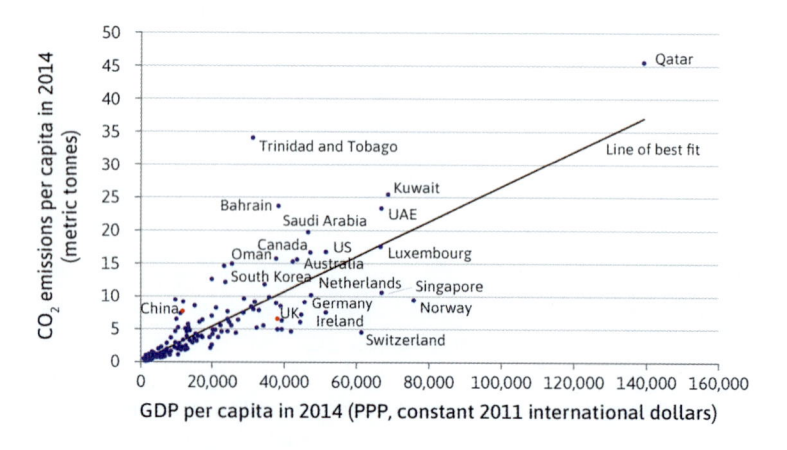

Figure 12.13 Carbon dioxide emissions are greater in richer countries, but countries of the same level of income differ greatly in how much they emit.

politics of lobbies representing the natural resource industries, including the gas, oil, and coal producers.

A similar contrast appears when we look at inequality, shown in Figure 12.14. Germany and the US have both experienced about the same rate of growth in GDP per capita over the past four decades, but they differ markedly in inequality of living standards, as can be seen by the much higher Gini coefficient for disposable income in the US. The comparison for the measure of intergenerational inequality is similar. Denmark, Sweden, and Finland are more equal by this measure than even Germany.

Many things could account for these differences. They are, at least in part, due to the greater political influence in Germany than in the US, of those who value sustaining a higher living standard for the least well off.

What can we learn from the comparisons in Figure 12.14 showing that high income countries with a similar growth in GDP per capita do not necessarily have similar levels of inequality.

Lessons from the experiences of different countries

One lesson, if we wish to address problems like climate change and unfair inequalities in living standards, is that for most countries it is possible to do a lot more than is currently being done. The fundamental forces contributing to inequality in the high-income countries—new technologies and growing imports (from China, for example) that make the skills of low-paid workers redundant—do not differ much among the high-income countries in Figure 12.14. The differences appear to be a matter of choices among the similar set of policies that are economically and administratively feasible, some countries opting for policies that sustain high levels of inequality, and others pursuing the goal of greater equality.

Chen Wang and Koen Caminada. 2011. 'Leiden Budget Incidence Fiscal Redistribution Dataset' (https://tinyco.re/9338721). Version 1. Leiden Department of Economics Research.

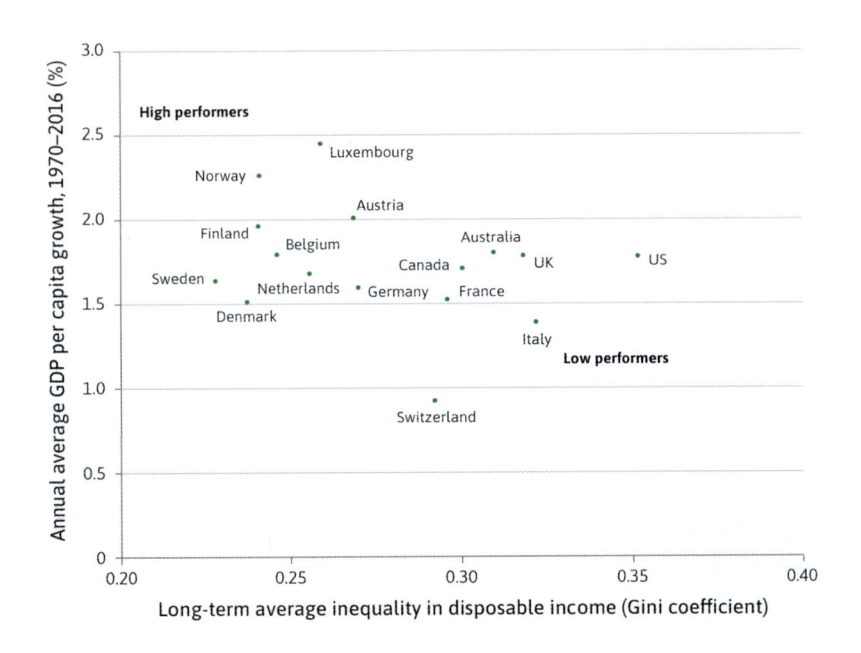

Figure 12.14 Greater equality in disposable income is not associated with slower growth in average income.

We also have a lot to learn from the top performers in these and similar figures, by studying the policies and institutions that appear to account for their success in addressing market failures and unfairness and in delivering public services.

For example, some countries have school systems that teach much more effectively than others. Because educational policies differ greatly among countries, we can get some idea of the importance of good policy by looking at differences among nations in performance on a mathematics test administered to 15-year-old students around the world.

You can access the data from a test at the OECD's Programme for International Student Assessment (https://tinyco.re/1018246).

Using the OECD data, let's compare two countries that are ethnically diverse and have about the same per capita income: the US and Singapore. The average maths score in Singapore was 20% higher than in the US. Even more striking, the student whose score placed them in the middle of the US students (the student with the median score) would have been in the bottom quarter of Singapore's students. A similar comparison would place the median American student in the bottom quarter of Japanese students, and just above the bottom quarter of Finland's students.

Not all policies and institutions that are effective in one country can be transferred to another. For example, a comparison between the innovation systems in Silicon Valley and in Germany in Section 21.2 (https://tinyco.re/2640737) of *The Economy* shows how different combinations of innovating firms, government policies, financial institutions, and social norms in these two regions produce effective solutions to the market failures associated with knowledge production. Neither would be easily adopted in the other country.

12.12 THE DISTRIBUTIONAL IMPACT OF PUBLIC POLICIES: EARLY CHILDHOOD EDUCATION

Harold Lasswell, a prominent mid-twentieth-century American political scientist, is best known for his book, *Politics: Who gets what, when and how* (https://tinyco.re/2227728). The title captures a basic point of this unit. Politics is all about:

- Who gets what.
- Who gets to be what.
- Who gets to do what.

Harold D. Lasswell. 1936. *Politics; who gets what, when and how* (https://tinyco.re/2227728). New York: Whittlesey House.

The reason is that political processes determine the rules of the game—the basic institutions that govern how we interact in the economy and other arenas of our society.

But politics is not simply about dividing up a pie, with the powerful getting the larger slice and the struggle for power sometimes resulting in a smaller pie. Well-designed government policies are also able to increase the size of the pie, improving living standards for the vast majority of people. Examples that you have already seen include the economic policies of the government of China, which since the 1980s resulted in the most rapid eradication of large-scale poverty ever witnessed in human history. Another example was the clean water and sanitation policies that were behind the global reduction in child mortality.

12.12 THE DISTRIBUTIONAL IMPACT OF PUBLIC POLICIES: EARLY CHILDHOOD EDUCATION

Schooling and inequality

Economic research has explored the question of how schooling and preschool experience affects inequality. In our 'Economist in action' video, James Heckman shows how economists can learn from experiments and other data about how to level the playing field for children growing up poor. You may also want to read his book *Giving kids a fair chance*.

His book begins by noting that: 'The accident of birth is a principal source of inequality in America today. American society is dividing into skilled and unskilled … birth is becoming fate.'

Heckman's 'strategy that works' to address this problem is based on the following logic: 'Both cognitive and socio-emotional skills develop in early childhood and their development depends on family environment.' Growing up poor deprives children of opportunities to develop these skills, and 'family environments in the US have deteriorated'.

In response, Heckman advocates 'early interventions', such as enriched preschool environments and home visits by professionals to assist parents, which his research shows can 'produce positive and lasting effects on children in disadvantaged families'.

Policies of the kind advocated by Heckman are being implemented in several countries, including Colombia, Jamaica, Chile, and in the state of Orissa in India. Teams of economists and experts in child development are rigorously evaluating them (https://tinyco.re/2744426) for their longer-term effects and to assess the feasibility of scaling them up from small pilot interventions.

We know that the kids of poor parents often grow up to be poor. We now also know that this has little to do with genetics, and more to do with the socio-emotional situation that poor parents and children experience. We now know of, and governments can implement, effective policy remedies to break this cycle of poverty.

In our 'Economist in action' video, James Heckman, a Nobel-prize-winning economist from the University of Chicago and a leader in this research, explores the question of how schooling and preschool experience affects inequality. https://tinyco.re/3964341

James J. Heckman. 2013. *Giving Kids a Fair Chance*. Cambridge, MA: MIT Press.

> **QUESTION 12.8 CHOOSE THE CORRECT ANSWER(S)**
> Watch the 'Economist in action' video (https://tinyco.re/3964341) of James Heckman. According to Heckman, which of the following individual attributes are NOT among the reasons for persistent poverty in a family from generation to generation?
>
> ☐ inherited IQ
> ☐ limited schooling
> ☐ race
> ☐ social behaviour

12.13 FREE TUITION IN HIGHER EDUCATION: CAN IT BE FAIR TO NON-STUDENTS?

As a person enters the labour force, education—its quality, amount and content—is an **endowment** that affects both their wage and the kinds of goods and services and possible innovations that the citizens of a nation can enjoy. Governments set aside tax revenues to fund higher education for both efficiency and fairness reasons.

Taking efficiency first, without government support people would have to pay for the costs of their own (or their children's) studies, and this would result in less higher education than economists think would be desirable for two efficiency-related reasons:

- *External benefits of education:* The benefits of a higher education are both private—accruing to the individual who gets the education—and public—accruing to the people with whom she works, neighbours, friends and others (these external benefits are similar to those studied in Unit 11 (page 512)). Because of the external benefits of higher education, the individuals acting on their own self-interest would not 'purchase' enough education in the absence of government policies to lower university fees or support scholarships.
- *Credit constraints:* It is also efficient for governments to support higher education because some families do not have the funds and cannot borrow sufficiently to support their children's university studies, even in cases where the private benefits exceed the private costs. This problem arises because, as we have seen in Unit 9 (page 416), there is a conflict of interest between the borrower (the student in this case) and the lender (a bank) because the bank cannot be sure the student will repay the loan later. A solution would be for the student to provide collateral but unlike the case of a mortgage loan for buying a home or vehicle, in which the house or the car is the collateral, there is no saleable collateral for a student loan in the event that the loan is defaulted on.

> **endowment** The facts about an individual that may affect his or her income, such as the physical wealth a person has, either land, housing, or a portfolio of shares (stocks). Also includes level and quality of schooling, special training, the computer languages in which the individual can work, work experience in internships, citizenship, whether the individual has a visa (or green card) allowing employment in a particular labour market, the nationality and gender of the individual, and even the person's race or social class background. See also: human capital.

EXERCISE 12.6 SOLUTIONS TO THE CREDIT CONSTRAINTS PROBLEM

The 'asset' acquired by attending a university is a person's knowledge, problem-solving abilities, contacts, gained as a result of higher education. Two ways to turn this asset into collateral (as with a car loan or home mortgage) are described below. Compare and evaluate these solutions to the credit constraints problem from the standpoint of efficiency and fairness.

1. One proposed solution to the credit constraints problem is that a company or other organization could select promising secondary school students and offer to pay their entire cost of higher education (the student's degree program chosen by the company) in return for the student's agreement to work for the company for ten years, on terms determined by the company.

2. During the nineteenth century many Europeans wishing to move to North America and lacking the funds and unable to borrow to pay for the trans-Atlantic voyage agreed to what is known as an indentured servitude contract. Their prospective North American employer would pay for the voyage, and in return the person would be obligated to work for the employer, perhaps for many years.

12.13 FREE TUITION IN HIGHER EDUCATION: CAN IT BE FAIR TO NON-STUDENTS?

Questions of fairness arise because many people consider education to be a merit good, namely one that should be available to all irrespective of their ability to pay.

In response to the fact that meeting two objectives—fairness and efficiency—requires some kind of government support, methods of funding higher education vary greatly around the world. For example:

- *No fees:* In many European countries, higher education is funded by the government and students pay no fees (or a very low fee).
- *High fees:* In others, students (or their families) pay a substantial fraction of the cost of a university education.

Where student fees are high, some families are able to pay. Students from other families take out loans for this purpose.

- *In the US or Thailand (and others):* Loans are repaid just as a mortgage on a house would be repaid.
- *In Australia and the UK (and others):* The amount that the student repays depend on how much they earn. Graduates in high-paying jobs pay the full amount they borrowed, but those with small incomes repay only a portion of the amount they borrowed, or even none at all. These are called 'income contingent' loans.
- *In the past:* In the UK and the US, for example, when higher education was entirely privately funded, and virtually all of the students were from wealthy families who paid their fees, and also paid the fees of expensive schooling that was effectively a prerequisite for admission.

Let's think about these five ways of financing higher education from the standpoint of efficiency and fairness (summarized in Figure 12.15 below).

1. *The entirely private funding of higher education by the families of students*: This is now considered unfair. It violates elementary principles of equality of opportunity and education as a merit good. Because as a result, the children of the high-paid and well-educated also then tend to be highly paid and well educated, it contributes to the perpetuation of income differences across families from generation to generation. It is inefficient because it restricts high-quality education to a small group, not all of whom are capable of benefiting, while denying higher education to the talented children of the less well off.
2. *The no-fees option:* This addresses the 'too little education' inefficiency of the entirely private funding option by removing the private costs of attendance. But it goes to the other extreme: motivating even those who expect to benefit very little from higher education to attend, at considerable cost to taxpayers. Also, many consider this option to be unfair because the students enrolled in higher education tend to come from families with much higher incomes than those without children in university, so the no-fees option is a free government service that is used disproportionately by well-off people.
3. *Private-credit-financed higher education:* This is an option, but this has never been a major source of funding. The reason is that unlike borrowing to purchase a home or a car, the borrower does not acquire an asset that can be used as collateral (insuring the lender against losses if the borrower cannot repay). The asset acquired are the skills embodied in

To see why many have decided that funding the full cost of higher education from general taxation is not fair, watch the video by the economist Nick Barr of the LSE: 'Why university isn't free'
https://tinyco.re/8500075

the person herself, and (because slavery is illegal) that person cannot sign over ownership of herself to the lender (see Exercise 12.6 (page 566) for more details).

4. *A government-backed student loan option with repayment contingent on income:* By making loans available to families who otherwise would be excluded from borrowing sufficient funds, this increases educational opportunity for the less well off. Because repayment depends (is 'contingent') on the income the student later earns, it also addresses two shortcomings of student loans. The first is that the income of a former student may vary from year to year, making repayment difficult during periods of low income (or unemployment).

CORE author Antonio Cabrales investigates with colleagues (https://tinyco.re/9545692) how an income-contingent loan system would work in Spain, where the labour market for young university graduates functions poorly.

The second shortcoming is that the obligation to repay a fixed amount unconditionally also leads students to major in subjects they think will allow a reliable high income, rather than studying subjects they like, or in which they are most talented. This results in a mismatch between the educational resources devoted to, say, an engineering education, and the students signing up for engineering studies, who might have been a better fit for the study of subjects associated with less well-paying jobs such as language or primary school teaching.

Those who take out income-contingent loans are shielded from the worst income shocks since there is a maximum proportion of a debtor's income required to be repaid in any year. In Australia and England, for example, this is 8% and 9%, so there is insurance against hardship and default. And because the amount repaid depends on your income, the student is not biased to major in high-income-earning subjects. In practice, neither kind of loan system covers the full cost of higher education and the gap is filled by a combination of general taxation and income from private university endowments.

5. *Free tuition with an income-contingent tax for graduates*: This is a proposal under which attending university would be free, but students would incur a tax obligation (later in life), the total revenues of which would fund higher education (either fully or more plausibly partially). As with income-contingent loans, the amount of tax paid would depend on the income earned. An effect would be to reduce the pressure that students feel to study 'high-earning subjects' so as to be able to pay off their loans (low-earning subjects would lead to jobs with lower graduate taxes).

Either income-contingent loans or free tuition with an income-contingent tax obligation are capable of addressing most of the shortcomings of the other systems, depending on how they are designed. For example, suppose policymakers or the electorate wanted to aggressively promote equal access to higher education without expanding the amount of public resources used. They could implement the free tuition option with a steeply graduated income contingent graduate tax. Those who receive high incomes following graduation pay more than their education cost, while those with low incomes pay very little.

12.14 THE DISTRIBUTIONAL IMPACT OF PUBLIC POLICIES: RENT CONTROL

Another policy that is frequently advocated on grounds of fairness is rent control. Rent control is a legally binding limitation on the rents that landlords can charge tenants. Landlords (owners of housing that is rented out) are typically much wealthier than the people they rent to. Rent control is advocated as a way to redistribute income from the landlords to the tenants. Adequate housing is also considered by many to be a merit good, available to all irrespective of their income, providing a second reason commonly proposed in support of rent control.

Rent control laws are common in some major cities in the US, including Los Angeles, San Francisco, New York and Washington DC. Rent control is typically bundled with restrictions on the conditions under which a landlord can evict a tenant.

In its economic logic, rent control is similar to the minimum wage: it seeks to improve the economic conditions of less well-off people (renters, low-wage workers) by imposing a price (a lower rent, a higher wage) that is favourable to their interests.

The rental housing market: Renters' surplus and landlords' surplus

We can use the model of supply and demand to study the impact of rent control. Recall that in Unit 7 (page 312) the model of the bread market allowed us to identify two components of the gains from trade:

- *Consumer surplus:* This is based on the fact that for most buyers their willingness to pay exceeded the price.
- *Producer surplus:* This is based on the fact that the price at which bread sold exceeds the marginal cost of its production for most bakeries, allowing a producer's surplus.

You can find an analysis of the minimum wage, along with an 'Economist in action' video (https://tinyco.re/3737648) by one of the leading researchers in this area in Unit 19 of *The Economy* (https://tinyco.re/2299150).

Policy	Efficiency	Fairness
Private universities funded by fees paid by the families of students	Too little education	Perpetuates unfair inequality (inheritance from parents)
Free universities funded by general taxation	Too much education	Unfair: it provides a free public service to rich families
Private universities as above but with students (and families) borrowing to pay	Too little education (credit constraints)	Unfair: parents or students who lack wealth cannot borrow.
Income contingent government loans to students	Depends on design	Depends on design
Free tuition with an income contingent graduates tax	Depends on design	Depends on design

Figure 12.15 Financing higher education.

Here we adapt those concepts to the rental market, giving us:

- *Renter surplus:* This arises because, for most renters, their willingness to pay for their apartment exceeds the rent they actually pay. So it is similar to consumer surplus.
- *Landlord surplus:* The rent that most landlords receive exceeds the marginal cost of providing a unit of housing to the market. In this way, it is similar to producer surplus.

Figure 12.16 illustrates these concepts at the equilibrium of a hypothetical rental market. To make sense of the model assume that there are two classes of people in a city: landlords and renters. The latter considerably outnumber the former, which in a democracy gives them the possibility of passing legislation limiting the rents that landlords can charge, much like the way that Angela and her colleagues in Unit 5 (page 209) voted to reduce the hours of work.

To explore all of the slides in this figure, see the online version at https://tinyco.re/6127678.

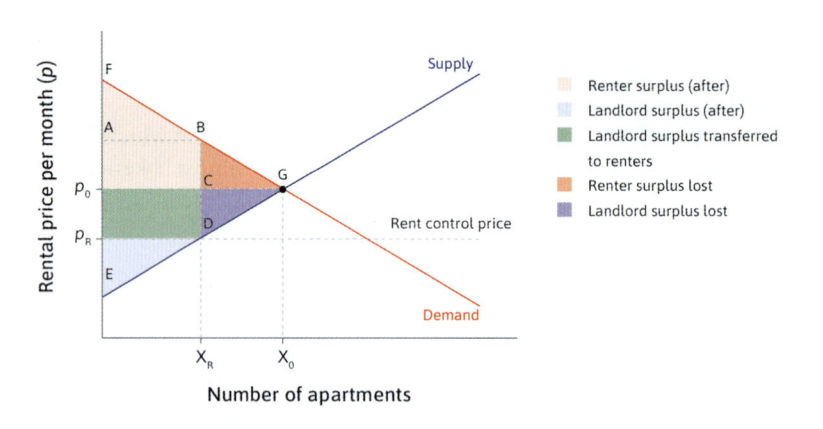

Figure 12.16 The rental market after rent control.

1. The rental market before rent control
The market is in equilibrium (point G), with X_0 apartments each rented at a price of p_0.

2. Renter surplus and landlord surplus before rent control
The light red area shows renter surplus, and the light blue area shows landlord surplus.

3. Rent control affects the equilibrium price and quantity
Rent control lowers the price of an apartment to p_R and reduces the number of units supplied to X_R.

4. Renter surplus and landlord surplus after rent control
Renter surplus is now the sum of the light red and green areas (FBDp_R), and landlord surplus is now the (smaller) light blue area (p_RDE).

5. Winners and losers from rent control
Rent control results in a redistribution of surplus from landlords to renters (the area p_0CDp_R), and deadweight losses for both renters and landlords (the areas BCG and CDG respectively).

12.14 THE DISTRIBUTIONAL IMPACT OF PUBLIC POLICIES: RENT CONTROL

The horizontal axis is the number of units of housing. To simplify, we assume they are all identical in quality and that landlords are unable to charge different rents to different people so there will be just a single rent, which is measured on the vertical axis. The supply curve tells you, for any given rent, how many units of housing will be offered. A higher price will bring more units onto the market, even in the short run, as landlords find ways of converting unused space into apartments. And in the long run, of course, higher rentals will raise the profitability of owning rental apartments and stimulate new construction.

The demand curve provides the answer to the question: if the rental price is p, how many units of housing will be demanded? At a lower rent, more units are demanded, as more people choose to live in the city, or not to live with their parents or roommates.

In the figure you can see that prior to the introduction of rent control, the rent was p_0 and the number of units rented was X_0, and the renters' surplus and the landlords' surplus are as shown by the shaded areas.

Rent control reduces the total surplus and rearranges who gets it

The introduction of the rent control reduces the rental price to p_R and the landlords respond by supplying fewer units, reducing the number available to X_R. With fewer units being rented, notice, the willingness to pay of the 'least willing' renter (the height of the demand curve at X_R), exceeds the marginal cost of putting additional units on the market. This being the case, there are people who would have been willing to rent units beyond the X_R, being offered at a price exceeding the marginal cost. So the demand for rent controlled housing exceeds the supply.

This has two effects:

- *Redistribution to renters*: A portion of what was before the landlords' surplus, is now part of the renters' surplus. This was the intended effect of the policy.
- *Reduction of the total surplus*: The deadweight loss (foregone surplus) resulting from the reduced supply of rental housing under rent control is partly lost by renters (the top triangle of the deadweight loss space) and partly by landlords' (the bottom triangle).

The net effect of these two changes is that landlords definitely lost. Their surplus is less than before for two reasons: first, they experienced some of the deadweight loss and second, they transferred some of what was before their surplus to the renters.

The effect on the renters is more complicated to evaluate. Like the landlords, they experienced some deadweight loss, but they also gained some of what was previously landlords' surplus. Their net gain is the green rectangle $p_0\text{CD}p_R$ minus the orange triangle BCG.

In the figure the surplus gained at the expense of the landlords is greater than the deadweight loss experienced by the renters. So, the policy benefited them, as intended, even though it reduced the supply of housing. Rent control is a way of dividing up a smaller pie, with a larger slice going to the renters.

Because the pie is smaller as a result of the deadweight loss, the surplus lost by the renters must be greater than the surplus gained by the renters. To see this:

$$\begin{aligned}
\text{Landlord surplus lost} = {} & \text{Landlord surplus transferred to Renters} \\
& (\text{rectangle } p_0\text{CD}p_R) \\
& + \text{Landlords' share of deadweight loss} \\
& (\text{triangle CDG}). \\
\text{Renter surplus gained} = {} & \text{Landlord surplus transferred to Renters} \\
& (\text{rectangle } p_0\text{CD}p_R) \\
& - \text{Renters' share of deadweight loss} \\
& (\text{triangle BCG}).
\end{aligned}$$

So:

$$\begin{aligned}
\text{Landlords' surplus lost} - \text{Renter's surplus gained} = {} & \text{Landlords' share of} \\
& \text{deadweight loss} \\
& (\text{triangle CDG}) \\
& + \text{Renters' share of} \\
& \text{deadweight loss} \\
& (\text{triangle BCG}) \\
= {} & \text{Total deadweight loss} \\
& (\text{triangle BDG}) > 0
\end{aligned}$$

Is there a better way to help the less well off?

It is also the case that rent control could hurt the less well off, rather than helping them as was the case in this example. The costs inflicted on the renters in the form of deadweight loss could have exceeded the gains they made by capturing some of what previously had been the landlords' surplus.

> **EXERCISE 12.7 DISTRIBUTION OF SURPLUS UNDER RENT CONTROL.**
> Using a diagram similar to Figure 12.16 (page 570), sketch supply and demand curves such that the costs experienced by renters (deadweight loss) will exceed their gains through gaining a larger share of the surplus.

Is there a better way to help the less well off? What can we learn from the experience of Angela and Bruno in Unit 5? Recall that Angela and her friends exploited their newly-won voting rights to impose legislation that resulted in an outcome that they preferred, but which was Pareto inefficient. From the new position of greater bargaining power that democracy had granted them, they had the idea that they might reach some agreement with Bruno (and the other members of Bruno's class) that compared to the new status quo would make all of them better off.

Let's modernize Angela and Bruno. They are now living in San Francisco and Bruno, a manager at Apple, is a landlord. Angela, a driver for Uber, is a renter. Both have learned a lot of economics, too, since Unit 5. So, when Angela goes to Bruno with Figure 12.16 she does not have to explain much. Angela has lost none of her assertiveness.

12.14 THE DISTRIBUTIONAL IMPACT OF PUBLIC POLICIES: RENT CONTROL

ANGELA: Look, Bruno, we are willing to vote to rescind the rent control if you and your landlord pals will simply transfer some money to us so that we are as well off or better than we are under rent control.

BRUNO: How much would you need?

Angela shows Bruno Figure 12.17.

From the table you can see that if the landlords transferred $137.5 million per month to the renters, the renters would be as well off as they would be under rent control, and the landlords would be much better off (paying $137.5 million directly to the renters is better than losing a total of $212.5 million in lower rents and deadweight losses). This would strike Bruno as a bargain.

Of course, Angela would be quick to point out that, were the landlords to transfer $212.5 million to the renters, then the landlords would be no worse off than they were under the rent control, and the renters much better off (getting a transfer of $212.5 million beats the net benefits to the renters from lower rents but on a reduced number of apartments rented).

The two might then bargain and agree on some intermediate amount, under which both landlords and renters would be better off.

This episode in the story of Angela and Bruno, like the others, is fanciful. It is difficult of think of ways that the kinds of transfers from landlords to renters could take place in any practical way. But it underlines an important objective: if possible, policies to grant a larger slice of the pie to the less well off should be designed to make the pie larger. Or, at least, not smaller.

The data in Figure 12.14 (page 563) shows that many countries have found ways to give a larger slice to the less well off while also growing the pie. By comparison to the US, France, and Italy, for example, Germany, Norway and Finland, have enjoyed both more rapid growth in average incomes and a larger share of income going to the less well off.

Weighing the gains and losses to different groups in society

What these countries have accomplished—granting a larger slice of a larger pie to the less well off—is impressive. But we do not conclude that policies that redistribute the pie, even while shrinking it should be ruled out. The fact that in the case of rent control, the surplus lost to landlords must exceed the surplus gained by renters is not a reason to oppose the policy: remember, it was intended to help the renters, and it did.

	Landlord (LL) and Renter (R) surplus gained or lost.	Area in Figure 12.16	Calculated area ($)	Amount ($ '000s)
1	Previously LL surplus, now R surplus	Rectangle p_0CDp_R	350,000 × 500	175,000
2	LL's share of deadweight loss	Triangle CDG	150,000 × 500 × 1/2	37,500
3	R's share of deadweight loss	Triangle BCG	150,000 × 500 × 1/2	37,500
4	LL surplus lost (net)	p_0CDp_R + CDG	Line 1 plus Line 2	212,500
5	R net surplus gained	p_0CDp_R − BCG	Line 1 minus Line 3	137,500

Figure 12.17 Monthly gains and losses compared to the no rent control market equilibrium. (Entries in the table are based on Figure 12.16, with p_0 = $1,500, p_R = $1,000, X_0 = 500,000, X_R = 350,000, and the price at A = $2,000.)

573

Policies to redistribute income are often advocated on the grounds that providing additional income to one group (typically less well off) is more highly valued than the incomes lost by some other (typically higher income). The basic idea here is that the utility of people can be compared, and the needs that will be met by the poor family—more adequate housing, for example—are more important than the reduction in spending—perhaps on a second home—that the well off will experience.

Returning to Figure 12.17 you can see that if we placed a value on the gains by the renters that is twice the value placed on the costs to the landlords then the former (2 × 137.5 million) greatly outweigh the latter (212.5 million).

> **EXERCISE 12.8 IMPLEMENTING RENT CONTROL**
> Imagine you are a policymaker considering imposing the rent control whose distributional effects are shown in Figure 12.17. You place a higher value on the gains to the renters than on the losses to the landlords, because you wish to raise the living standards of the less well off (the renters) even at a cost to those who are better off (the landlords). You just saw that if your value on the gains to the renters is twice your value on the losses to the landlords, then the benefits of the policy exceed the cost.
>
> What is the smallest value placed on the gains of the renters that would make the benefits of the policy exceed the costs?

12.15 CONCLUSION

Governments and markets are two major economic institutions today. Like other important economic institutions, such as families and firms, each has particular advantages and shortcomings in organizing economic activities.

Markets can allow large numbers of people to interact in mutually beneficial trades, relying on prices to convey information rather than centralized planning or coordination. However, markets are not ideal in the cases of **repugnant markets** or **merit goods**, and even for goods where markets are acceptable, **market failures** are common. Therefore, we need governments to produce and distribute some types of goods and to help address unfairness or inefficiencies resulting from market failure.

A **government** is distinct from other economic actors because it has the authority to act on behalf of all people within a given territory and to require citizens to abide by its decisions. These powers allow the government to be a successful problem solver, but also to become a problem itself. There are many examples in which governments were more concerned with earning **political rents** than serving the interests of their citizens.

In well-governed societies, democracy is a **political institution** that gives citizens the power to dismiss the government. This **political accountability** constrains what governments can do to further their private interests. Still, the **principal–agent relationship** between government officials and the citizens that exists because of differences in objectives means that some policies are not **politically feasible**.

Besides political feasibility, governments may fail to adopt policies that solve society's problems for two reasons. First, the policy may not be **economically feasible**, meaning that an efficient and fair outcome is not a Nash equilibrium. Second, the policy may not be **administratively feasible**, meaning that it is impossible for the government to implement it in practice, given the information available and its **fiscal capacity**. The extent to which governments can address problems of unfairness and inefficiency depends on the limits posed by economic, political, and administrative feasibility.

12.16 *DOING ECONOMICS*: GOVERNMENT POLICIES AND POPULARITY: HONG KONG CASH HANDOUT

In Sections 12.7–12.11, we looked at government spending priorities in different countries, and discussed how economic, administrative, and political feasibility influence government policy decisions.

An important role of the government is to use tax funds to provide goods and services for its citizens. When governments have a budget surplus (taxes exceed government spending), they may choose to increase spending on public programs or improve the goods and services provided to their citizens.

In *Doing Economics* Empirical Project 12, we will look at an unconventional policy adopted by the Hong Kong Government in 2011, which was to simply give a lump sum to every citizen aged 18 or above. We will assess the effects that this policy could have on inequality, and discuss some reasons why governments may choose this policy over other redistributive policies.

Go to *Doing Economics* Empirical Project 12 (https://tinyco.re/7482053) to work on this project.

> *Learning objectives*
> In this project you will:
>
> - draw Lorenz curves
> - assess the effect of a policy on income inequality
> - convert cells from text to number format
> - convert nominal values to real values (extension).

12.17 REFERENCES

Bakija, Jon, Lane Kenworthy, Peter Lindert, and Jeff Madrick. 2016. *How Big Should Our Government Be?* Berkeley: University of California Press.

Besley, Timothy, and Anne Case. 1995. 'Does electoral accountability affect economic policy choices? Evidence from gubernatorial term limits'. *The Quarterly Journal of Economics* 110 (3): pp. 769–98.

Besley, Timothy, and Torsten Persson. 2014. 'Why do developing countries tax so little?' (https://tinyco.re/3513621). *The Journal of Economic Perspectives* 28 (4): pp. 99–120.

Bonica, Adam, McCarty, Nolan, Poole, Keith T., and Howard Rosenthal. 2013. 'Why hasn't democracy slowed rising inequality?' (https://tinyco.re/5838764) *The Journal of Economic Perspectives* 27 (3): pp. 103–23.

Deaton, A. 2013. *The Great Escape: health, wealth, and the origins of inequality* (https://tinyco.re/5750302). Princeton: Princeton University Press.

Gilens, Martin, and Benjamin I. Page. 2014. 'Testing theories of American politics: Elites, interest groups, and average citizens' (https://tinyco.re/7911085). *Perspectives on Politics* 12 (03): pp. 564–81.

Hamilton, Alexander, James Madison, and John Jay. 1961. *The Federalist*. Middletown, Ct. Wesleyan University Press.

Heckman, James. 2013. *Giving Kids a Fair Chance: A Strategy That Works*. Cambridge, MA: MIT Press.

Kalla, Joshua L., and David E. Broockman. 2015. 'Campaign contributions facilitate access to congressional officials: A randomized field experiment' (https://tinyco.re/6564191). *American Journal of Political Science* 60 (3): pp. 1–14.

Lasswell, Harold D. 1936. *Politics; who gets what, when and how* (https://tinyco.re/2227728). New York: Whittlesey House.

Lindert, Peter. 2004. *Growing Public: Social Spending and Economic Growth since the 18th Century*. Cambridge: Cambridge University Press.

Martinez-Bravo, Monica, Miquel, Gerard P. I., Qian, Nancy, and Yang Yao. 2014. 'Political reform in China: The effect of local elections' (https://tinyco.re/6544486). NBER working paper, 18101.

Rasul, Imran, and Daniel Rogger. 2016. 'Management of bureaucrats and public service delivery: Evidence from the Nigerian civil service' (https://tinyco.re/1535739). *The Economic Journal* 128 (608): pp. 413–46.

Roth, Alvin E. 2007. 'Repugnance as a Constraint on Markets' (https://tinyco.re/2118641). *Journal of Economic Perspectives* 21 (3): pp. 37–58.

Sandel, Michael. 2009. *Justice*. London: Penguin.

Schumpeter, Joseph. 1918. 'The crisis of the tax state'. Reproduced in Swedberg R. (ed.) 1991. *Joseph A. Schumpeter, The Economics and Sociology of Capitalism.* Princeton University Press.

Shleifer, Andrei. 1998. 'State versus private ownership' (https://tinyco.re/4317440). *Journal of Economic Perspectives* 12 (4): pp. 133–50.

Walzer, Michael. 1983. *Spheres of Justice: A Defense of Pluralism and Equality*. New York, NY: Basic Books.

GLOSSARY

accountability The obligation of a decision-maker (or body) to be responsive to the needs and wishes of people affected by his, her or its decisions.

administratively feasible Policies for which the government has sufficient information and staff for implementation.

adverse selection The problem faced by parties to an exchange in which the terms offered by one party will cause some exchange partners to drop out. Example: The problem of asymmetric information in insurance. If the price is sufficiently high, the only people who will seek to purchase medical insurance are people who know they are ill (but the insurer does not). This will lead to further price increases to cover costs. Also referred to as the 'hidden attributes' problem (the state of already being ill is the hidden attribute), to distinguish it from the 'hidden actions' problem of moral hazard. *See also: incomplete contract, moral hazard, asymmetric information.*

allocation A description of who does what, the consequences of their actions, and who gets what as a result (for example in a game, the strategies adopted by each player and their resulting payoffs).

altruism The willingness to bear a cost in order to help another person. Altruism is a social preference. *See also: social preferences.*

antitrust policy Government policy and laws to limit monopoly power and prevent cartels. *Also known as: competition policy.*

arbitrage The practice of buying a good at a low price in one market to sell it at a higher price in another. Traders engaging in arbitrage take advantage of the price difference for the same good between two countries or regions. As long as the trade costs are lower than the price gap, they make a profit. *See also: price gap.*

artificially scarce good A public good for which it is possible to exclude some people from enjoying. *Also known as: club good. See also: public good.*

asset price bubble A sustained and significant rise in the price of an asset, fuelled by expectations of future price increases.

asset Anything of value that is owned. *See also: balance sheet, liability.*

asymmetric information Information that is relevant to all the parties in an economic interaction, but is known by some and not by others. *See also: adverse selection, moral hazard.*

average product Total output divided by a particular input, for example per worker (divided by the number of workers) or per worker per hour (total output divided by the total number of hours of labour put in).

balance sheet A record of the assets, liabilities, and net worth of an economic actor such as a household, bank, firm, or government.

bank money Money in the form of bank deposits created by commercial banks when they extend credit to firms and households.

bank run A situation in which depositors withdraw funds from a bank because they fear that it may go bankrupt and not honour its liabilities (that is, not repay the funds owed to depositors).

bank A firm that creates money in the form of bank deposits in the process of supplying credit.

bargaining power The extent of a person's advantage in securing a larger share of the economic rents made possible by an interaction.

base money Cash held by households, firms, and banks, and the balances held by commercial banks in their accounts at the central bank, known as reserves. *Also known as: high-powered money.*

behavioural experiment An experiment designed to study some aspect of human behaviour.

best response In game theory, the strategy that will give a player the highest payoff, given the strategies that the other players select.

biologically feasible An allocation that is capable of sustaining the survival of those involved is biologically feasible.

budget constraint An equation that represents all combinations of goods and services that one could acquire that exactly exhaust one's budgetary resources.

capital goods The equipment, buildings, and other durable inputs used in producing goods and services, including where applicable any patents or other intellectual

577

GLOSSARY

property that is used. Raw materials used in production are referred to as intermediate inputs.

capitalism An economic system in which the method of producing goods and services is centred on firms, which own and control the capital goods that are used in production. Private property, markets, and firms all play an important role in capitalism.

capitalist revolution Rapid improvements in technology combined with the emergence of a new economic system.

cartel A group of firms that collude in order to increase their joint profits.

causality A direction from cause to effect, establishing that a change in one variable produces a change in another. While a correlation is simply an assessment that two things have moved together, causation implies a mechanism accounting for the association, and is therefore a more restrictive concept. *See also: natural experiment, correlation.*

central bank The only bank that can create base money. Usually part of the government. Commercial banks have accounts at this bank, holding base money. *See also: base money.*

ceteris paribus Economists often simplify analysis by setting aside things that are thought to be of less importance to the question of interest. The literal meaning of the expression is 'other things equal'. In an economic model it means an analysis 'holds other things constant'.

club good *See also: artificially scarce good, public good.*

co-insurance A means of pooling savings across households in order for a household to be able to maintain consumption when it experiences a temporary fall in income or the need for greater expenditure.

collateral An asset that a borrower pledges to a lender as a security for a loan. If the borrower is not able to make the loan payments as promised, the lender becomes the owner of the asset.

commodities Physical goods traded in a manner similar to shares. They include metals such as gold and silver, and agricultural products such as coffee and sugar, oil and gas. Sometimes more generally used to mean anything produced for sale. *See also: share.*

common-pool resource A rival good that one cannot prevent others from enjoying. *Also known as: common property resource. See also: rival good.*

competition policy Government policy and laws to limit monopoly power and prevent cartels. *Also known as: antitrust policy.*

competitive equilibrium A market outcome in which all buyers and sellers are price-takers, and at the prevailing market price, the quantity supplied is equal to the quantity demanded.

complements Two goods for which an increase in the price of one leads to a decrease in the quantity demanded of the other. *See also: substitutes.*

conflict of interest The situation which arises if in order for one party to gain more from the interaction, another party must do less well.

conspicuous consumption The purchase of goods or services to publicly display one's social and economic status.

constant prices Prices corrected for increases in prices (inflation) or decreases in prices (deflation) so that a unit of currency represents the same buying power in different periods of time. *See also: purchasing power parity, real GDP.*

constant returns to scale These occur when doubling all of the inputs to a production process doubles the output. The shape of a firm's long-run average cost curve depends both on returns to scale in production and the effect of scale on the prices it pays for its inputs. *See also: increasing returns to scale, decreasing returns to scale.*

constrained choice problem This problem is about how we can do the best for ourselves, given our preferences and constraints, and when the things we value are scarce. *See also: constrained optimization problem.*

constrained optimization problem Problems in which a decision-maker chooses the values of one or more variables to achieve an objective (such as maximizing profit) subject to a constraint that determines the feasible set (such as the demand curve).

consumer durables Consumer goods with a life expectancy of more than three years such as home furniture, cars, and fridges.

consumer price index (CPI) A measure of the general level of prices that consumers have to pay for goods and services, including consumption taxes.

consumer surplus The consumer's willingness to pay for a good minus the price at which the consumer bought the good, summed across all units sold.

consumption (C) Expenditure on both short-lived goods and services and long-lived goods, which are called consumer durables. *See also: consumer durables.*

consumption good A good or service that satisfies the needs of consumers over a short period.

consumption smoothing Actions taken by an individual, family, or other group in order to sustain their customary level of consumption. Actions include borrowing or reducing savings to offset negative shocks, such as unemployment or illness; and increasing saving or reducing debt in response to positive shocks, such as promotion or inheritance.

contract A legal document or understanding that specifies a set of actions that parties to the contract must undertake.

cooperation Participating in a common project that is intended to produce mutual benefits.

cooperative firm A firm that is mostly or entirely owned by its workers, who hire and fire the managers.

copyright Ownership rights over the use and distribution of an original work.

correlation coefficient A measure of how closely associated two variables are and whether they tend to take similar or dissimilar values, ranging from a value of 1 indicating that the variables take similar values ('are positively correlated') to −1 indicating that the variables take dissimilar variables ('negative' or 'inverse' correlation). A value of 1 or −1 indicates that knowing the value of one of the variables would allow you to perfectly predict the value of the other. A value of 0 indicates that knowing one of the variables provides no information about the value of the other. *See also: correlation, causality.*

correlation A statistical association in which knowing the value of one variable provides information on the likely value of the other, for example high values of one variable being commonly observed along with high values of the other variable. It can be positive or negative (it is negative when high values of one variable are observed with low values of the other). It does not mean that there is a causal relationship between the variables. *See also: causality, correlation coefficient.*

creative destruction Joseph Schumpeter's name for the process by which old technologies and the firms that do not adapt are swept away by the new, because they cannot compete in the market. In his view, the failure of unprofitable firms is creative because it releases labour and capital goods for use in new combinations.

credit-constrained A description of individuals who are able to borrow only on unfavourable terms. *See also: credit-excluded.*

credit-excluded A description of individuals who are unable to borrow on any terms. *See also: credit-constrained.*

credit rationing The process by which those with less wealth borrow on unfavourable terms, compared to those with more wealth.

crowding out There are two quite distinct uses of the term. One is the observed negative effect when economic incentives displace people's ethical or other-regarding motivations. In studies of individual behaviour, incentives may have a crowding-out effect on social preferences. A second use of the term is to refer to the effect of an increase in government spending in reducing private spending, as would be expected for example in an economy working at full capacity utilization, or when a fiscal expansion is associated with a rise in the interest rate.

cyclical unemployment The increase in unemployment above equilibrium unemployment caused by a fall in aggregate demand associated with the business cycle. *Also known as: demand-deficient unemployment. See also: equilibrium unemployment.*

deadweight loss A loss of total surplus relative to a Pareto-efficient allocation.

decile A subset of observations, formed by ordering the full set of observations according to the values of a particular variable and then splitting the set into ten equally-sized groups. For example, the 1st decile refers to the smallest 10% of values in a set of observations. *See also: percentile.*

decreasing returns to scale These occur when doubling all of the inputs to a production process less than doubles the output. *Also known as: diseconomies of scale. See also: increasing returns to scale.*

default risk The risk that credit given as loans will not be repaid.

deflation A decrease in the general price level. *See also: inflation.*

demand curve The curve that gives the quantity consumers will buy at each possible price.

democracy A political system, that ideally gives equal political power to all citizens, defined by individual rights such as freedom of speech, assembly, and the press; fair elections in which virtually all adults are eligible to vote; and in which the government leaves office if it loses.

depreciation The loss in value of a form of wealth that occurs either through use (wear and tear) or the passage of time (obsolescence).

developmental state A government that takes a leading role in promoting the process of economic development through its public investments, subsidies of particular industries, education and other public policies.

difference-in-difference A method that applies an experimental research design to outcomes observed in a natural experiment. It involves comparing the difference in the average outcomes of two groups, a treatment and control group, both before and after the treatment took place.

differentiated product A product produced by a single firm that has some unique characteristics compared to similar products of other firms.

diminishing marginal product A property of some production functions according to which each additional unit of input results in a smaller increment in total output than did the previous unit.

diminishing marginal returns to consumption The value to the individual of an additional unit of consumption declines, the more consumption the individual has. *Also known as: diminishing marginal utility.*

diminishing marginal utility A property of some utility functions according to which each additional unit of a given variable results in a smaller increment to total utility than did the previous additional unit. *Also known as: diminishing marginal returns to consumption.*

discount rate A measure of a person's impatience: how much that person values an additional unit of consumption now relative to an additional unit of consumption later. It is the absolute value of the slope of a person's indifference curve for consumption now and consumption later, minus one. *Also known as: subjective discount rate.*

diseconomies of scale These occur when doubling all of the inputs to a production process less than doubles the output. *Also known as: decreasing returns to scale. See also: economies of scale.*

disequilibrium A situation in which at least one of the actors can benefit by altering his or her actions and therefore changing the situation, given what everybody else is doing.

disinflation A decrease in the rate of inflation. *See also: inflation, deflation.*

disposable income Income available after paying taxes and receiving transfers from the government.

disutility of effort The degree to which doing some task (effort) is unpleasant.

division of labour The specialization of producers to carry out different tasks in the production process. *Also known as: specialization.*

dominant strategy equilibrium An outcome of a game in which every player plays his or her dominant strategy.

dominant strategy Strategy that yields the highest payoff for a player, no matter what the other players do.

earnings Wages, salaries, and other income from labour.

economic accountability Accountability achieved by economic processes, notably competition among firms or other entities in which failure to take account of those affected will result in losses in profits or in business failure. *See also: accountability, political accountability.*

economic cost The out-of-pocket cost of an action, plus the opportunity cost.

economic inequality Differences among members of a society in some economic attribute such as wealth, income, or wages.

economic profit A firm's revenue minus its total costs (including the opportunity cost of capital).

economic rent A payment or other benefit received above and beyond what the individual would have received in his or her next best alternative (or reservation option). *See also: reservation option.*

economic system The institutions that organize the production and distribution of goods and services in an entire economy.

economically feasible Policies for which the desired outcomes are a Nash equilibrium, so that once implemented private economic actors will not undo the desired effects.

economics The study of how people interact with each other and with their natural surroundings in providing their livelihoods, and how this changes over time.

economies of scale These occur when doubling all of the inputs to a production process more than doubles the output. The shape of a firm's long-run average cost curve depends both on returns to scale in production and the effect of scale on the prices it pays for its inputs. *Also known as: increasing returns to scale. See also: diseconomies of scale.*

efficiency unit A unit of effort is sometimes called an efficiency unit.

efficiency wages The payment an employer makes that is higher than an employee's reservation wage, so as to motivate the employee to provide more effort on the job than he or she would otherwise choose to make. *See also: labour discipline model, employment rent.*

employment rate The ratio of the number of employed to the population of working age. *See also: population of working age.*

employment relationship The interaction between an employee and an employer in which the employer sets the hours and other conditions of work and the wage, directs the employee's activities and may terminate her employment, and the employee chooses how hard to work and whether to quit her job. The employee's level of effort, or her decision to remain in the firm, are determined by the choices made by the two parties—and are affected by the exercise of power by the employer and the social norms of both parties.

employment rent The economic rent a worker receives when the net value of her job exceeds the net value of her next best alternative (that is, being unemployed). *Also known as: cost of job loss.*

endogenous Produced by the workings of a model rather than coming from outside the model. *See also: exogenous*

endowment The facts about an individual that may affect his or her income, such as the physical wealth a person has, either land, housing, or a portfolio of shares (stocks). Also includes level and quality of schooling, special training, the computer languages in which the individual can work, work experience in internships, citizenship, whether the individual has a visa (or green card) allowing employment in a particular labour market, the nationality and gender of the individual, and even the person's race or social class background. *See also: human capital.*

entrepreneur A person who creates or is an early adopter of new technologies, organizational forms, and other opportunities.

equilibrium unemployment The number of people seeking work but without jobs, which is determined by the intersection of the wage-setting and price-setting curves. This is the Nash equilibrium of the labour market and product market where neither employers nor workers could do better by changing their behaviour. *See also: involuntary unemployment, structural unemployment, wage-setting curve, price-setting curve, WS/PS model, inflation-stabilizing rate of unemployment.*

equilibrium A model outcome that does not change unless an outside or external force is introduced that alters the model's description of the situation.

equity An individual's own investment in a project. This is recorded in an individual's or firm's balance sheet as net worth. *See also: net worth.* An entirely different use of the term is synonymous with fairness.

excess demand A situation in which the quantity of a good demanded is greater than the quantity supplied at the current price. *See also: excess supply.*

excess supply A situation in which the quantity of a good supplied is greater than the quantity demanded at the current price. *See also: excess demand.*

exogenous shock A sharp change in external conditions affecting a model.

exogenous Coming from outside the model rather than being produced by the workings of the model itself. *See also: endogenous.*

external benefit A positive external effect: that is, a positive effect of a production, consumption, or other economic decision on another person or people that is not specified as a benefit in a contract. *Also known as: external economy. See also: external effect.*

external cost A negative external effect: that is, the negative effect of production, consumption, or other economic decisions on another person or party, which is not specified as a liability in a contract. *Also known as: external diseconomy. See also: external effect.*

external diseconomy A negative effect of a production, consumption, or other economic decision, that is not specified as a liability in a contract. *Also known as: external cost, negative externality. See also: external effect.*

external economy A positive effect of a production, consumption, or other economic decision, that is not specified as a benefit in a contract. *Also known as: external benefit, positive externality. See also: external effect.*

external effect When a person's action confers a benefit or cost on some other individual, and this effect is not taken account of by the person in deciding to take the action. It is external because it is not included in the decision-making process of the person taking the action. Positive effects refer to benefits, and negative effects to costs, that are experienced by others. A person

GLOSSARY

breathing second-hand smoke from someone else's cigarette is a negative external effect. Enjoying your neighbour's beautiful garden is a positive external effect. *Also known as: externality. See also: incomplete contract, market failure, external benefit, external cost.*

fairness A way to evaluate an allocation based on one's conception of justice.

feasible frontier The curve made of points that defines the maximum feasible quantity of one good for a given quantity of the other. *See also: feasible set.*

feasible set All of the combinations of the things under consideration that a decision-maker could choose given the economic, physical or other constraints that he faces. *See also: feasible frontier.*

financial deregulation Policies allowing banks and other financial institutions greater freedom in the types of financial assets they can sell, as well as other practices.

firm A business organization which pays wages and salaries to employ people, and purchases inputs, to produce and market goods and services with the intention of making a profit.

fiscal capacity The ability of a government to impose and collect substantial taxes from a population at low administrative and other costs. One measure of this is the amount collected divided by the cost of administering the tax system.

Fisher equation The relation that gives the real interest rate as the difference between the nominal interest rate and expected inflation: real interest rate = nominal interest rate − expected inflation.

fixed costs Costs of production that do not vary with the number of units produced.

flow variable A quantity measured per unit of time, such as annual income or hourly wage. *See also: stock variable.*

free ride Benefiting from the contributions of others to some cooperative project without contributing oneself.

fundamental value of a share The share price based on anticipated future earnings and the level of risk.

gains from exchange The benefits that each party gains from a transaction compared to how they would have fared without the exchange. *Also known as: gains from trade. See also: economic rent.*

game theory A branch of mathematics that studies strategic interactions, meaning situations in which each actor knows that the benefits they receive depend on the actions taken by all. *See also: game.*

game A model of strategic interaction that describes the players, the feasible strategies, the information that the players have, and their payoffs. *See also: game theory.*

gender division of labour The ways men and women differ in how they spend their work time.

gig economy An economy made up of people performing services matched by means of a computer platform with those paying for the service. Workers are paid for each task they complete, and not per hour. They are not legally recognized as employees of the company that owns the platform, and typically receive few benefits from the owners, other than matching.

Gini coefficient A measure of inequality of any quantity such as income or wealth, varying from a value of zero (if there is no inequality) to one (if a single individual receives all of it).

global financial crisis This began in 2007 with the collapse of house prices in the US, leading to the fall in prices of assets based on subprime mortgages and to widespread uncertainty about the solvency of banks in the US and Europe, which had borrowed to purchase such assets. The ramifications were felt around the world, as global trade was cut back sharply. Goverments and central banks responded aggressively with stabilization policies.

governing elite Top government officials such as the president, cabinet officials, and legislative leaders, unified by a common interest such as membership in a particular party.

government bond A financial instrument issued by governments that promises to pay flows of money at specific intervals.

government failure A failure of political accountability. (This term is widely used in a variety of ways, none of them strictly analogous to market failure, for which the criterion is simply Pareto inefficiency). *See also: political accountability.*

government Within a given territory, the only body that can dictate what people must do or not do, and can legitimately use force and restraints on an individual's freedom to achieve that end. *Also known as: state.*

gross domestic product (GDP) per capita A measure of the market value of the output of the economy in a given period (GDP) divided by the population.

gross domestic product (GDP) A measure of the market value of the output of the economy in a given period.

gross income Income net of taxes paid. Includes depreciation. *See also: income, net income.*

hawk–dove game A game in which there is conflict (when hawks meet), sharing (when doves meet), and taking (by a hawk when it meets a dove).

hedge finance Financing used by firms to fulfil contractual payment obligations using cashflow. Term coined by Hyman Minsky in his Financial Instability Hypothesis. *See also: speculative finance.*

hidden actions (problem of) This occurs when some action taken by one party to an exchange is not known or cannot be verified by the other. For example, the employer cannot know (or cannot verify) how hard the worker she has employed is actually working. *Also known as: moral hazard. See also: hidden attributes (problem of).*

hidden attributes (problem of) This occurs when some attribute of the person engaging in an exchange (or the product or service being provided) is not known to the other parties. Example: an individual purchasing health insurance knows her own health status, but the insurance company does not. *Also known as: adverse selection. See also: hidden actions (problem of).*

homo economicus Latin for 'economic man', referring to an actor assumed to adopt behaviours based on an amoral calculation of self-interest.

human capital The stock of knowledge, skills, behavioural attributes, and personal characteristics that determine the labour productivity or labour earnings of an individual. It is part of an individual's

581

GLOSSARY

endowments. Investment in this through education, training, and socialization can increase the stock, and such investment is one of the sources of economic growth. *See also: endowment, labour productivity.*

impatience Any preference to move consumption from the future to the present. This preference may be derived either from pure impatience or diminishing marginal returns to consumption.

inactive population People in the population of working age who are neither employed nor actively looking for paid work. Those working in the home raising children, for example, are not considered as being in the labour force and therefore are classified this way.

incentive Economic reward or punishment, which influences the benefits and costs of alternative courses of action.

income effect The effect, for example, on the choice of consumption of a good that a change in income would have if there were no change in the price or opportunity cost.

income elasticity of demand The percentage change in demand that would occur in response to a 1% increase in the individual's income.

income net of depreciation Disposable income minus depreciation. *See also: disposable income, gross income, depreciation.*

income The amount of labour earnings, dividends, interest, rent, and other payments (including transfers from the government) received by an economic actor, net of taxes paid, measured over a period of time, such as a year. The maximum amount that you could consume and leave your wealth unchanged. *Also known as: disposable income. See also: gross income.*

incomplete contract A contract that does not specify, in an enforceable way, every aspect of the exchange that affects the interests of parties to the exchange (or of any others affected by the exchange).

increasing returns to scale These occur when doubling all of the inputs to a production process more than doubles the output. The shape of a firm's long-run average cost curve depends both on returns to scale in production and the effect of scale on the prices it pays for its inputs. *Also known as: economies of scale. See also: decreasing returns to scale, constant returns to scale.*

indifference curve A curve of the points which indicate the combinations of goods that provide a given level of utility to the individual.

Industrial Revolution A wave of technological advances and organizational changes starting in Britain in the eighteenth century, which transformed an agrarian and craft-based economy into a commercial and industrial economy.

inequality aversion A dislike of outcomes in which some individuals receive more than others. It is considered a social preference. *See also: social preferences*

inferior good A good whose consumption decreases when income increases (holding prices constant).

inflation-stabilizing rate of unemployment The unemployment rate (at labour market equilibrium) at which inflation is constant. Originally known as the 'natural rate' of unemployment. *Also known as: non-accelerating rate of unemployment, stable inflation rate of unemployment. See also: equilibrium unemployment.*

inflation An increase in the general price level in the economy. Usually measured over a year. *See also: deflation, disinflation.*

insolvent An entity is this if the value of its assets is less than the value of its liabilities. *See also: solvent.*

institution The laws and social customs governing the way people interact in society.

interest rate (short-term) The price of borrowing base money. This is a nominal interest rate.

interest rate The price of bringing some spending power forward in time. *See also: nominal interest rate, real interest rate.*

investment (I) Expenditure on newly produced capital goods (machinery and equipment) and buildings, including new housing.

invisible hand game A game in which there is a single Nash equilibrium and where there is no other outcome in which both players would be better off or at least one better off and the other not worse off. *See also: Nash equilibrium, Pareto efficient.*

involuntary unemployment A person who is seeking work, and willing to accept a job at the going wage for people of their level of skill and experience, but unable to secure employment is involuntarily employed.

irrational exuberance A process by which assets become overvalued. The expression was first used by Alan Greenspan, then chairman of the US Federal Reserve Board, in 1996. It was popularized as an economic concept by the economist Robert Shiller.

isocost line A line that represents all combinations that cost a given total amount.

isoprofit curve A curve on which all points yield the same profit.

joint surplus The sum of the economic rents of all involved in an interaction. *Also known as: gains from exchange.*

labour discipline model A model that explains how employers set wages so that employees receive an economic rent (called employment rent), which provides workers an incentive to work hard in order to avoid job termination. *See also: employment rent, efficiency wages.*

labour force The number of people in the population of working age who are, or wish to be, in work outside the household. They are either employed (including self-employed) or unemployed. *See also: unemployment rate, employment rate, participation rate.*

labour productivity Total output divided by the number of hours or some other measure of labour input.

lending rate (bank) The average interest rate charged by commercial banks to firms and households. This rate will typically be above the policy interest rate: the difference is known as the markup or spread on commercial lending. This is a nominal interest rate. *Also known as: market interest rate. See also: interest rate, policy (interest) rate.*

leverage ratio (for banks or households) The value of assets divided by the equity stake in those assets.

liability Anything of value that is owed. *See also: balance sheet, asset.*

liquidity risk The risk that an asset cannot be exchanged for cash rapidly enough to prevent a financial loss.

liquidity Ease of buying or selling a financial asset at a predictable price.

Lorenz curve A graphical representation of inequality of some quantity such as wealth or income. Individuals are arranged in ascending order by how much of this quantity they have, and the cumulative share of the total is then plotted against the cumulative share of the population. For complete equality of income, for example, it would be a straight line with a slope of one. The extent to which the curve falls below this perfect equality line is a measure of inequality. See also: *Gini coefficient*.

marginal cost The addition to total costs associated with producing one additional unit of output.

marginal external cost (MEC) The cost of producing an additional unit of a good that is incurred by anyone other than the producer of the good. See also: *marginal private cost, marginal social cost*.

marginal private benefit (MPB) The benefit (in terms of profit, or utility) of producing or consuming an additional unit of a good for the individual who decides to produce or consume it, not taking into account any benefit received by others.

marginal private cost (MPC) The cost for the producer of producing an additional unit of a good, not taking into account any costs its production imposes on others. See also: *marginal external cost (MEC), marginal social cost (MSC)*.

marginal product The additional amount of output that is produced if a particular input was increased by one unit, while holding all other inputs constant.

marginal rate of substitution (MRS) The trade-off that a person is willing to make between two goods. At any point, this is the slope of the indifference curve. See also: *marginal rate of transformation*.

marginal rate of transformation (MRT) A measure of the trade-offs a person faces in what is feasible. Given the constraints (feasible frontier) a person faces, the MRT is the quantity of some good that must be sacrificed to acquire one additional unit of another good. At any point, it is the slope of the feasible frontier. See also: *feasible frontier, marginal rate of substitution*.

marginal social benefit (MSB) The benefit (in terms of utility) of producing or consuming an additional unit of a good, taking into account both the benefit to the individual who decides to produce or consume it, and the benefit to anyone else affected by the decision.

marginal social cost (MSC) The cost of producing an additional unit of a good, taking into account both the cost for the producer and the costs incurred by others affected by the good's production. Marginal social cost is the sum of the marginal private cost and the marginal external cost.

marginal utility The additional utility resulting from a one-unit increase of a given variable.

market-clearing price At this price there is no excess supply or excess demand. See also: *equilibrium*.

market failure When markets allocate resources in a Pareto-inefficient way.

market power An attribute of a firm that can sell its product at a range of feasible prices, so that it can benefit by acting as a price-setter (rather than a price-taker).

market A way of connecting people who may mutually benefit by exchanging goods or services through a process of buying and selling.

maturity transformation The practice of borrowing money short term and lending it long term. For example, a bank accepts deposits, which it promises to repay at short notice or no notice, and makes long-term loans (which can be repaid over many years). Also known as: *liquidity transformation*.

mean A summary statistic for a set of observations, calculated by adding all values in the set and dividing by the number of observations.

median The middle number in a set of values, such that half of the numbers are larger than the median and half are smaller. Also known as: 50th percentile.

merit goods Goods and services that should be available to everyone, independently of their ability to pay.

minimum acceptable offer In the ultimatum game, the smallest offer by the Proposer that will not be rejected by the Responder. Generally applied in bargaining situations to mean the least favourable offer that would be accepted.

missing market A market in which there is some kind of exchange that, if implemented, would be mutually beneficial. This does not occur due to asymmetric or non-verifiable information.

money Money is something that facilitates exchange (called a medium of exchange) consisting of bank notes and bank deposits, or anything else that can be used to purchase goods and services, and is generally accepted by others as payment because others can use it for the same purpose. The 'because' is important and it distinguishes exchange facilitated by money from barter exchange, in which goods are directly exchanged without money changing hands.

monopolistic competition A market in which each seller has a unique product but there is competition among firms because firms sell products that are close substitutes for one another.

monopoly power The power that a firm has to control its own price. The fewer close substitutes for the product are available, the greater the firm's price-setting power. See also: *monopoly*.

monopoly rents A form of profits, which arise due to restricted competition in selling a firm's product.

monopoly A firm that is the only seller of a product without close substitutes. Also refers to a market with only one seller. See also: *monopoly power, natural monopoly*.

moral hazard This term originated in the insurance industry to express the problem that insurers face, namely, the person with home insurance may take less care to avoid fires or other damages to his home, thereby increasing the risk above what it would be in absence of insurance. This term now refers to any situation in which one party to an interaction is deciding on an action that affects the profits or wellbeing of the other but which the affected party cannot control by means of a contract, often because the affected party does not have adequate information on the action. It is also referred to as the 'hidden actions' problem. See also: *hidden actions (problem of), incomplete contract, too big to fail*.

GLOSSARY

mortgage (or mortgage loan) A loan contracted by households and businesses to purchase a property without paying the total value at one time. Over a period of many years, the borrower repays the loan, plus interest. The debt is secured by the property itself, referred to as collateral. *See also: collateral.*

mutual gains An outcome of an interaction among two or more people, in which all parties are better off as a result than they would have been without the interaction (or at least some parties are better off and none are worse off).

Nash equilibrium A set of strategies, one for each player in the game, such that each player's strategy is a best response to the strategies chosen by everyone else.

natural experiment An empirical study exploiting naturally occurring statistical controls in which researchers do not have the ability to assign participants to treatment and control groups, as is the case in conventional experiments. Instead, differences in law, policy, weather, or other events can offer the opportunity to analyse populations as if they had been part of an experiment. The validity of such studies depends on the premise that the assignment of subjects to the naturally occurring treatment and control groups can be plausibly argued to be random.

natural monopoly A production process in which the long-run average cost curve is sufficiently downward-sloping to make it impossible to sustain competition among firms in this market.

negative feedback (process) A process whereby some initial change sets in motion a process that dampens the initial change. *See also: positive feedback (process).*

net income Gross income minus depreciation. *See also: income, gross income, depreciation.*

net present value The present value of a stream of future income minus the associated costs (whether the costs are in the present or the future). *See also: present value.*

net worth Assets less liabilities. *See also: balance sheet, equity.*

network economies of scale These exist when an increase in the number of users of an output of a firm implies an increase in the value of the output to each of them, because they are connected to each other.

nominal interest rate The price of bringing some spending power (in dollars or other nominal terms) forward in time. The policy rate and the lending rate quoted by commercial banks are examples of nominal interest rates. *See also: real interest rate, interest rate, Fisher equation.*

nominal wage The actual amount received in payment for work, in a particular currency. Also known as: money wage. *See also: real wage.*

non-excludable public good A public good for which it is impossible to exclude anyone from having access. *See also: artificially scarce good.*

non-rival good A good that, if available to anyone, is available to everyone at no additional cost. *See also: rival good, non-excludable public good.*

normal good A good for which demand increases when a person's income rises, holding prices unchanged.

oligopoly A market with a small number of sellers of the same good, giving each seller some market power.

one-shot game A game that is played once and not repeated.

opportunity cost The opportunity cost of some action A is the foregone benefit that you would have enjoyed if instead you had taken some other action B. This is called an *opportunity* cost because by choosing A you give up the opportunity of choosing B. It is called a *cost* because the choice of A costs you the benefit you would have experienced had you chosen B.

Pareto criterion According to the Pareto criterion, a desirable attribute of an allocation is that it be Pareto efficient. *See also: Pareto dominant.*

Pareto dominant Allocation A Pareto dominates allocation B if at least one party would be better off with A than B, and nobody would be worse off. *See also: Pareto efficient.*

Pareto efficiency curve The set of all allocations that are Pareto efficient. Often referred to as the contract curve, even in social interactions in which there is no contract, which is why we avoid the term. *See also: Pareto efficient.*

Pareto efficient An allocation with the property that there is no alternative technically feasible allocation in which at least one person would be better off, and nobody worse off.

Pareto improvement A change that benefits at least one person without making anyone else worse off. *See also: Pareto dominant.*

Pareto inefficient An allocation with the property that there is some alternative technically feasible allocation in which at least one person would be better off, and nobody worse off.

participation rate The ratio of the number of people in the labour force to the population of working age. *See also: labour force, population of working age.*

patent A right of exclusive ownership of an idea or invention, which lasts for a specified length of time. During this time it effectively allows the owner to be a monopolist or exclusive user.

payment service Any service provided by a financial institution to allow one person or organization to pay another for a product or service.

payoff matrix A table of the payoffs associated with every possible combination of strategies chosen by two or more players in a game.

payoff The benefit to each player associated with the joint actions of all the players.

percentile A subset of observations, formed by ordering the full set of observations according to the values of a particular variable and then splitting the set into ten equally-sized groups. For example, the 1st percentile refers to the smallest 1% of values in a set of observations. *See also: decile.*

piece-rate work A type of employment in which the worker is paid a fixed amount for each unit of the product that the worker produces.

Pigouvian subsidy A government subsidy to encourage an economic activity that has positive external effects. Example: subsidizing basic research.

Pigouvian tax A tax levied on activities that generate negative external effects so as to

584

correct an inefficient market outcome. *See also: external effect, Pigouvian subsidy.*

policy (interest) rate The interest rate set by the central bank, which applies to banks that borrow base money from each other, and from the central bank. *Also known as: base rate, official rate. See also: real interest rate, nominal interest rate.*

political accountability Accountability achieved by political processes such as elections, oversight by an elected government, or consultation with affected citizens. *See also: accountability, economic accountability.*

political institution The rules of the game that determine who has power and how it is exercised in a society.

political rent A payment or other benefit in excess of the individual's next best alternative (reservation position) that exists as a result of the individual's political position. The reservation position in this case refers to the individual's situation were they to lack a privileged political position. *See also: economic rent.*

political system A set of principles, laws, and procedures that determine how governments will be selected, and how those governments will make and implement decisions that affect all or most members of a population.

politically feasible Capable of being implemented given the existing political institutions.

polluter pays principle A guide to environmental policy according to which those who impose negative environmental effects on others should be made to pay for the damages they impose, through taxation or other means. *See also: external cost.*

population of working age A statistical convention, which in many countries is all people aged between 15 and 64 years.

positional good A good—such as high status, conspicuous consumption, or power—which, if enjoyed by one member of a community is experienced negatively by others. The more one person benefits from this good, the more others are harmed.

positive feedback (process) A process whereby some initial change sets in motion a process that magnifies the initial change. *See also: negative feedback (process).*

power The ability to do (and get) the things one wants in opposition to the intentions of others, ordinarily by imposing or threatening sanctions.

preference Pro-and-con evaluations of the possible outcomes of the actions we may take that form the basis by which we decide on a course of action.

present value The value today of a stream of future income or other benefits, when these are discounted using an interest rate or the person's own discount rate. *See also: net present value.*

price discrimination A selling strategy in which different prices for the same product are set for different buyers or groups of buyers, or per-unit prices vary depending on the number of units purchased.

price elasticity of demand The percentage change in demand that would occur in response to a 1% increase in price. We express this as a positive number. Demand is elastic if this is greater than 1, and inelastic if less than 1.

price elasticity of supply The percentage change in supply that would occur in response to a 1% increase in price. Supply is elastic if this is greater than 1, and inelastic if less than 1.

price gap A difference in the price of a good in the exporting country and the importing country. It includes transportation costs and trade taxes. When global markets are in competitive equilibrium, these differences will be entirely due to trade costs. *See also: arbitrage.*

price markup The price minus the marginal cost, divided by the price. It is inversely proportional to the elasticity of demand for this good.

price-setting (PS) curve The curve—arising from the price-setting decisions of firms in markets for goods and services (the product market)—that gives the real wage paid when firms choose their profit-maximizing price.

price-taker Characteristic of producers and consumers who cannot benefit by offering or asking any price other than the market price in the equilibrium of a competitive market. They have no power to influence the market price.

principal–agent relationship This is an asymmetrical relationship in which one party (the principal) benefits from some action or attribute of the other party (the agent) about which the principal's information is not sufficient to enforce in a complete contract. *See also: incomplete contract. Also known as: principal–agent problem.*

prisoners' dilemma A game in which the payoffs in the dominant strategy equilibrium are lower for each player, and also lower in total, than if neither player played the dominant strategy.

private property The right and expectation that one can enjoy one's possessions in ways of one's own choosing, exclude others from their use, and dispose of them by gift or sale to others who then become their owners.

procedural judgements of fairness An evaluation of an outcome based on how the allocation came about, and not on the characteristics of the outcome itself, (for example, how unequal it is). *See also: substantive judgements of fairness.*

producer surplus The price at which a firm sells a good minus the minimum price at which it would have been willing to sell the good, summed across all units sold.

production function A graphical or mathematical expression describing the amount of output that can be produced by any given amount or combination of input(s). The function describes differing technologies capable of producing the same thing.

profit margin The difference between the price and the marginal cost.

property rights Legal protection of ownership, including the right to exclude others and to benefit from or sell the thing owned.

public bad The negative equivalent of a public good. It is non-rival in the sense that a given individual's consumption of the public bad does not diminish others' consumption of it.

public good A good for which use by one person does not reduce its availability to others. *Also known as: non-rival good. See also:*

585

non-excludable public good, artificially scarce good.

public goods game Similar to a prisoners' dilemma game with more than two people; the dominant strategy is not to contribute to the public good.

public policy A policy decided by the government. *Also known as: government policy*

purchasing power parity (PPP) A statistical correction allowing comparisons of the amount of goods people can buy in different countries that have different currencies. *See also: constant prices.*

pure impatience In a situation in which a person's endowment is the same amount of consumption this period and later, she would have this characteristic if she values an additional unit of consumption now over an additional unit later. It arises when a person is impatient to consume more now because she places less value on consumption in the future for reasons of myopia, weakness of will, or for other reasons. *See also: weakness of will.*

ratio scale A scale that uses distances on a graph to represent ratios. For example, the ratio between 3 and 6, and between 6 and 12, is the same (the larger number is twice the smaller number). In a ratio scale chart, all changes by the same ratio are represented by the same vertical distance. This contrasts with a linear scale, where the distance between 3 and 6, and between 6 and 9, is the same (in this case, 3). *Also known as a log scale (in for example, Microsoft Excel).*

real GDP An inflation-adjusted measure of the market value of the output of the economy in a given period. (GDP). *See also: inflation, constant prices, gross domestic product.*

real interest rate The price of bringing some real spending power forward in time. *See also: nominal interest rate.*

real wage The nominal wage, adjusted to take account of changes in prices between different time periods. It measures the amount of goods and services the worker can buy. *See also: nominal wage.*

reciprocity A preference concerning one's actions towards others that depends on an evaluation of the others' actions or character, for example, a preference to help those who have helped you or in some other way acted well (in your opinion), and to harm those who have acted poorly. It is considered a social preference. *See also: social preferences.*

repeated game A game in which the same interaction (same payoffs, players, feasible actions) may occur more than once.

repugnant market Buying or selling something that people believe ought not to be exchanged on a market.

research and development Expenditures by a private or public entity to create new methods of production, products, or other economically relevant new knowledge.

reservation indifference curve A curve that indicates allocations (combinations) that are as highly valued as one's reservation option. *See also: reservation option.*

reservation option A person's next best alternative among all options in a particular transaction. *Also known as: fallback option. See also: reservation price.*

reservation price The lowest price at which someone is willing to sell a good (keeping the good is the potential seller's reservation option). *See also: reservation option.*

reservation wage What an employee would get in alternative employment, or from an unemployment benefit or other support, were he or she not employed in his or her current job.

residual claimant The person who receives the income left over from a firm or project after the payment of all contractual costs (for example the cost of hiring workers and paying taxes).

risk aversion A preference for certain over uncertain outcomes.

rival good A good which, if consumed by one person, is not available to another. *See also: non-rival good.*

saving When consumption expenditure is less than net income, saving takes place and wealth rises. *See also: wealth.*

scarcity A good that is valued, and for which there is an opportunity cost of acquiring more.

separation of ownership and control The attribute of some firms by which managers are a separate group from the owners.

sequential game A game in which all players do not choose their strategies at the same time, and players that choose later can see the strategies already chosen by the other players, for example the ultimatum game. *See also: simultaneous game.*

share A part of the assets of a firm that may be traded. It gives the holder a right to receive a proportion of a firm's profit and to benefit when the firm's assets become more valuable. *Also known as: common stock.*

shock An exogenous change in some of the fundamental data or variables used in a model.

simultaneous game A game in which players choose strategies simultaneously, for example the prisoners' dilemma. *See also: sequential game.*

social dilemma A situation in which actions, taken independently by individuals in pursuit of their own private objectives, may result in an outcome that is inferior to some other feasible outcome that could have occurred if people had acted together, rather than as individuals.

social insurance Expenditure by the government, financed by taxation, which provides protection against various economic risks (for example, loss of income due to sickness, or unemployment) and enables people to smooth incomes throughout their lifetime. *See also: co-insurance.*

social interaction A situation in which the actions taken by each person affect other people's outcomes as well as their own.

social norm An understanding that is common to most members of a society about what people should do in a given situation when their actions affect others.

social preferences A person with social preferences cares not only about how her action affects her personally, but also about how it affects other people. *Also known as: other-regarding preferences.*

solvent A firm or individual for which net worth is positive or zero. For example, a bank for this assets are more than its liabilities (what it owes). *See also: insolvent.*

specialization This takes place when a country or some other entity produces a narrower range of goods and services than it consumes, acquiring the goods and services that it does not produce by trade.

GLOSSARY

speculative finance A strategy used by firms to meet payment commitments on liabilities using cash flow, although the firm cannot repay the principal in this way. Firms in this position need to 'roll over' their liabilities, usually by issuing new debt to meet commitments on maturing debt. Term coined by Hyman Minsky in his Financial Instability Hypothesis. *See also: hedge finance.*

stock exchange A financial marketplace where shares (also known as stocks) and other financial assets are traded. It has a list of companies whose shares are traded there. *See also: share.*

stock variable A quantity measured at a point in time. Its units do not depend on time. *See also: flow variable.*

strategic interaction A social interaction in which the participants are aware of the ways that their actions affect others (and the ways that the actions of others affect them).

strategy An action (or a course of action) that a person may take when that person is aware of the mutual dependence of the results for herself and for others. The outcomes depend not only on that person's actions, but also on the actions of others.

structural unemployment The level of unemployment at the Nash equilibrium of the labour and product market model.

subprime borrower An individual with a low credit rating and a high risk of default. *See also: default risk, subprime mortgage.*

subprime mortgage A residential mortgage issued to a high-risk borrower, for example, a borrower with a history of bankruptcy and delayed repayments. *See also: subprime borrower.*

substantive judgements of fairness Judgements based on the characteristics of the allocation itself, not how it was determined. *See also: procedural judgements of fairness.*

substitutes Two goods for which an increase in the price of one leads to an increase in the quantity demanded of the other. *See also: complements.*

substitution effect The effect for example, on the choice of consumption of a good that is only due to changes in the price or opportunity cost, given the new level of utility.

supply curve The curve that shows the number of units of output that would be produced at any given price. For a market, it shows the total quantity that all firms together would produce at any given price.

tangency When a line touches a curve, but does not cross it.

tax A compulsory payment to the government levied, for example, on workers' incomes (income taxes) and firms' profits (profit taxes) or included in the price paid for goods and services (value added or sales taxes).

technically feasible An allocation within the limits set by technology and biology.

technological progress A change in technology that reduces the amount of resources (labour, machines, land, energy, time) required to produce a given amount of the output.

technology A process taking a set of materials and other inputs, including the work of people and capital goods (such as machines), to produce an output.

too big to fail Said to be a characteristic of large banks, whose central importance in the economy ensures they will be saved by the government if they are in financial difficulty. The bank thus does not bear all the costs of its activities and is therefore likely to take bigger risks. *See also: moral hazard.*

total surplus The total gains from trade received by all parties involved in the exchange. It is measured as the sum of the consumer and producer surpluses. *See: joint surplus.*

trade union An organization consisting predominantly of employees, the principal activities of which include the negotiation of rates of pay and conditions of employment for its members.

trademark A logo, a name, or a registered design typically associated with the right to exclude others from using it to identify their products.

tragedy of the commons A social dilemma in which self-interested individuals acting independently deplete a common resource, lowering the payoffs of all. *See also: social dilemma.*

transaction costs Costs that impede the bargaining process or the agreement of a contract. They include costs of acquiring information about the good to be traded, and costs of enforcing a contract.

ultimatum game An interaction in which the first player proposes a division of a 'pie' with the second player, who may either accept, in which case they each get the division proposed by the first person, or reject the offer, in which case both players receive nothing.

unemployment benefit A government transfer received by an unemployed person. *Also known as: unemployment insurance.*

unemployment rate The ratio of the number of the unemployed to the total labour force. (Note that the employment rate and unemployment rate do not sum to 100%, as they have different denominators.) *See also: labour force, employment rate.*

unemployment A situation in which a person who is able and willing to work is not employed.

union voice effect The positive effect on labour effort (and hence labour productivity) of trade union members' sense that they have a say (a voice) in how the firm is run.

unit cost Total cost divided by number of units produced.

utility A numerical indicator of the value that one places on an outcome, such that higher-valued outcomes will be chosen over lower-valued ones when both are feasible.

Veblen effect A negative external effect that arises from the consumption of a positional good. Examples include the negative external effects imposed on others by the consumption of luxury housing, clothing, or vehicles.

verifiable information Information that can be used to enforce a contract.

wage labour A system in which producers are paid for the time they work for their employers.

wage-setting (WS) curve The curve—arising from the wage-setting decisions of firms in the labour market—that gives the real wage necessary at each level of economy-wide employment to provide workers with incentives to work hard and well.

wage subsidy A government payment either to firms or employees, to raise the wage received by workers or lower the wage costs paid by firms, with the objective of increasing hiring and workers' incomes.

weakness of will The inability to commit to a course of action (dieting or foregoing some other present pleasure, for example) that one will regret later. It differs from impatience, which may also lead a person to favour pleasures in the present, but not necessarily act in a way that one regrets.

wealth Stock of things owned or value of that stock. It includes the market value of a home, car, any land, buildings, machinery, or other capital goods that a person may own, and any financial assets, such as bank deposits, shares, bonds, or loans made to others. Debts to others are subtracted from wealth—for example, the mortgage owed to the bank.

willingness to accept (WTA) The reservation price of a potential seller, who will be willing to sell a unit only for a price at least this high. *See also: reservation price, willingness to pay.*

willingness to pay (WTP) An indicator of how much a person values a good, measured by the maximum amount he or she would pay to acquire a unit of the good. *See also: willingness to accept.*

worker-owned cooperative A form of business in which a substantial fraction of the capital goods are owned by employees rather than being owned by those who are not involved in production in the firm; worker-owners typically elect a manager to make day-to-day decisions.

worker's best response function (to wage) The amount of work that a worker chooses to perform as her best response to each wage that the employer may offer. *Also known as: best response curve.*

WS/PS model Model of the aggregate economy that combines wage-setting (WS) and price-setting (PS) decisions. Where the WS and PS curves intersect is the Nash equilibrium and determines structural unemployment and the real wage. *See also, wage-setting curve, price-setting curve, structural unemployment.*

yield The implied rate of return that the buyer gets on their money when they buy a bond at its market price.

BIBLIOGRAPHY

Acemoglu, Daron, and James A. Robinson. 2012. *Why Nations Fail: The Origins of Power, Prosperity, and Poverty*. New York, NY: Crown Publishing Group.

Aesop. 'Belling the Cat'. In *Fables*, retold by Joseph Jacobs. XVII, (1). The Harvard Classics. New York: P. F. Collier & Son, 1909–14; Bartleby.com (https://tinyco.re/6827567). 2001.

Aleem, Irfan. 1990. 'Imperfect information, screening, and the costs of informal lending: A study of a rural credit market in Pakistan' (https://tinyco.re/4382174). *The World Bank Economic Review* 4 (3): pp. 329–49.

Alvaredo, Facundo, Anthony B. Atkinson, Thomas Piketty, Emmanuel Saez, and Gabriel Zucman. 2016. *The World Wealth and Income Database (WID)* (https://tinyco.re/5262390).

Atkinson, Anthony B., and Thomas Piketty, eds. 2007. *Top Incomes Over the Twentieth Century: A Contrast between Continental European and English-Speaking Countries*. Oxford: Oxford University Press.

Bakija, Jon, Lane Kenworthy, Peter Lindert, and Jeff Madrick. 2016. *How Big Should Our Government Be?* Berkeley: University of California Press.

Banerjee, Abhijit V., Paul J. Gertler, and Maitreesh Ghatak. 2002. 'Empowerment and Efficiency: Tenancy Reform in West Bengal' (https://tinyco.re/9394444). *Journal of Political Economy* 110 (2): pp. 239–80.

Berger, Helge, and Mark Spoerer. 2001. 'Economic Crises and the European Revolutions of 1848'. *The Journal of Economic History* 61 (2): pp. 293–326.

Berghoff, Hartmut, and Uta Andrea Balbier. 2013. 'From Centrally Planned Economy to Capitalist Avant-Garde? The Creation, Collapse, and Transformation of a Socialist Economy'. In *The East German Economy, 1945–2010: Falling behind or Catching Up?* Cambridge: Cambridge University Press.

Besley, Timothy, and Anne Case. 1995. 'Does electoral accountability affect economic policy choices? Evidence from gubernatorial term limits'. *The Quarterly Journal of Economics* 110 (3): pp. 769–98.

Besley, Timothy, and Torsten Persson. 2014. 'Why do developing countries tax so little?' (https://tinyco.re/3513621). *The Journal of Economic Perspectives* 28 (4): pp. 99–120.

Bewley, Truman F. 1999. *Why Wages Don't Fall during a Recession*. Cambridge, MA: Harvard University Press.

Bonica, Adam, McCarty, Nolan, Poole, Keith T., and Howard Rosenthal. 2013. 'Why hasn't democracy slowed rising inequality?' (https://tinyco.re/5838764) *The Journal of Economic Perspectives* 27 (3): pp. 103–23.

Bowles, Samuel. 2006. *Microeconomics: Behavior, Institutions, and Evolution (The Roundtable Series in Behavioral Economics)*. Princeton, NJ: Princeton University Press.

Bowles, Samuel. 2016. *The Moral Economy: Why Good Incentives Are No Substitute for Good Citizens*. New Haven, CT: Yale University Press.

Braverman, Harry, and Paul M. Sweezy. 1975. *Labor and Monopoly Capital: The Degradation of Work in the Twentieth Century*. 2nd ed. New York, NY: Monthly Review Press.

Brunnermeier, Markus. 2009. 'Lucas roundtable: Mind the frictions' (https://tinyco.re/0136751). *The Economist*. Updated 6 August 2009.

Camerer, Colin, and Ernst Fehr. 2004. 'Measuring Social Norms and Preferences Using Experimental Games: A Guide for Social Scientists'. In *Foundations of Human Sociality: Economic Experiments and Ethnographic Evidence from Fifteen Small-Scale Societies*, edited by Joseph Henrich, Robert Boyd, Samuel Bowles, Colin Camerer, and Herbert Gintis. Oxford: Oxford University Press.

Carlin, Wendy, and David Soskice. 2015. *Macroeconomics: Institutions, Instability, and the Financial System*. New York, NY: Oxford University Press.

Carter, Susan Payne, and Paige Marta Skiba. 2012. 'Pawnshops, Behavioral Economics, and Self-Regulation' (https://tinyco.re/3000562). *Review of Banking and Financial Law* 32 (1): pp.193–220

Cassidy, John. 2010. 'Interview with Eugene Fama' (https://tinyco.re/0438887). *The New Yorker*. Updated 13 January 2010.

Churchill, Winston. 1946. 'Iron Curtain' speech (https://tinyco.re/6053919).

Clark, Andrew E., and Andrew J. Oswald. 2002. 'A Simple Statistical Method for Measuring How Life Events Affect Happiness'. *International Journal of Epidemiology* 31 (6): pp. 1139–44.

Coase, Ronald H. 1937. 'The Nature of the Firm' (https://tinyco.re/4250905). *Economica* 4 (16): pp. 386–405.

Coase, Ronald H. 1992. 'The Institutional Structure of Production' (https://tinyco.re/1636715). *American Economic Review* 82 (4): pp. 713–19.

Couch, Kenneth A., and Dana W. Placzek. 2010. 'Earnings Losses of Displaced Workers Revisited'. *American Economic Review* 100 (1): pp. 572–89.

Cournot, Augustin, and Irving Fischer. (1838) 1971. *Researches into the Mathematical Principles of the Theory of Wealth*. New York, NY: A. M. Kelley.

Deaton, A. 2013. *The Great Escape: health, wealth, and the origins of inequality* (https://tinyco.re/5750302). Princeton: Princeton University Press.

Drèze, Jean, and Amartya Sen. 2013. *An Uncertain Glory: India and its Contradictions*. Princeton, NJ: Princeton University Press: p. 2.

Easterlin, Richard. 1974. 'Does economic growth improve the human lot?' (https://tinyco.re/7453951) In M Abramovitz, P David & M Reder (Eds.), *Nations and Households in Economic Growth: Essays in Honor of Moses Abramovitz*. New York: Academic Press.

Edgeworth, Francis Ysidro. 2003. *Mathematical Psychics and Further Papers on Political Economy*. Oxford: Oxford University Press.

Ehrenreich, Barbara. 2011. *Nickel and Dimed: On (Not) Getting By in America*. New York, NY: St. Martin's Press.

Eisen, Michael. 2011. 'Amazon's $23,698,655.93 book about flies'. It is NOT junk. (https://tinyco.re/0044329). Updated 22 April 2011.

Fafchamps, Marcel, and Bart Minten. 1999. 'Relationships and Traders in Madagascar'. *Journal of Development Studies* 35 (6) (August): pp. 1–35.

Falk, Armin, and James J. Heckman. 2009. 'Lab Experiments Are a Major Source of Knowledge in the Social Sciences'. *Science* 326 (5952): pp. 535–538.

Farnie, Douglas A. 1979. *The English Cotton Industry and the World Market 1815–1896*. Oxford: Clarendon Press.

Feiwel, George R. (ed.). 1989. *Joan Robinson and Modern Economic Theory*. New York: New York University Press: p. 4.

Fligstein, N., and A. Roehrkasse. 2016. 'The causes of fraud in the financial crisis of 2007 to 2009'. *American Sociological Review* 81 (4): pp. 617–43.

Fogel, Robert William. 2000. *The Fourth Great Awakening and the Future of Egalitarianism: The Political Realignment of the 1990s and the Fate of Egalitarianism*. Chicago: University of Chicago Press.

Freeman, Sunny. 2015. 'What Canada can learn from Sweden's unionized retail workers' (https://tinyco.re/0808135). *Huffington Post Canada Business*. Updated 19 March 2015.

Friedman, Milton. 1953. *Essays in Positive Economics*. (7th ed.) Chicago: University of Chicago Press.

Giberson, Michael. 2010. 'I Cringe When I See Hayek's Knowledge Problem Wielded as a Rhetorical Club' (https://tinyco.re/9189202). Knowledge Problem. Updated 5 April.

Gilbert, Richard J., and Michael L. Katz. 2001. 'An Economist's Guide to US v. Microsoft' (https://tinyco.re/7683758). *Journal of Economic Perspectives* 15 (2): pp. 25–44.

Gilens, Martin, and Benjamin I. Page. 2014. 'Testing theories of American politics: Elites, interest groups, and average citizens' (https://tinyco.re/7911085). *Perspectives on Politics* 12 (03): pp. 564–81.

Graeber, David. 2012. 'The Myth of Barter' (https://tinyco.re/6552964). *Debt: The First 5,000 years*. Brooklyn, NY: Melville House Publishing.

Gross, David, and Nicholas Souleles. 2002. 'Do liquidity constraints and interest rates matter for consumer behavior? Evidence from credit card data'. *The Quarterly Journal of Economics* 117 (1) (February): pp. 149–85.

Hamilton, Alexander, James Madison, and John Jay. 1961. *The Federalist*. Middletown, Ct. Wesleyan University Press.

Hansmann, Henry. 2000. *The Ownership of Enterprise*. Cambridge, MA: Belknap Press.

Hardin, Garrett. 1968. 'The Tragedy of the Commons' (https://tinyco.re/4834967). *Science* 162 (3859): pp. 1243–48.

Harding, Matthew, and Michael Lovenheim. 2017. 'The effect of prices on nutrition: Comparing the impact of product- and nutrition-specific taxes' (https://tinyco.re/6153912). *Journal of Economics* 53(C): pp. 53–73.

Harford, Tim. 2012.'Still think you can beat the market?' (https://tinyco.re/7063932). *The Undercover Economist*. Updated 24 November 2012.

Harford, Tim. 2015. 'The rewards for working hard are too big for Keynes's vision' (https://tinyco.re/5829245). *The Undercover Economist*.

Hayek, Friedrich A. 1948. *Individualism and Economic Order* (https://tinyco.re/3958172). University of Chicago Press.

Hayek, Friedrich A. 1994. *The Road to Serfdom* (https://tinyco.re/0683881). Chicago, Il: University of Chicago Press.

Heckman, James. 2013. *Giving Kids a Fair Chance: A Strategy That Works*. Cambridge, MA: MIT Press.

Helper, Susan, Morris Kleiner, and Yingchun Wang. 2010. 'Analyzing Compensation Methods in Manufacturing: Piece Rates, Time Rates, or Gain-Sharing?' (https://tinyco.re/4437027). NBER Working Papers No. 16540.

Henrich, Joseph, Richard McElreath, Abigail Barr, Jean Ensminger, Clark Barrett, Alexander Bolyanatz, Juan Camilo Cardenas, Michael Gurven, Edwins Gwako, Natalie Henrich, Carolyn Lesorogol, Frank Marlowe, David Tracer, and John Ziker.

2006. 'Costly Punishment Across Human Societies' (https://tinyco.re/2043845). *Science* 312 (5781): pp. 1767–70.

Hirsch, Barry T. 2008. 'Sluggish institutions in a dynamic world: Can unions and industrial competition coexist?' *Journal of Economic Perspectives* 22 (1) (February): pp. 153–76.

Huberman, Michael, and Chris Minns. 2004. 'The Times They Are Not Changin': Days and Hours of Work in Old and New Worlds, 1870–2000' (https://tinyco.re/2758271). *Explorations in Economic History* 44 (4): pp. 538–67.

Jacobson, Louis, Robert J. Lalonde, and Daniel G. Sullivan. 1993. 'Earnings Losses of Displaced Workers'. *The American Economic Review* 83 (4): pp. 685–709.

Jaffer, S., N. Morris, E. Sawbridge, and D. Vines. 2014. 'How changes to the financial services industry eroded trust'. In *Capital Failure: Rebuilding Trust in Financial Services*, ed. N. Morris and D. Vines. Oxford: Oxford University Press.

Jensen, Robert. 2007. 'The Digital Provide: Information (Technology), Market Performance, and Welfare in the South Indian Fisheries Sector.' *The Quarterly Journal of Economics* 122 (3) (August): pp. 879–924.

Kalla, Joshua L., and David E. Broockman. 2015. 'Campaign contributions facilitate access to congressional officials: A randomized field experiment' (https://tinyco.re/6564191). *American Journal of Political Science* 60 (3): pp. 1–14.

Kay, John. 'The Structure of Strategy' (https://tinyco.re/7663497). Reprinted from *Business Strategy Review* 1993.

Keynes, John Maynard. 1963. 'Economic Possibilities for our Grandchildren' (https://tinyco.re/8213530). In *Essays in Persuasion*. New York, NY: W. W. Norton & Co.

Kindleberger, Charles P. 2005. *Manias, Panics, and Crashes: A History of Financial Crises* (https://tinyco.re/6810098). Hoboken, NJ: Wiley, John & Sons.

Kletzer, Lori G. 1998. 'Job Displacement' (https://tinyco.re/8577746). *Journal of Economic Perspectives* 12 (1): pp. 115–36.

Krajewski, Markus. 2014. 'The Great Lightbulb Conspiracy' (https://tinyco.re/3479245). *IEEE Spectrum*. Updated 25 September 2014.

Kroszner, Randall S., and Louis Putterman (editors). 2009. *The Economic Nature of the Firm: A Reader*. Cambridge: Cambridge University Press.

Landes, David S. 2003. *The Unbound Prometheus: Technological Change and Industrial Development in Western Europe from 1750 to the Present*. Cambridge: Cambridge University Press.

Lasswell, Harold D. 1936. *Politics; who gets what, when and how* (https://tinyco.re/2227728). New York: Whittlesey House.

Lazear, Edward P., Kathryn L. Shaw, and Christopher Stanton. 2016. 'Making Do with Less: Working Harder during Recessions'. *Journal of Labor Economics* 34 (S1 Part 2): pp. 333–60.

Leeson, Peter T. 2007. 'An-arrgh-chy: The Law and Economics of Pirate Organizations'. *Journal of Political Economy* 115 (6): pp. 1049–94.

Leigh, Andrew. 2007. 'How closely do top incomes shares track other measures of inequality?' *Economic Journal* 117: pp. 619-33.

Levitt, Steven D., and John A. List. 2007. 'What Do Laboratory Experiments Measuring Social Preferences Reveal About the Real World?' (https://tinyco.re/9601240). *Journal of Economic Perspectives* 21 (2): pp. 153–74.

Lindert, Peter. 2004. *Growing Public: Social Spending and Economic Growth since the 18th Century*. Cambridge: Cambridge University Press.

Lorenz, Max O. 1905. 'Methods of Measuring the Concentration of Wealth' (https://tinyco.re/0786587). *Publications of the American Statistical Association* 9 (70).

Lucas, Robert. 2009. 'In defence of the dismal science' (https://tinyco.re/6052194). *The Economist*. Updated 6 August 2009.

Malkiel, Burton G. 2003. 'The efficient market hypothesis and its critics' (https://tinyco.re/4628706). *Journal of Economic Perspectives* 17 (1) (March): pp. 59–82.

Marshall, Alfred. 1920. *Principles of Economics* (https://tinyco.re/0560708). 8th ed. London: MacMillan & Co.

Martin, Felix. 2013. *Money: The Unauthorised Biography*. London: The Bodley Head.

Martinez-Bravo, Monica, Miquel, Gerard P. I., Qian, Nancy, and Yang Yao. 2014. 'Political reform in China: The effect of local elections' (https://tinyco.re/6544486). NBER working paper, 18101.

Marx, Karl. (1848) 2010. *The Communist Manifesto* (https://tinyco.re/0155765). Edited by Friedrich Engels. London: Arcturus Publishing.

Marx, Karl. 1906. *Capital: A Critique of Political Economy*. New York, NY: Random House.

Mencken, H. L. 2006. *A Little Book in C Major*. New York, NY: Kessinger Publishing.

Micklethwait, John, and Adrian Wooldridge. 2003. *The Company: A Short History of a Revolutionary Idea*. New York, NY: Modern Library.

Mill, John Stuart. (1848) 1994. *Principles of Political Economy* (https://tinyco.re/9348882). New York: Oxford University Press.

Mill, John Stuart. (1859) 2002. *On Liberty* (https://tinyco.re/6454781). Mineola, NY: Dover Publications.

Miller, Grant. 2008. 'Women's suffrage, political responsiveness, and child survival in American history' (https://tinyco.re/5731666). *The Quarterly Journal of Economics* 123 (3): pp. 1287–1327.

Miller, R. G., and S. R. Sorrell. 2013. 'The Future of Oil Supply' (https://tinyco.re/6167443). *Philosophical Transactions of the Royal Society A: Mathematical, Physical and Engineering Sciences* 372 (2006) (December).

Morduch, Jonathan. 1999. 'The Microfinance Promise' (https://tinyco.re/2004502). *Journal of Economic Literature* 37 (4) (December): pp. 1569–1614.

Moser, Petra. 2013. 'Patents and Innovation: Evidence from Economic History' (https://tinyco.re/7074474). *Journal of Economic Perspectives* 27 (1): pp. 23–44

Moser, Petra. 2015. 'Intellectual Property Rights and Artistic Creativity' (https://tinyco.re/2212476). *VoxEU.org*. Updated 4 November 2017.

Nasar, Sylvia. 2011. *A Beautiful Mind: The Life of Mathematical Genius and Nobel Laureate John Nash*. New York, NY: Simon & Schuster.

New York Times. 1988. 'Ban greed? No: Harness it' (https://tinyco.re/9781012). 20 January: editorial page.

O'Reilly, Tim, and Eric S. Raymond. 2001. *The Cathedral & the Bazaar: Musings on Linux and Open Source by an Accidental Revolutionary*. Sebastopol, CA: O'Reilly.

Ostrom, Elinor. 2000. 'Collective Action and the Evolution of Social Norms' (https://tinyco.re/0059239). *Journal of Economic Perspectives* 14 (3): pp. 137–58.

Ostrom, Elinor. 2008. 'The Challenge of Common-Pool Resources' (https://tinyco.re/0296632). *Environment: Science and Policy for Sustainable Development* 50 (4): pp. 8–21.

Owen, Nick A., Oliver R. Inderwildi, and David A. King. 2010. 'The Status of Conventional World Oil Reserves—Hype or Cause for Concern?' (https://tinyco.re/8978100) *Energy Policy* 38 (8): pp. 4743–49.

Pencavel, John. 2002. *Worker Participation: Lessons from the Worker Co-ops of the Pacific Northwest*. New York, NY: Russell Sage Foundation Publications.

Pickard, J., and B Thompson. 2014. 'Archives 1985 & 1986: Thatcher policy fight over "Big Bang" laid bare' (https://tinyco.re/3866414). *Financial Times*. Accessed 7 August 2018.

Pigou, A. C. (editor). 1966. *Memorials of Alfred Marshall*. New York, A. M. Kelley. pp.427–28.

Pigou, Arthur. 1912. *Wealth and Welfare* (https://tinyco.re/2519065). London: Macmillan & Co.

Pigou, Arthur. (1920) 1932. *The Economics of Welfare* (https://tinyco.re/2042156). London: Macmillan & Co.

Piketty, Thomas. 2014. *Capital in the Twenty-First Century*. Cambridge, MA: Harvard University Press.

Plant, E. Ashby, Karl Anders Ericsson, Len Hill, and Kia Asberg. 2005. 'Why study time does not predict grade point average across college students: Implications of deliberate practice for academic performance' (https://tinyco.re/7875663). *Contemporary Educational Psychology* 30 (1): pp. 96–116.

Plummer, Alfred. 1971. *Bronterre: A Political Biography of Bronterre O'Brien, 1804–64*. Toronto: University of Toronto Press.

Rasul, Imran, and Daniel Rogger. 2016. 'Management of bureaucrats and public service delivery: Evidence from the Nigerian civil service' (https://tinyco.re/1535739). *The Economic Journal* 128 (608): pp. 413–46.

Rawls, John. 1985. 'Justice as Fairness: Political not Metaphysical'. *Philosophy and Public Affairs* 14 (3): pp. 223-51.

Raychaudhuri, Ajitava. 2004. *Lessons from the Land Reform Movement in West Bengal, India* (https://tinyco.re/0335719). Washington, DC: World Bank.

Reyes, Jose Daniel, and Julia Oliver. 2013. 'Quinoa: The Little Cereal That Could' (https://tinyco.re/9266629). The Trade Post. 22 November 2013.

Robbins, Lionel. (1932) 1984. *An Essay on the Nature and Significance of Economic Science* (https://tinyco.re/4615466). (3rd ed.) New York: New York University Press.

Robertson, Dennis. 1923. *The Control of Industry*. Hitchen: Nisbet.

Robinson, Joan. 1933. *The Economics of Imperfect Competition* (https://tinyco.re/1766675). London: MacMillan & Co.

Roth, Alvin E. 2007. 'Repugnance as a Constraint on Markets' (https://tinyco.re/2118641). *Journal of Economic Perspectives* 21 (3): pp. 37–58.

Sandel, Michael. 2009. *Justice*. London: Penguin.

Schumacher, Ernst F. 1973. *Small is Beautiful: Economics as if People Mattered* (https://tinyco.re/3749799). New York, NY: HarperCollins.

Schumpeter, Joseph. 1918. 'The crisis of the tax state'. Reproduced in Swedberg R. (ed.) 1991. *Joseph A. Schumpeter, The Economics and Sociology of Capitalism*. Princeton University Press.

Schumpeter, Joseph. (1943) 2003. *Capitalism, Socialism and Democracy* (https://tinyco.re/4138375). pp. 167—72. Routledge.

Schumpeter, Joseph A. 1949. 'Science and Ideology' (https://tinyco.re/4561610). *The American Economic Review* 39 (March): pp. 345–59.

Schumpeter, Joseph A. 1997. *Ten Great Economists*. London: Routledge.

Seabright, Paul. 2010. *The Company of Strangers: A Natural History of Economic Life* (Revised Edition). Princeton, NJ: Princeton University Press.

Shiller, Robert J. 2003. 'From Efficient Markets Theory to Behavioral Finance' (https://tinyco.re/3989503). *Journal of Economic Perspectives* 17 (1) (March): pp. 83– 104.

Shiller, Robert J. 2015. *Irrational Exuberance*, Chapter 1 (https://tinyco.re/4263463). Princeton, NJ: Princeton University Press.

Shleifer, Andrei. 1998. 'State versus private ownership' (https://tinyco.re/4317440). *Journal of Economic Perspectives* 12 (4): pp. 133–50.

Shum, Matthew. 2004. 'Does Advertising Overcome Brand Loyalty? Evidence from the Breakfast-Cereals Market' (https://tinyco.re/3909324). *Journal of Economics & Management Strategy* 13 (2): pp. 241–72.

Silver-Greenberg, Jessica. 2014. 'New York prosecutors charge payday loan firms with usury' (https://tinyco.re/8917188). *DealBook*.

Simon, Herbert A. 1951. 'A Formal Theory of the Employment Relationship' (https://tinyco.re/0460792). *Econometrica* 19 (3).

Simon, Herbert A. 1991. 'Organizations and Markets' (https://tinyco.re/2460377). *Journal of Economic Perspectives* 5 (2): pp. 25–44.

Skidelsky, Robert. 2012. 'Robert Skidelsky-portrait: Joseph Schumpeter' (https://tinyco.re/8488199).

Smith, Adam. 1759. *The Theory of Moral Sentiments* (https://tinyco.re/6582039). London: Printed for A. Millar, and A. Kincaid and J. Bell.

Smith, Adam. 1776. *An Inquiry into the Nature and Causes of the Wealth of Nations* (https://tinyco.re/9804148). New York: NY: Random House Publishing Group.

Smith, Adam. 1776. 'Of the profits of stock' (https://tinyco.re/9527891). In *An Inquiry into the Nature and Causes of the Wealth of Nations*.

Stevenson, Betsey, and Justin Wolfers. 2008. 'Economic growth and subjective well-being: Reassessing the Easterlin paradox' (https://tinyco.re/7219387). Brookings Papers on Economic Activity: pp. 1–87.

The CORE team. *The Economy* (https://tinyco.re/6612325). New York, NY: Oxford University Press.

The Economist. 2001. 'Is Santa a Deadweight Loss?' (https://tinyco.re/7728778) Updated 20 December 2001.

The Economist. 2014. Keynes and Hayek: Prophets for Today (https://tinyco.re/0417474). Updated 14 March 2014.

The Economist. 2017. 'Barclays and four former executives are charged with fraud'. 22 June: Finance and Economics section.

Toynbee, Polly. 2003. *Hard Work: Life in Low-pay Britain*. London: Bloomsbury Publishing.

Walzer, Michael. 1983. *Spheres of Justice: A Defense of Pluralism and Equality*. New York, NY: Basic Books.

Whaples, Robert. 2001. 'Hours of work in U.S. History' (https://tinyco.re/1660378). *EH.net Encyclopedia*.

Williamson, Oliver E. 1985. *The Economic Institutions of Capitalism*. New York, NY: Collier Macmillan.

World Bank, The. 1993. *The East Asian miracle: Economic growth and public policy* (https://tinyco.re/3040506). New York, NY: Oxford University Press.

COPYRIGHT ACKNOWLEDGEMENTS

Cover: Aerial view of a city, Magnifier / Shutterstock.com. **Unit 1:** Extreme wealth inequality in Mexico City, Santa Fe District: Johnny Miller / africanDRONE. Adam Smith: Etching created by Cadell and Davies (1811), John Horsburgh (1828) or R.C. Bell (1872). Joseph Schumpeter: Volkswirtschaftliches Institut, Universität Freiburg, Freiburg im Breisgau, Germany, https://goo.gl/ZlRjmG, licensed under CC BY-SA 3.0. **Unit 2:** Chinese men playing chess, zhuda/Shutterstock.com. Elinor Ostrom: Holger Motzkau 2010, Wikipedia/Wikimedia Commons (CC BY-SA 3.0). John Nash: Peter Badge/Typos1, https://goo.gl/vkcH9s, licensed under CC BY-SA 3.0. **Unit 3:** Scales of justice, r.classen/Shutterstock.com. Vilfredo Pareto: Paul Fearn/Alamy Stock Photo. **Unit 4:** Clock mechanism, MarkoV87 / Shutterstock.com. **Unit 5:** View of Macau old town, Prin Adulyatham/Shutterstock.com. **Unit 6:** Aerial view of office, Rawpixel.com / Shutterstock.com. Herbert Simon: AP/Shutterstock. Karl Marx: John Jabez Edwin Mayall, International Institute of Social History, Amsterdam, Netherlands. John Stuart Mill: Unknown author, Popular Science Monthly Volume 3. **Unit 7:** Warehouse shelving, SasinTipchai / Shutterstock.com. Augustin Cournot: Unknown author, Wikipedia/Wikimedia Commons. Joan Robinson: Punt / Anefo / Nationaal Archief. Alfred Marshall: Unknown author, *The Economic Journal* Vol. 34, No. 135 (Sep., 1924), pp. 311-372. **Unit 8:** Workers in a factory, Frame China / Shutterstock.com. **Unit 9:** Man in front of Moneyshop, Thinglass / Shutterstock.com. **Unit 10:** Abandoned housing development, Keshcarrigan, Ireland, Aidan Crawley / Bloomberg News. **Unit 11:** Factories emitting smoke, Balu / Shutterstock.com. Friedrich Hayek: LSE Library. Ronald Coase: Coase-Sandor Institute for Law and Economics, University of Chicago Law School. Arthur Pigou: Mary Evans Picture Library. **Unit 12:** Children lying on the floor of the Michigan Legislature, Lester Graham / Michigan Radio

We would like to acknowledge everybody who granted us permission to reproduce images, figures and quotations throughout this text. Every effort was made to trace copyright holders, but we will make arrangements to clear permission for material reproduced in this book with any copyright holders whom it has not been possible to contact.

INDEX

A
accountability 539, 574
active labour market policy 376
actors 431–2
administrative feasibility 555, 557–8, 562, 574–5
adverse selection 516–19, 520, 521, 522, 523, 524
advertising 277, 299, 327–8, 487
Aesop 52
affluence 1, 23, 30, 40
aggregate demand 381, 382
aggregate economy 337, 361–3, 364, 383–4
  see also WS/PS model
Airbnb 529
Akerlof, George 516, 517
Allende, Salvador 555–6, 561
allocation 99, 135, 136, 207, 213, 530
  competitive equilibrium 314–15
  fairness 116, 117
  kidney transplants 528–9
  Operation Barga 190
  Pareto efficiency 105–9, 110, 207, 212, 214, 227–8
  reservation indifference curve 201–2, 203–4
  scarce resources 528
  under the rule of force 194–9
altruism 69, 71, 72, 78, 92, 122
  positional goods 177
  reciprocity compared with 76, 79
  survey questions 68
Amazon 276
antibiotics 49–50, 51, 509
antitrust policy 297
apartheid 1–2, 16

Apple 231, 278, 279
arbitrage 435, 466
Argentina 34, 35
Ariely, Dan 111
Arrow, Kenneth 477
artificial scarcity 513
assets 412–15, 429, 431, 432–6, 478
  banks 440–1, 443, 444, 447–51, 474
  bubbles 463–8
  firms 452
  households 469
  markets 432
  risk and return 454–60, 478
  supply and demand 461–2
asymmetric information 234, 512, 516–21, 524, 525
auctions 300, 301
Australia
  carbon dioxide emissions 562
  climate change policy 562–3
  collective bargaining 364, 367
  democracy 40
  environmental protection 45
  governing elite 548
  higher education 567, 568
  inequality 222, 563
  labour market 335–6
  mining 332, 381
  unemployment 333
  unemployment benefits 375
  working hours 141
Austria
  collective bargaining 364, 367
  democracy 40
  inequality 222, 563
  unemployment benefits 375

authority 236–7
automation 334, 371–2
average cost curve 285, 345, 347–8
average product 164–6, 182, 346, 354, 359, 362–3, 369, 382

B
Bahrain 562
bailouts 430, 474, 476, 478
balance sheets 412–15, 438
  banks 440–1, 446–51, 478
  households 469
banana plantations 482–3, 493–6, 497, 499–502, 504–7, 509, 514
bank lending rate 445, 478
bank money 431, 439–40, 441–2, 443, 478
bank runs 443, 478
banks 264, 391, 429, 430–2, 439–43, 453, 478
  balance sheets 412–13, 440–1, 446–51
  definition of 431
  deregulation 470–1, 474–6, 478
  failures 448, 473–4
  financial crisis 413, 472–4, 479
  incomplete contracts 270
  liability-based money 438
  market failure 523
  moneylenders 388
  morals 474, 476–7
  mortgages 469
  risk-taking by 430
  'too big to fail' concept 36
  trust in 424, 436
Barclays 412, 413, 449–50, 467, 475

597

INDEX

bargaining 81–2, 185
  efficiency 211–12
  private 481, 497–503, 524, 525
  unions 364–70
bargaining power 191–9, 203, 206, 209–13, 214, 227
  competitive equilibrium 306
  definition of 188
  democracy 572
  employees 253
  gains from trade 289
  gig economy 267
  Keralan fish market 490–1
  large firms 278
  market power 295
  pesticide problem 499
  price-setting 292, 293
  ultimatum game 188, 190
  unions 365, 367, 370, 384
barter 436
base money 432, 439–40, 443–4, 446, 448, 453, 478
basic research 37, 46
bathtub model 390–1, 413–14, 431
Baxandall, Phineas 171
behavioural economics 233
behavioural experiments 69, 92
Belgium
  collective bargaining 367
  democracy 40
  GDP per capita 6
  inequality 222, 563
  unemployment benefits 375
  unpaid care work 175
  working hours 173
bell curve 110
Bentham, Jeremy 117
Besley, Tim 547
best response 59–60, 76, 92
  bargained wages 366
  conflicts of interest 84
  labour discipline model 250–2, 272
  Nash equilibrium 79–81
  unemployment 258–61
best response curve 251–3, 256–7, 259–61, 338–40, 368
Bewley, Truman 261–2
biological feasibility (biological survival constraint) 195–9, 201, 202, 204, 213
biosphere 91
Bisenius, Don 476
Blanchflower, David 341
BNP Paribas 471

boards of directors 234, 240
Boigny, Felix Houphouet 537
Bolivia 316, 317
bonds 391, 403, 431, 432–3
  debt financing 452
  government 445, 453, 454–9
  prices 434–6
  risk and return 454–9
borrowing 387–8, 391, 392–401, 452
  balance sheets 413–15
  banks 439–40, 445, 446–9, 453, 470
  constraints 416–19
  ease of 465
  housing 469
  inequalities 422–4
  for investment 409–11
  market failure 523
  microfinance 420
  mutual gains and conflicts 406–9
  tuition fees 566
  see also lending; loans
Botswana 3–5, 34, 35
Bowley, A. L. 304
Boyce, James K. 507
brand loyalty 299
Braverman, Harry 237
Brazil
  cooperation in fishing 69
  cotton production 489
  democracy 40
  GDP per capita 34, 35
  incomes 3–4
  inequality 222
  policy interest rate 445
  undemocratic government 39
breakfast cereals 279–80, 299
bribery 40, 97
British East India Company 18, 36
broad money 439, 442
Broockman, David 560
Brunnermeier, Markus 466
bubbles 429, 463–8, 469, 478
Burgoon, Brian 171
business cycles 534
buying power 411, 424
  see also spending power

C

Camerer, Colin 70
Canada
  carbon dioxide emissions 562
  collective bargaining 364, 367
  democracy 40

  inequality 222, 563
  unemployment benefits 375
  working hours 141
CAPE *see* cyclically adjusted price-to-earnings ratio
capital 1
capital goods 22–3, 28, 29
capitalism 2, 16, 191
  capitalist revolution 1, 23–9, 36, 37, 46
  creative destruction 28–9
  credit market 388
  definition of 23
  division of labour 272
  dynamism 35–7
  economic growth 29–33
  environmental impacts 40–1
  Hayek on 487
  inequality 37–8
  limits to government 538
  Marx on 235
  South Africa 16
  varieties of 34–7
carbon dioxide emissions 41–2, 45, 54, 74
  climate change game 87–9
  market failure 510, 515
  public policies 89–90, 562–3
  willingness to pay 525
  see also climate change
Cárdenas, Juan Camilo 69
care work 175
cartels 297, 315, 323, 327
Case, Anne 547
cash 431, 436, 448, 451, 453
Cassidy, John 467
Castro, Fidel 548
causation 29–31, 96, 97, 135
Ceausescu, Nicolae 537, 541
cell phones 491
central banks 429, 432, 453
  bubbles 466
  government intervention 536
  interest rates 444–6, 478
  money 438, 439
centralization 27, 46, 531
centrally planned economies 23, 31–3, 34, 236, 487, 489
ceteris paribus assumption 145, 146, 148–9, 182, 358
CFCs 54, 81
change 26, 235
checks and balances 538
cheques 430–1, 436, 437
chicken game 88

598

child mortality 97, 98, 534, 564
children's health 96–7, 98
Chile
   democracy 40
   early childhood education 565
   economic policies 555–6
   political limits to policies 561
   undemocratic government 39
   working hours 143
China
   base money 442
   capitalism 23
   carbon dioxide emissions 89, 562
   climate change game 87–9
   competition from 371–2
   developmental state 34
   economic growth 10, 12–14, 16
   economic policies 564
   GDP per capita 7
   incomes 3–4, 5, 15
   inequality 221, 222
   political competition 546
   salt tax 132
   undemocratic government 39
chlordecone 482, 505–7, 509, 522
Churchill, Winston 31
City of London 475–6
civil liberties 550
civil rights 535
climate change 41–3, 44, 46–7, 54, 91, 510
   Copenhagen summit 81, 90
   free riding 66
   game theory 86–90, 92
   public policies 89–90, 562–3
   willingness to pay for mitigation 525
   see also carbon dioxide emissions
club goods 513
Coase, Ronald 236, 497–9, 500–1, 530–1
Coasean bargaining 497–503, 525
coercion 535
Cohen, Jack 279
collateral 387, 417–18, 419, 425, 427
   bank loans 447
   borrowing for investment 409
   households 469, 478
   student loans 566
collective action 501
collective bargaining 364–70
Colombia 222, 565
commodities 461
commodity money 437, 438

common-pool resources 51, 64, 513, 514, 515, 523
   see also tragedy of the commons
common property 70–1, 99, 107
Communism 31, 32, 34, 236
compensation 108, 505, 506, 507, 510
competition 295–7, 327
   capitalist dynamism 37
   competitive pressures 345–6
   firms 27, 531, 551
   global 358
   Hayek on 487
   imperfect 523
   inequality 359, 362, 370, 371–2
   'invisible hand' 51
   labour market 378
   lack of 486
   markets 24, 46, 481
   monopolistic 294, 295, 296, 312, 331
   perfect 295, 315, 327, 551, 555
   political 546–51, 553
   price markups 373
   price-setting curve 350, 351, 383
   profit maximization 240
competition policy 36, 275, 296–7, 327, 536
competitive equilibrium 275, 305–6, 311–15, 327, 378, 487
complete contracts 378, 380
compound annual growth rate (CAGR) 10, 11–12
conflicts of interest 81–2, 92
   borrowing and lending 387, 395, 406, 416–18, 425, 427
   climate change 86–9
   employment relationship 241
   firms 231, 239
   Nash equilibrium 83–6
   principal–agent relationships 269, 425, 473
conspicuous consumption 176–7, 178, 179, 182
constant prices 6
constant returns to scale 284
constrained choice problems 162, 163, 164, 182, 227, 255
constrained optimization 327
consumer lifestyles 89
consumer price index (CPI) 341
consumers see customers
consumer surplus 289–90, 293, 296, 303, 569
   competitive equilibrium 312–13, 314, 315
   renter surplus 570, 572–3

consumption 139, 140, 389
   borrowing and lending 392–401, 407, 410–11, 426
   changing preferences 181
   choices 415
   conspicuous 176–7, 178, 179, 182
   free time and 182
   households 452
   as normal good 169
   oil 323, 325
   Pareto efficiency 492–3
   smoothing 396–7, 399, 402–5, 406, 426, 432
   Veblen effect 177
consumption goods 154
continuous change 26
contracts 229, 232–3, 237, 238
   complete 314, 378, 380
   enforcement of 492, 501, 511, 524
   external effects 481
   gig economy 267
   managers 240
   see also incomplete contracts
cooperation
   fishing 69
   informal agreements 71
   markets 24, 484
   public goods 68, 72–5, 81
   social preferences 53
cooperatives 229, 264–5, 272
coordination game 80, 92
coordination of work 233–4
Copenhagen climate change summit 81, 90
copyright 134–5, 299, 513, 514
Costa Rica 40
cost of job loss see employment rents
costs
   banana production 493–6
   banks 440
   economic 146–7
   economies of scale 275, 277–8
   of effort 254–6
   fixed 277, 290, 308, 327
   gains from trade 291–2
   gig economy 267
   isoprofit curves 290
   monopolies 538–9
   production 253, 276
   profits and 284–8
   transaction 498
   wage-setting 256, 272
   see also marginal cost; opportunity cost
cotton 488–9

INDEX

Cournot, Augustin 294
CPI *see* consumer price index
creative destruction 28–9, 37, 46
credit-constrained individuals 418–19
credit market 406–8
   constraints 416–19
   exclusion from the 411, 418, 422–3, 523
   inequalities 422–4
   labour market comparison 425–6
   see also borrowing; lending; loans
credit rationing 418–19, 427
crowding out 129, 135
cryptocurrencies 438
Cuba 548
culture
   East/West Germany comparison 31–2
   'permanent technological revolution' 30
   working hours 171, 173
customary rules 54
customers
   decision-making 383
   firm's relationship with 234
   gains from trade 289
   interaction in markets 275
   preferences 294–5
   price discrimination 282–3, 291–3
   willingness to pay 289–90, 291, 294–5, 300, 312–13, 317, 327
cyclically adjusted price-to-earnings (CAPE) ratio 467
cyclical unemployment 381–2
Czech Republic 367, 375

D

data collection 68–9, 93
Davenant, Charles 282
daycare centre fines 128–9, 130, 532
deadweight loss 275, 292, 293, 296, 327
   competitive equilibrium 313, 315
   rent control 570, 571–2
Deaton, Angus 16
debit cards 430
debt financing 452
debt-to-income ratio 470, 472
decentralization 27, 46, 531
   firms 238
   markets 233, 272
deciles 3
decision making 146–7
   firms 233–4, 236, 239, 273, 276, 383
   gender division of labour 174
   scarcity 161–4
decreasing returns to scale 278

default risk 442, 446, 478
defaults, strategic 476–7, 478
deflation 6
Deliveroo 242, 268
Dell 276
demand 276, 279–83, 300–26, 328
   assets 454
   bubbles 463, 465
   changes in 316–22
   economies of scale 278
   excess 305–6, 318–19, 380, 488, 490–1
   financial assets 461
   income elasticity of 325
   labour 332
   law of 282
   money markets 444
   oil 322–6
   price elasticity of 132, 133, 136, 295, 327
   shocks 275, 318
   unemployment 381–2
   willingness to pay 281–3
   see also elasticity of demand
demand curve 275, 279–83, 307, 315, 327, 328, 353
   competitive equilibrium 311–12, 314
   gains from trade 290, 291–2
   oil 323–4
   price elasticity of demand 295, 352
   price-setting 293, 327, 345, 347–9
   product selection 298
   profit maximization 286–7
   rent control 570–1
   shifts in supply and demand 320, 322
   wage-setting 344–5
   willingness to pay 289
democracy 2, 16, 46, 187, 191, 527, 539
   bargaining power 572
   environmental sustainability 45
   ideal 551
   India 188
   inequality 1, 38–40, 115
   political competition 546
   political influence 559
   political institutions 550, 574
   resistance to 549
   South Africa 2, 37, 39
   undermined by markets 532
   see also elections
Denmark
   collective bargaining 367
   democracy 40
   inequality 40, 222, 225, 563
   unemployment benefits 374, 375

wealth 39
working hours 143
deposits 431, 436, 444, 445
   balance sheets 448
   bank runs 443
   interest costs 446
   maturity transformation 442
depreciation 390–1, 392, 413
deregulation 470–1, 474–6, 478
derivatives 432, 476
derived demand for labour 381
deservingness 117
deskilling 237
developmental state 34
dictator game 188, 190
dictatorships 541–6, 549, 550, 551, 552, 561
difference-in-difference method 97
differentiated products 280–1, 299, 306, 314, 327
differentiation 275
dignity 115, 531, 532
diminishing marginal product 150–1, 182
diminishing marginal returns 252, 396, 397, 426
directives 120
discount rate 399, 400–1, 426, 445
discretionary time 170
discrimination 112, 117, 118
diseconomies of scale 278
disequilibrium 318, 327
disposable income 220–1, 223, 228, 390
disutility of effort 244, 250–1, 258, 272, 369
dividends 239, 449, 452
division of labour 90, 484–5, 524
   capitalism 46
   firms and markets 231, 272
   game theory 80, 82
   Smith, Adam 17–18
dominant strategy 59–60, 63, 68, 76, 79, 88, 92
dominant strategy equilibrium 59, 61, 63, 68, 79–80, 92
Duflo, Esther 97, 98
Durkheim, Emile 270

E

early childhood education 565
earnings 390
   see also incomes; wages
'Easterlin Paradox' 179
East Germany 23, 31–3, 34, 96
eBay 300, 301
economic accountability 539

600

INDEX

economic conditions 35, 36
economic cost 146–7
economic development 190, 552
economic feasibility 201–2, 205, 213, 227, 555–6, 562, 574
economic growth 10–18
    capitalism 29–33
    East/West Germany comparison 31–3, 96
    'permanent technological revolution' 19–21
    varieties of capitalism 34–7
economic inequality *see* inequality
economic models 30, 91, 139, 144–5, 172, 174, 191–3
    see also WS/PS model
economic outcomes 16, 105, 185, 213
economic rents 146, 198, 203, 206, 209–10, 227, 289, 327
economics 17, 46, 90–1, 93, 296
    behavioural 233
    definition of 17, 90
    efficiency 106
    experiments 69–70
    fairness 118
    game theory 82–3
    homo economicus 78
    marginal change 150
    rules of the game 136
    self-interest 61
    social dilemmas 50
    social preferences 53
economic security 534
economic systems 23, 24, 26–7, 31–3
economies of scale 275, 277–8, 327, 484
economy 90–1, 331, 530
    aggregate 337, 361–3, 364, 383–4
    economic models 144
Ecuador 316
Edgeworth, Francis 78
education 37, 46, 372–3, 527
    administrative feasibility 558
    differences between countries 564
    early childhood 565
    government spending 553
    higher education funding 566–8, 569
    incomplete contracts 270
    investment in 18
    merit goods 532–3, 537, 567
    Mill on 266
efficiency 95, 99, 105–10, 135
    bargaining 211–12, 227
    competitive equilibrium 314–15
    definition of 105–6

higher education funding 566, 567–8, 569
    Nash equilibrium 120–3
    Operation Barga 190
    policies 527
    trade-off with fairness 118, 136
    ultimatum game 102
    see also Pareto efficiency
efficiency units 253–4, 272
efficiency wages 255–7
efficient market hypothesis 465–6
effort
    disutility of 244, 250–1, 258, 272, 369
    employment rents 272
    labour discipline model 249–53, 272
    unemployment 261
    wage-setting 253–7, 272
Egypt 222, 488, 489
Ehrenreich, Barbara 237
80-20 rule 110
Eisen, Michael 306
elasticity of demand 275, 295, 298, 307, 352
    food taxes 132, 133, 136
    income 325
    price markups 294, 327, 346, 350
    profit margins 345
elasticity of supply 318
elections 38–9, 46, 527, 538, 546–8, 550, 559, 560
elites 527, 540, 547–9, 551
employees
    asymmetric information 234, 520
    bargained wages 364–70
    capitalism 26, 27
    conflicts of interest 231
    contracts 229, 237, 238, 242–3, 268, 270, 272
    cooperatives 264–5
    costs and benefits of employment 244, 245
    division of revenue 238
    economies of scale 278
    employment relationship 232, 241–3, 379
    employment rents 245–9, 250–1, 255, 257, 258–61, 262–3, 272, 342, 379, 540
    Firestone 230
    labour discipline model 249–53, 255, 257, 272
    market failure 523
    Mill on 266
    motivation 244, 245, 378
    power relations 234–8
    principal–agent relationship 269, 270, 417, 425–6
    productivity 261–2

    size of firms 276
    unemployment benefits 259–60
    see also labour; labour market; wages
employers
    bargained wages 364–70
    conflicts of interest 231
    contracts 229, 237, 238, 242–3, 268, 270, 272
    employment relationship 232, 241–3, 379
    employment rents 262–3
    labour discipline model 249–53
    power relations 188, 234–8
    principal–agent relationship 269, 270, 417, 425–6
    unemployment benefits 259–60
    wage-setting 229, 253–7, 377–8, 379, 380
    working hours 173
    see also firms; labour market
employment rate 335, 336, 338–9
employment relationship 232, 241–3, 379
employment rents 245–9, 258–61, 262–3, 272, 379, 540
    labour discipline model 250–1, 255, 257
    wage-setting curve 342
endowments 214, 393–4, 395, 398–9, 407
energy
    model of the economy 91
    renewable 44, 89–90, 91
Engels, Friedrich 235
entrepreneurs 28
environmental issues 40–5
    environmental protection 36–7
    environmental spillovers 496, 508, 523
    global problems 54
    influence of firms on regulation 327
    policies 536
    social dilemmas 51
    social preferences 53
    sustainable lifestyles 89
    see also climate change; pollution
equality, political 550
equal opportunity 117
equilibrium
    changes in demand 317–20
    competitive 275, 305–6, 311–15, 327, 378, 487
    dominant strategy 59, 61, 63, 68, 79–80, 92
    economic models 144
    involuntary unemployment 257, 272
    labour discipline model 255
    labour market 363, 378
    product market 362
    see also Nash equilibrium

601

INDEX

equilibrium price 302–3, 305, 324
equilibrium unemployment 355, 380, 382
equity 387, 417, 419, 427, 449, 469, 478
ethics 304, 531
Europe 320–1
European Commission 296–7
excess demand 305–6, 318–19, 380, 488, 490–1
excess supply 303, 305–6, 356, 380, 490–1
exchange-traded note (ETN) 467
excludability 513, 514, 515
exogenous shocks 320, 327
expected value 454–5
experiments 69–70, 72–5, 92, 93, 96, 128, 145
   see also natural experiments
external benefits 486, 504, 511–12, 515, 520, 523
   see also private benefits
external costs 486, 493, 496, 508, 511–12, 515, 520, 523
   see also marginal external cost; private costs
external diseconomies 509
external economies 509
external effects 45, 46, 92, 486, 510
   bank risk-taking 473
   external diseconomies 509
   incomplete contracts 510–11
   market failure 493, 496, 508, 514, 523, 524
   markets 481
   policies 504–5
   positional goods 176–7, 179, 182
   positive 502, 509, 515
   public goods 512–14
   social dilemmas 50, 51, 53
   social institutions 53–4

F

Fafchamps, Marcel 492
fairness 95, 99, 106, 111–19, 135
   competitive equilibrium 314–15
   economic outcomes 105
   government intervention 536
   higher education funding 566, 567–8, 569
   inequality 214
   institutions 213
   Operation Barga 190
   policies 527
   polluter pays principle 502
   rent control 569
   repugnant markets 532
   social preferences 49

   substantive and procedural judgements 116–18, 119, 135, 192
   trade-off with efficiency 118, 136
   ultimatum game 100, 101–3
   working hours 209
Falk, Armin 70
Fama, Eugene 465–6, 467
families
   family-based production 26, 27
   incomplete contracts 270
   model of the economy 91
   resource allocation 529
   rules of the game 483, 530
farming
   borrowing 387–8, 392, 409, 422, 423
   irrigation 54, 66–8, 92, 99, 510
   Operation Barga 189–90, 225
   quinoa production 316–22
Farnie, Douglas 489
feasible frontier 182, 192–3, 194, 207, 227
   asset risk and return 455–9
   bargaining power 210
   borrowing and lending 394–5, 400–1, 406, 407, 411, 426
   consumption 415
   investment 409, 410, 411
   labour discipline model 252
   political rents 544, 545
   reservation indifference curve 203, 205
   smoothing consumption 402, 403, 404–5
   study time 158–60, 161–2, 164
   technical feasibility 196–9
   wage-setting 256
   willingness to pay 281–2
   working hours 166–8, 172, 255
feasible set 158–61, 166, 167, 182
   asset risk and return 455–6
   borrowing 392, 394, 409, 427
   investment 409, 411
   labour discipline model 252
   lending 403
   willingness to pay 281–2
FedEx 275, 276, 277
Fehr, Ernst 70
fiat currency 438
financial assets 431, 432–6, 452, 478
   banks 447, 448
   government 453
   risk and return 454–60
   supply and demand 461–2
   value of 429
   see also assets

financial crisis 36, 261–2, 413, 478
   bank failures 448
   efficient market hypothesis 466
   lack of trust in banks 424
   mortgage defaults 476
   oil prices 322, 325
   role of banks 472–4, 479
   subprime housing crisis 471
financial deregulation 470–1, 474–6, 478
financial markets 430, 432, 465–6
fines 128–9, 130, 135, 532
Finland
   bubbles 468
   collective bargaining 367
   democracy 40
   educational performance 564
   government spending 553, 554
   incomes 5, 573
   inequality 222, 563
   unemployment benefits 375
   unpaid care work 175
   wealth 39
Firestone 229–30, 231, 249, 263
firms 229–74, 275–330
   aggregate economy 337
   bargained wages 364–70
   bonds 434
   capitalism 16, 23, 25, 26–7, 36, 46
   central planning 489
   competitive markets 300–26
   cooperatives 264–5, 272
   definition of 231
   demand curve 279–80
   economies of scale 277–8
   employee motivation 244, 245
   employment relationship 241–3
   employment rents 245–9, 262–3
   failure of 26
   gains from trade 289–93
   incomplete contracts 242–3, 263, 268–71
   involuntary unemployment 257
   labour discipline model 249–53, 255
   make or buy decisions 530–1
   model of the economy 91
   money 452
   ownership and control 238–40
   perfect competition 551
   power relations 234–8
   price-setting 289–93, 294–7, 327, 331, 337, 344–55, 383, 545
   product selection 298–9
   profits and costs 284–8
   resource allocation 529

INDEX

rules of the game 483, 530
setting wages to minimize costs 253–7
Simon on 231–3
size of 275–6, 277–8
tax avoidance game 124–7
tax policies 124
wage-setting curve 331, 337, 338–43, 353–5, 379, 383
see also employers
fiscal capacity 557, 575
Fisher, Irving 408
Fisher equation 408
fishing 54, 99, 490–1
cooperation 69
pesticide pollution 493–6, 497, 499–502, 504–7, 509, 511, 514
fixed costs 277, 290, 308, 327
flow variables 390
Fogel, Robert 170
Fong, Christina 113
food taxes 131–4, 135, 136
Ford 229–30, 276, 295
fossil fuels 41–2, 44, 87, 91
France
anti-obesity taxes 133
chlordecone contamination 482, 507, 522
collective bargaining 364, 367
democracy 40
inequality 222, 563
Loire Valley 551
Louis XIV 537, 541
salt tax 132
unemployment benefits 375
wealth 39
working hours 141–2, 143, 173, 178
Freddie Mac 476–7
freedom 115, 266
Freeman, Richard 278
free riding 51, 52, 66–8, 73, 92, 510
altruism 76
public policy 98–9
punishment of 71, 74, 77
reciprocity 77
shareholders 240
free time 140, 142–3, 146, 166–70, 182, 209–10
differences between countries 171
gender division of labour 174–5
independent producers 192–3
as normal good 169
study time trade-off 152–64
under rule of force 194, 195, 198–9

under rule of law 201–2, 204, 205
see also working hours
Friedman, Milton 172
fundamental value of a share 463, 478
future generations 45

G

gains from exchange 203
gains from trade 289–93, 299, 313, 493
Galton, Francis 460–1
game, definition of a 55
game theory 49, 55–90, 92
climate change 86–90
common property 71
coordination game 80, 92
dictator game 188, 190
hawk–dove game 87–9, 92
invisible hand game 56–61, 80, 81, 92, 120
labour discipline model 249–53, 255, 272
Nash equilibrium 79–86, 120–3
Pareto efficiency 107–9
public goods games 66–8, 72–5, 76, 81, 92, 378
tax avoidance game 124–7, 135
ultimatum game 95, 100–5, 119, 135, 188, 190, 200, 499
see also prisoners' dilemma
GDP *see* gross domestic product
gender
discrimination 112, 117
gender division of labour 174–5
inequality 228
unfairness 118
working hours 139, 174–5
see also women
General Electric 297
General Mills 280
General Motors 247, 487, 489
Germany
banks 424
carbon dioxide emissions 562
climate change policy 562–3
collective bargaining 364, 367
comparison of East and West 31–3
democracy 40
income growth 573
inequality 221, 222, 563
labour market 335–6, 337
unemployment 332–4, 357–9, 381
unemployment benefits 375
working hours 141, 143, 178
gig economy 229, 242, 267–8, 272, 370–1
Gini, Corrado 214

Gini coefficient 214–15, 217–27, 228, 331
aggregate economy model 361–3, 384
borrowing and lending 422–3
differences between countries 563
US rise in inequality 360, 371
global financial crisis *see* financial crisis
gold 437, 438
Golden Rule 53
goods
artificial scarcity 513
demand for 381
economic models 144
increase in consumption 140
inferior 169
merit 531, 532–3, 537, 567, 574
model of the economy 91
non-rival 512–14
normal 169
positional 176–9, 182
price-taking 306
governing elites 547–9
government 46, 527, 574–5
bank risk-taking 473, 474
borrowing 391
capitalist dynamism 36
central banks 438
definition of 535
as economic actor 534–40, 574
economic outcomes 16
feasibility of policies 555–61, 574–5
government failure 530, 531, 538–9
market failure 525, 530, 531
money 453
political competition 546–51, 553
pollution policies 504–5, 507
public and private goods 514
as rent-seeking monopolist 540–6
resource allocation 529
role in market systems 18
rules of the game 483, 530
spending 534, 552–4, 575
tax policies 124–7
government bonds 434, 445, 453, 454–9
Graddy, Kathryn 315
Graham, Andrew 430
Grameen Bank 420
Great Depression 486
Greece
collective bargaining 367
inequality 222
labour market 335
unemployment benefits 375
working hours 143

603

INDEX

greenhouse gases 91
Greenspan, Alan 467
Grey, Rob and Doug 332, 338, 381
gross domestic product (GDP)
   government spending 553
   production of 25
   tax revenues 535
   see also real GDP
gross domestic product (GDP) per capita
   capital accumulation 22
   definition of 6–7
   East/West Germany comparison 32, 33
   environmental issues 41
   growth 10–16
   varieties of capitalism 34–5
   wellbeing 183
   working hours 139, 142–3
Guadeloupe 482, 493, 505–6
Guatemala 222

H

happiness 115, 139, 178–9
Hardin, Garrett 51, 53, 55, 64, 71, 98–9
Harding, Matthew 133–4
Harford, Tim 140
Hargreaves, James 19
Harrison, George 118, 124
Hausman, Jerry 279
hawk–dove game 87–9, 92
Hayek, Friedrich 485, 486–7
health
   antibiotics 49–50
   children's 96–7, 98
   chlordecone contamination 482
   government spending 553
   inequalities 115
   merit goods 532–3
health insurance 516, 517–19, 523
Heckman, James 70, 565
Heinrich, Joseph 70
hidden actions 269, 272, 516, 519–20, 522, 523, 524
hidden attributes 516–19, 521, 524
higher education 566–8, 569
hockey stick 44
   capital goods 22–3
   capitalism 25, 29, 30
   economic growth 7, 13–14
   inequality 46
   population 42
   technology 19, 20
home production 174–5
homo economicus 78, 92

Honda 412, 413, 449–50
Hong Kong 575
households
   assets and liabilities 469
   bank loans 448
   bonds 434
   debt-to-income ratio 470, 472
   model of the economy 91
   money 452
housing 429, 431
   as an asset 469
   collateral 418
   financial crisis 413, 471, 472, 476
   market 432
   real estate bubbles 468
   rent control 569–74
   strategic defaults 476–7, 478
   subprime borrowers/mortgages 470, 471, 472, 478
Huberman, Michael 141
human capital 390, 426
human organ sales 532
Human Resources (HR) 337, 353–5, 383
human rights 535
Hungary 221, 222, 367, 375

I

Iceland 222, 468
impatience 396, 399, 402, 406, 426
imperfect competition 523
import tariffs 109
inactive population 334, 335, 336, 338–9
incentives 120, 128–9, 135, 355
   government intervention 537
   labour discipline model 249–53
   Nigeria 558
   piece rates 242
income elasticity of demand 325
incomes
   borrowing and lending 422
   definition of 390
   differences between countries 171
   disposable income 220–1, 223, 228, 390
   distribution of 9, 37, 331, 554
   drops in 15
   economic growth 10
   farming in India 189
   GDP per capita 6–7
   gender inequality 174
   growth in 573
   happiness and 178–9
   income effect 169, 170, 171, 182, 356–7
   income net of depreciation 390, 391, 392

inequality 3–6, 111–12, 115, 214–19, 220–7, 361–3
   Lorenz curve 216–17, 361–3
   median 140
   net and gross income 391
   net worth 413
   Operation Barga 225
   redistribution 113, 220, 228, 535, 569–74
   rich/poor ratio 8
   South Africa 2
   transfers 535, 537
   working hours 141–2, 178
   see also wages; wealth
incomplete contracts 378, 379, 380, 478
   asymmetric information 520
   borrowing and lending 417, 427
   employment 242–3, 263, 268–71, 272
   external effects 510–11, 514, 524
   labour 523
increasing returns to scale 277
   see also economies of scale
independence 191, 192–3, 208
India
   antibiotics 50
   British East India Company 18
   carbon dioxide emissions 89
   common irrigation projects 68
   cotton production 488, 489
   credit constraints 419
   democracy 40, 188
   early childhood education 565
   economic growth 12–14, 16
   fishing 490–1
   GDP per capita 6, 7
   governing elite 548
   incomes 3–5, 15
   inequality 221, 222
   Operation Barga 189–90, 225, 227
   salt tax 132
   women councillors 97, 98, 131
indifference curves 152–4, 161–2, 164, 182, 192–3
   asset risk and return 455–9, 478
   borrowing and lending 392, 400–4, 406, 415, 426
   investment 410
   isocost lines 254
   marginal rate of substitution 154–7, 160
   reservation indifference curve 201–5, 208, 209–10, 227, 398–9, 402, 411
   smoothing consumption 397, 399, 403–4
   working hours 167–8, 172, 255
Indonesia 3–4, 40

INDEX

Industrial Revolution 19, 22, 23, 30, 36, 141, 196
inequality 46, 115, 214–27, 334, 361–3
   borrowing and lending 388, 422–4
   capitalism 1, 37–8, 235
   comparisons between countries 220–3
   conflicts 68
   credit rationing 418–19, 427
   democracy 38–40, 45
   differences between countries 563
   education 565
   fairness 111–12, 115
   gender 174, 228
   institutions 185, 188
   measuring 3–6
   public policy 185
   rich/poor ratio 8
   rising 331, 359–60, 370–2
   rules of the game 136
   South Africa 2, 37
   WS/PS model 384
   see also Gini coefficient; Lorenz curve
inequality aversion 69, 76, 77, 78, 92
inferior goods 169
Infineon 231
inflation 6, 407–8
information
   administrative feasibility 557
   asymmetric 234, 512, 516–21, 524
   borrowing and lending 416
   government provision 536, 537
   market failure 522
   principal–agent relationship 269
   private bargaining 501
   verifiable 268, 511, 519
infrastructure 558
inheritance 418, 426
innovation 37, 89, 134, 135, 327, 564
insolvency 412, 413, 417, 448, 451, 472, 478
institutions 17, 185, 187–90, 213, 227, 483
   bargaining power 203
   capitalism 23, 34
   division of labour 485
   East/West Germany comparison 31–2
   Marx on 235
   'permanent technological revolution' 30
   political 550
   repugnant markets 532
   social 53–4
   see also rules of the game
insurance 270, 516, 519–20, 522, 523
Intel 275, 276, 277
intellectual property rights (IPR) 134–5, 431

interest rates 129, 393–5, 400–1, 426, 427
   banks 442, 443, 446, 478
   bonds 435
   central banks 444–6
   feasible frontiers 406
   inequality 424
   investment 409, 410
   lending risk 416
   moneylenders 388
   nominal 408, 431, 435–6
   policy interest rate 429, 432, 435, 444–6, 453, 478
   present value 433, 434
   profitability of lending 439
   real 407–8
   short-term 444
   smoothing consumption 403–5
International Labour Organization (ILO) 334, 336
intervention 536–7
investment 373, 391, 392, 409–11
   banks 429
   definition of 389
   financial assets 452
   government 18, 453
   Nash equilibrium 82
   net present value 434
'invisible hand' 17, 18, 51–2, 55, 78
invisible hand game 56–61, 80, 81, 92, 120
involuntary unemployment 257, 272, 332, 355–6, 382, 384
IOUs 437–8
Iowa Electronic Markets 461
iPad 278, 279
iPhone 231, 278, 279
IPR *see* intellectual property rights
Ireland
   bank strike 430, 431, 436
   bubbles 468
   carbon dioxide emissions 562
   collective bargaining 367
   house prices 472
   inequality 222
   unemployment benefits 375
irrational exuberance 467
irrigation 54, 66–8, 92, 99, 510
isocost lines 254–5, 256, 257, 272, 366, 368
isoprofit curves 284–8, 290–2, 327, 345, 347–9, 352, 545
isorent curves 544–6
Israel 222, 367, 375

Italy
   collective bargaining 364, 367
   democracy 40
   economic growth 12–14, 16
   GDP per capita 7
   inequality 222, 563
   labour market 335
   unemployment benefits 375
   working hours 143
Ivory Coast 537

J

Jacobson, Louis 248
Jamaica 565
Japan
   bubbles 468
   capital accumulation 22
   collective bargaining 364, 367
   democracy 40
   developmental state 34
   economic growth 12–14, 16, 32, 33, 34
   educational performance 564
   GDP per capita 7
   incomes 3–4
   inequality 40, 222
   interest rates 408
   undemocratic government 39
   unemployment benefits 375
   working hours 141, 143
job loss 248
John Lewis Partnership 264
joint access 107
joint surplus 203, 212, 227
   see also surplus

K

Kalla, Joshua 560
'keeping up with the Joneses' 176–7, 178, 181
Kenya 102–5, 173
Keynes, John Maynard 140, 170, 296, 487
kidney transplants 528–9
Kindleberger, Charles 468
King, Gregory 282
Kroszner, Randall S. 231
Krueger, Alan B. 230
Krugman, Paul 438
Kuwait 562
Kyoto Protocol 81

L

laboratory experiments 69–70, 145

INDEX

labour
    coordination of work 233–4
    derived demand for 381
    employment relationship 241–3
    model of the economy 91
    wage labour contracts 237
    see also employees
labour discipline model 249–53, 255, 257, 272, 339
labour force 334–5, 338–9, 342
labour market 26, 331–43
    aggregate economy 337
    credit market comparison 425–6
    differences between countries 335
    inequality 359–60, 361–3
    policies 372–7
    power relations 188
    price-setting curve 344–55
    unions 364–70
    wage-setting curve 338–43
    see also employees; employers; unemployment
labour productivity 164, 345–6
    price-setting curve 349–50, 351, 358, 383
    unions 369, 384
    see also productivity
Lalonde, Robert 248
land
    land ownership 216, 218, 219, 225
    model of the economy 91
Landes, David 19
Lasswell, Harold 564
Latin America 16
law of demand 282
lawyers 124–7
Lazear, Edward 261, 262
legal representation 532–3, 537
legislation 209, 210, 211, 213
leisure 140, 170, 182
'lemons problem' 516–19
lending 387–8, 391, 402–5, 406–8
    balance sheets 413–14
    banks 439–40, 441–3, 445, 446–9, 453, 470
    constraints 416–19
    inequalities 422–4
    Irish publicans 431
    market failure 523
    profitability 439
    risk 416
    see also borrowing; loans
Lesotho 5
leverage ratio 449, 450, 469, 471, 472, 478

Levitt, Steven D. 70
liabilities 412–15
    banks 440–1, 442, 443, 444, 446–51, 474
    households 469
liability-based money 438
life expectancy 16, 196, 534
lighting technology 20–1, 22, 44
Lincoln, Abraham 53, 488, 489
liquidity 448
    risk 442–3, 478
    transformation 442, 443
List, John A. 70
living standards 15, 16, 167
    centrally planned economies 34
    competitive equilibrium 314
    dynamic economies 35–6
    income transfers 537
    real GDP 183
    rise in 1, 14, 25, 30, 142
loans
    banks 429, 431
    cooperatives 264
    higher education funding 566, 567–8, 569
    incomplete contracts 270
    payday 388, 392, 409, 419, 439
    see also borrowing; lending
lobbying 40, 277
Lorenz, Max 216
Lorenz curve 216–19, 220–2, 224, 226, 228, 331
    aggregate economy model 361–3, 384
    borrowing and lending 422
    rise in profit share 371, 372
Louis XIV of France 537, 541
Lovenheim, Michael 133–4
Lucas, Robert 466
Luxembourg 367, 375, 562, 563
luxury items 176–7, 178, 183
Lyft 242, 267, 268

M

Madagascar 492
Madison, James 539
Malaysia 468
managers 238–40
    asymmetric information 234
    conflicts of interest 231
    cooperatives 264
    decision-making 273
    incomplete contracts 270
    power 233, 237
Mandela, Nelson 2
manufacturing 242

marginal change 150
marginal cost 275, 291–3, 303, 308–12, 353
    competitive equilibrium 313
    monopolies 539
    non-rival goods 514
    price markups 294
    price-setting curve 345, 346, 350
    social 486, 493–6, 500, 503, 504–7, 557
    see also unit costs
marginal external cost (MEC) 494, 495, 505, 506
marginal private benefit (MPB) 502, 504
marginal private cost (MPC) 493–6, 500, 503, 504–5, 506
marginal product 150–1, 163, 165, 166, 168, 182
marginal rate of substitution (MRS) 154–7, 160, 161–4, 167, 172, 182
    asset risk and return 457–8, 459
    borrowing 400, 401
    consumption 397, 399, 426
    feasible frontier 207
    independent producers 192–3
    investment 410
    isoprofit curves 287–8, 327
    isorent curves 546
    labour discipline model 252, 272
    Pareto efficiency curve 207–8, 212, 227–8
    reservation indifference curve 203, 204, 210
    smoothing consumption 403, 404
    survival constraint 197, 198, 199
    wage-setting 254–7
marginal rate of transformation (MRT) 160, 161–4, 166, 172, 182
    asset risk and return 456–7, 459
    borrowing 395, 400, 401
    consumption 426
    demand curve 283
    feasible frontier 207
    independent producers 192
    investment 409, 410
    isoprofit curves 287–8, 327
    isorent curves 546
    labour discipline model 272
    Pareto efficiency curve 207–8, 212, 227–8
    reservation indifference curve 203, 204, 210
    smoothing consumption 402, 403, 404, 405
    survival constraint 197, 198, 199
    wage-setting 255–7
marginal social benefit (MSB) 502, 504

INDEX

marginal social cost (MSC) 486, 493–6, 500, 503, 504–7, 557
marginal utility 303
market-clearing price 305, 327
market failure 275, 294, 477, 481, 492–3, 524–5, 574
   administrative feasibility 557
   asymmetric information 520
   bank risk-taking 473
   chlordecone contamination 482
   government failures 530, 531, 539
   policies 522–3
   pollution 493–6, 499–501, 504–7, 508, 514, 557
   public goods 512–14
   remedies 515, 522–3
   unfairness 554
market income 220–1, 223, 228
marketing departments 337, 353–5, 383
market power 295, 296, 298, 327
markets 18, 275, 276, 300–26, 481–526, 529–30, 574
   asset 432
   bubbles 463–8
   capitalism 16, 23, 24–5, 26–7, 36, 46
   decentralization of power 233
   division of labour 484–5
   financial 430, 432, 465–6
   kidney transplants 529
   'magic' of the market 486, 531, 557
   market for lemons 517, 518, 521
   Marx on 235
   missing 511, 519, 520, 523, 524
   politics and sociology of 379–80
   prediction 461
   private goods 514
   repugnant 531–2, 574
   Simon 233
markups 294, 327, 345, 346–7, 350–1, 352
   competition 373, 383
   inequality 359–60, 362–3, 370
marriage 187
Marsh, Rick 247
Marshall, Alfred 303–4, 306, 507
Martinique 482, 486, 493, 505–7
Marx, Karl 38, 234–5, 236–7
Mas, Alexandre 230
mathematics 145, 304
maturity 434–5
maturity transformation 442, 478
MBSs *see* mortgage-backed securities
McDonalds 276
mean 9

MEC *see* marginal external cost
Mechanical Turk 267
median 9, 460–1
Meidner, Rudolph 374–5
Mencken, H. L. 78
men's working hours 139, 174–5
merit goods 531, 532–3, 537, 567, 574
Mexico
   anti-obesity taxes 133
   bubbles 468
   democracy 40
   free time 171
   governing elite 548
   inequality 222
   working hours 143, 173
Micklethwait, John 231
microfinance 420
Microsoft 297
Mill, John Stuart 266
Miller, Grant 96
Miller, Helen 118
minimum acceptable offer 499
minimum wage 534, 536, 547, 569
mining 332, 381
Minns, Chris 141
Minten, Bart 492
Mirrlees Review (2010) 552
missing markets 511, 519, 520, 523, 524
modern slavery 188, 191
money 389, 429, 430–1, 432, 436–43
   bank money 431, 439–40, 441–2, 443, 478
   base money 432, 439–40, 443–4, 446, 448, 453, 478
   broad money 439, 442
   definition of 436
   key actors 452–3
moneylenders 387–8, 392, 416, 424, 439
money markets 432, 435, 444
monopolistic competition 294, 295, 296, 312, 331
monopoly 36, 294, 297, 327, 552
   inequality 371
   natural 538–9
   political 549–51
   rents 295
   Smith, Adam 18
Monopoly (game) 298, 299
Montreal Protocol 54, 81
moral hazard 516, 519–20, 522, 523, 524
morals 474, 476–7, 478
mortgage-backed securities (MBSs) 475

mortgages 413, 425, 432, 442
   collateral 469
   strategic defaults 476–7, 478
   subprime 471, 472, 478
Moser, Petra 134–5
motivation 69, 229, 244, 245, 263, 378
MPB *see* marginal private benefit
MPC *see* marginal private cost
MRS *see* marginal rate of substitution
MRT *see* marginal rate of transformation
MSB *see* marginal social benefit
MSC *see* marginal social cost
mutual gains 90, 185, 190, 202, 212–13, 378
   borrowing and lending 387, 406, 424, 427
   employment relationship 241
   government intervention 536
   voluntary exchanges 533
Myerson, Roger 83

N

Nasdaq Composite Index 461–2, 464
Nash, John 82–3
Nash equilibrium 79–86, 92, 95, 120–3, 378
   climate change game 88, 89
   competitive equilibrium 306
   labour discipline model 250, 255
   labour markets 374–7, 379
   markets 303
   policy feasibility 555
   positional goods 177–8
   public policy 129, 131, 562
   tax avoidance game 127
   unemployment 356, 381, 382
   wage-setting and price-setting 257, 272, 353–5, 383
natural experiments 30–3, 46, 96
   intellectual property rights 134, 135
   job loss 248
   political competition 547
   sugar tax 136
natural monopoly 538–9
Netherlands
   capitalism 39
   carbon dioxide emissions 562
   collective bargaining 364, 367
   democracy 40
   free time 171
   inequality 220, 222, 563
   unemployment benefits 374, 375
   working hours 141–2, 143, 178
net present value (NPV) 434
network economies of scale 278

INDEX

net worth 412–15, 440, 448
  banks 442, 449, 451
New England Program for Kidney Exchange (NEPKE) 529
News Corp 461–2
Newton, William 230
New Zealand 39, 40, 367, 375
Nicaragua 548
Niger 5, 10
Nigeria 3–6, 34, 35, 40, 558
90/10 ratio 5
nominal interest rates 408, 431, 435–6
nominal wage 350–1, 353
non-excludability 513, 514
non-rival goods 512–14
Nordhaus, William 20
Nordic countries 95
normal goods 169
North Korea 23, 188
Norton, Michael 111
Norway
  bubbles 468
  carbon dioxide emissions 562
  collective bargaining 364, 367
  democracy 40
  incomes 3–6, 573
  inequality 222, 563
  labour market 335–6
  pro-poor policies 95
  unemployment benefits 374, 375
  wealth 39
  working hours 143

O

Obama, Barack 547
obesity 131, 132–4, 135, 136
O'Brien, James Bronterre 38
oil 320, 322–6
oligarchs 537, 540–1
oligopoly 294, 323
Oman 562
one-shot games 56, 66, 76, 81, 92
OPEC *see* Organization of Petroleum Exporting Countries
open-access resources 71, 107
Operation Barga 225, 227
opportunity cost 146–7, 158, 159
  bank reserves 448
  borrowing 392
  marginal rate of transformation 160, 166, 182
  scarcity 163
  working hours 168

Organization of Petroleum Exporting Countries (OPEC) 297, 323–6
organizations 187, 232
Osram 297
Ostrom, Elinor 68, 70–1, 72
Oswald, Andrew 341
output 346–7, 351, 358, 362
  see also productivity
outsourcing 278
owners 238–40, 265
  asymmetric information 234
  conflicts of interest 231
  incomplete contracts 270
  Mill on 266
  power 233, 237
ownership 237, 238–40, 265, 272

P

Pakistan 387–8, 416
Pareto, Vilfredo 106, 109–10
Pareto criterion 106, 108, 111, 190
Pareto dominance 107, 109, 135, 203
Pareto efficiency 105–10, 120, 135–6, 190, 192, 227–8, 378
  banana production 494, 495–6, 500, 504, 505
  bargaining 211–12
  competitive equilibrium 313–15, 327
  distribution of surplus 207
  gains from trade 291–2
  inequality 214
  labour markets 379
  market failure 492–3
  Pareto efficiency curve 207–8, 212, 214, 228
  price-setting 327
  private bargaining 498, 500, 501
  private goods 514
  regulation 504
Pareto improvement 108, 190, 203, 207, 212, 213, 291
Pareto's law 110
Paris Agreement (2015) 90
Parker Brothers 298, 299
participation rate 334, 336
patents 134–5, 299, 431
pawnbrokers 417, 421
payday loans 388, 392, 409, 419, 439
payment services 440–1
payoffs 56–65, 67, 92
  climate change game 87–9
  conflicts of interest 84–5
  Nash equilibrium 80, 121–3

Pareto efficiency 108
  positional goods 176–7, 178
  reciprocity 77
  tax avoidance game 125–6
  tragedy of the commons 121
  ultimatum game 95, 100–5
pension funds 391, 432
perfect competition 295, 315, 327, 551, 555
performance-related pay 244
Peru 222, 316, 317
pesticides 482, 486, 493–6, 499–502, 508, 509, 514, 523
Philips 297
physical environment 91
piece rates 242
Pigou, Arthur 504, 507–8
Pigouvian tax 504, 507, 508, 509, 525
Piketty, Thomas 38
Pinochet, Augusto 561
piracy 185–6, 187, 216–17
Pitt, William 25, 537, 538
pleasure 146
Poland
  collective bargaining 364, 367
  democracy 40
  inequality 222
  unemployment benefits 375
police 532–3
policy *see* public policy
policy interest rate 429, 432, 435, 444–6, 453, 478
political accountability 539, 574
political institutions 187, 550, 574
political rents 540–6, 551, 574
political systems 16
politics
  campaign funding 560
  capitalist dynamism 35, 36–7
  India 190
  Lasswell on 564
  political competition 546–51, 553
  political feasibility 555, 559–61, 562, 574
  prediction markets 461
  revolutions 320–1
  working hours 173
pollution
  administrative feasibility 557
  external effects 493–6, 504–7, 509, 510, 514
  incomplete contracts 511
  model of the economy 91
  polluter pays principle 501–2
  private bargaining 499–502

608

INDEX

remedies 508
see also carbon dioxide emissions; environmental issues
population growth 41, 42
population of working age 334, 335, 336, 338–40
population size 3
Portugal 335, 367, 375
positional goods 176–9, 182
poverty 1, 532, 564, 565, v
power
   definition of 200
   democracy 38
   employment relationship 241
   firms 233, 234–8, 272
   institutions 185, 188
   labour discipline model 255
   market power 295, 296, 298, 327
   monopoly 371–2
   positional goods 176
   see also bargaining power
PPP *see* purchasing power parity
prediction markets 461
preferences 49, 52–3, 92, 152–7
   asset risk and return 457–8
   consumers 294–5
   crowding out 129, 135
   cultural 173
   definition of 152
   economic outcomes 185, 213
   government 535
   indifference curves 182
   scarcity 163
   smoothing consumption 403
   working hours 171, 181, 182
present value (PV) 433, 434–5, 445, 478
price discrimination 282–3, 291–3, 327
price elasticity of demand 132, 133, 136, 295, 327, 352
   see also elasticity of demand
price elasticity of supply 318
price markups 294, 345, 346–7, 350–1, 352
   competition 373, 383
   inequality 359–60, 362–3, 370
prices 128, 233, 279
   assets 429
   asymmetric information 517, 518, 519, 521
   bonds 434–6
   bubbles 463–8
   cartels 297
   competition 24
   constant 6

equilibrium price 302–3, 305, 324
food taxes 132, 133
gains from trade 291
gig economy 267
house 469, 470, 472
isoprofit curves 284–8, 290
'magic' of the market 557
market-clearing 305, 327
market-determined 481
as messages 485–6, 487, 488–91, 524
monopolies 538–9
oil 322–6
price-setting 275, 289–93, 294–5, 296, 327, 331
price-taking 275, 306, 307, 309, 313–14, 315, 327, 377, 380
reservation price 300–1, 302–3, 327
share prices 240, 461–2, 463, 466, 555–6
supply and demand 300–25
willingness to pay 281–3, 289–90, 291, 294–5, 300, 312–13, 317, 327
price-setting curve 331, 337, 344–55, 383
   downward shift 371
   inequality 361–3
   policies 372, 373
   unemployment 358–9, 382
   unemployment benefits 375–7
   union wage-setting 365–6, 369, 384
principal–agent relationship 269–71, 272
   banking 473, 474, 478
   borrowing and lending 387, 416–17, 419, 425–6, 427
   elected officials 559, 574
   labour market 425–6
   moral hazard 520
prisoners' dilemma 61, 64–6, 76, 92, 378
   'keeping up with the Joneses' 176–7
   Nash equilibrium 80
   outcomes 81
   Pareto efficiency 107
   tragedy of the commons 121
private bargaining 481, 497–503, 524, 525
private benefits 496, 502, 504, 508, 509, 515, 520, 523
   see also external benefits
private costs 509, 515, 520, 523
   see also external costs
private property 187, 200, 233
   capitalism 16, 23, 24, 26–7, 36, 37, 46
   fairness 117
   government acquisition of 538
   'invisible hand' 51
   markets 492

Pareto efficiency 107
   tragedy of the commons 99
   see also property rights
procedural judgements of fairness 116, 117–18, 119, 135, 192
Proctor and Gamble 276
producer surplus 289–90, 293, 303, 309, 569
   competitive equilibrium 312–13, 314, 315
   landlord surplus 570, 572–3
production
   costs 253, 276
   households 91
   Marx on 235
   oil 323, 325
   Pareto efficiency 492–3
production function 182, 227
   scarcity 163
   study time 149–51, 152, 158
   working hours 164, 167–8
productivity 164, 261–2, 353
   capitalism and economic growth 30
   creative destruction 28
   education and training 372–3
   impact of technology 20–1, 44
   inequality 362
   price-setting curve 331, 345–6, 349–50, 351, 358, 383
   solidarity wage policy 375–6
   specialization 17
   unions 369, 384
product market 331
   aggregate economy 337
   inequality 359–60, 361–3
   monopoly power 371–2
   price-setting curve 344–53
profit 25, 238, 241, 284–8, 452
   banana production 494, 500
   banks 442
   bargained wages 365–6, 368
   competition 551
   conflicts of interest 231, 239
   cooperatives 264, 265
   increase in 359–60
   inequality 370
   isoprofit curves 284–8, 290–2, 327, 345, 347–9, 352, 545
   labour discipline model 250
   lending 439
   Lorenz curve 371
   maximization 240, 253, 255, 256, 275, 286–7, 293
   net present value 434
   oil 324

609

INDEX

price elasticity of demand 352
price-setting curve 344–9, 351
price-taking 327
producer surplus 290
profit margins 294, 346, 347–8
supply and demand 308, 309
Tesco 279
wage-setting curve 338, 365
profit margins 345
prohibitions 120
property rights 29, 36, 191, 200, 213
   collective 70
   enforcement of 492, 524
   external effects 481
   fairness 99
   incomplete 511
   market failure 514
   private bargaining 498–9, 501
   see also private property
public bads 176, 179, 512–13, 515, 523
public goods 79, 81, 92, 378
   cooperation 72–5
   free riding 66–8
   health conditions 98
   non-rivalry 512–14
   social preferences 68–72, 76–7
public policy 95–137
   administrative feasibility 555, 557–8, 562, 574–5
   climate change game 89–90
   competition policy 36–7, 275, 296–7, 327, 536
   differences between countries 562–4
   early childhood education 565
   economic feasibility 555–6, 562, 574
   effectiveness 131–5
   fairness 95, 111, 118, 227, 527
   goals of 98–9
   higher education funding 566–8, 569
   implementation 120–3
   inequality 185
   labour market 372–7
   market failure 481, 522–3
   Pareto efficiency 108–9
   political feasibility 555, 559–61, 562, 574
   pollution 504–5
   positional goods 178
   private influence on 39–40
   redistributive 220, 228
   rent control 569–74
   responses to 95
   social dilemmas 50
   tax policy 124–7

unemployment 257, 258–62, 331
unintended consequences 129
see also regulation
public services 527, 532–3, 535, 541–6, 553
punishment 81
   free riding 71, 74, 77
   ultimatum game 101, 102
   unfair behaviour 95
purchasing power 436, 441
purchasing power parity (PPP) 7
pure impatience 396, 399, 402, 406, 426
Putin, Vladimir 537
Putterman, Louis 231

Q
Qatar 562
quinoa production 316–22

R
race 2, 113, 117, 118
Ramaphosa, Cyril 1–2, 16, 37
Rasul, Imran 558
ratio scales 13–15, 46
Rawls, John 116, 117, 519
raw materials 91
real estate 468
real GDP
   capital accumulation 22
   definition of 6
   East/West Germany comparison 32, 33
   environmental issues 41
   growth 10–12
   varieties of capitalism 34
   wellbeing 183
   working hours 139, 142–3
   see also gross domestic product
real interest rate 407–8
real wage 341–2, 344–51, 353, 357, 383
   inequality 362
   policies 372
   unemployment benefits 375, 376–7
recession 261–2, 471
reciprocity 49, 69, 76, 77, 78, 79, 92
redistribution 113, 124–7, 220, 228, 535, 569–74
regulation
   bargaining 81
   capitalist dynamism 36, 37
   government intervention 537
   importance of 478
   influence of firms on 327
   pollution 504, 506, 507
   see also public policy

Rehn, Gösta 374–5
renewable energy 44, 89–90, 91
rent control 527, 569–74
rent-seeking 540–6, 551, 552, 574
repeated games 66, 77, 79, 81, 92
repugnant markets 531–2, 574
research and development (R&D) 277, 299, 452, 453, 515, 536
reservation indifference curve 201–5, 208, 209–10, 227, 398–9, 402, 411
reservation option 195, 201, 203, 211, 213, 227, 374, 375, 499
reservation price 300–1, 302–3, 327
reservation wage 253, 256, 272, 377–8, 380
   employment rents 246–7
   labour discipline model 250
   unemployment 258–9
   union wage-setting 366, 368
   wage-setting curve 338–40
reserves 439, 448, 451, 453
residual claimants 238
resources, common-pool 51, 64, 513, 514, 515, 523
revenues
   banks 446
   firms 238, 452
   government 453
revolutions 320–1, 548
rich/poor ratio 8
Rio Declaration on Environment and Development 501
risk
   assets 429, 432–3, 454–60, 478
   bank risk-taking 430, 473, 475, 476
   default 442, 446, 478
   lending 416
   liquidity 442–3, 478
   risk aversion 458, 460, 478
risk-return schedule 455–7
rival goods 513, 515
Robbins, Lionel 173
Robertson, D. H. 236
Robinson, Joan 295, 296
Rogger, Daniel 558
Romania 537, 541
Rosling, Hans 8, 16, 20, 221
Roth, Alvin 529, 532
Royal Rover 185–6, 187, 188, 216–17
rule of 70 for growth rates 10, 11–12
rule of force 191, 194–9
rule of law 36, 46, 191, 200–6, 227, 543–4, 550

610

rules of the game 136, 187–90, 194–5, 296, 483, 530
   changing the 209
   fairness 116, 117–18
   gains from trade 289, 293
   political institutions 550
   political processes 564
   social institutions 53–4
   see also institutions
Russia
   GDP per capita 35
   inequality 222
   oligarchs 537, 540–1
   salt tax 132
   working hours 143
   see also Soviet Union

S

salaries 239, 240, 241, 264, 332
   see also wages
Samsung 278
Samuelson, Paul 296
Sandel, Michael 532
Saudi Arabia 562
saving 391, 432
   banks 445
   bonds 434
   definition of 391
   households 452
Scania 296–7
scarcity 139, 161–4
   allocation of scarce resources 528
   artificial 513
   marginal rate of substitution 155
   oil 323
   prices as messages 489, 491, 524
   social marginal cost 486
Schor, Juliet 181
Schumacher, Ernst F. 275
Schumpeter, Joseph 28–9, 486, 508, 552
Seabright, Paul 90
secondary trading 432
Second World War 31
self-employment 418
self-interest 92, 195, 200
   climate change 90
   common property 71
   game theory 49, 55, 59, 61
   homo economicus 78
   incentives 129
   markets 532
   prisoners' dilemma game 66
   public goods games 73, 77

Smith, Adam 17, 51
   social dilemmas 52
   social preferences 52–3, 76
   ultimatum game 102
separation of ownership and control 239, 240, 272
sequential games 92, 101, 135, 249
services
   demand for 381
   economic models 144
   increase in consumption 140
   model of the economy 91
shale oil 326
shareholders 240
shares 26, 239, 391, 431, 432–3
   banks 449
   bubbles 463, 466, 468, 478
   equity financing 452
   fundamental value of a share 463, 478
   managerial compensation 240
   risk and return 454–5, 458–9, 460
   stock exchange 461–2
Sharp 231
Shaw, George Bernard 236
Shiller, Robert 465, 466–7, 517
shocks 275, 318
   exogenous 320, 327
   oil prices 322, 325, 326
short-term interest rate 444
Shum, Matthew 299
Simon, Herbert 231–3, 238, 529, 530
simultaneous games 56, 92
Singapore 5, 10, 562, 564
Skidelsky, Robert 29
slavery 24, 141, 188, 191, 235, 488
Slovakia 367, 375
Slovenia 222
Smith, Adam 17–18, 51, 55, 78, 266
   capitalism 235
   credit rationing 418
   division of labour 484, 485
   managers 239
   monopolies 36
   self-interest 61
   specialization 26
Smith, Vernon 70
smoothing 396–7, 399, 402–5, 406, 426, 432
social dilemmas 49, 50
   chlordecone contamination 482
   economics 90
   free riding 66–8
   market failure 493
   resolution of 52–4

tragedy of the commons 51
   work and wellbeing 176–81
social insurance 553
social interactions 49–94
   bargaining 81–2
   conflicts of interest 81–90
   definition of 51
   economics 90–1
   Nash equilibrium 79–86
   social preferences 49, 52–3, 68–72, 76–7, 92, 129, 135
   types of 51–2
   ultimatum game 101
   see also game theory
socialism 486
social norms 72, 78, 92, 129, 430
   climate change 90
   common property 71
   employment relationship 241
   fairness 101
   farming in India 189
   financial deregulation 474
   gender division of labour 174
   institutions 187
   market failures 477
   markets 492
   ultimatum game 104–5
social preferences 49, 52–3, 68–72, 76–7, 92, 129, 135
   see also preferences
social security 552
social status 115, 139, 176, 182
solidarity wage policy 374–6
South Africa 1–2, 16
   base money 442
   democracy 39, 40
   governing elite 548
   inequality 37, 220, 221, 222
   undemocratic government 39
South Korea
   capitalist revolution 36
   carbon dioxide emissions 562
   collective bargaining 364, 367
   democracy 40
   free time 171
   GDP per capita 34, 35
   government spending 553, 554
   inequality 40, 221, 222
   unemployment benefits 375
   working hours 143, 171, 173
Soviet Union
   central planning 23, 486, 489
   dissolution of the 322

611

INDEX

GDP per capita 34, 35
see also Russia
Spain
  banks 424
  bubbles 468
  collective bargaining 364, 367
  economic growth 32, 33
  governing elite 548
  house prices 472
  inequality 222
  labour market 335–6, 337
  unemployment 332–4, 357–9, 381
  unemployment benefits 375
  working hours 143
specialization
  capitalism 1, 29, 46
  division of labour 484–5
  economies of scale 277
  Smith, Adam 17, 26
spending power 6, 407
  see also buying power
status symbols 176, 182
stereotypes 97
Stern, Nicholas 86
Stevenson, Betsey 179
stock exchange 461–2
stock market 239, 432, 461, 556, 561
stock variables 390
storing wealth 402–5
strategic interactions 55, 61–3, 92, 100, 101, 174
strategy 55, 92
  dominant 59–60, 63, 68, 76, 79, 88, 92
  tax avoidance game 125
strikes 364–5
structural unemployment 331, 344, 354–9, 369, 372, 374, 381–3
Stucke, Maurice 314
study time 148–64
Sturges v Bridgman (1879) 497–8
subprime borrowers 470, 478
subprime mortgages 471, 472
subsidies 95, 525
  government intervention 537
  polluter pays principle 502
  R&D 536
  wage 373
substantive judgements of fairness 116–17, 119, 135, 192
substitutes 295
substitution effect 169, 170, 171, 182, 356–7
sugar tax 131–4, 135, 136
Sullivan, Daniel 248

supervision 264
supply 300–26, 328
  changes in 316–22
  excess 303, 305–6, 356, 380, 490–1
  financial assets 461
  money markets 444
  oil 322–6
  price elasticity of 318
  shocks 275
supply curve 301–2, 307, 309–12, 315, 327, 328
  competitive equilibrium 314
  labour 356
  Marshall 303
  oil 323–5
  rent control 570–1
  shifts in supply and demand 318–20, 322
surplus 211, 212, 289–90, 492
  competitive equilibrium 312–13
  distribution of 207–8, 209
  gains from trade 289–90, 291–2
  government intervention 536
  mutual gains 213
  rent control 569–73
  see also joint surplus
surrogacy 532
surveys 68
sustainability 41, 45, 89
Sweden
  bubbles 468
  collective bargaining 364, 367
  democracy 40
  governing elite 548
  inequality 40, 221, 222, 563
  pro-poor policies 95
  unemployment benefits 374–6
  wealth 39
  working hours 141, 178, 181
Sweezy, Paul 237
Switzerland
  carbon dioxide emissions 562
  collective bargaining 367
  democracy 40
  incomes 5
  inequality 222, 563
  unemployment benefits 375
  working hours 141

T

Taiwan 22, 222
tangency 167, 255, 272, 404, 410
tariffs 109
TaskRabbit 267, 268

taxation 36–7, 95, 373, 527
  definition of tax 113
  dictatorships 541–6
  economic development 552
  elasticity of demand 275
  fairness 118
  fiscal capacity 557
  government intervention 537
  graduates 568
  inequality 40, 220, 228
  influence of firms on 327–8
  limits of governments 534
  luxury housing 178
  Nash equilibrium 122–3
  Pareto efficiency 109
  Pigouvian tax 504, 507, 508, 509, 525
  policy feasibility 555
  political competition 547, 549, 550
  pollution 502, 504, 506
  private property 233
  redistribution of income 113
  social preferences 53
  sugar tax 131–4, 135, 136
  tax avoidance game 124–7, 135
  UK tax revenues 535, 536
  unintended consequences 124–7
technical feasibility 196–9, 205, 213, 227, 291, 379
technology
  automation 334, 371–2
  capital goods 22
  capitalist revolution 1
  clean 89–90
  creative destruction 28
  definition of 19
  economic outcomes 185
  economies of scale 275, 277
  environmental issues 44
  'permanent technological revolution' 16, 19–21, 29, 30, 37, 44, 46
  tech bubble 464–7
  technical feasibility 196–9, 213, 227
  technological progress 19, 140, 164–9, 182
  wage-setting curve 383
termination of employment 241, 244, 365
Tesco 279
textiles 488–9
Thailand 468, 567
Thatcher, Margaret 475
Tirole, Jean 536
'too big to fail' concept 36
Toshiba 231, 278

INDEX

total surplus 289–90, 291–2, 312–13, 327, 492, 571
Toynbee, Polly 237
Toyota 298
trade liberalization 109
trademarks 431
trade-offs
   gender division of labour 174–5
   indifference curves 182
   risk and return 455–9
   study time 158–60, 161–3
   working hours 167–8
   see also marginal rate of substitution
trade unions 230, 331, 364–70, 384, 560
trading 465
tragedy of the commons 51–2, 53, 55, 64, 92
   fairness and efficiency 121–3
   Ostrom's work 70–1, 72
   public policy 98–9
training 372–3
transaction costs 498
Trinidad and Tobago 562
Trump, Donald 547
trust 430, 431, 436, 438, 492
tuition fees 527, 528, 566–8, 569
Turkey
   collective bargaining 367
   democracy 40
   free time 171
   unemployment benefits 375
   working hours 142, 143
turnover 263

U

Uber 242, 267, 268, 529
ultimatum game 95, 100–5, 119, 135, 188, 190, 200, 499
uncertainty 232, 268–9, 466
unemployment 229, 334–6, 555
   bargained wages 367, 369
   cyclical 381–2
   definition of 334
   demand 381–2
   differences between countries 332–4, 357–9
   employment rents 245–7, 248, 251, 262, 342
   equilibrium unemployment 355, 380, 382
   gig economy 268
   inequality 361, 370, 371, 372
   involuntary 257, 272, 332, 355–6, 382, 384
   labour discipline model 251, 253
   Nash equilibrium 82
   non-monetary costs 384
   price-setting curve 344
   public policy 257, 258–62, 372
   rate of 334, 335, 336, 338–9, 341
   structural 331, 344, 354–9, 369, 372, 374, 381–3
   wage-setting curve 331, 338–43
   wages related to 258–61, 332, 333
unemployment benefits 244, 258, 331
   employment rents 245–7, 249
   labour discipline model 250–1, 253
   level of 259–60, 358
   policy 373–7
   wage-setting curve 342, 343, 383
unethical behaviour 475, 476
unions 230, 331, 364–70, 384, 560
union voice effect 367–8, 369, 384
unit costs 284, 286, 290, 327, 345–6, 347–8
   see also marginal cost
United Arab Emirates (UAE) 562
United Kingdom
   base money 442
   British East India Company 18
   bubbles 468
   capital accumulation 22
   capitalism 39
   carbon dioxide emissions 562
   centralized production 236
   City of London 475–6
   collective bargaining 364, 367
   compulsory purchase orders 538
   cotton production 488, 489
   democracy 40
   economic growth 12–14, 16, 34
   GDP per capita 7
   higher education 567, 568
   incomes 3–4
   Industrial Revolution 19, 22, 36, 196
   inequality 220, 222, 563
   leverage ratio 471, 472
   Mirrlees Review 552
   Modern Slavery Act 191
   Pitt 537, 538
   policy interest rate 445
   rate of technological progress 140
   salt tax 132
   tax revenues 535, 536
   unemployment benefits 375
   wealth 39
   working hours 140–1, 143, 169–70
United States
   antitrust policy 297
   banks 424
   breakfast cereals 279–80, 299
   bubbles 468
   capital accumulation 22
   capitalism 23
   carbon dioxide emissions 89, 562
   centralized production 236
   child mortality 98
   climate change 87–9, 562–3
   collective bargaining 364, 367
   cotton 488–9
   credit rationing 418
   democracy 40
   distribution of wealth 110, 111–12, 115, 554
   division of labour 485
   educational performance 564
   financial crisis 413
   financial deregulation 470
   food taxes 133
   free time 171
   GDP production 25
   governing elite 547, 548
   government employees 535
   government spending 553, 554
   higher education 567
   house prices 472
   incomes 3–5
   inequality 220–1, 222, 331, 359–60, 370, 371, 563, 565
   inheritance of wealth 426
   job loss 248
   large firms 276
   leverage ratio 471
   median wage 140
   mortgage defaults 476–7
   payday loans 419
   piece rates 242
   political competition 547
   political influence 560
   poverty 534
   rate of technological progress 140
   redistribution of income 113
   rent control 569
   right of eminent domain 538
   shale oil 326
   ultimatum game 102–5
   unemployment benefits 249, 375
   unpaid care work 175
   wage-setting curve 341
   wealth 39
   women's voting rights 96–7
   worker productivity 261–2
   working hours 141–2, 143, 171, 178, 181

613

INDEX

universities 527, 528, 566–8, 569
unpaid care work 175
Upworkers 267
Uruguay 222
utilitarianism 117
utility 117, 152, 207
  employment 244
  indifference curves 153–4, 156, 161–2, 182, 398–9, 401, 426
  marginal 303
  redistribution of income 574
  smoothing consumption 403, 404
  worker's best response function 258
  working hours 167, 255

V

Van Reenen, John 376
Veblen, Thorstein 176
Veblen effects 177, 178, 179, 181, 182
veil of ignorance 116, 119, 136, 519
verifiable information 519
Vietnam 39
voluntary exchange 24, 117, 200–1, 203, 206, 213, 533
Volvo 296–7
voting 16, 549
  right to vote 38, 45, 191, 527, 550, 552–3
  women 96–7
vox populi 460–1

W

wage labour 237
wages 169, 229, 241
  cooperatives 264
  efficiency wages 255–7
  employment rents 246–8, 250–1, 257, 258, 262–3, 272
  fall in wage share 371, 372
  Firestone 230
  free time and 171
  impact of unemployment benefits 374, 375–7
  inequality 362
  involuntary unemployment 257
  labour discipline model 249–53, 272
  market failure 523
  median 140
  minimum wage 534, 536, 547, 569
  performance-related pay 244
  piece rates 242
  price-setting curve 331, 344–55
  principal–agent problems 417
  setting 253–7, 272, 327–8, 331, 344
  solidarity wage policy 374–6
  unemployment relationship 258–61, 332, 333
  unions 364–70
  wage subsidies 373
  see also incomes; real wage; reservation wage; salaries
wage-setting curve 331, 337, 338–43, 379, 383
  bargained 364–7, 369, 384
  downward shift 370–1
  inequality 361–3
  Nash equilibrium 353–5
  unemployment 356, 358–9, 382
  unemployment benefits 374, 375–7
Waldfogel, Joel 313
Walmart 233, 277, 535
Walras, Léon 303, 487
Walzer, Michael 532
war 534, 553
water 54, 91
wealth 389–90, 391, 392, 406
  assets 431
  credit market 406, 418, 419, 424, 425
  definition of 389
  distribution of 110, 111–12, 115, 222, 554
  expected value 454
  Gini coefficient 223
  inequality 37–8
  inheritance of 426
  Lorenz curve 216, 218, 222
  net worth 413
  political influence 559, 560
  share of the richest 39
  storing 402–5
  tax systems 535
  wealth creation 37
  see also incomes
wellbeing 117, 183
West Germany 31–3, 34, 96
Whaples, Robert 141

Whitlam, Gough 548
willingness to accept (WTA) 300–1, 327
willingness to pay (WTP) 281–3, 289–90, 291, 294–5, 300, 327
  climate change mitigation 525
  competitive equilibrium 312–13
  quinoa 317
  students 528
  unfairness 532
win-win agreements 211, 212
wisdom of the crowd 460–1
Wolfers, Justin 179
women
  Marshall on 304
  political representation 95
  village councils in India 97, 98
  voting rights 96–7, 550
  working hours 139, 174–5
  see also gender
Wooldridge, Adrian 231
work, coordination of 233–4
worker-owned cooperatives 264–5, 272
worker's best response function 251, 259, 272
working hours 139–43, 164–75, 192–3, 255
  bargaining 211–12
  changes in 169–70, 181
  conflicts of interest 231
  culture and politics 173
  differences between countries 171, 180
  fairness 209
  Firestone 230
  firms 241
  gender division of labour 174–5
  high incomes 178
  Pareto efficiency 207
  reservation indifference curve 203–5
  status symbols 176
  technical feasibility 196–9
  see also free time
WS/PS model 337–56, 357, 361–3, 369, 370, 383–4
WTA *see* willingness to accept
WTP *see* willingness to pay

Y

yields 435, 445